Frommer's®

Las Vegas with Kids

2nd Edition

by Bob Sehlinger
with Lisa Derrick

Here's what the critics say about Frommer's:

"Amazingly easy to use. Very portable, very complete."

—*Booklist*

"Detailed, accurate, and easy-to-read information for all price ranges."
—*Glamour Magazine*

"Hotel information is close to encyclopedic."
—*Des Moines Sunday Register*

"Frommer's Guides have a way of giving you a real feel for a place."
—*Knight Ridder Newspapers*

WILEY

Wiley Publishing, Inc.

About the Authors

Bob Sehlinger is the creator of the Unofficial Guide travel series and author or co-author of over 25 travel guides. He makes his home in Birmingham, Alabama, where the catfish are jumping and the cotton is high.

Lisa Derrick is a Los Angeles–based freelancer whose work has appeared in *Spin, Details, Nylon, Time Out,* and other national publications.

Published by:

Wiley Publishing, Inc.

111 River St.
Hoboken, NJ 07030-5774

Copyright © 2005 Wiley Publishing, Inc., Hoboken, New Jersey. All rights reserved. No part of this publication may be reproduced, stored in a retrieval system or transmitted in any form or by any means, electronic, mechanical, photocopying, recording, scanning or otherwise, except as permitted under Sections 107 or 108 of the 1976 United States Copyright Act, without either the prior written permission of the Publisher, or authorization through payment of the appropriate per-copy fee to the Copyright Clearance Center, 222 Rosewood Drive, Danvers, MA 01923, 978/750-8400, fax 978/646-8600. Requests to the Publisher for permission should be addressed to the Legal Department, Wiley Publishing, Inc., 10475 Crosspoint Blvd., Indianapolis, IN 46256, 317/572-3447, fax 317/572-4447, E-Mail: permcoordinator@wiley.com.

Wiley and the Wiley Publishing logo are trademarks or registered trademarks of John Wiley & Sons, Inc. and/or its affiliates. Frommer's is a trademark or registered trademark of Arthur Frommer. Used under license. All other trademarks are the property of their respective owners. Wiley Publishing, Inc. is not associated with any product or vendor mentioned in this book.

ISBN 0-7645-7765-4

Editor: Naomi P. Kraus
Production Editor: Erin Vorhies
Cartographer: Elizabeth Puhl
Photo Editor: Richard Fox
Production by Wiley Indianapolis Composition Services

For information on our other products and services or to obtain technical support, please contact our Customer Care Department within the U.S. at 800/762-2974, outside the U.S. at 317/572-3993 or fax 317/572-4002.

Wiley also publishes its books in a variety of electronic formats. Some content that appears in print may not be available in electronic formats.

Manufactured in the United States of America

5   4   3   2

Contents

List of Maps   vi

1   How to Feel Like a Las Vegas Family   1

1 Frommer's Favorite Las Vegas
Family Experiences   .5

2 Best Hotel Bets   .8

3 Best Dining Bets   .11

4 The Rest of the Best   .13

2   Planning a Family Trip to Las Vegas   15

1 Visitor Information   .15

*Destination: Las Vegas—
Red Alert Checklist*   .16

2 Money   .17

What Things Cost   .18

3 When to Go   .20

*Las Vegas Calendar of
Kid-Friendly Events*   .21

Major Convention Dates   .22

4 Getting the Kids Interested
in Las Vegas   .25

*Tips for Having a Great
Family Vacation*   .26

5 What to Pack   .27

*Using a Cellphone
on Your Trip*   .28

6 Insurance, Health & Safety   .29

*Curfew, According to the Law:
When and Where Children
Shouldn't Be Without
an Adult*   .31

7 Tips for Travelers with
Special Needs   .33

8 Getting There   .38

Flying with Film & Video   .40

9 Tips on Flying with
Your Children   .45

In-Flight Fun for Kids   .51

10 Package Tours for Independent
Travelers   .52

11 Planning Your Trip Online   .54

*Frommers.com: The Complete
Travel Resource*   .55

Online Traveler's Toolbox   .56

12 Tips on Accommodations   .58

13 Babysitters & Child-Care
Centers   .60

*What Parents Can Do in Vegas
if They Have a Sitter/
Child Care*   .62

14 Recommended Reading
for Adults   .63

3   Getting to Know Las Vegas   64

1 Visitor Information   .64

2 City Layout   .66

3 Getting Around   .67

Fast Facts: Las Vegas   .72

4   Family-Friendly Accommodations   75

1 South Strip 80

Cleaning Up 83

Nice Places to Visit (But You Wouldn't Want to Stay There) 88

2 Center Strip 90

3 North Strip 97

4 East of the Strip 101

5 West of the Strip 110

6 Outside of Las Vegas 113

5   Family-Friendly Dining   116

1 Tips for Dining in Las Vegas . . .117

Dining Out in Peace 118

2 Restaurants by Cuisine 119

3 South Strip 121

Tea for Two 128

Cheap Eats 130

Las Vegas's Chinatown 132

4 Center Strip 132

Sweets for the Sweet 135

The Kult of Krispy Kreme 136

5 North Strip 139

6 East of the Strip 141

7 West of the Strip 144

8 Downtown 144

9 Buffets 145

10 Just the Two of Us: Romantic Dining 149

6   What Kids Like to See & Do in Las Vegas   151

Suggested Itineraries 152

Free Attractions 154

1 Attractions for Kids 156

If I Could Talk to the Animals 158

Arcades Abound 164

2 Thrill Rides 166

3 Art Galleries & History Museums 168

Hey, Sport! 173

4 Factories & Food 175

Trivia: Viva Las Vegas 176

5 Kid-Friendly Tours 178

For Your Little Race Car Enthusiast 179

7   Las Vegas for the Active Family   181

1 Places to Run & Walk 181

2 Family Fun Centers & Indoor Playgrounds 184

3 Sports 184

Not for the Faint of Heart 185

For the Special-Needs Child . .188

4 Classes & Workshops 188

8   Shopping for the Whole Family   189

1 The Shopping Scene 190

2 Shopping A–Z 195

9 Entertainment for the Whole Family 213

1 What's Playing Where 214
   Buying Show Tickets 215
2 Major Production Shows 215
3 Headliner Showrooms 225
4 Comedy Clubs 227

5 Spectator Sports 228
6 Local Performing Arts 231
   Look & Listen 231
7 What to Do if You've Left
   the Kids with a Babysitter 232

10 Side Trips from Las Vegas 241

1 Hoover Dam & Lake Mead ...241
   Did You Know.............244
2 Valley of Fire State Park 250
   Take a Hike: Desert
   Hiking Advice 252
3 Red Rock Canyon 253
4 Bonnie Springs Ranch/
   Old Nevada 257

5 Spring Mountains National
   Recreation Area/Mount
   Charleston 260
6 Primm 261
7 The Grand Canyon:
   Grand Canyon West 262
8 Outdoor Activities &
   Tour Companies 266

Appendix A: For International Visitors 268

1 Preparing for Your Trip 268
2 Getting to the United States ..274
3 Getting Around the
   United States 275

Fast Facts: For the
International Traveler 277

Appendix B: Las Vegas in Depth 283

1 A Look at the Past 283
   Dateline 283

Farewell to Frank 289
2 Las Vegas Today 292

Index 293

General Index 293
Accommodations Index 302

Restaurant Index 302

List of Maps

Las Vegas & Environs   6

Las Vegas at a Glance   65

South Strip Accommodations   81

Center Strip Accommodations   91

North Strip Accommodations   99

Accommodations East
of the Strip   103

Accommodations, Dining &
Entertainment West
of the Strip   111

Accommodations, Dining &
Attractions in Henderson   114

South Strip Dining   123

Center Strip Dining   133

North Strip Dining   140

Dining East of the Strip   143

South Strip Attractions   157

Center Strip Attractions   163

North Strip Attractions   165

Downtown Attractions &
Dining   167

Attractions & Entertainment
East of the Strip   169

Las Vegas for the Active Family   182

Las Vegas's Shopping Scene   191

South Strip Shopping   197

Center Strip Shopping   199

North Strip Shopping   201

Shopping East of the Strip   203

Shopping West of the Strip   205

South Strip Entertainment   217

Center Strip Entertainment   219

North Strip Entertainment   221

Las Vegas's Sports Venues,
Stadiums & Local Performing Arts
Venues   229

Side Trips from Las Vegas   243

Lake Mead & Vicinity   247

Grand Canyon West &
Environs   263

Acknowledgments

Thanks to Mary Herczog for her overwhelming generosity and wisdom and to Rick Garman for living in Las Vegas. Thanks to Frommer's for the chance; Naomi Kraus for her bravery, perseverance, patience and diligence; and Catherine T. Schwenk for her attention to detail. Thanks also to project manager Christina Crowe and cartographer Steve Jones of Frommer's sister series, The Unofficial Guides.

This book would not have been possible without Mark Hechtman, the Clements, the Sparlings, the Whetstone-Gibsons, and all the amazing children of these wonderful folks.

Thanks to Lisa's family: Barry Devlin and Caroline Erskine; Erron Silverstein for repeatedly lending Maria to Lisa; M.V. Montgomery for her travel skills; Michael R. Goth; Corey and Marta Solomon; Mark Ebner; Vicky Adams and Jymie Darling; Abigail Bok; Hecate and Hermes.

An Invitation to the Reader

In researching this book, we discovered many wonderful places—hotels, restaurants, shops, and more. We're sure you'll find others. Please tell us about them, so we can share the information with your fellow travelers in upcoming editions. If you were disappointed with a recommendation, we'd love to know that, too. Please write to:

Frommer's Las Vegas with Kids, 2nd Edition
Wiley Publishing, Inc. • 111 River St. • Hoboken, NJ 07030-5774

An Additional Note

Please be advised that travel information is subject to change at any time—and this is especially true of prices. We therefore suggest that you write or call ahead for confirmation when making your travel plans. The authors, editors, and publisher cannot be held responsible for the experiences of readers while traveling. Your safety is important to us, however, so we encourage you to stay alert and be aware of your surroundings. Keep a close eye on cameras, purses, and wallets, all favorite targets of thieves and pickpockets.

Other Great Guides for Your Trip:

Frommer's Las Vegas

Frommer's Portable Las Vegas for Non-Gamblers

Las Vegas For Dummies

The Unofficial Guide to Las Vegas

Frommer's Irreverent Guide to Las Vegas

Frommer's California

Frommer's Utah

Frommer's Arizona

Frommer's U.S.A.

Frommer's Star Ratings, Icons & Abbreviations

Every hotel, restaurant, and attraction listing in this guide has been ranked for quality, value, service, amenities, and special features using a **star-rating system.** In country, state, and regional guides, we also rate towns and regions to help you narrow down your choices and budget your time accordingly. Hotels and restaurants are rated on a scale of zero (recommended) to three stars (exceptional). Attractions, shopping, nightlife, towns, and regions are rated according to the following scale: zero stars (recommended), one star (highly recommended), two stars (very highly recommended), and three stars (must-see).

In addition to the star-rating system, we also use **six feature icons** that point you to the great deals, in-the-know advice, and unique experiences that separate travelers from tourists. Throughout the book, look for:

Finds	Special finds—those places only insiders know about
Fun Fact	Fun facts—details that make travelers more informed and their trips more fun
Moments	Special moments—those experiences that memories are made of
Overrated	Places or experiences not worth your time or money
Tips	Insider tips—great ways to save time and money
Value	Great values—where to get the best deals

The following **abbreviations** are used for credit cards:

AE	American Express	DISC	Discover	V	Visa
DC	Diners Club	MC	MasterCard		

Frommers.com

Now that you have the guidebook to a great trip, visit our website at **www.frommers.com** for travel information on more than 3,000 destinations. With features updated regularly, we give you instant access to the most current trip-planning information available. At Frommers.com, you'll also find the best prices on airfares, accommodations, and car rentals—and you can even book travel online through our travel booking partners. At Frommers.com, you'll also find the following:

- Online updates to our most popular guidebooks
- Vacation sweepstakes and contest giveaways
- Newsletter highlighting the hottest travel trends
- Online travel message boards with featured travel discussions

How to Feel Like a Las Vegas Family

If you sprang for this guide, you no doubt have Las Vegas on the brain. Is it a good family destination? You're probably hoping the reply is yes. As it happens, the question is a lot more straightforward than the answer.

Las Vegas offers everything a family could want: world-class resorts; eye-popping neon; ersatz replicas of Egypt, Venice, Paris, ancient Rome, King Arthur's castle, and New York City; the most dynamic dining scene in America; top-notch entertainment for all ages; sports and outdoor recreational opportunities rivaled by few; and an assortment of attractions ranging from exploding volcanoes to the Hoover Dam. To ice the cake, all of this is available for a fraction of what you'd pay at most other destinations. Without spending a nickel in the casinos, you'll discover more to see and do in Las Vegas than a family can cram into 6 weeks.

But there, you see, is the rub. For many parents (perhaps including you), Las Vegas is on the short list for family vacation destinations precisely because mom and dad want to enjoy a little gambling. Gambling, after all, is what subsidizes those bargain hotel rooms, free pirate battles, and gut-busting buffets. It would seem almost un-American not to spend some time in the casino. Once you've started down that path, however, you're well on the way to taking the "family" out of "family vacation."

Gambling and spending time as a family are mutually incompatible. Children are not allowed in casinos. Period. So if you want to play some blackjack, the children will have to be someplace else. Where would that be exactly? Well, the 12-and-up crowd will eke out a couple hours a day at the pool (some pools require a parent present for children younger than 16); spend as much on buffets, burgers, and snacks as your budget allows; and then go cruising. This last consists of roaming up and down the Strip or Fremont Street ducking into arcades, gift shops, and hotels, riding the monorail, and checking out the freebie sex brochures available on street corners. Though cruising is good exercise, quite educational (every imaginable form of humanity is on display), and definitely horizon expanding, you might not be altogether pleased with the discoveries your children make.

For children aged 11 years and younger, your options are even more constrained. One spouse can watch the kids while the other gambles, or you can plop the kids in day care (generally not available on the Strip or downtown), or hire an in-room sitter. If you pick up the tab and sign some waivers, a number of in-room sitters will even take your kids out for sightseeing or other activities. The problem with all of these alternatives, however, is that they turn your family vacation into an occasionally overlapping medley of solitary pursuits. You've become, in effect, just like all the other adults in town—a person who has come to Las Vegas to get away from children.

Can you have it both ways? Of course. After all, it's essentially a matter of degree. Even at Walt Disney World parents hire sitters in order to enjoy an occasional adult night out. Problem is, in Las Vegas it's very easy to let that adult evening expand into an adult vacation with your grown-up agenda supplanting the family one.

WHO LOVES YOU, BABY?

Possibly the most effective PR campaign ever launched on behalf of Las Vegas was the **Las Vegas Convention and Visitors Authority (LVCVA)** broadside of the early '90s that attempted to recast Las Vegas as a family destination. Today, more than a decade later, the misconceptions planted by that nifty piece of marketing still run rampant.

LVCVA had a couple of objectives. First, it wanted bodies to fill all those hotel rooms that sat empty except on weekends. Second, it sought to make gambling seem more mainstream and wholesome, sort of like bowling. Because family vacations are generally a few days longer than the average Las Vegas stay, and because a high percentage of families travel during the hot summer (historically Las Vegas's slowest time of year), an ad campaign targeting families seemed like a perfect strategy for boosting occupancy rates and visitors' average length of stay.

LVCVA's logic seemed reasonable to most outsiders and was buttressed by the opening of the Excalibur, a resort that, like its older sister Circus Circus, actually pursued the family trade. Coming on line at about the same time was the new MGM Grand Resort & Casino with its on-site Grand Adventures theme park. The message could not have been clearer: "Families! Las Vegas is the place for you!" Unfortunately, though the hype for the new theme park was world class, the park itself was a total disaster. And while on the surface it appeared that the MGM Grand was targeting families, its actual position was one of confused ambivalence, an ambivalence that was resolved pretty quickly in the wake of the dud theme park. Of course, by the time these events had transpired, LVCVA had long since bought into its own press releases.

Though LVCVA's family campaign seemed cogent enough and was successful in stimulating a lot of families to consider Las Vegas, there was a very big pea under the proverbial mattress. It seems that LVCVA had failed to solicit the support of the casinos, and that likewise it had failed to take the views of the Las Vegas bread-and-butter adult visitor into account.

As for the resorts, the last thing they wanted was a bunch of kids tearing around the casino and roaming up and down the Strip. The casinos *had* bothered to consult their regular customers. These folks responded resoundingly and unambiguously that they came to Las Vegas to have an adult experience. As one recreational gambler put it, "When we want to be around kids we'll go to Disneyland." Looking at it from another angle, LVCVA failed to notice that there was no hospitality infrastructure to support a large population of vacationing families. When it launched its campaign, there were only two resorts that solicited family business. That should have been a clue. Today, more than a dozen years later, there are still only the same two resorts—Excalibur and Circus Circus—that greet families with a warm smile. As for LVCVA, it now works more cooperatively with casinos and pays more attention to the repeat adult visitor. To make amends for letting the "Families Welcome" monster out of the bag, LVCVA runs ads and commercials that depict Las Vegas as a lusty, 24-hour-a-day den of iniquity where adults can find just about any kind of action they're looking for.

THE BOTTOM LINE

For you, two questions are paramount: 1) What are the practical implications of not being wanted by the casinos; and 2) Can you have a great family vacation in Las Vegas? We'll take them one at a time.

In practical terms, casino resorts are open to the public. They may not want you, but they won't turn you away either. And once you're there they'll treat you cordially, just like any other guest. The business logic is straightforward. Once you've arrived, they want you to have a good experience, to recommend the resort to others (preferably to adults), and hopefully to come back someday without the children. Security will be none too gentle if they catch your kids in the casino, and other guests will demonstrate their displeasure if your little ones are disruptive at the pool or in other public areas.

If, however, your children are generally well behaved and comfortable around adults, you can expect smooth sailing. Be aware that casinos aren't the only game in town. There are also dozens of nongaming hotels and motels in Las Vegas. These properties range from budget to luxury, and, unlike the casinos, will be happy to have your entire family's business. You won't be able to sneak down to the craps table in the middle of the night, but you'll enjoy certain other benefits, such as easy access to your car, that are absent from the product mix of the large casino resorts.

On to question two. You can most definitely enjoy a whale of a vacation in Las Vegas if your real objective is to have fun as a family. The way to accomplish this, however, is to commit to being together, or, expressed differently, to pretty much swear off gambling. Go to Las Vegas with the attitude that you'll let the grinds and high rollers subsidize your bargain four-star resort, your endless buffets, and your lush Disneyesque swimming pool. The casinos are full of people busily losing money. Ride their coattails. Let them pick up the tab for the pirate battles, exploding volcanoes, and dancing fountains. Allow their losses to turn your beer budget into a champagne vacation.

BRING IT ON

Las Vegas is designed to separate you from your money, whether by gambling— the preferred manner—or spending, which does not offer quite as high a profit margin for proprietors. The malls of the resorts and hotels, as discussed in chapter 8, "Shopping for the Whole Family," are, for the most part, over-the-top castles of commerce. Though the city's exotic hotels are low priced in comparison to rooms in other destination locations, there are attractions (reviewed in chapters 6, 7, and 9) such as roller coaster and gondola rides, aquariums, dolphin habitats, IMAX movies, arcades, Humvee tours of the desert, simulated weightless flights, and numerous other (kid and adult) magnets that will nibble away at your vacation budget. That said, while some of Las Vegas's memorable experiences aren't exactly cheap, you can definitely have an amazing time whether you are on a budget-conscious vacation or a price-be-damned adventure.

Along with visiting the glitzy tourist attractions, consider discovering the city's past and present through its cultural offerings (also discussed in chapter 6), many of which are offered in settings that are a pleasant change from the man-made environments of the casino hotels. Hoover Dam, the Mormon Fort, and the Clark County Museum obviously provide very different views of the area than what you can garner "just" from the Strip.

The history and culture of Las Vegas are explored not only in museums and monuments, but also with diverse outdoor happenings. Rodeos, recreations of posse shootouts, and festivals celebrating the different traditions of the area's settlers help families explore Las Vegas's past. During the summer, there are opportunities to see classic family films screened outdoors under the stars. Nearby Nellis Air Force Base provides a chance to watch fighter jets up close, while those inclined toward the terpsichorean arts can see the ballet and/or a luau. Athletically inclined families can race BMX bikes and sports cars, or participate in or simply watch any number of indoor and outdoor sports. We were reminded by several locals that "kids under 12 fish free," meaning that fishing licenses are not required for that age group to try their hand at the fishing holes around town as well as at giant Lake Mead, which features fishing along with a slew of other water-related recreation. See chapters 6, 7, and 10 for more information on the many available activities and experiences in and around Las Vegas.

All that activity can build up an appetite, and though Las Vegas can be a gourmet's paradise of foie gras with chocolate sauce—something we actually saw on one restaurant's menu—feeding the kids something they'll like is no problem because every Strip hotel has a food court with a variety of quick meals and fast food. There are also the inevitable buffets and round-the-clock coffee shops, where your kids should be able to find *something* they'll like. We've made it a point to consider your family when reviewing the restaurants in chapter 5. Theme restaurants are a big draw here, especially for boys who can be coddled, entertained, *and* fed by the likes of NASCAR, Harley-Davidson, or ESPN. And while some fancy restaurants ban children under 5, others welcome children of all ages, going beyond offering booster chairs to actually making custom dishes for the little ones. Vegetarian or vegan family members will also find something for their dietary concerns on almost every menu.

Being a vegetarian in Vegas is easy, but being a teenager is always difficult, and in Vegas, it can be especially hard. Unless you are 21, you are not allowed on the casino floor, and if you look underage, trust us, you will be carded. There are less than a handful of all-age nightclubs, and none of those are located in the actual Las Vegas area. Teens and 'tweens are too old for day care at most hotels, yet too young to be allowed alone in the pool areas. They are not allowed on the Strip after 9pm, or in arcades unescorted during the late night/early morning hours. But do not despair; teens who live in Vegas manage to have plenty of fun, and so can yours. In fact, even the grumbling Goth, rebellious rocker, and truc-ulent teen should find something (they can choose from the likes of huge water parks, shows that will suit their tastes, arcades, movie theaters, malls, thrill rides, swimming pools, bookstores, record shops, comic book stores, and so much more) cool to do, see, eat, or buy in Las Vegas, which is saying a lot.

We are continually amazed at the number of fun activities for families in Las Vegas and even more impressed with the educational opportunities that can be cleverly disguised as fun. A trip to one museum lets you examine live, exotic desert creatures from just inches away, while a visit to another lets you explore sound waves and soap bubbles. In one casino hotel, you can take a quick trip to an Egyptian tomb, while others transport you to other distant times and places: Renaissance Venice, ancient Rome, the New York of the 1930s, a perfect Paris, and exotic deserts. Here in Vegas, you get quite a bang from your vacation buck!

When in Vegas, you won't be able to help noticing the number of tourists (from around both the country and the world) who have traveled to Vegas, kids in tow, to take advantage of both the adult- and child-oriented attractions the city offers. They know what you're about to find out: You can't help but be over-whelmed by the sheer amount of stuff to do and see in Las Vegas, but, then again, if all you like to do on vacation is relax and lounge around the pool, that, too, can be accomplished with minimum effort in this city, because, in reality, Las Vegas is a great family vacation spot, with something for everyone—just don't let the casino hotels in on the secret!

1 Frommer's Favorite Las Vegas Family Experiences

- **Watching the Free Bird Show at the Tropicana.** Tiana Carroll performs amazing stunts with her fine-feathered cast of amazing avians. They will entertain you with singing, dancing, riding a bicycle, flying through hoops on command, and juggling upside down. See p. 155.

- **Watching Statues at Caesars Palace.** The "statues" come astoundingly alive at two locations in Caesars Palace in the Forum Shops, accompanied by music, lasers, and fog, enthralling everyone around them. The Fountain Festival, the original statue show, stars Bacchus, the god of wine, and might actually get your children interested in Greco-Roman mythology. The newer show, more loosely drawn from classical literature, is full of explosions, thunder, and lightning. Both are huge favorites with children of all ages. For more information, see p. 156.

- **Lighting Up the Night at Fremont Street.** Fremont Street, the site of U2's video for "Still Haven't Found What I'm Looking For," is now closed to cars, and a projection canopy of 12.5 million LEDs electrifies the evening sky with brilliant changing colors. A 540,000-watt sound system accompanies the light-and-laser show. Between shows, which run five times a night, there are live music and entertainers performing along this 5-block-long promenade lined with shops and cafes. The Neon Museum provides additional glow with the original lamp from the Aladdin and other classic Vegas signs. See p. 157.

- **Exploring Lied Discovery Children's Museum.** Your entire family will have a blast piloting the Space Shuttle and composing tunes with your feet at this museum where over 100 exhibits are designed to be touched and played with. See p. 162.

- **Seeing the Pirate Battle at Treasure Island.** Five times nightly cannons boom as a ship of lusty sirens does battle with a rag-tag troop of pirates. The sirens, scantily clad, were substituted for the British Navy in an effort to make the pirate battle more adult. Though still pretty adolescent, the presentation features hard-driving music, some good choreography, and an arsenal of special effects. Swords are drawn, swashbucklers swash and buckle, plus there's fire and a sinking ship. All in all, it's a very satisfying experience (watch it from the simulated docks outside Treasure Island), and, for fun after the crowds have cleared, you can watch the sunken ship rise from the watery depths to do battle again. Alternatively, you can have dinner at Buccaneer Bay and see the whole thing from above. See p. 155.

- **Picnicking at the Family Film Fests.** You'll feel like a real local family when you grab some sandwiches and drinks from Capriotti's and, with a blanket wrangled from your hotel's housekeeping department, head out to one of several festivals held outdoors Thursdays, Fridays, and Saturdays at various park locations throughout the summer. The film fare tends toward newer releases, but they also screen Gen X adventure classics such as *Raiders of the Lost Ark* and musicals. And, if you tire of watching the stars on screen, you can lean back and count the ones in the sky. See p. 183 for more information on Las Vegas's parks.

- **Watching the White Tigers.** While visiting The Mirage,

Las Vegas & Environs

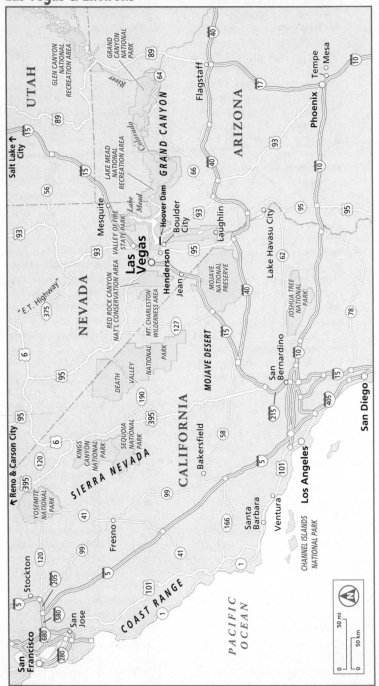

Siegfried and Roy's big cats stay in the White Tiger Habitat (yes, they are still there, despite the injuries one of them inflicted on Roy Horn during a tragic 2003 performance —it wasn't the tiger's fault—it acted like, well, a tiger), which is climate controlled and designed to replicate the tigers' natural environment. You can stay as long as you like waiting for the big cats to romp, roar, and roll. See p. 162.

- **Riding the Monorail.** Assuming that it's running (it's been experiencing some technical difficulties since its launch in 2004 and had just resumed operations at press time), take a ride from the MGM Grand to the Sahara on the Las Vegas Strip Monorail. The ride takes 14 minutes each way and affords behind-the-scenes glimpses of famous strip hotels before racing past the Wynn Las Vegas golf course and the Las Vegas Convention Center, to the end of the line at the Sahara. See p. 68.

- **Tossing Balls with the Dolphins at the Dolphin Habitat.** There is nothing cooler than playing ball with a water mammal. These dolphins don't do tricks, per se, but they will bounce balls back to you and their trainers, stand up on their tails, and do flips, not because they're trained to, but because they want to. See p. 162.

- **Counting the Moray Eels at Shark Reef, Mandalay Bay.** Supposedly, there are over 20 of the slinky, spotted sea creatures living in the vast coral reef here, but we only managed to count 8. It's also fun to give them names, because each has a distinctive look. Ella Eel, Elvis Eel, Irwin . . . you get the idea. See p. 164.

- **Feeling Brave After the Stratosphere Thrill Rides.** You'll bond on the adrenaline rush before,

during, and after a trip on the High Roller, the world's highest roller coaster; a drop on the Big Shot, a 160-foot free-fall ride on the Stratosphere's spire; and being dangled over the edge of the tower on X Scream. See p. 168.

- **Exploring the International Marketplace.** This vast warehouse, a secret to most visitors, stocks thousands of different foods from around the world. Gooey Japanese fruit candies in neon wrappers share space with tarragon soda pop from the Middle East and purple yam ice cream from the Philippines. See p. 208.

- **Racing Each Other in NASCAR Replicas.** At All-American Sports Park, families can race each other on one of three tracks in scaled-down NASCAR replicas. The Challenge track's two-seaters allow a parent or older child to drive with a passenger, while at the Sprint track, the small vehicles make it possible for younger kids to drive themselves. See p. 166.

- **Seeing the Dinosaurs Dance at the Las Vegas Natural History Museum.** Equipped with motion sensors, the recreations of *T. rex* and his dino buddies come alive, roaring and moving when you enter their display room. Live sharks swim in a nearby tank, and there's a cool collection of stuffed animals in displays designed to replicate their natural environment. See p. 172.

- **Traveling at Warp Speed.** If a trip to Vegas isn't out of this world enough for your family, try blasting off into hyperspace with the crew of the Enterprise at *Star Trek:* **The Experience.** Beam aboard, then save the universe. Even if you pass on the rides, you'll still get a kick out the History of the Future Museum, *Star Trek* memorabilia and themed shops, and a Trekker meal of Hamborger or Glop on a Stick in Quark's Bar. Yum. See p. 167.

- **Watching the Local Team Hit a Home Run.** Half the fun of going to a baseball game is eating hot dogs, popcorn, and peanuts. But at a Las Vegas 51s game, there's a good chance you'll see a budding baseball star hit his record-breaking run before he's called up to the majors; the 51s—who take their name from the alleged UFO-sighting ground Area 51 and have an alien as their logo—are the AAA (farm team) for the Los Angeles Dodgers. See p. 228.

- **Ordering in a Pizza.** Take a break from your sightseeing to relax in front of the TV and order up a pay-per-view movie. Then call out for a large pie from Metro Pizza, the city's best, who will actually deliver to your hotel room. Those ingredients should add up to decadent, silly fun that will help remind you of what being a family is all about. It will also hopefully revitalize you for your next adventure. See p. 142.

2 Best Hotel Bets

For the full descriptions of hotels below, please see chapter 4, "Family-Friendly Accommodations."

- **Most Family Friendly on the Strip:** Both **Excalibur,** 3850 Las Vegas Blvd. S. (℗ **877/750-5464** or 702/597-7777), and its North Strip sibling, **Circus Circus,** 2880 Las Vegas Blvd. S. (℗ **877/224-7287** or 702/734-0410), were designed with families in mind and feature regularly scheduled free entertainment and large arcades. Circus Circus also has its own theme park (with rides for all ages) and miniature golf. See p. 87 and 98, respectively.

- **Most Family Friendly off the Strip:** The **Orleans,** 4500 W. Tropicana Ave. (℗ **800/ORLEANS** or 702/365-7111), has a bowling alley and movie theaters and offers child care. **Sam's Town,** 5111 Boulder Hwy. (℗ **800/634-6371** or 702/456-7777), also features a multiplex theatre plus the free Sunset Stampede show and a large, beautiful indoor park with animatronic animals. See p. 112 and 109 respectively.

- **Best Suite Deals Close to the Strip: The Carriage House,** 105 E. Harmon Ave. (℗ **800/221-2301** or 702/798-1020), offers plenty of room for families in a nongaming environment 2 minutes from the Strip. A full kitchen in each suite also makes eat-in meals an option. And unlike hotels, there's full cable TV with over 40 channels, along with Nintendo at an hourly rate, plus free board games. See p. 102.

- **Best Suite Deals off the Strip:** A nongaming resort ideal for short- or long-term stays, **Desert Paradise,** 5165 S. Decatur Blvd. (℗ **877/257-0010** or 702/257-0010), offers complete apartments with their own washer/dryers, huge kitchens, full cable, and patio. With a barbecue area, lounge with large-screen TV, and a nice pool, this resort was designed with families in mind, and is a perfect getaway location. See p. 110.

- **Most Peace and Quiet on the Strip and the Most Child-Pampering Hotel:** You can't beat the nongaming **Four Seasons,** 3960 Las Vegas Blvd. S. (℗ **877/632-5200** or 702/632-5000), located at the southernmost tip of the Strip. The luxurious hotel pampers children as well as parents, providing small bathrobes and gift baskets for the kiddies. Rooms can be childproofed in advance of your arrival, ensuring your peace of mind. See p. 80.

- **Most Peace and Quiet off the Strip:** Staying in Henderson, at the ultrarestful **Green Valley Ranch** resort, 2300 Paseo Verde Drive (© **866/617-7777** or 702/782-9487), will give you plenty of peace and quiet in luxurious surroundings, plus many activities for the children. There's a casino on-site, but you can avoid it completely and just go to the on-site multiplex, play golf, or sun by the pool. See p. 113.

- **Best View:** Unless you are on a low floor, at night, you should get a view of something sparkling no matter where you stay. But the view standing on the tower atop the **Stratosphere,** 2000 Las Vegas Blvd. S. (© **800/998-6937** or 702/380-7777), located at the northernmost end of the Strip, tops them all. See p. 98.

- **When Price Is No Object: Caesars Palace,** 3570 Las Vegas Blvd. S. (© **800/634-6661** or 702/731-7110), with its hilarious Greco-Roman theme, provides an over-the-top vacation experience for all ages. And the Fountain Show and Forum Shops just add to the fun. See p. 90.

- **Best Lobby:** Huge statues of ancient Egyptian rulers greet you when you walk into the **Luxor,** 3900 Las Vegas Blvd. S. (© **800/288-1000** or 702/262-4000), making this a jaw-dropper for almost everyone. See p. 89.

- **Best Pool:** You can bob on a lazy river ride or body surf the gentle swells in the pools at both **Mandalay Bay,** 3950 Las Vegas Blvd. S. (© **877/632-7000** or 702/632-7000), or the **Monte Carlo,** 3770 Las Vegas Blvd. S. (© **800/311-8999** or 702/730-7777), but the best pool scene is at **The Flamingo Las Vegas,** 3555 Las Vegas Blvd. S. (© **800/732-2111** or 702/733-3111), where there are five pools, two whirlpools, a kiddie pool, and waterslides set in a tropical environment complete with exotic birds and koi ponds. See p. 89, 84, and 94 respectively.

- **Best Hotel Arcade:** Even though it's not a 24-hour game room, the Coney Island arcade in **New York–New York,** 3790 Las Vegas Blvd. S. (© **888/696-9887** or 702/740-6969), is the cleanest, best lit arcade in the entire city, with gleaming hardwood floors instead of the usual dark carpet. See p. 85.

- **Best Fitness Center:** Though **The Four Seasons,** 3960 Las Vegas Blvd. S. (© **877/632-5200** or 702/632-5000), is a very expensive hotel, unlike other casinos/resorts in the area, the use of their ultramodern, state-of-the-art health club is free. Other hotels, such as the **Fairfield Inn by Marriott,** 3850 Paradise Rd. (© **800/228-2800** or 702/791-0899), also offer free use of their exercise rooms, which, though small, can still make you break a sweat. For those who don't mind paying $25 a day for access to spa facilities, **The Venetian,** 3355 Las Vegas Blvd. S. (© **888/2-VENICE** or 702/414-1000), offers Canyon Ranch, a branch of what is considered one of the best spas in the United States. The fee gets you access to all the machines, saunas, and exercise classes Canyon Ranch offers, including yoga and Pilates. There's also a rock-climbing wall. See p. 80, 108, and 93, respectively.

- **Best Bathrooms:** Marvelous marble everywhere graces the very large bathrooms at **The Venetian,** 3355 Las Vegas Blvd. S. (© **888/2-VENICE** or 702/414-1000), but for sheer shower and bath opulence, we opt for **Mandalay Bay,** 3950 Las Vegas Blvd. S. (© **877/632-7000** or 702/632-7000), with glassed-in showers and sunken tubs, plus bathrobes available upon request. See p. 93 and 89, respectively.

- **Best Shopping Area:** While grown-ups may love the luxuries on display at **Via Bellagio** in the **Bellagio,** 3600 Las Vegas Blvd. S. (© **888/987-6667** or 702/693-7111), kids will have more fun at **Caesars Forum Shops** at **Caesars Palace,** 3570 Las Vegas Blvd. S. (© **800/634-6661** or 702/731-7110), **The Venetian's Grand Canal Shoppes,** 3355 Las Vegas Blvd. S. (© **888/2-VENICE** or 702/414-1000), or even the **Desert Passage** at the **Aladdin/Planet Hollywood,** 3667 Las Vegas Blvd. S. (© **877/333-WISH** or 702/785-5555), for their mix of family entertainment and eye candy. **Las Vegas Premium Outlets:** 875 S. Grand Central Pkwy., (© **702/474-7500**) located near downtown Las Vegas, offers 120 prestige-brand outlet stores. See p. 193, 195, and 192, respectively.

- **Best Hotel Coffee Shop:** Kids under 12 will enjoy the carousel theme of the **Pink Pony Cafe** inside **Circus Circus,** 2880 Las Vegas Blvd. S. (© **877/224-7287** or 702/734-0410), with its circus placemats and crayons. The hipster groove of **Mr. Lucky's 24/7** at the **Hard Rock Hotel & Casino,** 4455 Paradise Rd. (© **800/473-ROCK** or 702/693-5000), is more appealing to teens. But hands down, visitors go out of their way to visit **Calypsos** at the **Tropicana Resort & Casino,** 3801 Las Vegas Blvd. S. (© **888/826-8767** or 702/739-2222), a classic coffee shop, which allows you to build your own burger and features classic coffee

shop fare (try the slab of pound cake topped with fruit and frozen yogurt) in a tropical-themed environment. See p. 139, 142, and 129, respectively.

- **Best Hotel Restaurant for Kids:** The **Rainforest Cafe at MGM Grand,** 3799 Las Vegas Blvd. S. (© **800/929-1111** or 702/891-7777), features a kid's menu, crayons, good food, and, best of all, animatronic animals and thunderstorms, plus sleight-of-hand magicians at breakfast. See p. 128.

- **Best Hotel Kids' Program:** **KidQuest,** in the Sunset Station, 1301 W. Sunset Rd. (© **888/786-7389** or 702/547-7777) is a fun, safe place to tuck the kids for a while. See p. 62.

- **Best Hotel Pet Programs: Hawthorn Suites,** 5051 Duke Ellington Way (© **800/527-1133** or 702/739-7000), welcomes any size, well-behaved Fido. See p. 105.

- **Best Hotel Buffet: The Flamingo,** 3555 Las Vegas Blvd. S. (© **800/732-2111** or 702/733-3111), feeds kids under 12 for half price at breakfast, brunch, and dinner, with a view of birds, habitat, and fishponds. See p. 148.

- **Tops for Toddlers:** For convenience, the **Boardwalk Hotel & Casino,** 3750 Las Vegas Blvd. S. (© **866/915-3097** or 702/735-2400), wins hands down. The elevators are close to the main entrance and the casino is out of sight, making checking in and getting to your room a breeze. The self-parking is also very close to the entrance if you'd prefer to use that to its valets. But for sensory stimulation, **Circus Circus,** 2880 Las Vegas Blvd. S. (© **877/224-7287** or 702/734-0410), offers a midway, clowns, jugglers, and lots of flashing lights. The **Excalibur,** 3850 Las Vegas Blvd. S. (© **877/750-5464** or 702/597-7777), also has jugglers and throws in puppet shows and story times as well. See p. 86, 98, and 87, respectively.

- **Tops for Teens:** Staying at the **Hard Rock,** 4455 Paradise Rd. (© **800/473-ROCK** or 702/693-5000), can fill your teen with rock star dreams, plus *you'll* get points

for being cool. Young sophisticates will enjoy the **Monte Carlo Resort & Casino,** 3770 Las Vegas Blvd. S. (© **800/311-8999** or 702/730-7777), or **The Venetian,** 3355 Las Vegas Blvd. S. (© **888/2-VENICE** or 702/414-1000), with their luxurious European style. See p. 104, 84, and 93, respectively.

3 Best Dining Bets

For more information, please see chapter 5, "Family-Friendly Restaurants."

- **Best Burger:** Lots of folks love the 24-hour **Tiffany's Cafe at White Cross Drugs,** 1700 Las Vegas Blvd. S. (© **702/382-1733**), on the north end of the Strip, but we are actually partial to the juicy, and pricey, burger available at lunchtime only at **Delmonico Steakhouse** in The Venetian, 3355 Las Vegas Blvd. S. (© **702/414-3737**)—it's served with caramelized onions and Vermont cheddar, and made according to celebrity chef Emeril Lagasse's specifications. For drive-through, you can't beat **In-N-Out Burger,** 4888 Industrial Rd. at Tropicana (© **800/786-1000**), where vegetarians can order cheese only, and those on Atkins can get a protein burger (no bun). Many locals agree consider this the best burger joint in town. See p. 140, 133, and 129, respectively.
- **Best Kids' Menu:** Buffets that offer price breaks for kids, such as those at the **Luxor,** 3900 Las Vegas Blvd. S. (© **800/288-1000** or 702/262-4000), or **The Flamingo,** 3555 Las Vegas Blvd. S. (© **800/732-2111** or 702/733-3111), actually can give kids a feeling of empowerment as they choose their own meals. Children can eat for half price at the buffet and at Benihana in the **Las Vegas Hilton,** 3000 Paradise Rd.

(© **888/732-7117** or 702/732-5111), but the best actual kid's menu is at the **Verandah** at the **Four Seasons,** 3960 Las Vegas Blvd. S. (© **877/632-5000** or 702/632-5000), which offers lots of kids' favorites, including pizza, hot dogs, and PB&J sandwiches. See p. 145, 148, 149, and 128, respectively.

- **Best Tacos:** El Sombrero, at 807 S. Main St. (© **702/382-9234**), serves by far the best tacos in Las Vegas, and they have been doing so for more than 50 years. Ask for any kind you like; chef Jose will put them together for you. See p. 145.
- **Best Secret Meal:** It's not on the menu, and it's a real deal—steak and shrimp, a Vegas classic, for $7.77 at **Mr. Lucky's 24/7** in the Hard Rock, 4455 Paradise Rd. (© **800/473-ROCK** or 702/693-5592). Someone in your party should order it, just to prove that parents know cool stuff that isn't always written down. See p. 142.
- **Best Food Court:** Most of the hotels have the same offerings (McDonalds, Nathan's, Häagen-Dazs, Starbucks, and the like), so that it's nice to find some different options. The food court at the **MGM Grand,** 3799 Las Vegas Blvd. S. (© **800/929-1111** or 702/891-7777), has the usual suspects mentioned above, but also has

Mama Ilardo's Pizza, which does a nice slice, and Hamada Orient Express, which sells Chinese and Japanese food, including boxes of decent sushi. Menus are in Japanese and Mandarin, along with English, so you know it's the real deal. See p. 124.

- **Best Alternative Breakfast:** Some kids, and grown-ups, just don't like breakfast food. And even if you're a fan of eggs and waffles, that fare can get pretty dull day after day. Along with the usual morning meals, **Chin Chin,** in New York–New York, 3790 Las Vegas Blvd. S. (© **800/693-6763** or 702/740-6300), serves traditional Chinese breakfast foods such as *congee* (rice porridge) and *dim sum* (small individual dishes, like steamed dumplings filled with meat, vegetables, or seafood, and many other dishes), including the Chinese version of a barbecue sandwich, *cha su bao,* chunks of pork or chicken and sweet sauce tucked inside a white doughy bun. See p. 126.
- **Best Pizza:** Practically every hotel food court has a pizza stand, and there are also nouvelle-style places like **California Pizza Kitchen,** in The Mirage, 3400 Las Vegas Blvd. S. (© **702/791-7223**), and **Wolfgang Puck Cafe,** in the MGM Grand, 3799 Las Vegas Blvd. S. (© **800/929-1111** or 702/895-9653), throughout Vegas for fans of exotic toppings on their 'za. However, **Metro Pizza,** 1395 E. Tropicana Ave. (© **702/736-1955**), located about 15 minutes away from the Strip, not only serves up the best slice in town, but also delivers to all major hotels. See p. 138, 128, and 142, respectively.
- **Best Ice Cream: Olio Gelato,** in the MGM Grand (3799 Las Vegas Blvd. S.; © **800/929-1111** or 702/891-7777), serves up a low-fat, low-sugar version of ice cream in a space-age setting. **Schrafft's** in New York–New York, 3790 Las Vegas Blvd. S. (© **800/693-6763** or 702/740-6969), serves up frozen custard, along with their own brand of ice cream. See p. 135 and 85, respectively.
- **Best Place for Kids to Have an Exciting View While Dining: Buccaneer Bay Club** at Treasure Island, 3300 Las Vegas Blvd. S. (© **877/793-7111** or 702/894-7223), wins hands down with kids over 5 because they can watch the *Sirens of TI* battle from the window seats. If you don't manage to reserve one of these, the wait staff will announce "Pirate battle!" at the start of the combat, so you can rush to the windows and watch; they'll hold your order until you return. See p. 132.
- **Best Educational Restaurant: America,** located in New York–New York, 3790 Las Vegas Blvd. S. (© **800/693-6763** or 702/740-6451), features food from around the United States; each menu item is designated with its reputed place of origin. That alone makes for some interesting conversation, but the really neat (yet educational) feature is the 90 ft. × 20 ft. map of the United States, complete with geographic and topographic features. See p. 125.
- **Best Milkshake: Tiffany's Cafe at White Cross Drugs,** 1700 Las Vegas Blvd. S. © **702/382-1733**), on the North Strip, serves them cold, thick, and creamy. If you'd rather sample the fountain goods in a hotel coffee shop, **Roxy's Diner,** in the Stratosphere, 2000 Las Vegas Blvd. S. (© **800/998-6937** or 702/380-7777), pours a good one. See p. 140 and 98, respectively.
- **Best Thai: Lotus of Siam,** 953 E. Sahara Ave. (© **702/735-3033**),

located about 10 minutes east of the Strip, serves the best Thai food in the entire United States, according to food critics, both amateur and professional (*Gourmet* magazine's Jonathan Gold being one of the LoS's biggest fans). If you have a craving for satay, this is the place to sate it, because you won't find much Thai food at any of the casinos/resorts. See p. 141.

- **Best Hot Dog:** Ubiquitous Nathan's Hot Dogs, with their perfect texture, savory taste, and low cost make them a great snack or quick meal. You'll find a Nathan's at Monte Carlo, 3770 Las Vegas Blvd. S. (© **800/311-8999** or 702/730-7777), New York–New York, 3790 Las Vegas Blvd. S. (© **888/696-9887** or 702/740-6969), and MGM Grand, 3799 Las Vegas Blvd. S. (© **800/929-1111** or 702/891-7777). See p. 84, 85, and 82, respectively.

- **Best Selection:** The **Grand Lux Café** at The Venetian, 3355 Las Vegas Blvd. S. (© **888/2-VENICE** or 702/414-1000), gives you a choice of over 150 entrees, appetizers, salads, and desserts, all of which are big enough to split between two or three people. The cuisine jumps from Italian to pan-Asian to American, with stops in Europe, providing a huge, mostly very tasty

selection. Plus, there's a kids' menu, which your server will recite for you, because it's not printed in the book-sized menu you are handed at the table. See p. 137.

- **Best Romantic Outdoor Restaurant:** The patio at **Mon Ami Gabi** at Paris Las Vegas, 3655 Las Vegas Blvd. S. (© **702/944-4224**), faces the Bellagio waters show, making this French bistro the most romantic spot on the Strip as the fountains spray and dance in time to music. After a meal of oysters, grilled steak, or roasted chicken; wine; profiteroles; and espresso, stroll through the adjacent casino hotel. Then whisper in your beloved's ear, "We'll always have Paris . . . Las Vegas." See p. 134.

- **Best Romantic Restaurant View (for a Night When You Hired a Sitter):** The food at **Alizé** is as impressive as its view from three huge windows overlooking the Strip from atop the Palms Hotel, 4321 W. Flamingo Rd. (© **702/951-7000**). Chef Andre Rochat, from Andre's French Restaurant and Andre's at the Monte Carlo (two of city's most acclaimed French restaurants) and Chef Michael Demeres, formerly of Napa, continually create and execute meals of epicurean perfection. See p. 150.

4 The Rest of the Best

- **Best Place to Run Around:** Providing a variety of outdoor diversions, from picnicking to skateboarding and in-line skating, plus a dog park, a radio-controlled miniboat area, and a horseshoe pitch, **Sunset Park,** 2601 Sunset Rd. (© **702/455-8200**), located south of the Strip near McCarran International Airport, is a welcome respite from much of the city's artificial atmosphere. See p. 183.

- **Best Bookstore:** While both **Waldenbooks** in the Fashion Show Mall, 3200 Las Vegas Blvd. S. (© **702/733-1049**), and **Virgin Megastore** at Caesars, 3500 Las Vegas Blvd. S. (© **702/696-7100**), are easily accessed from the Strip, **Dead Poet Books**, 3874 W. Sahara Ave. (© **702/227-4070**), has a huge selection of used books for adults and children, and is the perfect place to fill up on literature at a discount. See p. 198 and 197, respectively.

- **Best Toy Store: FAO Schwarz,** located in the Forum Shops at Caesars Palace, 3500 Las Vegas Blvd. S. (© **702/796-6500**), is three stories of fabulous toys—including a room of Barbies for girls, action figures for boys, and the store's trademark supersoft stuffed animals—stocked in a section that replicates Homer's Trojan Horse. Plus, they can hold a birthday party for your wee one, which could include a sleepover in the tree house section of the store, if you want (and can afford it). See p. 211.

- **Best History Lesson:** Your child can join the posse and head out to hunt down the bad guy or watch the goofy Western melodramas

that are staged ever half-hour in **Old Nevada on the Bonnie Springs Ranch** (© **702/875-4191**). Explore Boot Hill Cemetery—and other locations that recreate pioneer icons—with your family. Along with the Western town, cowhands, and petting zoo, there's a caged collection of rescued wildlife and the most reasonably priced horseback rides in the Las Vegas area. See p. 257.

- **Best Place to Beat the Heat:** Head for **Mount Charleston** in the Spring Mountains 40 minutes to the northwest of Las Vegas. While everyone else is sizzling in the desert heat, you'll be walking among tall conifers and drinking in the cool mountain air. Best of all, it's free! See p. 260.

Planning a Family Trip to Las Vegas

Before any trip, you need to do some advance planning. In the pages that follow, you'll find everything you need to know to handle the practical details of planning your trip in advance: airlines and area airports, a calendar of events, a list of major conventions you may want to avoid, resources for those of you with special needs, what you can do to get your kids interested in a trip to Las Vegas, and much more.

We also suggest that you check out chapter 9, "Entertainment for the Whole Family," before you leave home; if you want to see the most popular shows, it's a good idea to call ahead and order tickets well in advance to avoid disappointment. The same goes if you want to dine in one of the city's top restaurants; head to chapter 5, "Family-Friendly Dining," for full restaurant reviews and contact information.

1 Visitor Information

For advance information, call or write the **Las Vegas Convention and Visitors Authority,** 3150 Paradise Rd., Las Vegas, NV 89109 (© **877/VISITLV,** 877/847-4858, or 702/892-7575; www.vegasfreedom.com). They can send you a comprehensive packet containing brochures, a map, a show guide, an events calendar, and an attractions list; help you find a hotel that meets your specifications (and even make reservations); and tell you if a major convention is scheduled during the time you would like to visit Las Vegas. Or, stop by when you're in town. They're open daily from 8am to 5pm.

Another excellent information source (more oriented toward local businesses rather than convention business) is the **Las Vegas Chamber of Commerce,** 3720 Howard Hughes Pkwy., #100, Las Vegas, NV 89109 (© **702/735-1616;** www.lvchamber. com). Ask them to send you their *Visitor's Guide,* which contains extensive

information about accommodations, attractions, excursions, children's activities, and more. They're open Monday to Friday 8am to 5pm.

For information on all of Nevada, including Las Vegas, contact the **Nevada Commission on Tourism** (© **800/638-2328;** www.travelnevada. com), which has a comprehensive information packet on Nevada.

There's also a lot of great information for visitors on the Internet, including specific Las Vegas websites dedicated to children. **Las Vegas Kids (www.las vegaskids.com)** lists basic information, including information on local child care and accommodations, and has an e-mail list that features family-related discounts.

Check out **I Love Las Vegas** (www. ilovelasvegas.com) to see the production shows and celebrity headliners that will be playing during your visit, and **Las Vegas Advisor** (www.lasvegas advisor.com) for meal deals, freebies, show reviews, and everything you'd want to know about gambling. Although it primarily covers all things Disney, **Mousesavers** (www.mouse savers.com) is the best site on the Internet for scoring great deals on rental cars. Similarly, **Travelaxe** (www. travelaxe.com) will make finding the best deals on lodging a breeze, especially in Las Vegas.

Destination: Las Vegas—Red Alert Checklist

- Did you bring copies of vaccination records if you plan on leaving your children at any of the hotel child-care centers?
- Did you bring copies of insurance cards for you and your children?
- Did you pack sunblock, sunglasses, and wide-brimmed hats for the entire group?
- Did you pack lightweight, long-sleeved, button-down shirts to keep off both the hot sun and the chilly casino air?
- Did you pack collared shirts and khakis or slacks for the men and a dress or nice blouse and pants or skirt for women for dinner in a finer, more expensive restaurant?
- Do any theater, restaurant, or travel reservations need to be booked in advance? If at all possible, Celine Dion, Cirque du Soleil's productions, the Blue Man Group, and other top attractions you may want to see should be booked well before you arrive in Las Vegas, as should restaurants like Buccaneer Bay, if you want a view of the pirate battle.
- Did you make sure that the attractions you want to see are open? Some attractions, such as the Hoover Dam observation decks, may be closed for security reasons. Also note that outdoor roller coasters and the *Sirens of TI* pirate battle close during windy and inclement weather. It's also possible that scheduled tours, festivals, and special events may be canceled or rescheduled. Additionally, you should double-check the opening and closing hours of places you really want to go.
- If you purchased traveler's checks, have you recorded the check numbers and stored the documentation separately from the checks?
- Did you pack your camera, an extra set of camera batteries, and purchase enough film? If you packed film in your checked baggage, did you invest in protective pouches to shield it from airport x-rays?
- Did you pack an extra battery and the charger for your cellphone?
- Do you have a safe, accessible place to store money?
- Did you bring your ID cards that could entitle you to discounts such as AAA and AARP cards, student IDs, etc.?
- Do your children who are old enough to need photo ID have theirs with them?
- Did you bring emergency drug prescriptions and extra glasses and/ or contact lenses?
- Do you have your credit card PINs?
- If you have an e-ticket, do you have documentation?
- Did you leave a copy of your itinerary with someone at home?

Websites maintained by the local papers will give you and your family an overview of Las Vegas's current events, politics, and entertainment. Check out the *Las Vegas Review-Journal* (**www. lvrj.com**) and the alternative newspaper, the *Las Vegas Mercury* (**www. lasvegasmercury.com**) for lots of information.

Citysearch offers comprehensive city information for hundreds of locations across America. Click onto www. lasvegas.citysearch.com for both real-people and professional critics' reviews of restaurants, shows, and other attractions. **Digitalcity** (www.digitalcity. com/lasvegas) is a similar city guide site.

Designed for travelers, **Vegas4Visitors** (www.vegas4visitors.com) offers reviews, articles, and commentary, with a special "for families" section. **Vegas. com** (www.vegas.com) reviews shows, adding a sidebar that comments on the age appropriateness and nudity factor.

Also see "Planning Your Trip Online," later in this chapter, which recommends more useful sites.

2 Money

ATMs

There is an ATM within feet of you at almost all times in Las Vegas; no one in the city wants you to find yourself without cash that you could lose in a slot! Beware of withdrawal charges, though, which can often run as high as $2 or $3 per transaction; the highest charges are usually for commercial machines in convenience stores and hotel lobbies. On top of this, the bank from which you withdraw cash may charge its own fee. Nevertheless, ATMs are a safe and convenient way of accessing cash while you're away from home.

Almost all of the ATMs in Las Vegas are linked to a national network that most likely includes your bank at home. **Cirrus** (© **800/424-7787;** www.mastercard.com) and **PLUS** (© **800/843-7587;** www.visa.com) are the two most popular networks; check the back of your ATM card to see which network your bank belongs to, and use the 800 numbers or Web addresses above to locate the ATMs closest to your Las Vegas destination.

Additionally, make sure you know your four-digit PIN before you leave home and find out your daily withdrawal limit before you depart: You can get cash advances on your credit card at an ATM, but keep in mind that credit card companies try to protect themselves from theft by limiting the funds someone can withdraw away from home. It's therefore best to call your credit card company before you leave and let them know where you're going and how much you plan to spend.

TRAVELER'S CHECKS

Traveler's checks are something of an anachronism from the days before the ATM made cash accessible at any time. Traveler's checks used to be the only sound alternative to traveling with dangerously large amounts of cash. They were as reliable as currency, but, unlike cash, could be replaced if lost or stolen.

Tips Small Change

Always keep some small bills on hand when you're in Las Vegas. Petty cash will come in handy for tipping and public transportation. Consider keeping your small bills separate from your larger bills, so they are readily accessible. This system will also help you become less of a target for theft.

What Things Cost	US$
Hot dog at hotel snack bar	2.00
Medium soda at hotel snack bar	1.50
Apple juice at hotel convenience store	2.00
Bottled water at hotel convenience store	2.00
Slice of cheese pizza at hotel food court	3.00
McDonald's Happy Meal	2.50
4-oz. jar baby food	0.80
Tube of sunblock	10.00
Package of diapers	7.00
Admission to movie:	
Child	5.50
Adult	8.75
Admission to Imperial Palace Auto Collection:	
Child	3.00
Student	3.00
Adult	6.95
Admission to *Tournament of Kings:*	
Child under 4	free
Ages 4 and above	50.00
Cab fare from Strip to Downtown	15.00
Trolley ride from Strip to Downtown	1.65
One game of bowling	2.00
One video game	1.00–2.00

These days, however, traveler's checks seem less necessary because most cities have 24-hour ATMs that allow you to withdraw amounts of cash as needed. And, naturally, in Las Vegas, the casinos have ATMs at every turn. However, keep in mind that you will likely be charged an ATM withdrawal fee if the bank is not your own (and in Las Vegas's casinos and hotels, the bank is *never* your bank), so if you're withdrawing money every day, you might be better off with traveler's checks—provided that you don't mind showing identification every time you want to cash one.

You can get traveler's checks at almost any bank. **American Express** offers denominations of $20, $50, $100, $500, and (for cardholders only) $1,000. You'll pay a service charge ranging from 1% to 4%. You can also get American Express traveler's checks over the phone by calling ✆ **800/221-7282;** Amex gold and platinum cardholders who use this number are exempt from the 1% fee.

Visa offers traveler's checks at Citibank locations nationwide, as well as at several other banks. The service charge ranges between 1.5% and 2%; checks come in denominations of $20, $50, $100, $500, and $1,000. Call ✆ **800/732-1322** for information. AAA members can obtain Visa checks without a fee at most AAA offices. **MasterCard** also offers traveler's checks. Call ✆ **800/223-9920** for a location near you.

Tips **Dear Visa: I'm off to Vegas!**

Some credit card companies recommend that you notify them of any impending trip so that they don't become suspicious when the card is used numerous times away from home and block your charges. Even if you don't call your credit card company in advance, you can always call the card's toll-free emergency number (see below) if a charge is refused—a good reason to carry the phone number with you. But perhaps the most important lesson here is to carry more than one card with you on your trip; a card might not work for any number of reasons, so having a backup is the smart way to go.

CREDIT CARDS

Credit cards are invaluable when traveling. They are a safe way to carry money and provide a convenient record of all your expenses. You can also withdraw cash advances from your credit cards at any bank (though you'll start paying hefty interest on the advance the moment you receive the cash). At most banks, you don't even need to go to a teller; you can get a cash advance at the ATM if you know your PIN access code. If you've forgotten yours, or didn't even know you had one, call the number on the back of your credit card and ask the bank to send it to you. It usually takes 5 to 7 business days, though some banks will provide the number over the phone if you tell them your mother's maiden name or pass some other security clearance. All credit cards—American Express, Diners Club, Discover, MasterCard, and Visa, along with their foreign counterparts such as JCB and Barclays—are accepted in Las Vegas.

WHAT TO DO IF YOUR WALLET IS LOST OR STOLEN

Be sure to tell all of your credit card companies the minute you discover your wallet has been lost or stolen and file a report at the nearest police precinct. Your credit card company or insurer may require a police report number or record of the loss. Most credit card companies have an emergency toll-free number to call if your card is lost or stolen; they may be able to wire you a cash advance immediately or deliver an emergency credit card in a day or two. Visa's U.S. emergency number is ✆ **800/847-2911** or 410/581-9994. American Express card-holders and traveler's check holders should call ✆ **800/221-7282.** MasterCard holders should call ✆ **800/307-7309** or 636/722-7111. For other credit cards, call the toll-free number directory at ✆ **800/555-1212.** If you choose to carry traveler's checks, be sure to keep a record of their serial numbers separate from your checks. You'll get a refund faster if you know the numbers.

If you need emergency cash over the weekend when all banks and American Express offices are closed, you can have money wired to you via **Western Union** (✆ **800/325-6000;** www.westernunion.com).

Identity theft or fraud are potential complications of losing your wallet, especially if you've lost your driver's license along with your cash and credit cards. Notify the major credit-reporting bureaus immediately; placing a fraud alert on your records may protect you against liability for criminal activity. The three major U.S. credit-reporting agencies are **Equifax** (✆ **800/766-0008;** www.equifax.com), **Experian** (✆ **888/397-3742;** www.experian.com), and **TransUnion** (✆ **800/680-7289;** www.transunion.

Tips According to the Record

Before you travel, take an inventory of the contents of your billfold. List the customer service and "lost card" numbers from the back of your credit cards, phone cards, and ATM cards, as well as the numbers of your frequent flyer accounts and important memberships such as AAA and AARP. Also record relevant info from your health insurance card and auto insurance card. Finally, make a copy of your driver's license and passport to have as a backup.

---

com). Finally, if you've lost all forms of photo ID call your airline and explain the situation; they might allow you to board the plane if you have a copy of your passport or birth certificate and a copy of the police report you've filed.

3 When to Go

Because most of a Las Vegas vacation is usually spent indoors, you can have a good time here year-round. That said, the most pleasant seasons here are spring and fall, especially if you want to experience the great outdoors.

Weekdays are considerably less crowded than weekends. Holidays are always a mob scene and come accompanied by high hotel prices. Hotel prices also skyrocket when big conventions and special events are taking place. The slowest times of the year are July and August, the week before Christmas, and the week after New Year's.

If a major convention is to be held during your trip, you might want to change your date because rooms will be hard to get and will be more expensive during that time. Check the box later in this section for convention dates, and contact the **Las Vegas Convention and Visitors Authority** (© **877/VISITLV,** 877/847-4858, or 702/892-7575; www.vegasfreedom. com), because convention schedules often change.

THE WEATHER

First of all, Vegas isn't always hot, but when it is, it's *really* hot. One thing you'll hear again and again is that even though Las Vegas gets very hot, the dry desert heat is not unbearable. This is true, except in most of the hotel pool areas, which are surrounded by massive hotels covered in mirrored glass, which acts like a giant magnifying glass on the antlike people below. Still, generally, the humidity in Vegas averages a low 22%, and even on very hot days, there's apt to be a breeze. Also, except on the hottest summer days, there's almost always relief at night when temperatures often drop by at least 20°F (–7°C).

But this is the desert, and it's not hot all year round. It can get quite cold, especially in the winter, when, at night, it can drop to 30°F (–1°C) and lower. In the winter of 1998 to 1999, it actually snowed in Vegas, dropping nearly 2 inches on the Strip. There's nothing quite like the sight of Luxor's Sphinx covered in snow. The breeze can also become a cold, biting, strong wind of up to 40 mph and more. And so, there are entire portions of the year when you won't be using that hotel swimming pool at all (even if you want to—be aware that most of the hotels close huge chunks of those fabulous swimming pool areas for "the season," which can be as long as Labor Day to Memorial Day). If you aren't traveling in the height of summer, bring something for warmth. Also,

Las Vegas's Average Temperatures (°F/°C)

	Jan	Feb	Mar	Apr	May	June	July	Aug	Sept	Oct	Nov	Dec
Average Temp. (°F)	47	52	58	66	75	86	91	89	81	69	55	47
(°C)	8	11	14	19	24	30	33	32	27	21	13	8
Avg. High Temp. (°F)	57	63	69	78	88	99	104	102	94	81	66	57
(°C)	14	17	21	26	31	37	40	39	34	27	19	14
Avg. Low Temp. (°F)	37	41	47	54	63	72	78	77	69	57	44	37
(°C)	3	5	8	12	17	22	26	25	21	14	7	3
Average Precip. (in.)	.59	.69	.59	.15	.24	.08	.44	.45	.31	.24	.31	.40

remember sunscreen and hats—even if it's not all that hot, you and your kids can burn very easily and very fast in these parts. You should see (and not be among!) all the lobster-red people glowing in the casinos at night.

LAS VEGAS CALENDAR OF KID-FRIENDLY EVENTS

You may be surprised to learn that Las Vegas actually does have annual community events. Granted, they don't have as many as most tourist cities, and the reason for that is Las Vegas's very raison d'être: the gaming industry. This town wants its visitors spending their money in the casinos, not at Renaissance fairs and parades. However, we know you'd like to spend your vacation doing fun things with your family, so we compiled a list of the best family-friendly events below.

When in town, check the local paper and call the **Las Vegas Convention and Visitors Authority** (© **877/VISITLV,** 877/847-4858, or 702/892-7575; www.vegas freedom.com) or the **Chamber of Commerce** (© **702/735-1616;** www.lv chamber.com) to find out about other events that may be scheduled during your visit.

The **Clark County Parks and Recreation Department** (© **702/455-8200;** www.co.clark.nv.us/parks/homepage.htm) also provides an excellent resource for children's activities and will, upon request, mail you a catalog of upcoming events. The city also has a Web page (**www.ci.las-vegas.**

nv.us), which lists local parks and has sidebars leading you to cultural and recreational events.

Additionally, Las Vegas is rich in performing arts organizations and has teams for all major sports, so there's almost always a performance or sporting event to be seen, if that's your family's cup of tea.

January

Martin Luther King, Jr., Parade. This lively parade along Fremont Street, held during the week surrounding MLK's birthday, January 15, is the culmination of a week-long celebration honoring the slain civil rights leader, which includes a gospel concert and poetry reading.

Chinese New Year. Las Vegas's Asian community comes out in full force for this lunar festival, with an all-day celebration that includes a parade, drummers, dancers, martial artists, and a large variety of Asian food. Held at Chinatown Plaza, 4255 Spring Mountain Rd., the New Year can fall between the last week of January and the third week of February. © **702/221-8448;** www.lvchinatown.com.

March

Great Las Vegas Craft Festival. One-of-a-kind arts and crafts are on display indoors at Cashman Field, a huge athletic park, during this semi-annual event (also held in

Major Convention Dates

Listed below are Las Vegas's major annual conventions for 2005 (30,000 and up expected visitors), with projected attendance figures; believe us, unless you're actually coming to town to attend them, you probably want to avoid the biggies. Contact the **Las Vegas Convention and Visitors Authority** (✆ **877/VISITLV**, 877/847-4858, or 702/892-7575; www.vegasfreedom.com) to double-check the latest info before you commit to your travel dates, because convention schedules frequently change.

Event	Dates	Expected Attendance
Consumer Electronics Show	Jan 6–9	115,000
World of Concrete Exposition	Jan 17–21	75,000
World Floor Covering Associates	Jan 26–28	41,000
Men's Apparel Guild in California (MAGIC)	Feb 14–17	90,000
Associated Surplus Dealers	Feb 27–Mar 3	52,000
Construction Expo	Mar 15–19	135,000
National Association of Broadcasters (NAB)	Apr 18–21	125,000
Kitchen/Bath Industry Show	May 10–12	70,000
JCK Show	June 3–7	40,000
Associated Surplus Dealers	Aug 14–18	52,000
Men's Apparel Guild in California (MAGIC)	Aug 29–Sept 1	90,000
AAPEX	Nov 1–4	130,000
Comdex	Nov 14–17	50,000

Nov), including handmade toys like kaleidoscopes, puppets, and whirly-gigs. Musicians and magicians perform throughout the 3-day event, which usually takes place on the second-to-last weekend in March. ✆ **702/386-7184;** www.stevepowers.com.

April

Clark County Rodeo and Fair. Riding and roping are just part of the fun at this traditional Western fair. There's also a junior rodeo, livestock shows, carnival food, talent shows, and best of all, pig races. The rodeo and fair is held in mid-April. ✆ **888/876-FAIR;** www.ccfair.com.

May

Cinco de Mayo Festival. This large fiesta, held in Lorenzi Park on one of the first weekends in the month, has a special children's area, plus crafts, music, and dancing, as well as food from almost two dozen vendors. ✆ **702/229-6792.**

Jazz in the Park. This free outdoor evening series, at the Clark County

Amphitheatre, runs through July, drawing all ages of jazz fans. Big names and local combos perform styles ranging from Chicago to New Orleans to West Coast jazz. The series is a good way to introduce your children to this truly all-American music genre. The series begins the second week in May. ℭ **702/455-8200;** www.co.clark.nv.us/parks/Events_Calendar.htm.

Pride Festival. Gay, lesbian, bi, and transgender families have their own groups marching in the parade along Fourth Street in Downtown, and the festival at the parade's end has a children's play area with clowns, magicians, and face-painting. Naturally, open-minded straight families are welcome to this celebration of unity in diversity, held in mid-May. ℭ **702/225-3389;** www.lasvegaspride.org.

June

Las Vegas Jazz Festival. World-class jazz musicians are invited to this relatively new but growing festival held at the Fremont Street Experience for 3 days, usually in early June. This rollicking event will get your family's toes tapping and spirits soaring. ℭ **800/249-3559;** www.vegasexperience.com.

Friday Family Film Fest. As the sun sets, the stars come out on-screen. Pack a picnic meal or grab snacks from the vendors and enjoy adventure and family films, all PG- or G-rated. The locations vary between various county parks; call for details, location, and screening schedule toward the beginning of May for the most up-to-date information for the Fest, which usually begins the first weekend in June. ℭ **702/455-8200;** www.co.clark.nv.us/parks/Events_Calendar.htm.

CineVegas International Film Festival. Ooh la la, Las Vegas shows its Cannes-do spirit with a variety of independent foreign and domestic films, both feature length and shorts, including those shot by University of Nevada, Las Vegas students, all screened during the second week of June. If you have a budding Spielberg at home, call ahead for the schedule and make sure to order tickets as quickly as you can—this festival has caught a buzz. Keep in mind that sometimes "independent" can be synonymous with a hard R-rating, so read over the film descriptions carefully, and call festival organizers if you have any questions about age-appropriate content. ℭ **702/992-7979;** www.cinevegas.com.

July

Family Film Festival. Families pull up their lawn chairs, pop open sodas, and settle in at Jaycee Park for a free family night at the movies. ℭ **702/229-6211.** Thursday nights July through late September.

September

Oktoberfest. Families will enjoy the folk dancers, singalongs around a roaring fire, special decorations, and Bavarian cookouts at the **Mount Charleston Resort** during this festival. On Sundays, the entertainment includes oompah bands, with accordions and brass, who play traditional Bavarian music. Visitors can also take advantage of the easy hiking trails on the resort's property, which provide a spectacular outdoors experience. This boisterous autumn holiday is celebrated on weekends from mid-September through the end of October. ℭ **800/955-1314** or 702/872-5408.

International Mariachi Festival. Mandalay Bay started hosting this worldwide Mariachi music festival almost a decade ago, and it has become one of the city's most eagerly anticipated events. The traditional, festive music of Mexico incorporates folk guitars and brass; the songs are sung in Spanish by colorfully costumed men and women. There are often mariachi groups of children as well. It is usually held the second week in September. Call the Mariachi Festival Hotline at ℂ **800/637-1006.**

San Gennaro Feast. New York's Little Italy comes to Vegas at this traditional festival, known as the Feast of Feasts. Celebrate Italian culture with plenty of pasta and pastries, sausage sandwiches, local headliners, games, rides, and a petting zoo. It's loud, lively, and fun, and held in mid-September at the Boca Park Center just off Summerlin Parkway. ℂ **702/286-4944;** www.royalfestivals.com.

Las Vegas Hot-Air Balloon Festival. Up, up, and away. Balloon enthusiasts and kite-fliers take to the air at this popular event, which benefits the Deaf Kids' Kamp. This festival begins at dawn, the second-to-last weekend in September. ℂ **702/247-6905;** www.smilerides. com.

All-You-Can-Eat Ice Cream Festival. The name says it all. Held at the end of September, this all-day event in Summerlin, about 20 minutes from the Strip, benefits the Nevada Ballet Theatre. Once there, you and yours can watch the ice cream eating contests or try your hand sampling cones, sundaes, and root beer floats; over 750 gallons of ice cream are served during the one-day event, which draws over 12,000 people. You'll also find entertainment from trained animals, clowns, musicians, and the Nevada Ballet, the beneficiary of the festival's proceeds. ℂ **702/791-4500;** www. summerlin.com/eventsframes.html.

October

Nevada Shakespeare in the Park. The enduring works of the Bard, performed by local theater actors, are featured at Liberty Point Park. The sword fights in *Romeo and Juliet* and the costumes and merry making in *A Midsummer Night's Dream* might keep kids interested. Even if you never go, it's nice to know it's there (for a weekend in mid-Oct). ℂ **702/384-8427;** www.artscouncilhenderson.org/ pages/SpInthePark.html.

Age of Chivalry Renaissance Festival. If visiting the Excalibur hasn't sated your child's passion for all things knightly, step back into the Middle Ages at this festival in Sunset Park, where crowds in T-shirts and jeans munch turkey legs and mingle with elaborately costumed lords and ladies. Jousting, battles, and pageants, plus artisans and others hawking their wares, can all be seen at this festival, which is held in mid-October. ℂ **702/455-8200;** www.lvrenfair.com.

November

Great Las Vegas Craft Festival. This event is held in mid-November. See information for this listing under "March," above.

December

Tree and Menorah Lighting Ceremonies. Fremont Street goes ablaze with holiday spirit in these two separate ceremonies, held in early December, proving that not all the lights in Vegas are neon. ℂ **800/ 249-3559;** www.vegasexperience. com.

National Finals Rodeo. This is the Super Bowl of rodeos, attended by close to 170,000 people each year (usually during the second week of Dec). The top 15 male rodeo stars compete in six different events: calf roping, steer wrestling, bull riding, team roping, saddle bronco riding, and bareback riding. And the top 15 women compete in barrel racing. An all-around "Cowboy of the Year" is also chosen here. In connection with this event, hotels book country stars in their showrooms, and there's a cowboy shopping spree—the **NFR Cowboy** **Christmas Gift Show,** a trade show for Western gear—at Cashman Field. The NFR runs for 10 days during the first 2 weeks of December at the 17,000-seat Thomas and Mack Center of the University of Nevada, Las Vegas (UNLV). Order tickets as far in advance as possible (✆ **888/NFR-RODEO;** http://nfr-rodeo.com.

4 Getting the Kids Interested in Las Vegas

To help children get interested in their upcoming trip, have them write, e-mail, or call the **Las Vegas Convention and Visitors' Authority,** 3150 Paradise Rd., Las Vegas, NV 89109 (✆ **877/VISITLV,** 877/847-4858 or 702/892-7575; www.vegasfreedom.com), or the **Las Vegas Chamber of Commerce,** 3720 Howard Hughes Pkwy., #100, Las Vegas, NV 89109 (✆ **702/735-1616;** www.lvchamber.com), and ask for its *Visitor's Guide,* which contains extensive information about accommodations, attractions, excursions, children's activities, and more.

For information on all of Nevada, including Las Vegas, they can contact the **Nevada Commission on Tourism** (✆ **800/638-2328;** www.travelnevada.com). It has a comprehensive information packet on Nevada. Your kids will get excited when they receive large envelopes and magazines addressed to them. Have them explore the kid-friendly Las Vegas websites listed above and make their own notes about what they want to see and do.

There are very few books for children about Las Vegas, but older children and teens may enjoy *Cult Vegas* by Mike Weatherford, entertainment reporter for the *Las Vegas Review-Journal,* which lays out the history and legends of Las Vegas. Packed full of facts and photos, this is a fun book.

On the cinematic front, Las Vegas has mainly been shown from an adult perspective. Films such as *Casino, Leaving Las Vegas,* and *Indecent Proposal* are geared for mature audiences. *Honeymoon in Las Vegas* and the Brad Pitt/George Clooney version of *Ocean's Eleven* are both good for those over 13; both show minimal sex, and have plenty of humor and excitement. And you can't go wrong with *Viva Las Vegas,* which can introduce your kids to Elvis Presley as well as providing a goofy glimpse of the city in the 1960s. Prehistoric Vegas appears in *The Flintstones Viva Rock Vegas,* suitable for preteens. If your children are old enough, the highly regarded TV crime series *CSI* takes place in Las Vegas.

Considering the rich imitation of cultures on display in Las Vegas, you'll want to get your children excited about Egypt and the legends of the Middle East, Medieval Europe, Paris, Rome, and New York City.

For a stay at the Luxor—along with history books about Egypt (*The Egyptians; The Cultural Atlas for Young People Series: Ancient Egypt;* and the very cool *Eyewitness: Ancient Egypt*)—consider fictional books: *Mara, Daughter of the Nile* by Eloise McGraw tells the story of Cleopatra's servant girl, and is good for reading levels 7 through 13. Award-winning children's author Zilpha Keatley Snyder has written about modern children incorporating Egyptian history into their daily lives in *The Egypt Game,* which will also entrance children in the 7 to 13 age range.

Tips for Having a Great Family Vacation

- Family vacations are about spending time together and having fun. It's not a marathon to cover as much territory as possible. Pick and choose what you're going to see and do judiciously, and keep in mind that you aren't going to see and do everything.
- Tired people, no matter their age, are difficult to deal with, so keep the pace slow on your trip, and make sure you schedule time to rest.
- Hungry people are even worse than tired people, so carry snacks (protein bars are a wise choice) if you can't manage to feed everyone at regular intervals.
- You may have arrived together, but you don't have to travel in a pack. If it's possible to split up the kids among the adults to give everyone a break, do so, even if it's just for an hour.
- Be flexible and maintain a sense of humor. If the line for a particular buffet or ride is too long, perhaps that's just nature's way of telling you to try something else.
- Ask your children what they would like to do during this trip. Give them some options, make a calendar, and follow through on some of their suggestions. This doesn't mean they are in charge. It means they get to participate in a bit of decision making. And if they want to ride the coaster six times in a row, why not? That could just be what great vacation memories and family stories are made of.

Additionally, the Elizabeth Taylor/Richard Burton cinematic epic *Cleopatra* is a beautiful and compelling spectacle, but some kids might find parts boring.

There are many versions of *1001 Tales of the Arabian Nights* in print for all ages. These stories include "Aladdin and his Magic Lamp," "Ali Baba and the 40 Thieves," and "The Adventures of Sinbad," among other favorites. These will give your kids some mythic context to the Aladdin/Planet Hollywood and the Sahara. Relating to Planet Hollywood's new ownership of the Aladdin, check out *The Mailroom: Hollywood History from the Bottom Up* by David Rensin.

In preparation for a stay at the Excalibur, consider movies about Robin Hood and his band of Merry Men. *Robin Hood, Prince of Thieves* with Kevin Costner, the comedy *Robin Hood Men in Tights,* and Errol Flynn's *Adventures of Robin Hood* are all easy to find on video. The recent release *A Knight's Tale,* with Heath Ledger, also gives a rollicking portrayal of the Middle Ages.

The classic books *The Story of Sir Lancelot and His Companions* and *King Arthur and the Knights of the Roundtable,* both written by Howard Pyle, are available in editions designed for various reading levels.

Older children can experience Paris before visiting Paris Las Vegas via the big screen extravaganza *Moulin Rouge,* while younger children will enjoy the Madeline series of books and videos.

A Visitor's Guide to Ancient Rome and *Coloring Book of Ancient Rome* are good places to start interesting younger kids on the subject and prepare them for a visit to the wonders of Caesars Palace, while preteens and teens may want to watch movies. *A Funny Thing Happened on the Way to the Forum* (fine for all ages) and the violent, albeit Oscar-winning movie, *Gladiator* each deliver decidedly different visions of Ancient Rome. The miniseries *I, Claudius* may prove popular with history buffs.

New York City has been captured in books and on film seemingly more than any other place on earth. *Eloise, Harriet the Spy,* and *A Cricket in Times Square* are excellent places to start with reading material for younger children, while older ones can discover the city by reading or watching *Breakfast at Tiffany's, On the Town, A Tree Grows in Brooklyn* (both book and film), and *One of a Kind Family* provide perspective on the lives of immigrants, visitors to the city, and first-generation Americans during the early part of the 20th century.

5 What to Pack

IN GENERAL

One of the most important articles of clothing you can pack is a lightweight, long-sleeved, button-down shirt, preferably in white or another light color, for you and your kids. This will keep the sun off while outside and will help you adjust to the often-chilly hotels.

If you're going to Las Vegas in the summer, pack for hot weather and balmy nights. Shorts on men and women are seen everywhere, as are tank tops, though sometimes it's not a pretty sight. Bring bathing suits, naturally, as well as cover-ups to get you from room to pool and back again, along with sandals for the same purpose.

Desert winters can be cold, so make sure you bring some warmer clothes with you. A hooded sweat jacket can be especially handy. In winter and spring, sudden downpours can strike, but when that happens, umbrellas and inexpensive plastic ponchos appear in almost every hotel gift shop and convenience store, so hardcore rainwear shouldn't be an issue.

You'll be doing plenty of walking in Las Vegas, so comfortable shoes are a must, as are wide-brimmed hats and sunglasses, even during the cooler winter months. Hikers will want their boots; rock climbers theirs.

At one time, gentlemen couldn't get into any show or a restaurant after 5pm without a jacket and tie, but these days, for the most part, Las Vegas has gone casual. At the most expensive restaurants, however, a jacket or collared shirt may still be required, along with long pants (khakis and chinos are fine; jeans are not), so if you're in doubt, call ahead. Women should pack one lightweight skirt or dress that can be worn to such a restaurant, if that's on your agenda, or a semidressy blouse to go with khakis. If dining out with your kids, they should have one nice but not-too-dressy outfit (sundress or khakis and a collared shirt) if you plan on taking them out for a "grown-up meal" at Buccaneer Bay, Mon Ami Gabi, or a similar restaurant.

You may want to leave your stroller at home and invest in a strap-on baby carrier, if you don't already have one, because strollers are frowned upon, if not banned, on the casino floors.

Tips **Quick ID**

Tie a colorful ribbon or piece of yarn around your luggage handle, or slap a distinctive sticker on the side of your bag. This makes it less likely that someone will mistakenly appropriate it. And if your luggage gets lost, it will be easier to find.

Tips Using a Cellphone on Your Trip

At this point, most wireless companies in North America provide roaming services, which means it's likely you'll be able to use your own cellphone on your trip. Check with your carrier and see if it offers discounted or free long-distance calling plans, so that you can use the cellphone to make local calls while in Las Vegas (otherwise roaming charges might cost you up to $1 a minute to make a local call).

If you don't own a cellphone, consider renting one before you leave. The phone is delivered to you via Federal Express, UPS, or the like and activated immediately. When you get home, you simply return the phone in the prepaid package provided for you.

Taking your cellphone, or bringing a rental, has its advantages, such as you knowing the phone number in advance to give to family and friends at home who might need to reach you; you familiarizing yourself with the phone before you leave home, instead of spending quality vacation time reading instructions; and your kids having more time to memorize the number.

Most wireless rental companies require a credit card deposit and bill the customer at the end of the trip. Although prices vary widely, in general, using a rented cellphone is more expensive than using a telephone calling card but cheaper than calling direct from your hotel room. Most companies charge a basic rental fee (which may include activation and shipping fees) of $40 to $75, plus a per-minute rate for both outgoing and incoming calls. In addition, airtime rates vary from network to network. Bottom line: Shop around for the best deal.

A highly recommended wireless rental company is **InTouch USA** (© **800/872-7626**; www.intouchusa.com).

So-called disposable cellphones, with a preprogrammed amount of minutes, can also be bought at some convenience stores. If you use a short-term phone, make sure your entire family has the number written down.

Some hotels ban strollers except for registered guests. Also, negotiating a stroller in a crowded mall or on the sidewalk can be burdensome. All hotels are close to 24-hour drugstores that stock major brands of disposable diapers, infant formula, and over-the-counter medications; some of these items can even be found at gas station minimarts and in the convenience stores of the hotels/resorts, so you shouldn't worry about forgetting the essentials—anything you forgot can be easily found here.

FOR TRAVEL WITH YOUR KIDS

If you're flying with kids, don't forget a deck of cards, coloring books and crayons, toys, magnetic board games, and chewing gum to help them relieve ear pressure buildup during ascent and descent. Let each child pack his or her own backpack with favorite toys. Kindly ask your kids to keep their Walkmen and GameBoys turned to a low volume out of courtesy to your fellow passengers. If your child is still in diapers, be sure to pack plenty of extras, plus baby wipes and plastic bags for wrapping up the used diaper before tossing it in the airplane bathroom's trash. When altitude is reached, you might want to hand out additional books about Las Vegas and the various cultures and histories represented there.

When driving to Las Vegas, make sure to have a cooler of snacks and plenty of water and diluted juice. Take time out to stretch your legs, or grab a snack at a local diner or even a fast-food joint. Again, baby wipes, paper towels, and plastic bags for trash are important, as well as plenty of extra diapers.

Playing road games such as license plate bingo and counting out-of-state cars can keep kids occupied, and so can magnetic board games, Game-Boys, coloring books, and radio/cassette/CD players with headphones. We know one mom who bought a cheap, portable DVD player to keep her young kids entertained on family road trips and swears that it makes driving a more pleasurable experience for both her and her kids.

6 Insurance, Health & Safety

Check your existing insurance policies and credit card coverage before you buy travel insurance. You may already be covered for lost luggage, canceled tickets, or medical expenses. The cost of travel insurance varies widely, depending on the cost and length of your trip, your age, your health, and the type of trip you're taking.

TRIP-CANCELLATION INSURANCE

Trip-cancellation insurance helps you get your money back if you have to back out of a trip, if you have to go home early, or if your travel supplier goes bankrupt. Allowed reasons for cancellation can range from sickness to natural disasters to the State Department declaring your destination unsafe for travel. (Insurers usually won't cover vague fears, though, as many travelers discovered who tried to cancel their trips in Oct 2001 because they were wary of flying.) In this unstable world, trip-cancellation insurance is a good buy if you're getting tickets well in advance—who knows what the state of the world, or of your airline, will be in 9 months? Insurance policy details vary, so read the fine print—and especially make sure that your airline or cruise line is on the list of carriers covered in case of bankruptcy. For information, contact one of the following insurers: **Access America** (© 866/807-3982; www.accessamerica.com); **Travel Guard International** (© 800/826-4919; www.travelguard.com); **Travel Insured International** (© 800/243-3174; www.travelinsured.com); and **Travelex Insurance Services** (© 888/457-4602; www.travelex-insurance.com).

MEDICAL INSURANCE

Most health insurance policies cover you if you get sick away from home—but check, particularly if you're insured by an HMO. If you require additional medical insurance, try **MEDEX International** (© 800/527-0218 or 410/453-6300; www.medexassist.com) or **Travel Assistance International** (© 800/821-2828; www.travelassistance.com; for general information on services, call the company's Worldwide Assistance Services Inc. at © 800/777-8710).

LOST-LUGGAGE INSURANCE

On domestic flights, checked baggage is covered up to $2,500 per ticketed passenger. If you plan to check items more valuable than the standard liability, see if your valuables are covered by your homeowner's policy, get baggage insurance as part of your comprehensive travel-insurance package, or buy Travel Guard's "BagTrak" product. Don't buy insurance at the airport, as it's usually overpriced. Be sure to take any valuables or irreplaceable items with you in your carry-on luggage, as many valuables (including books, money, and electronics) aren't covered by airline policies.

If your luggage is lost, immediately file a lost-luggage claim at the airport, detailing the luggage contents. For most airlines, you must report delayed, damaged, or lost baggage within 4 hours of arrival. The airlines are required to deliver luggage, once found, directly to your house or destination free of charge.

CAR-RENTAL INSURANCE

If you hold a private auto insurance policy, you are probably covered throughout the U.S. for loss or damage to the car and for liability in case a passenger is injured. The credit card you used to rent the car also may provide some coverage.

Car-rental insurance probably does not cover liability if you caused the accident. Check your own auto insurance policy, the rental company policy, and your credit card coverage for the extent of coverage: Is your destination covered? Are other drivers covered? How much liability is covered if a passenger is injured? If you rely on your credit card for coverage, you may want to bring a second credit card with you, as damages may be charged to your card and you may find yourself stranded with no money.

Car-rental insurance costs about $24 a day.

THE HEALTHY TRAVELER
STAYING HEALTHY

It can be hard to find a doctor you can trust when you're in an unfamiliar place. Try to take proper precautions the week before you depart to avoid falling ill while you're away from home. Amid the last-minute frenzy that often precedes a vacation, make an extra effort to eat and sleep well—especially if you feel an illness coming on. It's a drag to be sick on vacation, and a head cold can make a plane flight intolerable.

Once in Vegas, limit your exposure to the sun, especially during the first few days of your trip, and, thereafter, from 11am to 2pm. Use a sunscreen with a high protection factor and apply it liberally. Remember that children need more protection than adults do.

WHAT TO DO IF YOU GET SICK AWAY FROM HOME

If you worry about getting sick away from home, you may want to consider **medical travel insurance** (see "Medical Insurance," above). In most cases, however, your existing health plan provides all the coverage you need. Be sure to carry your identification card in your wallet.

If you suffer from a chronic illness, consult your doctor before your departure. For conditions such as epilepsy, diabetes, or heart problems, wear a **MedicAlert Identification Tag** (✆ 888/633-4298; www.medicalert. org), which will immediately alert doctors to your condition and give them access to your records through MedicAlert's 24-hour hot line.

Pack **prescription medications** in your carry-on luggage, and carry prescription medications in their original containers, with pharmacy labels—otherwise they won't make it through airport security. Also bring along copies of your prescriptions in case you lose your pills or run out. And don't forget an extra pair of contact lenses or prescription glasses.

If you do get sick, ask the concierge at your hotel to recommend a local doctor, even his or her own. You can also try the emergency room at a local hospital; many have walk-in clinics for emergency cases that are not life threatening. You may not get immediate attention, but you won't pay the high price of an emergency room visit (usually a minimum of $300 just for signing your name).

Also see the "Fast Facts" section in chapter 3, "Getting to Know Las Vegas." There, you'll find listings for hospitals, dental referrals, and even a clinic, right on the Strip.

The nearest poison control center is at **Humana Medical Center,** 3183 Maryland Pkwy. (℅ **800/446-6197**).

THE SAFE TRAVELER

Las Vegas has very strict laws regarding children. No one under 21 is allowed in casinos. Children may not watch you so much as drop a nickel in a slot machine. This law also covers infants

---

Curfew, According to the Law: When and Where Children Shouldn't Be Without an Adult

This is not a town for teens to explore on their own after dark: The fine for violating curfew is $300, and the offending juvenile will most likely be cited and taken into custody, then placed with juvenile services until his or her parents or guardians can be located. Some of Clark County's Codes on Minors and Curfews are listed below. For a full list, head to **http://municipalcodes.lexisnexis.com/codes/clarknv**. (Click on "Title 12" and then "Chapter 12.12" for the information you see listed below.)

It is unlawful for any child under the age of 18 to be without adult supervision in or upon the following streets or sidewalks adjacent thereto and all parking lots, driveways, and walkways which are open to the public and located on properties that adjoin such designated streets between the hours of 9pm and 5am of the succeeding day on Friday, Saturday, and legal holidays, and between 6pm on December 31 and 5am of the succeeding day:

- Las Vegas Boulevard South between Sahara Avenue and Sunset Road
- Harmon Avenue between Las Vegas Boulevard South and Koval Lane
- Dunes Road/Flamingo Road between I-15 and Koval Lane
- Spring Mountain Road/Sands Drive between Vegas Plaza Drive and Koval Lane
- Stardust Road between Industrial Road and Las Vegas Boulevard South
- Convention Center Drive
- Riviera Boulevard
- Circus Circus Drive

It is unlawful for any child under the age of 18 to be in or upon the following streets or sidewalks adjacent thereto and all parking lots, driveways, and walkways which are open to the public and located on properties that adjoin such designated streets between the hours of 6pm on the last Wednesday, Thursday, Friday, and Saturday in the month of April and 5am of the succeeding days:

- Casino Drive, from block number 1500 through block number 3000

Tips Don't Wear It Out

Children should never wear clothing with their names displayed. Doing so can put them at risk—a stranger can call them by name, thus establishing a level of trust with the child.

---

and babies in strollers. Additionally, strollers are not allowed on the casino floors. However, because in most hotels, you have to walk through the casino to get to your room, your child may walk *with you* to and from your room as long as you stay on "the path," usually designated by a different-colored strip of carpet.

The curfew in arcades for children under 18 unaccompanied by parents or a responsible adult over 21 is 10pm to 5am of the succeeding day, Sunday through Thursday; and from midnight to 5am of the succeeding day, Friday through Saturday. From Memorial Day through Labor Day and on school holidays, the start of curfew is extended until midnight.

The majority of arcades in hotels are monitored by security guards, who, by law, must patrol the arcade four times an hour. Some hotel arcades have full-time security present in the arcade, rather than quarter-hourly patrols. A very few arcades comply with security ordinances by relying upon video surveillance. These arcades will have a prominently featured sign indicating that security cameras are in use.

Pamphleteers who line the Strip passing out colorful ads for private exotic dancers and the like are not allowed to hand these to minors, and, thankfully, will probably ignore you as well if you are with your children. That said, discarded pamphlets often end up on the Strip's sidewalks and may give your child an unintended eyeful.

You will see people walking the streets with alcoholic drinks in hand. Yes, this is legal, and is one of Las Vegas's many draws for those who like that sort of thing.

For more ordinances regarding minors and other public safety issues, see **http://municipalcodes.lexisnexis. com/codes/clarknv**.

As in any location with vacationers, pickpockets try to work their skills. Keep your wallet in the front pocket of your pants, or firmly zipped inside your purse. Don't carry all your credit cards or cash with you. Also, see the "What to Do If Your Wallet Is Lost or Stolen" section above for more information.

The only part of downtown Las Vegas we recommend visiting, except during parades, is Fremont Street, which has been cleaned up and turned into a pedestrian mall. However, the rest of the area is seedy and is not suitable for families.

The streets of Las Vegas are very wide and full of tourists walking and driving. Only cross on the "walk" signal, even if you see the foolhardy folks next to you jumping off the curb against the light. Use the crosswalks; do not jaywalk! And you should hold the hands of younger children while crossing the street.

Hats on parents can help children spot them in a crowd, and brightly colored shirts also help family members find each other. Always make sure each child carries the name of your hotel on a piece of paper, along with your cellphone number.

If separated in a casino/resort, your child should immediately approach a uniformed security guard or other employee, including staff in a shop or restaurant, explaining that they are lost, and ask that you be paged.

No casino wants a stray child roaming about. Security can find your child anywhere in the building; those "eye in the sky" surveillance cameras are good for more than just catching card sharks.

7 Tips for Travelers with Special Needs

Because Las Vegas was designed for tourists, the city accommodates the majority of visitors with ease. Most hotels were built in the last 20 years, so tens of thousands of rooms are compliant with the Americans with Disabilities Act (ADA). The city actively woos seniors, who love to travel here. A single parent will have no trouble keeping kids busy and amused in Las Vegas because there are so many attractions that are kid-friendly. And nobody really notices or cares if you are gay, lesbian, bi, or transgender. This accommodating attitude makes Vegas a great place to visit, even though families will sometimes face obstacles to their fun, such as crossing large, smoky casinos to get to their rooms, no-stroller and no-children policies, and occasional hostile stares from those who don't think kids belong in Sin City. Don't let it get you down, however. There are plenty of families who live in Las Vegas, as well as those who visit, and they all enjoy a myriad of fun activities at this neon oasis.

TRAVELERS WITH DISABILITIES

Most disabilities shouldn't stop anyone from traveling. There are more options and resources out there than ever before.

On the one hand, the distance between each Vegas hotel (particularly on the Strip) makes a vehicle of some sort virtually mandatory for most of the disabled, and it may be extremely strenuous and time-consuming to get from place to place (even within a single hotel, because of the crowds). Additionally, the casinos can be quite difficult to maneuver in (particularly for a guest in a wheelchair) because they are crowded, and the machines and tables are often laid out close together, with chairs and such blocking easy access. You should also consider that it is often a long trek through larger hotels between the entrance and the room elevators (or, for that matter, anywhere in the hotel), and then add a crowded casino to the equation.

On the other hand, Las Vegas is fairly well equipped for the disabled, with virtually every hotel having accessible rooms, ramps, and other requirements. (If mobility is a problem, we suggest basing yourself in a South or Center Strip location.)

The city provides for disabled travelers with not only ADA rooms and TTY phones, but with ADA coordinators. You can get assistance in booking your room by voice or TTY from the Las Vegas Convention and Visitors Authority ADA Coordinator (© **800/884-2592** or 702/892-7406; www.onlylasvegas.com). Showrooms also have assisted listening devices as well as wheelchair seating.

All taxi vans have wheelchair access, casinos have roll-up tables and slot machines, and wheelchair seating is available at most restaurants.

The U.S. National Park Service offers a **Golden Access Passport** that gives free lifetime entrance to U.S. national parks and recreation areas (such as Lake Mead National Recreation Area; see chapter 10) for persons who are blind or permanently disabled, regardless of age. You may pick up a Golden Access Passport at any NPS entrance fee area by showing proof of a medically determined disability and eligibility for receiving benefits under federal law. Besides free entry, the Golden Access Passport also

> **Tips   Menus for the Blind**
>
> In 1999, activist Gordon De Witty formed Abilities 2000, an organization that works with hotels, resorts, and restaurants to provide Braille and large-print menus for the blind in accordance with the Americans with Disabilities Act, which mandates accessibility to goods and services for all. Thanks to his efforts, the Monte Carlo, Treasure Island, Excalibur, Stardust, The Riviera, Bally's, and Harrah's Las Vegas now offer these menus in their coffee shops, food courts, and other high-traffic restaurants. De Witty is also working with hotels and resorts to provide room service directories in Braille and large print.

offers a 50% discount on federal-use fees charged for such facilities as camping, swimming, parking, boat launching, and tours. For more information, click onto **www.nps.gov/ fees_passes.htm** or call ✆ **888/GO-PARKS.**

AGENCIES/OPERATORS

- **Flying Wheels Travel** (✆ **507/ 451-5005;** www.flyingwheels travel.com) offers escorted tours and cruises that emphasize sports and private tours in minivans with lifts.

- **Access Adventures** (✆ **589/889-9096**), a Rochester, New York–based agency, offers customized itineraries for a variety of travelers with disabilities.

- **Accessible Journeys** (✆ **800/ TINGLES** or 610/521-0339; www.accessiblejourneys.com) caters specifically to slow walkers and wheelchair travelers and their families and friends.

ORGANIZATIONS

- **The Southern Nevada Center for Independent Living Program,** 6039 Eldora St., Suite H8, Las Vegas, NV 89146 (✆ **702/ 889-4216**), can recommend hotels and restaurants that meet your needs, help you find a personal attendant, advise about transportation, and answer all sorts of other questions.

- The **Nevada Commission on Tourism** (✆ **800/638-2328;** www.travelnevada.com) offers a free accommodations guide to Las Vegas hotels that includes access information.

- **The MossRehab Hospital** (✆ **215/456-9603;** www.moss resourcenet.org) provides friendly, helpful phone assistance through its **Travel Information Service.**

- **The Society for Accessible Travel and Hospitality** (✆ **212/447-7284;** www.sath.org) offers a wealth of travel resources for all types of disabilities and informed recommendations on destinations, access guides, travel agents, tour operators, vehicle rentals, and companion services. Annual membership costs $45 for adults, $30 for seniors and students.

- **The American Foundation for the Blind** (✆ **800/232-5463;** www.afb.org) provides information on traveling with Seeing Eye dogs.

PUBLICATIONS & WEBSITES

For more information specifically targeted to travelers with disabilities, the community website **iCan (www.ican online.net/channels/travel/index. cfm)** has destination guides and several regular columns on accessible travel. Also check out the quarterly magazine *Emerging Horizons* ($15 per year, $20 outside the U.S.; www.emerginghorizons.com); and *Open World Magazine,* published by the Society for Accessible Travel and Hospitality (see above; subscription: $18 per year, $35 outside the U.S.).

SINGLE PARENTS

Single parents face special, unique challenges when they travel with their children. **Parents Without Partners** (© 561/391-8833; www.parents withoutpartners.org) provides links for numerous single parents' resources.

Single mom Brenda Elwell's website (**www.singleparenttravel.net**) is full of advice garnered from traveling around the world with her two children.

Single parents also can find travel tips at **www.solosingles.com**.

GAY, LESBIAN, BI & TRANS-GENDER (GLBT) FAMILIES

There are many gay, lesbian, bi, and transgender families living in Las Vegas. And the city's lack of judgment with regard to tourists makes this a great place for GLBT families to visit.

We Are Family (www.weare familylv.com) provides activities such as movie groups, outings, and socials for the area's gay, lesbian, bi, and transgender families. The organization also works to promote accurate messages about GLBT families within the southern Nevada area. Its website lists events and resources for the community.

The Gay and Lesbian Community Center of Southern Nevada, 953 E. Sahara Ave., Suite B-25 (© 702/733-9800; www.thecenter-lasvegas.com), provides another important resource, with links to Parents, Families & Friends of Lesbians & Gays (PFLAG) and other GLBT family organizations, including spiritual groups.

The International Gay & Lesbian Travel Association (IGLTA; © 800/ 448-8550 or 954/776-2626; www. iglta.org) links travelers up with gay-friendly hoteliers, tour operators, and airline and cruise-line representatives. It offers monthly newsletters, marketing mailings, and a membership directory that's updated once a year. Membership is $200 yearly, plus a $100 administration fee for new members.

AGENCIES/OPERATORS

- **Above and Beyond Tours** (© 800/397-2681; www.above beyondtours.com) offers gay and lesbian tours worldwide and is the exclusive gay and lesbian tour operator for United Airlines.
- **Now, Voyager** (© 800/255-6951; www.nowvoyager.com) is a San Francisco–based gay-owned and -operated travel service.
- **BluWay** (www.bluway.com) dedicates its Internet-exclusive travel service to the GLBT community.

PUBLICATIONS

The following publications are directed more toward the single or childfree GLBT traveler, but some of the information will apply to families.

- The *Las Vegas Bugle,* a biweekly magazine serving the gay community, provides information about bars, workshops, local politics, support groups, shops, events, and more. A subscription costs $20 for 12 issues. You can find the magazine in bars, music stores, and most libraries and bookstores. For details, call © 702/650-0636 or check its online edition at www.lvbugle.com.
- *Out and About* (© 800/834-6411 or 415/644-8044; www. outandabout.com) offers guidebooks and a newsletter 10 times a year packed with solid information on the global gay and lesbian scene.

- *Spartacus International Gay Guide* and *Odysseus* are good, annual English-language guidebooks focused on gay men, with some information for lesbians. You can get them from most gay and lesbian bookstores, or order them from **Giovanni's Room** bookstore, 1145 Pine St., Philadelphia, PA 19107 (℗ **215/923-2960;** www.giovannisroom.com).
- *Gay Travel A to Z: The World of Gay & Lesbian Travel Options at Your Fingertips,* by Marianne Ferrari (Ferrari Publications; Box 35575, Phoenix, AZ 85069) is a very good gay and lesbian guidebook series.

SENIOR TRAVEL

One of the benefits of age is that travel often costs less. Mention the fact that you're a senior citizen when you make travel reservations. Although all of the major U.S. airlines except America West have canceled their senior discount and coupon book programs, many hotels still offer discounts for seniors. In most cities, people over the age of 60 qualify for reduced admission to theaters, museums, and other attractions, as well as discounted fares on public transportation.

Members of **AARP** (formerly known as the American Association of Retired Persons), 601 E St. NW, Washington, DC 20049 (℗ **888/687-2277** or 202/434-2277; www.aarp.org), get discounts on hotels, airfares, and car rentals. AARP offers members a wide range of benefits, including *Modern Maturity* magazine and a monthly newsletter. Anyone over 50 can join.

The **Alliance for Retired Americans,** 888 16th St., NW, Washington, D.C. 20006 (℗ **202/974-8222;** www.retiredamericans.org), offers a newsletter six times a year and discounts on hotel and auto rentals; annual dues are $13 per person or couple. *Note:* Members of the former National Council of Senior Citizens receive automatic membership in the Alliance.

The **U.S. National Park Service** offers a **Golden Age Passport** that gives seniors 62 years or older lifetime entrance to U.S. national parks for a one-time processing fee of $10, which must be purchased in person at any NPS facility (Lake Mead National Recreation Area, p. 246, sells them) that charges an entrance fee. Besides free entry, a Golden Age Passport also offers a 50% discount on federal-use fees charged for such facilities as camping, swimming, parking, boat launching, and tours. For more information, head online to **www.nps.gov/fees_passes.htm** or call ℗ **888/GO-PARKS.**

AGENCIES/OPERATORS

Many reliable agencies and organizations target the 50-plus market. **Elderhostel** (℗ **877/426-8056;** www.elderhostel.org) arranges study programs for those aged 55 and over (and a spouse or companion of any age) in the United States and in more than 80 countries around the world. Most courses last 5 to 7 days in the United States (2–4 weeks abroad), and many include airfare, accommodations in university dormitories or modest inns, meals, and tuition. Its Las Vegas options include sessions on the city's entertainment, hotel, and gaming industries and, in a tip of the hat to top-ranked (and locally set) *CSI,* a program on criminal forensic science at UNLV.

PUBLICATIONS

Recommended publications offering travel resources and discounts for seniors include the quarterly magazine *Travel 50 & Beyond* (www.travel50andbeyond.com); *Travel Unlimited: Uncommon Adventures for the Mature Traveler* (Avalon); and *101 Tips for Mature Travelers,* available from Grand Circle Travel (© **800/ 959-0405** or 617/350-7500; www. gct.com).

ONLINE RESOURCES FOR FAMILY TRAVEL

- **Family Travel Network** (www.familytravelnetwork.com) offers travel tips and reviews of family-friendly destinations, vacation deals, and thoughtful features such as "What to Do When Your Kids Are Afraid to Travel."
- **Travel with Your Children** (www. travelwithyourkids.com) is a comprehensive site offering sound advice for traveling with children.
- **Family Travel Files** (www.the familytravelfiles.com) offers an online magazine and a directory of off-the-beaten-path tours and tour operators for families.

TRAVELING WITH PETS

Many of us wouldn't dream of going on vacation without our pets. Under the right circumstances, it can be a memorable experience. And these days, more and more lodgings and restaurants are going the pet-friendly route. Many hotel and motel chains, such as Best Western, Motel 6, Holiday Inn, and Four Seasons–Regent Hotels, welcome pets. Policies vary, however, so call ahead to find out the rules.

Frankly, bringing your pets to Las Vegas anytime from mid-May to early October is a bad idea because it's just too hot. The searing heat will cook their paws during walks on the endless hot cement, and forget about letting them run and frolic in the desert. In other words, there's nothing for them to do. But if you must, only one hotel in Vegas, the **Hawthorn Suites,** has no size limit on animals.

All city parks allow dogs on leashes, and **Sunset Park** has a special area set aside for off-leash dogs. There are also boarding kennels in the city. Make sure to bring copies of your pet's vaccination records with you, in case you encounter any problems.

An excellent resource is **www.pets welcome.com**, which dispenses medical tips, names of animal-friendly lodgings and campgrounds, and lists of kennels and veterinarians. Also check out *The Portable Petswelcome. com: The Complete Guide to Traveling with Your Pet* (Howell Book House), which features the best selection of pet travel information anywhere.

If you plan to fly with your pet, the FAA has compiled a list of all requirements for transporting live animals at **http://airconsumer.ost.dot.gov/ publications/animals.htm**. You may be able to carry your pet on board a plane if it's small enough to put inside a carrier that can slip under the seat. Pets usually count as one piece of carry-on luggage. Note that summer may not be the best time to fly with your pet: Many airlines will not check pets as baggage in the hot summer months. The ASPCA discourages travelers from checking pets as luggage at any time, as storage conditions on planes are loosely monitored, and fatal accidents are not unprecedented. Your

---

Tips The Peripatetic Pet

Never leave your pet inside a parked car in hot climates with the windows rolled up. It's a good idea never to leave a pet inside a hot car even with the windows rolled down for any length of time.

Make sure your pet is wearing a nametag with the name and phone number of a contact person who can take the call if your pet gets lost while you're away from home.

other option is to ship your pet with a professional carrier, which can be expensive. Ask your veterinarian whether you should sedate your pet on a plane ride or give it antinausea medication. Never give your pet sedatives used by humans.

Keep in mind that dogs are prohibited on hiking trails and must be leashed at all times on federal lands administered by the National Park Service national parks and monuments, including Red Rock Canyon and the Valley of Fire.

8 Getting There

BY PLANE

The following airlines have regularly scheduled flights into Las Vegas (some of these are regional carriers, so they may not all fly from your point of origin): **Air Canada** (© 888/249-2262; www.aircanada.ca) does not offer direct service but will book on partner airlines, usually with a change in San Francisco; **Alaska Airlines** (© 800/426-0333; www.alaskaair.com); **Allegiant Air** (© 877/202-6444; www.allegiant-air.com) has service only from Long Beach and Fresno, California; **Aloha Air** (© 916/484-4131; www.alohaairlines.com); **America West** (© 800/235-9292; www.americawest.com); **American/American Eagle** (© 800/433-7300; www.aa.com); **American Trans Air/Comair** (© 800/435-9282; www.ata.com or www.comair.com); **Continental** (© 800/525-0280; www.continental.com); **Delta/Skywest** (© 800/221-1212; www.delta.com); **Frontier Airlines** (© 800/432-1359; www.flyfrontier.com); **Hawaiian Airlines** (© 800/367-5320; www.hawaiianair.com); **Japan Airlines** (© 800/525-3663; www.jal.co.jp/en); **JetBlue** (© 800/538-2583; www.jetblue.com); **Midwest Express** (© 800/452-2022; www.midwestexpress.com); **Northwest** (© 800/225-2525; www.nwa.com); **Song** (© 800/359-7664; www.flysong.com); **Southwest** (© 800/435-9792; www.iflyswa.com); **Spirit Airlines** (© 800/772-7117; www.spiritair.com); **United** (© 800/241-6522; www.ual.com); **US Airways** (© 800/428-4322; www.usairways.com); and **Virgin Atlantic Airways** (© 800/862-8621; www.virgin-atlantic.com).

We've always enjoyed Southwest's relaxed attitude, and its service leaves few complaints. However, it mostly features first-come, first-served seating, so if you want to avoid that, try one of the other carriers.

In fact, now might be the time to talk about the spiffy new leather seat/DirecTV wonder that is JetBlue. First-time passengers usually turn into longtime converts (including a number of Frommer's editors, who swear by this airline). Currently, they fly to Vegas from Long Beach, California, and New York City, and often for very low prices. Delta's new Song airlines has also jumped on the DirecTV wagon and offers flights from several cities on the East Coast to Las Vegas.

GETTING INTO TOWN FROM THE AIRPORT

McCarran International Airport is just a few minutes drive from the southern end of the Strip, and minibuses run daily between McCarran to all major Las Vegas hotels and motels. One of the major providers, **Bell Trans** (© **702/739-7990**) provides transportation almost around the clock (4:30am–2am). There are several other companies that offer the same service as well, along with taxis. Cabs will cost $10 to $14 from the airport to South Strip hotels and $15 to $18 to Downtown, and carry up to five passengers, while the minivans charge $4 per person to the South Strip, $5 to Downtown, and will carry up to 20 passengers, stopping at hotels along the way. When your vacation comes to an end, make reservations the night before with a minivan company to pick your party up at least 2½ hours before your departure time. The hotel's concierge may be able to help you with this as well. Or take a cab from in front of the hotel.

All major car rental companies are represented in Las Vegas and at the airport, should you choose to rent one while in town. Once you pick up the keys at the desk, a shuttle will take you to the agency's lot. From there, it's usually a quick drive up Paradise Road, a left on Tropicana Avenue, and one very long block later, you are on the Strip.

For complete information on renting a car in Las Vegas, see "Renting a Car" in chapter 3.

AIR TRAVEL SECURITY MEASURES

With the federalization of airport security, security procedures at U.S. airports are more stable and consistent than ever. Generally, you'll be fine if you arrive at the airport **1 hour** before a domestic flight and **2 hours** before an international flight; if you show up late, tell an airline employee and he or she will probably whisk you to the front of the line.

Try **not to drive your car** to the airport because terminal access can be restricted at a moment's notice. If you do drive, be sure to allow extra time to get from the long-term parking lots to the main terminal, as these aren't always close to each other.

Bring a **current, government-issued photo ID** such as a driver's license or passport, and if you've got an e-ticket, print out the **official confirmation page;** you'll need to show your confirmation and your ID at the ticket counter to get a boarding pass. (Children under 18 do not need photo IDs for domestic flights, but the adults checking in with them need them.)

Security lines are getting shorter than they were a couple of years ago, but some doozies remain. We've heard reports of security checks and gridlocks causing delays of up to 4 and 5 hours, with plenty of missed flights as a result. If it's a busy convention or holiday weekend, you might want to plan accordingly. Better a long wait at the airport than a missed flight. If you have trouble standing for long periods of time, tell an airline employee; the airline will provide a wheelchair. Speed up security by **not wearing metal objects** such as big belt buckles or clanky earrings. If you've got metallic body parts, a note from your doctor can prevent a long chat with the security screeners. Keep in mind that only **ticketed passengers** are allowed past security, except for folks escorting passengers with disabilities, or children. If you're bringing a child who will be traveling solo to the airport, then be sure to call in advance to confirm the proper procedure.

Federalization has stabilized **what you can carry on** and **what you can't.** The general rule is that sharp things are out, nail clippers are okay, and food and beverages must be passed through the X-ray machine—but that security screeners can't make you drink from your coffee cup. Bring food in your carry-on rather than checking it, as explosive-detection machines used on checked luggage have been known to mistake food (especially chocolate, for some reason) for bombs. Travelers in the U.S. are allowed one carry-on bag, plus a "personal item" such as a purse, briefcase, or laptop bag. Carry-on hoarders can stuff all sorts of things into a laptop bag; as long as it has a laptop in it, it's still considered a personal item. The Transportation Security Administration (TSA) has issued a list of restricted items; check its website (**www.tsa.gov/public/index.jsp**) for details.

Flying with Film & Video

Never pack unprotected, undeveloped film in checked bags, which may be scanned. The film you carry with you can be damaged by scanners, too. X-ray damage is cumulative; the slower the film, and the more times you put it through a scanner, the more likely the damage. Film under 800 ASA is usually safe for up to five scans. If you're taking your film through additional scans, request a hand inspection. In domestic airports, the Federal Aviation Administration guarantees hand inspections. Keep in mind that airports are not the only places where your camera may be scanned: Highly trafficked attractions are X-raying visitors' bags with increasing frequency.

Most photo supply stores sell protective pouches designed to block damaging X-rays. The pouches fit both film and loaded cameras. They should protect your film in checked baggage, but they also may raise alarms and result in a hand inspection.

An organization called **Film Safety for Traveling on Planes, FSTOP** (© **888/301-2665;** www.f-stop.org), can provide additional tips for traveling with film and equipment.

You'll have little to worry about if you are traveling with **digital cameras.** Unlike film, which is sensitive to light, the digital camera and storage cards are not affected by airport X-rays, according to Nikon. Still, if you plan to travel extensively, you may want to play it safe and hand-carry your digital equipment or ask that it be inspected by hand. See "Digital Photography on the Road," p. 57.

Carry-on scanners will not damage **videotape** in video cameras, but the magnetic fields emitted by the walk-through security gateways and handheld inspection wands will. Always place your loaded camcorder on the screening conveyor belt or have it hand-inspected. Be sure your batteries are charged, as you may be required to turn the device on to ensure that it's what it appears to be.

In 2003 the TSA phased out **gate check-in** at all U.S. airports. Passengers with e-tickets and without checked bags can still beat the ticket-counter lines by using **electronic kiosks** or even **online check-in.** Ask your airline which alternatives are available, and if you're using a kiosk, bring the credit card you used to book the ticket. If you're checking bags, you will still be able to use most airlines' kiosks; again, call your airline for up-to-date information. **Curbside check-in** is also a good way to avoid lines, although a few airlines still ban curbside check-in entirely; call before you go.

Airport screeners may decide that your checked luggage needs to be searched by hand. You can now purchase luggage locks that allow screeners to open and relock a checked bag if hand-searching is necessary. Look for Travel Sentry certified locks at luggage or travel shops and Brookstone stores (you can buy them online at www.brookstone.com). These locks, approved by the TSA, can be opened by luggage inspectors with a special code or key. For more information on the locks, visit www.travelsentry.org. If you use something other than TSA-approved locks, your lock will be cut off your suitcase if a TSA agent needs to hand-search your luggage.

FLYING FOR LESS: TIPS FOR GETTING THE BEST AIRFARE

Passengers within the same airplane cabin are rarely paying the same fare. Business travelers who need to purchase tickets at the last minute, change their itinerary at a moment's notice, or get home for the weekend pay the premium rate.

Passengers who can book their ticket **long in advance,** who can **stay over Saturday night,** or who **fly midweek** or **at less-trafficked hours** will pay a fraction of the full fare. If your schedule is flexible, say so, and ask if you can secure a cheaper fare by changing your flight plans. *Note:* Southwest Airlines does not require you to stay over Saturday to obtain its lowest fares. It is thus often the best choice for business travelers and others whose schedules rule out a Saturday overnight.

Here are a few other easy ways to save:

- You can save on airfares by keeping an eye out in local newspapers for **promotional specials** or **fare wars,** when airlines lower prices on their most popular routes. You'll almost never see a sale during the peak summer vacation months of July and August, or during the Thanksgiving or Christmas seasons; but if you can travel in the off months, you may snag a bargain. If you already hold a ticket when a sale breaks, it may pay to exchange your ticket, even though that usually incurs a $100 to $150 charge.

   Note: The lowest-priced fares are often nonrefundable, require advance purchase of 1 to 3 weeks and a certain length of stay, and carry penalties for changing dates of travel.

- **Consolidators,** also known as bucket shops, are great sources for international tickets, although they usually can't beat the Internet on fares within North America. Start by looking in Sunday newspaper travel sections; U.S. travelers should focus on the *New York Times, Los Angeles Times,* and *Miami Herald.* For less-developed destinations, small travel agencies that cater to immigrant communities in large cities often have the best deals. *Beware:* Bucket-shop tickets are usually nonrefundable or rigged with stiff cancellation penalties, often as high as 50% to 75% of the ticket price, and some put you on charter airlines with questionable safety records. **Fly-Cheap** (© **800/FLY-CHEAP;** www.flycheap.com) is owned by package-holiday megalith MyTravel and so has especially good access to fares for sunny destinations. **Air Tickets Direct**

Travel in the Age of Bankruptcy

Airlines go bankrupt, so protect yourself by **buying your tickets with a credit card,** as the Fair Credit Billing Act guarantees that you can get your money back from the credit card company if a travel supplier goes under (and if you request the refund within 60 days of the bankruptcy). **Travel insurance** can also help, but make sure it covers against "carrier default" for your specific travel provider. And be aware that if a U.S. airline goes bust midtrip, a 2001 federal law requires other carriers to take you to your destination (albeit on a space-available basis) for a fee of no more than $25, provided you rebook within 60 days of the cancellation.

Tips Canceled Plans

If your flight is canceled, don't book a new fare at the ticket counter. Instead, find the nearest phone and call the airline directly to reschedule. You'll be relaxing while other passengers are still standing in line.

(© 800/778-3447; www.air ticketsdirect.com) is based in Montreal and leverages the currently weak Canadian dollar for low fares. And **TravelHub** (www. travelhub.com) represents nearly 1,000 travel agencies, many of whom offer consolidator and discount fares.

- Search **the Internet** for cheap fares. Great last-minute deals are available through free weekly e-mail services provided directly by the airlines. See "Planning Your Trip Online," later in this chapter, for more information.

- Book a seat on a **charter flight.** Discounted fares have pared the number available, but they can still be found. Most charter operators advertise and sell their seats through travel agents, thus making these local professionals your best source of information for available flights. Before deciding to take a charter flight, however, check the restrictions on the ticket: You may be asked to purchase a tour package, to pay in advance, to be amenable if the day of departure is changed, to pay a service charge, to fly on an airline you're not familiar with (this usually is not the case), and to pay harsh penalties if you cancel—but be understanding if the charter doesn't fill up and is canceled up to 10 days before departure. Summer charters fill up more quickly than others and are almost sure to fly, but if you decide on a charter flight, seriously consider buying cancellation and baggage insurance. Also be prepared for late departure hours and long airport delays, as charters usually do not have priority.

- Join a travel club such as **Moment's Notice** (© 718/234-6295; www.moments-notice.com) or **Travelers Advantage** (© 800/433-9383, or 877/259-2691 to join; www.travelersadvantage.com), which supply unsold tickets at discounted prices. You pay an annual membership fee to get the club's hot line number. Of course, you're limited to what's available, so you have to be flexible.

- Join **frequent-flier clubs.** Accrue enough miles and you'll be rewarded with free flights and elite status. It's free, and you'll get the best choice of seats, faster response to phone inquiries, and prompter service if your luggage is stolen, your flight is canceled or delayed, or if you want to change your seat. You don't need to fly to build frequent-flier miles—**frequent-flier credit cards** can provide thousands of miles for doing your everyday shopping.

- For many more tips about air travel, including a rundown of the major frequent-flier credit cards, pick up a copy of *Frommer's Fly Safe, Fly Smart* (Wiley Publishing, Inc.).

HOW TO HAVE AN (ALMOST) FIRST-CLASS EXPERIENCE IN COACH

Anyone who has traveled in coach or economy class in recent years can attest to the frustrating reality of cramped seating. But with a little savvy and advance planning, you can make an otherwise unpleasant coach experience downright comfy.

Here are some tips for finding the right seat:

- Your choice of airline and airplane will definitely affect your legroom. Find more details at **www.seat guru.com**, which has extensive details about almost every seat on six major U.S. airlines. For more legroom, check in early and ask for an aisle seat in an emergency-exit row or bulkhead. The former is often restricted to able-bodied adults, so your kids may not be able to sit in that row. The latter, however, is where the airlines tend to stick passengers traveling with bassinets.

- You also may want to reserve a window seat so that your child can watch the scenery, rest his head, and avoid being bumped in the aisle.

- If you're traveling with a single child, try and book an aisle and a window seat. Middle seats are usually booked last, so chances are good you'll end up with three seats to yourselves. And in the event that a third passenger is assigned the middle seat, he or she will probably be more than happy to trade for a window or an aisle.

- To sleep, avoid the last row or the row in front of the emergency exit, as these seats are the least likely to recline.

Here are some tips for making yourself comfortable during your flight:

- Wear comfortable, low-heeled shoes and dress in loose-fitting layers that you can remove as cabin temperature fluctuates. Don't underdress: Airline cabins can be notoriously chilly and blankets may be unavailable. Wear breathable natural fabrics instead of synthetics. Bring light, long-sleeved shirts for the kids.

- Hydrate before, during, and after your flight to combat the lack of humidity in airplane cabins—which can be as dry as the Sahara Desert. Bring a bottle of water on board. Sugary sodas and diet drinks don't count as water and can actually dehydrate you if they contain caffeine. Have the children drink club soda or diluted juice throughout the flight.

- Preorder special meals for some of your group if that option is available (most airlines no longer serve meals except in first class on short-haul flights). The airlines' vegetarian, high-protein, low-sodium, and kosher meals are usually fresher than standard plane fare, and you get served faster. By having a couple regular meals arrive as well, you'll be able to share desserts and other items that will vary from plate to plate. Or pack a lunch in each child's backpack, plus have some snacks in yours.

- Get up, walk around, and stretch every 60 to 90 minutes to keep your blood flowing. Escort your younger children to the bathroom so you get some exercise. This helps avoid **deep vein thrombosis,** or "economy-class syndrome," a potentially deadly condition that can be caused by sitting in cramped conditions for too long.

- Bring a toothbrush and moisturizer to stay fresh.

- When flying with kids, don't forget a deck of cards, toys, extra bottles, pacifiers, diapers, and chewing gum to help them relieve ear pressure buildup during ascent and descent. Let each child pack his or her own backpack with favorite toys.

- Ask about entertainment options. Many airlines offer seatback video systems where you get to choose your movies or play video games—but only on some of their planes.

- If you're flying with a cold or chronic sinus problems, use a decongestant 10 minutes before ascent and descent, to minimize pressure buildup in the inner ear.
- Try to acclimate yourself and your kids to the local time as quickly as possible. Stay up as long as you can the first day, and then try to wake up at a normal hour the next morning.

COPING WITH JET LAG

Jet lag is a pitfall of traveling across time zones. If you're flying north-south—say, from Canada to Chile—and you feel sluggish when you touch down, your symptoms will be the byproduct of dehydration and the general stress of air travel. When you travel east to west or vice versa, however, the bodily functions that operate cyclically—your hormone levels, blood pressure, body temperature, digestive enzymes, kidney, heart, and brain activity—fall into a sort of time warp. This is because they are, in part, someplace else, inclined to do the things they normally would have been doing back home. Traveling east, say, from Chicago to Paris, is more difficult on your internal clock than traveling west, say, from Atlanta to Hawaii. Traveling east, you lose time, whereas traveling west you gain time, and thus gain sleep, which will help your body recover more quickly. Children seem more affected by traveling long distances than adults, but maybe they are just excited about the trip.

Here are some tips for combating jet lag:

- **Drink lots of water** before, during, and after your flight.

- **Reset your watch** according to your destination time before you board the plane.
- **Avoid drinking alcohol** before and during your flight.
- **Exercise, sleep well, and eat especially healthy foods** during the few days before your trip.
- **Eat more lightly** than you would, both before and during your flight.
- When you reach your destination, **don't sleep longer than you normally would** to try to "catch up."
- **Daylight** is the key to resetting your body clock and your kids.' At the website for **Outside In** (www. bodyclock.com), you can get a customized plan of when to seek and avoid light.
- **Some doctors recommend melatonin for adults** 2 hours before bedtime. A natural, sleep-inducing hormone, it's thought that melatonin will trick your body into thinking night has fallen earlier and help you adjust to a new time zone. **Children usually sleep well on planes, and adjust to jet lag with Calms Forte,** an inexpensive homeopathic medication available over the counter at health food stores. Check, however, with your doctor before taking any over-the-counter medication.
- Remember that eating **carbohydrates** (such as pasta or whole-grain bread) **before bedtime** will allow you to sleep better. High-protein foods—such as meats, fish, eggs, and dairy products—eaten before bedtime will give you energy.

Tips **Under Pressure**

According to folk wisdom, ear pressure can be relieved by placing a hot, damp paper towel in a cup and holding it over the affected ear(s).

BY CAR

The main highway connecting Las Vegas with the rest of the country is I-15; it links Montana, Idaho, and Utah with southern California. The drive from Los Angeles is quite popular, and thanks to the narrow two-lane highway, can get very crowded on Friday and Sunday afternoons with hopeful weekend gamblers making their way to and from Vegas. By the way, as soon as you cross the state line, there are three casinos ready to handle your immediate gambling needs, as well as an outlet shopping mall, and most importantly for children, thrill rides and a video arcade.

From the east, take I-70 or I-80 west to Kingman, Arizona, and then U.S. 93 north to Downtown Las Vegas (Fremont St.). From the south, take I-10 west to Phoenix and then U.S. 93 north to Las Vegas. From San Francisco, take I-80 east to Reno and then U.S. 95 south to Las Vegas. If you're driving to Las Vegas, be sure to read the driving precautions in "Getting Around," in chapter 3.

Vegas is 286 miles from Phoenix, 759 miles from Denver, 421 miles from Salt Lake City, 269 miles from Los Angeles, and 586 miles from San Francisco.

For complete information on renting a car in Las Vegas, see the "Getting Around" section of chapter 3.

BY TRAIN

We don't really recommend this method if traveling with children because **Amtrak** (© **800/USA-RAIL;** www.amtrak.com) does not currently offer direct rail service to Las Vegas. If you take the train to Los Angeles or Barstow, Amtrak will get you to Vegas by bus. It's a long trip, and not a lot of fun. Plans have been in the works to restore the rails between Los Angeles and Las Vegas for years now. At press time, Amtrak wouldn't confirm a date.

---

9 Tips on Flying with Your Children

SAFE SEATS FOR KIDS

The practice of allowing children younger than 2 to ride for free on a parent's lap may be prohibited by the time you read this. At press time, the FAA was writing a rule that would require all children under 40 pounds to have their own tickets and be secured in a child seat.

All the major American airlines except Delta now offer discounted infant tickets for children 2 years of age or younger to make it more affordable for you to reserve a separate adjacent seat for your baby and a restraining device.

For now, if a seat adjacent to yours is available, your "lap child" can sit there free of charge. When you check in, ask if the flight is crowded. If it isn't, explain your situation to the agent and ask if you can reserve two seats—or simply move to two empty adjacent seats once the plane is boarded. (You might want to shop around before you buy your ticket and deliberately book a flight that's not very busy for this reason—ask the reservationist which flights tend to be most full and avoid those.) Only one extra child is allowed in each row, however, due to the limited number of oxygen masks.

On international journeys, children already can't ride free on parents' laps. On flights overseas, a lap fare usually costs 10 percent of the parent's ticket. Children who meet the airline's age limit (which ranges from 11–15 years old) can purchase international fares at 50% to 75% of the lowest coach fare in certain markets. Some of the foreign carriers make even greater allowances for children. Note, however, that children riding for free will usually not be granted any baggage allowance.

Kids with Colds

It's difficult for kids to make their ears pop during takeoff and landing, because the eustachian tube is especially narrow in children. This passage becomes even tighter when kids are sick and their mucous membranes are swollen, which can make ascent and descent on planes especially painful—even dangerous—for a child with congested sinuses. If your little one is suffering from a cold or the flu, it's best to keep him grounded until he recuperates, if that's an option. (If you simply must travel with your child as scheduled, give them an oral child's decongestant an hour before ascent and descent or administer a spray decongestant before and during takeoff and landing.)

Some airlines offer child meals, if requested in advance, for ticketed babies. All major airlines except Alaska and Southwest will warm bottles on request.

While Alaska Airlines lets babies fly as soon as they're born, most airlines require that an infant be 2 weeks old to travel, though American and Continental only require that the child be 7 days old. (Bring a birth certificate if you're traveling with a very young baby to avoid any possible problems.)

CHILD SEATS: THEY'RE A MUST

According to *Consumer Reports Travel Letter,* the National Transportation Safety Board says that, since 1991, the deaths of five children and injury to four could have been prevented had the children been sitting in restraint systems during their flights. Even in the event of moderate turbulence, children sitting on a parent's lap can be thrust forward and injured. When you consider that a commercial aircraft hits a significant amount of turbulence at least once a day on average, you'd do well to think about investing a few hundred dollars for a safety seat. In the event of an accident, unrestrained children often don't make it—even when the parent does. Experience has shown that it's impossible for a parent to hold onto a child in the event of a crash, and children often die of impact injuries. Sudden turbulence is a real danger to a child who is not buckled into his own seat belt or seat restraint. According to *Consumer Reports Travel Letter,* the most common flying injuries result when unanticipated turbulence strikes and hurtles passengers from their seats.

The FAA recommends that children under 20 pounds ride in a rear-facing child-restraint system and says children that weigh 20 to 40 pounds should sit in a forward-facing child restraint system. Children over 40 pounds should sit in a regular seat and wear a seat belt.

All child seats manufactured after 1985 are certified for airline use, but make sure your chair will fit in an airline seat—it must be less than 16 inches wide. You may not use booster seats or seatless vests or harness systems on airplanes. Safety seats must be placed in window seats—except in exit rows, where they are prohibited, so as not to block the passage of other travelers in the case of an emergency.

The airlines themselves should carry child safety seats on board. Unfortunately, most don't. To make matters worse, overzealous flight attendants have been known to try to keep safety seats off planes. One traveler recounts in the November 2001 issue of *Consumer Reports Travel Letter* how a Southwest attendant attempted to block use of a seat because the red label certifying it as safe for airline use had flaked off. That traveler won her case by bringing the owner's manual and appealing to the pilot—you should do the same.

Getting safety seats on an international flight may be even more difficult. Ask to make sure you can use your safety seat when you book a flight on a foreign airline.

Until the new FAA rule comes into effect, if you can't afford the expense of a separate ticket, book a ticket toward the back of the plane at a time when air travel is likely to be slowest—and the seat next to you is most likely to be empty. The reservationist should also be able to recommend the best (meaning the least busy) time for you to fly.

CHILDREN TRAVELING SOLO

Although individual airline policies differ (check with the specific airline for details), for the most part, children aged 5 to 11 pay the regular adult fare and can travel alone as unaccompanied minors on domestic flights only with an escort from the airlines—a flight attendant who seats the child, usually near the galley, where the flight crew is stationed; watches over the child during the flight; and escorts the child to the appropriate connecting gate or to the adult who will be picking up the child. Unaccompanied minors typically board first and disembark last.

On domestic flights, the service costs between $30 and $75, depending on the airline and whether the child will have to change planes. On all the major airlines, several children traveling together from the same family will only have to pay one fee.

Unaccompanied children are never left alone; escorts stay with them until turning them over to an escort on the connecting flight or to a designated guardian.

In order to accompany your solo traveling child to the gate you will need to obtain a gate pass from the check-in counter of your airline. Present the gate pass along with photo ID at the security checkpoint and you will be allowed onto the concourse. For questions concerning airport security contact the **Transportation Security Administration** at ✆ **866/ 289-9673** or check out **www.tsa.gov**.

Airlines require attending adults to furnish a name, address, and government-issued photo ID. The adult who drops the child off at the airport must designate then the name and address of the adult who is authorized to pick the child up. At the destination city, the airline will not release the child to anyone but the authorized adult, after receiving a signature and seeing a photo ID.

Children aged 5 to 7 generally may travel unaccompanied on direct and nonstop flights only; in other words, they're not allowed to change planes for connecting flights at that age (though Northwest and Delta do allow all children to travel on connecting flights). Children aged 8 to 11 may make connecting flights with an escort, with the exception of Southwest and America West, which do not allow any unaccompanied child under the age of 12 to take a connecting flight.

Children over the age of 12 are considered adults and may travel without an escort on every major carrier but Northwest, which requires escorts until age 14. However, even if the children are over age 12, they still qualify for assistance from the airline for the extra fee. Southwest is the only airline that does not allow children to use the escort service once they are able to fly without one, at age 12.

Because airlines want to avoid the responsibility of having to shepherd children overnight, minors are usually not allowed to take the last connecting flight of the day, when the risk of missed connections is greatest. Minors are usually not allowed to travel on standby, and they must have confirmed reservations.

On connecting flights, ask when you book if the child will be flying on more than one airline. (Due to airline code-sharing alliances, your child may end up on a Northwest aircraft, even though you booked the flight through Continental.) If so, make sure you know each airline's policy for unaccompanied minors. Once you receive the ticket, review it yourself to make sure the city of origin and the destination are accurate. Review the ticket carefully with your child and explain in simple terms how it works.

If you're booking a flight for your child, the airlines will request your name, telephone number, and address—along with the name, number, and address of the guardian who will meet your child at the destination city. An adult guardian must accompany the child to the gate or plane, furnish reasonable proof that another adult will meet the child at the final destination, and remain at the airport until the plane is in the air. The accompanying adult at the destination will have to sign a release form and furnish government-issued photo identification, such as a license or passport. If a child is unusually big or small, it's wise to bring a birth certificate to the airport as proof of age.

MINOR ORIENTATION

With stricter security measures at airports, parents must now get a gate pass from the ticket agent for permission to escort their children to the departure gate. (Adults picking up unaccompanied minors at arrival gates also need this pass.) If your child has never flown before, it makes sense to show up at the airport a little early to wander around, watch other planes take off and land, and prepare your child in advance for how flight is going to feel. Be sure to discuss the danger of talking to strangers—even if you have had the same discussion before. You will be allowed to escort your child to the gate, but not onto the plane.

Some airlines allow unaccompanied minors to board first, so the flight crew has more time to meet the child, orient the child to the location of bathrooms and emergency exits, store carry-ons, review safety procedures, and—kids love this part—introduce the child to the cockpit crew. Make sure minors understand that they should contact an attendant in case of any type of problem—from sickness, to a malfunctioning headset, to a bothersome neighbor. Be sure to introduce your child to the gate attendant and to ensure that he or she will receive help boarding if necessary.

Some airlines offer special meals for children, such as hamburgers, hot dogs, or peanut butter sandwiches, which must be ordered in advance, when you make the reservation. It's still wise to send your child off with a bagged lunch, snack, and drinks. Also pack books and other entertainment in a carry-on and make sure your child knows how to get at them on board the plane.

Additionally, make sure your child has cash and knows how to make a collect phone call. In one place, record your child's name, your own name, address, and phone number, along with the names and phone number of your child's hosts at the final destination. Review the information with your child and place it in a safe purse, pocket, or neck pouch. Be sure, however, that your child knows not to share this information with strangers—not even a friendly seat neighbor in the cabin.

If your child is taking medication, it may be wise to postpone the trip unless you are certain your child is responsible for self-administering dosages properly—flight attendants are not allowed to administer drugs to minors.

EASING TRAVEL WITH THE TOTS IN TOW

Several books on the market offer tips to help you travel with kids. *How to Take Great Trips with Your Kids* (The Harvard Common Press; $9.95) is full of good general advice that can apply to travel anywhere. Another reliable tome, with a worldwide focus, is *Adventuring with Children* (Avalon House; $15).

Family Travel Times (© 212/ 977-5524; www.familytraveltimes. com) is an excellent online newsletter updated twice monthly. Subscriptions are $39 a year, $49 for 2 years. Sample articles are available on the newsletter's website.

If you plan carefully, you can actually make it fun (or at least less stressful) to travel with kids.

- **Save yourself a good bit of aggravation by reserving a seat in the bulkhead** row. You'll have more legroom, and your children will be able to spread out and play on the floor underfoot. You're also more likely to find sympathetic company in the bulkhead area, as families with children tend to be seated there.

- **Be sure to pack items for your children in your carry-on luggage.** In case you're forced to check one of your carry-ons, consolidate the children's things in one bag or in your purse. If you're forced to check a carry-on, be sure to keep the one that holds the kid's things. When you're deciding what to bring, ready yourself for the worst: long, unexpected delays without food, bathrooms without changing tables, airline meals that feature your children's least favorite dishes, and more.

- **Have a long talk with your children** before you depart for your trip. If they've never flown before, explain to them what to expect. If they're old enough, you may even want to describe how flight works and how air travel is even safer than riding in a car. Explain to your kids the importance of good behavior in the air—how their own safety can depend upon their being quiet and staying in their seats during the trip.

- **Pay extra careful attention to the safety instructions** before takeoff. Consult the safety chart behind the seat in front of you and show it to your children. Be sure you know how to operate the oxygen masks, as you will be expected to secure yours first and then help your children with theirs. Be especially mindful of the location of emergency exits. Before takeoff, plot out an evacuation strategy for you and your children in your mind's eye.

- **Ask the flight attendant if the plane has any special safety equipment for children.** Make a member of the crew aware of any medical problems your children have that could manifest during flight.

- **Be sure you've slept sufficiently for your trip.** If you fall asleep in the air and your child manages to break away, there are all sorts of sharp objects that could cause injury. Especially during mealtimes, it's dangerous for a child to be crawling or walking around the cabin unaccompanied by an adult.

- **Be sure your child's seatbelt remains fastened properly,** and try to reserve the seat closest to the aisle for yourself. This will make it harder for your children to wander off—in case, for instance, you're taking the red-eye or a long flight overseas and you do happen to nod off. You will also protect your child from jostling passersby and falling objects—in the rare but entirely possible instance that an overhead bin pops open.

- **Try to sit near the lavatory,** though not so close that your children are jostled by the crowds that tend to gather there. Consolidate trips there as much as possible.

- **Try to accompany children to the lavatory.** They can be easily bumped and possibly injured as they make their way down tight aisles. It's especially dangerous for children to wander while flight attendants are blocking passage with their service carts. On crowded flights, the flight crew may need as much as an hour to serve dinner, so it's wise to encourage your kids to use the rest room as you see the attendants preparing to serve.

- **Be sure to bring clean, self-contained compact toys.** Leave electronic games at home. They can interfere with the aircraft navigational system, and their noisiness, however lulling to children's ears, will surely not win the favor of your adult neighbors (note, however that some airlines do offer personal video screens with in-flight games—check when you make your reservation). Magnetic checker sets, on the other hand, are a perfect distraction, and small coloring books and crayons also work well, as do card games like Go Fish.

- **Visit the library before you leave home and check out children's books about flying or airplane travel.** Geography-related books and coloring books that include their departure point and destination will also help engage them during air travel.

- **A portable CD or tape player with a few favorite recordings will also come in handy**—especially if you throw in some sleepy-time tunes. By all means, don't leave home without a favorite

blanket or stuffed animal—especially if it's your kid's best friend at bedtime.

- **Some airlines serve children's meals first.** When you board, ask a flight attendant if this is possible, especially if your children are very young or seated toward the back of the plane. After all, if your kids have a happy flight experience, everyone else in the cabin is more likely to as well.

- **You'll certainly be grateful to yourself for packing tidy snacks** such as rolled dried fruit, which are much less sticky and wet and more compact and packable than actual fruit. Blueberry or raisin bagels also make for a neat, healthy sweet and yield fewer crumbs than cookies or cakes. Ginger snaps, crisp and not as crumbly as softer cookies, will also help curb mild cases of motion sickness. And don't forget to stash a few resealable plastic bags in your bag. They'll prove invaluable for storing everything from half-eaten crackers and fruit to checker pieces and matchbox cars.

- **Juice or cookies** will not only keep your kids distracted during ascent and descent—often the scariest parts of flight for a child—they will also help their little ears pop as cabin air pressure shifts rapidly. Juice (paper cartons travel best) will also keep them swallowing and help them to stay properly hydrated. Avoid giving young children gum or hard candies because sudden turbulence may cause them to choke.

- **If your children are very young, bring pacifiers.** The act of sucking will keep their ears clear. By the same logic, takeoff and landing are the perfect time for feedings. Your kids will be distracted from the deafening cabin noise,

In-Flight Fun for Kids

With one of these children's game books on board, even the longest plane ride will go faster.

Gladstones Games to Go: Verbal Volleys, Coin Contests, Dot Duel, and Other Games for Boredom-Free Days
by Jim Gladstone
Retail price: $9.95
Ages 4 to 12
This book is full of entertaining educational games to help your kids while away the miles. Each game is highly engaging and entertaining and requires few materials and very little space.

Brain Quest for the Car: 1,100 Questions and Answers All About America
by Sharon Gold
Retail price: $11
Ages 7 to 12
This book features cards with questions about American geography, culture, and customs.

Vacation Fun Mad Libs: World's Greatest Party Game
by Roger Price
Retail price: $3.99
Ages 8 and up
As suggested by the title, this book is chock-full of Mad Libs. Your kids will want to keep playing even after you've touched down.

and their ears will pop more easily. If your schedule won't allow this, try placing drops of water on an infant's tongue, to facilitate swallowing. Don't forget to pack bottles and extra milk or formula as well, as these are unavailable on most aircraft. Many airlines prohibit flight attendants from preparing formula, so it's best to pack your baby's food premixed.

TASTELESS: DEALING WITH AIRLINE FOOD

Most airlines have cut back on food service recently—and even if you do get a "meal" on a domestic flight, it's likely to be a limp turkey sandwich. Your best bet is to brown-bag homemade sandwiches. Unlike fruit, for example, they have no leftover parts to throw away, and you won't have to tussle with airport security over silverware. But if you insist on eating economy-class cuisine, some tips follow:

- **Order a special meal.** Most airlines allow coach-class passengers to order from a range of special meals, including low-fat, low-cholesterol, vegetarian and children's meals (usually a hamburger or hot dog). These meals aren't necessarily fresher than the standard ones, but at least you'll know what's in them. Call your airline 2 days before your flight to secure your meal. Then double-check they're still available when you check in.

- **Become a vegetarian.** Dieticians and frequent flyers say vegetarian and vegan meals are often better than standard airline fare. Vegan meals skip cheese and sweets, leading to a healthier but more spartan platter.

In general, coach-class passengers now only get meals on flights crossing two-thirds of the country or more; everyone else gets peanuts or other minibags of snacks.

Most low-fare airlines generally only serve snacks, even on cross-country flights, though some sell heartier fare onboard for somewhat inflated prices. At press time, a "kids meal" on Song, for example, included Nabisco Teddy Grahams, Nabisco Fruit Snacks, Goldfish Crackers and Motts Strawberry Applesauce and cost $5.

THE ECONOMY-CLASS MEAL POLICIES OF MAJOR AIRLINES

- **Alaska:** Food served on flights of 4 hours or more. Meal times: breakfast 6 to 8:30am; lunch 10:30am to 1:30pm; dinner 4 to 7pm.
- **America West:** Food served only on selected flights depending on destination and flight time. Breakfast 6 to 9am; lunch 11am to 1pm; dinner 5 to 7pm.

- **American:** Food served only on flights of 4 hours or more. In-flight meals can be purchased before the flight and taken on board. Breakfast 5 to 8:30am; lunch noon to 1pm; dinner 5:30 to 7pm.
- **Continental:** Food served on flights of 2 hours or more. Breakfast 7 to 9am; lunch 11am to 1pm; dinner 5 to 7pm.
- **Delta:** Food served only on flights of more than 4 hours or 1,750 miles. Times vary according to flight time.
- **Northwest:** Meals are available for purchase on board selected flights. Breakfast 6 to 9:45am; lunch 11am to 1:15pm; dinner 4:30 to 7:15pm.
- **United:** Food served only on flights of more than 4 hours. Breakfast 5 to 10am; lunch 11am to 1:30pm; dinner 4:50 to 7:30pm.
- **US Airways:** Food served on most domestic flights over 700 miles (2 hr.). Breakfast 6 to 10am; lunch 11am to 1pm; dinner 4pm to 7pm.

10 Package Tours for Independent Travelers

Before you start your search for the lowest airfare, you may want to consider booking your flight as part of a travel package. What you lose in adventure, you'll gain in time and money saved when you book even food and entertainment, along with your flight.

Package tours are not the same thing as escorted tours. Package tours are simply a way to buy the airfare, accommodations, and other elements of your trip (such as car rentals, airport transfers, and sometimes even activities) at the same time and often at discounted prices—kind of like one-stop shopping. Packages are sold in bulk to tour operators—who resell them to the public at a cost that drastically undercuts standard rates.

RECOMMENDED PACKAGE TOUR OPERATORS

One good source of package deals is the airlines themselves. Most major airlines offer air/land packages, including **American Airlines Vacations** (✆ 800/321-2121; http://aav1.aavacations.com), **Continental Airlines Vacations** (✆ 800/301-3800; www.coolvacations.com), **Delta Vacations** (✆ 800/654-6559; www.deltavacations.com), **United Vacations** (✆ 888/854-3899; www.united

vacations.com), and **US Airways Vacations** (✆ 800/455-0123 or 800/422-3861; www.usairwaysvacations.com).

Another good bet is **Southwest Airlines** (✆ **888/423-5683;** www.swavacations.com), which has dozens of flights in and out of Las Vegas every day. Sheer volume of flights allows them to offer some relatively inexpensive vacation deals with lots of options in terms of travel time and hotels.

Vacation Together (✆ **800/839-9851;** www.vacationtogether.com) allows you to search for and book packages offered by a number of tour operators and airlines.

The **United States Tour Operators Association**'s website (www.ustoa.com) has a search engine that allows you to look for operators that offer packages to a specific destination. Travel packages are also listed in the travel section of your local Sunday newspaper.

Reservations Plus, 2275 A Renaissance Dr., Las Vegas, NV 89119 (✆ **800/805-9528;** www.resplus.com), runs a free room-reservation service, but it can also arrange packages (including meals, transportation, tours, show tickets, car rentals, and other features) and group rates.

Travel packages are also listed in the travel section of your local Sunday newspaper. **Liberty Travel** (✆ **888/271-1584;** www.libertytravel.com), one of the biggest packagers in the Northeast, often runs full-page ads in Sunday papers. Or check ads in the national travel magazines such as *Arthur Frommer's Budget Travel Magazine, Travel & Leisure, National Geographic Traveler,* and *Condé Nast Traveler.*

If you're unsure about the pedigree of a smaller packager, check with the Better Business Bureau in the city where the company is based, or go online to **www.bbb.org**. If a packager won't tell you where it's based, don't fly with them.

The biggest hotel chains, casinos, and resorts also offer package deals. If you already know where you want to stay, call the resort itself and ask if it offers land/air packages.

THE PROS & CONS OF PACKAGE TOURS

Packages can save you money because they are sold in bulk to tour operators, who sell them to the public. They offer group prices but allow for independent travel. The disadvantages are that you're usually required to make a large payment up front; you may end up on a charter flight; and you have to deal with your own luggage and with transfers between your hotel and the airport, if transfers are not included in the package price. Packages often don't allow for a wide range of choices (the hotels may be unremarkable and are usually located more for the packager's convenience than for yours), or have a fixed itinerary that doesn't allow for an extra day of shopping. Some packages offer a better class of hotels than others. Some offer the same hotels for lower prices than their competitors. Some offer flights on scheduled airlines while others book charters. In some packages, your choices of travel days may be limited. Some packages let you choose between escorted vacations and independent vacations; others allow you to add on a few guided excursions or escorted day trips (also at prices lower than if you booked them yourself) without booking an entirely escorted tour. Your choice of travel days may be limited as well. Which package is right for your family depends entirely on what you want. Prices vary according to the season, seat availability, hotel choice, whether you travel midweek or on the weekend, and other factors.

QUESTIONS TO ASK IF YOU BOOK A PACKAGE TOUR

- What are the **accommodations choices** available and are there price differences? Once you find out, look them up in a Frommer's guide and check their rates for your specific dates of travel online.

- What **type of room** will you be staying in? Don't take whatever is thrown your way. Request a nonsmoking room, a quiet room, a room with a view, or whatever you fancy.

- Look for **hidden expenses.** Ask whether airport departure fees and taxes are included in the total cost.

11 Planning Your Trip Online

SURFING FOR AIRFARES

Tip: When searching for good airfares, remember that (with the exception of citywide conventions) Las Vegas is a weekend town. You'll save yourself a bundle if you can arrange to fly in and out on a weekday.

The "big three" online travel agencies, **Expedia.com, Travelocity.com,** and **Orbitz.com,** sell most of the air tickets bought on the Internet. (Canadian travelers should try Expedia.ca and Travelocity.ca; U.K. residents can go for Expedia.co.uk and Opodo.co. uk.) Each has different business deals with the airlines and may offer different fares on the same flights, so it's wise to shop around. Expedia and Travelocity will also send you **e-mail notification** when a cheap fare becomes available to your favorite destination. Of the smaller travel agency websites, **SideStep** (www.sidestep. com) has gotten the best reviews from Frommer's authors. It's a browser add-on that purports to "search 140 sites at once," but in reality only beats competitors' fares as often as other sites do.

Tip: Keep in mind that because several airlines are no longer willing to pay commissions on tickets sold by online travel agencies, the online agencies may either add a $10 surcharge to your bill if you book on that carrier—or neglect to offer those carriers' schedules.

Also remember to check **airline websites,** especially those for low-fare carriers such as Southwest, JetBlue, or AirTran, whose fares are often misreported or simply missing from travel agency websites. Even with major airlines, you can often shave a few bucks from a fare by booking directly through the airline and avoiding a travel agency's transaction fee. But you'll get these discounts only by **booking online:** Most airlines now offer online-only fares that even their phone agents know nothing about. For the websites of airlines that fly to and from your destination, go to "Getting There," earlier in this chapter.

Great **last-minute deals** are available through free weekly e-mail services provided directly by the airlines. Most of these are announced on Tuesday or Wednesday and must be purchased online. Most are only valid for travel that weekend, but some (such as Southwest's) can be booked weeks or months in advance. Sign up for weekly e-mail alerts at airline websites or check megasites that compile comprehensive lists of last-minute specials, such as **Smarter Living** (http:// smarterliving.com). For last-minute trips, **site59.com** in the U.S. often has better deals than the major-label sites.

If you're willing to give up some control over your flight details, use an **opaque fare service** such as **Priceline** (www.priceline.com; www.priceline. co.uk for Europeans) or **Hotwire** (www.hotwire.com). Both offer rock-bottom prices in exchange for travel on a "mystery airline" at a mysterious time of day, often with a mysterious change of planes en route. The mystery airlines are all major, well-known carriers—and the possibility of being sent from Philadelphia to Las Vegas via Miami is remote; the airlines' routing computers have gotten a lot better than they used to be. But your chances of getting a 6am or 11pm flight are pretty high. Hotwire tells you flight prices before you buy; Priceline usually has better deals than Hotwire, but you have to play their "name our price" game. If you're new at this, the helpful folks at **Bidding-ForTravel.com** do a good job of demystifying Priceline's prices. Priceline and Hotwire are great for flights within North America and between the U.S. and Europe. But for flights to other parts of the world, consolidators will almost always beat their fares. *Note:* In 2004 Priceline added nonopaque service to its roster. You now have the option to pick exact flights, times, and airlines from a list of offers—or opt to bid on opaque fares as before.

For much more about airfares and savvy air-travel tips and advice, pick up a copy of *Frommer's Fly Safe, Fly Smart* (Wiley Publishing, Inc.).

SURFING FOR HOTELS

Shopping online for hotels is much easier in the U.S., Canada, and certain parts of Europe than it is in the rest of the world. Of the "big three" sites, **Expedia** may be the best choice, thanks to its long list of special deals. **Travelocity** runs a close second. Hotel specialist sites **hotels.com** and **hoteldiscounts.com** are also reliable. *Tip:* Always check the individual casino hotel websites, as they often feature deals you won't find anywhere else.

The best site for finding discounts on Las Vegas hotels is **Travelaxe.com.** Travelaxe allows you to download a free software program that compares room rates offered by more than a dozen of the top Internet discounters. You click on the price you like and the program will send you straight to the website offering it. And, unlike most websites, Travelaxe prices include hotel tax, so you actually see the total price of the room. Unfortunately the program works on PCs only.

Priceline and Hotwire are even better for hotels than for airfares; with both, you're allowed to pick the neighborhood and quality level of your hotel before offering up your money. Priceline's hotel product covers several of the major casino hotels, including

---

Frommers.com: The Complete Travel Resource

For an excellent travel-planning resource, we highly recommend **Frommers.com** (www.frommers.com), voted Best Travel Site by *PC Magazine.* We're a little biased, of course, but we guarantee that you'll find the travel tips, reviews, monthly vacation giveaways, bookstore, and online-booking capabilities thoroughly indispensable. Among the special features are our popular **Destinations** section, where you'll get expert travel tips, hotel and dining recommendations, and advice on the sights to see for more than 3,500 destinations around the globe; the **Frommers.com Newsletter,** with the latest deals, travel trends, and money-saving secrets; our **Community** area featuring **Message Boards,** where Frommer's readers post queries and share advice (sometimes even our authors show up to answer questions); and our **Photo Center,** where you can post and share vacation tips. When your research is done, the **Online Reservations System** (www.frommers.com/book_a_trip) takes you to Frommer's preferred online partners for booking your vacation at affordable prices.

Online Traveler's Toolbox

Veteran travelers usually carry some essential items to make their trips easier. Following is a selection of handy online tools to bookmark and use.

- **Airplane Seating and Food.** Find out which seats to reserve and which to avoid (and more) on all major domestic airlines at **www. seatguru.com**. And check out the type of meal (with photos) you'll likely be served on airlines around the world at **www.airline meals.com**.
- **Intellicast** (www.intellicast.com) and **Weather.com** (www.weather. com). Both sites give weather forecasts for all 50 states and for cities around the world.
- **Mapquest** (www.mapquest.com). This best of the mapping sites lets you choose a specific address or destination, and in seconds, it will return a map and detailed directions.
- **Time and Date** (www.timeanddate.com). See what time (and day) it is anywhere in the world.
- **Universal Currency Converter** (www.xe.com/ucc). See what your dollar or pound is worth in more than 100 other countries.
- **Visa ATM Locator** (www.visa.com), for locations of PLUS ATMs worldwide, or **MasterCard ATM Locator** (www.mastercard.com), for locations of Cirrus ATMs worldwide.

The Venetian, The Mirage, and MGM Grand. Be sure to do your research before putting in a bid, however, because their prices aren't always the best available in Vegas.

BiddingForTravel.com has an excellent Las Vegas board in its hotel section. If you plan on bidding on Priceline, it's a must-stop. It also frequently posts hotel discount codes and available packages.

SURFING FOR RENTAL CARS

Although it primarily covers all things Disney, **Mousesavers.com** is the best site on the Internet for scoring great deals on rental cars.

Other good deals can also be found at rental-car company websites, although all the major online travel agencies also offer rental-car reservations services. Priceline and Hotwire work well for rental cars, too; the only "mystery" is which major rental

company you get, and for most travelers the difference between Hertz, Avis, and Budget is negligible.

SMART E-SHOPPING

The savvy traveler is armed with insider information. Here are a few tips to help you navigate the Internet successfully and safely.

- **Know when sales start.** Last-minute deals may vanish in minutes. If you have a favorite booking site or airline, find out when last-minute deals are released to the public. (For example, Southwest's specials are posted every Tues at 12:01am CST.)
- **Go straight to the source.** After finding the best possible room rate on the Internet, check both the website and the reservations desk of the hotel in question. Ask if a better rate is available by booking direct. Always call the hotel's local

number as opposed to a chain's central reservation number. When speaking to the hotel reservations desk on the phone, be sure to ask about specials. Because a given hotel manages its room inventory almost on a minute-by-minute basis, you'll often bump into deals that will never be offered on the Web.

• **Shop around.** If you're looking for bargains, compare prices on different sites and airlines—and against a travel agent's best fare. Try a range of times and alternative airports before you make a purchase.

• **Stay secure.** Book only through secure sites. Look for a key icon (Netscape) or a padlock (Internet Explorer) at the bottom of your Web browser before you enter credit card information or other personal data.

• **Avoid online auctions.** Sites that auction airline tickets and frequent-flier miles are the number-one perpetrators of Internet fraud, according to the National Consumers League.

• **Maintain a paper trail.** If you book an e-ticket, print out a confirmation, or write down your confirmation number, and keep it safe and accessible—or your trip could be a virtual one!

INTERNET ACCESS AWAY FROM HOME
Travelers have any number of ways to check their e-mail and access the Internet on the road (and your teens may be horrified at the thought of forgoing e-mail nowadays). Of course, using your own laptop—or even a PDA (personal digital assistant) or electronic organizer with a modem—gives you the most flexibility. But even if you don't have a computer, you can still access your e-mail from cybercafes (or even from your own hotel room).

WITHOUT YOUR OWN COMPUTER
It's hard nowadays to find a city that *doesn't* have a few cybercafes, and Las Vegas has its share. Although there's no definitive directory for cybercafes—these are independent businesses, after all—three places to start looking are at **www.cybercaptive.**

Digital Photography on the Road
Many travelers are going digital these days when it comes to taking vacation photographs. Not only are digital cameras left relatively unscathed by airport X-rays, but with digital equipment you don't need to lug armloads of film with you as you travel. In fact, nowadays you don't even need to carry your laptop to download the day's images to make room for more. With a **media storage card,** sold by all major camera dealers, you can store hundreds of images in your camera. These "memory" cards come in different configurations—from memory sticks to flash cards to secure digital cards—and different storage capacities (the more megabytes of memory, the more images a card can hold) and range in price from $30 to over $200. (*Note:* Each camera model works with a specific type of card, so you'll need to determine which storage card is compatible with your camera.) When you get home, you can print the images out on your own color printer or take the storage card to a camera store, drugstore, or chain retailer. Or have the images developed online with a service like **Snapfish** (www.snapfish.com) for something like 25¢ a shot. See "Flying with Film & Video," p. 40.

com, www.netcafeguide.com, and www.cybercafe.com.

If you don't want to go looking for a cybercafe and don't feel like lugging your computer along on your family vacation, consider a stay at the Aladdin/Planet Hollywood, where all the guest rooms offer computer terminals with Internet and e-mail access for approximately $10 a day.

Most major airports now have **Internet kiosks** scattered throughout their gates. These kiosks, which you'll also see in shopping malls, hotel lobbies, and tourist information offices around the world, give you basic Web access for a per-minute fee that's usually higher than cybercafe prices. The kiosks' clunkiness and high price means they should be avoided whenever possible.

To retrieve your e-mail, ask your **Internet Service Provider (ISP)** if it has a Web-based interface tied to your existing e-mail account. If your ISP doesn't have such an interface, you can use the free **mail2web** service (www.mail2web.com) to access your home e-mail. For more flexibility, you may want to open a free, Web-based e-mail account with **Yahoo! Mail** (http://mail.yahoo.com) or **Microsoft's Hotmail** (www.hotmail.com). Your home ISP may be able to forward your e-mail to the Web-based account automatically.

12 Tips on Accommodations

For information on the various types of accommodations that you'll find in Las Vegas, see chapter 4, "Family-Friendly Accommodations."

TIPS FOR SAVING ON YOUR HOTEL ROOM

The rack rate is the maximum rate that a hotel charges for a room. It's the rate you'd get if you walked in off the street and asked for a room for the night. Hardly anybody pays these prices, however, especially in Vegas, where prices fluctuate wildly with demand, and there are many ways around them.

- **Don't be afraid to bargain.** Most rack rates include commissions of 10% to 25% for travel agents, which some hotels may be willing to reduce if you make your own reservations and haggle a bit. Get in the habit of asking for a lower price than the first one quoted. Always ask politely whether a less expensive room is available than the first one mentioned, or whether any special rates apply to you. You may qualify for corporate, student, military, senior, or other discounts. Be sure to mention membership in AAA, AARP, frequent-flier programs, or trade unions, which may entitle you to special deals as well. Find out the hotel policy on children—do kids stay free in the room or is there a special rate? If you belong to one of the slot clubs at a hotel casino, you may be able to secure a better deal on a hotel room. Of course, you will also be expected to spend a certain amount of time, and money, gambling there, which might not be practical with children. (See the "Sign Up to Save" box on p. 87 of chapter 4 for more details on slot clubs.)

- **Rely on a qualified professional.** Certain hotels give travel agents discounts in exchange for steering business their way, so if you're shy about bargaining, an agent may be better equipped to negotiate discounts for you.

- **Dial direct.** When booking a room in a chain hotel, compare the rates offered by the hotel's local line with that of the toll-free number. Also check with an agent and online. A hotel makes nothing on a room that stays empty, so the local hotel reservation desk may be willing to offer a special rate unavailable elsewhere.

- **Remember the law of supply and demand.** Las Vegas hotels are most crowded and therefore most expensive on weekends. So the best deals are offered midweek, when prices can drop dramatically. If possible, go then. Business hotels in downtown locations are busiest during the week, so you can expect discounts over the weekend. Avoid high-season stays whenever you can: Planning your vacation just a week before or after official peak season (or a large convention) can mean big savings. You can contact the **Las Vegas Convention and Visitors Authority** (© **877/VISITLV,** 877/847-4858, or 702/892-7575; www.vegasfreedom.com) to find out if an important convention is scheduled at the time of your planned visit; if so, you might want to change the dates of your trip. Some of the largest and most popular conventions are listed in the "Major Convention Dates" box earlier in this chapter.

- **Look into group or long-stay discounts.** If you come as part of a large group, you should be able to negotiate a bargain rate, because the hotel can then guarantee occupancy in a number of rooms. Likewise, if you're planning a long stay (at least 5 days), you might qualify for a discount. As a general rule, expect 1 night free after a 7-night stay.

- **Avoid excess charges.** When you book a room, ask whether the hotel charges for parking. Many hotels charge a fee just for dialing out on the phone in your room. Find out whether your hotel imposes a surcharge on local and long-distance calls. A pay phone, however inconvenient, may save you money, although many calling cards charge a fee when you use them on pay phones. Finally, ask about local taxes and service charges, which could increase the cost of a room by 25% or more.

- **Watch for coupons and advertised discounts.** Scan ads in your local Sunday newspaper travel section, an excellent source for up-to-the-minute hotel deals.

- **Consider a suite.** You can pack more people into a suite (which usually comes with a sofa bed), and thereby reduce your per-person rate. Remember that some places charge for extra guests.

- **Join hotel frequent-visitor clubs,** even if you don't use them much. You'll be more likely to get upgrades and other perks. A hotel-branded credit card usually gives its owner "silver" or "gold" status in frequent-guest programs for free.

- **Many hotels offer frequent-flier points.** Don't forget to ask for yours when you check in.

- **Investigate reservations services.** These outfits usually work as consolidators, buying up or reserving rooms in bulk, and then dealing them out to customers at a profit. You can get 10% to 50% off; but remember, these discounts apply to inflated rack rates that savvy travelers rarely end up paying. You may get a decent rate, but always call the hotel as well to see if you can do better.

Among the more reputable reservations services, offering both telephone and online bookings, are **Hotels.com** (© **800/2-HOTELS;** www.hotels.com); **Hotel Reservations Network** (© **800/715-7666;** www.hoteldiscounts.com or www.180096HOTEL.com); and **Quikbook** (© **800/789-9887,** includes fax-on-demand service; www.quik book.com). Online, try booking your hotel through **Frommers. com** (www.frommers.com).

LANDING THE BEST ROOM

Somebody has to get the best room in the house. It might as well be you.

Always ask about a corner room. They're often larger and quieter, with more windows and light, and they often cost the same as standard rooms.

When you make your reservation, ask if the hotel is renovating, pretty much a given in Las Vegas, where most of the hotels seem to have something old being torn out and something new going in its place. If this is the case, request a room away from the construction. Ask about nonsmoking rooms, rooms with views, and rooms with twin, queen-, or king-size beds. If you're a light sleeper, request a quiet room away from vending machines, elevators, restaurants, bars, and discos. Ask for one of the rooms that have been most recently renovated or redecorated, if that's possible. If you aren't happy with your room when you arrive, talk to the front desk. If they have another room, they may be willing to accommodate you. And, if you join the hotel's frequent visitor club, you may qualify for upgrades.

Some other questions you may want to ask before you book a room include:

- What's the view like? Cost-conscious travelers may be willing to pay less for a back room facing the parking lot, especially if they don't plan to spend much time in their room.
- Do the windows open? Few hotels have windows that open more

than just an inch, the notable exception being the Hard Rock Hotel.

- What is the noise level outside the room? Some hotels on the Strip can be noisy because of attractions on-site or close by. Rooms on lower floors, overlooking the Strip, can be loud, as can ones that open into the casino atrium.
- What's included in the price? Your room may be moderately priced, but if you're charged for sports equipment and other amenities, you could end up spending more than you bargained for.
- Is the hotel pool heated year-round? (Most pools in Las Vegas stop heating their pools in the fall and some close them down altogether in the winter.)
- Are airport transfers included in the price? Some Vegas hotels charge a small fee, per person, for shuttles to and from the airport, while others provide this service *gratis.*
- If it's off season, will any facilities be shut down while you're there?
- What programs are available for kids?
- How far is the room from the pool? From the elevator? We know one exercise fanatic who didn't mind skipping her workouts in Vegas because her room was almost a mile away (or felt like it), one-way, from the hotel's entrance. The distance issue will only be magnified when it comes to small kids (or parents who've been pushing strollers all day).
- What is the cancellation policy?

13 Babysitters & Child-Care Centers

BABYSITTERS

Major hotels can arrange a sitter for you from agencies with whom they frequently work; however, you may

prefer to screen the sitter yourself. Keep in mind that babysitters, like all casino employees, must have a sheriff's card, which proves that they have undergone a 10-year background check. Sitters requested by a hotel must check in with the concierge, who will verify her ID and sheriff's card with their files.

When calling an agency yourself, ask for faxed proof that all employees have been cleared by the health department, the Clark County Sheriff, and the FBI, and that they know CPR.

Along with watching kids in your hotel room, sitters can—with your permission—take children to the pool and to see kid-appropriate shows, shopping, or on outings to arcades. You may want to consider having a sitter accompany you if you take a tour or simply as you stroll about as a family, especially if you have more children than adults in your party.

Sitters base their rates on the number of children and by the number of families involved, meaning sets of parent(s). In other words, cousins don't count as the same family, but brothers, stepsisters, and half-siblings do. All services charge a 4-hour minimum.

Reputable sitters can be arranged by your hotel concierge: In order to work as a sitter in a casino hotel, like all casino employees, sitters must have a "casino card," a form of ID that proves they have been cleared by law enforcement agencies to work in casinos and that they have a "clean record." If your hotel doesn't offer this service, you can try one of the following sitter services:

- In business since 1987, **Around the Clock Child Care** (✆ **800/ 798-6768** or 702/365-1040) is a reputable company that clears its energetic, outgoing sitters with the health department, the sheriff, and the FBI, and carefully screens references. Charges for a sitter at most casino hotels are $48 for 4 hours for one or two children, $10 for each additional hour, with surcharges for additional children, children from different families, and on holidays. Sitters are on call

7 days a week, 24 hours a day, and they will come to your hotel. Call at least 3 hours in advance.

- For 16 years, **Four Season's Babysitting Service** (✆ **702/ 456-1175**), not affiliated with the hotel of the same name, has provided sitters for guests of casinos and resorts. According to the owner, all sitters are CPR-certified and have their sheriff's card. Charges at most of the casino hotels are $30 for 4 hours for one or two children, $10 for each additional hour, with surcharges for additional children, children from different families, and on holidays. Sitters are on call 7 days a week, 24 hours a day, and they will come to your hotel. Call at least 3 hours in advance.

- At **Grandma Dottie's Baby-sitting** (✆ **702/456-1175**), Grandma Dottie and her able crew of sitters—all with sheriff's cards and health cards—charge $40 for one or two children for the 4-hour minimum, and $8 for each additional hour, with surcharges for additional children, children from different families, and on holidays.

CHILD-CARE CENTERS

There are four supervised activity centers (run by two different providers) for children that serve casino hotel guests. Residents of Clark County must show current vaccination records; it's a good idea to have a copy of your child's with you. Your ID will be checked when you drop off and pick up your child. Under these facilities' licensing rules, at least one parent must stay on the gaming property while their child is at the center.

Rest assured that all staffs are trained and certified in CPR and first aid, and have undergone background checks. The maximum a child can stay at any supervised activity center is 5

What Parents Can Do in Vegas if They Have a Sitter/Child Care

Being a family is great, but sometimes parents want to have fun on their own, and Las Vegas is certainly the place to do it. Gambling is one of the first things that comes to people's minds when they think of Vegas (see our brief discussion on p. 233), so go ahead, drop a couple quarters in the one-armed bandit and see if you hit the jackpot. Chances are 1 in 8,000 that you will.

Or maybe you'd prefer to spend your time and money catching up on the spectacular adult-oriented shows for which Vegas is famous. If topless women in feather headdresses don't appeal to you, then perhaps you'd rather see *Mystère, O,* Celine Dion, or other headliners (see chapter 9, "Entertainment for the Whole Family," and especially the section called "What to Do If You've Left the Kids with a Babysitter," p. 232) as a couple, rather than in a group.

And then, of course, there's the food: Las Vegas has top-notch restaurants with plenty of romantic appeal (see chapter 5, "Family-Friendly Dining," and especially the section called "Just the Two of Us: Romantic Dining," p. 149), so take a night off and rediscover the fun of dating again. Enjoy!

hours. If you want your kids to munch on snacks (pizza, chips, sodas, juice, hot dogs), you can prepay for the food or trust your child with the cash.

KidQuest is a chain of supervised play centers, and its three Las Vegas outposts are located at **Texas Station Gambling Hall & Hotel,** 2101 Texas Star Lane (© **800/654-8888** or 702/631-1000); **Boulder Station,** 4111 Boulder Hwy. (© **800/683-7777** or 702/432-7777); and **Sunset Station,** 1301 W. Sunset Rd. (© **888/786-7389** or 702/547-7777). These casino hotels are way off the beaten path for most visitors, but locals visit them regularly to bowl, go to the movies, and to gamble.

A fun, safe place to leave children for a few hours, KidQuest has a giant soft slide/jungle gym, plus computers, games, and toys. For safety reasons, all children receive a sticker with their name and a SKU bar code, which is copied onto the parent's receipt. The hourly rate for children from 3 to 12

years old is $6 per hour from Monday to Thursday. Friday through Sunday, it costs $7 per hour, with a 2-hour minimum. Reservations must be made for children 6 weeks to 2½ years old, and their rate is $6.25 per hour with a 2-hour minimum from Monday through Thursday and $7.25 per hour with a 2-hour minimum from Friday though Sunday. KidQuest is open Sunday through Thursday from 9am to 11pm and Friday through Saturday from 9am to 1am.

Note: The **South Coast Hotel & Casino** (© **702/796-7111**), set to open on the Strip in November 2005, will have a Kids Tyme Child Care Facility available to its guests. At press time, it was being described to us as an in-house babysitting service with a 3-hour maximum, though games and a climbing gym will be available for the kids to use.

Accepting children ages 2½ to 12 years old, the child-care center at the **Orleans Hotel & Casino,** 4500 W.

Tropicana Ave. (© **800/675-3267** or 702/365-7111), has the most reasonable rates, and allows you to leave your children for as little as 15 minutes. Their maximum is 3½ hours. Children must be completely toilet trained: no pull-ups or diapers allowed. Hourly rates are $5.40 per child, no minimum stay; you'll get a $1 per hour discount if you show an Orleans gaming card at checkout. Facilities include a movie room, supervised arts and crafts, a jungle gym, a playroom, and a small games arcade.

14 Recommended Reading for Adults

If you believe in "reading more about it," here are a select few of our favorites you might turn to:

- Castleman, Deke, *Whale Hunt in the Desert—The Secret Las Vegas of Superhost Steve Cyr* (Huntington Press, 2004). If you've ever wondered how super-rich gamblers ("whales") get treated in Las Vegas, this book contains all the answers. Interwoven is an interesting high-roller history of the city.
- Fleming, Charles, *The Ivory Coast* (St. Martin's, 2002). A fictionalized look at Las Vegas in the glamour and glory years of the mid-'50s, centered around segregation. The Ivory Coast represents, and is loosely modeled after, the Moulin Rouge, which opened in 1955 and was the only black-owned Las Vegas casino until Don Barden bought Fitzgeralds more than 45 years later.
- Martinez, Andrez, *24/7 Living It Up and Doubling Down in the New Las Vegas* (Villard, 1999). A former Ivy League lawyer uses his $50,000 book advance to live it up in Vegas for a month. A true story, it reads like the best in modern surrealist fiction.
- Ridley, John, *Everybody Smokes in Hell* (Ballentine, 1999). John Ridley has written some big-name screenplays (*Three Kings* comes to mind), and his books are mordant slices of tragic lives. In *Everybody,* a loser, possessing the only extant tape of a dead superstar rocker, runs into the underside of Vegas with bad guys on his trail.
- Swain, James, *Grift Sense* (Pocket Books, 2001). A senior citizen/former cop gets hauled out of retirement in Florida to investigate some shady doings at a major Vegas casino. The book has good insider info in addition to laughs and action. It may be fiction, but the background material is all fact.
- Thompson, Hunter S., *Fear and Loathing in Las Vegas* (Random House, 1971). A gonzo journalist and his Samoan lawyer head to Sin City for the all-time binge.
- Wilkerson, W.R. III, *The Man Who Invented Las Vegas* (Circo Books, 2000). This book, written by the son of Billy Wilkerson II, a Hollywood restaurant and nightclub owner, presents compelling evidence that Wilkerson envisioned and launched construction of The Flamingo in 1945. Subsequently, Benjamin Siegel not only stole the hotel from Wilkerson, but actually hoodwinked history into crediting him with the idea.

3

Getting to Know Las Vegas

Las Vegas means "the meadows" in Spanish, and though it's hard to believe, as you look at the vast expanses of asphalt and concrete, this entire area was once just another valley—albeit a large one—among the hundreds of valleys in this corner of the American Southwest. The largest city in Nevada, Las Vegas is located in the southernmost area of that wide, flat valley.

The Anasazi first settled this area in a small central portion of the valley, surrounding a water hole. They were followed by Paiute Indians, pioneers, and eventually by ranchers, and then, in the 20th century, by gamblers and developers who built casinos, resorts, and housing.

One of the fastest growing cities in America, Las Vegas has concentrated the majority of tourist attractions in a centrally located area along Las Vegas Boulevard South, known as the Strip; this is the portion of the city you see in movies and on television, sparkling with bright and colorful lights. But there is more to Vegas than just the Strip, and while we do concentrate heavily on those few glittering miles in this book, we've also found a variety of attractions for families that will take you off that beaten, bedazzling path.

To the east of the Strip lies the Convention Center and a number of hotel chains focused on the business traveler, while to the west there are a few resorts/hotels, several residential motels, plus stores, strip malls, and a family recreation center, as well as Las Vegas's Chinatown. Downtown, though it's been spruced up in recent years, is still oriented more for the hard-core gambler than for families.

1 Visitor Information

All major Las Vegas hotels provide comprehensive tourist information at their reception and/or sightseeing and show desks.

Other good information sources are: the **Las Vegas Convention and Visitors Authority,** 3150 Paradise Rd., Las Vegas, NV 89109 (© **877/VISITLV** or 702/892-7575; www.vegasfreedom.com), open daily from 8am to 5pm; the **Las Vegas Chamber of Commerce,** 3720 Howard Hughes Pkwy., Las Vegas, NV 89109 (© **702/735-1616;** www.lvchamber.com), open Monday to Friday 8am

---

Impressions

A few centuries from now archaeologists, studying the ruins of our civilization, will no doubt determine that Las Vegas was an important religious center, boasting dozens of massive temples to which pilgrims from afar brought bountiful offerings.

—Andres Martinez, *24/7: Living It Up and Doubling Down in the New Las Vegas*

Las Vegas at a Glance

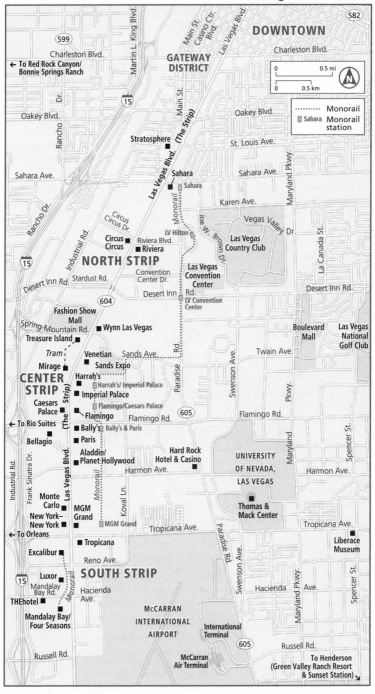

To Red Rock Canyon/
Bonnie Springs Ranch

599

Charleston Blvd.

GATEWAY
DISTRICT

DOWNTOWN

582

Charleston Blvd.

Oakey Blvd.

15

Stratosphere

St. Louis Ave.

Oakey Blvd.

Sahara Ave.

Rancho Dr.

Sahara

Sahara

Sahara Ave.

Karen Ave.

Vegas Valley Dr.

Circus
Circus Dr.

LV Hilton

Riviera Blvd.

Las Vegas
Country Club

Circus
Circus

Riviera

NORTH STRIP

15

Stardust Rd.

Desert Inn Rd.

Industrial Rd.

Convention
Center Dr.

Las Vegas
Convention
Center

Desert Inn Rd.

604

Desert Inn Rd.
LV Convention
Center

Fashion Show
Mall

Boulevard
Mall

Las Vegas
National
Golf Club

Spring Mountain Rd.

Wynn Las Vegas

Treasure Island

Twain Ave.

Tram

Venetian

Sands Ave.

Mirage

Sands Expo

CENTER
STRIP

Harrah's

Harrah's/ Imperial Palace

Imperial Palace

Caesars
Palace

Flamingo/Caesars Palace

Flamingo

Flamingo Rd.

605

Flamingo Rd.

To Rio Suites

Bally's

Bally's & Paris

Bellagio

Paris

Aladdin/
Planet Hollywood

Hard Rock
Hotel & Casino

UNIVERSITY
OF NEVADA,
LAS VEGAS

Harmon Ave.

Harmon Ave.

Monte
Carlo

MGM
Grand

MGM Grand

New York–
New York

To Orleans

Thomas &
Mack Center

Tropicana Ave.

Tropicana

Tropicana Ave.

Liberace
Museum

Excalibur

Reno Ave.

SOUTH STRIP

15

Luxor

Mandalay
Bay Rd.

Hacienda
Ave.

THEhotel

Hacienda Ave.

Mandalay Bay/
Four Seasons

McCARRAN
INTERNATIONAL
AIRPORT

International
Terminal

Russell Rd.

Russell Rd.

McCarran
Air Terminal

605

To Henderson
(Green Valley Ranch Resort
& Sunset Station)

0   0.5 mi
0   0.5 km

······· Monorail
Sahara Monorail
station

to 5pm; and, for information on all of Nevada, including Las Vegas, the **Nevada Commission on Tourism** (© **800/638-2328;** www.travelnevada.com), open daily 24 hours.

Free magazines such as *What's On* and *Show Biz,* available at hotel front desks or in-room, are loaded with information and discount coupons to shows, museums, and other attractions, along with articles about current performers and events.

2 City Layout

There are two main areas of Las Vegas: the **Strip** and **Downtown.** For the purposes of your family trip, we will be focusing on the Strip and the areas around it, where the majority of attractions are located. Shuttles, tours, cabs, or trolleys can take tourists wherever they want to go outside this area, while visitors with cars should be able to quickly navigate their way to outlying sites.

Las Vegas Boulevard South (the Strip) is the starting point for addresses; any street crossing it will start with 1 East and 1 West (and go up from there) at its intersection with the Strip. Tropicana Boulevard is a major east-west route, as are Flamingo Road and Sahara Avenue.

Almost every new Strip hotel has a road named after it, which should make finding the turnoff for your hotel easy.

Downtown has the Fremont Street Experience light and sound show, but that's the only attraction for families. There are no other amusements for children.

Confining yourself to the Strip is fine for the first-time visitor, but repeat customers (and you will be) should get out farther out and explore.

THE STRIP

The Strip is probably the most famous 4-mile stretch of highway in the nation. Officially called Las Vegas Boulevard South, it contains most of the top hotels in town and offers almost all of the major showroom entertainment. First-time visitors will, and probably should, spend the bulk of their time on the Strip.

For the purposes of organizing this book, we've divided the boulevard into three sections. The **South Strip** can be roughly defined as the portion of the Strip south of Harmon Avenue, including Aladdin/Planet Hollywood, MGM Grand, Mandalay Bay, Monte Carlo, New York–New York, Luxor, and several other megaresorts.

Center Strip is a long stretch of the street between Harmon Avenue and Spring Mountain Road, including Bellagio, Caesars, The Mirage, Treasure Island, Bally's, Paris Las Vegas, The Flamingo Las Vegas, and Harrah's, among other hotels and casinos.

North Strip stretches north from Spring Mountain Road all the way to the Stratosphere Tower and includes Wynn Las Vegas (opening Apr 2005), Stardust, Sahara, The Riviera, and Circus Circus, to name just a few of the accommodations and attractions.

EAST OF THE STRIP/CONVENTION CENTER

Paralleling the Strip to the east is Paradise Road, connected to the Strip by the Las Vegas Strip Monorail—which runs from Koval Lane to Sahara Avenue—as well as by road. The Las Vegas Convention Center is located on Paradise Road, as are the Hard Rock Hotel and the Las Vegas Hilton, among others.

Because Las Vegas is one of the nation's top convention cities (attracting more than 3.5 million conventioneers each year), the area around the Convention Center has really developed lately. The major hotel in this section is the Las

---

> (*Fun Fact* **Bright Lights, Sin City**
>
> More than 15,000 miles of neon tubing is used to light up the Strip and Downtown Vegas!

Vegas Hilton, but you'll find many excellent smaller hotels and motels southward along Paradise Road. They offer close proximity to the Strip.

East of Paradise, along Sahara Boulevard, you'll find the Commercial Center, a large shopping center where many fine ethnic restaurants are located, along with an Asian market.

WEST OF THE STRIP

Hotels such as the Rio, Palace Station, Palms, Gold Coast, and the Orleans, along with timeshare developments, shops serving locals, and a family-fun center are in this area, which includes Industrial Road and Decatur Boulevard. This is a far more suburban section of Las Vegas and, accordingly, the hotels and motels here can offer lower rates than those on the Strip. Running parallel to the Strip, Industrial Road provides a good north-south shortcut to avoid the often-clogged Strip. The fabulous International Marketplace (p. 208) is also located in this area.

BETWEEN THE STRIP & DOWNTOWN

The area between the Strip and Downtown is a seedy stretch dotted with tacky wedding chapels, bail-bond operations, pawnshops, and cheap motels.

However, the area known as the **Gateway District** (roughly north and south of Charleston Blvd. to the west of Las Vegas Blvd. S.) is slowly but surely gaining a name for itself as an actual artists' colony. Studios, small cafes, and other signs of life are springing up, and we hope this movement will last.

DOWNTOWN

With the advent of the **Fremont Street Experience** (p. 157), Downtown has experienced a revitalization, though its hotels don't offer much in the way of anything for kids, so we don't recommend staying in this location with your family. Also, while there has been a strong effort to keep out unsavory elements, the area can still attract some unpleasant types. Nevertheless, the area is clean, the crowds are low-key and friendly, and the light and music show—millions of light-emitting diodes (LEDs) attached to a 90-foot-tall, 4-block-long canopy, erupting to music throughout the evening—is as ostentatious as anything on the Strip. Las Vegas Boulevard runs all the way into Fremont Street Downtown, and beyond into North Las Vegas.

3 Getting Around

For information on getting into town from the airport, see section 8, "Getting There," in chapter 2.

Once in town, it shouldn't be too hard to navigate your way up and down the Strip, because the hotels themselves are such noticeable landmarks. Luxor's pyramid is to the south and the Stratosphere, with its 1,149-foot-tall tower, is at the Strip's north end.

That said, just because you know where you're going doesn't mean that it's easy to get there: Always allow plenty of time to travel to where you want to go, because sometimes just getting from your room to another part of your hotel

---

> *Tips* **Staying off the Street**
>
> To make crossing the Strip safer and to help prevent traffic gridlock, pedestrian bridges and people movers have been built to help speed tourists on their way. Raised walkways, accessed from the street by escalators and elevators and from the mezzanine floors of many hotels, provide excellent photo opportunities. People movers, like those linking the Excalibur and the Luxor, glide tourists from hotel to hotel with a minimum amount of exertion, while monorails transport guests from property to property. Thanks to good city planning, it's possible to go from Mandalay Bay all the way to the Sahara without setting foot on the sidewalk!

---

can take 10 minutes or more, especially with children in tow. Outside your hotel, moving around is even more time consuming: Resort properties are huge and what looks like it's just across the street is actually quite a distance. This, coupled with crowds wanting to see everything, can make walking along the Strip a slow process.

BY PUBLIC TRANSPORTATION

There are a number of free transportation services, courtesy of the casinos. A free elevated tram connects Mandalay Bay with Luxor and Excalibur; another connects Bellagio with the Monte Carlo; still another links The Mirage and Treasure Island. Given how far apart even neighboring hotels can be, thanks to their size, and how they seem even farther apart on really hot days, these are blessed additions—and the more tourists who take them, the less traffic there might be on the Strip.

The $650-million **Las Vegas Strip Monorail (www.lvmonorail.com),** after numerous delays, finally began running in July 2004—and then promptly shut down again in September due to maintenance and safety concerns. It was up and running again in December 2004, but prepared for temporary or long-term service outages until the kinks are worked out. The fully automated public-transportation system is one of the most sophisticated in the world. It runs between MGM Grand and the Sahara, with stops at Bally's-Paris, Flamingo-Caesars, Harrah's–Imperial Palace, Convention Center, Las Vegas Hilton, and the Sahara. Covered walkways connect all the stations to the hotels and Convention Center. Tickets cost $3 one-way, $5.50 for two rides, $10 for an all-day pass (the full 24 hr.), $20 for 10 rides, and $25 for a 3-day pass. This is an extremely convenient and comfortable way to travel along the Strip, though the North Strip casinos from The Riviera and Circus Circus are marginally served; it's a long walk from the monorail to the North Strip. Because the monorail stations are located 400 yards or more to the east of the Strip casinos they serve, expect a bit of a hike to access the stations (strollers might be in order for the smallest tykes or your little ones might be exhausted by the time you get to your destination).

Alternatively, you can hop aboard a classic streetcar replica run by **Las Vegas Strip Trolley (ⓒ 702/382-1404).** These old-fashioned dark-green vehicles have interior oak paneling and are comfortably air-conditioned. The trolleys run northward from Hacienda Avenue, stopping at all major hotels en route to the

Sahara, and then loop back from the Las Vegas Hilton. They do not, however, go to the Stratosphere Tower or Downtown. Trolleys run about every 15 minutes daily between 9:30am and 1:30am. The fare is $1.65 (free for children under age 5), and exact change is required.

The no. 301 bus operated by **Citizens Area Transit** (© 702/CAT-RIDE) plies a route between the Downtown Transportation Center (at Casino Center Blvd. and Stewart Ave.) and a few miles beyond the southern end of the Strip. The fare is $2 on the Strip, $1.25 off the Strip, 60¢ for seniors and children 6 to 17, and free for children 5 and under. CAT buses run 24 hours a day and are wheelchair accessible. Exact change is required, but dollar bills are accepted.

BY TAXI

Because cabs line up in front of all major hotels, they are an easy way to get around town. Cabs charge $3 at the meter drop and 20¢ for each additional ⅓ mile. A taxi from the airport to the Strip will run you $10 to $15, from the airport to Downtown $15 to $20, and between the Strip and Downtown about $10 to $12. You can often save money by sharing a cab with someone going to the same destination. (Up to five people can ride for the same fare.)

If you want to call a taxi, any of the following companies can provide one: **Desert Cab Company** (© 702/386-9102), **Whittlesea Blue Cab** (© 702/384-6111), and **Yellow/Checker Cab/Star Company** (© 702/873-2000).

BY CAR

If you won't have your own car in Las Vegas, we recommend renting one. Your best bet for doing things together as a family is to get away from the Strip. Certainly there are family-friendly attractions on the Strip, but they're expensive and somewhat limited in number, especially if you're staying for more than a couple of days. Having a car will allow you to see the Hoover Dam, Bonnie Springs, Mount Charleston, Red Rock Canyon, Lake Mead, and dozens of other truly memorable sights for less than you'd spend to ride two or three Strip roller coasters. You'll be able to sample some of the excellent local restaurants if you have a car, and economize on snacks and even meals by shopping at a grocery. Many families stock a cooler in their hotel room with milk and orange juice so they can enjoy breakfast in their hotel room. You can also rent a refrigerator at many of the major casino hotels for that purpose.

We should warn you that Las Vegas's growing population means a proportionate increase in the number of cars on its streets. Traffic is getting worse, and it's harder and harder to get around town with any certainty of swiftness. A rule of thumb is to avoid driving on the Strip whenever you can, and avoid driving at all during peak rush hours (8–9:30am and 4:30–6pm). You should note that places with addresses some 60 blocks east or west from the Strip are actually less than a 10-minute drive away—provided there is no traffic.

⌐*Tips* **Quick Exits**

When visiting another hotel, tell the valet that you'll only be an hour, and politely ask him "to keep it on the pad," then tip him a couple dollars as he takes your car. This usually ensures that you won't have to wait as long as a nontipper for you to get your vehicle back—a bonus with small children or in hot weather. Also, kindly tip the valet who returns your wheels. It's worth it!

Parking is usually a pleasure, because all casino hotels offer valet service. That means that for a mere $1 to $2 tip you can pull up right to the door (though the valet usually fills up on busy nights). In those cases, you can use the gigantic, free self-parking lots that all hotels have.

RENTING A CAR

National companies with outlets in Las Vegas include **Alamo** (© 877/227-8367; www.goalamo.com), **Avis** (© 800/230-4898; www.avis.com), **Budget** (© 800/527-0700; www.budgetrentacar.com), **Dollar** (© 800/800-3665; www.dollar.com), **Enterprise** (© 800/736-8227; www.enterprise.com), **Hertz** (© 800/654-3131; www.hertz.com), **Payless** (© 800/729-5377; www.payless carrental.com), and **Thrifty** (© 800/847-4389; www.thrifty.com).

Car-rental rates can vary even more than airline fares. The price you pay will depend on the size of the car, where and when you pick it up and drop it off, the length of the rental period, where and how far you drive it, whether you purchase insurance, and a host of other factors. A few key questions could save you hundreds of dollars.

- Are weekend rates lower than weekday rates? Ask if the rate is the same for pickup Friday morning, for instance, as it is for Thursday night.
- Is a weekly rate cheaper than the daily rate? Even if you only need the car for 4 days, it may be cheaper to keep it for 5.
- Does the agency assess a drop-off charge if you don't return the car to the same location where you picked it up? Is it cheaper to pick up the car at the airport compared to a Downtown location?
- Are special promotional rates available? If you see an advertised price in your local newspaper, be sure to ask for that specific rate; otherwise you may be charged the standard cost. Terms change constantly, and reservations agents are notorious for not mentioning available discounts unless you ask.
- Are discounts available for members of AARP, AAA, frequent-flyer programs, or trade unions? If you belong to any of these organizations, you may be entitled to discounts of up to 30%.
- How much tax will be added to the rental bill? Local tax? State use tax?
- What is the cost of adding an additional driver's name to the contract?
- How many free miles are included in the price? Free mileage is often negotiable, depending on the length of your rental.
- How much does the rental company charge to refill your gas tank if you return with the tank less than full? Though most rental companies claim these prices are "competitive," fuel is almost always cheaper in town. Try to allow enough time to refuel the car yourself before returning it.

Some companies offer "refueling packages," in which you pay for an entire tank of gas up front. The price is usually fairly competitive with local gas prices, but you don't get credit for any gas remaining in the tank. If a stop at a gas station on the way to the airport will make you miss your plane, then by all means take advantage of the fuel purchase option. Otherwise, skip it.

Many packages are available that include airfare, accommodations, and a rental car with unlimited mileage. Compare these prices with the cost of booking airline tickets and renting a car separately to see if these offers are good deals. See section 10, "Package Tours for Independent Travelers," in chapter 2 for more information on package deals.

Internet resources can also make comparison shopping easier. See section 11, "Planning Your Trip Online," in chapter 2, for tips on helpful websites.

⌒Tips Driving Safety

Because driving on the outskirts of Las Vegas—for example, coming from California or visiting Red Rock Canyon—involves passing through long stretches of uninhabited desert, you should take certain precautions: It's a good idea to check your tires, water, and oil before leaving; take at least 5 gallons of water in a clean container that can be used for either drinking or the radiator; pay attention to road signs that suggest when to turn off your car's air-conditioner; and don't push your luck with gas— it may be 35 miles, or more, between stations. If your car overheats, do not remove the radiator cap until the engine has cooled. Once the temp had dropped, remove the cap slowly and add water to within an inch of the top of the radiator.

Demystifying Renter's Insurance

Before you drive off in a rental car, be sure you're insured. Hasty assumptions about your personal auto insurance or a rental agency's additional coverage could end up costing you tens of thousands of dollars—even if you are involved in an accident that was clearly the fault of another driver.

If you already hold a **private auto insurance** policy, you are most likely covered in the United States for loss of or damage to a rental car and liability in case of injury to any other party involved in an accident. Be sure to find out whether you are covered in the area you are visiting, whether your policy extends to all persons who will be driving the rental car, how much liability is covered in case an outside party is injured in an accident, and whether the type of vehicle you are renting is included under your contract. (Rental trucks, sports utility vehicles, and luxury vehicles such as a Jaguar may not be covered.)

Most **major credit cards** provide some degree of coverage as well—provided they were used to pay for the rental. Terms vary widely, however, so be sure to call your credit card company directly before you rent.

If you are **uninsured,** your credit card may provide primary coverage as long as you decline the rental agency's insurance. This means that the credit card will cover damage or theft of a rental car for the full cost of the vehicle. If you already have insurance, your credit card may provide secondary coverage—which basically covers your deductible. *Credit cards will not cover liability,* or the cost of injury to an outside party and/or damage to an outside party's vehicle. If you do not hold an insurance policy, you may seriously want to consider purchasing additional liability insurance from your rental company. Be sure to check the terms, however: Some rental agencies only cover liability if the renter is not at fault; even then, the rental company's obligation varies from state to state. Bear in mind that each credit card company has its own peculiarities; call your own credit card company for details before relying on a card for coverage.

The basic insurance coverage offered by most car rental companies, known as the **Loss/Damage Waiver (LDW)** or **Collision Damage Waiver (CDW),** can cost as much as $20 per day. It usually covers the full value of the vehicle with no deductible if an outside party causes an accident or other damage to the rental car. In all states but California, you will probably be covered in case of theft as well. Liability coverage varies according to the company policy and state law, but the minimum is usually at least $15,000. If you are at fault in an accident, however, you will be covered for the full replacement value of the car but not for liability. In Nevada, you can buy additional liability coverage for such cases. Most rental companies will require a police report in order to process any claims you file, but your private insurer will not be notified of the accident. Check your own policies and credit cards before you shell out money on this extra insurance, because you may be already covered.

FAST FACTS: Las Vegas

American Express There are about a dozen offices in town, but the closest one to the Strip is located inside the MGM Grand Hotel at 3799 Las Vegas Blvd. S. (corner of Tropicana; ℂ **702/739-8474**), which is open daily from 8am to 6pm.

Babysitters See section 13, "Babysitters & Child-Care Centers," in chapter 2.

Banks Banks are generally open from 9 or 10am to 5 and sometimes 6pm, and many have Saturday hours. ATMs are plentiful all around town. Also see "Cash & Credit," below.

Car Rentals See "Renting a Car," under section 3, "Getting Around," earlier in this chapter.

Cash & Credit It's extremely easy to obtain cash in Las Vegas. Most casino cashiers will cash personal checks and can exchange foreign currency, and just about every casino has a machine that will provide cash on a wide variety of credit cards.

Conventions Las Vegas is one of America's top convention destinations. Much of the action takes place at the **Las Vegas Convention Center,** 3150 Paradise Rd., Las Vegas, NV 89109 (ℂ **702/892-7575**), which is the largest single-level convention center in the world. Its 3.2-million square feet include 144 meeting rooms. This immense facility is augmented by the **Cashman Field Center,** 850 Las Vegas Blvd. N., Las Vegas, NV 89101 (ℂ **702/386-7100**). Under the same auspices, Cashman provides another 98,100 square feet of convention space. Additionally, there are massive convention facilities at many of the big hotels, including the MGM Grand, Mirage, Mandalay Bay, The Venetian, and more.

Dentists & Doctors Hotels usually have lists of dentists and doctors should you need one. In addition, doctors and dentists are listed in the Centel Yellow Pages. Also see "Hospitals," below.

For physician referrals, call the **Desert Springs Hospital** (ℂ **702/733-8800**). Hours are Monday to Friday 8am to 5pm.

Drugstores & Pharmacies There's a 24-hour **Walgreen's** (which also has a 1-hr. photo) at 3765 Las Vegas Blvd. S. (ℂ **702/739-9638**), almost directly across from the Monte Carlo. **Sav-On** is a large 24-hour drugstore and pharmacy close to the Strip at 1360 E. Flamingo Rd., at Maryland Parkway (ℂ **702/731-5373** for the pharmacy, 702/737-0595 for general merchandise). **White Cross Drugs,** 1700 Las Vegas Blvd. S. (ℂ **702/382-1733**), open daily 7am to 1am, will make pharmacy deliveries to your hotel during the day.

Dry Cleaners Most hotels provide dry cleaning services with a 24-hour or less turnaround, but charge an arm and a leg.

Emergencies Dial ⓒ **911** to contact the police or fire departments or to call an ambulance. This is a free call.

Highway Conditions For recorded information, call ⓒ **702/486-3116.** You can also tune your radio into 970 AM for traffic news or 1610 AM for highway reports.

Hospitals Emergency services are available 24 hours a day at **University Medical Center,** 1800 W. Charleston Blvd., at Shadow Lane (ⓒ **702/383-2000**); the emergency room entrance is on the corner of Hastings and Rose streets. **Sunrise Hospital and Medical Center,** 3186 Maryland Pkwy., between Desert Inn Road and Sahara Avenue (ⓒ **702/731-8080**), also has a 24-hour emergency room.

A branch of the **Fremont Medical Center** is located close to the Strip. The Wynn Road center, 4880 S. Wynn Rd., at Tropicana Ave. (ⓒ **702/871-5005**), is a 24-hour facility.

Hot Lines Emergency hot lines include the Rape Crisis Center (ⓒ **702/366-1640**), Suicide Prevention (ⓒ **702/731-2990**), and Poison Emergencies (ⓒ **800/446-6179**).

Liquor & Gambling Laws You must be 21 to drink or gamble in the United States; proof of age is required and often requested at bars, nightclubs, and restaurants, so it's always a good idea to bring ID when you go out, especially if you look young. There are no closing hours in Las Vegas for the sale or consumption of alcohol, even on Sunday. Beer, wine, and liquor are all sold in all kinds of stores pretty much around the clock; trust us, you won't have a hard time finding a drink in this town. It's even legal to have an open container on the Strip. However, don't even think about driving while you're under the influence of alcohol or if you have an open container of alcohol in your car. You will not be shown any tolerance if caught.

Newspapers & Periodicals There are two Las Vegas dailies: the *Las Vegas Review-Journal* and the *Las Vegas Sun.* The *Review-Journal*'s Friday edition has a helpful "Weekend" section with a comprehensive guide to shows and buffets. Additionally, there are three free, weekly alternative papers, *City Life, Las Vegas Weekly,* and *Las Vegas Mercury,* with club listings and many unbiased restaurant and bar reviews. And at every hotel desk you'll find dozens of free local magazines, such as *Vegas Visitor, What's On in Las Vegas, Showbiz Weekly,* and *Where to Go in Las Vegas,* which are chock-full of helpful information—even though almost all of it comes from paid advertising.

Parking Valet parking is one of the great pleasures of Las Vegas, and it's well worth the dollar tip (given when the car is returned) to save walking a city block from the far reaches of a hotel parking lot, particularly when the temperature is over 100°F (38°C). Another summer plus: The valet will turn on your air-conditioning so that you don't have to get into an "oven on wheels."

Police For nonemergencies, call ⓒ **702/795-3111.** For emergencies, call ⓒ **911,** which is a free call.

Post Office One convenient post office is immediately behind the Stardust Hotel at 3100 Industrial Rd., between Sahara Avenue and Spring

Mountain Road (© **702/735-8519**). It's open Monday to Friday from 8:30am to 5pm. You can also mail letters and packages at your hotel, and there's a full-service U.S. Post Office in the Forum Shops in Caesars Palace.

Safety In Las Vegas, vast amounts of money are always on display, and criminals find many easy marks. Don't be one of them. At gaming tables and slot machines, men should keep wallets well concealed and out of the reach of pickpockets, and women should keep handbags in plain sight (on laps). If you win a big jackpot, ask the pit boss or slot attendant to cut you a check rather than give you cash—the cash may look nice, but flashing it can attract the wrong kind of attention. Outside casinos, popular spots for pickpockets and thieves are restaurants and outdoor shows, such as the volcano at The Mirage or the Treasure Island pirate battle. Stay alert. Unless your hotel room has an in-room safe, check your valuables in a safe-deposit box at the front desk.

Show Tickets See chapter 9, "Entertainment for the Whole Family," for details on obtaining show tickets.

Taxes Clark County hotel room tax is 9%; in Henderson, it's 10%. The sales tax in Las Vegas is 7%.

Time Zone Las Vegas is in the Pacific Standard Time zone, 3 hours earlier than the East Coast and 2 hours earlier than the Midwest. For exact local time, call © **702/248-4800**.

Veterinarian If Fido or Fluffy gets sick while traveling, go to the **West Flamingo Animal Hospital**, 5445 Flamingo Rd., near Decatur Boulevard (© **702/876-2111**). Open 24 hours, they take Discover, MasterCard, Visa, and they have an ATM machine.

Weather See "The Weather" under section 3, "When to Go," in chapter 2. For local weather information, call © **702/248-4800**. The radio station 970 FM also gives regular weather reports for Vegas.

Weddings Las Vegas is one of the easiest places in the world to tie the knot. There's no blood test or waiting period, the ceremony and license are inexpensive, chapels are open around the clock, and your honeymoon destination is right at hand. More than 140,000 marriages are performed here each year. Get a license Downtown at the **Clark County Marriage License Bureau**, 200 S. 3rd St., at Bridger Avenue (© **702/455-3156**), which is open Monday to Thursday 8am to midnight, and from 8am Friday through midnight on Sunday. On legal holidays, it's open 24 hours. The cost of a marriage license is $50; the cost of the ceremony varies depending on where you go to have it done.

4

Family-Friendly Accommodations

With more than 130,000 rooms for rent, including those in 18 of the world's 21 largest hotels, Las Vegas should have more than enough room for you and your brood. But when a convention, holiday, fight, or other major event happens—and they do, almost weekly—all of a sudden, the rooms evaporate into the desert air, or at least skyrocket in price. However, with advance planning, you should be able to choose your vacation in a Vegas version of Paris, Venice, New York, ancient Rome, King Arthur's England, Egypt of the Pharaohs, or simply a pleasant hotel with a gorgeous pool.

Hotel rooms in Vegas are low priced compared to similar rooms in other vacation locations, but there are some drawbacks. Most hotels are casino/resorts, which means huge premises with long walks, through often-smoky casinos, to get between your room and anywhere else on the grounds. Minors cannot be unaccompanied at any time in casino areas, meaning that you'll have to walk with them whenever they want to go to the pool, the arcade, or the animal attractions.

Nongaming properties (yes, some places in Vegas actually do not have casinos) are located off the main drag, requiring a bit of planning and a car or cab in order for you and your kids to make it over to the Strip so that you can gape at all the wonderment it offers, such as volcanoes and talking statues. While these nongaming resident and apartment-style hotels, where each room comes with a fully equipped in-room kitchen, make it easy to cut meal costs by preparing food en suite, again, you will need a car to get to the market or convenience stores in order to take advantage of the pots, pans, and plates these hostelries provide.

Las Vegas's new identity as a resort location has yet to settle in completely. The pools at the self-proclaimed luxury resorts are often chilly, close early in the evening, and at most properties may partially shut down for half the year. Plus, some kids can quickly get bored with the whole pool experience, in which case, staying in a place with cool stuff to do, or at least an arcade and a lot of television stations to keep them preoccupied, is a good idea. Keep in mind that though these properties bill themselves as getaway locations with astounding shopping opportunities, there's only one real bookstore in a hotel mall (at Mandalay Bay), so if your child likes to devour books on vacation, you should plan ahead and bring a supply or be prepared to drive to the nearest bookshop. The same situation applies to CD stores, so it's a good idea to load up on music in advance.

The most important factors, after your family's needs and interests, naturally, are location and price, because at a certain point, most hotel rooms are surprisingly similar. Granted, some rooms are larger than others and some have nicer furnishings, but basically, your room is only a place to rest between sightseeing adventures.

Most of the time in Las Vegas, the difference between paying $69 for a

---

Tips **Check In**

While checkout time is 11am in most hotels, your check-in time is usually 3pm. You can try to arrange an early check-in, but that isn't always an option. Conveniently, though, you can leave your baggage with the bellman, then go sightseeing, either in your hotel or nearby, until it's time to check in. Once in your room, call for your bags, and don't forget to tip when they come.

---

room and $250 for the same bed/bathroom/TV combo is the date you plan to stay, because Las Vegas has incredibly fluid room prices. Be aware that there is no standard for what is considered a "child." Some hotels charge an extra person fee for anyone over 7; others feel the cut-off age is 17, and some grinches will charge no matter how old or young the extra person. At certain properties, the extra person fees are seasonal or changeable, based on "specials." Don't be afraid to ask.

One thing you'll notice is that while, in many cities, hotel chains have the corner on ultraluxurious or at least large, substantial properties, in Las Vegas, with its abundance of over-the-top, supersize resorts, the usual, standard-name hotels recede into the background. Sure, they are still nice (especially if you are on one of their frequent-visitor programs and get points for laying your head on the pillow), but they do pale by comparison to the pyramids and palaces that are almost minicities unto themselves.

The one thing that is fixed about room prices is the tax; as of press time, you will pay an additional 9% tax in Clark County (where you'll find the major Strip hotels), and 10% in nearby Henderson for hotel room taxes.

You should know that price might not have anything to do with the quality of the hotel's other clientele. Even the nicest hotels can have rowdy—well, let's be blunt, drunken—guests, especially if there's a holiday, convention, or big sporting event in town.

And because the rooms are mass produced—no matter how nice the hotel—you will hear plumbing noises, conversations (and sometimes more) from next door, along with the pitter-patter of little feet in the room above you.

Many of the classic Las Vegas hotels have fallen to the wrecking ball and demolition experts, or have been renovated so they no longer resemble their old images. In their places are the new kids on the block, bigger, but not necessarily better.

Everyone thought entrepreneur Steve Wynn was nuts when he envisioned, then built, the huge Mirage, with its jungle foliage and erupting volcano. But the naysayers were mistaken; The Mirage was a success, and the race to build successively more stupendous resorts was on. Circus Circus, Excalibur, the MGM Grand, and Treasure Island began courting families, until the bottom-line executives realized that Las Vegas was never going to be the next Orlando. Wynn, in a firm antikid move, built Bellagio, which, though its gift shop has some cool stuff for kids, isn't the most kid-friendly place to stay. The MGM Grand, which also owns New York–New York, banished their kiddie-oriented ethos and, upon the taking over of Wynn's Mirage group (Bellagio, Treasure Island, and The Mirage), it revised the welcome with regards to families at those properties as well.

Meanwhile, Downtown, which had gotten progressively shabbier, underwent a major revitalization, thanks in great part to the Fremont Street Experience, a multimillion-dollar light show that draws crowds nightly to what is now a pedestrian promenade lined with kiosks and street entertainers. It's a nice place to visit but we still don't suggest you stay there with your family.

Both the Stratosphere Hotel and Sam's Town Hotel & Gambling Hall have undergone major redos. In the case of the former, most people feel the current semitheme of upscale amusement park coupled with a decent, low-cost hotel works as well as anything could, given the hotel's location at the north end of the Strip. But many regular visitors bemoan the changes at Sam's Town, including the loss of its diner with tasty, traditional food.

Steve Wynn has now gone off on his own, to build anew. His latest project, a hotel called Wynn Las Vegas, will stand on the location of the old Desert Inn. It promises to out-Bellagio Bellagio, with 3,000 rooms, a 15-story mountain, a 150-acre championship golf course, three showroom extravaganzas, and a whopping $2.7-billion price tag.

One hotel-casino, the Southcoast, is currently also under construction at the far south end of Las Vegas Boulevard, and a new 500-room Station casino, the Red Rock Station on the far western end of town, is ready to break ground. In addition, Wet 'n Wild, the venerable water park on the North Strip, has closed to make way for an Australian-themed casino called Palace of the Sea, and both the Tropicana and Stardust could meet their destinies with a "controlled demolition" implosion in the near future.

Planet Hollywood has taken over the Aladdin. Colony Capital has taken over the Las Vegas Hilton. Harrah's has taken over Binion's Horseshoe. Two 30-something dot.com superstars have taken over the Golden Nugget. Harrah's Entertainment is currently aiming to buy Caesar's Entertainment, and MGM MIRAGE is attempting to buy Mandalay Resort Group (both purchases have yet to be approved by the Department of Justice and it's likely the merged companies will have to divest properties in order to prevent antitrust issues from sinking the buy-outs, so there may be even more casino hotels changing hands over the next couple of years). Nothing and no one stands still in this City of Perpetual Change.

The majority of visitors with families stay on the Strip, because that's where most of the attractions can be found. Downtown is not a suitable location for families—trust us on that one. Both to the east and west of the Strip you'll find decent to fine hotels, but you'll need transportation to get you there and back. And while staying on the Strip provides you with heaps to do and see, keep in mind that the hotels are farther apart than they appear, especially while walking in 100°F (38°C) weather or on a cold, windy night, with children in tow.

The price guidelines that follow are rough, given the flexible nature of Vegas's room rates. But that doesn't

---

⌒ Tips Beating the Heat

The hottest months in Las Vegas—July, August, and September—are the least popular months for travel to the desert—no doubt because the weather can get up to 118°F (48°C). However, because those are the most convenient months to travel with children, you can take advantage of the hotels' empty rooms, and, with a few phone calls, find the best possible deal.

Las Vegas's Spas & Gyms

Hotel	Phone	Hours	Gym/Workout Room Fee	Min. Age	Spa Hours	Name	Notes
Aladdin/ Planet Hollywood	702/785-5772	6am–7pm	$25	18	8am–6pm	Elemis	$30 for nonhotel guests, multiple-day passes available; can use gym at 16+, but must have parent present if 16–17
Bally's	702/967-4366	6am–7:30pm	$20	18	6am–7pm	The Spa at	Women's spa completely remodeled in 2001
Bellagio	702/693-7111	6am–8pm	$25	18	6am–8pm	Spa Bellagio	Must be 18 (16+ for workout room with parent); registered hotel guests only
Caesars Palace	702/731-7776	6am–8pm	$24	18	8am–6pm	The Spa at	Nonhotel guest can use gym Mon–Thurs; $30
Flamingo Las Vegas	702/733-3535	7am–8pm	$20	18	7am–8pm	The Spa at	
Four Seasons	702/632-5000	6am–9pm	free	18	8am–8pm	The Spa at	Gym is free to hotel guests or those with spa service appt.; 16+ can use workout room with parent present
Green Valley Ranch	702/617-7777	7am–9pm	free	12	7am–9pm	The Spa at	$25 to use gym if nonhotel guest
Hard Rock	702/693-5000	6am–8pm	$18	18	8am–8pm	Rock Spa	$25 if not staying at hotel
Harrah's	702/369-5489	6am–8pm	$15	18	9am–6pm	The Spa at	3 days/$30; same fees for nonhotel guests; gym free with spa service; platinum players card can use gym for free

Hotel	Phone	Hours	Gym/Workout Room Fee	Min. Age	Spa Hours	Name	Notes
Las Vegas Hilton	702/732-5648	6am–8pm	$20	16	6am–8pm	The Spa at	2 days/$36, 3 days/$51, 4 days/$64, 5 days/$75
Luxor	702/262-4000	24 hr.*	$20	18	8am–2am or 6am	Oasis	*Closed 11:30pm Tues–6:30am Wed; $30 nonguest
Mandalay Bay	877/632-7777	5am–10pm	$27	18	6am–10pm	Spa Mandalay	$30 if nonhotel guest
MGM	702/891-1111	6am–8pm	$25	18	6am–7pm	Grand Spa	Gym for hotel guests only
Mirage	702/791-7472	6am–7pm	$20	18	8am–5:30pm	Spa & Salon	Facials start at 9am
Monte Carlo	702/730-7777	6am–9pm	$19	18	8am–8pm	The Spa at	$22 for gym and spa
New York–New York	702/740-6955	6:30am–7pm	$20	18	8am–6:30pm	Spa	Multiple day rates available
Palms	866/942-7777	6am–8pm	$20	18	7am–8pm	Palms Spa	Pool/gym open to hotel guests only
Paris Las Vegas	702/946-7000	6am–7pm; Fri–Sat 6am–9pm	$25	18	6am–7pm	Spa by Mandara	Service of $50 or more includes comp use of gym
Rio	702/777-7777	6am–8pm	$20	18	8am–7pm	Spa & Salon	Can use gym 3 consecutive days for $50
Treasure Island	702/894-7474	7am–7pm	$20	18	7am–7pm	The Spa at	Appt. available to nonhotel guests Mon–Thurs, subject to availability; can use gym 3 consecutive days for $50; spa treatments include use of workout room
The Venetian	702/414-3610	5:30am–10pm	$30	18	8am–8pm	Canyon Ranch	Gym and spa open to nonguests

All hours shown are 7 days a week unless otherwise noted.

Fun Fact **Rapid Rate Changes**

At larger hotels such as the MGM Grand, room rates can change hourly, based on demand. Special employees (called rate clerks) track the demand for rooms the way brokers watch the stock ticker, and alter the room rates according to the number of bookings.

---

mean that you shouldn't call the hotels directly to see what kind of rates you can get.

We classified the recommended hotels below based on the average rack rate you can expect to be quoted on an average night, not when huge conventions are in town. Expect to pay a bit less than rack rates Sunday through Thursday, and a bit more on Friday and Saturday nights.

For more tips on accommodations, see p. 58.

1 South Strip

Staying on the South Strip puts you right in the heart of the most extravagantly kid-friendly hotels, along with providing you with plenty of eye candy, courtesy of hotels such as the Luxor, the Excalibur, and New York–New York. Many family-oriented attractions can also be found here, and, additionally, this is where you'll find the largest range of rates in this section of Las Vegas.

VERY EXPENSIVE

The Four Seasons ★★★ If you crave pure, unabashed luxury, the Las Vegas branch of this famously plush hotel is exactly where you belong. You'll be pampered like royalty in rooms decorated in quiet good taste with quality furnishings. Located on the top five floors of Mandalay Bay, with a separate driveway, entrance, and registration area, the nongaming Four Seasons' rates are higher for a basic room than any other hotel in town. But included in those rates are amenities for which most hotels charge, making the calm, peaceful Four Seasons a relative bargain amongst Las Vegas luxury resorts. Use of both the large health club (with weight training and cardio machines) and the hotel's private pool cabanas (at least $75 at most hotels) are free. Room amenities—including incredibly fluffy feather pillows, down comforters, and plush robes—are definitely a step up from the Vegas standard. Children get their own robes, and rooms are childproofed in advance. Use of strollers, highchairs, and playpens are complimentary, and all the hotel's restaurants, as well as their room service, have children's menus. Best of all, children get a welcome package at check-in, which includes popcorn and soda for teens and toys and cookies for smaller kids. And if you'd like to body surf, guests have access to all the pools at Mandalay Bay (p. 89), but the Four Seasons also has its own pool.

3960 Las Vegas Blvd. S., Las Vegas, NV 89119. (C) **877/632-5200** or 702/632-5000. Fax 702/632-5222. www.fourseasons.com. 424 units. $229–$500 double; from $400 suite. Extra person $35. Children under 18 stay free in parent's room. Cribs/rollaways free. AE, DC, DISC, MC, V. Free self- and valet parking. Pets under 25 lb. only. **Amenities:** 2 restaurants (Continental, American); heated outdoor pool with free cabanas; health club (free to guests); spa; concierge; car-rental desk; courtesy car; full 24-hr. business center with faxing, delivery, and secretarial service; 24-hr. room service; in-room massage; babysitting; overnight laundry service; overnight dry cleaning; nonsmoking rooms; executive-level rooms. *In room:* A/C, TV w/pay movies, dataport, minibar, fridge, coffeemaker, hair dryer, iron/ironing board, safe.

Aladdin/Planet Hollywood
Resort & Casino **1**
Boardwalk Hotel & Casino **2**
Excalibur **6**
The Four Seasons **10**
Hotel San Remo **8**

Luxor Las Vegas **9**
Mandalay Bay **10**
MGM Grand Hotel/Casino **5**
Monte Carlo Resort & Casino **3**

New York–New York
Hotel & Casino **4**
Tropicana Resort & Casino **7**

EXPENSIVE

Aladdin/Planet Hollywood Resort & Casino ⭐ The Aladdin/Planet Hollywood has its pluses for families: You could stay here for a week and never know that there's a casino on-site, which is a rarity in Las Vegas. Additionally, each room is no more than seven doors away from an elevator. And then there's the mall.

The decor of the original building is Disney-fied exotic, lumping together Egyptian, Moroccan, Turkish, Arab, Indian, and Persian styles, though Planet Hollywood, which assumed control of the hotel in September 2004, plans to retheme the place over the next several years. The fairytale Middle Eastern atmosphere is most prevalent in the Desert Passage, an Arabian Nights–themed shopping mall with belly dancers, jugglers, and spicy smells, designed to evoke the essence of the Silk Road, Scheherazade, and all that. (Make shopping there a learning experience for your kids by pointing out that the Desert Passage is a sort of historical perspective on shopping centers, in that bazaars and souks were early versions of their hometown malls.) Despite all the bells and whistles, however, the stores here are pretty much the same as in every other hotel mall (with the exception of the gourmet cookware shop **Sur La Table** and the only free-standing **Clinique Boutique** in the world). One nice touch, though, is the pedicabs that haul you from Ben and Jerry's Ice Cream Store to the Desert Passage's "harbor," where a rainstorm complete with thunder, lightning, wind, and "rain" occurs with astounding regularity.

Tips Fighting the Crowds

Boxing matches draw huge crowds to Las Vegas, which, according to newspaper reports, have been known, from time to time, to attract unsavory, organized criminal groups who flock to Strip hotels during these times. If there's a fight scheduled during your trip, you may want to book a hotel off the Strip, and plan an activity for fight night that will keep you away from Las Vegas Boulevard.

Rooms are nice, serviceable, and forgettable, barely distinguishable from other hotel rooms in the same price range. However, the large bathrooms do stand out—the rooms' separate showers and baths as well as an enclosed toilet area are features usually found at more expensive hotels.

The two pools are pleasant, and there's a vast selection of restaurants in the Desert Passage, including a branch of New Orleans' much-lauded Commander's Palace (perfect for grown-ups), along with over a dozen other options. If you get tired of the Aladdin's own buffet, there's always **Todai**'s sushi and seafood buffet (p. 122) and **Crustacean,** a fusion French-Vietnamese restaurant and late-night hot spot, both in the Desert Passage Mall.

3667 Las Vegas Blvd. S., Las Vegas, NV 89109. ⓒ 877/333-WISH (333-9474) or 702/785-5555. Fax 702/785-5558. www.aladdincasino.com. 2,567 units. $99 and up double. Extra person $30. Children under 12 stay free in parent's room, depending on season. Cribs/rollaways free. AE, DC, DISC, MC, V. Free self- and valet parking. **Amenities:** 13 restaurants (all major cuisines); 6 bars/lounges; casino; showroom; performing arts center; 2 outdoor pools; health club; spa; Jacuzzi; sauna; watersports equipment/rental; concierge; tour desk; car-rental desk; business center; 24-hr. room service; in-room massage; babysitting; laundry service; dry cleaning; nonsmoking rooms; executive-level rooms. *In room:* A/C, TV w/pay movies, dataport, high-speed Internet access (for a fee), hair dryer, iron/ironing board, safe.

MGM Grand Hotel/Casino ⭐⭐⭐   The MGM Grand was once the flagship of kid-friendly Vegas, but oh how times have changed. While we were researching this book, a PR rep went out of her way to let us know that the MGM Group did not wish to be known as family oriented. The amusement park, which used to be in the back—one of the true kid-friendly spots on the Strip—closed and was replaced by the new pool, convention center, and luxury highrise condo towers. Even so, though it may talk the not-for-children talk, this hotel, more than any of the other MGM holdings—Treasure Island, The Mirage, and the oh-so-children-unwanted Bellagio—(p. 95 and 88 respectively) is a wonderful place for families to stay, with plenty for children to do and see.

Boasting more ATMs than any other building on earth, the MGM Grand takes its name seriously—it's enormous, with 5,034 rooms. The hotel's theme is the City of Entertainment, and the rotunda (with its lavish use of frosted glass frescos, marble, and wood) carries out the theme of truly historic Hollywood elegance at its most extravagant. The balcony above the rotunda, overlooking the casino, is an excellent place for children and their parents to watch the live entertainment (often free!) on the lounge stage. Even if your little darlings could care less about the Golden Age of the silver screen or the platinum age of rock, there are plenty of distractions to keep them busy, interested, and amused, some of which won't cost you a dime.

For starters, there's the **Lion Habitat** (p. 155) and **CBS Television City,** where children ages 10 and older can play critic—attending screenings of new television programs (with a parent) and rating shows. The pool area, where not-for-free artists will braid hair into elaborate styles and apply temporary tattoos, sits on 6.6 landscaped acres. Along with a Jacuzzi and standard pools, the MGM Grand also boasts the longest lazy river ride in Vegas; flotation devices are available for rent, along with cabanas. There's an arcade (p. 160), a food court with plenty of options, and restaurants such as **Wolfgang Puck Café, Emeril's** (Creole/Cajun), and **Nob Hill.** These, along with the buffet, **Stage Deli,** and the **Rainforest Cafe,** are reviewed in Chapter 5. For nighttime entertainment, the hotel offers the adults-only *La Femme,* a headliner showroom, and an event area for sporting matches and larger concerts. Add in a convenient location and helpful staff and you have a complete city of entertainment for the wee and teen ones, and for those who pay for them.

The MGM Grand also boasts the luxurious **Grand Spa,** an Asian-themed retreat that offers massages, high-priced pedicures, facials, aromatherapy scrubs, and other treatments. The health club—$25 a day, with a discounted rate after 6pm—has a full complement of equipment, ranging from weights to state-of-the-art computerized cardio machines.

However, all of this fun, fun, fun needs to be housed in a large, large, large area, and alas, the signage is hard to read, so getting around inside this monstrosity can become a Sisyphean task. We "lost" the elevators to our room several times, though the attentive staff luckily recognized our befuddled expression and pointed us in the right direction. Also, getting from room to pool can take awhile, especially if the hotel is crowded, because, this being Vegas, the pathway circumnavigates the casino.

The rooms at the MGM Grand are done in a vaguely mid-'30s style, with light wood and neutral camel tones. Black-and-white photos of stars, lions, and celebrities decorate the walls, and there are plenty of lamps. The bathrooms are a good size; however, the bathtubs are small. Children should be reminded that

---

Fun Fact **Cleaning Up**

- The MGM Grand launders 12,000 bath towels, 18,000 washcloths, 11,000 sheets, and 15,000 pillowcases every day. Kids should be glad they don't have to make the beds here! MGM launders more than 29 million pounds of sheets annually for its guests in the largest privately owned laundry in Nevada: It takes an average of 22 miles of sheets each day to freshen the beds!

- Bellagio, one of MGM Grand's sister hotels, generates 44,000 pounds of dirty linen daily, including 10,000 king-size sheets, 10,000 pillowcases, 7,500 bath towels, 9,000 washcloths, and 4,000 bath rugs.

- In 1 month, Circus Circus sends 403,000 bath towels, 357,000 hand towels, and 800,000 sheets to its laundry service, Mission Industries, to be cleaned for the hotel's 3,770 rooms.

- A tablecloth lasts about 35 washes, sheets about 100 washings, and towels 60. Approximately 25% of MGM Grand's linen that has been deemed unserviceable is recycled; sheets become pillowcases, towels become cleaning rags, etc.

—from the *Las Vegas Review-Journal*

Fun Fact **Plenty of Room at the Inn**

The MGM Grand is one of the world's largest hotels, with more than 5,000 rooms. It would take a person 13 years and 8 months to sleep in every one of them!

---

the retractable clothesline is not a toy. The premier suites boast a far nicer array of toiletries than the standard rooms and bungalow suites, and unless you stay in the premier suites, you must request turndown service. *Note:* The MGM Grand's Emerald Tower rooms, which had gotten rather shabby, are in the process of being refurbished from head to toe. When the tower reopens in late 2005, it will have a new (though as yet unknown) name.

The MGM Grand also has a service to ease your travel experience; it's one of several hotels to offer airport reservations and check-in at Las Vegas's McCarran International Airport. This satellite desk, located in south baggage claim, near the exit from the C and D gates, is open from 9am to 11pm. There you can also make reservations for shows at both the MGM Grand and New York–New York, and, for an extra fee, shuttle and luggage transportation can be arranged to either hotel.

3799 Las Vegas Blvd. S. (at Tropicana Ave.), Las Vegas, NV 89109. © **800/929-1111** or 702/891-7777. Fax 702/891-1030. www.mgmgrand.com. 5,034 units. $89–$329 double; $129–$2,500 suite. Extra person $25. Children under 13 stay free in parent's room. Cribs free; rollaways $25 per night. AE, DC, DISC, MC, V. Free self- and valet parking. **Amenities:** 16 restaurants (all major cuisines); casino; events arena; showroom; cabaret theater; 2 wedding chapels; outdoor pool; health club; spa; Jacuzzi; sauna; concierge; tour desk; car-rental desk; business center; 24-hr. room service; in-room massage; babysitting; laundry service; dry cleaning; nonsmoking rooms; executive-level rooms. *In room:* A/C, TV w/pay movies, dataport, hair dryer, iron/ironing board, safe.

Monte Carlo Resort & Casino ★★   At first look, this hotel with its marble lobby looks imposing and too formal for children, especially with the slightly suggestive statues out front. Additionally, depending on season and availability, there may be an extra charge for children staying in their parent's room. But despite those slight negatives, this is a kid-friendly place to stay, especially for older children and teens. The rooms, accessible without going through the casino, are spacious and decorated in traditional European style. And while there's no discount at the **Monte Carlo Buffet** (p. 146), and none of the hotel's restaurants offer children's menus, the restaurants—including **Dragon Noodle Co.** (p. 126) and the **Monte Carlo Pub & Brewery** (p. 131)—have a large selection that kids will find appealing. Standard options—pizza, burgers, hot dogs, ice cream—are available at the food court.

The main attraction for children, aside from master magician **Lance Burton** (p. 220) and an adequate arcade, is the huge pool area, which includes a kiddies' pool, a lazy river, and a wave pool.

Parents will appreciate that the health club charges a very reasonable (for Vegas) $19 a day for use of the large and well-maintained facilities, including steam rooms and whirlpools. Those priming themselves for Wimbledon, or who just want to practice their backhands, can take advantage of the three tennis courts, lit for night use.

3770 Las Vegas Blvd. S. (between Flamingo Rd. and Tropicana Ave.), Las Vegas, NV 89109. © **800/311-8999** or 702/730-7777. Fax 702/730-7250. www.monte-carlo.com. 3,002 units. Sun–Thurs $69–$179 double; $149–$279 suite; Fri–Sat $109–$269 double, $189–$469 suite. Extra person $25. Children under 12 stay free in parent's room, depending on season. Cribs/rollaways free. AE, DC, DISC, MC, V. Free self- and valet parking. **Amenities:** 7 restaurants (all major cuisines); casino; showroom; wedding chapel; large wave pool with lazy river and separate kiddie pool; 3 night-lit tennis courts with full services and equipment rental; health club; spa; Jacuzzi; sauna; watersports equipment/rental; video arcade; concierge; tour desk; business center; 24-hr. room service; in-room massage; babysitting; laundry service; dry cleaning; nonsmoking rooms; executive-level rooms. *In room:* A/C, TV w/pay movies, dataport, hair dryer, iron/ironing board.

New York–New York Hotel & Casino ⚆ New Yorkers will tell you that, for the most part, this hotel is nothing like their city, and some seem to almost resent this cartoon version of their hometown. But people from everywhere else love this place, especially since the terrorist attacks of September 11, 2001. Within days of that tragedy, a spontaneous tribute—T-shirts from hundreds of police and fire departments—covered the shrubbery around the miniature New York Harbor (complete with fireboats that shoot water) in front of the hotel. Since then, New York–New York has installed a permanent memorial to the lives lost, including two large flags that can be seen from the roller coaster as it whizzes by.

A complete refurbishing of the smallish guest rooms in a '40s-inspired decor was completed in August 2004. There are 64 different room layouts, and all of them have attractive though dinky bathrooms that may disappoint parents, as will the fact that each extra person is $20, no matter what their age, but what the heck, it's a vacation right, and kids love the New York–New York experience. There's the aforementioned roller coaster, the Manhattan Express, which zips around miniature Manhattan landmarks, and loads of junk food including pizza, candied apples, hot dogs, and ice cream. They'll also be able to see one-third replicas of Rockefeller Plaza, a subway station, and Central Park as you escort them about. The **Coney Island arcade** (p. 164) is the best hotel arcade in town—large, clean, and well lit, with both traditional boardwalk and video games as well as really nice tiled bathrooms.

While only the **ESPN Zone** restaurant offers a children's menu, **America** and **Chin Chin** (all reviewed in chapter 5) have kid-friendly and vegetarian food, as do **Gonzalez Y Gonzalez** and **Il Fornaio. Schrafft's** features great frozen custard that's especially popular with the kid set. Additionally, the spectacular Greenwich Village–themed **Village Eateries** food court offers up pizza, smoothies, and other snacks.

The major drawback—aside from the not-so-big health club and the surcharge for children—is that the bland pool is right next to the parking lot. *Tip:* Rooms next to the roller coaster tend to rumble.

3790 Las Vegas Blvd. S. (at Tropicana Ave.), Las Vegas, NV 89109. ⓒ **888/696-9887** or 702/740-6969. Fax 702/740-6920. www.nynyhotelcasino.com. 2,033 units. Sun–Thurs from $99 double; Fri–Sat from $249 double. Extra person $30. No discount for children. Cribs/rollaways free. AE, DC, DISC, MC, V. Free self- and valet parking. **Amenities:** 9 restaurants (all major cuisines); casino; showrooms; roller coaster; outdoor pool; small health club and spa; Jacuzzi; sauna; video arcade with carnival midway games; concierge; tour desk; 24-hr. room service; laundry service; dry cleaning; nonsmoking rooms; executive-level rooms. *In room:* A/C, TV w/pay movies, dataport, hair dryer, safe.

The Tropicana Resort & Casino ⚆ A great pool, decent rooms, kid-friendly food and shows, and a prime location add up to make the Tropicana a perfectly fine, dependable place to stay. There have been rumblings for a while now that this venerable Strip hotel may soon be remodeled or expanded, but those radical changes have yet to materialize. However, one favorite kid-friendly attraction, the **Wildlife Walk,** which had tropical birds, animals, and amphibians, has been replaced by kiosks and carts selling touristy items.

The outside of the hotel vaguely resembles a Swiss village in the summer, though locals assure us that it's meant to be a Caribbean town. Whatever. Rooms suffer from the same split personality. The small Island Tower rooms have an overgrown tropical theme going on, while the Paradise Tower rooms drift toward French provincial. Both are a bit of a trek from the lobby. *Note:* The so-called "Garden Rooms" extending into the Trop's parking lot are downright awful and should be avoided at all costs.

The pool, with its waterfall, is large and partially indoors, partially outdoors. In the winter, a wall comes down, and the pool becomes half its size and completely indoors, staying mostly warm and sheltered from desert winds. Considering that most Vegas hotels don't bother to heat their pools during the colder months, this feature is a bonus for winter vacationers.

Calypsos, a gussied-up coffee shop (p. 129), and the **Tropicana Island Buffet** are reliable places for a meal, while **Mizuno's** Japanese restaurant (p. 125) provides a minishow with dinner, along with kids' menus. For a fun snack or a quick PB&J, try **Legends Deli** (p. 130).

The **Casino Legends Hall of Fame Museum** (p. 170), is a fun, dare we say educational, way to spend an hour or so. *The Illusionary Magic of Rick Thomas* (p. 220) and the *Tropicana Bird Show* (p. 223) are great shows for the whole family, while parents may enjoy the classic Vegas kitsch of *Folies Bergere,* one of the last production shows (read: lots of sequins and very little clothing) left in Las Vegas.

3801 Las Vegas Blvd. S. (at Tropicana Ave.), Las Vegas, NV 89109. (C) **888/826-8767** or 702/739-2222. Fax 702/739-2469. www.tropicanalv.com. 1,878 units. $79–$229 double. Extra person $20. Children under 18 stay free in parent's room. Cribs free; rollaways $20. AE, DC, DISC, MC, V. Free self- and valet parking. **Amenities:** 7 restaurants (buffet, American, Chinese, Japanese); lounges; casino; showrooms; wedding chapel; 3 outdoor pools; small health club and spa; video arcade; concierge; tour desk; car-rental desk; 24-hr. room service; laundry service; dry cleaning; nonsmoking rooms; executive-level rooms. *In room:* A/C, TV w/pay movies, dataport; minifridge (in some units), hair dryer, iron/ironing board.

MODERATE

Boardwalk Hotel & Casino 🎭🎭   Formerly a Holiday Inn, this hotel is now part of the "we don't want to be known as family oriented" MGM MIRAGE group. Unlike its crankier stepsisters, Boardwalk isn't high concept or fancy, and it doesn't suffer from antikiditis either. For the price, you can't beat the location, on the Strip less than a block from the Monte Carlo, Aladdin/Planet Hollywood, New York–New York, Paris Las Vegas, and Bellagio. We also like that the entrance is just a few yards away from the elevators, making getting to your room a quick, air-conditioned breeze. The valets are speedy, and the self-parking is very close to the hotel's front. The casino is contained to one side of the building and can be avoided completely as you enter and exit.

Disappointingly, the roller coaster, part of the early-20th-century Coney Island facade, doesn't actually work. The American carnival imagery of beachside clowns and acrobats, however, does carry on throughout the property with murals, posters, and paintings.

The rooms have been updated, some with a pleasant pastel color scheme, others in more lively shades. They are perfectly serviceable and nice, especially if you can snag a room at the lower end of the rack rates. The pools are clean, cool, and inviting, though not as glamorous as those at the glitzier neighbors.

Some families may like that the Boardwalk has the only 24-hour buffet in Las Vegas (p. 146), along with a 24-hour coffee shop.

3750 Las Vegas Blvd. S. (between Harmon and Tropicana aves.), Las Vegas, NV 89109. © **866/915-3097** or 702/735-2400. Fax 702/730-3166. www.boardwalklv.com. 653 units. $45–$139 double; $295–$495 1-bedroom suite; $495–$895 2-bedroom suite. Extra person $15. Children under 13 stay free in parent's room. Cribs free; rollaways $10. AE, DC, DISC, MC, V. Free self- and valet parking. **Amenities:** 5 restaurants (American, buffet); casino; showroom; outdoor pools; small exercise room; tour desk; car-rental desk; room service; laundry service; dry cleaning; nonsmoking rooms; coin-op washers and dryers. *In room:* A/C, TV w/pay movies, dataport, coffeemaker, hair dryer, iron/ironing board.

Excalibur ★★   This medieval-themed hotel was built with families in mind—it's full of things for kids to see and do, and "The Realm" concept definitely produces some "whoas" from children. Excalibur's decor is based on the romantic ideals of the Middle Ages, filtered through fairy tale cartoons, sword-and-sorcery movies, and 1980s postmodern design. In other words, it's a Middle Ages mishmash that manages to capture the essence of life in a medieval village—loud, claustrophobic (low ceilings in the hallways and guest rooms), and crowded. Thankfully, the resemblance ends there; unlike a feudal village, Excalibur is neither plague ridden nor stinky.

We must stress that this hotel—along with its sister up the Strip, Circus Circus—is still going strong by catering to families (offering lots for kids to do in a pretty cool environment) at a time when many over-the-top Vegas hotels are going out of their way to be kid unfriendly. Along with an IMAX movie theater, there is a well-stocked **arcade** full of the latest video games and the dinner show *Tournament of Kings* (p. 164 and 224, respectively). Excalibur also offers a pool, free juggling, magic, and puppet acts, plus story time every 45 minutes on the **Jester's Stage,** located on the second floor. Known as the Village Square, this level has meandering streets and Ye Olde Shoppes selling plastic viking helmets and swords, princess hats, and a variety of other appropriately themed souvenirs.

Kids and adults alike get excited over the **Krispy Kreme** factory (p. 136) on the second floor. And though enthralled throngs watch in fascination as the fried dough chunks slide from racks into their sugar-glaze bath, alas, there are no free samples. The second floor also hosts the hotel's restaurants, including a food court, the **Round Table buffet** (p. 147), the **Regale Italian Eatery,** and **The Steakhouse at Camelot,** a pricey hearty-eaters prime rib and steakhouse that is really more of an adult dining option. This floor also has the entranceway to the people mover (really, a moving sidewalk) to the **Luxor.** There's also a free tram to the **Luxor** and **Mandalay Bay,** which is a lot of fun to ride.

Tips **Sign Up to Save**

Almost every hotel with a casino in Las Vegas has a slots club or another similar type of frequent-gambling program. Once you sign up, you'll receive a plastic card with a magnetic strip, which you insert in the slot machines, or, if you are playing the tables, hand to your dealer. The card functions as a sort of tracking device, notifying the casino how much you are spending and what your gambling habits are. At the tables, you may need to place a large bet, say over $20 a hand, to rate, but at the slots, you rack up points by your length of play and the amount of money you feed into the machine. What are the advantages? Well, simply by signing up, you can end up with a mailbox full of offers to stay in Vegas again at significantly discounted rates. If you plan on returning to Vegas within a year, it's a good use of your time to stand in the line at the promotions desk and join the club.

Nice Places to Visit (But You Wouldn't Want to Stay There)

Bellagio   3600 Las Vegas Blvd. S., at the corner of Flamingo Road (© 888/987-6667 or 702/693-7111; www.bellagio.com). This is a beautiful hotel, designed for the rich and those who would prefer not to come in contact with children. The hotel states on their website, on the phone, and in person, that persons under the age of 18 are not permitted on the premises—even with their guardians—unless they're guests of the hotel, or have tickets or reservations for a show or restaurant. This harsh rule seems flexible: On our visits we saw slews of kids with adults moving through the lobby and Via Bellagio (p. 193). A casino security person told us that for the most part, they practice don't-ask-don't-tell with regards to escorted, well-behaved children. Other folks have reported that they have seen families without room keys turned away at the hotel's revolving door. If you want to visit the conservatory or see Cirque du Soleil's *O* (p. 218), be prepared to answer staff's questions and possibly encounter hostile glares from guests who were promised a childfree zone.

Hotel San Remo   115 E. Tropicana Ave., just east of the Strip (© 800/522-7366 or 702/739-9000; www.sanremolasvegas.com). A cheap prime rib buffet makes this an attractive place for a meal, but they don't want children staying here. And San Remo will be even less inviting to families with children when it's transformed into the world's first Hooters Hotel Casino—yes, an expanded version of the infamous restaurant chain of the same name—in 2005.

Imperial Palace   3535 Las Vegas Blvd. S., between Sands Avenue and Flamingo Road (© 800/634-6441 or 702/731-3311; www.imperialpalace.

Rooms have noticeably low ceilings, and the windows have curved arches above them on the outside, blocking out a small portion of the view. On the lower floors, these factors can make for an exceptionably Rapunzel-like closed-in feeling. The rooms are decorated primarily in earth and woodsy tones, with Arts and Crafts–style bedspreads, faux-antique furniture, and heraldic art hung on the walls. Without dust ruffles on the beds, we got a nice view of the box springs. And there are no bathtubs, so keep this in mind if your little ones are bathers. Some guests who have stayed in Tower 2 have complained about noise from the roller coaster at New York–New York across the street, which runs from 10am through 11pm. Though we experienced no problems during our stay, you might want to take the coaster into consideration if you or your children are light sleepers. Note also that cellphones do not work well on the lower floors, which might make dial-happy teenagers unhappy.

If the rooms aren't exactly stellar, the staff is incredibly accommodating, moving us twice after we had been assigned problematic accommodations. Staff members are generally friendly and very kid tolerant, because families are the hotel's bread and butter.

3850 Las Vegas Blvd. S. (at Tropicana Ave.), Las Vegas, NV 89109. © 877/750-5464 or 702/597-7777. Fax 702/597-7009. www.excalibur.com. 4,008 units. $69–$159 double. Extra person $15. Children under 13 stay com). If your child is 6 or older your room will be an extra $15 per night, and depending on who's at the front desk, the crib and rollaway rentals can be either $15 or free, so even if you can get the lowest rate of $29, you're not saving much. Because there's little for kids to enjoy here, just drop in to see the Auto Collections (p. 168) or the *Legends in Concert* impersonators show (p. 221). During the summer there's a Hawaiian luau. But basically this hotel is for gamblers, not families.

Mandalay Bay   3950 Las Vegas Blvd. S., at Hacienda Avenue (© **877/ 632-7000** or 702/632-7000; www.mandalaybay.com). Despite the fabulous pool area with waves for body surfing and boogie boarding, this is not the place to stay with children. The hotel, with its beautiful Southeast Asian decor, cultivates a hip, adults-only clientele, emphasized by its room policy: Any extra person, be they 7 months or 7 years old, costs an extra $35 a night. Add in the crib or rollaway rental ($20), and you might as well stay at the far kid-friendlier Caesars, Venetian, or Monte Carlo. Plus the food selection for children is virtually nil. However, the Shark Reef aquarium (p. 164) is worth a visit.

Rio All-Suite Hotel & Casino   3700 W. Flamingo Rd., at I-15 (© **888/ 752-9746** or 702/777-7777; www.playrio.com). While the idea of an "all-suite hotel" may seem appealing, in the Rio's case this just means larger rooms with unusual-for-Vegas refrigerators. Rollaways are free, but each extra person runs $30 per night, no matter how old the child. Cribs are also free, but the hotel has a limited number available, and there's no guarantee one will be available for you. Stay elsewhere and visit for the buffet (p. 149) or the free *Masquerade in the Sky* show (p. 155).

free in parent's room. Cribs/rollaways free. AE, DC, DISC, MC, V. Free self- and valet parking. **Amenities:** 5 restaurants (buffet, American, Italian, more); casino; showrooms; wedding chapel; outdoor pool; video arcade; concierge; tour desk; car-rental desk; 24-hr. room service; laundry service; dry cleaning; nonsmoking rooms. *In room:* A/C, TV w/pay movies, dataport, hair dryer.

Luxor Las Vegas ✦✦✦   Luxor's theme is all Egypt, all the time, and there's no skimping on the cornucopia of Cleopatrania contained within. You can't miss the Luxor as you drive or fly into town; it's that big black pyramid at the south end of the Strip. At night, balls of light roll down its sides and the top of the pyramid shoots out a giant 315,000-watt light beam—supposedly representing the ancient Egyptians' belief that the soul ascends to Heaven on a beam of light—which is the world's brightest, according to the hotel's talking animatronic camels, located in the Giza Gallery of shops. Yes, that's right, talking camels! Kids love them, and so do adults for that matter, and it's rare to find the gabbing dromedaries without a cluster of tourists hanging on their every word and jostling to take their photos.

The hotel's main entrance, on the casino level, is breathtaking. As you enter the lobby through the pyramid, you are greeted by a fountain with a giant statue of Ramses or some other suitable pharaoh. The lobby itself is a mix of Art Nouveau and Art Deco—beautiful and soothing, full of marble and dark wood, with hanging glass lamps and wall sconces. There's a less fancy, smaller lobby on the north side by the towers for tour group check-in only, but they didn't snarl at us when we used it accidentally.

The pyramid guest rooms open onto the huge open-air atrium, and the windows slant, which is sort of cool, but naturally, the higher you go, the more they slant, which could get a bit frustrating for the taller folks in your group. These rooms have shower-only bathrooms, making baths a nonoption. ("But mom, doesn't using the pool count as a bath?") Very cool for kids are the 39-degree high-speed inclinators—that's what an elevator is when it works inside a pyramid. (Really, they are part conveyance, part thrill ride—check out that jolt when they come to a halt!) The larger tower rooms do indeed have baths (some are of the wonderful whirlpool variety), though in family travel mode, you may not want one of the suite options, which have the tub in the bedroom under the window. All rooms are decorated in an Egyptian motif, but oddly, there were no bedside lamps, which made the in-bed reading of Shakespeare's *Antony and Cleopatra* a bit difficult. But the mattresses were comfy and the room was quiet.

The hotel is great for kids with an interest in mummies—they're everywhere, from the gift shops to the **Pharaoh's Pheast** buffet (p. 145). There are also enough attractions to keep the kids amused: There's a fantastic **arcade** and an **IMAX theater** with several films, plus an excellent motion simulator, *In Search of the Obelisk;* the amazing **Blue Man Group** (p. 216); and **King Tut's Tomb & Museum** (p. 159). Reliable family dining spots include **Hamada** (p. 124) and **La Salsa** (p. 129). The Egyptian theme stops poolside, but the pool area is really nice, with four dunking options, all of which accept kids. There are lifeguards on duty, but as with all hotels, a parent or other responsible adult must be present.

3900 Las Vegas Blvd. S. (between Reno and Hacienda aves.), Las Vegas, NV 81119. ✆ **800/288-1000** or 702/262-4000. Fax 702/262-4452. www.luxor.com. 4,400 units. Sun–Thurs $79–$259 double, Fri–Sat $109 and up double; $149 and up whirlpool suite; $249–$800 other suites. Extra person $25. Children under 12 stay free in parent's room. Cribs $15; rollaways $25. AE, DC, DISC, MC, V. Free self- and valet parking. **Amenities:** 10 restaurants (all major cuisines); casino; showrooms; 4 outdoor pools; health club and spa; 18,000-sq.-ft. video arcade with the latest Sega and more; concierge; tour desk; car-rental desk; courtesy car or limo; business center; shopping arcade; 24-hr. room service; dry cleaning; nonsmoking rooms; executive-level rooms. *In room:* A/C, TV w/pay movies, hair dryer, iron/ironing board.

2 Center Strip

Center Strip boasts 10 of the world's largest and most famous hotels, along with Las Vegas's most concentrated shopping opportunities, with three major malls and numerous retail promenades. Center Strip also features the finest pools in town (at The Flamingo, The Mirage, and Caesars), white tigers, a sirens-vs.-pirates live extravaganza, a regularly erupting volcano, a larger-than-life dancing-waters show, and even an exact half-size replica of the Eiffel Tower. Despite the visual stimuli, however, Center Strip megaresorts are less family oriented than those along the South Strip.

VERY EXPENSIVE

Caesars Palace ⭐⭐⭐   Now this is Vegas—over the top, goofy, and kitschy. In the past few years, Caesars has actually toned its theme down a bit; some of its previous obvious vulgarity has been sacrificed on the altar of restraint, much to our disappointment. But really, do your children need mirrors over the bed? We thought not. You might, so if planning on separate rooms from the kids, ask what they can do for you at the front desk. Gladiators greet you on arrival,

Bally's Las Vegas **11**
Bellagio **10**
Caesars Palace **8**
The Flamingo Las Vegas **9**
Harrah's Las Vegas **4**
Imperial Palace **5**

The Mirage **3**
Palms Resort & Casino **6**
Paris Las Vegas **12**
Rio All-Suite Hotel & Casino **7**
TI–Treasure Island Las Vegas **1**
The Venetian **2**

cocktail waitresses wear togas, and everywhere there are arches, statues, and columns. Chariots and temples line the entranceways, and it's all gloriously silly. But historical and educational, too. Really.

Like the Caesars' empire, this hotel is vast and sprawling, making navigation a bit difficult, especially because there's just so much to gape at. But once you get the hang of following the signage, you'll be moving as quickly as the bow to Nero's fiddle. Rooms, occupying four towers (a fifth is under construction), tend toward classical themes—Greco-Roman statues and architectural details (and the aforementioned mirrored ceilings in some rooms). The newer rooms are less neo-Roman in their decor and are very nicely appointed with great views. All bathrooms have oversize tubs and marble floors. You should make sure that your room doesn't have a tub in the center of the room—that detail could make getting bathed a bit too much of a family experience for anyone's taste.

With nine restaurants and a food court in the hotel, plus eight more in the Forum Shops, you won't be at a loss to take care of your hungry brood. Along with the hotel's buffet, Caesars features Bradley Ogden's, winner of the prestigious 2004 James Beard award for "Best New Restaurant." Additionally, **Spago** (perfect for your gourmets-to-be) can be found in the Forum Shops, along with **La Salsa,** the **Cheesecake Factory,** and the **Stage Deli,** all of which are reviewed in chapter 5. There's also a 24-hour coffee shop, Café Lago, in the hotel proper.

Located in the Garden of the Gods, the pool area features attractive granite mosaics, seahorses and griffins, and a **Snackus Maximus.** If you'd prefer not to

---

Fun Fact **Darling, You Look Marble-ous**

The majority of the art in the Caesars Palace casino replicates master-pieces created centuries after the fall of Rome. Most of the marble stat-ues there are replicas of classic Renaissance works, including Michelangelo's *David*. There is, however, one non-European style statue gracing the property—the golden statue of *Brahma,* the Hindu god of good fortune, which was donated by a Thai gambler.

---

rest on your laurels poolside, there are also tennis courts and a $24-a-day health club with a rock-climbing wall and state-of-the-art machines.

The Forum Shops features laser shows, animatronic statues, and high-end clothes and accessories, along with kiosks of children's gladiator costumes, toga sleep shirts, and assorted schlock. But then, without schlock, it wouldn't really be Vegas, would it?

3570 Las Vegas Blvd. S. (just north of Flamingo Rd.), Las Vegas, NV 89109. © **800/634-6661** or 702/731-7110. Fax 702/731-6636. www.caesars.com/caesars/lasvegas. 2,471 units. From $99 standard double, $109–$500 "run of house deluxe" double; $549–$1,000 suite. Extra person $20. Children under 18 stay free in parent's room. Cribs free; rollaways $20. AE, DC, DISC, MC, V. Free self- and valet parking. **Amenities:** 18 restaurants (all major cuisines); casino; wedding chapel; 3 outdoor pools; health club and spa; concierge; tour desk; car-rental desk; business center; shopping arcade; 24-hr. room service; laundry service; dry cleaning; nonsmoking rooms; executive-level rooms. *In room:* A/C, TV w/pay movies, dataport, hair dryer, iron/ironing board, safe.

Paris Las Vegas ✦✦   *Zut alors!* Not content with miniaturizing Rome, Egypt, and New York, Las Vegas turned its eyes to gay Paree, and before you could say *"vive la différence,"* there was a half-scale replica of the Eiffel Tower, a *petit* Louvre (sans artwork) and *demi*-Arc de Triomphe, fountains, and other landmarks higgledy-piggledy heaped about with no sense of the real city's geog-raphy. Nor of its language. Kindly point out to your children that "le car rental" is not real French. However, along with these pseudo-*français* touches—includ-ing the staff uttering *"bonjour"* and *"merci"* at every turn—there is real attention to detail and comfort here.

The lobby, designed to replicate chunks of Versailles, glistens under ornate crystal chandeliers. The Eiffel Towerette's legs rest on the casino floor; its spire, from whence you can gaze on the Strip or dine at the *très* overpriced Eiffel Tower restaurant, shoots upward. It's always a lovely twilight in this fantasy Paris; streetlights gleam along the cobblestone paths that wind through the casino and Le Boulevard shopping area.

The theme fades slightly at the rooms, which are luxurious with thick carpets and drapes and plenty of marble, but only with the faintest hint of a French accent. The bathrooms are attractive, with larger-than-average tubs; but, frankly, the public *pissoirs* off the casino have more of the flavor (though, thankfully, not the scent) of Paris. Rooms that face west will give you a great view of Bellagio's fountains, though the water jets and music can be noisy.

In the real Paris, tourists can eat cheaply at local cafes and patisseries. Oh, that this were true here. Because Paris Las Vegas's perfectionist bakers feel that the Nevada water is not perfect for their art, H_2O is imported from the City of Lights for all the bread and pastries, which are baked on-site. You may not be able to taste the difference, but your wallet will feel it. **Le Village Buffet** and **Mon Ami Gabi** (p. 147 and 134, respectively) are not inexpensive, but they do offer decent to fine versions of French food. There are also several cafes that offer basic sandwiches and salads, plus a branch of the Paris sweet and pastry shop, **Lenôtre** (p. 138).

The second-floor 2-acre pool, nestled between the Eiffel and hotel towers and surrounded by trees and marble planters, is a lovely place to spend an afternoon soaking up the rays and the view.

3655 Las Vegas Blvd. S., Las Vegas, NV 89109. ℂ 888/BONJOUR (266-5687) or 702/946-7000. Fax 702/967-3836. www.parislv.com. 2,916 units. $99–$269 double; $350 and up suites. Extra person $30. Children under 18 stay free in parent's room. Cribs free; rollaways $10. AE, DC, DISC, MC. V. Free self- and valet parking. **Amenities:** 11 restaurants (French, American, Italian, more); casino; showrooms; 2 wedding chapels; outdoor pool; health club and spa; concierge; tour desk; business center; shopping arcade; 24-hr. room service; laundry service; dry cleaning; nonsmoking rooms; executive-level rooms. *In room:* A/C, TV w/pay movies, dataport, hair dryer, iron/ironing board, safe.

The Venetian ★★★   European glamour abounds at this ornate casino resort. Outside, you can frolic along the Bridge of Sighs and take photos of the Campanile and Doge's Palace. The beautiful lobby's recessed ceiling is covered with hand-painted copies of Venetian art, surrounded by elaborate gold-leaf frames, but if you spend too much time staring upward, you'll miss out on the marble floors, aged stone, and statues. And you'll probably get lost, too. We visited several times and always got turned around, lost, or generally disoriented.

The luxurious decor in the main parts of the hotel carries through to the large rooms. All are suites, decorated with richly patterned fabrics. The sitting room, with a foldout couch, is a few steps down from the sleeping area. There's even a half-canopy over the bed, adding to the European feel. The sumptuous marble bathrooms have two sinks, make-up areas, deep tubs, separate showers, and enclosed toilets. West-facing rooms will give you a view of the sirens-and-sailors show across the street at Treasure Island, but the sounds will also leak in; the fracas ends at midnight. Also, under *no circumstances* should you or your kids touch, jiggle, or fiddle with anything in the minibar—you will be charged for simply moving items about (trust us—there are computer sensors under each item). The hotel will, however, provide a fridge free of charge, along with devices for the hearing impaired. ***Note:*** The new Venezia Tower rooms have their own check-in desk and are even more luxe than the regular ones (kids will find the plasma TV in the bathroom quite cool).

Several good choices for kid-type food here include the **Grand Lux Café** (p. 137), which has over 150 choices of (oversize) plates from which to choose, along with a good food court featuring Nathan's hot dogs, Italian food, and sandwiches. There are also two Chinese restaurants, Noodle Asia and the very pricey and not-very-kid-friendly Royal Star (p. 135).

While the hotel is elaborately detailed, the five pools are disappointingly stark in comparison. Located on the fourth-floor roof, they offer a view, with minimal shade and plantings.

Parents looking to get away from it all should try the lavish **Canyon Ranch SpaClub,** the finest hotel spa in town. You'll find nutritionists, physical

---

***Tips* Surfing for Savings**

Before you take your trip to Vegas, go online and sign up at the casino websites to be notified of promotional deals by e-mail. And, again, we strongly recommend that once you've arrived in Vegas, you should join the slot clubs at every casino you visit. Before long, you'll be getting glossy postcards in your mailbox with deals to lure you back to Sin City.

therapists, and acupuncturists on the staff, and vibrating massage chairs that you rest in during pedicures—what more could you want? The $30-a-day fee is high, but it does include a full day's worth of classes ranging from regular aerobics to yoga, Pilates, rock climbing, and dance.

The **Grand Canal Shoppes** is a stupendous mall complete with nearly four-score stores, seven eateries, costumed performers, and gondola rides. *Tip:* This is the only hotel on the Strip without a buffet. Plan your eating accordingly.

3355 Las Vegas Blvd. S., Las Vegas, NV 89109. ℂ **888/2-VENICE (283-6423)** or 702/414-1000. Fax 702/414-4805. www.venetian.com. 3,000 units. $179–$399 double. Extra person $35. Children under 13 stay free in parent's room. Cribs free; no rollaways. AE, DC, DISC, MC, V. Free self- and valet parking. **Amenities:** 16 restaurants (all major cuisines; no buffet); casino; showroom; wedding chapel; 5 outdoor pools; health club and spa; video arcade; concierge; tour desk; car-rental desk; business center; shopping arcade; 24-hr. room service; laundry service; dry cleaning; nonsmoking rooms; executive-level rooms. *In room:* A/C, TV w/pay movies, fax, dataport, fridge, hair dryer, iron/ironing board, safe.

EXPENSIVE

The Flamingo Las Vegas ★★★   The best pool in town and a generous discount for kids at the buffet make this a swell choice for your family, especially if you can land a good discount. The Flamingo rose to fame as the first Vegas hotel built with the mob's money (in 1946)—and eventually Bugsy Siegel's blood. The hotel has been renovated numerous times, and Bugsy's suite, with its secret panels and hidden doors was torn out with no regard for history (welcome to Las Vegas).

The hotel's giant pink facade, with the glowing lotus, is one of the most famous landmarks in Vegas, but negotiating the driveway under it leading to the valet can be confusing. Once inside, the hotel is nice, bright, and light, but a bit overwhelmed by the casino: The gaming area spreads throughout the property, winding about like a cash-hungry python.

The rooms have no set or consistent style, because there have been so many additions and renovations over the years. Room configurations vary depending on the era in which the tower was built, but most rooms tend to be slightly larger than the Vegas norm, decorated in either beach-toned pastels or deeper jewel colors (ask for a recently renovated room—most have been redone in the past couple of years). The bathrooms are everything you'd expect in a standard hotel: nothing to complain about, nothing to rave about, either.

The pool area is truly a wonder—15 acres of trees and tropical foliage with river rides, water slides, a kiddie pool, whirlpools, and spray misters to keep you cool. Islands are the homes to birds like ducks, swans, African penguins (they can stand the desert heat), spoonbills, and naturally, flamingos. The penguins are fed at approximately 3pm daily, and it's really fun to watch them dive and goggle their fishy meal. There are also ponds with turtles and koi. Window seats in the buffet provide an up-close view of much of the wildlife.

The **buffet** (p. 148) is half price for children, truly a bargain in Las Vegas. There are seven other dining choices, including a ubiquitous steakhouse. **Lindy's** is a decent deli with sandwiches, soups, and salads, while **Hamada** is reviewed on p. 124.

3555 Las Vegas Blvd. S. (between Sands Ave. and Flamingo Rd.), Las Vegas, NV 89109. ℂ **800/732-2111** or 702/733-3111. Fax 702/733-3353. www.flamingolasvegas.com. 3,642 units. $69–$299 double; $250–$580 suite. Extra person $20. Children under 18 stay free in parent's room. Cribs/rollaways free. Inquire about packages and timeshare suites. AE, DC, DISC, MC, V. Free self- and valet parking. **Amenities:** 8 restaurants (American, Italian, Chinese, buffet, more); casino; showrooms; outdoor pool; 4 night-lit tennis courts; health club and spa; small video arcade; tour desk; car-rental desk; business center; shopping arcade; 24-hr. room service; in-room massage; babysitting; laundry service; dry cleaning; nonsmoking rooms; executive-level rooms. *In room:* A/C, TV w/pay movies, dataport, hair dryer, iron/ironing board, safe.

Tips **Keep Them Out!**

At most hotels, children under 12 are forbidden to use the whirlpool—heed the warnings and keep your kids out, as violations are likely to attract the ire of adults seeking some sanctuary in the pool area. Anyway, the high heat is not healthy for your tots.

The Mirage   Tigers and dolphins are the main reasons to stay here, but overall, there are many better locations for families. Not that we don't adore the verdant tropical foliage, the huge aquarium at the check-in desk, the lush pool area, and the vanilla-scented air that floats throughout the property, but kids just aren't a high priority at The Mirage, as demonstrated by their charging an extra $30 per person per room, regardless of age, though cribs and rollaways are free.

If you decide to stay here because you love the animals and the location, and price is no object, here's a hint: Ask for what you want. For example, you'll want to ask for a room on the seventh floor or higher so you'll have a view of something aside from a wall; you should also ask for a room close to the elevators, or you'll be exhausted before you get out of the hotel; and finally, if you want it, ask for a room with a view of the volcano. But if you don't get a volcano room, fret not, you can watch the four-times-an-hour lava flow free from the street.

The rooms are decorated in camel and beige with red-toned accent colors—sort of dull, but tasteful nevertheless, while bathrooms sport the "see-we-have-marble-even-though-we're-small" theme. If we have one complaint it's that you can get better bang for your room buck elsewhere. The service here, however, is quite good and the staff pleasant enough.

The pool area is wonderfully landscaped, but you have to traipse through the casino to get to it from your room, which can be tiresome for smaller kids. The health club costs $20 per day, and for that you get saunas, juice bar, lockers, machines, and free weights. Expect to pay $35 and up, plus tip, for treatments such as manicures and pedicures.

3400 Las Vegas Blvd. S. (between Flamingo Rd. and Sands Ave.), Las Vegas, NV 89109. (☎) **800/627-6667** or 702/791-7111. Fax 702/791-7446. www.mirage.com. 3,044 units. Sun–Thurs $99–$399 double; Fri–Sat and holidays $129–$399 double; $250–$3,000 suite. Extra person $30. No discount for children. Cribs/rollaways free. AE, DC, DISC, MC, V. Free self- and valet parking. **Amenities:** 12 restaurants (American, French, Italian, Brazilian, buffet, more); casino; showrooms; beautiful outdoor pool; health club and spa; concierge; tour desk; car-rental desk; business center; shopping arcade; 24-hr. room service; laundry service; dry cleaning; non-smoking rooms; executive-level rooms. *In room:* A/C, TV w/pay movies, dataport, hair dryer, iron/ironing boards.

TI–Treasure Island Las Vegas   TI? What's up with the new name? Why, Vegas grew up, that's what. Though Treasure Island is a good choice for families who want to stay on the Center Strip, that doesn't mean it welcomes kids with open arms (at least not until they grow up and learn to drink and gamble). In fact, you might feel a bit pillaged when hit with the $25 per-extra-person charge, with no discount for children. But, like its next-door sister The Mirage, the cribs and rollaways are free. And Treasure Island is a lot more fun, at a little less cost, than The Mirage, while not quite as kitschy as Excalibur.

Originally conceived (or so the legend goes) as a family-oriented alternative to The Mirage, Treasure Island tried to shed its family-fun-zone vibe when it was acquired by MGM, but luckily, it kept the pirate theme intact. Skulls, crossbones, treasure chests, and other booty—appropriately gilded and marbled—are scattered all over the property. We especially like the seaside village that fronts the hotel along the lagoon where the free spectacle, *Sirens of TI,* is performed nightly. This new sirens-and-sailors show, which replaced the original pirates-vs.–British Navy extravaganza, is a bit risqué, earning a PG-13 rating.

The guest rooms are pretty spacious—bigger than those at next-door-neighbor Mirage—and are appropriately decorated in gold tones and a French Regency style. What they aren't is tacky. In fact, the rooms are surprisingly classy, with ultracomfortable beds and excellent lighting (a problem in many other Strip hotels). What there isn't is drawer space; there are only a measly two drawers, so be advised that you'll either be living out of your suitcase or the closet. The big marble bathrooms feature large soaking tubs and an abundance of counter space. *Warning:* The tub in our room didn't have handrails and the tub bottom was slippery—a bad combination for young kids. If you have older kids, try to get a Strip-side room facing the sirens show—which goes on every evening until midnight. If your kids, however, go to bed early, note that some of the goings-on can get a bit noisy.

The pool is small (just 3½ ft. deep), amoeba-shaped, and pretty bland by Vegas standards (the staff didn't even bother to check our room keys the last time we were there—a sure sign of mediocrity). There's a small kiddie pool, but most kids tend to congregate in the main pool (much to the consternation of many adults).

When it comes to food, you'll find a **buffet** (p. 148), plus a deli, a coffee shop, **Ben & Jerry's Ice Cream Store, Krispy Kreme Doughnuts,** and the **Buccaneer Bay Club** (p. 132), which provides a view of the sirens show. *Warning:* Children under 5 are not allowed in Buccaneer Bay, so plan your battle watching accordingly.

Shops are housed in a mock village, but aside from some cool skull-themed items, there's nothing outstanding—souvenirs, T-shirts, and some jewelry. Shrug. You're better off spending your window-shopping time across the street at The Venetian. The small, dark arcade will, however, keep kids (who are old enough to wander) busy long enough so you can have a romantic drink and watch the sirens show together from a table on the patio at **Tangerine,** TI's new ultralounge, like a real date.

Moms and dads looking for more escape time can go to the full-service spa and health club with a complement of machines, plus sauna, steam, whirlpool, massage, on-site trainers, TVs and stereos with headsets, and anything else you might need (including Sebastian grooming products in the women's locker room). It's $20 per day to use the facilities. Note that many of the spa services are ridiculously and outrageously overpriced: They charge $50 for a pedicure!

The greatest—albeit pricey—treat for kids at Treasure Island: The Cirque du Soleil production *Mystère.* The $90-a-ticket cost is prohibitive for most families, and it's probably too sophisticated for young kids (think 10 and over), but it is a very memorable experience, and adults and older children and teens usually rave about it.

Tip: A free tram travels between Treasure Island and The Mirage almost around the clock.

3300 Las Vegas Blvd. S. (at Spring Mountain Rd.), Las Vegas, NV 89177-0711. ✆ 800/944-7444 or 702/894-7111. Fax 702/894-7446. www.treasureisland.com. 2,900 units. From $89 double; from $149 suite. Extra person $25. No discount for children. Cribs/rollaways free. Special promotions on the Web. Inquire about packages. AE, DC, DISC, MC, V. Free self- and valet parking. **Amenities:** 11 restaurants (American, Chinese,

Italian, buffet, more); casino; showrooms; outdoor pool; health club and spa; very well-equipped game and video arcade; concierge; tour desk; car-rental desk; business center; shopping arcade; 24-hr. room service; laundry service; dry cleaning; nonsmoking rooms; executive-level rooms. *In room:* A/C, TV w/pay movies, fax, dataport, hair dryer, iron/ironing board, safe.

3 North Strip

The North Strip offers thrill rides at the Sahara and Stratosphere, a huge indoor amusement park, and big-top acts at Circus Circus, all of which can keep your children amused for hours, if not days.

MODERATE

Sahara Hotel and Casino　At first glance, this venerable gem seems a real bargain, especially if you have a NASCAR fan in the family, because one of the main lures is the Speed Zone, featuring a **NASCAR Cafe,** simulated races, and Speed—The Ride roller coaster (p. 166). However, if you need a crib or rollaway bed, you'll pay for it, and any child over 12 also hikes up your rates. And it should be noted that the Sahara feels it is not as well equipped as other hotels for children and discourages you from bringing yours—and yet, they added a roller coaster. Go figure.

The hotel is old school, a holdout from the glory days of the Rat Pack. It's not as shiny as some of its southerly neighbors, especially when compared to the similarly themed Luxor, but there is a certain amount of charm to the Moroccan decor—colored tiles and filigreed metalwork set with glowing red and blue gems are a nice touch, but the "midnight at the oasis" concept is left at the door to your room (and the bedspreads at the Sahara are notorious for their unattractiveness). Bathrooms are clean, serviceable, and just fine. Hopefully, if you've got a room here, it's just to sleep in, because that's pretty much what they're designed for—and under those not-our-taste-at-all bedspreads are some of the comfiest mattresses in town, which is an unexpected and welcome bonus.

The hotel features a buffet and the NASCAR Cafe (p. 139), along with Mexican food, a coffee shop, and the inevitable steakhouse, all of which provide sustenance.

The Olympic-size pool, located at the foot of the parking garage, is heated only during the summer months, a drawback and chilly disappointment for those visiting during the winter holidays. But even without a pool, kids will have things to do; there's an arcade in the hotel, a roller coaster in the front yard, plus the NASCAR attractions. The **Adventuredome** at Circus Circus (p. 166) is just minutes away. *Tip:* Get a bellman when checking in; it's a long trek from valet parking's domed driveway to the front desk.

2535 Las Vegas Blvd. S. (at E. Sahara Ave.), Las Vegas, NV 89109. ℰ **888/696-2121** or 702/737-2111. Fax 702/791-2027. www.saharavegas.com. 1,720 units. $39 and up double. Extra person $15. Children under 12 stay free in parent's room. Cribs/rollaways $15. AE, DC, DISC, MC, V. Free self- and valet parking. **Amenities:** 5 restaurants (American, buffet, Mexican, more); casino; showrooms; outdoor pool; Jacuzzi; tour desk; car-rental desk; business center; shopping arcade; limited room service; laundry service; dry cleaning; nonsmoking rooms; executive-level rooms. *In room:* A/C, TV w/pay movies, hair dryer, iron, ironing board.

Tips　Extra! Extra!

Because most rooms are stocked for only two guests, you may want to request enough towels and toiletries for your entire family before you arrive.

Fun Fact **Officer Dex, the K-9 Cop**

In December of 2001, Officer Dex, a then 2-year-old German shepherd, joined the security team at the Stratosphere, making him the only K-9 casino security officer in Las Vegas. Dex is trained in article and person search, obedience, scouting, and tracking. He and his handler, Officer Lieberman, are available to assist local and federal officers as well as security teams at other gaming properties, but what they really enjoy doing is interacting with guests. If you see Dex on duty, ask Officer Lieberman if it's all right to pet him or have your photo taken together.

Stratosphere Las Vegas ⭐   Yes, it's a bit far from the rest of the Strip, but the Stratosphere, the tallest building west of the Mississippi at 1,149 feet, has incredibly thrilling rides, amazing views, a fabulous pool, and reasonable rates.

The rooms are nice, with touches of cherrywood and the usual hotel amenities. Some suites offer window-side Jacuzzis, but this might not be the right way to go with your family. The bathrooms in the standard rooms are just fine; the ones in the suites are larger.

Along with dining at the high-priced, high-in-the-sky Top of the World on the 106th floor of the tower, you can stave off your hunger at **Hamada** (p. 124) or at the ubiquitous **buffet.** Bless **Fellini's Ristorante** for offering half-size, half-priced portions for both children and adults. **Roxy's** features singing waitresses in poodle skirts serving diner food. **Lucky's** coffee shop is open 24 hours and also has a retro feel. And then there's a food court with a Mickey D's, plus a steakhouse and a Mexican grill–oyster bar combo.

Indoor and outdoor observation decks offer the most stunning city views you will ever see, especially at night. The pool, located on the eighth floor overlooking the Strip, is big and beautiful, a perfect place to relax after a wild ride on the **High Roller** roller coaster (909 ft. above ground), or the **Big Shot** bungee-style ride that takes you to the top of the Strat's 1,149-foot tower, or **X-Scream,** a ride that rolls you over the edge and back. All three thrill rides are reviewed on p. 168.

The hotel also offers two shows that some deem acceptable for kids, *Viva Las Vegas,* the longest running afternoon show in the city, and the impersonator show, *American Superstars,* reviewed on p. 225 and p. 216, respectively.

2000 Las Vegas Blvd. S. (between St. Louis St. and Baltimore Ave.), Las Vegas, NV 89104. © **800/99-TOWER (998-6937)** or 702/380-7777. Fax 702/383-5334. www.stratospherehotel.com. 2,500 units. Sun–Thurs $39 and up double, Fri–Sat $79 and up double; $89 and up suite. Extra person $15. Children 12 and under stay free in parent's room. AE, DC, DISC, MC, V. Free self- and valet parking. **Amenities:** 9 restaurants (American, buffet, Italian, Asian, more); casino; showrooms; business center; large new pool area with great views of the Strip; children's rides and games located at the base of the Tower; concierge; tour desk; car-rental desk; shopping arcade; 24-hr. room service; laundry service; dry cleaning; nonsmoking rooms; executive-level rooms. *In room:* A/C, TV w/pay movies, dataport, hair dryer, iron/ironing board, safe.

INEXPENSIVE

Circus Circus ⭐⭐   With free circus acts and a huge indoor amusement park, this place is an awesome spot for all but the most jaded and cynical of today's youth. Of course, the latter could be your kids, in which case, you may want to just turn them loose at the **Adventuredome** (p. 166) anyway and see if a spin on the Chaos roller coaster will knock some fun into them.

Circus Circus **4**
Palace Station **1**
Sahara Hotel and Casino **3**
Stardust Resort & Casino **6**
Stratosphere Las Vegas **2**
Westward Ho
   Hotel & Casino **5**

Circus Circus is unique among all of Vegas's casino hotels in that, according to placards placed throughout the property, children 13 and older can move freely about the property except in the casino, where they are forbidden. Those under 13 must be accompanied by an older child. The curfew laws regarding arcades, however, still apply, and troublemakers can get themselves and their parents into all kinds of hot water.

Circus Circus was the first family-oriented casino in Las Vegas, and when it opened, the color scheme ran toward bilious and bright. One wag commented that the carpet was louder than the casino, and he wasn't far from the truth.

Fun Fact **You Learn Something New ...**

You won't find record producer Sean "P. Diddy" Combs staying at Circus Circus; he allegedly suffers from coulrophobia, fear of clowns.

Renovations completed in 1998 have toned things down a bit, though the over-all atmosphere of hectic fun remains. The midway level features dozens of car-nival games, a large arcade (more than 300 video and pinball games), trick mirrors, and ongoing circus acts under the big top from 11am to midnight daily. The world's largest permanent circus (according to the *Guinness Book of World Records*), it features renowned trapeze artists, stunt cyclists, jugglers, magicians, acrobats, and high-wire daredevils. Spectators can view the action from much of the midway or get up close and comfy on benches in the performance arena. There's a "be-a-clown" booth where kids can be made up with washable clown makeup and red foam-rubber noses. They can grab a bite to eat in McDonald's (also on this level), and since the mezzanine overlooks the casino action, they can also look down and wave to Mom and Dad—or more to the point, Mom and Dad can look up and wave to the kids without having to stray too far from the blackjack table. (For better or worse, this is the only hotel that will let you leave your brood unattended in the main area of the property, making losing money at the casino not the only risk you may be taking here!) Circus clowns wander the midway creating balloon animals and cutting up in various ways.

Rooms here come in three varieties and price ranges. The cheapest and least attractive, the Manor rooms, are housed in low three-story buildings off of the main hotel. Guests park in front of their building. A gate to the property that can only be opened with your room key ensures your safety, but you'll get what you pay for in terms of quality. The Skyrise Tower includes two pools and a casino, and these rooms are decorated in deep jewel tones. The West Tower, which houses the central registration desk and the shopping arcade, is connected to the Adventuredome theme park. These rooms are decorated in the same color scheme as those in the Skyrise Tower. The Casino Tower, where the circus acts perform, has rooms with darker earth tones. The bathrooms in every section are basic, clean, and serviceable, and they all have tubs and showers, except for a few designed for those with physical disabilities. The thousands of rooms here occupy sufficient acreage to warrant a free Disney World–style aerial shuttle (another kid pleaser) and minibuses connecting its many components.

Adjacent to the hotel is **Circusland RV Park,** with 384 full-utility spaces and up to 50-amp hookups. It has its own 24-hour convenience store, swimming pools, saunas, whirlpools, kiddie playground, fenced pet runs, video-game arcade, and community room. The rate is $17 and up Sunday to Thursday, $19 and up Friday and Saturday.

The **Pink Pony** coffee shop and the **buffet** (p. 139 and 148, respectively) are popular with the kids, and the eponymous Steakhouse has proven a consistent favorite with locals for a number of years, though a lot of people we know don't think it's all that good. **Stivali** Italian restaurant (p. 139) offers children's specials.

2880 Las Vegas Blvd. S. (between Circus Circus Dr. and Convention Center Dr.), Las Vegas, NV 89109. ℭ 877/224-7287, 800/634-3450, or 702/734-0410. Fax 702/734-5897. www.circuscircus.com. 3,744 units. Sun–Thurs $39 and up double; Fri–Sat $69 and up double. Extra person $12. Children under 18 stay free in parent's room. Cribs/rollaways $12. AE, DC, DISC, MC, V. Free self- and valet parking. **Amenities:** 7 restaurants (American, buffet, Italian, Mexican, more); casino; wedding chapel; circus acts; 2 outdoor pools; midway-style carnival games; video arcade; tour desk; car-rental desk; shopping arcade; 24-hr. room service; laundry service; dry cleaning; nonsmoking rooms; executive-level rooms. *In room:* A/C, TV w/pay movies, hair dryer, safe.

Westward Ho Hotel & Casino
Located next door to Circus Circus, this large motor inn houses its clean but plain motel rooms in two-story buildings that extend back several city blocks behind the casino. Twenty-four hours a day, a free bus shuttles guests between their rooms and the gaming area. Cost and the

proximity to the Adventuredome are the main reasons to stay here—the two bedroom suites have 1½ baths, fold-out couches, refrigerators, and sleep six. This is the home of the notorious Mega-Dog, over a half pound of hot dog for only $1.49; there's also a coffee stand with nickel cups of Joe, along with a small buffet in the coffee shop.

2900 Las Vegas Blvd. S. (between Circus Circus Dr. and Convention Center Dr.), Las Vegas, NV 89109. ✆ 800/634-6803 or 702/731-2900. www.westwardho.com. 777 units. $44–$65 double; $76 suite. Extra person $10. No discount for children. Cribs/rollaways free. MC, V. Free parking at your room door. **Amenities:** Restaurant (coffee shop/buffet); casino; showroom; 3 outdoor pools; tour desk; car-rental desk; nonsmoking rooms. *In room:* A/C, TV w/pay movies.

4 East of the Strip

This area is close to both the Convention Center and the Strip, especially if you have a car. There are many chain hotels in this area in all price ranges, as well as some standout resorts like the Hard Rock and the Las Vegas Hilton. You will need a car, however, or have to use cabs to get to the Strip.

EXPENSIVE

AmeriSuites ✪ *Value* Every AmeriSuite property is designed to look alike so that repeat guests will be able to find their way about with a minimum of thought or effort. So if you've seen one, you've seen them all. Not that that's a bad thing, just a bland one, especially in this town, where unique, theatrical hotels are the norm. Catering to business travelers, high school groups, and college sports teams, this corporate hotel offers large rooms in dark tones with microwaves, utensils, fridges, and foldout couches in all rooms. The TCB suites are larger, with a desk and workspace, but, alas, minus the Vegas-appropriate photos of Elvis wearing the lightning bolt symbol engraved with the anagram for his slogan, "Takin' care of business." Such levity might distract from the regulation room styles, causing some poor AmeriSuite-conditioned traveler to lose his way to the vending machines.

There's nary a slot machine on-site, but free shuttles can take you over to the centrally located Aladdin/Planet Hollywood Resort & Casino so you can experience the Strip in all its neon glory. We like that they provide *USA Today* gratis, which is more than can be said for the glitzier casino/hotels, whose attitude seems to be that you can't gamble if you're reading the paper.

Occasional weekend and manager's specials (the law of supply and demand) can bring the rates significantly lower than the rack prices, and the large complimentary breakfast buffet helps offset the cost of the rooms. Every Wednesday, you can drop in on the manager's reception and gobble up the hot and cold hors d'oeuvres and soft drinks. Some kids may appreciate that Nintendo is available (for an hourly fee) and that the hotel is across the street from the Hard Rock Hotel. It's also close to the Strip. The pool is heated and basic. This isn't the most glamorous place to stay, but it definitely does the job.

4520 Paradise Rd., Las Vegas, NV 89109. ✆ 702/369-3366. Fax 702/369-0009. www.amerisuites.com. 202 units. $79 and up double. Extra person over age 18 $10. Children under 18 stay free in parent's room. Cribs free; no rollaways. AE, DC, DISC, MC, V. Free self-parking. **Amenities:** Outdoor pool; fitness room; concierge; tour desk; laundry service; dry cleaning; nonsmoking rooms; free airport shuttle; vending machines. *In room:* A/C, TV w/pay movies, dataport, high-speed Internet access (for a fee), hair dryer, iron/ironing board.

Atrium Suites ✪ Here's a way to have all the benefits of the Hard Rock without any of the issues that might arise when your just-turned-teenagers start hanging out with the cool college kids at the Hard Rock pool. Located next to the Hard Rock but minus the swim-up blackjack tables and visible body

---

Tips Know Your Room's Limits

Most of the hotels oriented toward long-term stays and most all-suite hotels allow a maximum number of people to stay in a room, all for one fee, regardless of age. If you have five people in your party, no matter what their ages, you will have to get a room that sleeps six, rather than a room that sleeps four with a rollaway and an extra-person fee. Of course, desk staff and on-duty managers can be flexible at times, but it is best to assume that they will hold hard and fast to the guests-per-room maximum.

---

modifications on the guests, the Atrium Suites is sedate, with a center atrium and waterfall. All rooms are suites, though some tend to be on the small size, and come equipped with a fridge, microwave, and coffeemaker, along with a wet bar. Small pets are permitted on the first floor. The fitness room is open 24 hours, so you can squeeze in a few minutes on the exercycle while the kids sleep in. The pool is plain, with a Jacuzzi.

4255 Paradise Rd. (north of Harmon Ave.), Las Vegas, NV 89109. © **800/330-7728** or 702/369-4400. Fax 702/369-4330. www.atriumsuiteshotel.com. 201 units. $120–$200 double. Children under 19 stay free in parent's room. Cribs free; rollaways $10. AE, DC, DISC, MC, V. Free self-parking; no valet parking. Pets under 25 lb. okay. **Amenities:** Restaurant (American); outdoor pool; small exercise room with Nautilus, weights, and treadmills; Jacuzzi; sauna; concierge; business center; limited room service; dry cleaning; nonsmoking rooms; executive-level rooms; airport shuttle. *In room:* A/C, TV w/pay movies, dataport, fridge, coffeemaker, hair dryer, iron/ironing board.

Carriage House ★★★ *Finds* This might seem an expensive place to stay when compared to some hotels on the Strip, but the rack rates are often deeply discounted, putting the Carriage House into the same category as many of the Strip hotels. The Carriage House is actually a timeshare, but at any given time, up to 50 units are available for rent, which translates into family-oriented vacation comfort. All suites have full kitchens, including cookware and dishes. While the least expensive suites sleep only two, the larger units (deluxe and one- and two-bedroom condominium suites) sleep four to eight, making this a great option for larger families. And they *are* roomy—one-bedroom condos range in size from 660 to 700 square feet; the two bedrooms are 1,200 square feet.

The rooms are decorated with a casual, summery feel in beiges, greens, and gold. Great care has been taken with the design of the furnishings—armchairs are built so that there's no strain on the body when standing up, especially good for seniors and those with back problems. The nice-size bathrooms are very clean; shower chairs are available for those who might need them.

There's a standard-size pool, whirlpool, and a basketball and paddle tennis court, with equipment available for free at the front desk. Complimentary movies and VCRs are also available, as well as board games. Family bingo takes places on Thursday afternoons.

But who needs vending machines when there's a twice-a-week courtesy van to a supermarket, so you can bring back goodies to prepare in your well-appointed kitchen? Shuttles are also available to the **Las Vegas Outlet Center** (p. 192) and the Strip.

For those looking for a family atmosphere away from the smoky casinos yet close enough to easily see the sights, this is a perfect choice. *Tip:* If you can't find a parking place in the covered parking lot, park as close to the tennis courts as possible to take advantage of the shade.

AmeriSuites **15**
Atrium Suites **11**
Best Western Mardi Gras Inn **5**
Candlewood Suites **8**
Carriage House **13**
Clarion Hotel and Suites
  Emerald Springs **10**
Courtyard by Marriott **4**
Fairfield Inn by Marriott **6**
Hard Rock Hotel and Casino **12**

Hawthorn Suites **16**
La Quinta Inn **7**
Las Vegas Hilton **1**
Marriott Suites **3**
Motel 6 **17**
Residence Inn by Marriott **2**
St. Tropez **14**
Sam's Town Hotel
  & Gambling Hall **18**
Terrible's **9**

105 E. Harmon Ave. (at Koval Lane), Las Vegas, NV 89109. (C) 800/221-2301 or 702/798-1020. Fax 702/798-1020, ext 112. www.carriagehouselasvegas.com. 155 units. Guest rooms and studio suites $160 (2 people maximum); suites $185–$300 (4–8 people maximum). Ask for discounted rates. Cribs, highchairs, and roll-aways free. AE, DC, DISC, MC, V. Free self- and valet parking. **Amenities:** Tour desk; car-rental desk; 24-hr. room service; laundry service; dry cleaning; nonsmoking rooms, airport shuttle. *In room:* A/C, TV w/pay movies, VCR and games, dataport, hair dryer, full kitchen.

Courtyard by Marriott ★★

One of the many Marriotts in Las Vegas, this upscale hotel is fresh and clean. Its location, rather a ways from the Strip, means more quality time together around the sparkling pool. Rooms are comfortable and bathrooms a nice size in this three-story, attractively landscaped building. Most rooms have king-size beds, and all have balconies or patios. It's bland compared to the snazzy Strip hotels that cost about the same or less, no doubt because this hotel is more for the business traveler rather than the vacationer.

3275 Paradise Rd. (between Convention Center Dr. and Desert Inn Rd.), Las Vegas, NV 89109. (C) 800/321-2211 or 702/791-3600. Fax 702/796-7981. www.courtyard.com. 149 units. Sun–Thurs $129 and up double, Fri–Sat $149 and up double; $119 and up suite. No charge for extra person above double occupancy. Cribs/rollaways free. AE, DC, DISC, MC, V. Free parking at your room door. **Amenities:** Restaurant (American); outdoor pool; small exercise room; Jacuzzi; business center; limited room service; laundry service; dry cleaning; nonsmoking rooms; executive-level rooms; coin-op washers and dryers. *In room:* A/C, TV w/pay movies, dataport, coffeemaker, hair dryer, iron/ironing board.

Hard Rock Hotel and Casino ★★

If you worry that your children might be growing up too fast, you should steer clear of this hip hotel designed for MTV-viewing, Gen X demographic, piña-colada-sucking vacationers who want to rock 'n' roll all night and party every day. But if the only way you'll have peace on vacation is to indulge your offspring, no doubt the Hard Rock will have your teens screaming that you are hip to be cool, while secretly wishing they'd brought fake IDs.

Keep in mind that if a calm vacation's all you ever wanted, you won't find it here. The casino, with its rock-star themed versions of games (White Rabbit slot machines and Jimi Hendrix gambling chips, for instance), sits smack in the center of the main floor, and music blasts over the jingle-jangle of the slots. Everyone here—well, almost everyone—looks as if they stepped out of a casting call for *Blind Date* or the latest Vin Diesel action flick—think thousand-dollar tattoos and other surgical body modifications, tight T-shirts, skimpy skirts, and the chance to spot Ben Affleck, Lenny Kravitz, and Pamela Lee (or reasonable facsimiles thereof) at the craps table.

Enclosed in glass cases that ring the casino are costumes, instruments, and other rock memorabilia, including a floor-to-ceiling Beatles display and a collection of rock-star dolls and lunch boxes. Kurt Cobain, No Doubt, and the Rolling Stones are three of the many artists represented here. Over by the elevators, there's one large display of women who rock, which seems to marginalize the chicks—don't each of them deserve as much floor space as some of their male counterparts?

Check-in is easy: just turn left as you walk in the front door. Rooms have that slacker-chic, *Lost* (Hipster Generation) in Space vibe popularized by movies such as *Drugstore Cowboy, Austin Powers,* and *Swingers.* The newer rooms are larger, with bigger bathrooms than the older rooms, and all have French doors (a unique touch in this city), and larger-than-the-Vegas-norm TV sets with specialty music channels. On a high note, the beds have feather pillows, and mattresses are surprisingly comfortable.

Restaurants include the **Hard Rock Cafe** (in another building), **Nobu, Mr. Lucky's 24/7,** and the smarmily named **Pink Taco** (reviewed on p. 141, 142, and 144, respectively). The sundries shop has all manner of hipness—including Dirty Girl soap, Kama Sutra body oil, and pill cases shaped like prescription drug capsules. There's also a Hard Rock souvenir shop.

Girls—and guys—just wanna have fun by the pool, which features a swim-up (21-and-over) blackjack table, and a sandy beach where lithe tan bodies splash in the cool, shallow water. And we do mean cool—rock music is piped into the pool, so you've got the beat while breast stroking. Daily, over 1,600 piña coladas are served poolside, so the atmosphere can be a bit raucous, with more than a tinge of "let's hook up" hovering about.

If you are not a good sport or a suburban version of the Osbournes, you might hate the Hard Rock as a place to stay, especially when you factor its distance from the Strip (they have shuttles to take you there) and the prices. But you can always drop in for a visit.

4455 Paradise Rd. (at Harmon Ave.), Las Vegas, NV 89109. ⓒ 800/473-ROCK (473-7625) or 702/693-5000. Fax 702/693-5010. www.hardrockhotel.com. 657 units. Sun–Thurs $89 and up, Fri–Sat $150 and up double; from $250 suite. Extra person $35. Children under 13 stay free in parent's room. Cribs $25 per night; roll-aways free, available in suites only. AE, DC, MC, V. Free self- and valet parking. **Amenities:** 6 restaurants (American, Japanese, Mexican, more); casino; showroom; 2 outdoor pools with a lazy river ride and sandy beach bottom; small health club and spa; concierge; tour desk; 24-hr. room service; laundry service; dry cleaning; nonsmoking rooms; executive-level rooms. *In room:* A/C, TV w/pay movies, dataport, high-speed Internet access (for a fee), hair dryer, iron/ironing board.

Hawthorn Suites ⚜⚜ *(Finds* A good location, full kitchens, reasonable rates for this city, and it takes pets of any size—this place is a lifesaver for families. Just 1 block away from the intersection of Las Vegas Boulevard and Tropicana Avenue, this all-suite hotel is one of Las Vegas's best-kept secrets. The good-size suites are decorated in jewel tones, and all feature a fold-out couch in the living room. Bathrooms are clean and serviceable, and each room has a balcony, a unique feature in Las Vegas, where you're usually lucky if your hotel window slides open even 2 inches. Every morning, there's a complimentary breakfast buffet with hot and cold dishes, plus an evening social hour with snacks. Families can splash in the large pool, play volleyball, or shoot hoops.

5051 Duke Ellington Way, Las Vegas, NV 89119. ⓒ 800/527-1133 or 702/739-7000. Fax 702/739-9350. www.hawthorn.com. 280 units. $79–$109 1-bedroom suite (4 people maximum); $109–$169 2-bedroom suite (6 people maximum). Rates include complimentary breakfast. Cribs free; no rollaways. AE, DC, DISC, MC, V. Free outdoor parking. Pets accepted. **Amenities:** Complimentary breakfast and afternoon snacks; outdoor pool; small exercise room; Jacuzzi; laundry service; dry cleaning; nonsmoking rooms; coin-op washers and dryers. *In room:* A/C, TV w/pay movies, dataport, hair dryer, iron/ironing board, full kitchen.

La Quinta Inn ⚜⚜ The California Mission exterior of this hotel makes it stand out along this section of Paradise Road, and once on the grounds, you'll feel an instant sense of relaxation. The staff is terrific—friendly and incredibly helpful. Families will appreciate the barbecue grills and picnic tables along with the attractive pools. The clean, pleasant rooms are spacious, and each has an oversize whirlpool tub in the bathroom. Executive rooms feature one queen-size bed, along with a minifridge, a wet bar, and a microwave, while the double queens are larger but have no kitchen facilities. Two-bedroom suites are perfect for families; they have full kitchens, a dining area, and a living room. Ground-floor accommodations have patios.

3970 Paradise Rd. (between Twain Ave. and Flamingo Rd.), Las Vegas, NV 89109. ⓒ 800/NV-ROOMS or 702/796-9000. Fax 702/796-3537. www.laquinta.com. 251 units. $79 and up standard double; $89 and up executive queen; $115 and up suite. Extra person $10. Children under 18 stay free in parent's room. Rates include complimentary breakfast. Cribs free; rollaways $10. Inquire about seasonal discounts. AE, DC, DISC, MC, V. Free self-parking. **Amenities:** Complimentary continental breakfast; outdoor pool; Jacuzzi; tour desk;

car-rental desk; nonsmoking rooms; free Strip shuttle; coin-op washers and dryers. *In room:* A/C, TV w/pay movies, dataport, coffeemaker, hair dryer, iron/ironing board.

Marriott Suites 🌟   Extra-large comfortable rooms make this a good choice for families who don't want to experience the smoke and noise of the casino hotels, but still want to be close enough to visit the attractions. You will want to take a cab to the Strip in hot weather or if you have children who won't want to, or can't, make the long 3-block walk. The University of Nevada and the Convention Center are also nearby. Rooms are attractively decorated, and French doors separate the sitting area from the bedroom. This is a fine choice if you want to stay off the Strip and don't mind paying high prices for the care and standards provided by a national chain.

325 Convention Center Dr., Las Vegas, NV 89109. (✆ **800/627-6667** or 702/650-2000. Fax 702/650-9466. www.marriott.com. 278 units. $159 and up suites (4 people maximum). Cribs free; no rollaways. AE, DC, DISC, MC, V. Free outdoor parking. **Amenities:** Restaurant (American); outdoor pool; small exercise room; Jacuzzi; tour desk; car-rental desk; business center; 24-hr. room service; laundry service; dry cleaning; nonsmoking rooms; executive-level rooms; coin-op washers and dryers available at Residence Inn next door. *In room:* A/C, TV w/pay movies, dataport, minifridge, coffeemaker, hair dryer, iron/ironing board, safe.

Residence Inn by Marriott 🌟   Located on 7 acres of beautifully landscaped lawns, with tropical foliage and gardens, this link in the Marriott chain is a popular choice for business travelers and families. Most accommodations have working fireplaces—not that you'll need them in the summer, though during winter, it can actually get quite chilly in this desert town—along with their own patio or balcony. Studio suites, all with armchairs and queen-size beds, have adjoining sitting rooms with single-person fold-out sofas; these suites can sleep up to three, plus fit a crib. The deluxe penthouse suites add an upstairs bedroom with two queen-size beds, along with a bathroom, TV, and radio. These penthouses, which also have a dining room, sleep up to five, plus a crib. All accommodations have fully equipped kitchens, complete with dishwashers. Guests receive a complementary basket of microwave popcorn and coffee.

3225 Paradise Rd. (between Desert Inn Rd. and Convention Center Dr.), Las Vegas, NV 89109. (✆ **800/ 331-3131** or 702/796-9300. www.marriott.com. 192 units. $139 and up studio (3 people maximum); $169 and up penthouse (6 people maximum). Rates include continental breakfast. Cribs free. AE, DC, DISC, MC, V. Free self-parking. **Amenities:** Continental breakfast and free buffets in lobby lounge; outdoor pool; guests have access to small exercise room next door at the Marriott Suites; Jacuzzi; nonsmoking rooms; coin-op washers and dryers. *In room:* A/C, TV w/pay movies, dataport, kitchenette, coffeemaker, hair dryer, iron/ironing board.

St. Tropez 🌟🌟 *Finds*   Small, restful, and fairly secluded, this European style, all-suite hotel is worlds away from the glitter of the Strip, yet in reality, the Hard Rock is across the street and the Trop and MGM are just a few long blocks to the west.

Rooms are large, almost Venetian in size, but without the Venetian prices. You have your choice of either a king or two double beds, with either a "private

---

> *Tips* **Always Ask**
>
> "Suite" can mean a number of things in Las Vegas, and frequently translates to "slightly larger room, with a Jacuzzi tub, and maybe a fold-out couch." Less frequently, a suite will have either a partial kitchen with a minifridge and microwave or even a full kitchen. When unsure about what a hotel means by "suite," ask for specifics.

sleeping area" (the bed is to one side) or the "separate sleeping area," a suite that has the bed in a second room. Some suites come with an in-room whirlpool tub, and all have nice-size bathrooms. Rooms are tastefully decorated in subdued warm tones.

Lush landscaping surrounds the free form pool and Jacuzzi, and there's a small fitness room. The grassy courtyard offers plenty of space for kids to run about, and you can often see them playing Frisbee and tag on the lawn. Free continental breakfast, with lots of doughnuts and pastries, is served daily. *Tip:* Off-season rooms can be half price here.

455 E. Harmon Ave. (at Paradise Rd.), Las Vegas, NV 89109. ℂ 800/666-5400 or 702/369-5400. Fax 702/369-1150. www.sttropezlasvegas.com. 149 units. $100 and up double (5 people maximum). Children under 12 stay free in parent's room. Cribs/rollaways free. AE, DC, DISC, MC, V. Free self-parking. **Amenities:** Outdoor pool; fitness room; concierge; tour desk; free airport shuttle. *In room:* A/C, TV w/pay movies, fridge, coffeemaker, hair dryer, iron/ironing board.

MODERATE

Best Western Mardi Gras Inn *(Value)*   Located a block from the Convention Center and a quick few blocks by car from the Strip, this well-run, clean casino hotel is a reasonable choice for families, especially if parents want to do a little light gambling while the kids, who are old enough to be alone, play games or watch movies in the room. All accommodations are queen-bedded minisuites with sofa beds in the living room and eat-in minikitchens with wet bars, fridges, and coffeemakers. The quarters were recently redone so the furnishings and so forth should be fresh. The grounds are nicely landscaped, and the inexpensive restaurant serves basic coffee-shop fare.

3500 Paradise Rd. (between Twain Ave. and Desert Inn Rd.), Las Vegas, NV 89109. ℂ 800/634-6501 or 702/731-2020. Fax 702/731-4005. www.mardigrasinn.com. 314 units. $69 and up double. Extra person $10. Children under 18 stay free in parent's room. Cribs free. AE, DC, DISC, MC, V. Free parking at your room door. **Amenities:** Restaurant; free continental breakfast; small casino; outdoor pool; Jacuzzi; tour desk; car-rental desk; free airport shuttle; business center; limited room service; nonsmoking rooms; coin-op washers and dryers. *In room:* A/C, TV w/pay movies, dataport, fridge, coffeemaker, iron/ironing board, kitchenette.

Candlewood Suites 🎄   If you're planning on staying a week or longer in Las Vegas, this clean, well-appointed hotel can be a real deal; stay for a month, and it's sinfully cheap. However, you'll want a car if you plan to do any sightseeing—it's relatively far from the action of the Strip, though the Hard Rock is close by. The bland rooms are decorated in grays and blues, the beds are reasonably comfortable, and the bathrooms are clean. Studios sleep two people maximum, a one-bedroom sleeps four or less, and every room has a fully equipped kitchen, along with TV, VCR, and CD player. Kids will especially like the honor-system convenience store, stocked with microwavable goodies. Canned ravioli and soup, boxed macaroni and cheese, plus a cooler of drinks and a freezer full of frozen treats beckon from the store, accessible by room key and supervised by video surveillance. Prices are marked, and you pay by placing your money in an envelope, filling out your room number, and dropping the packet down a slot. You can also fax and copy for free at the front desk. *Note:* While this hotel is very expensive (for Vegas) if you only stay for one day, the longer you stay, the cheaper it becomes.

4303 Paradise Rd. (north of Harmon Ave.), Las Vegas, NV 89109. ℂ 888/226-3539 or 702/836-3660. Fax 702/836-3661. 227 units. $69–$149 daily, weekly $49–$74 per day, monthly $39 per day studios (2 people maximum); $99–$189 daily, weekly $60–$104 per day, monthly $59 per day 1-bedrooms (4 people maximum). Cribs free. AE, DC, DISC, MC, V. **Amenities:** Pool; weight room; Jacuzzi; nonsmoking rooms; free washers and dryers on each floor; honor-system convenience store. *In room:* A/C, TV w/pay movies, dataport, hair dryer, iron/ironing board, full kitchens.

Clarion Hotel & Suites Emerald Springs ⚛ This is a friendly, low-key alternative to the Strip, though some parents may not like that a "gentlemen's club," i.e., strip club, has opened up next door, though its signage is fairly well shielded from the hotel by tall plants. The hotel itself is pleasant, with a waterfall in the lobby, along with a sitting area that features a fireplace and TV. Typical of the inn's hospitality, there is a bowl of apples for the taking at the front desk, something we usually only see in more expensive hotels. Rooms are clean and nice, with bleached wood and a calming color scheme. Even the smallest accommodations (studios) offer small sofas, desks, and armchairs with hassocks. The pool is large, and there's a small exercise room.

325 E. Flamingo Rd. (between Koval Lane and Paradise Rd.), Las Vegas, NV 89109. ℂ 800/732-7889 or 702/732-9100. Fax 702/731-9784. www.choicehotels.com. 150 units. $79 and up studio; $99 and up whirlpool suite, $159 and up hospitality suite. Extra person $15. Children under 19 stay free in parent's room. AE, DC, DISC, MC, V. Free self-parking. **Amenities:** Restaurant (coffee shop); outdoor pool; small exercise room; Jacuzzi; concierge; tour desk; car-rental desk; courtesy limo to airport or Strip; nonsmoking rooms; executive-level rooms. *In room:* A/C, TV w/pay movies, dataport, kitchenette or wet bar, coffeemaker, hair dryer, iron/ironing board.

Fairfield Inn by Marriott ⚛ Cheerful rooms and a comfortable lobby make this a pleasant place to stay. Units with king-size beds offer sofa beds, and up to five people are permitted in each room. The pool will keep you cool between sightseeing jaunts; and complimentary pastries, yogurt, fruit, and juices are served every morning in the lobby, while coffee, tea, and hot chocolate are provided all day. From this hotel, you can walk to several restaurants, and the Strip is just minutes away.

3850 Paradise Rd. (between Twain Ave. and Flamingo Rd.), Las Vegas, NV 89109. ℂ 800/228-2800 or 702/791-0899. Fax 702/895-9810. www.fairfieldinn.com. 129 units. $69 and up (up to 5 people). Cribs/rollaways free. AE, DC, DISC, MC, V. Free self-parking. **Amenities:** Complimentary continental breakfast; outdoor pool; small exercise room; Jacuzzi; tour desk; car-rental desk; airport shuttle; dry cleaning; nonsmoking rooms. *In room:* A/C, TV w/pay movies, dataport, iron/ironing board.

Las Vegas Hilton ⚛ This classic Las Vegas hotel is where Elvis Presley performed during the last 8 years of his life. At the entrance, a giant bronze bust of the King commemorates the man whose name is synonymous with enormous excesses and Vegas style—and one of his sequined jumpsuits is enshrined near the entrance. Though it used to be a family-friendly hotel, the Hilton is now less sybaritic, designed more for the business traveler. (The Convention Center is next door.) Now that Colony Capital, an L.A.-based real-estate investment trust, has taken it over from Hilton, it's being turned into a convention hotel. The clean, well-maintained rooms have marble touches and marble in the bathrooms. There are small dressing areas off the bathroom in each room, another plus when several people are sharing a room. The rooms are nothing special in terms of decor, but some do have views of the adjacent 18-hole golf course.

Along with the buffet (p. 149), there's Mexican and Japanese food, as well as a food court with pizza, frozen yogurt, and sandwiches.

A big draw here for teens and Trekkers is the well-designed *Star Trek:* **The Experience** (p. 167), which most kids will find out of this world.

Active families will want to check out the 8-acre recreation deck on the third floor, with a swimming pool, six tennis courts lit for night play, Ping-Pong, and a putting green. Also on this level is a luxurious 17,000-square-foot state-of-the-art health club offering Nautilus equipment, Lifecycles, treadmills, rowing machines, three whirlpool spas, steam, sauna, massage, and tanning beds. There's a $20-per-day fee to use the facilities, but guests are totally pampered:

All toiletries are provided; there are comfortable TV lounges; and complimentary bottled waters and juices are served in the canteen.

3000 Paradise Rd. (at Riviera Blvd.), Las Vegas, NV 89109. © **888/732-7117** or 702/732-5111. Fax 702/794-3611. www.lvhilton.com. 3,174 units. $69 and up double. Extra person $30. Children under 18 stay free in parent's room. Cribs free; rollaways $30 if you are not paying the extra person charge. AE, DC, DISC, MC, V. Free self- and valet parking. **Amenities:** 10 restaurants (American, Japanese, buffet, Mexican, more); casino; showrooms; outdoor pool; golf course adjacent; 6 tennis courts (4 night-lit); health club and spa; Jacuzzi; car-rental desk; business center; shopping arcade; 24-hr. room service; laundry service; dry cleaning; nonsmoking rooms; executive-level rooms. *In room:* A/C, TV w/pay movies, dataport, hair dryer, iron/ironing board.

Sam's Town Hotel & Gambling Hall ⭐⭐⭐

Off the beaten track, Sam's Town is a local favorite situated 5 miles from the Strip, which can be a hassle if you don't have a car. On the other hand, this casino hotel does provide shuttles to the Strip and has a variety of entertainment to keep kids and adults busy. Along with the pool, Sam's Town has a 56-lane bowling alley and an 18-screen, all-THX, all-stadium-seating multiplex, showing the latest releases. The main attraction here is the hotel's giant atrium, which combines real trees and fountains with animatronic animals. The splashing water *is* loud, but, nevertheless, we find it far more restful than the usual casino sounds of clanging slot machines. Wander about this seminatural environment before taking in the Sunset Stampede at Mystic Falls: Four times a day, at 2, 6, 8, and 10pm, the wolf atop the waterfall howls, and the show, with lights and sounds, begins. It lasts for 10 minutes, and younger kids will enjoy it, especially if you get there a few minutes early for a good spot close up.

The adequately sized rooms have a Western theme, and you can choose from mountain views (ask for a higher floor to take advantage of this) or a room with a view of the atrium, which the children will probably enjoy more.

There are nine dining choices here to keep you and yours sated, including the **Firelight Buffet** (p. 149), which features a different theme nightly.

5111 Boulder Hwy. (at Flamingo Rd.), Las Vegas, NV 89122. © **800/634-6371** or 702/456-7777. Fax 702/454-8014. www.samstownlv.com. 650 units. $50 and up double; $140 and up suite. Extra person $10. Children under 16 stay free in parent's room. Cribs/rollaways free. AE, DC, DISC, MC, V. Free self- and valet parking. **Amenities:** 9 restaurants (American, Italian, buffet, more); huge casino; showrooms; outdoor pool; video arcade; tour desk; car-rental desk; shuttle to Strip and Downtown; laundry service; nonsmoking rooms. *In room:* A/C, TV w/pay movies, dataport.

INEXPENSIVE

Motel 6 This reliable chain hotel accepts small pets, making it a good choice for families traveling with Fluffy or Fido. Its location, right next to the MGM Grand and only seconds away from the Strip, also makes it convenient for families who want access to the main drag without the hassle or expense. Finally, this is also a good call if other, nearby, big-name hotels are booked, as this is the largest Motel 6 property in the country, with a large lobby and bland but very clean rooms set inside two-story buildings. If you need a tub, be sure to ask for one, as some rooms are shower only. Two pools will keep you busy and cool when you're not taking in the sights.

195 E. Tropicana Ave. (at Koval Lane), Las Vegas, NV 89109. © **800/4-MOTEL-6 (466-8356)** or 702/798-0728. Fax 702/798-5657. 608 units. Sun–Thurs from $35 single; Fri–Sat from $58 single. Extra person $6. Children under 17 stay free in parent's room. AE, DC, DISC, MC, V. Free parking at your room door. Small pets accepted. **Amenities:** 2 outdoor pools; Jacuzzi; tour desk; nonsmoking rooms; coin-op washers and dryers. *In room:* A/C, TV w/pay movies.

Terrible's ⭐ *Finds*

One of the best reasons to stay here is so that for years to come, you'll have a family joke about how your hotel in Las Vegas was Terrible's.

Are you laughing? Well, you should be—laughing all the way to the bank with the money you'll save by staying here. Seriously. This is a nice, cheap, clean, and "just-fine" hotel that gives the impression of being darn family friendly. The place gets its name from Ed "Terrible" Herbst, who owns a chain of local gas stations, and he's spent tons of money to upgrade what was once a flea trap into a decent place to stay with large rooms, pleasant bathrooms, and a serviceable pool. It's a cheap cab ride or short drive to the Strip and the airport, and the restaurants on the property are adequate.

4100 Paradise Rd. (at Flamingo), Las Vegas, NV 89109. © **800/640-9777** or 702/733-7000. Fax 702/691-2423. www.terribleherbst.com/ett-gaming/casino-hotel. 400 units. Sun–Thurs $29 and up double; Fri–Sat $59 and up double. Extra person $10. Children under 13 stay free in parent's room. Cribs/rollaways $10. AE, DC, DISC, MC, V. Free self- and valet parking. **Amenities:** 3 restaurants (American, buffet, fast food); outdoor pool; 24-hr. room service; laundry service; nonsmoking rooms. *In room:* A/C, TV w/pay movies, dataport, coffeemaker, hair dryer, pay-per-use Nintendo.

5 West of the Strip

There's not much to do in this area, which, fortunately, is a short cab or car ride to the Strip. However, the Orleans does provide plenty of entertainment for families.

EXPENSIVE

Desert Paradise ★★★ *Finds*   A really nice timeshare that rents out units, Desert Paradise offers apartment living, and we mean living large, for families. Big one-bedroom apartments sleep four; the bigger two-bedroom apartments sleep six, and each unit has a small patio or balcony (with sliding doors), covered parking (a bonus in the summer), its own washer and dryer, along with a full-size kitchen and breakfast nook—truly roomy accommodations, all decorated in sand and beige. The overall impression is "wow, this is huge," except for the bathrooms, which are smallish in comparison to the rest of the place, though the dressing area/vanity mitigates that to some extent. The beds, including the fold-out couch in the living room, are comfy, and there is a TV both in the living and the sleeping quarters.

A barbecue area and picnic tables further enhance the family-resort atmosphere. The verdant lawns provide a great place for kids to frolic (there were plenty of well-behaved children with parents and grandparents on-site when we stayed), while in the main building, a large-screen TV lounge allows guests to gather for the news or sports events. There are frequent manager's receptions, and continental breakfast is served daily. The atmosphere is relaxing and family oriented, making this a great place for spending quality time, while its proximity to the Strip allows for sightseeing and exploring.

5165 S. Decatur Blvd, Las Vegas, NV 89118. © **877/257-0010** or 702/257-0010. Fax 702/257-0363. 152 units. $85–$145 1-bedroom (4 people maximum); $99–$199 2-bedroom (6 people maximum). Cribs/rollaways free. AE, DC, DISC, MC, V. Free self-parking. **Amenities:** Complimentary continental breakfast; outdoor pool and spa; concierge; nonsmoking rooms. *In room:* A/C, TV with full cable, VCR, hair dryer, full kitchen.

MODERATE

Budget Suites of America   This hotel is conveniently located across from the wonders of the Orleans (see below), and if there's no place else to stay and you don't mind that all the rooms allow smoking, this could be an option for you and yours. The good-size rooms are all very, very clean, though they do reek of smoke. But not to be ultrafussy (okay, we are, but that's because we have your children to think about), they are all ultimately sort of depressing, with bright teal carpet and boring beige furniture. Not even the full-size stove and fridge or

Accommodations, Dining & Entertainment
West of the Strip

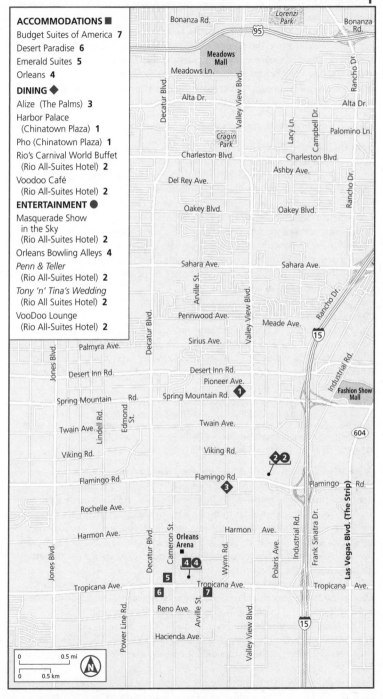

ACCOMMODATIONS ■
Budget Suites of America **7**
Desert Paradise **6**
Emerald Suites **5**
Orleans **4**

DINING ◆
Alize (The Palms) **3**
Harbor Palace
(Chinatown Plaza) **1**
Pho (Chinatown Plaza) **1**
Rio's Carnival World Buffet
(Rio All-Suites Hotel) **2**
Voodoo Café
(Rio All-Suites Hotel) **2**

ENTERTAINMENT ●
Masquerade Show
in the Sky
(Rio All-Suites Hotel) **2**
Orleans Bowling Alleys **4**
Penn & Teller
(Rio All-Suites Hotel) **2**
Tony 'n' Tina's Wedding
(Rio All Suites Hotel) **2**
VooDoo Lounge
(Rio All-Suites Hotel) **2**

the groovy rock-formation outdoor decor could brighten our spirits about staying there, and, frankly, it's actually because these aren't really hotels or time-shares; they are, for the most part, places for people to live who can't or won't, for any number of reasons, get apartments. Granted, some families with kids do stay here, especially in the summer. But unless you've exhausted all other options, do you really want to stay in a place that has to state on its prerecorded reservation line that they do not accept collect or third-party phone calls?

4205 W. Tropicana Ave. (at Wynn). © **888/611-0414** or 702/889-1700. Fax 702/227-8099. www.budget suites.com. 1-bedroom (3 people maximum) $69 and up daily, $229 and up weekly; 2-bedroom (5 people maximum) $119 and up daily, $289 and up weekly. AE, DC, DISC, MC, V. Free parking at your room door. **Amenities:** Outdoor pool; Jacuzzi; coin-op washers and dryers. *In room:* A/C, TV w/pay movies.

Emerald Suites   If your hotel of choice is full, you can always check into this clean, all-suite hotel across from the Orleans (see below). But if you need a crib or a rollaway, you won't get them here for love or money. This hotel, like the nearby Budget Suites, has weekly and monthly rates, and this being Vegas, some people—and families—live here for long periods of time for all sorts of reasons. The Emerald Suites designates some rooms as nonsmoking, though management points out that it's difficult to enforce the rule, so you might end up with a nonsmoking room with a stale-smoke stench. That said, and all things being equal, if you are hard up for a place to stay, this hotel will do you just a bit better that the nearby Budget Suites; though, like its neighbor, the Emerald does not accept third-party or collect calls.

Bright colors and sort of Swedish modern carpets and fabrics set this apart from other similar suite hotels with their bland decor. Additionally, there's a fully equipped kitchen. The pool doesn't have much shade. Thankfully, the Orleans (see below), with its many family-oriented activities, is close by, and the Strip is 4 blocks away. But unless the Consumer Electronics Show or other huge convention is in town, you should be able to find hotels with more kid-friendly amenities in this price range.

4777 S. Cameron St., Las Vegas, NV 89103 © **702/365-5500.** Fax 702/216-5547. www.emeraldsuites.com. 1-bedroom suite (3 people maximum) $79 and up daily; $279 and up weekly; 2-bedroom suite (5 people maximum) $99 and up daily, $319 and up weekly. Children stay free. No cribs or rollaways. AE, DC, DISC, MC, V. Free self-parking; no valet parking. **Amenities:** Outdoor pool; Jacuzzi; nonsmoking rooms; coin-op washers and dryers. *In room:* A/C, TV w/pay movies, dataport, full kitchen, hair dryer, iron/ironing board.

Orleans 🎭🎭   Now here's something for everyone—bowling, movies, gambling, a showroom, an events arena, two pools, child care, restaurants, a food court, a shuttle to the Strip—all at a reasonable price, mainly because there are nearly 1,500 rooms, it's too far from the Strip to walk, and there's really nothing much else nearby. But then some may say, "With this wealth of distractions around us, why go elsewhere?" Kids will enjoy getting the free Mardi Gras beads that are handed out in the restaurants, and parents will enjoy the decent prices for room and board.

The hotel is decorated to resemble the New Orleans of MGM musicals and Disneyland, more faux than French Quarter. Nevertheless, check out the mannequins leaning over balconies, frozen in a perpetual celebration.

The L-shaped rooms feature brass headboards on the beds, plenty of floral prints, and lace curtains to create a New Orleans–1880s feel. The bathrooms are large, though a closet, rather than a rod for hanging one's clothes, would be nice. Suites are larger, with dark wood, oval tubs in the bathrooms, and something families with several kids may or may not find pleasant—four TVs! A new tower opened in 2004, adding an additional 460 rooms and suites to the property's mix.

The two outdoor pools will do a fine job of keeping you cool; they are nowhere near as elaborate as those at the Strip resorts, but you aren't paying Strip prices.

With 70 lanes, the bowling alley (p. 185) is more like a super highway, but the size ensures that you can almost always get rolling without a wait. A megaplex theater screens a variety of new movie releases, at least one of which will usually fall within your approved ratings scale. If your kids are sports nuts, there's a new 9,000-seat arena for a minor-league hockey team and other sporting events. Take advantage of the Kids Tyme child-care center and enjoy up to 3 hours of childfree time in the casino, the showroom, or your own room. If you feel like dining on the premises, there are a dozen restaurants, including a fairly authentic Cajun/Creole place and a buffet. Children may enjoy **Don Miguel's,** a basic but satisfying Mexican restaurant, where you can watch tortillas being made.

4500 W. Tropicana Ave. (west of the Strip and I-15), Las Vegas, NV 89103. © **800/ORLEANS** (800/675-3267) or 702/365-7111. Fax 702/365-7500. www.orleanscasino.com. 1,886 units. $39–$89 standard double; $175–$225 1-bedroom suite. Extra person $10. Children under 15 stay free in parent's room. AE, DC, DISC, MC, V. Free self- and valet parking. **Amenities:** 9 restaurants (American, French, Italian, Cajun/Creole, buffet, more); casino; events arena; showroom; 18 movie theaters; 2 outdoor pools; health club; Kids Tyme children's center offering amusements and day care for kids under 13; video arcade; concierge; tour desk; car-rental desk; airport shuttle; 24-hr. room service; laundry service; dry cleaning; nonsmoking rooms; executive-level rooms; 70-lane bowling center. In room: A/C, TV w/pay movies, dataport, hair dryer, iron/ironing board.

6 Outside of Las Vegas

HENDERSON
EXPENSIVE

Green Valley Ranch ✦✦✦   This is a resort in every sense of the word. Located in Henderson, about 25 minutes southeast of Las Vegas and closer if coming from the airport, this luxurious getaway combines Strip action (gambling, grown-up nightclub, and fine dining) with kid-friendly fun (movie theaters, arcade, and a beach pool—which has sand instead of concrete around the edges). The casino is located on one side of the property, so it can be completely avoided. Wood, stone, and plush drapes and carpets give this resort (part of the huge Station Casinos chain) a high-end feel that rivals Bellagio, without the attitude or prices.

Rooms have big closets, and the bathrooms have big bathtubs. The beds are supercomfy and the bathrobes are soft. There's no charge to use the well-appointed health club, and there are great, though sometimes smoggy, views of the Las Vegas Valley from the pools (which are closed Nov–Apr). One pool is for all guests; the private pool is for those who rent cabanas, but even at the non-cabana pool, you'll enjoy large chaise lounges and wide beds (designed for poolside reclining and sprawling) in a sunscreen-soaked daze.

Panda Express and **Villa Pizza,** in the food court, and **Original Pancake House** and **Il Fornaio** provide a variety of family-friendly food. Steak-and-seafood **BullShrimp** is as good as, if not better than, many of the more expensive steak and seafood houses on the Strip. And **China Spice** is one of the best Chinese restaurants in a casino in town.

The Dolphin Spa offers treatments such as massage therapies, facials, body wraps, exfoliation, and the like. At the salon, you can get manicures, pedicures, and the usual hairstyling.

Accommodations, Dining & Attractions in Henderson

2300 Paseo Verde Dr. (at I-215), Henderson, NV 89012. ℂ 866/617-7777 or 702/782-9487. Fax 702/617-7778. www.greenvalleyranchresort.com. 247 units. Sun–Thurs $159 and up double; Fri–Sat $209 and up double. Extra person $12. Children under 12 stay free in parent's room. Cribs/rollaways free. AE, DC, DISC, MC, V. Free self- and valet parking. **Amenities:** 9 restaurants (all major cuisines); nightclub; casino; outdoor pool; health club and spa; Jacuzzi; sauna; concierge; business center; 24-hr. room service; in-room massage; laundry service; dry cleaning; nonsmoking rooms; executive-level rooms. *In room:* A/C, TV w/pay movies, dataport, high-speed Internet access (for a fee), coffeemaker, hair dryer, iron/ironing board, safe.

INEXPENSIVE

Sunset Station ⌾   Located about 25 minutes from the Strip, in the bedroom community of Henderson, close to **Ethel M's Chocolate Factory and Cactus Gardens** (p. 175) and **Ron Lee's World of Clowns** (p. 178) as well as the **Sport-Center** family sport park (p. 184), Sunset Station isn't really a major destination hotel, but it's good to know about in case your other options are booked. By Vegas standards, it's pricey for what you get (a basic hotel that charges $15 for cribs and rollaways and an additional $15 for an extra person), but it can be a good option if you place a high priority on accommodations that offer child care. Though it's far from the maddening crowds of tourists, expect to find plenty of locals here for both the food and gambling; they definitely make use of the available child-care facilities. The entire hotel is done in a vaguely Mediterranean, south-of-Spain theme—soft ochers, warm earth tones—carried through to the standard-size rooms with basic, clean bathrooms, and to two of the nine restaurants: **Capri** serves Italian food, **Casa del Sol** specializes in seafood. The outside pool does its job for daytime enjoyment; the fitness room, while nothing ultrafancy, is perfectly adequate, while 13 movie screens and a decent arcade can keep you and your family entertained in the evening.

1301 W. Sunset Rd., Henderson, NV 89014. ⓒ **888/786-7389** or 702/547-7777. Fax 702/432-7730. www. sunsetstation.com. 457 units. Sun–Thurs $49–$79; Fri–Sat $99–$139. Extra person $15. Cribs/rollaways $15. AE, DC, DISC, MC, V. Free self- and valet parking. **Amenities:** 9 restaurants (all major cuisines); food court; nightclub; casino; 13 movie theaters; outdoor pool; fitness room; concierge; 24-hr. room service; child care (for a fee); nonsmoking rooms. *In room:* A/C, TV w/pay movies, dataport, high-speed Internet access (for a fee), hair dryer, iron/ironing board.

5

Family-Friendly Dining

In the past decade, Las Vegas has experienced a restaurant boom, with celebrity chefs opening outposts in almost every hotel. Once purely a destination for gamblers, partiers, and wedding parties, the Strip is now the new Mecca for curious palates weaned on, and educated by, the Food Channel. Food used to be cheap in Vegas because the casinos a) wanted you to spend most of your money gambling and b) wanted you to feel like you'd gotten something—like a surf-and-turf special or an all-you-can-eat spread—for a bargain, so that your inevitable losses didn't seem so tragic. Then came food awareness—let's call it cuisine consciousness—and Vegas's entrepreneurs saw an opportunity to lure high rollers and their appetites, along with garden-variety gourmands, into the brand-new casino/resorts.

In came name chefs—Wolfgang, Emeril, Bradley Ogden, Bobby Flay—plus upscale, high-priced eateries such as **Lutèce, Picasso,** and **Alizé**—the list is mouthwateringly, and expensively, long.

At first glance, it seems that there are now fewer low- to midpriced options, and that it's easier to go broke at the dinner tables than at the gaming tables. Oh sure, you can eat three meals a day at food courts—**McDonald's, Nathan's Hot Dogs,** and pizza are staples at most of the hotels, with **Krispy Kreme Doughnuts** a popular choice for breakfast and dessert—but at a certain point, you may want, or need, some variety. With a little

forethought, the average visitor—especially ones with hungry mouths to feed—can find a cornucopia of reasonably priced eats. And that's where the Las Vegas gourmet boom has its advantages.

Buffets, once a stolid bastion of plain food, now offer international dishes and "stations" for Asian, Mexican, Italian, Middle Eastern, and other cuisines, along with large salad bars. Lunch menus, lower-priced gourmet cafes, and cantinas also provide a way for you and yours to sample celebrity chefs' cooking without squandering your children's college fund on the experience.

And while certain restaurants decline to seat families with children under 5 years old, most are more than happy to accommodate all ages, providing children's menus, highchairs, and booster seats. Some even go so far as to cook special, off-menu dishes to order for your children. Upscale chain restaurants such as **P.F. Chang's China Bistro** and the **Cheesecake Factory** offer dependable choices and large portions, while the themed chains—**Rainforest Cafe, ESPN Zone, NASCAR Cafe,** and similarly souvenir-slinging restaurants—provide varying levels of food in an entertaining environment. So grab a fork, tie on your napkin, and dive in. Bon appetite!

Note: In the listing descriptions after each review, following the website (or phone number if the restaurant doesn't have a website listed), we detail whether a restaurant has a children's menu and whether it's equipped with highchairs and booster seats. If any of these amenities is missing from the listing description, it means the restaurant doesn't offer that particular service.

1 Tips for Dining in Las Vegas

GETTING IN

The most logical, time-tested advice is that if you are planning to watch the *Sirens of TI* show from **Buccaneer Bay,** want to celebrate your budding Iron Chef's birthday at **Nobu,** or just want to eat at a specific place at a specific date and time, you should make reservations immediately after you make your hotel reservation, giving both your hotel and home phone number, and confirm your reservation once you arrive in town. Or you can have the concierge at your hotel call and make reservations for you. You should probably always make a reservation, no matter what, just to be safe, though we must say that during the down season (midsummer)—even with a chef's convention of more than 1,000 all staying at a hotel where we wanted to try out some of the restaurants—we still had no problem walking in and getting seated. Again, we don't recommend chancing it, but if you do, here are our hints for getting a table:

- **Go early,** right at opening, for lunch and dinner. Prime time for lunch is between 12:30 and 2pm, but restaurants open for lunch at 11 or 11:30am. Your best bet for dinner is arriving between 5:30 and 6pm.
- **Dress nicely.** That means shirts with collars (polo or button-down) on men and boys, no shorts or jeans for men, and nice blouses or casual dresses for women and girls. Also for the ladies, a lightweight sweater is advisable because it can sometimes get chilly in restaurants.
- **Take whatever seats are available.** Remember that you are walking in without a reservation and that you have kids, so don't be surprised if you are seated a bit away from the center of the action; other tables may have been already reserved.

SAVING MONEY

You can spend upwards of $200 a day on food for a family of four without ever having a memorable meal. And that bites. But with a small amount of planning, there's no reason that you won't be able to sample some celebrity-chef fare without busting the bank, or at least keep your food costs at a manageable level. One way is to get your rooms off the Strip at a place offering complimentary continental breakfasts, or at an apartment-style hotel, where you can use the in-room kitchen facilities for some of your meals. Granted, staying away from the main section of the city requires some planning and usually a car, or you could end up spending what you were trying to save in food costs on cab fares to and from the Strip.

Keep in mind that on the Strip, food-court stands such as Nathan's offer breakfast specials of standards such as pancakes, eggs, and bacon. Buffets are best saved for a late breakfast or an early lunch; kids can stuff themselves, then maybe rest in the room watching TV or playing games for a couple of hours during the hottest part of the day, emerging refreshed and still semifull in time for more sightseeing and an early dinner. Dinner can be as simple as appetizers and dessert or as elaborate as you like. Most restaurants offer kids' menus for all meals, though the lunch and dinner selections of pizza and chicken fingers may get repetitive for some children.

Tips Dining Out in Peace

Bring pencils or pens and paper with you, so the kids have something to do while waiting for their food. This is also a great time for them to write postcards, so keep some handy. If you get caught without even a crayon and the waiter won't lend you a pen, have a few word games at your disposal—I Spy, for example, or have someone choose a category (movies, actors, food, and so on) and, in turn, each person must name something in the category. The catch is that the person with the next turn must name something that starts with the last letter of the previous answer. (Example: orange, eggplant, tomato, onion . . .)

We're sure your kids have lovely manners, but if you happen to be ferrying around a child who decides to make a ruckus at the table, try a trick that's worked for us. Promptly remove him or her from the premises for a supervised time-out. Don't yell, don't threaten, just quietly keep a beady eye on the tyke until he calms himself down. It's highly effective for the majority of kids and makes a lasting impression on siblings. After the third time-out on the pavement, we promise you that you won't have to do it again.

Bend the rules. If you don't usually let your children drink soda pop, perhaps, as a treat when out for a meal (or behind your back—we're realists!), you can let them have some. And letting the kids order a Shirley Temple or Roy Rogers (7-Up or cola and grenadine with a cherry) always adds importance to a night out.

Think ahead before venturing out for dinner. If your little ones have had a long day seeing the sights, make time for them to nap before you go out to eat. (You won't mind the chance to put your feet up either.) You're on vacation, so don't dine early unless you plan to eat at a restaurant where reservations are hard to come by. There is no joy in returning to a hotel room to watch TV. With everyone relaxed and happy, mealtime can be a leisurely and enjoyable way to recap the adventures of day. Encourage each of the children to tell what they enjoyed best that day and discuss the family's plans for tomorrow.

Some fine restaurants—**Emeril's, Delmonico Steakhouse,** and **Mon Ami Gabi,** for example—offer lunch menus, providing an alternative, dare we say cheaper, way to sample their cuisines. Others, such as **Border Grill, Chinois,** and **Spago,** have more casual spin-offs that serve signature dishes at a far lower price.

We wish that more hotels had minibars and fridges so we could take doggie bags back to our rooms, because the portions are huge at many restaurants, most notably **Stage Deli, Cheesecake Factory,** and its sister, **Grand Lux Café.** Sharing an order—if you can come to a consensus—is a great way to eat. You can, however, rent small fridges at most hotels for $10 and up per day. Consider appetizers as main courses—many, such as the quesadillas at **Border Cantina,** are large enough for two. Family-style dining is expected at Asian restaurants such as **Chin Chin, P. F. Chang's,** and **Lotus of Siam**—considered by some to be the best Thai restaurant in the United States. Order a couple of dishes and

---

> ⌐*Tips* **Stock Up on Staples**
>
> If you have a car, you can use it to stock up on staples that you'd pay inflated prices for on the Strip. Drive just a couple miles into the suburbs to a big supermarket and stock up on soft drinks, snacks, cereal, bananas, and other foodstuffs, so you don't have to pay the inflated prices in the resorts. It may be worth your while to bring a cooler along to keep things cold in your room. Highways 159 and 160 west are littered with Albertson's, Smith's, and Raley's, and the Maryland Parkway is loaded with strip malls and discount stores.

---

some rice, and you've got a complete meal for a reasonable price. Dim sum—small Chinese dishes of many varieties—is a filling and inexpensive breakfast/lunch option available at several Chinese restaurants.

And then there's that old standby, pizza—try the gourmet versions at **Wolfgang Puck** or **California Pizza Kitchen,** go for a standard pie picked up from the nearest food court, or have **Metro Pizza** (p. 142) deliver to your room.

ABOUT PRICE CATEGORIES

The restaurants in this chapter are arranged first by location, then by the following price categories (based on the average cost of a dinner entree): **Very Expensive,** where most entrees cost more than $20; **Expensive,** where the majority of entrees are $15 to $20; **Moderate,** where the majority of entrees are $10 to $15; and **Inexpensive,** where entrees are under $10 (sometimes well under). We've also made sure to provide you with children's menu information, where applicable. In Very Expensive and Expensive restaurants, expect to spend no less than twice the price of the average entree for your entire meal with a tip; you can usually get by on a bit less in moderate and inexpensive restaurants. Dessert-restaurant pricing is based on the cost of one dessert. Buffets and Sunday brunches are gathered in a separate section at the end of this chapter.

2 Restaurants by Cuisine

AMERICAN

America (South Strip, $, p. 125)

Buccaneer Bay Club ⊛ (Center Strip, $$$$, p. 132)

Cheesecake Factory ⊛ (Center Strip, $$, p. 135)

ESPN Zone (South Strip, $$, p. 127)

Hard Rock Cafe (East of the Strip, $, p. 141)

Harley-Davidson Cafe (South Strip, $$, p. 127)

In-N-Out Burger ⊛ (South Strip, $ p. 129)

Monte Carlo Pub & Brewery ⊛⊛⊛ (South Strip, $, p. 131)

NASCAR Cafe (North Strip $, p. 139)

Nob Hill ⊛⊛⊛ (South Strip, $$$$, p. 122)

Rainforest Cafe ⊛ (South Strip, $$, p. 128)

Verandah ⊛ (South Strip, $$$$, p. 128)

ASIAN

Chinois Café ⊛⊛⊛ ($$, Center Strip, p. 137)

Dragon Noodle Co. ⊛ (South Strip, $$, p. 126)

Grand Wok and Sushi Bar ⊛ (South Strip, $$$, p. 124)

Key to Abbreviations: $$$$ = Very Expensive $$$ = Expensive $$ = Moderate $ = Inexpensive

BUFFETS/BRUNCHES

Bally's Big Kitchen Buffet ⍟
(Center Strip, $$, p. 147)

Boardwalk Casino & Hotel
(South Strip, $, p. 146)

Circus Circus (North Strip, $,
p. 148)

Excalibur's Round Table Buffet
(South Strip, $, p. 147)

Flamingo Paradise Garden
Buffet ⍟ (Center Strip, $,
p. 148)

Las Vegas Hilton Buffet ⍟
(East of the Strip, $, p. 149)

Luxor's Pharaoh's Pheast
Buffet ⍟⍟ (South Strip, $,
p. 145)

MGM Grand Buffet (South Strip,
$, p. 146)

Mirage Cravings Buffet ⍟⍟
(Center Strip, $$$, p. 147)

Monte Carlo Buffet ⍟ (South
Strip, $, p. 146)

Paris's Le Village Buffet ⍟⍟⍟
(Center Strip, $$$, p. 147)

Rio's Carnival World Buffet ⍟
(West of the Strip, $$$, p. 149)

Sam's Town Firelight Buffet ⍟
(East of the Strip, $, p. 149)

Treasure Island Buffet ⍟
(Center Strip, $, p. 148)

CALIFORNIA

California Pizza Kitchen
(Center Strip $, p. 138)

Spago ⍟⍟⍟ (Center Strip, $$$$,
p. 134)

Wolfgang Puck Cafe ⍟⍟
(South Strip, $$, p. 128)

CHINESE

Chin Chin (South Strip, $, p. 126)

Harbor Palace (West of the Strip,
$, p. 132)

168 Shanghai ⍟ (West of the
Strip, $, p. 132)

P.F. Chang's Chinese Bistro
(South Strip, $$, p. 127)

Royal Star ⍟ (Center Strip, $$$,
p. 135)

DELI

Legends Deli (South Strip, $,
p. 130)

Stage Deli ⍟ (Center Strip, $$,
p. 138)

DESSERTS

Cocolini Gelato (Center Strip, $,
p. 135)

Krispy Kreme (various locations, $,
p. 136)

Lenôtre ⍟⍟⍟ (Center Strip, $,
p. 138)

Olio Gelato ⍟ (South Strip, $,
p. 135)

Voodoo Café (West of the Strip, $,
p. 144)

DINER/COFFEE SHOP

Calypsos (South Strip, $, p. 129)

Legends Deli (South Strip, $,
p. 130)

Mr. Lucky's 24/7 ⍟⍟ (East of the
Strip, $, p. 142)

Pink Pony ⍟ (North Strip, $,
p. 139)

Tiffany's Café at White Cross
Drugs ⍟ (North Strip, $,
p. 140)

FRENCH

Alizé ⍟⍟⍟ (West of the Strip,
$$$$, p. 150)

Bouchon ⍟⍟⍟ (Center Strip,
$$$$, p. 150)

Mon Ami Gabi ⍟⍟ (Center Strip,
$$$$, p. 134)

Picasso ⍟⍟ (Center Strip, $$$$,
p. ###149

INTERNATIONAL

Grand Lux Café ⍟ (Center Strip,
$$, p. 137)

ITALIAN

Metro Pizza ⍟ (East of the Strip,
$, p. 142)

Stivali ⍟ (North Strip, $, p. 139)

JAPANESE

Dragon Sushi (West of the Strip,
$, p. 132)

Hamada ⍟ (various locations, $$$,
p. 124)

Mizuno's ✩✩ (South Strip, $$$, p. 125)

Nobu ✩✩✩ (East of the Strip, $$$$, p. 141)

Todai ✩ (South Strip, $$$$, p. #122)

MEXICAN

Border Grill ✩✩ (South Strip, $$$, p. 123)

Border Grill Cantina ✩✩ (South Strip, $, p. 126)

El Sombrero ✩ (Downtown, $, p. 145)

La Salsa (various locations, $, p. 129)

Pink Taco (East of the Strip, $, p. 144)

ROMANTIC DINING

Alizé ✩✩✩ (West of the Strip, $$$, p. 150)

Bouchon ✩✩✩ (Center Strip, $$$$, p. 150)

Lutèce ✩ (Center Strip, $$$, p. 150)

Mon Ami Gabi ✩✩ (Center Strip, $$$$, p. 134)

Picasso ✩✩ (Center Strip, $$$$, p. 149)

SANDWICHES

Capriotti's ✩ (North Strip, $, p. 139)

SEAFOOD

Second Street Grill ✩ (Downtown, $$$, p. 144)

SOUTHERN/CAJUN/CREOLE

Delmonico Steakhouse ✩✩ (Center Strip, $$$$, p. 133)

Emeril's New Orleans Fish House ✩✩ (South Strip, $$$$, p. 121)

House of Blues ✩ (South Strip, $$$, p. 125)

THAI

Lotus of Siam ✩✩✩ (East of the Strip, $, p. 141)

VIETNAMESE

Pho (West of the Strip, $, p. 132)

3 South Strip

VERY EXPENSIVE

Emeril's New Orleans Fish House ✩✩ SOUTHERN/CAJUN/CREOLE
Many of the kids we know, ages 4 on up, think Emeril is the bam. One cooking-show-addicted mom of our acquaintance swears that her baby's first words were "pork fat," but she might just be exaggerating the teeniest bit. No matter, it proves the point: Emeril Lagasse is a bona fide superstar with a young following; he even has his own line of children's cookware and a cookbook for kids. If your child is as nuts about him as some of the ones we know, you'll definitely want to treat the little one—and yourself—to a meal here. To eat at one of his restaurants is to understand why he inspires such a passionate following. We sampled tasty double-cut pork chops with gnocchi and mushrooms, plus Cajun-spiced rib-eye steak with Emeril's trinity of spices, and his famous smashed potatoes, along with fish dishes. You may want to consider coming at lunch, rather than at the busier, and more expensive, dinner seating.

But if you eat at this restaurant (designed to look like a sidewalk cafe in New Orleans—replete with vines and Spanish moss) rather than at Emeril's Delmonico Steakhouse (p. 133) up the way at The Venetian, it should be because you really want to try what Emeril does with fish—such as the jumbo Gulf shrimp wrapped in bacon or the seared salmon with Louisiana crawfish ragout. Share some awesome appetizers—think crab cakes or sinfully good Creole marinated fried calamari. The gumbo, served at both lunch and dinner, is thick with seafood and is rich, redolent, and dark with spices, and there's a winning selection of salads at both lunch and dinner.

Try to save room for dessert—there's banana cream pie with banana crust and caramel sauce, and individual lemon-pudding cakes with just the perfect balance of sweet and tart—edible sunshine, seriously. Chocolate freaks should delve into the lethal double-chocolate walnut brownie stack with Bailey's ice cream and warm fudge sauce. This is a perfect place for a fancy dessert with the kids no matter where you've eaten dinner.

In the MGM Grand, 3799 Las Vegas Blvd. S. © 702/891-7374. www.emerils.com. Highchairs, boosters. Reservations required. Main courses $12–$18 at lunch, $20–$38 at dinner (more for lobster). AE, DC, DISC, MC, V. Daily 11am–2:30pm and 5:30–10:30pm.

Nob Hill ★★★ Finds AMERICAN   This is a pricey, adult-looking restaurant, but, surprisingly, it's rather kid friendly, and good to boot. "We're a neighborhood restaurant," explained one of the staff members. "And we don't like to leave out any of the family." Indeed, we were delighted to see a family with a 5-year-old and a 7-year-old happily eating away in the modern yet comfortable room. When we inquired, our server told us that parents regularly bring their children here, and that most kids order the chicken tetrazzini (cream sauce, chicken, noodles, and black truffles!) and the appetizer sampler, which features fried shrimp, a mushroom egg roll, and a foie gras pot sticker.

Executive chef Wayne Alcaide will also specially make pasta or other entrees for children who might not want to try seasonal dishes such as pork loin with mission fig sauce or quail served with asparagus and *panzetta,* an Italian bread salad. And the wee ones can always happily dig away at the whipped potato sampler, featuring five types of spuds emulsified with tasty things such as cheese and bacon, garlic, and mushrooms.

This is a serious restaurant, make no mistake, but it's nice that the entire staff realizes that children of fine diners will most likely grow up to be as enthralled by food as their parents—and the parents we spied on were encouraging this by sharing bites of their potato-encrusted sand dabs, bouillabaisse, and fried soft-shell crab with their well-behaved offspring. Children aren't the only ones catered to at Nob Hill; upon placing our order, we were asked if we had any allergies or if we had reservations for a show, in order to allow the chef to adjust to our needs.

The theme of the chef/proprietor Michael Mina's restaurant is San Francisco, with its wealth of seafood and agricultural abundance, emphasizing organic vegetables and fruits and the free-range poultry and meats of Northern California. Appetizers included a charcuterie plate, seared foie gras with raspberry jam, and a crab Louis salad. The desserts are splendid as well—caramel pot au crème with a trio of hand-dipped biscotti, a custom-made miniature Tarte Tatin with mission figs, and a selection of homemade ice creams. Ask in advance for the special glass-enclosed booths, which look like old-style private train cars, for a truly intimate family dining experience.

In the MGM Grand, 3799 Las Vegas Blvd. S. © 702/891-7337. Highchairs, boosters. Reservations recommended. Main courses $23–$40. AE, DC, MC, V. Daily 5:30am–10:30pm, last seating at 10pm.

Todai ★ JAPANESE   Instead of basing the children's menu on age, Todai, a Japanese sushi/seafood buffet chain, takes a different tact—the charge for your children depends on their height. At any one time, Todai offers over 40 different types of sushi and rolls along with a wide variety of hot dishes, including teriyaki, tempura, dumplings, chicken wings, fried rice, and vegetables. Plus, there are salads ranging from the basic potato with mayo to the hot pickled cabbage, *kimchi.* There's an endless array of desserts including a couple very odd

RESTAURANTS

America (New York-
New York) **6**
Border Cantina
(Mandalay Bay) **11**
Border Grill
(Mandalay Bay) **11**
Calypsos (Tropicana) **9**
Chin Chin (New York-
New York) **6**
Dragon Noodle Co.
(Monte Carlo) **3**
Emeril's New Orleans
Fish House
(MGM Grand) **7**

ESPN Zone (New York-
New York) **6**
Grand Wok and Sushi Bar
(MGM Grand) **7**
Hamada (Luxor) **10**
Hamada (MGM Grand) **7**
Harley Davidson Café **4**
House of Blues
(Mandalay Bay) **11**
In-N-Out Burger **5**
La Salsa (Aladdin/
Planet Hollywood) **1**
La Salsa (Luxor) **10**

Legends Deli (Tropicana) **9**
Mizuno's (Tropicana) **9**
Monte Carlo Pub &
Brewery (Monte Carlo) **3**
Nob Hill (MGM Grand) **7**
Olio Gelato (MGM Grand) **7**
P.F. Chang's China Bistro
(Aladdin/Planet
Hollywood) **1**
Rainforest Café
(MGM Grand) **7**
Todai (Aladdin/
Planet Hollywood) **1**

Verandah (The Four
Seasons) **11**
Wolfgang Puck Café
(MGM Grand) **7**
BUFFETS
Boardwalk Casino
& Hotel **2**
Excalibur's Round
Table Buffet **8**
Luxor's Pharaoh's
Pheast Buffet **10**
MGM Grand Buffet **7**
Monte Carlo Buffet **3**

ones—green tea cheesecake and piña colada tofu—along with cookies, flourless chocolate cake, and puddings. We like it here, but sushi purists complain that the rice for the sushi is extruded and formed by machine. Nevertheless, this is the best bet for families who want an unlimited Asian food feast.

In Aladdin/Planet Hollywood, 3667 Las Vegas Blvd. S. ✆ **702/892-0021.** Highchairs, boosters. Reservations accepted for large parties. Children 5 ft. and under half price; 4 ft. and under $6.95. Lunch Mon–Thurs $16, Fri–Sun $18; dinner Mon–Thurs $28, Fri–Sun $30. AE, DC, DISC, MC, V. Lunch daily 11:30am–2:30pm; dinner Sun–Thurs 5:30–9:30pm, Fri–Sun 5:30–10pm.

EXPENSIVE

Border Grill ★★ MEXICAN The *Two Hot Tamales* television program is no longer aired, but long before there were hundreds of cable channels, Mary Sue Milliken and Susan Fenniger carved out an empire making fresh, light Mexican food with a *nuevo* twist. The Vegas outpost of their most famous restaurant is every bit as yummy as the ones in Santa Monica and Pasadena, and there's even a lower-priced cantina that serves a truncated, less expensive menu (p. 126). The location, at Mandalay Bay, the southern most point of the Strip, puts it a bit out of the way, but for devotees or the curious, it's worth a special trip. The prices and the hours at both locations also make this a sound choice for families staying next door at the Four Seasons or who've come to view Shark Reef.

We loved the enchiladas, made with citrus-marinated chicken and a poblano chile sauce, and our test child went wild over the chicken *chilaquiles,* a casserole made with corn tortillas, cheese, and different salsas. The tacos were a successful choice, as were all the appetizers, though 8 bucks was a steep tariff for guac and chips. Sharing a plate of assorted tamales and a salad is enough food for two any-sized people, but our portion-control issues may be different than yours. Order-ing off the children's menu gives kids the option of tacos, tamales, grilled turkey, or fish. Desserts for kids include cookies and ice cream, but we preferred the flan and the Mexican chocolate pie.

In Mandalay Bay, 3950 Las Vegas Blvd. S. ⓒ **702/632-7403**. www.mandalaybay.com. Kids' menu, high-chairs, boosters. Reservations recommended. Main courses $15–$20. AE, DC, DISC, MC, V. Sun–Thurs 11:30am–10pm; Fri–Sat 11:30am–11pm.

Grand Wok and Sushi Bar ⭑ ASIAN   This is one of the only places you'll find Thai food on the entire Strip, and you'll pay dearly for it by comparison to the Thai joints along Sahara Boulevard. No matter, the pad Thai noodles are light and sweet, perfectly seasoned, served with garnishes of shredded cabbage, carrots, and chopped peanuts. The red curry with coconut is tasty, with just the right amount of heat. Portions—especially the soups—are large enough to share, so you'll be able to sample several items from the extensive Pan-Asian menu. Along with Thai food, there are traditional Chinese dishes, Vietnamese rice noodle soup (*pho,* pronounced "fuhr"), Indonesian dishes, and sushi. Kids get a kick out of the minced shrimp "lollipops" on sugar-cane sticks. Adults may want to try one of the fine sakes with their meal. This restaurant is very popular with the MGM Grand's Asian clientele, which is always a good sign.

In the MGM Grand, 3799 Las Vegas Blvd. S. ⓒ **702/891-7777**. www.mgmgrand.com. Highchairs, boosters. Reservations not accepted. Main courses $8.95–$30; sushi $4.50–$14. AE, DC, DISC, MC, V. Restaurant Mon–Thurs 11am–10pm; sushi bar 5–11pm; both open Fri–Sat 11am–midnight, Sunday 11am–10pm.

Hamada ⭑ JAPANESE   This reliable restaurant has several branches scattered about Las Vegas's hotels, and has been rated as the Top Japanese Restaurant in Nevada by Zagat's, and by the readers of the *Las Vegas Review-Journal.* Hamada serves good, dependable Japanese food. There's nothing earthshakingly amazing about the food, served in bamboo-decorated rooms festooned with hanging banners, but there's a certain confidence in knowing you'll get the same food every time. The sushi is fresh, basic, standard stuff with a few now-traditional rolls (think California roll, dragon roll, and their siblings) thrown in. Tempura, teriyaki, and sukiyaki, along with noodle dishes, form different combos.

Lunch specials served in *bento* boxes—lacquered wooden platters with sepa-rate areas for each item, not unlike upscale TV-dinner plates—include teriyaki, tempura, sushi, and, inexplicably, potato salad, along with fruit, miso soup, and salad. They're definitely a bargain, but only the Luxor Hamada is open for lunch. This Luxor location has a sushi bar and dining room, while the dinner-only Hamada at The Flamingo (3555 Las Vegas Blvd. S.; ⓒ **702/733-3455**) also features a *teppan* grill for searing and stir-frying food before your eyes. The Hamada Asian Village at the Stratosphere (2000 Las Vegas Blvd. S.; ⓒ **702/ 380-7777**) also features a *teppan* grill and serves Chinese as well as Japanese food. Both of the latter locations are open from 5 to 11pm, daily. All locations serve *udon* soup—huge bowls of fat noodles with tempura shrimp and vegeta-bles floating in a clear broth. The MGM Grand's Hamada (3799 Las Vegas Blvd. S.; ⓒ **702/891-7349**), in the food court, is the least expensive of all, and its noodles, soups, sushi, and salads are a welcome change from the usual food court fare; it's open from 8am to midnight, daily.

In the Luxor, 3900 Las Vegas Blvd. S. ⓒ **702/262-4548**. www.hamadaofjapan.com. Highchairs, boosters. Main courses $15–$30; sushi $4–$10. AE, DC, DISC, MC, V. Lunch daily 11am–4:30pm; dinner daily 4:30pm–midnight.

Tips If Your Kids Are Really Picky . . .

Many Las Vegas restaurants will fax you their menus, so you and your kids can agree, in advance, where you'd like to have special, or just regular, meals.

House of Blues ★ SOUTHERN/CAJUN/CREOLE   The blues and folk music meet Disneyland with a New Age overlay here. Decorated with folk art, outsider art, and found art, this huge, funky shack serves up a (loud) all-ages gospel brunch buffet with eggs, fried chicken, bourbon-glazed ham, salads, and way too much other stuff in the main showroom every Sunday. The restaurant, separate from the nightclub so that all ages can dine here, provides regular meals. We like the burgers the best of everything on the regular menu, and we'd love it if the Sunday brunch fried chicken migrated over to the main menu. Along with ribs and gumbo, they serve catfish, grilled tuna, steak, and salads. It's above adequate for a chain, with some interesting selections (andouille sausage po' boys), but sometimes it seem like they're trying too hard (those andouille sausage po' boys again). The children's menu, which is fine for light eaters or the superfussy, features a grilled-cheese sandwich, pasta, or chef salad. Blah. Kids might be happier with the main-menu burger, or the rib "fingers" from the appetizer menu. Desserts are nothing special. For lunch, spend your money at one of Emeril's places instead: You'll get better, more original food for your money.

In Mandalay Bay, 3950 Las Vegas Blvd. S. *C* 702/632-7600. www.mandalaybay.com. Kids' menu, high-chairs, boosters. Main courses $11–$20; kids' menu $4.95. AE, DC, DISC, MC, V. Breakfast daily 8–11am; full meals Mon–Thurs 11am–midnight, Sat–Sun 11am–1am. Gospel brunch in the showroom Sun (2 seatings) 10am and 1pm.

Mizuno's ★★ JAPANESE   Mizuno's is the perfect place to take fussy eaters, budding gourmands, and vegetarians. The food is fresh and fun, and because this is Vegas, you get quite a show to go along with your meal. Guests are seated around a tabletop grill, called *teppan,* where your personal chef arrives with cleaver in hand to prepare your *teppanyaki* (stir-fried) meal. You can choose either the one-meat-item Samurai dinner or the two-item combo Shogun, with reduced price options for children under 12; vegetarians get sautéed veggies. All dinners come with miso soup and a small salad. Fried rice is made as you watch. There's sushi and *gyoza* (steamed then fried dumplings, aka pot stickers) for appetizers, but you'll want to save room for the light and tasty entrees. Want chicken with extra garlic? No problem. Like extra onions, or no onions with your steak? Your chef is happy to oblige as he rapidly chops, sautés, and stirs ingredients together. The strobe lights start as he tosses shakers and juggles knives, giving a real showbiz feel to the whole meal. It's satisfyingly flashy, and satisfyingly good as well. One dad told us that Mizuno's is the only place in all of Vegas where his two kids will actually eat their veggies and that they beg to come here. Now that's an endorsement!

In the Tropicana Resort & Casino, 3801 Las Vegas Blvd. S. *C* 702/739-2713. www.tropicanalv.com. Kids' menu, highchairs, boosters. Reservations recommended. Full Samurai dinners mostly $17–$25; shogun combination dinners $26–$79; kids' menu $9.95. AE, DC, DISC, MC, V. Daily 5–10:45pm.

MODERATE

America AMERICAN   Take a gastronomic tour of the USA at this brightly colored restaurant. Your kids can practice their geography and cultural history while ordering Buffalo wings—they're from upstate New York, not the prairies—and Cobb salad, which comes from Hollywood. The menu features American food, with a dish's point of origination spelled out next to each item. Some of these are a bit random, such as the fried mozzarella sticks from Santa Monica and the Laguna Nigel salade niçoise. And our neighbors down Mexico way might be a bit surprised to find out that America, the restaurant, has annexed Tijuana, the city, for America, the country, via the Caesar salad. On the main wall, a 90×20-foot map of the United States (complete with mountains, rivers, and forests) provides distraction and/or nonchalant education opportunities. The food is good, especially for such an ambitious concept.

In New York–New York, 3790 Las Vegas Blvd S. ⓒ **800/693-6763** or 702/740-6451. www.nynyhotel casino.com. Highchairs, boosters. Main courses $9–$23. AE, DC, DISC, MC, V. Daily 24 hr.

Border Grill Cantina ⭐⭐ MEXICAN   No kids' menu, but you don't really need it; you can share dishes, sampling the quesadillas, tacos, and empanadas also found at the Border Grill. We liked the chicken mole quesadilla, but alas, the complex dark sauce was not a child pleaser. Our test child much preferred the *carne asada* (steak) and the grilled fish tacos, and, naturally, the *taquitos*— corn tortillas rolled around shredded beef, deep fried, and served with guacamole and salsa. No desserts that we could find, but adults may appreciate the margaritas and fine tequilas on hand.

In Mandalay Bay, 3950 Las Vegas Blvd. S. ⓒ **702/632-7403.** www.mandalaybay.com. Highchairs, boosters. Reservations not accepted. Main courses $9–$14. AE, DC, DISC, MC, V. Daily 11:30am–7:30pm.

Chin Chin CHINESE   *Chin chin* means "to your health" in Chinese, and this chain, which got its start on chic Sunset Plaza in West Hollywood, uses no added MSG in the preparation of their fresh, light food. Along with noodles, which symbolize longevity to the Chinese, Chin Chin serves salads, wokked meats and veggies, plus dim sum (small and various dishes of Chinese food); a filling meal anytime of day. At breakfast, a traditional eggs, waffles, and bacon buffet shares space with dim sum, noodles, and *congee,* a rice porridge, which can be ordered off the menu. The light and airy room features an open kitchen, so kids can watch their food being prepared.

In New York–New York, 3790 Las Vegas Blvd S. ⓒ **800/693-6763** or 702/740-6300. www.nynyhotel-casino.com. Highchairs, boosters. Main courses $9–$14. AE, DC, DISC, MC, V. Sun–Thurs 8am–11pm; Fri–Sat 8am–midnight.

Dragon Noodle Co. ⭐ ASIAN   Sushi and Chinese food come together in this campily decorated restaurant (think lots of red paint, dragons, and hanging, fringed lamps). Food is cooked in an open kitchen, something kids love to watch, especially when the wok flares up. Everything can be prepared for take out, though unless you're staying in the Monte Carlo, it could be cold by the time you get back to your place. And forget about carrying sushi around in 100°F (38°C) weather. We really like the Chinese food here—the chow fun with beef and chop suey are solid choices, as are the kid-pleasing lemon chicken (battered and fried with a lemon sauce), the orange chicken (battered and fried with a chile-orange sauce), and the honey chicken (more battered and fried chicken morsels, this time with a honey glaze). If you'd like to throw in a vegetable or two (please do), there's spinach with soy and garlic and Chinese broccoli with oyster sauce, along with a selection of tofu dishes that even most nonvegetarians will like. Fried rice, egg rolls, wontons, and soups are traditional hunger busters that won't bust your budget. The barbecued pork appetizer is tasty, and the fried chicken and noodle salad are light and refreshing. Menu items can be modified and ingredients adjusted to your desires. Sushi is served Tuesday through Sunday evenings from 5pm until closing.

In the Monte Carlo Resort & Casino, 3770 Las Vegas Blvd. S. (between Flamingo Rd. and Tropicana Ave.). © 702/730-7965. www.monte-carlo.com. Highchairs, boosters. Main courses $7–$22 (many under $10); sushi $5 and up. AE, DC, DISC, MC, V. Sun–Thurs 11am–11pm, Fri–Sat 11am–midnight; sushi bar Tues–Thurs 5–10pm, Fri–Sun 5–11pm.

ESPN Zone AMERICAN   Sports enthusiasts will thrill to this theme chain, where some sporting event is always airing on the TVs and memorabilia lines the walls. The food is all-American armchair-quarterback fare—think burgers, grilled steaks, fried chicken fingers, and the ever-popular cheese fries, though they have tried to hit a home run with the health conscious by including grilled fish, pasta, and a subpar apple, blue cheese, and walnut salad, with the inexplicable addition of roasted red peppers. Kids under 10 have their own menu, which includes a drink with their order of chicken tenders, PB&J, hot dog, grilled cheese, pasta, or miniburgers. The same miniburgers, called sliders, are on the appetizer menu in a "cluster of six," while nachos, called Zone Queso Chips, have bacon on them for an extra-cholesterol kick (as do the aforementioned cheese fries). Desserts are big enough for two or three adults. When the kids are done eating, send them upstairs to play video games, so you can share a peaceful moment together watching bass fishing. This is Vegas—be prepared for the sports souvenir shop right outside the door.

In New York–New York, 3790 Las Vegas Blvd S. © 702/933-3776. www.espnzone.com. Kids' menu, highchairs, boosters. Main courses $12–$26; kids' menu at lunch and dinner $5.99. AE, DC, DISC, MC, V. Mon–Thurs 11:30am–11pm; Fri 11:30am–midnight; Sat 11am–midnight; Sun 11am–11pm.

Harley-Davidson Cafe AMERICAN   Harley-Davidson motorcycles were once the hog of choice for one-percenters—the outcasts of society, the rebels, the grungy, leather-clad bad asses you wouldn't want your kids to grow up and be. But now, doctors, lawyers, and other "upstanding" citizens—many of whom spend upwards of $18,000 for their hog—head on down the highway, riding America's number-one motorcycle for fun. Let your kids take an up-close gander at the motorcycle memorabilia as they sink into black simulated leather booths and chow down on sloppy Joes, Roadhouse Chicken Wings, and, of course, the Harley Hog sandwich. There are also salads as well as vegetarian fare on the menu, no doubt because the demographics and image of bikers has changed so much during the past 2 decades. But not to give short shrift to Harley-Davidson's rowdy history, there is a menu of over 20 hard liquor drinks available in souvenir glasses.

3725 Las Vegas Blvd. S. (between Harmon and Tropicana aves.). © 702/740-4555. Highchairs, boosters. Reservations accepted. Main courses under $10–$20. AE, DC, DISC, MC, V. Daily 11am–midnight.

P.F. Chang's China Bistro CHINESE   With menu items developed in conjunction with acclaimed chef Barbara Tropp (San Francisco's China Moon Café and author of *China Moon Cookbook* and *Modern Art of Chinese Cooking*), P.F. Chang's China Bistro serves a decent selection of favorite Chinese dishes. While you won't find exotic items such as shark fin or birds nest on the menu, you will get sizable portions of traditional Chinese restaurant items: Mongolian beef, orange-peel chicken, and sweet-and-sour pork, along with egg rolls, Peking duck, noodle dishes (we liked the Singapore street noodles with shrimp and curry, but kids might find its yellow color and spiciness a bit off-putting), cashew chicken, and the signature lettuce wraps. It's all good, even the nontraditional desserts—Great Wall of Chocolate Cake and the deep-fried banana rolls with coconut ice cream. The room itself (with replicas of Xian statues—life-size terracotta warriors found in an emperor's gravesite) is lovely.

In the Aladdin/Planet Hollywood Resort & Casino, 3667 Las Vegas Blvd. S. (at Harmon Ave.). © 702/ 836-0955. Highchairs, boosters. Reservations accepted. Main courses $8–$18 (many under $10), some less at lunch. AE, DC, DISC, MC, V. Sun–Thurs 11:30am–midnight; Fri–Sat 11:30am–1am.

Rainforest Cafe ⚜ AMERICAN   Part of a chain, this ecologically themed restaurant is entirely smoke-free—a rarity in Vegas. Animatronic animals (including a misplaced dinosaur) blink, roar, and twitch their ears and tails as a rainstorm passes overhead. There's a huge saltwater aquarium and a waterfall, and at breakfast, magicians from Houdini's Magic Store wander around performing sleight-of-hand and close-up magic. And yes, there's a souvenir shop with T-shirts, safari clothes, stuffed animals, and coffee mugs. We scored a very cool leopard-spotted onesie jumper from a rack next to a winking gorilla. But back to the food—which is really pretty good; for once, the owners seem to have paid just as much attention to it as to the decor.

   In keeping with the tropical theme, the food has exotic names cloaking its mostly kid-friendly ingredients, but the dishes are all described in detail, so you and your family can easily decide more easily. Some items, such as the Rasta Pasta with walnuts, broccoli, and red peppers may be a little too way out for some kids, but there are pizza, Buffalo wings, fried chicken, and pot roast, along with ribs, and large salads for the finicky. The 12-and-under set can choose from the kids' menu, which comes with a soda, milk, or juice. The most awesome kids' meal was Jurassic Chicken Tidbits—dinosaur-shaped deep-fried nuggets— but the Rainforest Rascal burger plate was also a good choice. Vegetarian adults and kids will find something for them on both menus, and the desserts are huge.

In the MGM Grand, 3799 Las Vegas Blvd. S. © 800/929-1111 or 702/891-8580. www.mgmgrand.com. Kids' menu, highchairs, boosters. Reservations accepted. Main courses $12–$15; kids' menu $5.99. AE, DC, DISC, MC, V. Sun–Thurs 8am–11pm; Fri–Sat 8am–midnight.

Wolfgang Puck Cafe ⚜⚜ CALIFORNIA   This branch of the celebrity-chef's populist chain is bright and lively, featuring the famous multicolored

---

Moments **Tea for Two**

High tea—with its dainty finger sandwiches, scones thickly slathered with clotted cream, and tiny frosted cakes, not to mention a choice of different teas, served with either milk or lemon—is a lovely and relaxing way to spend an afternoon with your children, especially if they are Anglophiles or prone to throwing tea parties with their dolls and pets. The **Verandah** ⚜ at the child-loving Four Seasons serves high tea daily from 2 to 5pm, replete with the requisite cucumber and cress sandwiches, scones, and pastries. You might want to pack ladylike hats and gloves and plan to make this a dress-up playtime by inviting any historical personages or invisible princesses and fantasy friends from your child's imagination. And if high tea's not your cup of tea, the Verandah offers children's menus for breakfast, lunch, and a dinner buffet. (In the Four Seasons, 3960 Las Vegas Blvd. S., © 877/632-5000 or 702/632-5000; www.fourseasons.com. Afternoon tea $23.75 per person. AE, DC, DISC, MC, V.)

mosaics designed by Puck's artistically ambitious wife Barbara Lazaroff and his even more famous huge wood-burning pizza ovens. This is an affordable choice for parents who want to have a gourmet-lite experience with their kids without breaking the bank, especially during happy hour, when appetizers are available at reduced prices. Well, okay, maybe your kids aren't into pesto pizza or goat cheese, but the ravioli is good and the salads are large and fresh, making it a welcome change from the food court, coffee shop, or from buffet fare. Puck's signature Chinese chicken salad is full of crunchy fried wontons and cabbage, and the basic Caesar salad is large enough for two. Another good option for sharing is the trio of spring rolls, featuring chicken, shrimp, and vegetable deep-fried egg rolls with hot mustard and sweet dipping sauces.

In the MGM Grand, 3799 Las Vegas Blvd. S. (℃) **800/929-1111** or 702/895-9653. www.mgmgrand.com. Highchairs, boosters. Reservations not accepted. Main courses $13–$29. AE, DC, MC, V. Mon–Fri 11:30am–11:30pm; Sun 11:30am–10pm.

INEXPENSIVE

Calypsos DINER/COFFEE SHOP   Building your own burger is one of the prime attractions at this cheery coffee shop, which also features salads, including a dessert camouflaging itself amongst the leafy-green offerings: melon balls heaped atop pound cake, served with frozen yogurt. For the adventurous, there's a Mediterranean chopped salad with shrimp and the Thai shrimp satay, but we prefer the classic coffee shop fare such as the burger with barbecue sauce, grilled onions, bacon, and pineapple, followed by a fudge sundae. Your kids will, too.

In the Tropicana Resort & Casino, 3801 Las Vegas Blvd. S. (℃) **702/739-2222**. Highchairs. Reservations not accepted. Main courses $5.95–$17. AE, MC, V. Daily 24 hr.

In-N-Out Burger (★) (*Value*) AMERICAN   This Southern California classic roadside, family-owned, drive-through burger chain has always made a point of serving fresh, high-quality fast food. Potatoes for the fries are hand cut at each location; the meat is always fresh, not frozen; shakes are made with real ice cream; and all burgers can be customized for your desires. None of the special variations are listed on the menu, but have gained mythic stature amongst those in the know. Try the Animal Style—grilled onions, extra sauce, and pickles—or the protein, which comes wrapped in lettuce with no bun; or the Wish Burger, which has no burger, just cheese, lettuce, and tomatoes. A Flying Dutchman has two slices of cheese and two patties with nothing else; if you just want mustard and ketchup with your meat and cheese, ask for the Old Fashioned. Along with their "secret items," the chain has a couple other peculiarities: Numbers of certain Bible chapters and verses (Revelation 3:20, John 3:16, Proverbs 3:15, and Nahum 1:7) are printed on the underside of soda cups, malt cups, and burger wrappers, which may be disturbing to some; and no phone numbers are listed for individual locations—they can only be reached through the 800 number. In addition to the Strip-side In-N-Out, you can find this quirky drive-through on the road to Nellis Air Force Base (51 N. Nellis Blvd.), west of the North Strip (2900 W. Sahara Blvd.), and on the east end of town (4705 S. Maryland Pkwy.).

4888 Industrial Rd. (at Tropicana). (℃) **800/786-1000**. www.inandout.com. Highchairs, boosters. Reservations not accepted. Main courses $1.45–$5.50. Cash only, no credit cards; ATM on-site. All branches Sun–Thurs 10:30am–1am; Fri–Sat 10:30am–1:30am.

La Salsa (*Value*) MEXICAN   This pioneering chain of Mexican fast food/casual dining restaurants created the concept of the salsa bar, where different types of fresh salsas can be self-served onto your freshly made tacos and burritos. La Salsa was also the first fast-food Mexican chain to grill chicken and beef for tacos and

Value Cheap Eats

Gone are Vegas's days of **super-cheap buffets**, but there are a few holdouts, places that offer meals for a bit less than the Strip average (though most really cheap dining establishments are in ickyish, smoky, old hotels). Also note that these places cut no discount for children; even kindergartners will pay full price. Nevertheless, if you feel that you *must* experience this vestige of old Las Vegas, try one of the below.

At its two locations, **Arizona Charlie's** buffet, 740 Decatur Blvd. ((C) **702/258-5200**), and 4575 Boulder Hwy. ((C) **702/951-9000**; www. arizonacharlies.com), offers basic food at cheap prices—breakfast for $4.99, lunch for $5.99, and dinner for $7.99. Children 2 and under eat free. The **Gold Coast** buffet, 4000 W. Flamingo Rd. ((C) **702/367-7111**), provides seven serving stations. Breakfast is $5.45, lunch $6.95, dinner and Sunday brunch $10.45, Sunday steak night will set you back $14.95, and Thursday seafood night is $14.95. Children 2 and under eat free. **Main Street Station,** 200 Main St. ((C) **702/387-1896**; www. mainstreetcasino.com), is 2 blocks from the Fremont Street Experience and offers a buffet with a variety of cuisines. Breakfast is $5.75, lunch $7.75, dinner $10.79. The Tuesday night T-bone special is $12.98, and Sunday brunch runs $9.95. Children 2 and under eat free. **The Orleans,** 4500 W. Tropicana Ave. ((C) **702/365-7111**; www.orleanscasino.com), also delivers low-price buffets of cuisines of the world. Breakfast is $5.95, lunch $6.95, and dinner $11.95. Children 2 and under eat free.

Hot dog lovers should check out **Westward Ho Hotel & Casino,** 2900 Las Vegas Blvd. S. ((C) **702/731-2900**; www.westwardho.com), which offers the Mega-Dog, a huge half pound of processed meat for a mere

is credited with popularizing soft tacos, *carne asada* (grilled steak), and black beans, all of which were quite an innovation when the chain launched more than 20 years ago. Its Vegas locations mean that vegans can eat vegetable, rice, and lard-free bean burritos or tacos, and that no one has to worry about the food being too spicy, because you can choose your salsas, all of which are rated by heat. An order of tacos comes two to a plate, burritos are large, and the chips good and fresh. All food can be custom-ordered—we overheard one slinky teen asking for a rice, tomato, and lettuce taco. Whatever! Along with this branch, you can find this popular taco stand at the Aladdin/Planet Hollywood Desert Passage Shops (3663 Las Vegas Blvd. S.; (C) **702/892-0645**), Caesars Palace (3570 Las Vegas Blvd. S.; (C) **702/735-8226**), and at the Neonopolis downtown (450 Fremont St.; (C) **702/384-1720**).

In the Luxor Las Vegas, 3900 Las Vegas Blvd. S. (C) **702/739-1776**. www.luxor.com. Reservations not accepted. Main courses $3–$9. AE, DC, DISC, MC, V. All branches open daily 11:30am–10pm.

Legends Deli DELI/DINER/COFFEE SHOP   After a tour of the Casino Legends Hall of Fame (p. 170) next door, fans of Elvis—or kids who just like trying food they may not get at home—will want to sample the King's favorite, a peanut butter, jelly, and banana sandwich—fried, of course. It's very good in a

$1.49. At the **Gold Coast Casino**, 3959 Las Vegas Blvd. S. (© **702/367-7111**; www.goldcoast.com), a dog from the cart near the sports bar is 75¢. **Slots A Fun Casino**, 2890 Las Vegas Blvd. S. (© **702/734-0410**; www.casinocity.com), has a much-lauded hot dog, which made it into a PBS special on the best hot dogs in all of the United States (though some people we know don't think they're anything particularly special!). These casinos allow children, accompanied by their parents, to go to the snack bars.

Beef eaters can find a $1.99 burger at **Key Largo**, 377 E. Flamingo Rd. (© **702/733-7777**; www.keylargocasino.com), available 24 hours a day. A complete sirloin steak dinner for $4.95 is served day and night at nearby **Ellis Island** (© **702/733-8901**; www.super8lasvegas.com). And a $7.77 steak and shrimp dinner can be had 24/7 at the Hard Rock's **Mr. Lucky's** coffee shop (© **702/693-5000**; www.hardrockhotel. com).

You can also save big at hotel food courts (with McDonald's, Nathan's, and more adventurous fare), which offer inexpensive alternatives to buffet or restaurant breakfasts. MGM Grand, Monte Carlo, and The Venetian have particularly good food courts with lots of interesting choices. You can save big bucks at breakfast, and the kids will be happy with familiar choices. On the other hand, buffets can be good value at lunch or dinner for kids under 10 because of the desserts—they're part of the buffet and you can eat as much as your stomach (or parent!) allows. Note also that children under 10 are charged half price at many Strip hotel buffets.

really decadent, trailer-park way. Other sandwiches—the main food item served here—include hot dogs, Philly cheese steak, tuna salad, plus a basic PB&J, without the added Elvisian touches. Though it's not listed on the hotel's website, you can find this fun snack spot, and the museum, near the sports bar.

In the Tropicana Resort & Casino, 3801 Las Vegas Blvd. S. © 702/739-2222. www.tropicanalv.com. Highchairs. Reservations not accepted. Main courses $5–$8. AE, MC, V. Daily 9am–9pm.

Monte Carlo Pub & Brewery ★★★ *(Value* AMERICAN   Huge, loud, and fun, this brewpub features pizzas, burgers, and salads, along with a half-dozen highly recommended local beers. TVs are tuned to different stations, so guests can watch (forget about hearing) sports, news, and other programs. Exposed bricks, copper tubing, and brew vats add to the casual and lively decor. Kids are welcome until 9pm, when live music begins. We really liked the barbecued chicken pizza, house salad, juicy cheddar burger, and the jalapeño poppers that literally popped with flavor. Pass on the Buffalo wings, which came soaked in a thin, unpleasant, vinegary pepper sauce. The nachos are large enough for a family of four, plus Spot the dog. Did we mention chicken fingers? Yum! There's ice cream, cheesecake, and a huge chocolate brownie smothered in ice cream and fudge sauce for dessert. This informal, reasonably priced hotel-dining barn is a

Las Vegas's Chinatown

Las Vegas's Chinatown (4255 Spring Rd.; www.lvchinatown.com) is an under-10-minute drive from Treasure Island, but almost a world away, despite its strip-mall atmosphere. Along with stores carrying a variety of exotic goods, there are over half-a-dozen family-friendly restaurants serving food from the Far East. **Pho** (② **702/227-8618**), a Vietnamese soup shop named for the soup itself, serves a big hot-pot with raw beef (it cooks instantly in the hot broth), bean sprouts, leaves, and lime, along with a regular menu of Vietnamese dishes like spring rolls wrapped in a delicate rice paper and stuffed with shrimp, noodles, and herbs. **Dragon Sushi** (② **702/889-4336**) offers sushi as well as basic Japanese foods.

Both **168 Shanghai** 🍴 (② **702/889-8700**) and **Harbor Palace** (② **702/ 253-1688**) serve dim sum from the traditional metal carts that are pushed through the restaurant, stopping at each table. Your waitress will lift up each dish, showing you the contents, which can range from the not-for-the squeamish (chicken feet) to the most sedate and succulent items such as *shu mai*—thin-skinned dumplings filled with shrimp—or fluffy *cha su bao,* the Chinese barbecued-pork sandwich. Each diner is given a small dish of mustard and hot sauce for dipping; the addition of soy sauce is at your discretion. The dim sum dishes for vegetarians are meager (Chinese broccoli, no oyster sauce, please), but the regular menu offers some options.

great change of pace from buffets and coffee shops with enough choices on the menu for everyone. We loved it, and so did the other families scattered about.

In the Monte Carlo Resort & Casino, 3770 Las Vegas Blvd. S. (between Flamingo Rd. and Tropicana Ave.). ② **702/730-7777.** www.monte-carlo.com. Highchairs, boosters. Reservations not accepted. Main courses $7–$18 (most under $10). AE, DC, DISC, MC, V. Sun–Thurs 11am–3am; Fri–Sat 11am–4am.

4 Center Strip

VERY EXPENSIVE

Buccaneer Bay Club 🍴 *(Moments* AMERICAN   You'll feel like you're dining in a pirate's lair in this elegant room decorated with swords, blunderbusses, and conquistadors' helmets. Treasure chests spill their bounty from nooks and crannies, and the many windows, albeit small, overlook the pirate battle that rages every hour and a half in the Sirens Cove lagoon below. The wait staff will alert you when the battle is on and kindly holds your order until the fracas is over. One of the best-kept secrets on the Strip, this restaurant serves meat, fowl, and seafood with a few surprises—like spice-rubbed quail and grilled prime rib of buffalo—along with the standard items, including hot and cold appetizers. If your child has an urge to try escargot, indulge him or her here—the garlicky morsels are baked in brioche, emerging tender and succulent. Portions, like those in almost every Vegas restaurant, are large and could overwhelm a child. You may want to stick to ordering appetizers and dessert while watching the pirate battle. And why not, when the final course includes warm Valrona chocolate cake, and delicate, perfect soufflés. A fancy, dress-up place to bring children

RESTAURANTS

Bouchon
(The Venetian) **2**
Buccaneer Bay Club
(Treasure Island) **1**
California Pizza Kitchen
(The Mirage) **3**
Cheesecake Factory
(Caesars Palace) **5**
Chinois Café
(Caesars Palace) **5**
Delmonico Steakhouse
(The Venetian) **2**
Grand Lux Café
(The Venetian) **2**
Lenôtre
(Paris Las Vegas) **7**
Lutece
(The Venetian) **2**

Mon Ami Gabi
(Paris Las Vegas) **7**
Royal Star
(The Venetian) **2**
Spago
(Caesars Palace) **5**
Stage Deli
(Caesars Palace) **5**

BUFFETS
Bally's Big Kitchen
Buffet **6**
Flamingo Paradise Garden
Buffet **4**
Le Village Buffet **7**
Mirage Cravings Buffet **3**
Treasure Island Buffet **1**

older than 5 for a special occasion, Buccaneer Bay may set you back a few dou-
bloons, but the view and the food make it worthwhile.

In Treasure Island, 3300 Las Vegas Blvd. S. ✆ **877/793-7111** or 702/894-7223. Boosters. Reservations recommended. Main courses $20–$35. AE, DC, DISC, MC, V. Wed–Sun 5–11pm. Children 5 and older only.

Delmonico Steakhouse ★★ SOUTHERN/CAJUN/CREOLE You may
want to save dinner here for the adults and bring your Emeril-adoring offspring
for lunch, because the food at Delmonico is very adult, as are the prices.
Lunchtime features a juicy burger with bacon, Swiss cheese, caramelized onions,
and truffle emulsion. The shredded barbecue-pork sandwich with A.O.K. sauce
is the most upscale barbecue food ever. For good measure, throw in some truffle Parmesan potato chips or smashed potatoes, and your child won't mind fore-
going dinner. Appetizers—including the barbecue shrimp in tangy sauce with a
rosemary biscuit and the creamy salmon cheesecake—are served at both lunch
and dinner, as are soups and salads. A true Emerilphile should go for the gumbo,
and the kid-pleasing French onion soup comes with an English muffin smothered in Swiss cheese. Desserts, especially the flourless chocolate–peanut butter
cake with peanut butter mousse, fudge sauce, and toasted peanuts, are rich, fla-
vorful, luxurious, and satisfying.

In The Venetian, 3355 Las Vegas Blvd. S. ✆ **702/414-3737.** www.emerils.com. Highchairs, boosters. Reservations strongly recommended for dinner. Lunch $11–$39; dinner $25–$44. AE, DC, DISC, MC, V. Daily
11:30am–2pm; Sun–Thurs 5:30–10:30pm; Fri–Sat 5:30–11pm.

Mon Ami Gabi ★★ *Moments* FRENCH   Tile floors and dark wood booths enhance the feeling of dining in a Parisian bistro, circa 1909, and the menu is traditional French grill food, such as steaks, soups, and salads, served in an elegant and charming atmosphere. Come early and make sure to ask for patio seating, where you are slightly elevated above the Strip and can watch the passersby. While there is no children's menu, young ones will find a variety of soups, salads, crepes, quiches, omelets, and sandwiches at lunch; at dinner, more adult food comes into play, though soups and sides can certainly fill young one's tummies. At both, guests are presented with a baguette of freshly baked bread upon being seated, and our waiter steadily brought us more as needed.

The portions are massive, even by Vegas standards, so once again, sharing is a wise option. We especially liked the pepper steak and the roasted duck, along with the endive and the frisee salads. Desserts, naturally, are big enough for four. Even though the menu has less for children at dinner, nighttime on the Strip patio offers a wonderful view of the water ballet across the street at the Bellagio. Every 15 minutes, the fountains dance and cascade in time to classical and pop music as you savor your fine meal, making this a romantic spot for couples, but without the formality of other adult restaurants.

In Paris Las Vegas, 3655 Las Vegas Blvd. S. ✆ **702/944-4224**. www.monamigabi.com. Highchairs, boosters. Reservations recommended, though you cannot specifically reserve a table on the patio. Lunch $9.95–$27; dinner $26–$49. AE, DC, DISC, MC, V. Lunch Mon–Fri 11:30am–3:30pm, Sat–Sun 11am–3:30pm; dinner Mon–Fri 5–11pm; Sat–Sun 5pm–midnight.

Spago ★★★ CALIFORNIA   Spago for kids? Sure, why not treat them, if you think they'd enjoy beets layered with goat cheese, crispy Asian duck, or any other of Wolfgang Puck's signature dishes? If you're not ready to commit to the more expensive indoor restaurants (reservations, please), grab a seat at the less formal "outdoor" cafe overlooking the Forum Shops and order up the Jewish pizza. (Yes, that's its creator's designation.) You'll have to ask for it by name, because this dish—crème fraîche and salmon on a thin, wood-fired pizza crust—is not on the menu. Puck's signature Chinois chicken salad can be found here (as well as at Wolfgang Puck Cafe at the MGM Grand and, of course, Chinois, also at Caesars), but its omnipresence in Vegas doesn't detract from its wonderfulness—soy mustard dressing, crisp wontons, and lettuces tossed with roasted chicken. For the less adventurous, there's meatloaf, pasta, and fish, all treated with herbs and seasonings in a way that will make you rethink food. The desserts, including homemade sorbets and the brownie sundae, are luxurious. If you think that the prices are more than you'd like to spend on the kids, then consider getting a sitter or ordering a pay-per-view movie for them and treating yourselves to this gourmet experience.

In Caesars Palace, 3570 Las Vegas Blvd. S. ✆ **702/369-6300**. Highchairs, boosters. Reservations recommended for the dining room; not accepted at the cafe. Dining room main courses $25–$42; cafe main courses $16–$27. AE, DC, DISC, MC, V. Dining room Sun–Thurs 5:30–10pm, Fri–Sat 5:30–11pm; cafe Sun–Thurs 11am–11pm, Fri–Sat 11am–midnight.

Tips **Call in Advance**

When making reservations, reserve the highchairs and booster seats you'll need, making it easier for the staff to accommodate you; some restaurants have limited numbers.

Sweets for the Sweet

Traditional gelato is a low-fat, low-sugar version of ice cream, made without eggs, and whipped to a dense, rich texture. Gelato Las Vegas–style takes the health kick a bit further; it's made without any milk products at all, so that lactose-intolerant individuals and vegans can enjoy a creamy, smooth frozen dessert. The base of this miracle dessert is vegetable oils and cellulose, a plant fiber: Think tofu, in a good way; in a very, very good way—whipped, sweetened, and fabulously flavored. Some flavors are also made sugar free, using Splenda, maltose, or aspartame—ask your server.

At The Venetian, **Cocolini Gelato** (3555 Las Vegas Blvd. S.; ℂ **888/ 283-6423** or 702/414-1000) scoops up brilliant, surreally colored gelatos and sorbets (made out of fruit juices) from their food court stand that also serves cappuccinos and Krispy Kreme Doughnuts. They are open from 11am to 11pm, daily. **Olio Gelato** ⚘, open Sunday through Thursday from 11am to 10pm, and Fridays and Saturdays from 11am to 11pm, in the MGM Grand (3799 Las Vegas Blvd. S.; ℂ **800/929-1111** or 702/891-7777), takes the frozen concept to its most Vegasy extreme— beautiful women in space-age, silver minidresses loll about in front of a wall of gelato and sorbet; each drawer is a freezer displaying a round photo of the flavor therein. Both the pseudo-Barbarellas and their far less flashier counterparts at Cocolini Gelato will happily supply you with sample after sample of the over 30 flavors (make sure to tip) until you come to a decision. (They stock almost the same choices.) We like *baci* (hazelnuts in a chocolate base), the summery peach, and tart green apple sorbets, but the espresso and the vanilla bean gelatos are also favorites. What the heck, there's half the calories in this stuff than in regular ice cream—get two scoops.

EXPENSIVE

Royal Star ⚘ CHINESE   This gem is hidden down a hallway at The Venetian; if you want a fine, authentic Chinese seafood meal, this is the place to search out. The food is fresh, clean, and tasty, with shrimp, crabs, and lobster plucked live from tanks and cooked to order. Seafood lovers should try the lettuce cups— sautéed fresh seafood served in leaves of lettuce and a plum sauce. Children will be happy with the crispy shrimp rolls, Peking duck, and fried rice. Vegetarians will have plenty to choose from including tofu dishes, both mild and spicy. Especially tasty is the Ivory Jade Buddha—spinach and tofu poached in vegetable broth. Portions from the main menu are large enough for a family to share. The dim sum here makes for an excellent snack, but be prepared—a quick afternoon nosh could set you back upward of $20, per person, in no time.

In The Venetian, 3355 Las Vegas Blvd. S. ℂ 702/414-1888. www.venetian.com/dining. Highchairs, boosters. Reservations recommended for dinner. Main courses $10–$28; lunch dim sum $4 and up per order. AE, DC, DISC, MC, V. Daily 11am–3pm and 5–11pm.

MODERATE

Cheesecake Factory ⚘ AMERICAN   Be prepared, the portions are huge here—even the lunch-sized portions of pasta and salads are too much for most

The Kult of Krispy Kreme

Part of Krispy Kreme's original attraction was its elusiveness. For decades, these doughnuts were legendary across the United States for their sweet coating and crisp, golden crust that gave away into the fluffy, but not too yeasty, interior. Visitors to the South, the only region in the United States where Krispy Kremes were sold, were urged by friends and family to bring back a box, usually of the Original Glazed doughnuts, as a delicious souvenir.

But by 1996, Krispy Kreme had migrated to New York City, in 1999 it arrived in California, and today there's at least one Krispy Kreme shop in almost every state. So elusiveness may no longer be the magnet, but you'll still see lines of people waiting for their dozen hot and fresh treats no matter which branch you head to.

Why? Aside from the great taste, another part of Krispy Kreme's attraction is the immediacy of a sinfully indulgent (and fresh!) experience. Each store that makes the doughnuts cooks two runs a day, one in the morning and one in the late afternoon. You really, really want to be there then to grab a hot, fresh Original Glazed right off the rack and feel it melt in your mouth. Luckily, Las Vegas, a city known for allowing—nay, encouraging—decadent behavior, has plenty of Krispy Kreme outlets to satisfy your cravings: **The Venetian,** 3355 Las Vegas Blvd. S. (© **702/414-4308**) in the food court, open 7am until midnight; **Treasure Island,** 3300 Las Vegas Blvd. S. (© **702/894-7223**), **Circus Circus,** 2880 Las Vegas Blvd. S. (© **702/733-9944**); and **Fitzgeralds,** 301 Fremont St. (© **702/366-0150**).

True Krispy Kreme connoisseurs head for the **Excalibur,** 3850 Las Vegas Blvd. S. (© **702/736-5235**), where the shop is open 24 hours a day, and doughnuts are made from 6 to 11am and again from 6 to 10pm. The real thrill about the Excalibur's Krispy Kreme, located on the second floor of the hotel, is that you can stand slack jawed in anticipation in front of a glass wall, watching the raw doughnuts flip into the hot grease then flip back out cooked and golden onto the tray where they are drenched with a warm, damp sugary coating before arriving in the cases for your buying and eating pleasure.

adults, and if you have guilt issues about leaving food on your plate, you may want to eat elsewhere. Their slogan is NO ONE GOES HOME HUNGRY FROM HERE, and they're right. Most people go home overstuffed. With more than 200 items on the menu (well, that includes desserts, too), everyone should find something pleasing in this faux-bistro-styled restaurant. The food is dependable, especially if you stick to the more basic items, though maybe you think avocado-stuffed, deep-fried egg rolls are a good idea. We preferred the standard burger, the Santa Fe salad, and the tacos to the more highfalutin attempts (miso-glazed salmon, for instance). The room is loud, loud, loud, so kids aren't frowned upon in the least, though you won't find an actual children's menu. There are also dozens of flavors of cheesecake for dessert; being purists, we opted for the basic plain and loved it.

In Caesars Palace, 3570 Las Vegas Blvd. S. ℂ **702/792-6888**. www.cheesecake-factory.net or www. caesars.com/caesars/lasvegas. Highchairs, boosters. Reservations accepted. Main courses $10–$20. AE, DC, DISC, MC, V. Mon–Thurs 11:10am–11:30pm; Fri–Sat 11:10am–12:30am; Sun 10:10am–11:30pm.

Chinois Café ★★★ (Value) ASIAN

Once he conquered Italian food and created gourmet pizza, Wolfgang Puck, like Caesar, did not rest on his laurels; he forayed into the realm of Chinese cooking; blended it with French, and Chinois was born. This outpost of Puck's famous Santa Monica eatery is divided into a pricey downstairs restaurant and a more playful, less expensive cafe upstairs, which is where we suggest you and your family eat. We like the Mongolian lamb chops, pink inside, crusted with herbs on the outside, the duck with plum sauce served with ginger and scallion pancakes, and the baby pork ribs in a sweet, tangy sauce, all served family style for sharing. The vegetable fried rice is light and fluffy, probably the best we've ever had, and the garlic tofu is deeply satisfying. The yummy sushi selection is very extensive.

In the Forum Shops at Caesars Palace, 3570 Las Vegas Blvd. S. ℂ **702/737-9700**. www.wolfgangpuck.com. Highchairs, boosters. Reservations recommended. Main courses $9–$32. AE, MC, V. Daily 11am–9pm.

Grand Lux Café ★ INTERNATIONAL

The Cheesecake Factory's not-so-little sister joins the international set, with an equally large menu of gargantuan dishes served 24 hours a day, every day. Art Nouveau styling gives the Grand Lux the feel of a Viennese cafe circa 1900, but the choices scream, "Welcome to the 21st century!" Asian nachos—fried wonton skins topped with peanut sauce, chicken, wasabi, and cheese—stand out as an egregious example of a food consultant run amok, as do the coconut–macadamia nut–crusted chicken skewers and the Santa Fe roll—sort of a Southwestern egg roll meets deep-fried burrito concept. Ugh. There's also a caramel-coated, fried chicken claiming Thai flavors (garlic and ginger), which just screams insulin and cholesterol overload. However, the Vietnamese summer roll, which is one of the few relatively greaseless appetizers, is good, as are the salads, many of which are carried over from the Cheesecake Factory. We liked that the waiter and the kitchen were able to handle a complex variation of Madeira chicken for our fussy eater who wanted no cheese, no mushrooms, no asparagus, and no sauce, and got exactly what he ordered—a plain chicken breast with plain mashed potatoes. Vegetarians will find a decent selection, plus sides (mashed sweet potatoes—yum). Desserts are big enough for three adults; we appreciated the fresh baked chocolate chip cookies, a whole dozen of them; they were simple and are probably the best item on the menu. There's a kid-size breakfast available, and if you ask your server, she or he may be able to work with you on a lunch or dinnertime meal customized for your kid.

In The Venetian, 3355 Las Vegas Blvd. S. ℂ **888/2-VENICE** or 702/414-1000. www.venetian.com. Highchairs. Reservations accepted. Main courses $9–$26 (most under $15). AE, DC, DISC, MC, V. Daily 24 hr.

(Tips) Chillin' Out

If your hotel does not provide a fridge in your room, inquire about renting one. The cost runs about $10–$15 a day for a small icebox. Because cold bottled water costs $2 at hotel convenience stores, you could easily save the rental charge by buying water, juice, and sodas outside the hotel and chilling them in your room. Plus, you'll have a place to stash leftovers for a quick breakfast—cold chow mein, anyone?

Stage Deli ⭐ *Finds* DELI You'd think a place with this many food items, at these reasonable prices, would be jammed, but it's not—especially at breakfast, when you can find a huge variety of morning foods at reasonable prices, making this a welcome option for those staying here and nearby at The Mirage and Treasure Island. The atmosphere is very New York. Kids will love the faux-graffitied walls and the plates of pickles served on every table. Those pickles are flown in daily from New York, along with bagels, lox, spicy mustard, and the bread for the Stage's famous 5-inch-high stacked sandwiches. The fountain selection features classics like egg creams, shakes, and malts. For dessert, try the chocolate rugelach or the New York cheesecake.

In Caesars Palace, 3570 Las Vegas Blvd. S. ℂ 702/893-4045. www.arkrestaurants.com or www.caesars. com/caesars/lasvegas. Highchairs, boosters. Reservations accepted for large parties only. Main courses $10–$14.50; sandwiches $6–$14. AE, DC, DISC, MC, V. Sun–Thurs 7:30am–11pm; Fri–Sat 7:30am–midnight.

INEXPENSIVE

California Pizza Kitchen CALIFORNIA Bright, light, and loud, this chain caused a sensation when it opened over 20 years ago—finally, gourmet food mainstreamed out of chic celebrity chefs' open kitchens and into the malls, eventually landing in the freezer section of your local supermarket. Here is a plethora of pizza—Thai pizza, Peking duck pizza, barbecued chicken pizza, pizza with odd sauces, tandoori chicken, stinky cheese, peanuts, potatoes, and just to keep the traditionalists at bay, pepperoni. All are good, depending on where your taste lies. The basic five-cheese is always going to make someone happy; you can order cheeseless if that's your choice, and should you prefer salads to slices, they have those too. We like the Southwestern-style salad with corn, beans, and chicken. It's a chain, so it's reliable. It's full of families (there's even a special kids section on the chain's website at **www.cpk.com/cpkids**), so yours is welcome. The California pizzas and pastas are large enough to share between two adults, as are the Neapolitan pizzas with thin crusts and more traditional toppings; salads come in (large) half and (even larger) full portions. The kids' menu features kid-sized pasta, salads, and a variety of pizzas, including the barbecue chicken pizza; all kids' meals come with a drink.

In The Mirage, 3400 Las Vegas Blvd. S. ℂ 702/791-7223. www.cpk.com. Kids' menu, highchairs, boosters. Main courses $7–$18; kids' menu $4.99. AE, DC, DISC, MC, V. Sun–Thurs 11am–midnight; Fri–Sat 11am–2am.

Lenôtre ⭐⭐⭐ *Finds* DESSERTS Oooo-la-la. Desserts made the Parisian way—delicious and decadent. Please thank Paris Las Vegas for bringing you this branch of the famous French cafe/shop (run by world-renowned pastry chef Gaston Lenôtre), which also makes smooth, rich chocolate candies and breakfast pastries. Try their most popular dessert: chocolate mousse surrounding pistachio cream filling dubbed the Millennium—though they might want to rethink that name. If you feel that fruit might be a more salubrious sweet, the charlotte features strawberries, along with vanilla custard supported by a ladyfinger crust. There's also Tarte Tatin (a caramelized apple tart) and other seasonal fruit tarts, plus heaps of chocolatey goodness. You can start your morning at Lenôtre in a more sensible fashion, with a cheese croissant, baguette, or apple turnover; the fresh desserts get loaded into the cases around 9:30am.

In Paris Las Vegas, 3655 Las Vegas Blvd. S. ℂ 702/946-7000. www.paris-lv.com. Reservations not accepted. Pastries $3–$7. AE, DC, DISC, MC, V. Daily 7am–11pm.

5 North Strip

INEXPENSIVE

Capriotti's ⭐ *Value* SANDWICHES   A favorite with locals, Capriotti's certainly builds the best and most eclectic selection of sandwiches on the Strip, and at the best prices. Along with traditional Italian subs, cheese steaks, and hot-sausage sandwiches, you'll find veggie burgers and a tofu "turkey" sub. Try the much-loved Bobbie (real turkey, cranberry sauce, and dressing) or any of the other of Cap's specials. Keep in mind that these sandwiches are very large; the so-called "small" is 9 inches long, while the large tops out at almost 20 inches. If you're planning a side trip or picnic, this is where you should pick up your victuals. *Note:* There are several branches of this restaurant scattered around town, though this one is our favorite; check the website for other locations.

322 W. Sahara Ave. ℂ 702/474-0229. www.capriottis.com. Reservations not accepted. Sandwiches $3–$12. AE, DC, DISC, MC, V. Mon–Sat 10am–7pm; Sun 10am–5pm.

NASCAR Cafe AMERICAN   Concept over content here—this is all-American food, with a slight Southern twist; after all, NASCAR got its start in the South, back in the days of moonshining, when bootleggers would build super-charged stock cars to outrun the revenuers. The food here is not bad, just not great, but the atmosphere makes up for it—race memorabilia festoons the walls and NASCAR races play on video screens. Race fans will love to look at all the photos, autographed items, and car parts while downing burgers and ribs—check out Carzilla, the largest NASCAR ever built, which serves as the bar downstairs. If you don't know Dale, Jr., from Michael Schumacher, or the Daytona 500 from the Monaco Grand Prix, you're better off elsewhere.

In the Sahara, 2535 Las Vegas Blvd. S. ℂ 702/734-7223. www.saharavegas.com. Highchairs, boosters. Reservations not accepted. Main courses $7–$18. AE, DC, DISC, MC, V. Sun–Thurs 11:30am–9pm; Fri–Sat 11am–10pm.

Pink Pony ⭐ DINER/COFFEE SHOP   Kid friendly is the operative theme at this coffee shop, where your children will get crayons and a circus placemat to color. The striped walls and circus paintings will delight, as will the prices. The food is fine for kids and for those who have grown tired of standing in lines and want a simple meal.

In Circus Circus, 2880 Las Vegas Blvd. S. ℂ 877/224-7287 or 702/734-0410. www.circuscircus.com. Kids' menu, highchairs, boosters. Main courses $6–$15; kids' menu $3–$6. AE, DC, DISC, MC, V. Daily 24 hr.

Stivali ⭐ ITALIAN   Locals love Stivali, and for good reason. This family-oriented Italian restaurant makes it easy for parents with half orders of pasta, full orders, and the mind-numbing all-you-can-eat pasta dinner. Parties of four can share multiple entrees, allowing everyone to pick and choose something that will satisfy their taste buds. The food is good Italian fare with some unexpected finds such as *osso buco.* Appetizers include *bruschetta,* calamari, and mozzarella marinara. There's a good selection of salads and an overwhelming amount of main courses, ranging from pasta and pizza to veal piccata. Entrees come with a dauntingly "endless" soup or salad starter, plus a side dish of pasta. The room is warm and cozy.

In Circus Circus, 2880 Las Vegas Blvd. S. ℂ 877/224-7287 or 702/734-0410. www.circuscircus.com. Highchairs, boosters. Main courses $6.95–$21. Children under 10 eat free with paying adult 5–7pm daily. AE, DC, DISC, MC, V. Wed–Fri and Sun 5–10pm; Sat 5–11pm.

North Strip Dining

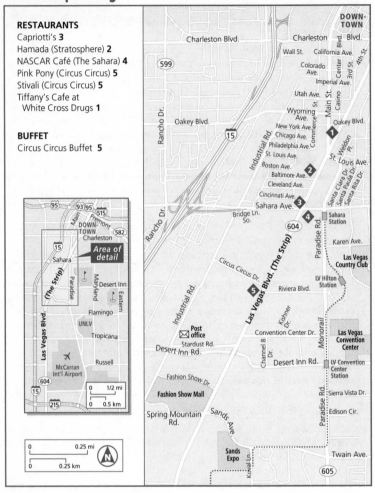

RESTAURANTS
Capriotti's **3**
Hamada (Stratosphere) **2**
NASCAR Café (The Sahara) **4**
Pink Pony (Circus Circus) **5**
Stivali (Circus Circus) **5**
Tiffany's Cafe at
   White Cross Drugs **1**

BUFFET
Circus Circus Buffet **5**

Tiffany's Cafe at White Cross Drugs ✿ DINER/COFFEE SHOP   Just a close walk from the Stratosphere, this is a real, old-fashioned coffee shop/diner that's been in business for over 60 years. Open 24 hours, it's located inside a pharmacy, so picturesque it isn't. Take your kids here, pull up to the fountain, and order thick creamy shakes (the best in Vegas), ⅕-pound burgers, slices of pie, or meatloaf, so they can see what all the other retro diners are merely *trying* to be. The food is good, plus, it's a bargain. *Note:* The neighborhood here remains stubbornly rough in appearance, and that can be a turnoff. Keep alert if you come here at night.

In White Cross Drugs, 1700 Las Vegas Blvd. S. ✆ **702/382-1733**. 1 highchair. Reservations not accepted. Main courses $3–$9. No credit cards. Daily 24 hr.

6 East of the Strip

VERY EXPENSIVE

Nobu ★★★ JAPANESE   If you want to experience a modern gourmet Japanese restaurant, this is the place, but if dragon rolls and volcanoes are more your sushi speed, go elsewhere. Nobuyuki Matsuhisa is the reigning king of modern Japanese cooking, whose acclaimed restaurants—Nobu, Ubon (Nobu backwards), and Matsuhisa—serve both the raw and the cooked in a delicate fusion of Japanese, Peruvian, and French cuisine. The Nobus in New York, Malibu, Miami, and London are very, very good restaurants, and, luckily, the landlocked Las Vegas version lives up to its heritage. Leave behind your expectations of standard Japanese cuisine when you enter this beautiful room, with its black-rock sculpture and bamboo walls. This is sushi supreme (the fish is flown in daily from Tokyo), and you'll want to taste the yellowtail with jalapeño, the tuna sashimi salad with ponzo dressing, and Kobe beef *carpaccio,* along with the changing *omatase* (chef's taste) dinners, which can feature items like seared Kobe with foie gras or seared salmon in a delicate sauce. Well-behaved children are welcome (there is chicken teriyaki on the menu for the fussy eater), but you may want to get a sitter, allowing you to savor this restaurant as a romantic, gourmet getaway.

In the Hard Rock Hotel, 4455 Paradise Rd. (✆) **702/693-5090**. www.hardrockhotel.com. Highchairs. Reservations suggested. Main courses $20–$50; sushi $5 and up per order. AE, DC, DISC, MC, V. Daily 6–11pm.

INEXPENSIVE

Hard Rock Cafe AMERICAN   Give this place the dubious respect it deserves; the Hard Rock was the progenitor of the theme restaurant as we know it today. Full of rock souvenirs like scarves, jackets, guitars, hats, and platinum records from bona fide superstars as well as those who made the grade if only for a moment, the Hard Rock serves decent burgers, good salads, and huge desserts, along with loud music and a party atmosphere. If your kids love rock music, they'll love this place. You, on the other hand, may not.

In the Hard Rock Hotel, 4455 Paradise Rd. (✆) **800/473-7625** or 702/733-8400. www.hardrockhotel.com. Kids' menu, highchairs, boosters. Main courses $8–$18; kids' menu $6.95. AE, DC, DISC, MC, V. Sun–Thurs 11am–11pm; Fri–Sat 11am–midnight.

Lotus of Siam ★★★ *(Value* THAI   There's virtually nowhere on the Strip to get Thai food, so a visit to Lotus of Siam is worth the cab fare for a *prik king* (a seasoned curry with green beans) fix. When *Gourmet* magazine's Jonathan

---

⎛Fun Fact⎞ Did You Know?

Celebrity watchers know that Nobuyuki Matsuhisa counts many stars as guests at his restaurants, some of whom are occasionally spotted dining at Nobu in Las Vegas, and that actor Robert DeNiro is an investor. Fans of the Iron Chef cooking show will also recognize the name Nobu—New York's Nobu restaurant is where Japanese Iron Chef Masaharu Morimoto worked as executive chef—when not performing as the Iron Chef in Kitchen Stadium—until he opened his own eponymous restaurant, Morimoto, in Philadelphia in 2002. At Nobu, he carried on and advanced founder Matsuhisa's vision, creating some of the signature dishes for the Nobu restaurants worldwide.

Commercial Center

The appropriately named Commercial Center at 953 E. Sahara Ave., just west of Maryland Parkway, features numerous authentic Korean and Thai restaurants, along with the plainly, but perfectly, named Asian Market, which is full of unique delicacies like *poki-poki*—thin cookies rolled around a sweet filling, then dipped in frosting.

Gold declared this small Thai restaurant (in a giant shopping center loaded with other Asian eateries) the best Thai restaurant in America, some locals were stunned, while others crowed rapturously that they'd known it all along. Luckily, Lotus of Siam has pretty much ignored the hype and hoopla—with the exception of reprinting reviews and posting them on their walls—and instead has stayed focused on its cooking. The lunch buffet at $6.99 is one of the best around, with more than a dozen dishes, including fried spring rolls and garlicky chicken wings, two soups, salad, vegetarian specialties (we loved the glass noodles with tofu and mushrooms), pad Thai, and several curries (which were warm and flavorful with spices, but not hot at all). Desserts included sliced fruits and delicious deep-fried banana rolls. If you'd like to order off the menu, you can adjust the spiciness to your comfort level, but be prepared, the higher range of hotness is truly, tearfully painful.

953 E. Sahara Ave. #A-5. (✆) **702/735-3033.** Highchairs, boosters. Reservations strongly suggested for dinner. Lunch buffet $6.99; other dishes $5–$15. AE, MC, V. Daily 11:30am–2:30pm and 5–9:30pm.

Metro Pizza ⭐ ITALIAN   Consistently voted Best Pizza by the citizens of Las Vegas in polls from the *Las Vegas Review-Journal,* Citysearch.com, and Zagat's, Metro features a variety of pizzas—"regular" with crisp crusts; stuffed, which sandwiches layers of cheese and toppings between two crusts, then tops with sauce; specialty pizzas like barbecued chicken and a sauceless white pizza; and East Side pizzas, which have slices, rather than a blanket, of cheese—along with calzones, baked ziti, and their highly addictive garlic Romano or spicy Atomic french fries. Meat eaters can dig into the Stockyard pizza, while vegetarians will appreciate the Casa Verde pizza, with veggies, and the Wrigley Field stuffed pizza with broccoli, green peppers, and mushrooms. Vegans will groove the cheeseless La Costa, topped with mushrooms, tomatoes, and broccoli. They also feature dine-in specials and desserts from Ferrara's of Little Italy. But best of all—they deliver to hotels!

1395 E. Tropicana Ave. (✆) **702/736-1955.** Highchairs, boosters. No reservations. Main courses and pizzas $5.95–$22. AE, DISC, MC, V. Mon–Thurs 11am–11pm; Fri–Sat 11am–11:30pm; Sun noon–10pm.

Mr. Lucky's 24/7 ⭐⭐ DINER/COFFEE SHOP   This is, in our opinion, the best hotel coffee shop for families in Las Vegas, if only because pop-cultured kids will like the groovy blue-and-orange menus, the blaring rock music, and overhead TVs playing videos. Feel like a Vegas insider by asking for the secret, off-the-menu steak and shrimp special, offered at $7.77. The burgers are good, and breakfasts are filling. We liked the pancakes and the omelets, as well as the smoothies. Salads are huge. Afterward, stroll around the hotel and take in the collections of rock memorabilia.

In the Hard Rock Hotel & Casino, 4455 Paradise Rd. (✆) **800/473-ROCK** or 702/693-5592. www.hardrock hotel.com. Kids' menu, highchairs, boosters. Reservations not accepted. Main courses $8–$16; kids' menu $5–$7. AE, DC, DISC, MC, V. Daily 24 hr.

Dining East of the Strip

RESTAURANTS
Hard Rock Café **4**
In–N-Out Burger **5**
Lotus of Siam **1**
Metro Pizza **6**
Mr. Lucky's 24/7 **4**
Nobu **4**
Pink Taco **4**

BUFFETS
Las Vegas Hilton Buffet **2**
Sam's Town
  Firelight Buffet **3**

Pink Taco MEXICAN   The loud rock music might make you want to turn away, but then you'd miss out on good Mexican food (tamales, quesadillas, tacos, and the like) served in a large room nicely decorated with folk art. Take a hint from us: Come early and sit on the patio, where you'll be far away from the margarita-maddened crowd. If you want to take advantage of half-priced appetizers to fill your family, happy hour runs Monday through Friday from 4 to 7pm. Along with the price-break on starters, they also offer two-for-one "beer's [sic] and margaritas," and half-off appetizers meaning the bar area and main room can get raucous. Again we stress: Retreat to the patio.

In the Hard Rock Hotel & Casino, 4455 Paradise Rd. (✆ **702/693-5525**. www.hardrockhotel.com. Highchairs, boosters. Reservations not accepted. Main courses $7.50–$13. AE, DC, DISC, MC, V. Sun–Thurs 11am–10pm; Fri–Sat 11am–midnight; bar open until 3am Fri–Sat.

7 West of the Strip

INEXPENSIVE

Voodoo Café *Moments* DESSERTS   Perfect for older kids, the Voodoo Café offers a spectacular view from the 50th floor of the Rio, coupled with a selection of tempting desserts in a setting straight out of *I Walked with a Zombie* or *The Serpent and the Rainbow.* The voodoo vibes are emphasized with elaborate *veves* (symbols) painted on the walls of the purple, black, and red room. The *veves* are accurately executed and designed to invoke or celebrate the different gods—known as *loas*—of success, happiness, love, luck, and wealth (all appropriate for a casino).

Avoid the entrees, which are large, spicy, and not the best Cajun food in Vegas. Instead, grown-ups should relax while enjoying an exotic drink such as the Headshrinker or Witch Doctor, while 'tweens and teens take in the spooky atmosphere, astounding view, and virgin cocktails with ghost-shaped stirrers. The bananas Foster are flambéed at the table—very flashy and fun, though you may want to make sure your server has flamed off all the alcohol before the kids sample it. The plate of chocolate desserts features flourless chocolate cake, homemade chocolate ice cream, a chocolate cookie, and a minimilkshake; ask that they make the milkshake without alcohol if the kids are having it. At night, the upstairs level becomes a bar/nightclub, strictly off limits for those under 21, and there is a dress code (no shorts, no jeans, no tank tops on men) for the restaurant and nightclub.

In the Rio All-Suite Hotel & Casino, 3700 W. Flamingo Rd. (✆ **702/252-7777**. www.playrio.com. Highchairs, boosters. Reservations recommended. Desserts $6–$9. AE, DC, MC, V. Daily 5–11pm.

8 Downtown

Note: Restaurants in this section can be found on the "Downtown Attractions & Dining" map on p. 167.

EXPENSIVE

Second Street Grill *Finds* SEAFOOD   Though the Grill is tucked away in an obscure corner of Downtown's obscure Fremont hotel, it's one of the great seafood restaurants in Las Vegas. What's more, though it's been around for nearly 15 years, it's one of Vegas's greatest unknown restaurants; if you're stuck for a nice place to eat, you can almost always get in here on short notice. The seafood served at the Second Street Grill is flown in fresh from around the Pacific Rim and that region's influence is felt throughout the menu. The blackened ahi and mahimahi might not be to kids' tastes, but the filet mignon smothered with Maui onion rings will be. There are also rib-eyes, pasta, and a bargain special. Appetizers include shrimp and duck tacos, crab cakes, and chicken wrapped in lettuce. For dessert, try some mango sorbet or the Hawaiian pineapple boat (floating with tropical fruit); kids will love the banana lumpia (a cinnamoned banana wrapped in an egg roll and deep-fried, served with vanilla ice cream with a honey-balsamic glaze).

In the Fremont Hotel & Casino, 200 E. Fremont St. (C) **800/634-6182** or 702/385-3232. www.fremont-casino.com. Boosters. Entrees $13–$32. AE, DC, MC, V. Sun–Mon and Thurs 6–10pm; Fri.–Sat 6–11pm.

INEXPENSIVE

El Sombrero (★) MEXICAN   At first glance, this squat adobe building, with bars across tiny windows and a heavy security door, looks like a Juárez jailhouse. But the neon sign gives it away: This is El Sombrero, the first Mexican cantina and the oldest restaurant in Las Vegas (opened in 1950). What's more, only two chefs have overseen things here in its entire 55-year history; the current one, Jose Aragon, has run the kitchen since 1976 and the menu has barely changed since then. Huevos are available for lunch and dinner; they're served ranchero style (covered with salsa) and with chorizo. The house special is a burrito enchilada-style (floating in red or green sauce), otherwise known as "smothered." Other entrees include *carne asada* (steak), *chile verde* and *colorado* (pork with green or red sauce), and *camarones* (shrimp). If you need to get away from it all and pretend you're anywhere but Vegas, this is the place to do it.

807 S. Main St. (C) **702/382-9234**. Reservations not accepted. Booster, highchairs. Entrees $6–$11.50. MC, V. Daily 11am–10pm.

9 Buffets

Most buffets are great deals for families. You get a vast amount of food for the money, the majority offer discounts for children, and you only need tip about a dollar per person, rather than 15% of the bill. In addition, you can have food on the table in a matter of a minute or two, handy especially for very young and hungry kids. Selections are varied, so you can almost always find something for everyone, and drinks and desserts are included in the price. Lunch buffets are the most cost effective; there's little difference in quantity from dinner, but the price is always lower. Consider having your largest meal mid-day (as recommended by most nutritionists), followed by a lighter less pricey supper. Las Vegas buffets used to be homogenous, without much to recommend one over another, but today the differences, both in quality and price, are more discernible.

SOUTH STRIP

For a map of the buffets below, see the "South Strip Dining" map on p. 123.

MODERATE

Luxor's Pharaoh's Pheast Buffet (★★)   As well as being fresh and tasty, this is a really fun buffet whose King Tut decor matches that of the hotel, giving you something to look at and talk about during the wait for your meal. The whole effect is very Indiana Jones, with servers in khaki uniforms and mummies and other artifacts artistically strewn about under "wooden" support beams. And the food is pretty darn good, too, including plenty of fresh salads (the tabbouleh and hummus were especially yummy) plus delectable Korean-style short ribs. The Chinese and pasta stations doled up some fine, ethnic options with several choices (important for kids); and the Mexican was surprisingly good, with an

---

Tips **Beware Buffet Lines**

At the more popular buffets, beware of humongous, ridiculous buffet lines, especially on weekends or in high season. Basic strategy is to arrive early for breakfast and early or late for lunch or dinner. If you arrive at prime time, resign yourself.

---

actual kick of spice to it (important for some adults). There wasn't enough chocolate for us on the dessert bar, but the mini crème brûlées were nice, and there are sugar-free desserts as well. This is a popular buffet, so lines can get ferociously long. *Tip:* The menu is posted at the entrance, so you can decide whether you want to eat here before you make the trudge down the ramp.

3900 Las Vegas Blvd. S. ℭ **800/288-1000** or 702/262-4000. www.luxor.com. Highchairs, boosters. Breakfast $10.75; lunch $11.25; dinner $16.95; children under 4 eat free; half price for children 4–10. AE, DC, DISC, MC, V. Daily 6:30am–11pm.

MGM Grand Buffet   At breakfast, omelet and Belgian waffle stations provide variety to this otherwise average buffet. If you ask nicely, the staff will get you plain yogurt instead of the sweeter berry flavors on display. Lunch and dinners have the usual carving stations, veggies, and salad bar. The children's prices and the selection make it a good choice for family lunches or dinners. Also available: low-fat, sugar-free desserts. At all meals, you get a full pot of coffee on your table.

3799 Las Vegas Blvd. S. ℭ **702/891-7777**. www.mgmgrand.com. Highchairs, boosters. Breakfast $11.99; weekend brunch $14.99; lunch $14.99; dinner $21.99 except Fri–Sat $24.99; children 3 and under eat free; children 4–12 breakfast $5.99, lunch $6.59, dinner $11.99. AE, DC, DISC, MC, V. Daily 7am–10pm.

Monte Carlo Buffet ⧳   A "courtyard" under a painted sky, the Monte Carlo's buffet room has a Moroccan market theme with murals of Arab scenes, Moorish archways, oriental carpets, and walls hung with photographs of, and artifacts from, Morocco. Dinner includes a rotisserie (for chicken and pork loin or London broil), a Chinese food station, a taco/fajita bar, a baked potato bar, numerous salads, and more than a dozen desserts, plus frozen yogurt and ice-cream machines. Lunches are similar. At breakfast, the expected fare is supplemented by an omelet station, and choices include crepes, blintzes, and corned beef hash. Fresh-baked New York–style bagels are a plus.

3770 Las Vegas Blvd. S. ℭ **702/730-7777**. www.monte-carlo.com. Highchairs, boosters. Breakfast $10.50; lunch $10.95; dinner $15.95; Sun brunch $16.95; children under 3 eat free; $7.25 for children 3–12. AE, DC, DISC, MC, V. Daily 7am–10pm; Sun brunch 7am–3pm.

INEXPENSIVE

Boardwalk Casino & Hotel   Remarkable because it's the only buffet now open around the clock, the Boardwalk offers a basic spread with prices that evoke the Vegas of old, with steak and eggs served from 11pm 'til 6am. A lengthy brunch/lunch period means sleepyheads can still get their adequate pancakes and sausages, while an equally adequate (read: not anything to write home about) dinner, with a selection of beef, chicken, and vegetables, as well as carbs, lasts until late in the evening.

3750 Las Vegas Blvd. S. ℭ **702/735-2400**. www.boardwalklv.com. Highchairs, boosters. $7.99 11pm–6am; $9.99 10am–4:30pm; $11.99 4:30–11pm; midnight steak and eggs $7.99; children under 4 eat free. AE, DC, DISC, MC, V. Daily 24 hr.

Excalibur's Round Table Buffet One of the nicest features of this bustling buffet is that the menus for the day's meals are posted overhead before you get to the entrance so that you can decide if you really want to eat here. The large room resembles a hospital cafeteria enlivened by heraldic flags draped about. The food is adequate and heavy on the starch.

3850 Las Vegas Blvd. S. (✆ 702/597-7777. www.excaliburlasvegas.com. Highchairs, boosters. Breakfast $9.99; lunch $10.99; dinner $14.49; children under 3 eat free; $2 off for children 4–12. AE, DC, DISC, MC, V. Daily 6:30am–10pm.

CENTER STRIP

For a map of the buffets below, see the "Center Strip Dining" map on p. 133.

EXPENSIVE

The Mirage Cravings Buffet 👫👫 Completely remodeled and retooled in summer 2004, The Mirage Cravings provides the best value among the Center Strip "gourmet buffets," such as Le Village at Paris and the ultraexpensive (and more-for-adults) Bellagio Buffet. The room has a high-tech feel with its stainless steel, brass, and a couple of dozen video monitors out front playing sensual video loops of food. Open and airy, the traffic flow is well designed, so you can usually get in and out of the serving stations without much waiting. Dim sum is served at every meal, along with abundant seafood, bagels and lox at breakfast, good sushi, wood-fired pizzas, on-site smoked meats, and gelato for dessert.

3400 Las Vegas Blvd. S. (✆ 800/791-7111. www.mirage.com. Highchairs, boosters. Breakfast $12.50, lunch $17.50, dinner $20.50, brunch $20.50; all meals free for children under 5; age 5–10 breakfast $8.50, lunch $12.50, dinner $14.50, brunch $14.50. AE, DC, DISC, MC V. Mon–Sat 7am–10pm; Sun 8am–10pm.

Paris's Le Village Buffet 👫👫👫 This is the only buffet in Las Vegas that successfully carries out its host hotel's theme in its entirety. As well as incorporating the hotel's decor into the buffet area, Le Village Buffet has based the entire spread, from salad to sugary finale, around the hotel's *parlez-vous* premise. All of France is represented at Le Village Buffet, in two-thirds replica of a French village that is charming in that Vegas-y fake way, but is the nicest buffet dining room in the entire city. If you want to sample all the cuisine of France without a vacation to five or so regions of that country, this is the place to do it. Though this is the second-most expensive buffet in town, for the variety and the well-executed concept, it's worth it.

Each buffet station reflects the specialties of a specific French region. In Brittany, you have crepes made to order, while Normandy features seafood and quiche. Burgundy, known for its farming and hunting, serves up the carving station with chateaubriand sauce and cherry sauce Escoffier. Hearty Alsace serves stews, while the Mediterranean region of Provence features made-to-order pastas. Be sure to sample a crepe from Le Village's one-of-a-kind cooked-to-order crepe station. Desserts include tarts, pastries, and bananas Foster.

3665 Las Vegas Blvd. S. (✆ 702/946-7000. www.paris-lv.com. Highchairs, boosters. Breakfast $12.95, lunch $17.95, dinner $24.95, brunch $24.95; children 3 and under eat free, $3 off for children 4–9. AE, DC, DISC, MC, V. Mon–Sat breakfast 7–11:30am, lunch 11:30am–5:30pm, dinner 5:30–10pm; Sat–Sun brunch 11:30am–4:30pm, dinner 4–10:30pm.

MODERATE

Bally's Big Kitchen Buffet 👫 This is a sort of old Las Vegas smorgie, where the dining room is separate from the serving area, so it's like going to the kitchen for your food. It's quieter in the dining room, too. The selection isn't as large as the newer superbuffets with all their specialized serving islands and vast variety, but the food here is consistently high quality and the service, for some reason, is always superb. The plentiful seafood will please adults; the baked-potato bar and soft-serve ice cream will satisfy the kids.

3645 Las Vegas Blvd. S. © 800/739-4111. www.ballyslasvegas.com. Highchairs, boosters. Brunch $12.95; dinner $17.95; all meals free for children 4 and under; 5–8 half price. AE, DC, DISC, MC V. Daily 7am–2pm, 4–10pm.

INEXPENSIVE

Flamingo Paradise Garden Buffet ★ *Value*   This is one of the nicest buffet rooms in Las Vegas, especially if you can be seated by the large windows over-looking the fish ponds and waterfalls. Watch the swans and ducks swim lan-guidly by as you eat selections chosen from the soup/salad/pasta bar, stir-fry station, or from the international food stations offered at lunch and dinner (their offerings change monthly). Desserts include sugar-free options, along with cookies, cakes, and really good brownies. Breakfast includes fresh-baked breads and the ubiquitous omelet station. The low prices for families, plus the view, make this a great place to eat.

3555 Las Vegas Blvd. S. © 800/732-2111 or 702/733-3111. www.flamingolv.com. Highchairs, boosters. Champagne breakfast/brunch $10.95; lunch/dinner $15.95; children under 3 eat free; half price for children 3–12. Prices may be higher on holidays. AE, DC, DISC, MC, V. Daily breakfast 6–11:30am, lunch 11:30am–2:30pm, dinner 4:30–10pm.

Treasure Island Buffet ★   Feel like a real pirate as you peel the shells from the tangy, tasty, all-you-can-eat shrimp under flags of the 13 colonies in the New Orleans room, strewn with antiques (or their replicas) from the period of Jean Lafitte. You'll be able to sample the thankfully not-too-salty Chinese food, cheeses, cold cuts, a salad bar, the decent hot dishes (chicken, beef, fish), fruits, and veggies in both this room and the adjoining one, designed as a Tuscan town plaza, with twinkling lights. Lunch and dinner in both rooms are stocked with identical, average-but-okay/passable, foods, including a large selection of desserts, so you can eat lunch in the bayou one day and dinner in Italy another. Breakfast packs no surprises, though on Sundays, there's unlimited champagne with brunch.

3300 Las Vegas Blvd. S. © 702/894-7111. www.treasureisland.com. Highchairs, boosters. Breakfast $10.99; lunch $13.99; dinner $17.99; Sun brunch $17.99; children under 4 eat free; half price for children 4–11. AE, DC, DISC, MC, V. Mon–Sat 7–10:45am and 11am–3:45pm; daily 4–10:30pm; Sun 7:30am–3:30pm.

NORTH STRIP

For a map of the buffets below, see the "North Strip Dining" map on p. 140.

INEXPENSIVE

Circus Circus   There are over 50 choices at this, the Strip's cheapest buffet, so kids can have a blast sampling everything from the steam tables. For the most part, adults rate it in a word: cheap. Low price, low quality. It's been remodeled a few times over the years, but the food seems never to change. Think of it as fuel for your next adventure, rather than as a dining experience.

2880 Las Vegas Blvd. S. © 877/224-7287 or 702/734-0410. www.circuscircus.com. Highchairs, boosters. Breakfast $7.99; lunch $8.99; dinner $9.99; Sat–Sun brunch $8.99; champagne brunch $24.95 (no discounts for children at any meal). AE, DC, DISC, MC, V. Mon–Fri 7–11:30am, noon–4pm, and 4:30–10pm; Sat–Sun 7am–4pm and 4:30–11pm.

EAST OF THE STRIP

For a map of the buffets below, see the "Dining East of the Strip" map on p. 143.

INEXPENSIVE

Las Vegas Hilton Buffet ⟨★⟩   As at all restaurants at the Hilton, children 12 and under eat at half price. Gone is the old sports theme, replaced with a sort of a generic outdoorsy look, but luckily, the kitchen still serves good food. Prime rib is served at lunch and dinner; the salad bar is fresh; and the desserts tasty and not overwhelmingly sugary. At dinner, there's the addition of an all-you-can-eat crab and shrimp station, while on Fridays there are additional seafood selections.

3000 Paradise Rd. © **888/732-7117** or 702/732-5111. www.lv-hilton.com. Highchairs, boosters. Breakfast $9.99; lunch $10.99; dinner $14.99; weekend brunch $14.99 (includes unlimited champagne); children under 2 free; half price for children 3–12. DC, DISC, MC, V. Daily 7am–2:30pm and 5–10pm.

Sam's Town Firelight Buffet ⟨★⟩   The huge wall of flames here is really impressive, and the room is open to the atrium with its Sunset Stampede light show, making this a nice room, especially for kids. Along with the usual food choices, there's a Mexican and Chinese food station, and it's fun to get your ice cream scooped at the dessert station. Prices are higher on Wednesday night for steak night and for the Friday night seafood buffet.

5111 Boulder Hwy. © **702/456-7777**. www.samstownlv.com. Highchairs, boosters. Lunch $7.99 adults, children $5.49; dinner Sat–Tues and Thurs $11.99, children 4–8 $7.99; dinner Wed $13.99, children 4–8 $10.49; dinner Fri $17.99, children 4–8 $13.49; Sat–Sun brunch $9.99, children 4–8 $6.99; all meals free for children under 4. AE, DC, DISC, MC, V. Mon–Fri 11am–3pm; Sat–Sun 10am–3pm; Mon–Sun 4–9pm.

WEST OF THE STRIP
EXPENSIVE

Rio's Carnival World Buffet ⟨★⟩ *Overrated*   Gorge yourself with food from around the world, if you (and more importantly, your kids) can stand to wait in line. Locals have long voted this one of the best buffets in town, but unless you're coming for the *Masquerade in the Sky* (p. 155), it's not really worth going out of your way; the food isn't good enough to pay off for the long lines. If you do want to try beating the crowd, plan on a late lunch at 2 or 3pm or an early dinner starting about 4 or 5pm. Remodeled and reopened in summer 2004, stations now include Chinese, Italian, Mexican, seafood, American, sushi, baked potato, barbecue, pizza, *teppanyaki,* and a unique Oriental noodle-soup bar, with *pho,* hot and sour *tom yum* soup, and more. Low-fat and sugar-free desserts are included along with the full-strength cakes, pies, and puddings.

In the Rio All-Suite Hotel & Casino, 3700 W. Flamingo Rd. © **888/752-9746** or 702/252-7777. www. playrio.com. Highchairs, boosters. Breakfast $12.99; lunch $14.99; dinner $22.99; champagne brunch $22.99; Village Seafood $34.99 adults, $22.99 children; children under 3 eat free; $3 off for children 4–8. AE, DC, MC, V. Daily 7am–10pm.

---

10 Just the Two of Us: Romantic Dining

Where to go when it's just the two of you? Try any of the below romantic restaurants, all of which happen to be French.

While we think the patio of **Mon Ami Gabi** (p. 134) is the most casual and affordable romantic dining spot in Las Vegas, other passionate couples who've snagged a sitter for the night may wish to indulge themselves at the incredibly romantic **Picasso** ⟨★★⟩, in the Bellagio, 3600 Las Vegas Blvd. S. (© **702/693-7111;** www.bellagio.com). Tables overlook the Bellagio fountains and are themselves surrounded by $30 million dollars worth of Picasso artwork. Chef Julian Serrano's prix-fixe dinners and tasting menus hold their own in this elegant environment, where attentive servers pamper you without intruding.

The new **Bouchon** ⭐⭐⭐, in The Venetian, (3355 Las Vegas Blvd. S.; ℂ **702/414-6200;** www.bouchonbistro.com), offers up an elegant and intimate French bistro setting (there's also lovely outside patio dining available in good weather)—and genius Thomas Keller, arguably the best chef in the United States. The classic menu changes daily, but expect such delicacies as pâté, Snow Creek oysters, and caviar.

High style and haute cuisine are the outstanding characteristics of **Lutèce** ⭐ (The Venetian, 3355 Las Vegas Blvd. S.; ℂ **702/414-2220**), where small nooks overlooking the Strip provide romantic dining spots. The emphasis here is also on French food, but with a lighter, more modern touch than at Le Cirque. Truffles, halibut, filet, baby vegetables, and other beautifully prepared foods are presented in an elegant (but not stuffy), minimalist decor.

Alizé ⭐⭐⭐ (Palms, 4321 W. Flamingo Rd.; ℂ **702/951-7000**), opened by the former chef at Napa, and freshly launched at the Palms, has received ecstatic reviews as the best restaurant in Las Vegas, which is saying a lot. The view, coupled with the superlative food (think jumbo prawns with ricotta dumplings, Muscovy duck with Moroccan spices, a palate-cleansing sorbet course, and voluptuous chocolate desserts), creates the most fabulously romantic dining experience in the whole city.

Reservations are a must for any of the above-mentioned restaurants.

For information on babysitters and child-care services, see section 13 of chapter 2, "Planning a Family Trip to Las Vegas," beginning on p. 60.

What Kids Like to See & Do in Las Vegas

The overwhelming number of attractions and distractions for tourists in the touristy parts of Las Vegas serve to enhance the city's reputation as an escape from reality and an oasis of nonstop fun. However, despite Las Vegas's emphasis on grown-up pleasures, there is a surprising amount of child-friendly activities, many free or low cost, and some even educational, to be found in what wags call Sin City.

Cruising the Strip hotels is a great pastime, especially during the heat of the day. You and your kids can stroll through a Middle Eastern bazaar while a simulated storm rolls overhead or experience the same-style deluge in a mall that replicates the Grand Canyon. Where else but in Las Vegas can you explore ancient Rome and Egypt in a day, then frolic down the Champs Elysée and through Greenwich Village, followed by a trip through deep space with an alien crew? If the around-the-world-in-80-hours experience gets to be too much, there are also parks, playgrounds, and wetlands awaiting you and your picnic basket. And let's not forget Las Vegas's museums—ranging from the silly and serious to the enlightening and the ludicrous—as well as the factory tours where you can see how candy and vitamins, clowns and cars are all made.

First-time visitors, or those with limited time, will definitely want to spend most of their stay exploring the Strip, perhaps concentrating on one section a day, if possible. (We've divided the itineraries by sections of the Strip.) One of the kindest things casino planners did was to provide free amusements. And while we doubt they had altruistic aims, it's a bonus for families, particularly those on a budget, or otherwise. We'd recommend that any itinerary you come up with should include an animal attraction, several of which are free, and a free show such as the statues at Caesars or *Masquerade in the Sky* at the Rio.

Older kids should take a roller coaster ride; coasters can be found at several hotels, giving kids and their families an adrenaline-pumping charge. The **Adventuredome,** the world's largest indoor amusement park, offers a couple of thrill rides, as well as more sedate rides for younger kids. With rides, games, attractions, and a miniature tour of the world, both ancient and modern, the Strip can keep a visitor occupied for a week, but with judicious planning and use of people movers, trams, the monorail, and taxis, the highlights of these few miles of many marvels can be seen in a day, if you want to rush from one end of the Strip to the other.

Getting around the Strip is simple, but the crowds can be overwhelming. Cabs are useful for getting places in relatively good time (except on weekend nights), and they are always air-conditioned. Consider them for trips from one end of the Strip to another, or if the little ones and you are exhausted. The monorail (when it's up and running—not always a given after a few false starts) is also good for longer Strip trips, though it can be a hike from the west side of the Strip. Rental cars can be handy, especially because valet parking is free, as are the parking garages; just drive to one hotel, see the nearby sites, and leave for the next stop.

If you have an extra day, a drive out to Red Rock Canyon, Hoover Dam, or Old Nevada/Bonnie Springs Ranch offers a stunning contrast to the neon-soaked cityscape. Getting to these locations is simple with a car, but tours can easily be arranged through your hotel. *A reminder:* Be prepared—Las Vegas is a huge, huge place. Just getting from your room to the sidewalk can take 20 minutes, easily tiring out even the hardiest of underage adventurers. With younger children, your best bet is to pick an area of the Strip (South, Center, or North) and stay within in it for the day. Not that that's a tall order; there's plenty to do and see at every hotel, and the flashing lights and ringing bells hypnotize youngsters as well as adults.

Of course, during the hot summer months, your hotel's pool and air-conditioned arcade may be the main attractions for the kids!

SUGGESTED ITINERARIES

For Toddlers to Age 6

If you have 1 day Because distances are far and casinos are large, not to mention the weather, which can be sizzling, pouring, or freezing, we've grouped the major Vegas sites and things to do by location. You know your toddlers better than we do; if you think they can handle the trek from one location to another, you may wish to expand your day to include more than one location.

If you are staying on the South Strip, take your wee ones over to Excalibur to watch performers on the **Jester's Stage,** where jugglers, magicians, storytellers, and puppeteers perform throughout the day. Then stroll over to the MGM Grand to watch the big cats in the **Lion Habitat** and eat at the **Rainforest Cafe** before taking the tram to Mandalay Bay to visit **Shark Reef.**

If you are on the North Strip, the circus acts and the Adventuredome indoor park, which has rides suitable for small children (both at **Circus Circus**), should certainly keep your children thrilled.

Guests staying on the Center Strip can visit the white tigers at **The Mirage,** either at the free viewing area or at the **Dolphin Habitat and Secret Garden,** keeping in mind that only registered guests are allowed to bring strollers into the hotel. However, **Caesars Palace** will provide strollers for families wishing to explore the Forum Shops, an excellent place to take children of all ages. Definitely plan on eating dinner at a buffet in the resort closest to where you wind up; because you can't beat the variety and because at most of them, children under 4 eat free.

If you have 2 days Make a point to wander through the **Flamingo Wildlife Habitat** that surrounds The Flamingo Hotel's pool area so your kiddies can spot flamingos, penguins, swans, and koi fish, or eat at the buffet seated by the window so you can watch the birds. Afterwards, hit anything you missed the day before. Those staying on the North Strip should venture south to see some of the offerings on the South Strip, such as Excalibur's Jester's Stage and MGM Grand's Lion Habitat, while South Strip guests should explore Circus Circus's free big-top circus acts and the Adventuredome indoor amusement park.

If you have 3 days Along with the above itineraries, toss in a visit to the **Lied Discovery Children's Museum,** located north of the Strip, where kids are encouraged to poke, touch, and yell. Consider a sitter at night so the adults can enjoy a show or a romantic dinner.

If you have 4 days Located about half an hour outside of Las Vegas, **Bonnie Springs Ranch/Old Nevada** is a combination petting zoo and Wild West theme park. The zoo is free; admission to Old Nevada is not, and you may not think that the shoot-out and simulated hanging are appropriate entertainment for your little ones. The town, however, is a nice replica of a Wild West frontier village.

For Ages 7 to 9

If you have 1 day Start your day with breakfast at the MGM Grand's **Rainforest Cafe,** check out the **Lion Habitat,** then stroll to the Tropicana for the free *Bird Show,* followed by an hour at the **New York–New York Coney Island arcade.** Taller children should take a trip on the **Manhattan Express** roller coaster at New York–New York, along with catching other South Strip sights, including the **Shark Reef** at Mandalay Bay and the wonder of **Luxor,** or the medieval merriment at **Excalibur.** Head to the North Strip and spend awhile watching the circus acts at **Circus Circus,** and make a point to see the view from the top of the **Stratosphere,** and braving the rides there. The **fountain shows** at the Forum Shops in Caesars Palace are a must. Eat at the buffet or try one of the many restaurants in the casino or mall. If your children want even more nightlife after all this, fit in a viewing of **The Mirage's volcano** and the **dancing fountains** at Bellagio.

If you have 2 days Visit Paris and ancient Egypt via **Paris Las Vegas** and **Luxor.** Explore the history of M&Ms and Coca-Cola at the **Showcase Mall.** Then visit the white tigers at **The Mirage** or take a trip to the **Lied Museum,** plus go for a nighttime stroll Downtown for the **Fremont Street Experience.** Consider either the magic of **Mac King (Harrah's)** or **Rick Thomas (The Tropicana)** if you'd like to see an inexpensive afternoon show. Substitute the early show of **Blue Man Group, O, Lance Burton,** or *Mystère* for Fremont Street if you've got money to burn.

If you have 3 days No question about it—head for **Adventuredome** on Day 3. Five acres of rides and attractions makes this the largest indoor amusement park on earth. After a day riding roller coasters and flume rides and playing laser tag, order up a pay-per-view movie along with a pizza or room service, then have the kids rest with a sitter while you parents enjoy a grown-up few hours on the town.

If you have 4 days **Red Rock Canyon,** located less than half an hour from Las Vegas, offers stunning desert landscapes. Take the 13-mile loop when the park first opens, and follow up with a jaunt to **Old Nevada/Bonnie Springs Ranch,** where you can watch live action melodramas and explore the zoo.

For Ages 10 to 13

If you have 1 day Follow the Day 1 itinerary for 7- to 10-year-olds and add in an evening trip to GameWorks or a show, if the kids, and you, have the stamina.

If you have 2 days Follow Day 2's itinerary for 7- to 10-year-olds, but add in *Star Trek:* The Experience at the Hilton if you have a sci-fi fan among your brood.

Value Free Attractions

It's easy to spend a small fortune on vacation, especially in this tourist town where almost everything—from slot machines to shopping malls—seems geared to separating you from your Benjamins as quickly as possible. But don't despair, you can find plenty of fun on— or near—the Strip for free.

Air Play at the Tropicana   Slot machines serve as a makeshift stage for a variety of acts performed by singers, dancers, and aerialists who spin and fly just inches above the whirring machines. Daily at 11am, 1pm, 3pm, and 7pm. (3801 Las Vegas Blvd. S., at Tropicana Ave., Las Vegas, NV 89109; ✆ **888/826-8767** or 702/739-2222).

Bellagio Fountains   Set to a wide variety of music ranging from opera to pop songs and classical to Broadway, the fountains at Bellagio erupt up to 240 feet in the air and dance every half-hour Mondays through Fridays from 3 to 8pm, Saturdays and Sundays from noon to 8pm, and every 15 minutes nightly from 8pm to midnight (3600 Las Vegas Blvd. S.; ✆ **888/987-6667** or 702/693-7111; www.bellagio.com).

Circus Circus   Clowns, acrobats, and jugglers perform every half-hour from 11am to midnight (2880 Las Vegas Blvd. S.; ✆ **877/224-7287**or 702/734-0410; www.circuscircus.com).

Desert Passage at Aladdin/Planet Hollywood   Jugglers and belly dancers vie for your attention as a desert rainstorm rages every hour at the Aladdin/Planet Hollywood Resort & Casino (3667 Las Vegas Blvd. S.; ✆ **877/333-9474** or 702/785-5555; www.aladdincasino.com).

Everything Coca-Cola and **M&Ms World**   Located in the Showcase Mall, these are quick, self-guided tours of the American icons' histories. You can also experience a desert rainstorm every 45 minutes at the Showcase Mall souvenir shop (3785 Las Vegas Blvd. S.; ✆ **702/597-3122**).

Fremont Street Experience   Downtown spiffed up its image by installing a canopy with 12 million light-emitting diodes and a sound system and turning Fremont Street into a pedestrian walkway. Four times nightly, the neon goes off and the LEDs display broad-quality and spectacular light shows. (Fremont St. between Main St. and Las Vegas Blvd.; www.vegasexperience.com).

The Grand Canal Shoppes   Vaguely historical (performers in Renaissance costumes and replicas of the Bridge of Sighs and St. Mark's Place, complete with real, bossy pigeons), this mall masquerades as Venice in its heyday. It's relaxing to sit under the blue faux sky and watch the singing gondoliers steer their fares along the waterway (3355 Las Vegas Blvd. S.; ✆ **888/283-6423** or 702/414-1000; www.venetian.com).

Jester's Stage   Located on the second floor of Excalibur, this stage features jugglers, storytellers, puppets, and other kiddie-pleasing acts every half-hour (3850 Las Vegas Blvd.; ✆ **877/750-5464** or 702/597-7777; www.excalibur.com).

Lion Habitat and **Royal White Tiger Habitat**   Both the MGM Grand, 3799 Las Vegas Blvd. S. (© **800/929-1111** or 702/891-7777; www.mgm grand.com) and The Mirage, 3400 Las Vegas Blvd. S. (© **800/627-6667** or 702/791-7111; www.mirage.com) display big beautiful cats sure to provoke plenty of oohs and aahs. The lions are on duty at the MGM Grand daily from 11am to 10pm, while the tigers at The Mirage are on display from 10am to 10pm daily.

Masquerade in the Sky   Seven times a day, from 3 to 9:30pm, Mardi Gras–styled floats move along tracks suspended from the ceiling at the Rio All-Suite Hotel & Casino, while costumed participants toss beads from the floats and lip-sync to the songs, followed by a stage-show extravaganza on the casino floor, complete with a giant peacock and sequin-covered dancers. Best place to watch is from the second-floor balcony (3700 W. Flamingo Rd.; © **888/752-9746** or 702/777-7777; www.playrio.com).

Mirage Volcano   The volcano in front of The Mirage erupts four times an hour from 6pm through midnight (3400 Las Vegas Blvd. S.; © **800/627-6667** or 702/791-7111; www.mirage.com).

Paris Las Vegas   You may not be able to see Paris in the springtime, but Paris Las Vegas is available anytime, complete with cobblestone streets and twinkling streetlamps (3655 Las Vegas Blvd. S.; © **888/ BONJOUR [266-5687]** or 702/946-7000; www.parislv.com).

Sirens of TI   This is the retooled pirate battle that raged outside Buccaneer Bay in front of Treasure Island for 10 years. The new show, performed at 7, 8:30, 10, and 11:30pm, is somewhat sexier, with "sirens" luring the pirates off their ship and into Sirens Cove for what can only be some X-rated activity. There are some fireworks and explosions that all kids will enjoy, but it might be tough to explain to the younger ones just what's going on. Also, the new show is nearly 20 minutes longer than the defunct 8-minute pirate battle—a long time to stand squashed in a crowd with a 40-pound kid on your shoulders—the only way the short ones can see a thing. (3300 Las Vegas Blvd. S.; © **800/ 944-7444** or 702/894-7111; www.treasureisland.com).

Sports Hall of Fame   Sports fans will love this huge collection of athletic items displayed throughout the ground floor of the Las Vegas Club in the Las Vegas Hotel and Casino downtown. It's available for viewing around the clock. The collection includes signed bats used in the World Series, autographed photos, T-shirts, and much more (18 Fremont St.; © **800/634-6532** or 702/385-1664; www.vegasclub casino.net).

Tropicana Bird Show   This show, starring colorful talented birds (p. 223), runs three times daily at the Tropicana: 11:30am and 1:30 and 2:30pm in the Tropics Lounge. (3801 Las Vegas Blvd. S.; © **888/826- 8767** or 702/739-2222; www.tropicanalv.com).

If you have 3 days Adventure-dome will keep your child busy for hours. Then head over to the Rio for the *Masquerade in the Sky* show, or just go back to your hotel, where the kids can watch TV and rest. Consider a sitter so you can explore adult Las Vegas.

If you have 4 days Hoover Dam and **Boulder City** are (oh no) educational and impressive. If your kids balk at the idea of an hour-long tour of the dam, just let them look at rushing water and read the information at the visitor center, then head off to explore Boulder City or **Valley of Fire State Park.**

For Kids Over 13

The same itineraries as for the 10- to 13-year-olds, but consider adding in or substituting **Madame Tussaud's Celebrity Encounter, Elvis-A-Rama,** the **Hard Rock Casino exhibits,** and one of the many **impersonator shows** as options for the star-struck. Of course, an unlimited game pass at **GameWorks** might be just as much fun for some.

1 Attractions for Kids

Luckily, most of Las Vegas's attractions appeal to all ages, and most accept children of every age group. Many are free (see "Free Attractions," above), and some can almost be construed as educational. But no matter what, they are all fun.

Big-Top Acts and Midway at Circus Circus ⊛⊛ **All ages,** though older kids may want to go play the arcade games. Parents who can trust their teenagers will appreciate the philosophy of this family-oriented hotel: Kids over 13 can explore the arcade and midway, watch the big-top acts without adults, and are allowed to supervise younger children, as long as they all stay off the casino floor. This allows the adults to escape for a brief time. But you should spend some time with your children, watching the acrobats, jugglers, and clowns in the world's largest indoor circus; the performers are all good and you could easily use up 2 hours just watching the shows and another strolling the midway; your video gamers will be kept amused for at least that long. The games, not unlike the adult versions on the casino floor below, will suck up plenty of quarters as your kids try to win tickets redeemable for gewgaws and gimcracks. There's also a face-painting booth, where little ones can get made up like clowns, and a McDonald's for the peckish. The entire arcade and big-top area are nonsmoking zones, though, at times, the drift of cigarette smoke from the casino below can sort of defeat the concept. Older kids may get bored because the acts aren't that daring—no juggling of chainsaws—but they'll enjoy watching for a bit until the pull of the arcade becomes too insistent.

Tip: The stairs up to the arcade and circus viewing area can be difficult for toddlers to manage on their own (we saw one little girl trying futilely to catch up with her mom), so you may want to hold on to them while going up or down.

In Circus Circus, 2880 Las Vegas Blvd. S. ℂ 877/224-7287 or 702/734-0410. Free admission. Daily 10am–midnight.

Fountain Shows at the Forum Shops **Ages 4 & up.** Every hour on the hour, two sets of fountains at the Forum Shops come alive for 10 minutes with lasers, fog, and moving, talking statues. In the original wing, the Bacchus fountain's statues bring Greek myths to life, while in the second wing, the Battle for Atlantis pits two bratty god children—one fire, one water—against each other in a battle for their father's kingdom, Atlantis. *Warning:* The loud noises and

Harmon Ave.

15

Tompkins Ave.

Palms Center Dr.

Rue de Monte Carlo

Tropicana Ave.

Reno Ave.

Ali Baba Ln.

Hacienda Ave.

Mandalay Bay Rd.

Diablo Dr.

Dewey Dr.

Russell Rd.

Quail Ave.

Oquendo Rd.

Frank Sinatra Dr.

Las Vegas Blvd. (The Strip)

Giles St.

Valley View Blvd.

Procyon

Polaris Ave.

Industrial Rd.

15

604

❶ Harmon Ave.

MGM Grand Station

Tropicana Ave.

Reno Ave.

Hacienda Ave.

❷ ❸ ❹ ❺ ❻ ❼ ❽

McCARRAN INTERNATIONAL AIRPORT

International Terminal

Wayne Newton Blvd.

McCarran Air Terminal

McCarran Exit Rd.

❾

Paradise Rd.

Airport Connector

0   0.5 mi
0   0.5 km

······· Monorail

Sunset Rd. ❿

Sunset Rd.

Arcade at Excalibur **5**	Jester's Stage (Excalibur) **5**
Bird Show (Tropicana) **6**	King Tut's Tomb & Museum (Luxor) **7**
Casino Legends Hall of Fame Museum (Tropicana) **6**	Lion Habitat (MGM Grand) **4**
Coney Island Emporium Arcade (New York-New York) **3**	M&M World **2**
Desert Passage (Aladdin/Planet Hollywood) **1**	Manhattan Express (New York-New York) **3**
Everything Coca-Cola Las Vegas **2**	National Vitamin Company Factory **10**
GameWorks **2**	Shark Reef at Mandalay Bay **8**
Howard W. Cannon Aviation Museum **9**	

explosions of the shows may be too much for younger kids. The Forum Shops are a pleasant way to pass an afternoon browsing, especially if you have little ones; strollers are provided gratis.

In Caesars Palace, 3570 Las Vegas Blvd. S. ⓒ **800/634-6661** or 702/731-7110. www.caesars.com. Free admission. Daily every hour.

Fremont Street Experience ⚑ **All ages.** Up until the mid-'90s, Fremont Street, aka Glitter Gulch, was a grubby and gritty old downtown area. But then, the street was closed, and a huge canopy light show was developed by a private corporation and funded by 10 downtown hotels. Today, Fremont Street, a pedestrian walkway that takes about 20 minutes to stroll and people-watch, boasts a grid-work of 12 million LEDs, strobes, robotically controlled mirrors, and a 540,000-watt sound system. Five times a night, a 6-minute spectacle of light and sound floods the promenade. Music from the 218 speakers plays throughout the evening, enhancing your stroll through the cafes and shops. Look for the old neon signs from casinos of the past, which the Neon Museum has restored and displayed.

Fremont St. (between Main St. and Las Vegas Blvd.), Downtown. www.vegasexperience.com. Free admission. Shows nightly.

GameWorks **Ages 6 & up.** This chain arcade is youth-action central with video games designed by Steven Spielberg and his DreamWorks team. Kids will love the Jurassic Park game, virtual racing, a virtual reality batting cage, and

If I Could Talk to the Animals

Animal lovers will have a field day in Las Vegas, where a large variety of animals, including rare big cats, piranhas, penguins, flamingos, hammerhead sharks, and more are part of the attractions. Regional fauna are also well represented at local museums and zoos.

See the Feathered and Furry for Free! Three times a day, Tiana Carroll and her avian friends delight all ages at the Tropicana, 3801 Las Vegas Blvd. S. (℡ **888/826-876** or 702/739-2222; www.tropicanalv.com). The big cats at the Lion Habitat at the MGM Grand, 3799 Las Vegas Blvd. S. (℡ **800/929-1111** or 702/891-7777; www.mgmgrand.com), sleep and frolic as you stroll through a clear tub. Look up, one might even be walking over your head. White tigers recline in their habitat at The Mirage, 3400 Las Vegas Blvd. S. (℡ **800/627-6667** or 702/791-7111; www.mirage.com), twitching their tails and padding about like giant tabby cats. At The Flamingo, 3555 Las Vegas Blvd. S. (℡ **800/732-2111** or 702/733-3111; www.flamingolv.com), hundreds of birds, including the hotel's namesake in addition to penguins, wander about on their own islands surrounding the pool area. All of these attractions are free.

Play with the Dolphins and Observe the Big Cats At The Mirage, 3400 Las Vegas Blvd. S. (℡ **800/627-6667** or 702/791-7111; www.mirage.com), dolphins swim and frolic in a huge pool, bouncing balls back to their trainer and to children who squeal with delight. The animals in the Secret Garden change regularly, but can include black panthers, white tigers, snow leopards, and even an elephant. Admission is $12 for those over 10 years old and is free for those under 10.

other distracting, and somewhat pricey, video games. Cash is not accepted for play; you'll have to buy a game card. With the standard version, $15 gets you $15 in game play, $20 gets you $25, or $25 gets you $35. Alternately, you can purchase a block of time ($20 for 1 hr., $25 for 2 hr., $27 for 3 hr., or, if you get there at opening or closing, you can buy 2 hr. for $20). Your payment goes on a debit card that is then inserted into the various machines to activate them. Games average $1.50 each. For a separate fee, there's also a rock-climbing wall in the center of the arcade, where climbers are cheered on by their friends and bystanders. When the climb is completed, the successful climber gets a T-shirt. Adults who wish to have a cocktail and snacks can do so at the Arena Bar and the Hopscotch Lounge, while kids will find burgers, pizza, and other child-friendly food at either Jax Grill or the GW Grill.

Adults should supervise younger children, but those 10 and older should be able to handle the complex games, most of which are geared for junior high schoolers and older. This is a very popular spot with both locals and visitors. We were unhappy about the litter on the floor and the deplorable state of the women's bathroom on one evening visit, but found the place more pleasant in the day. You're probably better off playing earlier rather than the later night hours, when it gets very crowded.

Shark Reef   Along with watching sharks (including one of the world's only hammerheads in captivity), moray eels, and piranhas go about their fishy business, visitors to the Shark Reef at Mandalay Bay, 3950 Las Vegas Blvd. S. (© **877/632-7000** or 702/632-7000; www.mandalaybay. com), can participate in educational programs offered weekdays that include a 1-hour guided tour. Admission is $16 for adults, $10 for children 5 to 12; those under 4 are free. Open daily 10am–11pm.

Meet the Locals   Check out the region's reptiles and other critters at the **Southern Nevada Zoological-Botanical Park,** 1775 N. Rancho Dr. (© **702/647-4685**), a quaint old-fashioned zoo. Here you will find Midas and Maniac Girl, a pair of lions born in 1998, along with a family of rare Barbary apes and swamp wallabies, as well as sidewinders, coyotes, and cougars. Admission is $7 for those over 12; admission for children 2 to 12 is $5, and children under 2 are free. It's open daily 9am to 5pm. Admission is free at the **Marjorie Barrick Museum,** at the University of Nevada, Las Vegas, 4505 Maryland Pkwy. (© **702/895-3381**), which has a collection of live, local reptiles. The Wild Nevada Room at the funky **Las Vegas Museum of Natural History,** 900 Las Vegas Blvd. N. (© **702/ 384-3466**), displays a tableaux of different desert environments, complete with sights, sounds, and smells. It also has dioramas of taxidermied animals from around the world, a tank of live sharks, and animatronic dinosaurs. Admission is $6 for those over 18, $5 for children 11 to 18, and $2 for children 3 to 11; those under 3 get in for free.

In the Showcase Mall, 3785 Las Vegas Blvd. S. © **702/432-GAME.** www.gameworks.com. AE, DC, DISC, MC, V. Sun–Thurs 10am–midnight; Fri–Sat 10am–1am. Hours may vary.

Gondola Ride   **All ages.** This slow cruise through the Grand Canal Shoppes is no thrill ride, but it is an experience. If you're lucky, you'll be serenaded by your own gondolier, but if you are a party of just two, you may end up sharing the four-seater boats with another couple. Small children will be more excited than teens to pass under bridges and to be looked at by groups of people dining, shopping, and, occasionally, just staring. The long lines, especially on weekends, however, can be overwhelming, especially because the ride lasts just a few minutes.

In The Venetian, 3355 Las Vegas Blvd. S. © **888/2-VENICE (283-6423)** or 702/414-1000. www.venetian. com. Admission: Indoor $15 adults, $8 children 2–12; outdoor $13 adults, $5 children 2–12, free for children under 2. AE, DC, DISC, MC, V. Open Sun–Thurs 10am–11pm; Fri–Sat 10am–midnight.

King Tut's Tomb & Museum   **All ages.** Some kids think it's "real neat" that the ancient Egyptians pulled out the guts of their dead and put them in special containers. Others won't notice that grisly (but cool) detail and will simply be astounded by the replicas of the solid-gold toys and other goodies buried with

Las Vegas's Arcades

Hotel	Phone	Name	Hours	Notes/Special Features
Bally's	702/739-4111	The Arcade Room	Sun–Thurs 9am–10pm; Fri–Sat 9am–midnight	Normal arcade
*Circus Circus	702/734-0410	no name, just an area on the Midway	Sun 9:30am–11:30pm; Mon–Thurs 11am–11pm; Fri 11am–12:30am; Sat 9:30am–1am	200+ games, plus the Midway and a McDonald's; children under 13 must be accompanied by a child over 13 or an adult; children 13 and over can play on their own
*Excalibur	702/597-7700	Wizard's Arcade	Mon–Thurs 10:30am–11pm; Fri–Sat 10am–1am; Sun 10am–midnight	Current arcade games and carnival games of skill and chance; Magic Motion Rides (70mm film, 5-channel Dolby stereo sound, specially designed seats that move in sync with the on-screen action.)
The Flamingo Las Vegas	702/733-3111	The Arcade	Daily 11am–10pm	"Very small area," according to the hotel
*GameWorks	702/432-4263	GameWorks	Sun–Thurs 10am–midnight; Fri–Sat 10am–2am	47,000 sq. ft.; 250+ games; world's tallest free-standing rock-climbing structure (75 ft.)
Green Valley Ranch Resort	702/617-7777	The Arcade	Daily 10am–midnight	"Just a normal video arcade"
Las Vegas Hilton	702/732-5111	Sports Zone	Daily 8am–midnight	Video and virtual reality games; smallish area, licensed out to Abel Amusements
Monte Carlo	702/730-7777	Backstreet Arcade	Daily 10am–10pm	60 video and redemption games
Las Vegas Hilton	702/732-5111	Sports Zone	Sun–Thurs 10am–10pm; Fri 10am–midnight; Sat 8am–midnight	Video and virtual reality games
*Luxor	702/262-4000	Games of the Gods	Sun–Thurs 9am–11pm; Fri–Sat 9am–midnight	Video, pinball, and interactive and simulator games/rides; includes a roller coaster simulator where you ride on a coaster you design yourself

Hotel	Phone	Name	Hours	Notes/Special Features
MGM Grand	702/891-7777	no name, just an area	Daily 10am–10pm	Skill, redemption, video and virtual reality games; also games geared for the 12-and-under set
The Mirage	702/791-7111	The Arcade	Sun–Thurs 10am–10pm; Fri 9am–midnight; Sat 9am–midnight	Video games only; small area near pool
Monte Carlo	702/730-7777	Backstreet Arcade	Daily 10am–10pm	60 video and redemption games
*New York–New York	702/736-4100	Coney Island Emporium Arcade	Sun–Thurs 9am–1am; Fri–Sat 9am–2am	32,000 sq. ft., midway games, laser tag, 8-person Daytona racing simulator, 200+ coin-op games; starting point for the Manhattan Express roller coaster; unaccompanied minors under 18 not allowed Sun–Thurs after 10pm, Fri–Sat and school holidays after midnight; and from Memorial Day to Labor Day, after midnight
Palms	702/942-7777	no name, just an area	Daily 6am–11pm	Video games only
Rio	702/777-7777	Fun & Games Arcade	Mon–Fri 11am–midnight; Sat–Sun 10am–midnight	Video, virtual reality, and redemption games
*Sahara	702/734-7223	Pit Pass Arcade	Varies according to season	120 interactive games, redemption and standard video games; part of the NASCAR Cafe; also available: Cyber Speedway racing simulators and Speed—The Ride roller coaster
*Stratosphere	702/380-7777	The Arcade	Daily 10am–midnight	Video games, some mechanical redemption games, and virtual soccer
Treasure Island	702/894-7111	no name, just an area	Sun–Thurs 9am–10pm; Fri–Sat 9am–midnight	Video games and a few games for children; considerably downsized from previous incarnation

Notable arcades noted by asterisk; all minors must be accompanied by parents/adult 21 or over unless noted; no video arcades: Aladdin/Planet Hollywood, Bellagio, Four Seasons, Hard Rock Casino, Harrah's, Mandalay Bay, Paris, The Venetian.

young Tut. The taped audio tour with individual tape players allows kids to take their time and listen at each exhibit, but unlike the audio wands with numbered buttons at Shark Reef and Secret Garden, kids must push pause and start buttons, making them unwieldy for the young ones and for less-adept adults. All in all, however, this is a great, inexpensive, educational, and fun attraction, which takes about 15 minutes, maximum, to go through.

In the Luxor Las Vegas, 3900 Las Vegas Blvd. S. ✆ **800/288-1000** or 702/262-4000. www.luxor.com. Admission $5. AE, DC, DISC, MC, V. Sun–Thurs 9am–11pm; Fri–Sat 9am–11:30pm.

Lied Discovery Children's Museum ★★★ *Finds* Ages 3 months–10 years.

Designed specifically for children, this hands-on museum makes learning fun with interactive exhibits that let kids touch, poke, and prod to their hearts content. Parents with babies and toddlers will especially appreciate the Baby Oasis, with special toys to encourage little brains and bodies, and the Parents' Resource Room. Children 5 and under can play in the Desert Discovery area, playing with soft boulders, pulleys, and shovels as they "build" a desert. Older kids can bang on steel drums, see what its like to play basketball from a wheel chair, and stand inside a giant soap bubble. All of this can keep you busy for at least 2 hours. Creativity Workshops, free with admission, allow kids to drop in and make cool stuff. These are offered Tuesday through Friday 12:30 to 4pm, Saturday 11am to 4:30pm, and Sunday 2 to 4pm.

833 Las Vegas Blvd. N. (½ block south of Washington, across the street from Cashman Field). ✆ **702/382-3445**. www.ldcm.org. Admission $7 adults, $6 seniors, military, and children 1–17. AE, DC, DISC, MC, V. Tues–Sun 10am–5pm.

Madame Tussaud's Celebrity Encounter ★ All ages. Oh, don't your chil-

dren yearn to throw their arms around Brad Pitt or go up for a rebound against Shaquille O'Neal? Well, Madame Tussaud's allows just this kind of horseplay. In fact, they encourage it by selling you overpriced cameras and film at the entrance. Don't be a sucker—stock up in advance at a local convenience store or pharmacy. Trust us; you'll want snapshots of your child with at least one of the waxy statues that pack the place. Hopefully, your children will recognize some of the older mannequins, so you won't feel like a geezer trying to explain Frank Sinatra and Tony Bennett, or even Elvis.

Alas, for the gruesomely inclined children, there's no Chamber of Horrors like the one in London's Tussaud's (it's historical, really!), but there are some pretty horrifyingly realistic figures, especially the Reverend Schuller statue which was so lifelike it scared the be-je—the be-jones—out of us, and the minuscule Prince (the Artist Who Preferred to Be Known as a Symbol). Princess Di is there, along with Joan Rivers, Madonna, Elvis, George W. Bush, and sports figures such as Michael Jordan. A guest book at the end of the self-guided tour (which takes anywhere from 15–45 min.) allows you to vote for the next star to be preserved in paraffin. Just so you don't feel like you have totally gone pop-culture crazy, there's also an educational display, which explains the history of the museum's founder Madame Tussaud (a feminist role model if ever there was one) and how the dummies, I mean celebrity figures, are made.

In The Venetian, 3355 Las Vegas Blvd. S. ✆ **702/990-3530**. Admission $21 adults, $15 seniors and Nevada residents, $10 children 3–12. AE, DC, DISC, MC, V. Daily 11am–7pm; summer hours 10am–11pm.

Siegfried & Roy's Secret Garden and Dolphin Habitat ★★★ *Value* All

ages. These two attractions in one are among the best bargains in Las Vegas, because once you pay, you can stay as long as you like wandering between the cages of large, exotic cats in the Secret Garden and watching the dolphins play,

Center Strip Attractions

Automobile Collection
at the Imperial Palace
(Imperial Palace) **4**
Bellagio Fountains
(Bellagio) **7**
Bellagio Gallery of
Fine Art (Bellagio) **7**
Flamingo Wildlife Habitat
(The Flamingo) **5**
Fountain Shows
at the Forum Shops
(Caesars Palace) **6**
Gondola Ride
(The Venetian) **2**
Grand Canal Shoppes
(The Venetian) **2**
Guggenheim and
Guggenheim Hermitage
Museums
(The Venetian) **2**

Houdini Museum
(The Venetian) **2**
Madame Tussaud's
Celebrity Encounter
(The Venetian) **2**
Mirage Volcano
(The Mirage) **3**
Paris Las Vegas **8**

Royal White Tiger
Habitat (The Mirage) **3**
Siegfried & Roy's
Secret Garden and
Dolphin Habitat
(The Mirage) **3**
Sirens of TI
(Treasure Island) **1**

and because it's a relatively cheap attraction and kids under 10 get in for free. Besides, what kids don't love animals?

Siegfried & Roy's famous white tigers recently became rather infamous when one of them either did what tigers all do, eventually, and attacked his beloved owner/trainer, or—depending on whether you buy this story—helped said beloved owner/trainer when the latter was having a medical emergency. Either way this story is played, it explains why the Secret Garden habitat is still up; no matter what, the tiger is not to blame (this may provide a good opportunity to discuss with your kids the dangers inherent in interacting with wild animals). In addition to the white tigers, you'll find dozens of the dynamic duo's animals exhibited amid lush landscaping. Because the animals—including black panthers, white lions, a snow leopard, and an elephant—are rotated between the Garden and the couple's home/game preserve, the inhabitants can vary from visit to visit. An audio wand allows you to learn more about the huge felines as they sleep, play, and wrestle just a few feet away from you. The close-up atmosphere gives perspective on the actual size and ferocity of these endangered species.

In the Dolphin Habitat, you'll watch the dolphins leap, cackle, and bounce balls to their handlers (or to the lucky kids in the audience who get to toss the balls back to the sea mammals). These dolphins are not "trained" like those at certain parks; instead, they act out of their own desire to play and have fun. All the dolphins in this exhibit have been born in captivity; none have been taken

Arcades Abound

A handful of hotels on the Strip have video arcades, and a few have put extra thought into their execution of a room that holds so much importance to both kids and adults. By far the nicest, cleanest, and most varied is the **Coney Island Emporium Arcade** in **New York–New York**, 3790 Las Vegas Blvd. S. (© 702/736-4100; www.nynyhotelcasino), open 9am to 1am Sunday through Thursday, and 9am to 2am Fridays and Saturdays. Along with video games, there are numerous board-walk-style games, all housed in a bright, light room with hardwood floors. Another plus: You board the Manhattan Express roller coaster from a corner in this arcade. The **Wizard's Arcade**, 3850 Las Vegas Blvd. (© 702/597-7700; www.excaliburlasvegas.com) is open Monday through Thursday from 10:30am to 11pm, Friday and Saturday from 10am to 1am, and Sunday from 10am to midnight. You can try out motion rides there and experience 70mm Dolby, with seats that move in synch with the onscreen action. The **Luxor Arcade**, 3900 Las Vegas Blvd. S. (© 702/262-4000; www.luxor.com)—located next to King Tut's Museum and the IMAX theaters—is packed with games and full of children and teens busily dropping quarters into race rides and other video-themed amusements Sunday through Thursday from 9am to 11pm, and Fridays and Saturdays from 9am until midnight. One special feature is a virtual roller coaster, which you get to design and then virtually ride. **Circus Circus**, 2880 Las Vegas Blvd. S. (© 702/734-0410; www.circuscircus.com), open Sunday from 9:30am to 11:30pm, Monday through Thursday from 11am to 11pm, Friday from 11am to 12:30am, and Saturday from 9:30am to 1am, surrounded a big-top show with midway games and a separate room for video and pinball, featuring over 200 machines, along with a McDonald's. At the midway, children under 13 must be accompanied by someone older than 13, but those over 13 can play on their own. For more on Las Vegas's arcades (names, hours, phone numbers, comments), see the arcade chart on p. 160.

from the ocean, and they seem to be quite happy here, breeding regularly and behaving in what their handlers feel is a natural manner. The large dolphin pool, which holds 2.5 million gallons of seawater, is designed so you can watch the dolphins interact with their human guardians, then walk below ground to observe them playing in the depths. *Tip:* Only registered guests may use strollers inside The Mirage, so if you have a baby, consider using a papoose-style carrier.

In The Mirage, 3400 Las Vegas Blvd. S. © 800/627-6667 or 702/791-7111. www.mirage.com. Admission $12, free for children under 10 if accompanied by an adult. AE, DC, DISC, MC, V. Weekdays 11am–7pm; weekends and major holidays 10am–7pm; last admission 6:30pm. Hours subject to change and vary by season.

Shark Reef at Mandalay Bay ★★ **All ages.** It's entirely appropriate that a Las Vegas casino celebrates sharks and other man-eaters, dontcha think? Ironic, cynical adult observations aside, this is a perennial fave with kids because there's nothing cooler than seeing plenty of flesh-eating, living, swimming death machines up close. Along with sharks, there are moray eels, stingrays, and a

Adventuredome
  (Circus Circus) **4**

Big Top Acts and Midway
  at Circus Circus **4**

Elvis-A-Rama **5**

Guinness World Records
  Museum and Gift Shop **3**

Speed—The Ride
  (The Sahara) **2**

Speedworld (The Sahara) **2**

Stratosphere Thrill Rides
  (Stratosphere) **1**

school of piranhas, which luckily have a naturalist-type guide standing next to the open tank to keep out curious fingers. Feeding time is usually around 2pm, but there are no guarantees, so don't plan your visit in the hopes of (or desire to avoid) seeing the South American killers swarm on hapless goldfish. The free audio devices provide plenty of prerecorded information, and the guides throughout the attraction are very helpful, answering questions about all of the finny beasts. We have only two complaints and those are minor: The "sunken temple" is a mite confusing, especially because some of the fish—most notably the famous piranhas—have nothing to do with the Asian artwork surrounding them; and some people, especially those with mobility issues, may find it a bit of a trek from the rest of the resort/casino. ***Tip:*** Don't go right after having your hair done; it's very humid inside.

In Mandalay Bay, 3950 Las Vegas Blvd. S. ℂ **877/632-7800** or 702/632-7777. Admission $16 adults, $10 children 5–12, free for children under 4. AE, DC, DISC, MC, V. Daily 10am–11pm.

2 Thrill Rides

Adventuredome ★★ **All ages.** Enclosed in this big pink dome are 5 acres of fun, including a miniature golf course, the world's largest indoor roller coaster, a flume ride, a rock-climbing wall, and a trampoline jump, plus virtual reality games. Toddlers can ride with their parents on four rides, including a Ferris wheel, along with watching clown acts and puppet shows. Some rides are designed for children 33 to 54 inches tall, while others restrict riders to those over 42 or 48 inches. The Rim Runner roller coaster is a real heart stopper and the flume ride gets you very wet if you ride in the front. One virtual-reality game/ride involves yelling, clapping, and stomping your feet while wearing VR goggles and responding to your "host," who can actually see you and direct your actions while it feels as though you're moving through 3-D rooms of a castle, trying to escape, while winning as many points as possible. Almost as much fun is watching the folks play the game, as they kick and flail in their seats, shouting and laughing. There's also the inevitable arcade for video-game junkies. Expect to spend at least 3 hours here.

2880 Las Vegas Blvd. S. (behind Circus Circus). ✆ **877/224-7287** or 702/794-3939. www.adventuredome. com. Free admission; pay per ride $4–$6; daily pass $22 adults, $14 children 33–47 in.; children under 33 in. ride some attractions free with parents. AE, DC, DISC, MC, V. Park hours vary seasonally but usually Mon–Thurs 10am–6pm; Fri–Sat 10am–midnight; Sun 10am–8pm.

Manhattan Express ★★ Blaze through the boroughs of New York, whip by the Statue of Liberty, and take the world's first "heartline" twist and dive roll, which allows the rider to feel negative g's by simulating a barrel roll in a jet fighter. With drops of 144 feet, speeds up to 67 mph, and one long rush along the 203-foot Coney Island–style coaster at New York–New York, this is considered one the best attractions in the city. The height restrictions may upset smaller kids who'll want to sit in the cool yellow taxicabs and race above the Strip and through the casino. Take them to the midway and let them play video games instead.

3790 Las Vegas Blvd. S. ✆ **800/693-6763** or 702/740-6969. www.nynyhotelcasino.com. $12 per ride; $35 all-day pass. Sun–Fri 10am–11pm; Sat 10am–11:30pm. Must be 54 in. or taller to ride.

Speed—The Ride ★ This is a monster roller coaster that uses electromagnetic "slingshot" technology to propel you from 0 to 35 mph in 2 seconds flat. You've never felt such acceleration (unless you're an astronaut). You roar out of the NASCAR area inside the Sahara and make an immediate sharp right turn to travel parallel to the Strip, zip through a misty tunnel, and go around a 360-degree loop. From there, you accelerate again from 35 to 70 mph to climb up a 224-foot-tall needle, straight up, before dropping down and replaying the entire tire in reverse. The whole thing takes 90 seconds at most, but it'll then require another 60 minutes for you to regain any steadiness on your feet.

Sahara Hotel & Casino, 2535 Las Vegas Blvd. S. ✆ **888/696-2121** or 702/737-2111. www.saharavegas.com. Single ride $10; all-day ride pass $20. Sun–Thurs 11am–midnight; Fri–Sat 11am–1am.

Speedworld ★ Riders on the Cyber Speedway must be 54 inches or taller to hop into these 7/8 replica NASCAR racers, which rock 'n' roll as they speed down a video version of the Las Vegas Speedway or the Strip itself. Drivers can adjust the tire pressure, aerodynamic wing angles, horsepower, braking response, transmission torque, and suspension before the race starts. The separate 3-D motion simulator with goggles will take you on a jostling race experience as you zoom along at what feels like 200 mph.

1 (2 miles)

93
15

Main St.

4
2 **3**
6
5

Cashman
Field Center

ATTRACTIONS ●
Cashman Field **6**
Fremont Street
  Experience **9**
Heritage Park **5**
Las Vegas Museum
  of Natural History **3**
Lied Children's
  Discovery Museum **2**
Old Las Vegas
  Mormon Fort **4**
Reed Whipple
  Cultural Center **7**
Southern Nevada
  Zoological-Botanical
  Park **1**
Sports Hall of Fame **8**
DINING ◆
El Sombrero **11**
Second Street Grill **10**

Bonanza Rd.

Reed Whipple
Cultural Center
7

Harris

Bell

Maryland Pkwy.

Bonanza Rd.

515 95 93

Stewart

SQUIRES
PARK

Ave.

Mesquite Ave.

Area of
detail

8

Main St.

9 **10**
Fremont St.

Ogden Ave.

95

93 95 515

DOWNTOWN

582

■ Bus
  Depot

Carson Ave.

Charleston

Casino Center Blvd.

Lewis Ave.

1st St.

3rd St.

4th St.

Las Vegas Blvd.

Bridger Ave.

7th St.

8th St.

Charleston Blvd. (The Strip)

15

Sahara

Maryland

Paradise

Desert Inn

Eastern

Clark Ave.

6th St.

9th St.

Flamingo

UNLV

Bonneville

Las Vegas Ave.

Tropicana

Commerce St.

Main St.

11

Garces Ave.

Gass Ave.

Hoover Ave.

604

McCarran
Int'l Airport

Russell

Charleston Blvd.

0   0.25 mi
0   0.25 km

Fremont Street
Experience

15

215

0   1/2 mi
0   0.5 km

Sahara Hotel & Casino, 2535 Las Vegas Blvd. S. ⓒ **888/696-2121** or 702/737-2111. www.saharavegas.com.
Single ride $10; all-day ride pass $20. Mon–Thurs noon–9pm; Fri noon–10pm; Sat 11am–10pm; Sun
11am–9pm.

Star Trek: The Experience ⓖ **Ages 6 & up.** More than just rides, this section of the Las Vegas Hilton is a complete world, including sci-fi, light-beam
activated slot machines for mom and dad, and a "History of the Future" display.
As you wait in line, clips from *Star Trek* episodes play on TV screens, somewhat distracting you from the often-long wait. Then, in the original attraction,
Klingon Encounter, you're beamed aboard the *Enterprise* (very cool) and help the
crew battle the evil Klingons. The motion ride itself is a jostling, rumbling,
stomach-churning romp, and you'll be wearing heavy visors that sometimes
need to be held on your head, especially if you wear glasses.

In 2004, a sister *Star Trek* attraction, *Borg Invasion 4-D,* was added. In this
one, the sinister Borg attack your spaceship and chase you to an escape craft
(actually a theater) where you'll see a 3-D movie in which your spacecraft helps
defeat the Borg. The special effects are good, but the plot is a little fuzzy for
those not already familiar with the Borg. All you really need to know is that the
Borg drill out your brain and take over your body.

After the Borg have excavated your brain (resistance is futile!), it's in perfect
shape to proceed to Quark's Bar for spacey food and two souvenir shops with
plenty of *Star Trek* merchandise. Actors in *Star Trek* outfits populate the Experience, adding to the atmosphere.

Tip: Both *Klingon Encounter* and *Borg Invasion 4-D* are about 22 minutes long. The best time to check out *Star Trek:* The Experience is on weekdays from 12:30 to 2pm or after 4:30pm.

In the Las Vegas Hilton, 3000 Paradise Rd. 🕐 **888/GO-BOLDLY.** www.ds9promenade.com. Dual Mission tickets (includes both rides) are $35, $32 seniors 65 and older and children 12 and under; children under 42 in. free. AE, DC, DISC, MC, V. Daily 11am–11pm.

Stratosphere Thrill Rides 🐸🐸 **Ages 9 & up.** Calling these heart-stoppers "thrill rides" is a bit of an understatement; two of them are downright frightening, providing an adrenaline rush unlike anything we've ever experienced. The **High Roller,** the world's highest roller coaster, wraps around the Stratosphere's tower, 909 feet above the ground, while the 32-degree angles over the edge give you quite a scare. As you stand in line for the **Big Shot,** keep in mind that soon you will be strapped onto a tiny seat at the top of the tallest building west of the Mississippi, and thrust approximately 16 stories straight up the needle. You pause at the top for a split second, then are dropped like a rock (your stomach stays at the top). Both rides are great, fun, and will provide quality bonding time with your kids if you ride them together. A third thrill ride, **X Scream,** is a giant teeter-totter-style device that propels you in an open car off the side of the 100-story tower and lets you dangle there weightlessly before returning you to relative safety. It's tame and not in the same category as the first two; give it a pass. Children under 48 inches not allowed on any of the rides.

Atop the Stratosphere Las Vegas, 2000 Las Vegas Blvd. S. 🕐 **800/99-TOWER (998-6937)** or 702/380-7777. Admission for the Tower $9; individual ride tickets $5–$15; combo package (Tower and rides) $25 (if you dine in the buffet room or Top of the World, there's no charge to go up to the Tower). AE, DC, DISC, MC, V. Sun–Thurs 10am–1am; Fri–Sat 10am–2am. Hours vary seasonally. Minimum height requirement for rides is 48 in.

3 Art Galleries & History Museums

When Steve Wynn opened Bellagio he stocked it with art—real art: Millions of dollars worth of Impressionist masterpieces, plus Picassos, Matisses, and Warhols. Like everything Wynn did, the concept was a success. Riding on the concept that Vegas visitors wanted cultcha along with all-you-can-eat-shrimp buffets, the Guggenheim came to The Venetian, followed by the separate Guggenheim and Hermitage collaboration in the same hotel. When the MGM Group bought The Mirage and ousted Steve Wynn, he took most of his artwork with him, to be displayed in Wynn Las Vegas.

Along with the art galleries and museums in these relative newcomers to the Vegas cultural scene, there are museums celebrating the city, its history, and its denizens, including Elvis, Liberace, and the Mormons. And, of course, no tourist town would be complete without a Guinness World Records Museum, which, in this town of superlatives, seems almost superfluous. The world's largest collection of automobiles is at the Imperial Palace, while the Liberace Museum boasts the world's largest rhinestone. See below for more information.

Auto Collections at the Imperial Palace 🐸🐸 **All ages.** Antique, vintage, rare, and notable—or notorious—cars make up this huge, beautifully displayed collection of automobiles. The collection is so large that the exhibits are changed regularly, but expect to see several Dusenbergs (the museum has the world's largest collection, valued at over $50 million), JFK's 1962 "bubbletop" Lincoln Continental, and Cadillacs belonging to FDR and Herbert Hoover. Other cars of the stars and celebrities of bygone days include Al Capone's and Marilyn Monroe's Cadillacs, and Howard Hughes's 1954 Chrysler, which was installed

Attractions & Entertainment East of the Strip

Clark County Museum **6**

Donna Beam Fine Art Gallery
  (University of Nevada Las Vegas) **4**

Hard Rock Casino **2**

Liberace Museum **5**

Marjorie Barrick Museum
  (University of Nevada Las Vegas) **3**

Star Trek: The Experience (Las Vegas Hilton) **1**

with a special air-purification system that cost more than the car itself. Over 200 vehicles are on display, including one of only 51 revolutionary Tucker automobiles ever manufactured.

In the Imperial Palace Hotel, 3535 Las Vegas Blvd. S. 𝒞 800/634-6441 or 702/794-3174. www.auto collections.com. Admission $6.95 adults, $3 seniors and children under 12, free for children under 4 and AAA members. Check website and ever-present hawkers in front of Imperial Palace for free admission coupon. AE, DC, DISC, MC, V. Daily 9:30am–9:30pm.

Bellagio Gallery of Fine Art ⟨★⟩   **Ages 10 & up.** First, the drawback: According to Bellagio, children under 18 are not permitted in the hotel unless their families are registered guests, or tickets have been purchased in advance for a gallery or show, or if reservations are already made at a restaurant. Now, when we were there, we saw many a youngster traipsing about with an adult in tow, and somehow it just didn't seem like all those families were staying there or had tickets for the Cirque de Soleil show *O*. The security person we spoke to said there's an unofficial "don't-ask" policy as long as kids stay well behaved, but on the other hand, we were told—both on the phone and in person—that children under 18 were verboten.

Now for the good part: This is an important gallery, even though its originator, Steve Wynn, is no longer associated with Bellagio. Past exhibits have included Impressionists; the mobiles of Alexander Calder; the art of Fabergé, jeweler to the Imperial Court of Russia, which featured many of his intricately designed and bejeweled eggs; Andy Warhol celebrity portraits; and a large exhibit of Monets.

The museum gift shop next door is stocked full of great gift and craft items, most of which are designed for children, which is odd, given the hotel's seeming antipathy toward them. And then there's that ticket price. Do let us point out that the Louvre and London's National Gallery collections—both of which are, needless to say, quite a bit larger and both of which, one can safely say, do have some notable works—cost a whole lot less as a family excursion.

In Bellagio, 3600 Las Vegas Blvd. S. 𝒞 877/957-9777 or 702/693-7871. www.bellagio.com. Admission $15 adults, $12 students with ID, $12 Nevada residents. Reservations suggested, but walk-ins taken every 15 min. AE, DC, DISC, MC, V. Daily 9am–9pm.

Casino Legends Hall of Fame Museum ⟨★⟩ *(Finds)*   **Ages 6 & up.** This is the "most visited museum in Nevada," according to its curator, who is understandably proud of the museum's collection of gaming memorabilia including chips, dice, swizzle sticks, matches, and china of 550 long-gone hotels. Over 180 current hotels are represented in their various incarnations, all of which might sound boring for kids, until they get a guided tour from a former—and very self-effacing and funny—showgirl, or settle down to watch videotaped implosions, explosions, and the exploits of gangsters. Outfits of Vegas notables are on display, along with the elaborate costumes worn by dancers and showgirls. (Some weigh almost 100 lb.!) A dress of sequins, fabric, boning, and farthingales, topped with a feather headdress, seems more suited for dancing the minuet at Versailles than sashaying on the stage at the *Folies Bergere*. A replica of a backstage dressing room is set up in this area, while another section is devoted to mobsters. Ephemera include contracts between entertainers and the casinos, pay stubs, and posters. The large gift shop sells postcards, gambling chips, T-shirts, and the like from old casinos. Nevada's sleazy side comes out on some of the chips on sale from various brothels and bordellos. *Tip:* Free passes are often available in many local magazines.

In the Tropicana, 3801 Las Vegas Blvd. S. ⓒ **888/826-8767** or 702/739-5444. www.tropicanalv.com. Admission $7, seniors $6. AE, DC, DISC, MC, V. Daily 9am–9pm.

Clark County Museum ⭐⭐⭐ Finds **Ages 5 & up.** One of the high points of this unique museum is Heritage Street, where historic homes from important periods of Clark County history have been restored to recreate the lifestyles of their times. There's also a mining exhibit, a ghost town, and a pueblo, making this an educational yet fun place to spend an afternoon walking about. Strollers can be easily accommodated, which is good, because young children may tire of walking around and looking at old buildings.

1830 S. Boulder Hwy., E. Las Vegas. ⓒ **702/455-7955.** www.co.clark.nv.us/parks/clark_county_museum. htm. Admission $1.50 adults, $1 seniors, military, and children 3–15. AE, DC, DISC, MC, V. Daily 9am–4:30pm.

Donna Beam Fine Art Gallery ⭐ Finds **Ages 10 & up.** Located on the campus of the University of Nevada, Las Vegas, this gallery displays traveling exhibitions, as well as works by UNLV's students and faculty. It also serves as a training ground for students studying gallery management. Exhibits change 7 to 15 times a year. Children who are fascinated by art will definitely enjoy this; the other 99% of kids will find it dull.

University of Nevada, Las Vegas, Alta Ham Fine Arts Building, 4505 Maryland Pkwy. ⓒ **702/895-3893.** www.unlv.edu/Colleges/Fine_Arts/Facilities/Donna_Beam_Gallery. Free admission. Mon–Fri 9am–5pm; Sat 10am–2pm.

Elvis-A-Rama **Ages 2 & up.** There's a whole lotta shakin' going on at Elvis-A-Rama, the all-Elvis-all-the-time museum. Elvis paraphernalia includes the King's handwritten love letter to the girl back home scrawled while he was in the army—hopefully, for the sake of chivalry—before he met Priscilla, the future Mrs. Presley. His driver's license, his little black book (presumably pre- or post-Priscilla), a Cadillac, sheet music, and more are displayed behind glass in vaguely chronological order. This museum's highest point of kitsch is the martial exhibit containing Elvis' karate outfit and a video display of the King going through his karate moves set to the song "Kung Fu Fighting." We gaped in speechless amazement that anyone would actually think that this was a good idea, then watched the video two more times, trying not to laugh. Unfortunately, unless your kids know who Elvis is and how he changed the face of music throughout the world—emphasize to your kids that we wouldn't have the Beatles, Nirvana, or the Hard Rock Casino if it weren't for Elvis and his swiveling hips—this museum won't really help them understand The Man, The Myth, and The Music, but it will show them how to write "Elvis" in over 60 languages. Prepare beforehand with a video of *Viva Las Vegas* before leaving home. Kids of all ages may enjoy the free Elvis impersonator, performing every hour; he looks, sounds, and moves almost like the real thing.

3401 Industrial Rd. ⓒ **702/309-7200.** www.elvisarama.com. Admission $9.95 adults, $7.95 seniors, students with ID, and Nevada residents, free for children under 12. Admission includes a 20-min. Elvis impersonator show, held 7 times daily. AE, DC, DISC, MC, V. Daily 10am–8pm. Call for free shuttle bus pickup at your hotel; shuttle will return you or drop you at another location after your tour.

Guggenheim and Guggenheim Hermitage Museums ⭐⭐ **Ages 5 & up for the Guggenheim, 10 & up for the Guggenheim Hermitage.** The Guggenheim Las Vegas opened in 2002 with its Art of the Motorcycle show, which closed in early 2003. The Frank Ghery–designed museum has hosted a couple of exhibits since, though not on any regular schedule. However, the collaboration between the Guggenheim and the State Hermitage Museum in St. Petersburg (which is a different museum from "just" the Guggenheim)—called,

appropriately enough, the Guggenheim Hermitage—has been reliable since it opened, also in 2002. The collaboration between the venerable Russian museum and the Guggenheim has resulted in paintings never seen outside of Russia (okay, some have appeared in books). At press time, the exhibit at the Guggenheim Hermitage was the Pursuit of Pleasure, featuring works of art from the two major sponsoring museums as well as the Kunsthistorisches Museum in Vienna. Depicting the art of leisure (an art Vegas knows quite well), the exhibition featured masterpieces by such painters as Degas, Picasso, Titian, and Rubens. Ask for self-guided activity books for children, which are geared for ages 9 and up.

In The Venetian, 3355 Las Vegas Blvd. S. ℂ **866/484-4849** or 702/414-2440. Individual museum passes $15 adults, $11 students with ID, $7 children 6–12, free for children under 6. AE, DC, DISC, MC, V. Daily 9:30am–8:30pm.

Houdini Museum *Finds* **Ages 8 & up.** This small museum, in the Grand Canal Shoppes, squeezed into a space barely the size of a hotel room, is the least expensive museum on the Strip, but if your kids don't care about magic or know who Harry Houdini was, it's a pretty pointless venture. Those fascinated by legerdemain and stage magic will certainly want to absorb every news article and gaze at all the manacles, ropes, and assorted other devices the great escape artist used in his acts. Next door is a branch of Houdini's Magic Shop, where kiddies can have the sales staff perform tricks for them and purchase gag items (black soap, foaming sugar, hand buzzers, whoopee cushions, and more) as well as actual magic tricks with instructions.

In The Venetian, 3355 Las Vegas Blvd. S. ℂ **877/DINI-WHO (346-4946)** or 702/798-4789. www.houdini. com. Admission $2 adults, $1 children under 12, $5 families. Pay admission at the shop next door. AE, DC, DISC, MC, V. Daily 10am–11pm.

Howard W. Cannon Aviation Museum ★ *Finds* **All ages.** Open 24 hours a day, this free museum at McCarran Airport is located on level 2, above baggage claim, and details the history of aviation in Nevada from the first flight to the introduction of the commercial jet. Plane fans will love it and plain folks will learn a little something. Plus, it's a better, more family-oriented way to kill time at the airport than pulling slots.

5757 Wayne Newton Blvd. ℂ **702/455-7968.** Free admission. Daily 24 hr.

Las Vegas Museum of Natural History ★ **All ages.** "Cool, totally cool," lauded one preteen, entranced by the shark tank with its undulating, sharp-toothed denizens. The slightly old and dusty taxidermy displays of bears, wolves, and the like also got high marks, as did the motion detector-activated dinosaurs, which roar and move when you enter the room. (Some smaller kids startle because of this, so you may want to explain the situation first.) This is a fun museum in the old-school diorama style and is definitely worth checking out, especially because it is located next to the Mormon Fort (p. 174) and close to the Lied Museum (p. 162). The Out of Africa exhibit details the fossils of primitive man found on the continent; one high point are the replica skulls enclosed in light boxes that illuminate when you press a button. Nifty. Make sure you visit the desert environment, complete with sights, sound, and smells of the living desert. The sharks are fed Monday, Wednesday, and Friday at 2pm—if that's the sort of thing you'd like to enjoy watching as a family.

900 Las Vegas Blvd. N. ℂ **702/384-3466.** www.lvnhm.org. Admission $6 adults; $5 seniors, students with ID, and military; $3 children 3–11; free for children under 2. AE, DC, DISC, MC, V. Daily 9am–4pm.

Hey, Sport!

Sports are a major part of the American psyche and Las Vegas plays right into it. Here are some activities and attractions your young sports fans will like:

Eat at ESPN Zone   You'll be surrounded by sports-themed items and souvenirs while you munch sports-fan food (New York–New York, 3790 Las Vegas Blvd. S.; ✆ **702/933-3776**; www.espnzone.com). See p. 127.

Visit the Sports Hall of Fame   This is the world's largest personal collection of athletic memorabilia, including Muhammad Ali's boxing gloves, baseball cards, and bats from the World Series (Las Vegas Club Hotel and Casino, 18 Fremont St.; ✆ **702/385-1664**; www.vegasclub casino.net). See p. 155.

Watch a Local Team Play   Whether it's baseball, basketball, or hockey, college or pro, Las Vegas has plenty of sports all year round. (See p. 228 for a complete listing of teams and their contact numbers.)

Visit the SportCenter   Whether your sports fans yearn for batting cages or rock-climbing walls, they'll find it here, along with golf and go-kart racing (121 E. Sunset Rd.; ✆ **702/317-7777**; www.sportcenter lasvegas.com). See p. 184.

Play Sport-Themed Arcade Games at GameWorks   State-of-the-art video games allow players to kick soccer balls, swing bats, and perform other sporty feats in the comfort of their local arcade (in the Showcase Mall, 3785 Las Vegas Blvd. S.; ✆ **702/432-GAME**). See p. 157.

Browse at Field of Dreams   This chain boutique offers a variety of autographed sports items, including photos, jerseys, cards, and balls (Rio, 3700 W. Flamingo Rd.; ✆ **702/221-9144**; or at Caesars Palace, 3500 Las Vegas Blvd. S.; ✆ 702/792-8233). See p. 210.

Liberace Museum and Center for the Arts 🎩🎩 **All ages.** "He was Grandma's Elton John." That's the easiest way to explain Liberace to your children, and we can't think of a kid who won't be excited over some part of the monumental (even by Vegas standards) excesses displayed here. The first half of the museum is dedicated to Liberace's life, his cars, and his pianos. His story is indeed a distillation of the American dream—son of immigrants, Lee (nee Walter) Liberace vowed to become "the most famous pianist in the world." And boy howdy, did he succeed! His first entry in the Guinness Book of World Records was as the world's fastest pianist; he also set records in his time as the most highly paid. Even today, his name lives on as a symbol of kitsch and flamboyance.

The men in your family will no doubt be awestruck by the late pianist's collection of automobiles, including a rhinestone-encrusted limousine, a replica of a London taxicab, and a red, white, and blue Rolls-Royce used in the 1976 Bicentennial celebration. Check out the pink Volks Royce, a customized version of a VW bug with a Rolls-Royce grille. The piano collection features a rhinestone-covered piano and many rare antique models, but this will probably bore most kids; even we were a little ho-hum over this part. A video program and photographic chronology of Liberace's life, his cars, and pianos are housed in the front part of the museum.

Fun Fact Muy Macho

Lest anyone call Liberace a sissy for wearing ermine and pearls, point out that his furs alone could weigh up to 200 pounds and he would stride out on stage wearing a huge fur cape and fling it open, revealing a heavy and elaborately sparkling ensemble. After accepting his applause, the fur would be driven off stage by a "show-fur" in the custom Volks Royce, and then Lee would begin to play the piano in his bejeweled garb, his fingers encumbered by the massive rings now on display at the museum. Now that's a macho man!

The real wows, however, are heard in the second museum building—the one that has the musical score to "Beer Barrel Polka" laid out in mosaic. That's where Lee's clothes and jewels, including the world's largest rhinestone—do we sense a theme here?—are displayed. And what a Barbie doll fantasy closet—multicolored, high-collared, insanely spectacular, sequined, spangled, and rhinestoned within an inch of their seams clothes! Amongst the splendor and sparkle, there's a monkey fur jacket, a green Chinese-style number, and a striking black and red outfit that will make any Gothy teen perk up. A small display of Las Vegas historical artifacts, a cafe, and a gift shop round out the visit.

1775 E. Tropicana Ave. (at Spencer St.). © 702/798-5595. www.liberace.com. Admission $12 adults, $8 seniors over 65 and students 6 "through college," free for children under 6. AE, DC, DISC, MC, V. Mon–Sat 10am–5pm; Sun 1–5pm.

Marjorie Barrick Museum **All ages.** Previously known as the Marjorie Barrick Natural History Museum at UNLV, the name has been shortened and altered, which makes it more easily distinguished from the Las Vegas Natural History Museum. Located on the UNLV campus, this free museum offers examples of Mexican folk art, Native America pottery, traveling art exhibits (changed every 8 weeks), and other worthwhile, somewhat dry, displays based around the collections and interests of the museum's patroness, Marjorie Barrick. For kids, the real thrill is getting close to the glass cages of the live snakes (who, if you are lucky— or unlucky, depending on your view—will be dining on mice when you drop by), lizards, and tortoises on display. Remind younger kids to please not tap the glass.

On the UNLV campus, 4505 S. Maryland Pkwy. © 702/895-3381. http://hrcweb.nevada.edu/Museum/exhibits.html. Free admission. Mon–Fri 8am–4:45pm; Sat noon–4pm.

Old Las Vegas Mormon Fort **All ages.** It's hard to believe that from this tiny structure sprang the glittering giant that is Las Vegas today, but in 1855, Mormons moving westward stopped here because of the fresh water springs, and stayed, in what was then an oasis, to build a fort, with a post office and other buildings that became a way station for travelers. Within 2 years, the hot weather and a dispute between two church leaders caused a schism, and the Mormons sold their land to a rancher. Eventually, the area was deeded to the San Pedro, Los Angeles, and Salt Lake Railroad. In 1905, trains came to Vegas, and the town was finally born around the remnants of this adobe fort. This is a good place to stop and take a look on the way to or from the Lied Museum (p. 162) or the Natural History Museum (p. 172). It is outdoors, so make sure you have hats and sunblock.

500 E. Washington Blvd. © 702/486-3511. www.state.nv.us/stparks/olvmf.htm. Admission $3 adults, $2 children 6–12, free for children under 5. Daily 8am–4:30pm.

4 Factories & Food

IN LAS VEGAS

Everything Coca-Cola Las Vegas *Overrated* **All ages.** The giant Coke-bottle-shaped window indicates you're in the right place to purchase everything Coca-Cola. Or, at least almost everything. From key chains to T-shirts, postcards, and replicas of vintage glasses and trays, this monofocused monolith is here to sell Coke. Upstairs you can taste samples of Coke from around the world, plus buy items with the Coke logo in different languages.

In the Showcase Mall, 3785 Las Vegas Blvd. S. ✆ 702/597-3122. Free admission. Daily 10am–11pm.

M&Ms World ✮ **All ages.** Along with being a store full of all things M&Ms (including giant canisters of the candy-coated chocolate in a rainbow of colors—they all taste the same, though—pajamas, and lunch boxes), this multistoried building also serves as a 3-D movie theater. The half-hour movie, *I Lost My M in Las Vegas,* stars (plain) Red M and (peanut) Yellow M, which all ages will enjoy. Expect to be badgered into buying lavender or pastel pink M&Ms; you can mix and match colors by weight. Or, if you like, try a box of the Mars Company's upscale chocolate, Ethel M's, also conveniently available in the gift shop.

In the Showcase Mall, 3785 Las Vegas Blvd. S. ✆ 702/736-7611. Free admission. Daily 9am–11pm; movie screens continuously every 30 min. Sun–Thurs 10am–6pm, Fri–Sat 10am–8pm.

National Vitamin Company Factory **All ages.** Advertised in all the local tourist attraction magazines, this quick, self-guided tour takes you through a vitamin and cosmetic company, giving you a behind-the-scenes look at how the stuff is made and packaged. There are also educational displays, and, afterward, you get free samples. This being Vegas, there's also a gift shop where you can buy hair-care products, herbs, and vitamins. The smoothie bar is considered by locals to make one of the best such drinks in the West. This place is especially good for the budding scientist or cosmetic collector.

7440 S. Industrial Rd. ✆ 866/897-4712. www.nationalvitamin.com. Free admission. Tours during business hours 6am–6pm, with limited runs on Sun.

IN NEARBY HENDERSON

There are two factories about 6 miles from the Strip in the town of Henderson that offer free tours, and if that's your kind of thing, well, you won't be entirely alone on your visit; they are a favorite with tour groups. If you do put these factories on your to-do list, it's best to see them on a weekday, when they're fully operative.

To get to Henderson, drive south on Las Vegas Boulevard South to Sunset Road. Then, continue straight on Sunset Way, rather than following Sunset Road to the right. Turn left onto Cactus Garden Drive. You will soon see Ethel M's Chocolates, a good place to begin. Ron Lee's World of Clowns is approximately 3 miles away from Ethel M's. To get there, turn right off Cactus Garden Drive onto Sunset Way, then left onto Sunset Road. Follow Sunset Road south to Stephanie. Turn right on Stephanie and left on Warm Springs Road. Drive past the light at Marks to Carousel Parkway, a long driveway on your right.

Ethel M's Chocolate Factory and Cactus Gardens **All ages.** This is a self-guided tour, with audio and visual explanations of the processes involved in creating sweet treats. The mixtures bubble and boil before you, separated from hungry faces by a thick glass wall. The candy bits travel down conveyer belts where they are covered in chocolate and gently jiggled before being boxed by

Fun Fact **Trivia: Viva Las Vegas**

1. Gambling was legalized in Nevada in:
    a. 1931
    b. 1918
    c. 1877
    d. 1849

2. Fremont Street was the site of Las Vegas's first:
    a. elevator
    b. paved street
    c. first streetlight
    d. all of the above

3. McCarran International Airport is the nation's seventh-busiest airport. It averages how many flights a day?
    a. 210
    b. 540
    c. 720
    d. 980

4. Though Las Vegas is known for its casinos, it also has numerous churches, synagogues, and other places of worship. Approximately how many?
    a. 1,200
    b. 500
    c. 140
    d. 70

5. The Spanish words "las vegas" means:
    a. "the winners"
    b. "the meadows"
    c. "the sands"
    d. "the losers"

6. Las Vegas is famous for its neon. How many miles of neon tubing are along the Strip and in Downtown?

hand, an absolutely hypnotizing process. Kids should also like watching the employees behind the glass and trying to figure out what they are saying. After you finish this brief portion of the tour, you get to watch a kindly factory worker demonstrate up close how the chocolate-enrobing machines work. (Enrobing is the candy-making word for "covering.") After, you'll get a piece of freshly enrobed candy. Then comes the really fun part—a trip to the chocolate shop for a free sample, plus plenty of sweet goodies to buy, including ice cream. We were happy to note that the shop sells both sugar-free candy and ice cream. There's also a picture of the actual Ethel M, Ethel Mars, the mom of the founder of Mars Candy, making this a nice addition to your trip to M&Ms World (p. 175).

The factory is surrounded by a **2½-acre cactus and wetlands garden,** which features 350 species of rare and exotic cacti from the arid areas of South and Central America, with signs provided for self-guided tours. The showpiece of the cactus garden is the water-reclamation plant. Built on ecological principles, only natural means—meaning algae, fish, and plants—are used to clean all the water

a.   15,000 miles
b.   400 miles
c.   1,500 miles
d.   4 miles

7. There are how many hotel swimming pools in the Las Vegas area?
a.   17
b.   27
c.   35
d.   50+

ANSWERS

1: a
Gambling was legalized in 1931. In 1909, the state passed a no-gambling law, which forbade even flipping a coin for the cost of a drink; no one in Las Vegas, however, really paid much attention to the law.

2: d
Fremont Street was also the location of the city's first hotel, Hotel Nevada, opened in 1905.

3: d
On average, McCarran International Airport handles 980 flights a day at 94 gates.

4: b
Over 40 faiths are served at 500-plus places of worship.

5: b

6: a
15,000 miles of neon tubing makes nighttime Las Vegas one of the most recognizable cityscapes in the world.

7: d
There are over 50 hotel pools; unfortunately, most close (or aren't heated) in the winter.

used at the candy factory. The cleaned water is then used to irrigate the cactus garden and the wetlands area. Any extra water goes to local water companies for nonpotable uses. This section is a really neat way to show how Mother Nature can be used to undo some of mankind's messes. Plus, the fish are fun to watch.

Tip: If you get there at opening, not a lot of candy is being made; the factory gets busier as the day goes on, but by 2:30pm, production has slowed back down. The early bird does catch the worm, or chocolate in this case; we were given multiple samples because nobody else was there, or maybe they just thought we looked hungry. You may not, however, want to have your darlings eating multiple helpings of toffee and truffles at 9am. Bottom line—if you want to see full production, aim for arrival between 10am and 1pm, but if you'd like an extra helping of chocolate, go at opening.

2 Cactus Garden Dr. (just off Mountain Vista and Sunset Way in the Green Valley Business Park), Henderson. © 702/435-2655. www.ethelm.com. Free admission. Daily 8:30am–7pm. Closed Dec 25.

Ron Lee's World of Clowns   **All ages.** If your kids like clowns, this small factory is worth a quick tour, especially because it's just a little ways from Ethel M's. Along with making clowns, it also manufactures figures for Disney. Much like the candy factory, this self-guided tour consists of simply looking in windows as people mold and paint. The real attraction (aside from a beautiful carousel) is the gift shop, with a nearly limitless supply of high-quality figurines, primarily with a clown motif.

330 Carousel Pkwy., Henderson. ℂ 800/829-3928 or 702/434-3920. www.ronlee.com/factorytour/index. html. Free admission. Mon–Fri 8:30am–4:30pm.

5 Kid-Friendly Tours

If you'd rather relax and leave the driving to someone else or if you'd like to try something more daring in sightseeing, almost every hotel in Las Vegas has a sightseeing desk where clerks can arrange any kind of tour you'd like to anywhere you want to go, whether you want to travel by helicopter, limo, horse, Humvee, foot, or bus.

COACH USA   This company (ℂ **888/COACHUSA;** www.coachusa.com) offers a rather comprehensive roster, including:

- Several 3½-hour **city tours,** with various itineraries, including visits to Ethel M's Chocolates (p. 175), the Fremont Street Experience (p. 157), the Liberace Museum (p. 173), and the Casino Legends Hall of Fame Museum (p. 170).
- Half-day excursions to **Hoover Dam, Mount Charleston,** and **Red Rock Canyon** (p. 242, 260, and 253, respectively).
- A full-day excursion to **Valley of Fire** and **Lake Mead** (p. 250 and 246, respectively).
- A 13-hour **Grand Canyon excursion** (p. 262).

Call for details or inquire at your hotel sightseeing desk, where you'll also find free magazines with coupons for discounts on these tours.

GRAND CANYON TOURS   The Grand Canyon is hundreds of miles away from Las Vegas, so if you happen to pass it on your way in or out of town, it's—to put it mildly—worth a stop. If experiencing the natural wonder is an important part of your trip, and you want to make the huge detour, there are dozens of sightseeing tours departing from the city daily. In addition to the Coach USA tours mentioned above, the major operator of Grand Canyon tours, **Scenic Airlines** (ℂ **800/634-6801** or 702/638-3300; www.scenic.com), runs full-day and overnight tours with hiking, along with their deluxe, full-day guided air-ground tours starting at $219 per person ($189 for children 2–11); the price includes a bus excursion through the national park, a flight over the canyon, and lunch. All their tours include flightseeing.

Scenic Airlines also offers tours to other points of interest and national parks, including Bryce Canyon and Monument Valley. Ask for details when you call.

UNIQUE DESERT TOURS   If you would like a personalized tour of Las Vegas, one that takes you off the beaten path, then call **Creative Adventures** 🌟🌟🌟 (ℂ **702/361-5565**). Founder and tour guide Char Cruze really knows the city and its outlying areas. Whether you would like to take one of her structured tours, or work with her to devise one suited to your family's interests and tastes, Char can deliver. A fourth-generation Las Vegan whose family has been here since 1855, and who can tell you firsthand about the opening of The

For Your Little Race Car Enthusiast

Race car fans are a very specific subset of sports fans, and Las Vegas has everything race-car themed you could want to get your kid revved up—from food to actual drivable scale models of NASCAR vehicles, virtual car races, an amazing auto museum, a tour of a race car factory, and more. Listed below are some of the best race car–related activities in town.

Eat at the NASCAR Cafe   Theme aplenty here, with autographed team jackets, actual cars, and a genuine love of NASCAR. *Tip:* Eat *after* the rides (Sahara Hotel, 2535 Las Vegas Blvd. S.; © **888/696-2121** or 702/737-2111; www.saharavegas.com)!

Watch the Races at the Las Vegas Motor Speedway   Weekly events here include stock car races, motocross, and hot rod races, but this is also a major stop on the NASCAR circuit. Some of the top races in the country are held here from March through December, with tickets at this 250,000-seat race course at times exceeding $100. But January and February, you can see races for under $10. There are tours available when races aren't on. The action takes place at 7000 Las Vegas Blvd. N. (© **800/644-4442**; www.lvms.com).

Tour the Shelby American Sports Car Museum and Assembly Area   Located next to the Las Vegas Motor Speedway, this free museum displays a dozen classic Shelby American cars (the Shelby Cobra is considered by enthusiasts to be the finest American sports car ever built—designer Carroll Shelby also worked for Ford and created the Mustang Cobra for that company), while the working auto assembly plant shows cars in every stage of production. The museum is located at 6755 Speedway Blvd. (© **702/942-7325**; www.shelbyamerican.com).

Visit the Liberace Museum   While the ladies ooh and aah over the world's largest rhinestone, check out the customized cars that Liberace collected (1775 E. Tropicana Ave.; © **702/798-5595**; www.liberace. com).

Explore the Auto Collections at the Imperial Palace   This constantly changing display features Dusenbergs, vintage commercial vehicles, cars owned by presidents, and, most impressively, a Tucker, one of the 51 manufactured before the company went out of business (Imperial Palace Hotel, 3535 Las Vegas Blvd. S.; © **702/794-3174**; www.auto collections.com).

Race on a Track   SportCenter, 121 E. Sunset Rd. (© **702/317-7777**; www.sportcenterlasvegas.com) offers a go-kart track, allowing kids over 58 inches to zip around. Those 33 inches and up can ride as passengers. **Las Vegas Mini Grand Prix**, 91401 N. Rainbow Blvd. (© **702/259-7000**; www.lvmgp.com), has go-karts and mini Grand Prix racers.

Flamingo, Char has extensively studied southern Nevada's geology and desert wildlife, its regional history, and its Native American cultures. And the thrilling stories she tells are all factual as well as fun.

From haunted mines to mobsters, Char takes you there literally and figuratively as you visit sacred Paiute land, ghost towns, ancient petroglyphs, and many historical landmarks in the city. Along with her storytelling skills, Char brings along visual aids, such as a board of labeled rocks to help illustrate her lecture on local geography. Prompt, knowledgeable, and thoughtful, Char provides tours unlike any other in Las Vegas and is well worth the expense. If you don't have a vehicle with you, Char can rent transport according to the size of your group. She is also knowledgeable about handling clients with disabilities.

Depending on your itinerary, the cost is $125 for a 4-hour tour and $30 per hour for additional hours; transportation is extra. Obviously, if you use your own car, you'll save the cost of the rental vehicle. This is an economical tour option, as well as a unique way of seeing the area. It's a good idea to make arrangements with her prior to leaving home to ensure she's available.

Las Vegas for the Active Family

Both tourist and local families take advantage of the variety of indoor and outdoor sports and activities in greater Las Vegas. Family fun centers and sports parks provide a variety of rides and activities, while parks—city, county, and state—offer recreational activities ranging from swings to horseshoes. You'll also find educational aspects to several parks, because they're often home to museums, historical sites, and ecological preserves.

Expect to drive or taxi to most of the in-city locations. Recreational sports such as rock climbing, cycling, horseback riding, and hiking happen in areas well outside the city—Bonnie Springs, Lake Mead, Mount Charleston, Red Rock Canyon, and Valley of Fire—and are covered in chapter 10, "Side Trips from Las Vegas."

1 Places to Run & Walk

Sometimes it seems as though the only walking anyone does in Las Vegas is to and from their room and up and down the Strip, but the city does have beautiful botanical gardens and public parks. Keep in mind, however, that most parks are not located close to the expensive real estate on the Strip.

NATURE WALKS & BOTANICAL GARDENS

The Gardens at Springs Preserve 😊😊 **All ages.** A public service of the Southern Nevada Water Authority, these gardens, covering 2.4 acres, were designed to educate the public on xeriscaping (creating drought-resistant landscapes). More than 180 species of plants—including cacti, grasses, flowering plants, and succulents—are sectioned into 11 different areas that ripple and explode with flora's bizarre shapes and vibrant colors. Would that the casino plantings on the Strip were so inspired.

3701 W. Alta Dr. ✆ **702/258-3205.** www.springspreserve.org. Free admission. Daily 8am–5pm except holidays. Docents available for guided tours Thurs and Sat 9am–1pm.

University of Nevada, Las Vegas 😊 **All ages.** The beautifully landscaped desert garden, in front of the Marjorie Barrick Museum on the university's campus, is at its most colorful from February through May, when the flowers bloom. But all year-round, the strange and wonderful plants in this xeriscape make for a scenic walk through a surreal landscape. Free brochures about the plants are available in the museum's gift shop. Throughout the campus are trees and other plants with labels. By the concert hall, a stand of weeping willows provides shade for a picnic or rest.

4505 Maryland Pkwy. ✆ **702/895-3381.** Free admission. Daily dawn–dusk.

Wetlands Nature Preserve 😊 **All ages.** Five miles of trails—including walking trails, dirt trails, a concrete ADA trail, and crossover trails—weave through this 130-acre nature preserve where wildlife roams, and indigenous and

Las Vegas for the Active Family

Washington Ave.

1 (3 miles)

2 (1/10 mile)

4 (3 miles)

← To The Meadows

Washington Ave.

6 **5**

Bonanza Rd.

93

Bonanza Rd.

95

599

Alta Dr.

7
(2 miles)

Fremont St.
Experience

Ogden Ave.
Fremont St.

515

95 93

DOWNTOWN

582

8
(3 miles)

← To Red Rock Canyon/
Bonnie Springs Ranch

Charleston Blvd.

**GATEWAY
DISTRICT**

Charleston Blvd.

Oakey Blvd.

Oakey Blvd.

St. Louis Ave.

15

0   0.5 mi

0   0.5 km

N

········· Monorail

▪ Sahara Monorail
station

Sahara Ave.

Sahara Ave.

9

10 →
(5 miles)

604

Sahara

Karen Ave.

LV Hilton

Vegas Valley Dr.

Circus
Circus Dr.

Circus Circus ▪

**NORTH
STRIP**

Stardust Rd.

Riviera
Blvd.

11 **12**

Convention
Center Dr.

13

Desert Inn Rd.

**Las Vegas
Convention
Center**

LV Convention
Center

**Las Vegas
Country Club**

Desert Inn Rd.

14

**Fashion Show
Mall**

**CENTER
STRIP**

Sands Ave.

**Sands
Expo**

▪ Harrah's/ Imperial Palace

▪ Flamingo/Caesars Palace

605

Flamingo Rd.

▪ Bally's & Paris

15

17

**Boulevard
Mall**

Twain Ave.

**Las Vegas
National
Golf Club**

Flamingo Rd.

16 →
(2 miles)

**Hard Rock
Hotel & Casino**

18

**UNIVERSITY
OF NEVADA,
LAS VEGAS**

Harmon Ave.

To Henderson

24 →
(7 miles)

23 (2 miles)

19

**MGM
Grand**

MGM
Grand

Tropicana

20
(1/2 mile)

Tropicana
Ave.

Reno Ave.

**SOUTH
STRIP**

Mandalay
Bay Rd.

15

Russell
Rd.

21

22

A.J. Hackett Bungy **11**
Angel Park Golf Club **1**
Bali Hai Golf Course **21**
Bally's **17**
Craig Ranch Golf Club **3**
The Gardens at Springs Preserve **7**
Desert Rose Golf Club **10**
Escape Adventures/The Cyclery **8**
Flamingo Las Vegas **15**
Flyaway Indoor Skydiving **13**
Heritage Park/Old Mormon Fort **5**
Las Vegas Mini Gran Prix **4**
Las Vegas National Golf Club **14**

Lied Children's Museum
Discovery Zone **6**
Lorenzi Park **2**
Monte Carlo Hotel & Casino **19**
Orleans Hotel & Casino **20**
Powerhouse Indoor Climbing **8**
Riviera Hotel & Casino **12**
Royal Links Golf Club **10**
Sam's Town **16**
Scandia Family Fun Center **9**
Sportcenter **22**
Sunset Park **23**
University of Nevada–Las Vegas **18**
Wetlands Nature Preserve **24**

migratory birds flock. Rare fossilized footprints of a dinosaur are displayed at the visitor center. Picnicking is allowed; plan to spend at least 2 hours strolling along the trails and watching the birds.

7050 Tropicana Blvd. E. ℂ **702/455-7522.** www.co.clark.nv.us/parks/Wetlands/Wetlands_Nature_Preserve. htm. Free admission. Daily dawn–dusk. Visitor center daily 10am–4pm.

PARKS & PLAYGROUNDS

Clark County has over 50 parks and playgrounds, and the City of Las Vegas administers to an additional 50. A complete listing can be found at **www.co. clark.nv.us/parks/homepage.htm**. State parks can be found online at **www. state.nv.us/stparks**. The following are the largest parks in the city, with a variety of activity areas, and are the sites of many festivals and events.

Heritage Park/Old Mormon Fort   All ages. The Old Mormon Fort, part of the Old Las Vegas Mormon State Historic Park, adjacent to the city's Heritage Park, draws tourists, historians, and field trips, but locals come here for the Heritage's playgrounds and picnic grounds. There's also a desert demonstration garden, also known as a xeriscape, which displays different drought-resistant plants. Tour the fort, and then have a picnic lunch.

500 E. Washington Ave. ℂ **702/486-3511.** www.parks.nv.gov/olvmf.htm. Free admission to Heritage Park. Admission to Old Mormon Fort $3 adults, $2 children 6–12, free for children under 5. Park daily 7am–9pm. Fort daily 8am–4:30pm.

Lorenzi Park ⚘ **All ages.** With picnic and barbecue areas along with slides and swings, sports fields, tennis courts, and a wheelchair fitness course, this park is a favorite for local families. The artificial lake is stocked with fish for catching or feeding, and waterfowl will beg for the crumbs you scatter. This is the site of the annual Sammy Davis, Jr., Festival, which honors the performer and civil rights pioneer. There is also a unique garden for the blind, with scented and textured plants, that the sighted will also enjoy. The Nevada State Museum (ℂ **702/ 486-5205**) is also located on the park grounds, allowing you to fit a picnic and play time in with a trip to the museum, which is stuffed full of taxidermied animals and a variety of other features, such as a replica of Bugsy Siegel's hotel suite and Paiute Indian artifacts.

3333 W. Washington Ave. ℂ **702/229-6297.** Free admission. Hours vary by area and season.

Sunset Park ⚘ **All ages.** This huge park (and lake!) features something for almost everyone, with multiuse fields and areas dedicated to specific sports including disc-golf, horseshoes, and radio-controlled boating. Residents of Las Vegas make good use of the ball fields, a swimming pool, tennis courts, and the walking/jogging track. The lake is available on a year-round basis for fishing. The State of Nevada Department of Fish and Wildlife stocks the lake with trout in the cooler winter months and catfish in the summer months; a fishing license, with a trout stamp, is required for anyone 13 and older. The Renaissance Festival–Age of Chivalry event is held here annually.

2601 E. Sunset Rd. ℂ **702/455-8200.** www.co.clark.nv.us/parks/Urban_Locations.htm. Free admission. Hours vary by area and season.

⌐*Tips* **License Required**

For fishing licenses, required for those 13 and older, and for more fishing information, contact the Department of Wildlife at ℂ **702/486-5127.**

2 Family Fun Centers & Indoor Playgrounds

Las Vegas Mini Gran Prix **Ages 4 and up.** The main attraction at this 7-acre family fun center with a roller coaster, slide, arcade, and snack bar is the opportunity to race on four different minitracks. Height requirements vary from ride to ride, but children must be at least 36 inches for any of the attractions. Children 42 inches to 54 inches can drive themselves on the Kiddie Karts (two rides per ticket), while taller kids can speed around on go-karts. There's also a mini Grand Prix course for those 16 and older. On the roller coaster, adults ride free with a paying child (who gets two rides per ticket); for the mini Grand Prix cars, children ride for free with a paying adult. Yes, it's a bit confusing, but you will have fun.

1401 N. Rainbow Blvd. ℂ **702/259-7000** or 702/259-7001. www.lvmgp.com. Rides $5.50 each, $25 for 5. Mon–Thurs 10am–10pm; Fri–Sun 10am–11pm.

Scandia Family Fun Center ★ *Value* **Ages 4 and up.** You can play miniature golf, ride the bumper boats, or race go-karts at this easily accessed, much-beloved family amusement center. Just off the Strip, Scandia provides hours of amusement for the younger set, though kids in their teens may start getting antsy after a bit. There's nothing thrilling or astounding here—just wholesome family entertainment that runs 24/7 when school is not in session. Granted, the place is a bit used and worn, and the games in the arcade are nowhere as flashy as those at GameWorks, but the miniature golf courses are cute, and smaller kids ride free with adults on the bumper boats and go-karts. This is a perennial favorite with locals and visitors who want to entertain their wee ones for a few hours and don't want to go broke in the process.

2900 Sirius Ave. (at Rancho Dr., just south of Sahara Ave.). ℂ **702/364-0070.** Free admission; differing prices for each game or activity, free for children under 6; Super Saver Pass $12 (includes 1 round of miniature golf, 2 rides, and 5 game tokens); Unlimited wristband package $18 (includes unlimited bumper boat and car rides, unlimited miniature golf, and 10 tokens for batting cages or arcade games). June to mid-Aug daily 24 hr.; mid-Aug to May Sun–Thurs 10am–midnight, Fri–Sat 10am–2am.

SportCenter ★ **Ages 4 and up.** Almost all things sporting can be played at this vast theme park. Indoors, the AllSport Arena, complete with bleachers and video screen, hosts events such as league competition pee-wee football on the convertible, multipurpose area, while the Rockreation Sport Climbing Wall, reputed to be one of the best in the city, looms 40 feet up. Golfers can practice putting on an 18-hole indoor putts-only course, whose water features and other challenges make this an authentic short game. Fresh air fans can find it here in Major League Stadium, which features 16 batting cages with various speeds for all levels of baseball and softball, and a home run walk at the far end featuring scenes from famous ballparks for that homer-at-Yankee-Stadium feel. Race fans love zipping around the outdoor go-kart track in NASCAR-replica vehicles. (Drivers must be over 58 in., while passengers must be 36 in. or taller.) Naturally, there is also a video arcade here.

121 E. Sunset Rd. ℂ **702/317-7777.** www.sportcenterlasvegas.com. $7 rock climbing, $5 racing, $2 for 20 pitches. Mon–Thurs batting cages only 3–8pm; entire park Fri 3–9pm, Sat noon–9pm, Sun 2–8pm.

3 Sports

BICYCLING The **Las Vegas Valley Bicycle Club** (ℂ **702/897-7800**) hosts rides throughout the week. A prerecorded message will fill you in on the itineraries, which can be anywhere from 13 to 45 miles. The length of the rides may

Not for the Faint of Heart

If the thrill rides weren't exciting enough for your teenagers, they might want to try bungee jumping. Children ages 13–18 must have their parents—with ID—sign them up to take this not-for-the-fainthearted plunge. **A. J. Hackett Bungy,** 810 Circus Circus Dr. (© 702/385-4321; www.aj-hackett.com), provides the know-how—a worldwide chain, they've helped over a million satisfied customers make the (very secure) leap of faith from a 175-foot tower. The first jump is $59, jumps two and three are $29 each; the fourth is free. Expect a wait of up to an hour.

To experience another form of weightlessness, but this time indoors, check out **Flyaway Indoor Skydiving,** 200 Convention Center Dr. (© 877/545-8093 or 702/731-4768; www.flyawayindoorskydiving.com), where you don a special flight suit and receive a 20-minute training session in weightless movement before a jet engine under the floor blasts on, keeping you hovering above the ground for another 15 minutes in its exhaust (no fumes, just air). There are no age requirements, but you must be between 40 and 230 lbs. Look for coupons in tourist magazines for discounts on the $50 ticket price. Open daily 10am to 7pm.

make them impractical for some kids; however, they are welcome with their guardians. Helmets are required, and you will need a bike; all manner of bike equipment can be rented from **Escape Adventures,** 8221 W. Charleston Blvd. (© **702/838-6966;** www.escapeadventures.com), starting at $35 first day; $30 for half-day or an additional day. If biking around the city doesn't strike your fancy, Escape Adventures also provides guided bike and hiking tours of the desert areas outside of Las Vegas.

BOWLING   Bowling is astoundingly popular in Las Vegas. The 56-lane alleys at **Sam's Town & Gambling Hall,** 5111 Boulder Hwy. (© **702/456-7777;** www.samstownlv.com), are open 24 hours, while the 70-lane **Orleans,** 4500 W. Tropicana Ave. (© **702/365-7111;** www.orleanscasino.com), offers child care (for league bowlers) for up to 3 hours. Bowling costs at each facility vary depending on day and time, but expect to pay about $2.75 a game, per person, plus $2.25 for shoe rental; midnight bowling for $1 per game per person is offered from Monday through Thursday, midnight to 8am.

GOLF   Desert golfing strikes something atavistic in even the highest-scoring duffer, and Las Vegas, with 63 courses—32 of which are public, resort, or semi-private—is a world-class location for teeing off. Players who have designed courses include greats Arnold Palmer, Jack Nicklaus, and Chi Chi Rodriguez. If you have any doubt about golf's impact on Las Vegas, consider this: The University of Nevada, Las Vegas offers a bachelor's degree in recreation with a PGA-approved emphasis on professional golf management. Greens fees can range from as low as $37 upward into the hundreds of dollars for a round of golf, depending on the course, season, and time of day you choose to play. You should also factor in renting a cart, because you won't want to carry your bags in the heat. Golf is a great family activity; all ages can play (little ones should have their own clubs) on the Vegas courses, and many courses offer reduced rates for junior golfing in the afternoon. (Juniors must walk.)

Serious golfers should contact **American Golf** (© **800/468-7918;** www. americangolf.com), a nationwide reservations service that's based in Arizona. They can help you arrange golf packages and book hard-to-get tee times in Las Vegas.

Local favorite **Angel Park Golf Club,** 100 S. Rampart Blvd. (© **888/ 446-5358** or 702/254-4653; www.angelpark.com), is a 36-hole par-70/71 public course. Arnold Palmer originally designed the Mountain and Palm courses; several years later, the Palm course was redesigned by Bob Cupp. The Palm Course, with gently rolling fairways, offers golfers of all abilities a challenging yet forgiving layout. The Mountain Course has rolling natural terrain and gorgeous panoramic views. In addition to these two challenging 18-hole courses, Angel Park offers a night-lit Cloud 9 Course (12 holes for daylight play, 9 at night), where each hole is patterned after a famous par-3. You can reserve tee times up to 60 days in advance with a credit card guarantee. Greens fees run between $65 and $160, with discounted twilight rates available. Juniors, those golfers under 17, can call the club daily and find out when "they are letting the juniors out." This arcane phrase means that once the course clears out from duffers finishing up their rounds (usually about 3 hr. before dark), the youngsters can come on for a quick 18 holes. However, all juniors, who pay the incredibly low rate of $15, must walk the course—no carts are allowed. Under 17s can also play at reduced rates throughout the day with a paying adult; they should ask for the "junior card holder rate." **Bali Hai Golf Club,** 5160 Las Vegas Blvd. S. (© **888/397-2499;** www.waltersgolf.com), is one of the area's newest and most exclusive golf addresses. This multimillion-dollar course, built in 2000, is located on the Strip just south of Mandalay Bay. Done in a wild South Seas theme, the par-72 course has over 7 acres of water features, including an island green, palm trees, and tropical foliage everywhere you look. All golf carts are equipped with global positioning satellite (GPS) tracking systems. And celebrity chef Wolfgang Puck opened his newest Vegas eatery here. All this glamour will cost you; greens fees run from $175 to $295, and even at those prices, tee times are often booked 6 months in advance. Unfortunately, they do not offer junior rates, but, as with all courses, all ages are allowed to golf here.

Two new greens have recently been added to **Black Mountain Golf & Country Club,** in nearby Henderson at 500 Greenway Rd. (© **702/565-7933;** www. golfblackmountain.com); an 18-hole, par-72 semiprivate course, which requires reservations 4 days in advance. Unpredictable winds can make your game a challenge on this course, which has greens fees ranging from $45 to $75. Expect to see wildlife here, including roadrunners. Juniors can walk the course from noon on for $10.

Greens fees are a bargain at **Craig Ranch Golf Club,** 628 W. Craig Rd., between Losee Road and Martin Luther King Boulevard (© **702/642-9700**), a flat, 18-hole, par-70 public course with many trees and bunkers, where both narrow and open fairways feature Bermuda turf. You can reserve tee times 7 days in advance, and expect to pay $18 walking, $26 with cart. Juniors can walk on after 12pm for a $15 fee. Another public course accepting tee time reservations 7 days in advance is the 18-hole, par-71 **Desert Rose Golf Club,** 5483 Clubhouse Dr., 3 blocks west of Nellis Boulevard, off Sahara Avenue (© **702/431-4653**). Built in 1963 and designed by Dick Wilson and Joe Lee, the course's narrow fairways feature Bermuda turf. Renting a cart adds an additional $12 to the greens fees, which can range from $53 to $75. Juniors can start walking at 2pm for only $5.

The 1996 Las Vegas Invitational, won by Tiger Woods, was held at the **Las Vegas National Golf Club,** 911 Desert Inn Rd., between Maryland Parkway and Eastern Avenue (© **877/378-6033**), an 18-hole, par-72 public course. The steep greens fees of $180 include cart rental. The classic layout of this course includes over half a dozen water hazards. Discounted tee times are often available. Reservations are taken up to 60 days in advance for a $5 to $7 fee. There is no junior rate.

Legendary Scottish golf holes, including St. Andrews Road Hole and the Postage Stamp at the Royal Troon, are among the famous fairways on the British Open tour that are faithfully re-created at the **Royal Links Golf Club,** 5995 East Vegas Valley, east of Boulder Highway, between Flamingo and Sahara (© **702/450-8000**), making for a unique game and an interesting history lesson. The 19th hole is designed to resemble a medieval castle, complete with an English Pub inside. You can expect to pay $135 to $250 for the greens fee; there is no junior rate here.

ROCK CLIMBING If you want to try your hand at this strenuous desert sport, which works out both the mind and body, see p. 267 for more information on outdoor rock climbing in the Las Vegas area. However, you should consider practicing at an indoor climbing facility before scrambling up the walls of Red Rock Canyon. **Rockreation Sport Climbing Wall** at SportCenter (p. 184) offers a 40-foot challenge, while both **GameWorks** (p. 157) and **Adventuredome** (p. 166) have smaller versions in amusement zone environments. True indoor climbing enthusiasts will want to head to **Powerhouse Indoor Climbing Center,** 8201 Charleston Blvd. (© **702/254-5604**), where textured terrain mimics caves, roofs, buttresses, and other rock formations. The floor is padded, and shoes and a harness can be rented. First timers will pay $40, which includes a lesson and rental of the harness and shoes. More experienced climbers can pay $14 for a day pass, with an $8 shoe and harness fee. Acrophobes may want to buy a boulder pass for $10, which will keep them climbing at a lower height.

TENNIS Tennis buffs should choose one of the many hotels in town that have tennis courts because locals keep the public courts in the parks busy. You should reserve a hotel court when you make your room reservations. Some hotels beyond those in this section do have tennis courts, but because they're not particularly child friendly, we didn't list them in the accommodations chapter or here.

Bally's (© **702/739-4111;** www.ballyslv.com) has eight night-lit hard courts and a pro shop. Fees per hour range from $10 to $15 for guests, $15 to $20 for nonguests. Hours vary seasonally. Reservations are required at **The Flamingo Las Vegas** (© **702/733-3444;** www.caesars.com), which has four outdoor hard courts, all lit for night play. Open to the public daily from 7am to 7pm (closes 6pm Sat–Sun), rates are $20 per hour for nonguests, $12 for guests. Lessons are available, and there's also a pro shop. The **Monte Carlo Hotel & Casino** (© **702/730-7777;** www.montecarlo.com) has three night-lit courts available to the public for $15 per hour. **The Riviera Hotel & Casino** (© **702/734-5110**) has only two courts, both available for night play; for nonguests the charge is $10 an hour, while hotel guests play free.

In addition to hotels, the **University of Nevada, Las Vegas (UNLV),** Harmon Avenue just east of Swenson Street (© **702/895-0844;** www.unlv.edu), has a dozen courts (all lit for night play) that are open weekdays from 6am to 9:45pm, weekends 8am to 9pm. Rates are $5 per person per day. You should call before going to find out if a court is available.

For the Special-Needs Child

The **Adaptive Recreation Center** (℃ 702/229-6704; www.ci.las-vegas. nv.us/1481_1486.htm) is a service of the city of Las Vegas and is the only Adaptive Recreation Program in the state. As of this writing, the center is open only to residents of Nevada. Designed for those with special needs, the recreation program offers after-school activities for ages 7 to 21, while ages 14 to 21 can participate in the Dynamic Teen Recreation program. There are also additional individual and team sports activities offered. For additional information, write to ARP, 749 Veterans Memorial Dr., Las Vegas, NV 89101.

Lorenzi Park, 3333 W. Washington Ave., where the Adaptive Recreation Program bases most of its activities, features a wheelchair fitness course and a garden for the blind, both of which are open to the public.

4 Classes & Workshops

Throughout the year, there are numerous free and low-cost activities for children and families available through **Clark County Parks and Community Services** ℃ **702/455-8200;** www.co.clark.nv.us/parks/homepage.htm). They offer a changing calendar of classes, workshops, and activities for children of all ages— as well as for adults and seniors—at locations throughout the greater Las Vegas area. Recent offerings included laser tag, fossil hunting, and horseback riding. Workshops for teens emphasize academic and leadership skills. Teens and 'tweens can attend seasonal dances and parties, while younger kids can participate in classes such as Alphabet Art, music, dance, and gymnastics. E-mail or call for a brochure, published four times a year, outlining what's available.

Lied Discovery Children's Museum 😊😊   **Ages 10 and under.** This innovative museum (p. 162) provides two workshops a day, Tuesday through Sunday. In the morning, children 5 and under can do seasonal arts and crafts in Explorative Play, while in the afternoon, those 6 and older work on more age-appropriate projects called Creative Experiences. Both are geared toward learning, with an emphasis on fun and a subtext of developing skills. These programs are free with admission. There are also Saturday workshops. At press time, the museum, in conjunction with Las Vegas Library Young People's Department, offered the Little Learners program, with classes in home science experiments as their Saturday events. There are also family theater workshops offered. Toddlers can play in the Desert Discovery area, while parents with babies are invited to play in the Baby Oasis.

833 Las Vegas Blvd. N. (½ block south of Washington, across the street from Cashman Field). ℃ **702/382-3445.** www.ldcm.org. Admission $7 adults, $6 seniors and children 1–17. AE, DC, DISC, MC, V. Tues–Sun 10am–5pm.

Shopping for the Whole Family

Shopping in Las Vegas falls into two categories—tourist and local. Tourists tend to stick to the hotel shopping malls and retail areas to sate their spending urges, while locals flock primarily to the malls, which—as in any urban center—are vast. You'll find many of the same large chain shops (such as bebe, Banana Republic, and Gap) in both styles of shopping venues, but local malls also host numerous department stores ranging from Sears to Neiman Marcus in addition to branches of national retail shops.

Fashion Show Mall, the only hotel-less shopping mall located on the Strip, underwent a massive renovation (completed in fall of 2003), which added more stores, including New York's venerable Bloomingdale's and a Nordstrom. The expansion makes Fashion Show Las Vegas's largest mall, at 2 million square feet, even eclipsing the Boulevard Mall, another Vegas

supershopping structure, which boasts 1.2 million square feet of shopping space.

Outlet shopping has become a big business in Las Vegas; there are regularly scheduled tours to both the Primm outlets and the closer Las Vegas Outlet Center, where consumers can find deep discounts on clothing, accessories, and household goods. A second related venue, Las Vegas Premium Outlets, opened near downtown in early 2004, with 120 outlet shops. Las Vegas is also a popular spot for collectors who search for finds along Charleston Boulevard, starting in the middle of the 1600 block of East Charleston Boulevard, where little stores in old houses dating from the 1930s line the street.

The majority of stores throughout Las Vegas accept American Express, Discover, MasterCard, and Visa, in addition to debit cards with a Visa or

Top Toys for Kids

In Vegas, logos are everywhere, and most souvenirs are nothing more than overpriced junk with a logo stamped on it. But you will find some cool stuff for kids, if they don't find it first. Here are our favorite Vegas children's toys:

- Excalibur's **Princess Hats:** These cone-shaped hats come in fuchsia, royal blue, and gold and silver, and from the cone hangs a neat veil ($9). Our 7-year-old wore hers all day long.
- The Mirage's **Stuffed White Tigers:** They come in a number of sizes; the $22 version is absolutely irresistible and is of good quality.
- The Luxor's **King Tut doll** ($30) or **Plush Camel** ($17).
- Of course, you can't go wrong with two of the cheapest gifts in the hotel gift stores: **used casino dice** ($1–$2) and **playing cards** (75¢–$1.50).

MasterCard logo, and traveler's checks. Some stores also accept traditional ATM cards requiring a PIN.

Most traditional stores in Las Vegas open at 10am and close at 7pm. Malls, whose openings and closings vary by location, have expanded hours on weekends and holidays; mall stores generally follow the hours of the mall itself. The physical spaces of hotel arcades are always open to tempt wee-hour window shoppers, but their actual hours vary from shop to shop, hotel to hotel, with some shops keeping traditional hours and others open around the clock.

The sales tax in Las Vegas is 7%.

1 The Shopping Scene

SHOPPING DISTRICTS

For the most part, Las Vegas's main shopping districts are the malls and hotel shopping promenades (see below), with the notable exception of Maryland Parkway, a long swath that runs parallel to the Strip to the east. There, in addition to the huge Boulevard Mall, you'll find drugstores, a Toys "R" Us, and vintage shops, hipster clothing emporia, and tattoo parlors.

MALLS

Boulevard Mall   Anchored by Sears, JCPenney, Macy's, Dillard's, and Marshalls, the Boulevard's 170-plus stores are geared to the average consumer. The wide variety of shops—offering moderately priced shoes and clothing for the entire family, books and gifts, jewelry, and home furnishings, plus more than a dozen fast-food eateries—means you can find just about find anything you need here. The shops and restaurants are arranged in arcade fashion on a single floor occupying 1.2 million square feet. There's free valet parking. The mall is open Monday through Saturday from 10am to 9pm, and Sunday from 11am to 6pm. 3528 S. Maryland Pkwy. (between Twain Ave. and Desert Inn Rd.). 🕐 702/732-8949. www.blvdmall.com.

Fashion Show Mall   Presently comprising more than 200 shops, restaurants, and services, this luxurious and centrally located mall is anchored by Neiman Marcus, Saks Fifth Avenue, Macy's, Robinsons-May, Dillard's, Bloomingdales and Nordstrom. Thanks to a $300-million expansion completed in the fall of 2003, Fashion Show now sports a wild, high-tech Strip entrance. The centerpiece of the expansion is the Cloud, the largest stainless-steel screen in existence: 479 feet long, 160 feet wide, up to 21 feet thick, and 182 feet tall. The 900-ton structure is actually a video screen, running ads from stores inside the mall, complete with a concert-quality sound system. Valet parking is available, and you can even arrange to have your car hand-washed while you shop. The mall is open Monday through Friday from 10am to 9pm, Saturday from 10am to 8pm, and Sunday from 11am until 6pm. 3200 Las Vegas Blvd. S. (at the corner of Spring Mountain Rd.). 🕐 702/369-0704. www.thefashionshow.com.

The Meadows   Fountains and trees enhance The Meadows' ultramodern, high-ceilinged interior, comprising 144 shops, services, and eateries, anchored by four department stores: Macy's, Dillard's, Sears, and JCPenney. In addition, there is full array of apparel for the entire family (including maternity wear, petites, and large sizes), 15 shoe stores, an extensive food court, and shops purveying toys, books, CDs and tapes, luggage, gifts, jewelry, home furnishings, and accessories. Thankfully, there are a few comfortable conversation/seating areas for resting your feet between purchases. The Meadows is open Monday through Friday from 10am to 9pm, Saturday from 10am to 9pm, and Sunday from 10am to 6pm. 4300 Meadows Lane (at the intersection of Valley View and U.S. 95). 🕐 702/878-4849. www.themeadowsmall.com.

Las Vegas's Shopping Scene

Washington Ave.

Lied Discovery Children's Museum ■

Washington Ave.

Bonanza Rd.

Bonanza Rd.

Fremont St. Experience

← To The Meadows

❶ (1 mile)

DOWNTOWN

Alta Dr.

Bonneville

Ogden Ave. Fremont St.

❷

Charleston Blvd.

GATEWAY DISTRICT

← To Red Rock Canyon/ Bonnie Springs Ranch

Oakey Blvd.

Charleston Blvd.

Oakey Blvd.

| 0 | | 0.5 mi |
| 0 | | 0.5 km |

St. Louis Ave.

❸

Sahara Ave.

Sahara Ave.

······· Monorail

▯ Sahara Monorail station

Sahara

Karen Ave.

Vegas Valley Dr.

LV Hilton

Las Vegas Country Club

Circus Circus Dr.

Riviera Blvd.

❺

❹

NORTH STRIP

Stardust Rd.

Convention Center Dr.

Las Vegas Convention Center

Desert Inn Rd.

LV Convention Center

Desert Inn Rd.

Fashion Show Mall ❻

■ Wynn Las Vegas

Boulevard Mall

❼

Las Vegas National Golf Club

❽

Tram

Mirage ■

Sands Expo ❾

Sands Ave.

Twain Ave.

CENTER STRIP

❿

Harrah's/ Imperial Palace

← ⓫

⓬ ⓭

Flamingo/Caesars Palace

Flamingo Rd.

Flamingo Rd.

⓯ ⓮

Bally's & Paris

Harmon Ave.

⓰

UNIVERSITY OF NEVADA, LAS VEGAS

⓱

⓲ MGM Grand

To Henderson (Green Valley Ranch Resort & Sunset Station)

← To Orleans

⓳

Tropicana Ave.

Reno Ave.

SOUTH STRIP

Mandalay Bay Rd.

⓴

㉑

McCARRAN INTERNATIONAL AIRPORT

Russell Rd.

㉒ (3 miles)

Avenue Shoppes (Bally's) **14**

Boulevard Mall **7**

Carnaval Court (Harrah's) **10**

Circus Circus **5**

Crystal Court (The Flamingo) **13**

Desert Passage (Aladdin/Planet Hollywood) **16**

Excalibur **19**

Fashion Show Mall **6**

Forum Shops (Caesars Palace) **12**

Giza Galleria (Luxor Las Vegas) **20**

Grand Canal Shoppes (The Venetian) **9**

Las Vegas Outlet Center **22**

Las Vegas Premium Outlets **2**

Mandalay Place **21**

Masquerade Village (The Rio) **11**

The Meadows **1**

The Monte Carlo **17**

The Riviera **4**

Star Lane Shops (MGM Grand) **18**

Tower Shops (The Stratosphere) **3**

Treasure Island **8**

Via Bellagio **15**

FACTORY OUTLETS

Las Vegas has two big factory outlet centers, one just a few miles past the southern end of the Strip (see below) and the other just off I-15 near Charleston Boulevard on the way to downtown.

Dedicated bargain hunters may want to make the roughly 40-minute drive along I-15 (there's also a $10 shuttle from New York–New York) to the Fashion Outlet at Primm (© **888/424-6898;** www.fashionoutletlasvegas.com), right on the border of California and Nevada. On your left will be a large factory outlet with some designer names prominent enough to make that drive well worthwhile—Kenneth Cole, Donna Karan, even Williams-Sonoma, among several others (p. 261).

Las Vegas Outlet Center You'll save up to 75% off retail prices here, where 155 air-conditioned outlets vie for your cash and credit cards. This bargain shopper's heaven features kids clothes at Oshkosh B'Gosh, along with offerings from Danskin, Casual Corner, Liz Claiborne, Perry Ellis, Calvin Klein, Levi's, Nike, Dress Barn, Leggs/Hanes/Bali, Esprit, Reebok, Jockey, Oneida, Van Heusen, and Tommy Hilfiger. Housewares and home goods include Bose (electronics), Royal Doulton, Waterford (crystal), and Black & Decker (tools). Children will enjoy the carousel; there is also a food court. Open Monday through Saturday from 10am to 10pm and Sunday from 10am to 9pm. 7400 Las Vegas Blvd. S. (at Warm Springs Rd.). © **702/896-5599.** www.premiumoutlets.com.

Las Vegas Premium Outlets The sister mall to the Las Vegas Outlet Center, this one is more accessible but potentially uncomfortable in the deep of winter and height of summer: It's not enclosed, so you walk from store to store exposed to the elements. You'll save between 20% and 65% at 120 stores, including Armani Exchange, Coach, Guess, and Polo Ralph Lauren at the high end, and Bass, Levi's, Rave, and Eddie Bauer in the midrange. The food court has both indoor and outdoor munching. Open Monday to Saturday 10am to 10pm, Sunday 10am to 9pm. 875 S. Grand Central Pkwy. (near Charleston), © **702/474-7500.** www.premiumoutlets.com.

HOTEL SHOPPING PROMENADES

Just about every Las Vegas hotel offers some shopping opportunities. The following have the most extensive areas. The physical spaces of these shopping centers are always open, but individual stores keep unpredictable hours. All hotels have convenience stores, which should be able to provide you with film, batteries, and disposable cameras.

Note: The Forum Shops at Caesars, the Grand Canal Shoppes at The Venetian, and the Desert Passage at the Aladdin/Planet Hollywood—as much sightseeing attractions as shopping opportunities—are in the must-see category.

ALADDIN/PLANET HOLLYWOOD The stores in Desert Passage, the Vegas version of a Middle Eastern souk, are an assortment of the usual-suspect mid- and high-end name brands, including Sur La Table, a cookware and kitchen supply boutique—no doubt for those who have just hit the jackpot and would rather buy expensive enamel pots and ceramic knives instead of expensive jewelry. Desert Brats has clothes for kids, which are far more charming than the store's name. Sharper Image, a national chain, features upscale items, including nose-hair trimmers, travel clocks, and ionizing pet brushes. Re-creations of the romantic, mystical architecture of Egypt, Morocco, and Turkey provide the backdrop for your browsing while, hourly, the painted-desert sky clouds hover and a "thunderstorm" rages. Don't worry—the rain only falls over the simulated lake. Acrobats, jugglers, and belly dancers all add to the visuals, and the scents

Hey, Big Spenders!

This is the perfect vacation. My husband likes to gamble; we like to shop. And trust me, my daughters and I can do more damage in an hour at a Vegas mall than he can in an hour on the tables!

—Laura, mother of 13- and 16-year-old girls

of perfume and spices float about, evoking bazaars of Babylon, minus the camel dung and flies. If your packages become too heavy, take the pedicabs—bicycle-powered carts pedaled by youths who gratefully accept tips. *Note:* Despite Planet Hollywood's purchase of the Aladdin, the Desert Passage should remain largely as is.

BALLY'S   You can always dispatch the kids to the video arcade while you shop in the Avenue Shoppes, which include several gift shops, art galleries, and a pool-wear shop. The offerings are meager by comparison to other hotel arcades, but the recent addition of a walkway to neighbor Paris has added more stores and restaurants.

BELLAGIO   Via Bellagio, in Las Vegas's most notoriously kid-unfriendly hotel, features the most glamorous and expensive collection of stores in any hotel. Armani, Chanel, Prada, Hermès, and Gucci are among the clothiers featured here. Fred Leighton, with its impressive selection of vintage and modern gems, and American standard-bearer Tiffany provide additional sparkle. Children of guests should be accompanied by parents prepared to whip out the platinum card. Otherwise, spend your time shopping someplace fun.

CAESARS PALACE   Even if you don't like to shop, Caesars Palace's shopping areas are a must-see. The Appian Way, an impressive selection of shops, is highlighted by an 18-foot-high Carrara-marble replica of Michelangelo's *David*. But the real draw are the fabulous **Forum Shops** ✸. Independently operated, this 250,000-square-foot Rodeo-Drive-meets-the-Roman-Empire affair overwhelms visitors who enter through a 48-foot triumphal arch entranceway. Beneath the painted Mediterranean sky that changes as the day progresses from rosy-tinted dawn to twinkling evening stars, you'll find acres of marble, lofty Corinthian columns with gold capitals, and a welcoming goddess of fortune under a central dome. The architecture and sculpture here span a period from 300 B.C. to A.D. 1700, framing 70 prestigious emporia including Louis Vuitton, Plaza Escada, Bernini, Christian Dior, A/X Armani Exchange, bebe, Caché, Gucci, Ann Taylor, and Gianni Versace, along with many other clothing, shoe, and jewelry stores. Every hour on the hour, the Festival Fountain show commences, when seemingly immovable "marble" animatronic statues of Bacchus (a bit tipsy), a lyre-playing Apollo, Pluto, and Venus come to life for a 7-minute revel with dancing waters and high-tech laser effects.

In 1998, the Forum Shops added an extension. The centerpiece is a giant Roman Hall, featuring a 50,000-gallon circular aquarium and another fountain that also comes to life with a show of fire (don't stand too close—it gets really hot), dancing waters, and animatronic figures as the mythical continent of Atlantis rises and falls every hour.

In this shopping area, you'll find a number of stores for adults, including a DKNY, Emporio Armani, Niketown, Fendi, Polo for Ralph Lauren, and Guess. Kids' Castle stocks clothes for the wee ones. Virgin Megastore, the only record/bookstore on the Strip, is also here. Also in the shops are Wolfgang Puck's Chinois Café (p. 137) and the Cheesecake Factory (p. 135).

One more expansion is underway as you read this: Another 175,000 square feet of space between the existing building and the Strip, featuring a three-story open courtyard, debuted in late 2004.

The shops at Caesars are open Sunday to Thursday from 10am to 11pm and Friday and Saturday from 10am to midnight. Strollers and wheelchairs are available, free of charge.

CIRCUS CIRCUS   Between the casino and Adventuredome (p. 166), about 15 shops offer a wide selection of gifts and sundries, logo items, toys and games, jewelry, liquor, resort apparel for the entire family, T-shirts, homemade fudge/candy/soft ice cream, and, appropriately, clown dolls and puppets. The newer shopping arcade, adjacent to the Adventuredome, is themed as a European village with cobblestone walkways and fake woods, decorated with replicas of vintage circus posters.

EXCALIBUR   Kids will enjoy shopping for plastic swords, the perfect accessory for horned viking hats and princess crowns also available in the shops of The Realm. Dragon's Lair features items ranging from pewter swords and shields to full suits of armor. Merlin's Mystic Shop carries crystals, luck charms, and gargoyles. Other shops carry more conventional wares: gifts, candy, jewelry, women's clothing, and Excalibur logo items. At Fantasy Faire, you can have your photo taken in Renaissance attire. And, most important, they have a branch of Krispy Kreme Doughnuts!

THE FLAMINGO LAS VEGAS   The Crystal Court shopping promenade here accommodates men's and women's clothing/accessories stores, gift shops, and a variety of other emporia selling jewelry, beachwear, Southwestern crafts, fresh-baked goods, logo items, children's gifts, toys, and games.

HARRAH'S   Harrah's has an outdoor shopping center called Carnaval Court with a bandstand and a bar. It's small and crowded, especially when a band is playing and the margaritas are flowing. The highlight is a Ghirardelli Chocolate store, a branch of the famous San Francisco–based chocolate company.

LUXOR   The Giza Galleria is a 20,000-square-foot shopping arcade with eight full shops, including the kids' shop Tiny Tuts, a tie and sock shop, plus a metaphysical gimcracks shop, a place to purchase logo items (your name in hieroglyphics on mugs and T-shirts), and more. Adjacent to the Giza Gallery is the Cairo Bazaar with plenty of Egyptian-themed statuary, jewelry, and knickknacks.

MANDALAY BAY   Mandalay Place is a small boutique mall in an expansion of Mandalay Bay on a sky bridge between Mandalay Bay and Luxor. Its 100,000 square feet house 40 or so shops, including 55 Degrees, a wine shop; Nike Golf; Oilily, an interesting children's store from Holland; Chocolate Swan; and the Burger Barn, which serves a $60 Kobe beef and foie gras hamburger. Mandalay Place also boasts The Reading Room, the only bookstore in a casino hotel mall anywhere.

MGM GRAND   You can still find the semibanished figures from the hotel's original *Wizard of Oz* diorama along Star Lane Shops, more than a dozen upscale emporia, which line the corridors en route from the parking garage. Studio Walk is another shopping area, adjacent to the main casino, which features some upscale boutiques, souvenir shops, and several restaurants.

MONTE CARLO   An arcade of retail shops here includes several upscale clothing, timepiece, eyewear, and gift boutiques plus a Lance Burton magic paraphernalia shop, and the unfortunately named Brats, a kids' clothing shop.

THE RIO   The 60,000-square-foot, two-story Masquerade Village is done up as a European village. It features a wide variety of shops, including the nation's largest Nicole Miller and the N'awlins store, which includes "authentic" voodoo items, Mardi Gras masks, and so forth.

THE RIVIERA   The Riviera has a fairly extensive shopping arcade comprising art galleries, jewelers, a creative photographer, and shops specializing in women's shoes and handbags, clothing for the entire family, furs, gifts, logo items, toys, phones and electronic gadgets, and chocolates.

THE STRATOSPHERE   The internationally themed second-floor Tower Shops promenade, housing more than 50 stores, is entered via an escalator from the casino. Some shops are in "Paris," along the Rue Lafayette and Avenue de l'Opéra (there are replicas of the Eiffel Tower and Arc de Triomphe in this section), while others occupy Hong Kong and New York City streetscapes. It's fine for shopping if you are staying there, but pales by comparison to Caesars, The Venetian, Paris Las Vegas, and Aladdin/Planet Hollywood.

TREASURE ISLAND   Doubling as a portrait gallery of famed buccaneers, Treasure Island's shopping promenade has wooden ship figureheads and battling pirates suspended from its ceiling. The Treasure Island Store, a basic hotel gift/sundry shop, also offers a good amount of pirate-themed merchandise, including some cool skull stuff, which kids may like. Fans of Cirque du Soleil will find their logo items at the Crow's Nest, en route to The Mirage monorail, and also in a shop near the ticket office.

THE VENETIAN 🐾   Directly accessible from the outside, so you can avoid the casino and other hotel distractions, the Grand Canal Shoppes are a direct challenge to Caesars's shopping eminence. You'll find the usual high- and medium-end brand names: Jimmy Choo, Mikimoto, Movado, New Balance, Davidoff, Lana Marks, Kieselstein-Cord, Donna Karan, Ludwig Reiter, Kenneth Cole, Ann Taylor, BCBG, bebe, Banana Republic, and more, plus Venetian glass and paper makers under a painted, cloud-studded blue sky. As you stroll through Renaissance-era Venice, gondoliers float by and sing. If you pay them (p. 159), you can take the lazy ride down and back, serenaded by your gondolier, who has perfected his Italian accent to ensure your illusion remains in place. Along the way, actors pose as living statues. The stroll (or float) ends at a miniature (though not by all that much) version of St. Mark's Square, the central landmark of Venice. Here, you'll find opera singers, strolling musicians, glass blowers, and other bustling marketplace activity. The Venetian's "Phase Two" hotel addition, the Venezia Tower, opened in late 2003 and adjoins the Canal Shoppes at the far end of St. Mark's Square.

2 Shopping A–Z

We've tried to keep you as close to the Strip as possible with these shops, but for some items, you may need to venture further afield. For stores with multiple locations, we've listed those nearest the Strip.

ANTIQUES & COLLECTIBLES

Academy Fine Books and Antiques   These shops, arranged in a square, are nothing much to look at, but inside, if you have the patience, you'll find some treasures; kids who have an interest in cool old stuff will enjoy looking at, well, cool old stuff. Individual store hours vary, but most are closed on Sunday and Monday. 2014–2034 Charleston (at Eastern Ave.). ✆ 702/471-6500.

Antique Sampler Shoppes   Over 200 dealers and small shops are located here, under one roof, offering a diversity of antiques and collectibles ranging from china and silver to *Star Wars* memorabilia and '50s prom dresses for kids who like to collect. Changing selections mean you can never guarantee what will be available, but count on antique clothing and shoes, lamps, antique furniture, flatware, and china, along with toys, saltshakers, and rugs. The displays are well labeled and well laid out, making it easy to take in all the antiques. The oldest antiques, from the mid-1800s, range in price from $100 to $4,000. Open Monday through Saturday from 10am until 7pm, Sunday from noon until 7pm. 6115 W. Tropicana Ave. ✆ 702/368-1170. www.antiquesampler.com.

Antiques at the Market   This is another group of antique shops lurking in minimall formation. The market consists of a number of individuals operating stalls under one roof, each with their own specialty, though, at times, some stalls look more like gussied-up garage sales. If your family enjoys rummaging around for treasures, oddities, or just something unique, you might get lucky here. Open Monday through Saturday from 9am until 5pm, Sunday from noon until 5pm. 6663 S. Eastern Ave. (between Sunset and Warm Springs Rd.). ✆ 702/307-3960.

Red Rooster Antique Mall   Individual stalls fill this mall, which sometimes offers real finds for collectors of all ages. Individual store hours vary. 307 W. Charleston Blvd. (at I-15). ✆ 702/382-5253.

ARTS & CRAFTS

Jo-Ann   Whether its beading, sewing, decoupage, or any other number of arts and crafts, Jo-Ann has the supplies you'll need, plus a helpful staff to guide you. Open Monday through Saturday from 9am to 9pm and Sunday 10am until 6pm. 4628 W. Sahara Ave. ✆ 702/878-9549. www.joann.com.

BABY & PRESCHOOLER CLOTHES AND ITEMS

Babies "R" Us   The name says it all. Clothes, toys, strollers, car seats, furniture, disposable diapers, cribs—everything you'll need for babies and toddlers at this branch of the nationwide chain. Open daily from 9:30am until 9:30pm. 2150 N. Rainbow Blvd. ✆ 702/647-8565. www.babiesrus.com.

Brats   Cute, fashionable clothes for children of all ages, along with some shoes, toys, and accessories. This store has many good siblings, too, including Brats at Monte Carlo and Desert Brats at Aladdin/Planet Hollywood. Open Monday through Friday from 10am until 9pm, Saturday from 10am to 7pm, and Sunday from noon until 6pm. Fashion Show Mall, 3200 Las Vegas Blvd S. ✆ 702/735-2728.

BOOKS

Albion Books *Value*   Six thousand square feet of used books, including first editions, vintage children's books, pop and sci-fi, pulp fiction, and bestsellers, both hard and paperback. You're welcome to take a seat and browse through your finds before purchasing. Open daily from 10am until 6pm. 2466 E. Desert Inn Rd. ✆ 702/792-9554. www.abebooks.com/home/albionbco.

B. Dalton   This nationwide chain sells a wide selection of books on all subjects. It stocks bestsellers and has a large children's section. 3680 S. Maryland Pkwy. ✆ 702/735-0008.

Barnes & Noble   Books on every subject for all ages, plus bestsellers are offered at this branch of the nationwide chain. Open Monday through Saturday, 9am to 10pm, and Sunday 9am to 9pm. 3860 Maryland Pkwy. ✆ 702/734-2900. www. barnesandnoble.com.

Harmon Ave. | **1** Harmon Ave. | Koval Ln. | Paradise Rd.

15

Tompkins Ave. | Rue de **2** Monte Carlo | **3** | UNIVERSITY OF NEVADA, LAS VEGAS
Palms Center Dr. | **4** | MGM Grand Station | **605**
| **5** | **6**

Tropicana Ave. | Tropicana Ave.

Reno Ave. | Reno Ave.

Ali Baba Ln.

Hacienda Ave. | Mandalay Bay Rd.

Frank Sinatra Dr. | Las Vegas Blvd. (The Strip) | Giles St. | Procyon Ave. | Polaris Ave. | Industrial Rd.

Charleston | **95** | **93 95** | **515** | Main | Fremont | DOWNTOWN | **582**

Dewey Dr.

Russell Rd. | Russell Rd. | **15** | Sahara | Maryland | Desert Inn | Eastern

Oquendo Rd. | Paradise | **604**

15 | **604** | Area of detail | Tropicana

······· Monorail

0 | 0.5 mi
0 | 0.5 km

McCarran Int'l Airport | Russell
0 | 1/2 mi
0 | 0.5 km
15
215

Sunset Rd. | Sunset Rd.

Brats at the Monte Carlo (Monte Carlo) **2**
Build-a-Bear Workshop (Aladdin/Planet Hollywood) **1**
Desert Brats (Aladdin/Planet Hollywood) **1**
Eddie Bauer (Aladdin/Planet Hollywood) **1**
Endangered Species (Aladdin/Planet Hollywood) **1**
Gallery of Legends (Aladdin/Planet Hollywood) **1**
Houdini's Magic Shop (MGM Grand) **6**
Houdini's Magic Shop (New York–New York) **5**
Lucky Brand (Aladdin/Planet Hollywood) **1**
M&M World **4**
The Magic Shop (Monte Carlo) **2**
Napoleon (Aladdin/Planet Hollywood)
Sephora (Aladdin/Planet Hollywood) **1**
Sharper Image (Aladdin/Planet Hollywood) **1**
Showcase Mall **4**
Sur La Table (Aladdin/Planet Hollywood) **1**
Walgreen's **3**

Bell Book & Candle *Finds*   This musty, dusty shop, a Las Vegas landmark, stocks books on witchcraft, along with herbs, expensive aromatherapy oils, and candles. Kids who are into this sort of stuff will appreciate the spooky vibes; atheists, skeptics, and the religiously strict will not. We found the free "lucky beans" improved our wins at the slots; maybe they help with math tests, too! Open daily 11am to 7pm. 1725 E. Charleston Blvd. ✆ **702-386-2950.** www.lasvegasbbc.com.

Borders   Along with a huge selection of books and magazines for all ages, this branch of the nationwide chain also has a decent cafe. Open Monday through Saturday 9am to 11pm, Sunday 9am to 9pm. 2323 S. Decatur Blvd. ✆ **702/258-0999.** www.borders.com.

Dead Poet Books *Finds*   The owners of this used bookstore wanted to name the store after the man from whose estate they bought their start-up stock, but they never did get his name, so they just called him the "dead poet." The unknown gentleman's good taste in books lives on at this store, a book lover's haven, with a large selection for children and young adults. This place is a good, low-cost way to start a young book-lover's library. Open Monday through Saturday from 10am to 6pm, Sunday from noon to 5pm. 3874 W. Sahara Ave. ✆ **702/ 227-4070.** www.abebooks.com/home/scalzi.

Learning Is Fun   Teachers and parents will find books, toys, learning games, and supplies—including posters, bulletin boards, paints, and paper—to help expand their children's minds and skills. It's a perfect place to load up at before a long road trip. Open Monday through Friday from 10am to 7pm, Saturday from 10am until 6pm, and Sunday from noon until 5pm. 290 S. Decatur Blvd. ℂ 702/258-5437.

Psychic Eye More a metaphysical minimall than a bookshop, you'll find crystals, T-shirts, candles, and tabletop fountains along with actual reading material here, making this a good stop for children into glittery gewgaws, crystals, and Indian-print fabrics, as well as the more mystical in books. Both branches keep the same hours; Monday through Friday 10am to 9pm, Saturday 10am to 8:30pm, Sunday 11am to 6pm. 2250 E. Tropicana Ave. ℂ 702/369-6622. 6848 W. Charleston Blvd. ℂ 702/255-4477. www.pebooks.com.

Virgin Megastore The only store for records and one of three for books in any hotel on the Strip, and boy, were we glad when it opened in Caesars' Forum Shops—and we're happy that it stays open late, as well. Not much for kids, but teens into rock and pop culture will find something to read. They also stock some bestsellers, mysteries, and cookbooks. Open daily from 10am to midnight. In Caesars Palace, 3500 Las Vegas Blvd S. ℂ 702/696-7100. www.virginmega.com.

Waldenbooks Before Virgin Megastore and Mandalay Bay's The Reading Room opened, Walden's, located in the Fashion Show Mall, was the only bookstore on the Strip. This national chain has books for all ages and is more of a complete bookstore than the Virgin Megastore; you'll find a large selection of all subjects here, plus a children's section as well as bestsellers. Open Monday through Saturday from 10am to 9pm, and Sunday from 12pm until 6pm. The Fashion Show Mall, 3200 Las Vegas Blvd. S. ℂ 702/733-1049. www.waldenbooks.com.

CANDY, CHOCOLATE & SWEETS
Godiva Sinful, rich, decadent chocolates in gleaming gold boxes, the perfect pick-me-up after a hard day shopping. All casino locations are open Sunday through Thursday from 10am to 11pm, Friday and Saturday from 10am until midnight. In Caesars Palace, 3570 Las Vegas Blvd S. ℂ 702/734-8855. Desert Passage, 3570 Las Vegas Blvd. S. ℂ 702/731-6798. The Venetian, 3377 Las Vegas Blvd. S. ℂ 702/732-1577. www.godiva.com.

M&Ms World The sheer volume of chocolate overwhelms here; along with candy (Mars products, all shades of M&Ms, and the upscale boxed Ethel M. brand), you can purchase M&M-themed pajamas, T-shirts, mugs, and other souvenirs. You can also see a 3-D movie starring the M&Ms. Open Sunday through Thursday from 9am to 11pm, Friday and Saturday from 9am to midnight. In the Showcase Mall, 3785 Las Vegas Blvd. S. ℂ 702/736-7611.

COMICS
Alternate Reality Comics This is the place in Vegas for all your comic book needs. They have a nearly comprehensive selection, with a heavy emphasis on the underground comics. But don't worry—the superheroes are here, too. Open Monday through Saturday from 11am until 7pm and Sunday from noon to 6pm. 4800 S. Maryland Pkwy. ℂ 702/736-3673.

Cosmic Comics Superheroes share shelf space with the antiheroes of underground and alternative comics providing local kids—and grown-ups—an escape from the omnipresent desert environment into fantasy. Open Monday through Saturday from 11am to 7pm and Sunday from 11am to 5pm. 3330 E. Tropicana Ave. ℂ 702/451-6611. http://jbrocius.home.mindspring.com.

Abercrombie & Fitch
  (Caesars Palace) **2**
Banana Repubic
  (Caesars Palace) **2**
Bernini Collection
  (Caesars Palace) **2**
Disney Store
  (Caesars Palace) **2**
Endangered Species
  Store (Caesars Palace) **2**
FAO Schwarz
  (Caesars Palace) **2**
Field of Dreams
  (Caesars Palace) **2**
Gap (Caesars Palace) **2**
Godiva (Caesars Palace) **2**
Godiva (The Venetian) **1**

Houdini's Magic Shop
  (The Venetian) **1**
Jimmy Choo
  (The Venetian)
Kenneth Cole
  (The Venetian)
New Balance
  (The Venetian) **1**

Nike Town
  (Caesars Palace) **2**
Sephora
  (The Venetian) **1**
Sport Logo
  (Caesars Palace) **2**
Virgin Megastore
  (Caesars Palace) **2**

Silver Cactus Comics   About 10 minutes from the Strip, this well-stocked shop features rare collectible comics, current issues, and hard-to-find action figures. (Never, never call them dolls!) Open Monday through Saturday from 11am until 8pm, Sunday noon to 6pm. 480 N. Nellis Blvd. ☎ **702/438-4408**. www.silvercactuscomics.com.

COOKWARE
Sur la Table   If you or your honey wins big and you've been craving a duck press, a lemon peeler, or a complete set of matching stainless steel pots and pans, this is the place. Aprons, potholders, seasonal cookie cutters, coffee mugs, plus kid-oriented gear and baking kits can also be found here. Open Sunday through Thursday from 10am to 11pm, Friday and Saturday from 10am until midnight. Aladdin/Planet Hollywood, Desert Passage, 3663 Las Vegas Blvd. S. ☎ **702/732-2706**. www. surlatable.com.

COSMETICS
Sephora   This branch of the famous chain has any color of nail polish you can imagine, every color of lipstick you could desire, and much more. Teen and 'tween girls will go nuts here. Indulge them with the store's own brand, which comes in small trial sizes, or load up on the cutting-edge colors from the likes of Urban Decay and Benefit. Fans of Chanel products should try Bourjois, a French company that is astoundingly similar in quality, yet far less expensive. For the

younger, pre-make-up set, there are cool hair clips, headbands, and ponytail hold-ers. The spa and body care kits—perfect for slumber parties or as birthday gifts—can keep girls (and women) of all ages busy in their hotel room. Both stores are open Sunday through Thursday from 10am until 11pm, and Friday and Satur-day from 10am until midnight. Desert Passage, 3663 Las Vegas Blvd. S. ℰ **702/737-0550.** The Venetian, 3377 Las Vegas Blvd. S. ℰ **702/735-3896.** www.sephora.com.

COSTUMES

Halloween Experience *Finds* A favorite with local Goths, it's Halloween 365 days of the year at this warehouse full of costumes and masks for all ages, plus props and all your haunted house needs. Other holidays don't get the short shroud, uh, shrift, here, either. They also stock Christmas lights, Santa suits, Easter bunny outfits, and more. Open daily 9am to 5pm. 5800 S. Valley View Blvd. ℰ **702/740-4224.**

Party City Every day is a party at Party City, which features costumes at Hal-loween, plus all the things you'll need for a baby shower, birthday party, or even a tiki-themed party. Open Monday through Friday from 9:30am until 9pm, Sat-urday from 8:30am until 9pm, and Sunday from 10:30am until 6pm. 4020 Mary-land Pkwy. ℰ **702/893-4600.**

Serge's Showgirl Wigs Both this shop and the less pricey Serge's Wig Out-let, across the way, offer an astounding array of hirsute replicas, ranging from the elaborate to the subtle. This is where showgirls get their glossy locks. Serge's can also make custom wigs and toupees and carries hair-care products. Children are welcome at both stores, though they may enjoy seeing (and trying out) the more colorful, goofier wigs at the outlet rather than the towering showgirl versions. Open Monday through Saturday, from 10am until 5:30pm. 953 E. Sahara Ave. ℰ **702/732-1015.** www.showgirlwigs.com.

DEPARTMENT STORES

Dillard's You'll find apparel for the entire family plus shoes, accessories, and more at this stolid retailer. All locations are open Monday through Saturday from 10am to 9pm and Sunday from noon until 6pm. Fashion Show Mall, 3200 Las Vegas Blvd S. ℰ **702/733-2008.** The Meadows, 4200 Meadows Lane. ℰ **702/870-2039.** Boule-vard Mall, 3700 S. Maryland Pkwy. ℰ **702/734-2111.** www.dillards.com.

Kmart This retailer (which can get pretty crowded on weekends) offers inexpen-sive clothing for the whole family, along with household items and small appliances. Open daily 8am until 10pm. 2975 E Sahara Ave. ℰ **702/457-1037.** www.kmart.com.

Macy's Quality clothes for teens, adults, and children, along with china, sheets, towels, and other household good from this New York–based retailer. The latest fashions, top designers, and classic styles can all be found here. All locations are open Monday through Friday 10am to 9pm, Saturday from 10am to 8pm, and on Sunday from 11am to 7pm. Fashion Show Mall, 3200 Las Vegas Blvd S. ℰ **702/731-5111.** The Meadows, 4100 Meadows Lane. ℰ **702/258-2100.** The Boulevard, 3634 S. Maryland Pkwy. ℰ **702/791-2100.** www.macys.com.

Marshalls Adult and children's clothing, plus housewares, are sold at this nationwide discount store. Open Monday through Saturday from 9:30am to 9:30pm and Sunday from 11am to 7pm. Boulevard Mall, 3740 S. Maryland Pkwy. ℰ **702/ 737-1117.** www.marshallsonline.com.

Mervyn's All ages will find clothes and housewares at reasonable prices at this nationwide discount store. Open Monday through Saturday from 9am to 10pm

North Strip Shopping

Academy Fine Books and Antiques **4**
Along Came a Spider (Fashion Show Mall) **9**
Arts Factory Complex **3**
The Attic **1**
Bell Book & Candle **5**
Bonanza Gift and Souvenir Shop **7**
Dillards (Fashion Show Mall) **9**
Disney Store (Fashion Show Mall) **9**
Gap (Fashion Show Mall) **9**
Gymboree (Fashion Show Mall) **9**
Neiman Marcus
  (Fashion Show Mall) **9**
Red Rooster Antique Mall **2**
Robinson's May
  (Fashion Show Mall) **9**
Sak's Fifth Avenue
  (Fashion Show Mall) **9**
Talbots (Fashions Show Mall) **9**
Waldenbooks
  (Fashion Show Mall) **9**
Walgreen's **6**
Walgreen's **8**

and Sunday 9am to 9pm. The Meadows, 4700 Meadows Lane. ✆ **702/870-9000.** www.target.com/mervyns.

Neiman Marcus   Expect to find one-of-a-kind pieces of jewelry to accessorize your designer clothes at this high-end retailer. Expect to swoon over the shoes. Teens who love to shop will be especially enthralled by the high fashions. Open Monday through Friday from 10am to 8pm, Saturday from 10am until 7pm, and Sunday from noon to 6pm. Fashion Show Mall, 3200 Las Vegas Blvd. S. ✆ **702/731-3636.** www.neimanmarcus.com.

Robinson's May   Midrange retailer with plenty to choose from, including trendy clothes and classic styles. Open Monday through Thursday 10am to 9pm, Friday from 10am to 10pm, Saturday 9am to 9pm, and Sunday from 11am to 7pm. Fashion Show Mall, 3200 Las Vegas Blvd. S. ✆ **702/737-8708.** www.mayco.com.

Saks Fifth Avenue   New York comes to Las Vegas; you'll find a large and high-end selection for all ages and tastes here. Open Monday through Wednesday from 10am to 8pm, Thursday and Friday from 10am to 9pm, Saturday from 10am to 7pm, and Sunday 10am to 6pm. Fashion Show Mall, 3200 Las Vegas Blvd. S. ✆ 702/733-8300. www.saks.com.

Sears   They stock everything here, from power tools to perfume, dresses to drills, boots to lingerie—bless them! Open Monday through Friday 10am to 9pm, Saturday 10am to 8pm, and Sunday 10am to 7pm (to 6pm Sun for Boulevard Mall location). The Meadows, 4000 Meadows Lane. ✆ 702/259-4200. Boulevard Mall, 3450 S. Maryland Pkwy. ✆ 702/894-4200. www.sears.com.

T. J. Maxx   This is where clothes and housewares go for discounting; you'll find some buys here for everyone. Open 9:30am to 9:30pm Monday through Saturday, Sunday 11am to 6pm. 4000 S. Maryland Pkwy. ✆ 702/733-7730. www.tjmaxx.com.

Target   Loved by young and old alike, this discount retailer stocks everything, from cool clothes and hip housewares (including goods designed by Phillipe Starck) to cans of bug spray and boxes of detergent. Open Monday through Saturday from 8am until 10pm and Sunday 8am to 9pm. 4001 S. Maryland Pkwy. ✆ 702/732-2218. www.target.com.

Wal-Mart   If you need it, they probably have it—and at low prices. Open daily, 24 hours. 3075 E. Tropicana Ave. ✆ 702/451-8900. www.walmart.com.

DRUGSTORES

Rite Aid   This national chain has all your over-the-counter needs such as cosmetics, formula, and disposable diapers, plus a pharmacy. Store open daily from 8am to 11pm, pharmacy hours from 9am to 9pm. 2905 S. Maryland Pkwy. ✆ 702/735-9195. www.riteaid.com.

Sav-On   Over-the-counter medications, cosmetics, baby needs, and more, along with a pharmacy. Store open 8am to 10pm Monday through Saturday, Sunday 8am to 7pm. Pharmacy open Monday through Friday from 8am to 9pm, Saturday 9am to 6pm, and Sunday from 10am to 6pm. 2555 S. Maryland Pkwy. ✆ 702/735-2201. 4600 Meadows Lane. ✆ 702/870-5003. www.savon.com.

Walgreens   Convenient locations open 24 hours, with pharmacies open around the clock, and pharmacists on staff throughout the day and night. Well stocked for baby needs, cosmetics, over-the-counter medications, and much more. We love it. 3025 Las Vegas Blvd. S. ✆ 702/836-0818. 3765 Las Vegas Blvd S. ✆ 702/739-9638. 1101 Las Vegas Blvd. S. ✆ 702/471-6840. 4905 W. Tropicana Ave. ✆ 702/889-0911. www.walgreens.com.

ELECTRONICS

Best Buy   If you can plug it in, they have it, along with cellphones, cameras, games, CDs, DVDs, and more. Open Monday through Saturday 10am to 9pm, and Sunday from 10am until 7pm. 3820 S. Maryland Pkwy. ✆ 702/732-8283. www.bestbuy.com.

Circuit City   Televisions, stereos, video players, and DVD players, plus cameras and cellphones tempt those who love their gadgets. Open Monday through Thursday from 10am until 9pm, Friday and Saturday 10am to 10pm, and Sunday from 11am to 7pm. 5055 W. Sahara Ave. ✆ 702/367-9700. www.circuitcity.com.

Good Guys   Home and personal electronics, including rows of televisions, videos and DVD players, cellphones, and cameras. Tower Records is in the same building, so you can buy something to play on your new toys. Open daily from 10am until midnight. 4850 W. Sahara Ave. ✆ 702/364-2500. www.goodguys.com.

Shopping East of the Strip

Albertsons Food & Drugs **15**
Albion Books **5**
Alternate Reality Comics **16**
Antiques at the Market **19**
Asian Market **1**
Barnes & Noble **9**
Best Buy **8**
Bike World **13**
Buffalo Exchange **14**
Casey's Sports Cards **17**
Cosmic Comics **17**
Dillards (The Boulevard Mall) **7**
Footlocker & Lady Footlocker
 (The Boulevard Mall) **7**
GapKids (The Boulevard Mall) **7**

Gymboree
 (The Boulevard Mall) **7**
India Bazaar **1**
Kmart **4**
Macy's
 (The Boulevard Mall) **7**
Marshall's
 (Boulevard Mall) **7**
Party City **12**
Psychic Eye **18**

Rite Aid **6**
Sav-On **2**
Sears (The Boulevard Mall) **7**
Serge's Showgirl Wigs **1**
Silver Cactus Comics **3**
T.J. Maxx **10**
Target **11**
Toys "R" Us/Kids "R" Us **10**
Wal-Mart **17**

Sharper Image   This nationwide chain features upscale electronics for those with disposable income. Nose-hair trimmers, ionizing pet brushes, white noise generators, and so on, make perfect gifts for those who have everything. Open Sunday through Thursday from 10am until 11pm and Friday and Saturday from 10am until midnight. Desert Passage, 3663 Las Vegas Blvd S. ✆ **702/732-2505.** www.sharperimage.com.

EVERYDAY CLOTHING FOR CHILDREN

GapKids   Cute and classic are the key notes of this global chain, with over 500 stores worldwide. Jeans, shirts, dresses, skirts, and accessories—all your kid-clothing needs can be met easily here. Designed with both form and function in mind, the clothes here won't fall apart if and when they fall out of style. The staff is helpful and patient. Open Monday through Friday 10am to 9pm, Saturday 10am to 8pm, and Sunday 10am to 6pm. Boulevard Mall, 3610 S. Maryland Pkwy. ✆ **702/734-7077.** www.gap.com.

Gymboree   This chain store stocks sturdy play clothes for toddlers to age 7. The stretchy solids and patterned separates are designed to mix, match, coordinate, and, most importantly, hold up. The Fashion Show Mall location is open Monday through Saturday 10am to 9pm, and Sunday 10am to 6pm. The Boulevard Mall location is open Monday through Friday 10am to 9pm, Saturday 10am to 8pm, and Sunday 10am to 6pm. The Meadows location is open Monday through Friday 10am to 9pm, Saturday 10am to 8pm, and Sunday 10am to 6pm. Fashion Show Mall, 3200 Las Vegas Blvd. S. ✆ **702/369-8909.** Boulevard Mall, 3680 S. Maryland Pkwy. ✆ **702/369-4055.** The Meadows, 4300 Meadows Lane. ✆ **702/880-4228.** www.gymboree.com.

Kids "R" Us   Located in the same building as Toys "R" Us (p. 212), next to The Meadows mall, this vast nationwide chain store sells shoes and clothes, both casual and formal, for toddlers on up to age 12-ish, along with some cribs and a small selection of cars seats. Open Monday through Saturday from 9:30am to 9:30pm and Sunday from 11am until 6pm. 4550 Meadows Lane. ✆ **702/877-9070.** www.kidsrus.com.

EVERYDAY CLOTHING FOR TEENS & ADULTS

Abercrombie & Fitch   This national retailer has caught a lot of flack for its racy catalogs and its unpleasant, inappropriate thong underwear for 7-year-olds. That aside, A&F stocks Ts, jeans, skirts, and shirts that are comfy and low-key, many of which are emblazoned with their logo. Both locations open Sunday through Thursday 10am to 11pm, Friday and Saturday from 10am until midnight. Caesars Palace, 3500 Las Vegas Blvd. S. ✆ **702/731-0712.** www.abercrombie.com.

Banana Republic   Banana Republic's clothes feature classic lines, but with a fashionable edge for both men and women, including slacks, sweaters, shirts, and skirts in the latest shades and fabrics. Sizes favor the lean; girls and women over size 12 may be disappointed to find few items that work for them, aside from scarves and hats. Open Sunday through Thursday 10am to 11pm, Friday and Saturday from 10am until midnight. Caesars Palace, 3500 Las Vegas Blvd. S. ✆ **702/650-5623.** The Venetian, 3377 Las Vegas Blvd. S. ✆ **702/733-1566.** www.bananarepublic.com.

Eddie Bauer   By shopping here, you can look outdoorsy and never leave the house, but the clothes are more than just for show; designed for outdoors men and women, they do hold up under the elements. The colors are low-key, the styles classic. Open Sunday through Thursday 10am to 11pm, Friday and Saturday from 10am until midnight. Desert Passage, 3663 Las Vegas Blvd. S. ✆ **702/892-8192.** www.eddiebauer.com.

Shopping West of the Strip

Antique Sampler
  Shoppes **14**
B. Dalton
  (The Meadows) **2**
Babies "R" Us **1**
Borders **8**
Circuit City **9**
Dead Poet Books **12**
Desert Outfitters **7**
Dillards (The Meadows) **2**
Escape Adventures
  Bike Shop and
  Tour Center **4**
Fantasy Toys
  (The Meadows) **2**
Field of Dreams **13**
Footlocker &
  Lady Footlocker
  (The Meadows) **2**
GameKeeper
  (The Meadows) **2**
Gap (The Meadows) **2**
Good Guys **10**
Gymboree
  (The Meadows) **2**
Halloween Experience **17**
International
  Market Place **16**
Jo-Ann **11**
Kid's Kloset **5**
Learning Is Fun **6**
Macy's (The Meadows) **2**
Men's Wearhouse **9**
Mervyn's (The Meadows) **2**
Psychic Eye **3**
Sears (The Meadows) **2**
Tower Records **10**
Trader Joe's **7**
Walgreen's **15**

Gap   The original standard bearer for egalitarian fashion is allegedly moving away from their brief dalliance with low-rise pants cut for scrawny, hipless waifs paired with belly-bearing tops, and back (thankfully) to its bread and butter—some of which includes clothes that fit girls and women over size 8 and men's fashions for a variety of shapes and sizes. As always, the Gap stocks jeans, khakis, and Ts, as well as basics in the latest fashion shades, plus accessories. For hours of each of Vegas's five Gap branches, check the mall hours in which they're located. Caesars Palace, 3500 Las Vegas Blvd. S. ℂ 702/737-1550. The Meadows, 4300 Meadows Lane. ℂ **702/878-2446.** Boulevard Mall, 3580 S. Maryland Pkwy. ℂ **702/734-6620.** Fashion Show Mall, 3200 Las Vegas Blvd. S. ℂ **702/796-0010.** www.gap.com.

Lucky Brand   Incredibly hip, expensive jeans and T-shirts let your teens tell the world that you care enough to spend your hard-earned cash on their trends. The lining inside the fly of some styles reads LUCKY YOU. Maybe your kids should wait until they're 18 for these. Open Sunday through Thursday 10am to 11pm, Friday and Saturday from 10am until midnight. Desert Passage, 3663 Las Vegas Blvd. S. ℂ **702/733-6613.** Fashion Show Mall, 3200 Las Vegas Blvd. S. ℂ **702/369-4116.** Forum Shops at Caesars, 3500 Las Vegas Blvd. S. ℂ **702/369-2536.** www.luckybrandjeans.com.

Talbots   Restrained good taste in an East Coast preppy style is the hallmark of this store. Open Monday through Friday from 10am to 9pm, Saturday 10am to 7pm, and noon to 6pm Sunday. Fashion Show Mall, 3200 Las Vegas Blvd S. ℂ **702/893-1706.** www.talbots.com.

FASHION CLOTHING FOR CHILDREN

Along Came a Spider   Suits, ties, dressy dresses, along with miniature versions of the latest adult styles, including camouflage and animal prints, as well as accessories and toys can be found here. Sizes range from toddlers to up to sizes 7 to 12 in boys and 16 for girls. We love the clothes here. The same store reappears as **Desert Brats** in Aladdin/Planet Hollywood's **Desert Passage,** 3663 Las Vegas Blvd. S. (ℂ **702/862-4949**) and as the far more charmingly dubbed **Kids' Castle** in **Caesars' Forum Shops** at Caesars Palace, 3500 Las Vegas Blvd. S. (ℂ **702/369-5437**). **Brats** at the Monte Carlo, 3770 Las Vegas Blvd. S. (ℂ **702/730-7165**) and **Kids' Karnival** in The Venetian's **Grand Canal Shoppes,** 3377 Las Vegas Blvd. S. (ℂ **702/414-3800**) stock more of the same cool kid clothes. If you prefer to go to the **Fashion Show Mall, Brats** is open there Monday through Friday from 10am until 9pm, on Saturday from 10am to 7pm, and Sunday from noon until 6pm. Fashion Show Mall, 3200 Las Vegas Blvd S. ℂ **702/735-2728.**

FASHION CLOTHING FOR TEENS AND ADULTS

A prowl through The Venetian, Desert Passage, Caesars Palace, or the Fashion Show mall will turn up any number of chic boutiques and chains, including **Armani Exchange** (ℂ 702/733-1666), **bebe** (ℂ 702/735-8885 or 702/892-0406), **Diesel** (ℂ 702/791-5927), **DKNY** (ℂ 702/650-9670), and **BCBG** (ℂ 702/737-0681 or 702/735-2947), all of which can put you and your teens in the latest au courant styles for a pretty penny, and whose hours mirror those of the mall in which they are located.

GIFTS & SOUVENIRS

Hotel logo shops and sundry stores offer a variety of Vegas-themed items that strive for good taste—and often come up just a little short, but, alas, not enough to make them appallingly fabulous. If you wish to move beyond your hotel, we offer the following suggestions.

Arts Factory Complex   This is a gift shop full of pink flamingos and Vegas-specific items. There should be something here for every camp fancy; take pleasure in the fact your children may not yet recognize the ironic aspect to these iconic souvenirs. The galleries also stock paintings and other art by local artists. Open Tuesday through Saturday noon until 4pm, but call before your make the trip, as hours can vary. 103 E. Charleston Blvd. ℂ **702/382-3886.**

Bonanza Gift and Souvenir Shop   Filled with items such as earrings made out of poker chips, snow domes, clocks with dice for numbers, fake turquoise, gold flakes in bottles, and more, this shop, in other words, has plenty of kitsch. Open daily 8am until midnight. 2460 Las Vegas Blvd. S. ℂ **702/384-0005.**

Showcase Mall   Native Americana (think kachina dolls, feathered dream catchers, and pottery) to all-American bad taste (dice clocks, again), this mall has it all. Every Vegas souvenir you could imagine—and some you'd prefer not to imagine—are here for your buying pleasure. But it's not only a mall; it's an "experience," in that very special Las Vegas way. Not to be outdone by Caesars, Aladdin/Planet Hollywood, and The Venetian, the Showcase has installed a Grand Canyon simulacrum where every 45 minutes, the clouds roll in and a thunderstorm erupts, only to be gradually replaced with a gentle sunrise and the sounds of chirping birds. There's also a rope bridge you can walk over. Open 8am until 1am daily. 3785 Las Vegas Blvd. S. ℂ **702/597-3122.**

GROCERY STORES & MARKETS

Albertsons Food and Drugs   This grocery store can meet all your food needs. It also has sundries, over-the-counter medications, pet food, disposable diapers, and more. Both stores are open daily 24 hours. 1300 E. Flamingo Rd. ℂ **702/733-2947.** 2300 E. Tropicana Ave. ℂ **702/739-8461.** www.albertsons.com.

Trader Joe's *Finds*   This store sells gourmet food—fresh, frozen, and canned—at budget prices. Trader Joe's carries its own line of comestibles, including sodas and juices, plus international treats, a large range of desserts, and candies, along with unique products from small manufacturers. Trader Joe's emphasizes making and keeping food as wholesome and natural as possible; the dairy products are hormone-free, and preservatives are nonexistent or kept at a minimum. The refrigerated selection of sandwiches and salads is great for picnics. Open daily 9am to 9pm. 2101 S. Decatur Blvd. ℂ **702/367-0227.** www.traderjoes.com.

INTERNATIONAL GROCERIES

Asian Market   Japanese food items dominate in this good-sized market full of *poki-poki* (rolled cookies dipped in chocolate and filled with creamy goop), colorful jelly candies, and ice cream, plus rice, noodles, frozen fish, sauces, and other exotic items. Open daily from 9am to 9pm. Commercial Center, 953 E. Sahara Blvd. ℂ **702/734-7653.**

India Bazaar   This shop carries Indian spices, sweets, and foodstuffs. Try the packaged curry snacks or the gooey candies. While it's nice to know it exists, most kids may find the flavors a bit too funky for their liking. Vegetarians, however,

Souvenir Savvy

My favorite souvenir is my T-shirt from MGM Grand with the picture of the lion and the words, "Here human, human, human."

—Victoria, 12

will appreciate the selection of lentils, pulses, and grains. Look for henna for authentic at-home *mendhi* (hand and body painting). Open 11am to 8pm Thursday through Tuesday. Commercial Center, 953 E. Sahara Ave. ℂ **702/892-0720.**

International Marketplace *(Finds)* The International Marketplace is the biggest, most fabulous food store in all of Las Vegas (we think). A world, literally, of food is for sale here. Items from England (burdock root soda, teas, chocolates, beans, cookies, and so on) share shelf space with Indonesian and Dutch delicacies. There is an astounding array of Indian curry mixes, Armenian foods, teas and coffees from around the globe, Middle Eastern breads and spices and their uniquely flavored, shockingly green drink, tarragon soda. The refrigerated food section stocks items as diverse as goose uterus (don't ask), steak, chicken, and cuttlefish. You'll also find Hawaiian hot dogs, Mexican sausages, and Filipino ice cream (including purple yam, cheese and corn, and durian flavors) in the freezer; and Japanese vegetable chips, plus strange, brightly glowing candies, Asian sauces and soups, dried fungus, juices, sodas, and more on the shelves lining this warehouse-sized market. Kids will be wowed by the colorful selection of snacks in their neon packaging. Give them a budget of $5 and they'll go wild buying things to share—and maybe learn a little bit about different cultures while they're at it. The International Marketplace also stocks woks, specialty stoves, and ovens. If you plan to load up on exotic items, or to spend more than $20, it's probably worth paying for a $10 membership card, which gives you discounts. Open Monday through Friday from 9am to 6pm, Saturday and Sunday from 9am to 6pm. 5000 S. Decatur Blvd. ℂ **702/889-2888.**

MAGIC & GAGS

Houdini's Magic Shop The staff at these magic emporia is more than happy to demonstrate their wares. Expect to have coins and cards pulled from behind ears and to see plenty of ring and scarf tricks. Buying a trick here and having to learn it and then perform it seamlessly will impress upon children that practice does make perfect. For slackers, there's a huge selection of gags including foaming sugar, soap that turns your hands black, and that perennial favorite, the whoopee cushion. The Houdini Museum (p. 172) is located next door to The Venetian's shop. Shop hours mirror those of their respective malls. New York–New York, 3790 Las Vegas Blvd. S. ℂ **702/740-6418.** Desert Passage, 3663 Las Vegas Blvd. S. ℂ **702/314-4674.** Venetian, 3377 Las Vegas Blvd. S. ℂ **702/796-0301.** MGM Grand, 3799 Las Vegas Blvd. S. ℂ **702/736-2883.** www.houdini.com.

The Magic Shop Located close to magician Lance Burton's theater in the Monte Carlo, this magic shop has plenty of tricks up its sleeve, along with Lance Burton–related items. A staff member can demonstrate the sleight of hand. And we're happy to say that there's nary a whoopee cushion or squirting flower in sight. Open daily 9am until midnight. In the Monte Carlo, 3770 Las Vegas Blvd. S. ℂ **702/730-7518.**

MEN'S WEAR

Bernini Collection High fashions and basics for the preening male. Think chinchilla baseball jackets, leather pants, and other Liberace-esque items. Open daily from 10am to midnight. Caesars Palace, 3500 Las Vegas Blvd. S. ℂ **702/893-1786.**

Men's Wearhouse Low prices, good service, and a quick turnaround on alterations make this national chain a favorite with fashion-conscious men old enough to care about such things. This store doesn't carry jeans or T-shirts, but it does have a large selection of suits, ties, and casual wear in name brands and quality fabrics. Open Monday through Friday from 10am to 9pm, Saturday from 9:30am to 6pm, and Sunday from 11am to 5pm. 4750 W. Sahara Ave. ℂ **702/878-4330**. www.menswearhouse.com.

Napoleon   Despite the name's connotations, this shop does not handle clothes purely for men under 5 feet 7 inches tall. In actuality, Napoleon carries a fine selection of menswear for all shapes and sizes in good fabrics, cuts, and colors. Open Sunday through Thursday from 10am to 11pm, Friday and Saturday from 10am until midnight. Desert Passage, 3663 Las Vegas Blvd. S. ℂ **702/733-6005**.

MUSIC

Tower Records/Video/Books   This vast emporium stocks new releases and standards, plus all genres of music, along with a good selection of videos and DVDs. Books tend towards rock bios and pop culture. This store shares space with a Good Guys electronics store, so you can buy a CD player to go with that complete Twisted Sister boxed set if you so desire. Open daily 10am to midnight. 4580 W. Sahara Ave. ℂ **702/364-2500**. www.towerrecords.com.

Virgin Megastore   Music of all genres, plus computer games, DVDs, and a good selection of pop culture books fill this vast emporium, the only multimedia store on the Strip. Open daily from 10am to midnight. Caesars Palace, 3500 Las Vegas Blvd. S. ℂ **702/696-7100**. www.virginmega.com.

SHOES

Department stores in the major shopping malls (p. 190) carry a wide selection of children's shoes. The following are specialty shops, some of which are sized more for teens than children.

Footlocker & Lady Footlocker   All manner of athletic shoes are sold here, which your child may prefer as fashion statements instead of for the purpose for which they were designed. The Meadows location is open Monday through Friday from 10am to 9pm, Saturday from 10am to 7pm, and Sunday from 10am to 6pm. You can visit the Maryland Parkway location from 10am to 9pm Monday through Friday, Saturday from 9:30am to 6pm, and Sunday from 11am to 5pm. The Meadows, 4300 Meadows Lane. ℂ **702/878-8226**. 3500 S. Maryland Pkwy. ℂ **702/731-3639**. www.footlocker.com.

Jimmy Choo   Popularized by the gals in *Sex and the City*, these pricey shoes, most with high heels, are only for girls whose feet have finished growing. And even then, at $300 and up, does she really need them? We were secretly relieved when the lusted-for pair didn't fit, and thanked our wide-footed genes. Open Sunday through Thursday from 10am to 11pm, Friday and Saturday from 10am until midnight. The Venetian, 3377 Las Vegas Blvd. S. ℂ **702/733-1802**. www.jimmychoo.com.

Kenneth Cole   These stores carry hip men's and women's shoes, along with other products such as jackets, purses, and belts. While you won't find any kid's shoes here, your bigger 'tweens and most teens can be fitted in a variety of shoes in the latest styles. Open Sunday through Thursday 10am to 11pm, Friday and Saturday from 10am to midnight. Caesars Palace, 3500 Las Vegas Blvd. S. ℂ **702/794-2653**. The Venetian, 3377 Las Vegas Blvd. S. ℂ **702/836-1916**. www.kennethcole.com.

New Balance   This athletic shoe store carries its own brand, in various styles, for infants, children, and adults, in widths ranging from AA to EEEE. Along with athletic shoes, including cross trainers and running shoes, New Balance carries an adult line called Dunhams, which are basic, casual shoes. What you don't see in stock can be ordered and shipped. Both locations are open Sunday through Thursday from 10am to 11pm, Friday and Saturday from 10am until midnight. The Venetian, 3377 Las Vegas Blvd. S. ✆ 702/733-4947. www.newbalance.com.

SPORTING GOODS & SPORTSWEAR

Bike World Bikes for everyone—from the 2-year-old to the 80-year-old—along with bike gear, clothes, helmets, and accessories are for sale at this professional and friendly shop. Open Monday through Friday from 10am to 6pm, Saturday from 10am until 5:30pm, and Sunday 10am to 5pm. 2320 E. Flamingo Rd. ✆ 702/735-7551.

Desert Outfitters Stop here for almost all your desert hiking, backpacking, and camping needs, including hats, tents, canteens, and the like (but you'll have to find the shoes elsewhere). If you feel like prospecting for gold, this is the place to load up on maps, tools, and local lore. Open Monday through Friday 10am until 6pm, 10am to 5pm Saturday. 2101 S. Decatur Blvd. ✆ 702/362-7177.

Escape Adventure Bike Shop and Tour Center Whether you want to buy a high-end racing bike a la Lance Armstrong or are just looking for a new set of spokes for your Schwinn , the Cyclery has it. The shop also does repairs and rents bikes, and is the headquarters for Escape Adventure tours. Open Monday through Friday from 9am until 6pm, Saturday 10am to 6pm, and Sunday from 10am until 4pm. 8221 W. Charleston Blvd. ✆ 702/596-2953. www.escapeadventures.com.

Niketown Sports clothes and shoes by Nike for men, women, and children, including the latest in superquick dry fabrics. Every Wednesday at 6pm, the Nike running club meets here to stretch out and warm up for 3- and 6-mile runs, followed by snacks. Open Sunday through Thursday from 10am to 11pm, Friday and Saturday from 10am until midnight. Caesars Palace, 3500 Las Vegas Blvd. S. ✆ 702/650-8888. http://niketown.nike.com.

Sport Logo Whether you're a fan of the Ravens, the Cardinals, or Raptors, you'll find your team's emblems emblazoned on shirts, hats, and other paraphernalia here. Open Sunday through Thursday 10am to 11pm, Friday and Saturday from 10am until midnight. Caesars Palace, 3500 Las Vegas Blvd. S. ✆ 702/792-2338.

SPORTS MEMORABILIA

Casey's Sports Cards With hundreds of thousands of sports cards in stock, this store deals to both the serious collector and the hobbyist. It's handled some of the world's hardest-to-find cards. Open Sunday through Friday 11am to 5pm, Sunday 11:30am to 4:30pm. 3421 E. Tropicana Ave. ✆ 702/458-6394.

Field of Dreams Framed and mounted sports memorabilia, including autographs, photos, balls, gloves, and players cards, all with certificates of authenticity, are sold here. They have Michael Jordan; they can get you Babe Ruth. Excellent for browsing and for boning up on sports history. The shop in the Rio is open daily from 10am to midnight. The Caesars store hours are Sunday through Thursday 10am to 11pm, Friday and Saturday from 10am until midnight. Rio, 3700 W. Flamingo Rd. ✆ 702/221-9144. Caesars Palace, 3500 Las Vegas Blvd. S. ✆ 702/792-8233. www.fieldofdreams.com.

Gallery of Legends Even more sports memorabilia—signed, sealed, and delivered with certificates of authenticity in a 1,200-square-foot store. When do these superstars have time to play? Don't their hands get tired from all that signing? Overwhelming. Sunday through Thursday 10am to 11pm, Friday and Saturday from 10am until midnight. Desert Passage, 3663 Las Vegas Blvd. S. ℂ **702/471-8300.** www. galleryoflegends.net.

TOYS & GAMES

Build-a-Bear Workshop   This is just too cute. You select an empty fur husk that will become your bear's body (they also have tigers, horses, and other cute critter skins), which is then stuffed with fluff before you give it a (plastic) heart and a name. Then you pay. Your bear is registered, and then you can buy heaps of clothes and accessories for him/her/it. It's oddly compelling for adults (people have proposed via the bears), and kids love it, too. Sunday through Thursday 10am to 11pm, Friday and Saturday from 10am until midnight. Desert Passage, 3663 Las Vegas Blvd. S. ℂ **702/836-0899.** www.buildabear.com.

Disney Store   This chain store carries all things Disney, but with an emphasis on the more modern creations, including *Little Mermaid, Beauty and the Beast,* and whatever else the studio has recently released or rereleased. You will find some of the classics—Mickey, Minnie, Pluto, and Goofy—but they are overwhelmed by The Incredibles and their ilk, making this more for pop-encultured kids than their nostalgic parents. The Caesars Palace store is open Sunday through Thursday 10am to 11pm, Friday and Saturday from 10am until midnight, while the Fashion Show location is open from 10am to 6pm daily. Fashion Show Mall, 3200 Las Vegas Blvd. S. ℂ **702/737-5400.** Caesars Palace, 3500 Las Vegas Blvd. S. ℂ **702/732-9560.** www.disneystore.com.

Endangered Species Store   Stuffed animals, T-shirts, puzzles, and games designed to increase awareness of the earth's rapidly disappearing fauna fill the shelves here. A portion of the sales from this store goes to organizations dedicated to saving endangered creatures. Both casino locations are open Sunday through Thursday 10am to 11pm, Friday and Saturday from 10am until midnight. Caesars Forum Shops, 3500 Las Vegas Blvd. S. ℂ **702/794-4545.** Desert Passage, 3663 Las Vegas Blvd. S. ℂ **702/794-0220.**

FAO Schwarz   From outside, the giant Trojan horse nods his head to welcome you into the ultimate toy store for kids and adults. If you can tear yourself and your children away from the store's own line of stuffed animals—some of the softest, most plush, loveable animals ever—you'll find three levels to explore. Along with a room dedicated solely to all things Barbie, there is a special area for Gene—a glamorous 1940s movie star doll—and her friends, a *Star Wars* boutique, G.I. Joes, electronic games, plus thousands of offerings from Steiff, Fisher-Price, and other well-known manufactures. A special section is dedicated to costumes, while another area holds trains and erector sets. You can walk around inside the Trojan horse, which is set up like a tree house, and if your children are really, really good, you can arrange for them to have a birthday party or sleepover at the store. This is one of our favorite places to spend hours and money. *Note:* Though many FAO Schwarz branches closed across the country when the company declared bankruptcy, this branch is supposed to remain open for the foreseeable future. Caesars Palace, 3500 Las Vegas Blvd. S. ℂ **702/796-6500.** www.fao.com.

Fantasy Toys   At this store, you can indulge your child's desire to be a child. The "fantasy" here means your little one's imagination, rather than weirdly costumed action figures from a grisly blockbuster sci-fi movie. You'll find mind-stimulating gifts for all age groups from newborns to 'tweens, including mobiles, Lincoln Logs, Tinkertoys, and even motor scooters here. The Meadows, 4300 Meadows Lane. ℂ **702/258-7448.**

GameKeeper Dedicated game players will find a wide selection of board games, plus Dungeons & Dragons, card games, strategy games, and more at this shop. There's also a selection of handheld electronic games and books on gaming. The Meadows, 4300 Meadows Lane. ✆ **702/878-1188.**

Toys "R" Us Toys, toys, toys: Battery operated, wind-up, push, pull, and stationary. It's huge, it can be loud (especially on weekends and around the holidays, when it can, at times, resemble a personal definition of hell), and though it's not as posh as FAO Schwarz, they do have sales and specials, and children will be busy for hours looking at all the stuff they'll want you to buy them. It's a good place for preplanning your holiday and birthday gift buying, so bring paper and pencil. Batteries are thoughtfully sold here for the toys that need them. Kids "R" Us, a clothing and kid supply store (p. 204), is on the same property. Both locations are open 9:30am to 9:30pm daily. 4000 S. Maryland Pkwy. ✆ **702/732-3733.** 4550 Meadows Lane. ✆ **702/877-9070.** www.toysrus.com.

VINTAGE & USED SHOPS

The Attic The former star of a Visa commercial, The Attic shares a large space with Cafe Neon, a coffeehouse that also serves Greek-influenced cafe food (so you can take a break during your shopping). The store offers plenty of clothing choices on many racks. Expect that all your child's dress-up desires will be met or surpassed here. Open Monday through Thursday from 10am until 5pm, Friday from 10am until 6pm, and Saturday from 11am until 6pm. 1018 S. Main St. ✆ **702/388-4088.** www.theatticlasvegas.com.

Buffalo Exchange Though this is actually a branch of a chain of stores spread out across the western United States, you shouldn't let the chain part keep you away; this store has plenty of cool stuff and good prices. Staffed by plenty of incredibly hip alt-culture kids, it is stuffed with dresses, shirts, pants, and so forth, both vintage and slightly worn, as well as remainder and discontinued fashions. We've seen Prada, Donna Karan, and other designers come through in addition to 1960s golf sweaters, retro cocktail dresses, and the like. But like any vintage shop, the contents are hit or miss, though the large stock ensures the chance of finding something. The store is open Monday through Saturday from 11am to 8pm and Sunday from noon until 7pm. 4110 S. Maryland Pkwy. (at Flamingo). ✆ **702/791-3960.** www.buffaloexchange.com.

Kids Kloset _Value_ Whether you need a preowned bassinette or are looking for back-to-school clothes for your rapidly sprouting 5-year-old, Kids Kloset can help. Featuring clothes and accessories for the newborn to size 7 child, the shop takes care to only buy clothes in good condition and resells them at reasonable prices, so that children can get clothes that are cool, while parents are pleased with their savings. 4250 S. Rainbow Blvd. ✆ **702/368-1983.**

Entertainment for the Whole Family

During its first few decades as Sin City, Las Vegas had a great formula for entertaining visitors; they'd deliver one or more of the following: pretty girls dancing in skimpy, sparkling outfits; a comedian; or a big-name star (though in later years, it became formerly big-name stars) headlining. Then, they'd run the show and get their guests in and out of the showroom and back to the gambling tables in less than 2 hours.

During the building boom of the '90s and the advent of the megacasino, many of the huge new hotels sought to lure guests through larger-than-life, fanciful themes and a confusing array of outdoor spectacles ranging from pirate battles to fire-belching volcanoes to dancing fountains. Coming at the same time as the hollow campaign to represent Las Vegas as a family destination, the themes and street extravaganzas were misinterpreted as proof that the major hotels were getting behind the family-friendly press releases. But alas, the over-the-top themes and colossal outdoor productions were about market share pure and simple, about getting more adults into the casino. Though the come-ons were in fact pretty juvenile, establishing a family clientele was the last thing the casinos intended.

The one-upmanship along the Strip was also manifest in the showrooms. Modest headliner and production shows gave way to eye-popping presentations with huge casts, staged in custom theaters seating audiences numbering in the thousands.

You can still see showgirls in their daring outfits (or without them, for that matter), but now they have full-blown productions behind them involving fire, ice, and light shows. These days, headliners are signed to 2-year contracts, Broadway shows come through town and land at hotel resorts, and some top-flight performances such as Cirque du Soleil's *Mystère* and Blue Man Group draw visitors to Vegas just to see their shows.

There's no longer any doubt that one of Las Vegas's biggest draws is its entertainment. Really! It has internationally known headline acts, local favorites, showgirls, comics, impersonators—both the female drag version and the faux-celebrity types—animals, and magicians appearing at hotels throughout the city. Add to all those stage shows the sporting events; rock concerts; Broadway shows; local, community-supported orchestras, dance, and theater (all of which can make a pleasant change from the onslaught of sequins and disappearing doves that are the staple of most resort shows); and much, much, more, and you can begin to understand the allure of all of Vegas's entertainment possibilities.

Of course, the options are more numerous for adults, but don't fret—Vegas also has entertainment that's quite suitable for the whole family, most notably magicians using animals, ranging from the afternoon delights of

Mac King and Rick Thomas to the over-the-top effects of Cirque du Soleil's *O*. And parents who don't object to their kids watching Christina Aguilera and Britney Spears videos may not mind taking their kids to *Folies Bergere*'s early show, though, for some kids, seeing semi-nude women dancing in real life while seated next to their parents might be disconcerting or uncomfortable; you may feel the same degree of discomfort, too.

For families, an evening out at a big ticket, major production show can run into the hundreds of dollars. There are, however, lower-priced options that provide a decent entertainment value, though you will not be seeing the same level of showmanship and production as you would at, say, Celine Dion. Will your kids enjoy the lower-priced shows? Most likely, especially your younger ones. Will you? Sure, especially if your children are having fun.

Sporting events in Las Vegas range from university football, basketball, and volleyball games to major boxing and golf matches, national rodeo finals, and local minor league baseball games.

The local performing arts scene also provides families with opportunities to see ballet, symphony orchestras, and plays. The Rainbow Company Children's Theatre and the Nevada Ballet perform regularly, and the Las Vegas Philharmonic works hard to prove that there's more to Vegas than the jingle of slot machines and the purr of Elvis impersonators.

Las Vegas, with both its production shows and local performing arts groups, offers opportunities for families to share time together, whether they're seeing a tiger disappear or watching a ballet troupe interpret Pink Floyd. Whatever you choose, know that spending an afternoon or evening at a show with your family (whatever that show may be) will almost definitely provide for many lasting memories for you and your family.

1 What's Playing Where

Most acts in Las Vegas sign a contract their first time in the city. If all goes well, they'll renew and extend their contract. If things go really well, they'll last forever or may move to a different, bigger location. Some shows eventually close for any number of reasons, including lack of interest from the general public. Las Vegas is showbiz Darwinism at its most refined, though what passes as the fittest is sometimes baffling, though always amusing. The following section will describe each of the major production shows appropriate for families currently playing in Las Vegas, arranged alphabetically by the title of the production. But first, here's a handy list arranged by hotel:

- **Bellagio:** Cirque du Soleil's *O* (unique circus-meets-performance-art theatrical experience; ages 5 and up)
- **Caesars Palace:** Celine Dion (music and variety; ages 12 and up)
- **Excalibur:** *Tournament of Kings* (medieval-themed revue; all ages)
- **Harrah's:** *Mac King Comedy Magic Show* (comedy and magic; all ages); Clint Holmes (music and variety, impersonations; ages 5 and up)
- **Imperial Palace:** *Legends in Concert* (musical impersonators; ages 5 and up)
- **The Luxor:** Blue Man Group, *Live at Luxor* (hilarious performance art; ages 5 and up)
- **Mandalay Bay:** *Mamma Mia* (musical based on the works of pop group ABBA; ages 5 and up)
- **Monte Carlo:** *Lance Burton: Master Magician* (magic show and revue; ages 5 and up)

Buying Show Tickets

Las Vegas shows, once a great bargain, are now pretty expensive. Before plunking down your cash, check the freebie visitor magazines for discount coupons. Also check the half-price ticket outlet in the Showcase Mall just north of the MGM Grand called **Tickets2Nite.** This discounter sells tickets for same-day shows for half price plus a $3 service fee. Open 2 to 9 pm, it's first come, first serve. Generally speaking, you won't find tickets available for top-tier productions such as the Cirque du Soleil shows, Blue Man Group, Danny Gans, and Celine, because, among other reasons, they sell out every night. Many, if not most of the other shows, turn up at Tickets2Nite, some routinely, some periodically. Tickets2Nite has a website, **www.Tickets2Nite.com**, but it doesn't list what shows are available on a particular day. According to Tickets2Nite, "agreements with the shows restrict us from disclosing that information except on our menu boards after 1:45 pm daily." So, yes, that means you have to troop over to the Tickets2Nite box office in person to see what's available.

A second half-price outlet is **Tix4Tonight,** located next door to the Harley-Davidson Cafe on the Strip. Tix4Tonight operates in pretty much the same way as Tickets2Nite, but often offers more shows than Ticket2Nite, and charges a lower handling fee. Tix4Tonight and Tickets2Nite sell largely the same shows, but each handles a number of shows the other doesn't sell. The two discounters are located so close together that it's easy and convenient to comparison shop.

If you're nervous about waiting until the last minute to purchase your tickets, most tickets are now available from **Ticketmaster** at **702/474-4000** or online at **www.ticketmaster.com**. Expect to pay full price, however.

- **Paris:** *We Will Rock You* (musical based on the songs of the rock band Queen; ages 10 and up)
- **Rio:** *Penn & Teller* (sarcastic, abrasive magic show; ages 5 and up); *Tony 'n' Tina's Wedding* (lighthearted comedy; ages 10 and up); *Scintas* (music and variety, impressions; ages 5 and up); Ron Lucas (comedy and ventriloquism; ages 5 and up)
- **Stratosphere:** *American Superstars* (an impression-filled production show; ages 7 and up); *Viva Las Vegas* (Las Vegas–style revue; ages 7 and up)
- **Treasure Island:** Cirque du Soleil's *Mystère* (unique circus performance; ages 10 and up)
- **Tropicana:** *Folies Bergere* (Las Vegas–style revue; 7:30pm show only for families, ages 8 and up; all other shows feature topless numbers, ages 16 and up)

2 Major Production Shows

Note: Although every effort has been made to keep up with the volatile Las Vegas show scene, keep in mind that the following reviews may not be indicative of the actual show you'll see, but the basic concept and idea will most probably be

---

The Wisdom of Youth

Las Vegas is better than Disneyworld, a hundred times! There's so much cool stuff! Wednesday, Dad and Susan got married; last night we saw Blue Man Group; and, tomorrow, we're going to O. I love it here, all of us do!

> —Kasey, age 9, in Las Vegas with her three siblings, her two stepsiblings, her dad, stepmom, and her stepgrandparents

---

the same. What's more, shows can close without warning, even ones that have been running just shy of forever, so it's a good idea to always call the venue ahead of time to check if it's open and what the show really is. And while you have them on the phone, find out if ticket prices include tax or drinks, just so you know which potential hidden costs you might be slammed with when you show up.

American Superstars   **Ages 5 and up.** Impersonator shows allow the audience to experience almost seeing their favorite stars in real life, but without having to pay a fortune and traipse all over to do so. (And, anyway, in the case of someone like Elvis, it would be pretty darn impossible, anyway, to catch the King in concert.) Here, Madonna, Ricky Martin, Christina Aguilera, and Michael Jackson (not maybe the best idea given Jacko's unfortunate publicity) are all re-created, live, in their most iconic phase (no lip-syncing allowed!), in all their pop glory—sparkling costumes, beards, sunglasses, whatever it takes to make sure you know who's being impersonated. The show is opened by a good Elvis, followed by a Ricky Martin who shakes his bon-bon quite credibly. Madonna is from the lingerie era of her career, and the version of modern poptress Aguilera is spot-on. Country fans will appreciate the fine voice and fiddling of Charlie Daniels. The Michael Jackson impersonator is good, but we found ourselves asking why and cringing a bit when watching that one. If your kids are fans of one or more of these performers in real life, or are just pop music fans, then they're more than likely to enjoy this show, and you will, too, as the skills of the impersonators will no doubt impress you, at least a bit! (While this show focuses more on pop music, the *Legends in Concert* show—see below—is geared more toward rock musicians such as Bruce Springsteen, Rod Stewart, and Little Richard. However, both shows deliver solid entertainment, so it's more about what your kids would prefer when choosing a show instead of which is better.) Shows are Sunday through Tuesday at 7pm, Wednesday, Friday and Saturday at 6:30 and 8:30pm. In the Stratosphere Las Vegas, 2000 Las Vegas Blvd. S. ✆ **800/99-TOWER** or 702/380-7711. www.statospherehotel.com. Tickets $39 adults, $28 children 5–12 (including tax and gratuity); $47 for show, buffet, 2 drinks, and tower pass (including tax and gratuity).

Blue Man Group: ***Live at Luxor***   **Ages 5 and up.** Kids will love this, period. Three men painted all blue ("I want to be one for Halloween," we overheard one tyke proclaiming afterward) do outrageous things with breakfast cereal, Jell-O, Twinkies, marshmallows, and more. The blue men—sort of innocent aliens/curious children/gentle beings from another place and time—make percussive music by playing PVC pipes and generally spread merriment and mischief using everyday objects during the 1¼ hour show (which some have said seemed longer). We found it to be a thought-provoking, uplifting, light-hearted experience, and the kids around us were spellbound. As an adult, you might find yourself squirming at times, especially if high-concept performance art is not your bag (until the uplifting, hysterical finale), but you and your children will

Aladdin Casino **1**
Blue Man Group:
  Live at Luxor
  (Luxor Las Vegas) **7**
Excalibur Casino **5**
Folies Bergere
  (Tropicana) **6**
House of Blues
  (Mandalay Bay) **8**
*The Illusionary Magic
  of Rick Thomas*
  (Tropicana) **6**
La Femme!
  (MGM Grand) **4**
Lance Burton:
  Master Magician
  (Monte Carlo) **2**
Luxor Las Vegas Casino **7**
Mamma Mia
  (Mandalay Bay) **8**
Mandalay Bay Casino **8**
MGM Grand Casino **4**
Monte Carlo
  Pub & Brewery
  (Monte Carlo) **2**
New York–New York
  Casino **3**
rumjungle
  (Mandalay Bay) **8**
Steve Wyrick (Aladdin/
  Planet Hollywood) **1**
Tournament of Kings
  (Excalibur) **5**
Tropicana Bird Show
  (Tropicana) **6**
Zumanity (New York–
  New York) **3**

surely discuss the show at length afterward. Be warned—the front rows get wrapped in waterproof plastic for a reason. Shows are Tuesday and Thursday at 7pm; Monday, Wednesday, and Friday at 7 and 10pm; Saturday at 4, 7, and 10pm; and Sunday at 7pm. *Note:* Just as this book went to press, the Blue Man Group announced it would be relocating to the Venetian in late 2005. In the Luxor Las Vegas, 3900 Las Vegas Blvd. S. © **800/288-1000** or 702/262-4000. www.blueman.com. Tickets $94 (including tax and gratuity).

Celine Dion: *A New Day*   **Ages 12 and up.** Celine Dion's Las Vegas production, created by Cirque du Soleil visionary Franco Dragone, blends a whopping 22 of Dion's songs with the surreal characters, imagery, and athletic (often acrobatic) choreography that distinguishes Cirque du Soleil. *A New Day*'s amazing costumes and sets are augmented by an enormous LED screen, the largest in the world, that wraps around the entire rear of the stage in a sweeping half circle. On it are displayed razor-sharp moving images, both powerful and hypnotic, that add haunting texture and context to what is happening on stage. The cast alone could carry *A New Day*, but the incorporation of this technological marvel exponentially leverages their considerable talent, wowing audiences in the same way that the introduction of sound or color once amazed moviegoers. *A New Day* is not just another Las Vegas spectacle, though as a production show it's truly groundbreaking in its special effects and choreography. What makes it transcendent is a diva who has the chutzpah to share the stage with such technology and talent. There are times, literally, when the dancing and LED images (everything from

Times Square to a passing storm) are so compelling that you momentarily forget Celine Dion is singing. But when you refocus your attention on her, you begin to understand the seamless way the elements of this production are integrated. Shows are Wednesday through Sunday at 8:30 pm. In the Colosseum Showroom at Caesars Palace, 3570 Las Vegas Boulevard S. ② **702/731-7333** or 877/4-CELINE. www.caesars.com. Tickets $7.50–$225 including tax and gratuity (children under 3 free).

Cirque du Soleil's *Mystère* **Ages 8 and up.** Part circus, part surrealist stage show, Cirque du Soleil's performances have defied description since the Canadian troupe first began performing their strange blend of dance, acrobatics, and mime over 20 years ago. When *Mystère* opened a decade ago in Vegas, there was nothing like it on the Strip, and even today, with its sibling *O* (at the Bellagio; see below) and the performance group the Blue Man Group at the Luxor (see above), *Mystère* is still a standout: Acrobats and gymnasts twirl, contort, and float through the air to the strains of haunting music; performers drop from giant bungee cords and scale vertical poles; and stilt-walkers prowl the stage in this show, considered by many to be the best production in Las Vegas. Children and adults alike will be awestruck by the feats of the 72 performers who bend and twist, defying physics and gravity. Plus there's a clown and a giant snail. Though all ages are admitted, this show is more suited for older children and teens; it can be a little scary at times, with some erotic overtones. The best view is from the center rows. Shows are Wednesday, Saturday, and Sunday at 4:30, 7:30, and 10:30pm. In Treasure Island, 3300 Las Vegas Blvd. S. ② **800/288-7206** or 702/894-7722. www.treasureisland.com. Tickets $95 (plus tax and surcharge).

Cirque du Soleil's *O* **Ages 5 and up.** This astounding show features a 1½-million-gallon pool of water into which performers dive, out of which they rise, and above which they fly, making *O* (a homophone of the French word *eau*, meaning water, and of the gasps you'll hear from the audience) a cross between a Busby Berkeley musical and a surrealist montage. There is a plot (our hero loses his red scarf and experiences many strange adventures trying to retrieve it), but it's secondary to the action on stage, which includes carousel horses descending from the ceiling, synchronized diving, a water ballet, and a fountain that erupts during the hour-and-a-half show. This is truly phenomenal entertainment for all ages, which, like *Mystère,* defies description; you must see it and experience the dreamlike world into which the performers draw you. You'll get the best view from the center seats somewhat up from the floor. Shows are Wednesday through Sunday at 7:30 and 10:30pm. In the Bellagio, 3600 Las Vegas Blvd. S. ② **888/488-7111** or 702/693-7722. www.bellagiolasvegas.com/pages/ent_main.asp. Tickets $99–$150 (including tax and surcharge). Children under 18 must be accompanied by an adult.

Danny Gans: *The Man of Many Voices* **Ages 10 and up.** Affable, talented Gans may be the man of many voices, but, unfortunately, unless your children are retro-buffs, they will not recognize many of the impressions he does so well. They may, however, laugh at some of the jokes. Gans can impersonate over 400 celebrities and on any given night, he'll perform about 80 or so of them, depending on the crowd. Teens may recognize Bruce Springsteen, but be baffled by the Spencer Tracy/Katherine Hepburn dialogue spouting from Gans's talented throat. The "Twelve Days of Christmas," sung in 12 different voices, will make kids laugh even if they don't recognize Paul Lynde or Woody Allen. His speech at the end about his inspiration to perform may inspire some but make older kids roll their eyes. If your child is an aspiring actor, or has a good background in vintage film and television, this might be a good call. Otherwise, you

Bellagio Casino **8**
Caesars Palace Casino **7**
Celine Dion: *A New Day*
(Caesars Palace) **7**
Cirque du Soleil's *Mystere*
(Treasure Island) **1**
Cirque du Soleil's *O* (Bellagio) **8**
Cleopatra's Barge Nightclub
(Caesars Palace) **7**
Danny Gans: *The Man of Many Voices*
(The Mirage) **3**
Eiffel Tower Bar (Paris Las Vegas) **10**
Imperial Palace Luau (Imperial Palace) **5**
Jubilee! (Bally's Las Vegas) **9**
Legends in Concert (Imperial Palace) **5**

Mac King Comedy Magic Show
(Harrah's) **4**
The Mirage Casino **3**
Second City (The Flamingo) **6**
The Venetian Casino **2**
Venus and Tiki Bar Lounge
(The Venetian) **2**
We Will Rock You
(Paris Las Vegas) **10**

may be better off spending an evening at a show they can relate to. The showroom has good seating throughout, and you're really there to hear (not see) him, anyway. Shows are Tuesday through Thursday and Saturday and Sunday at 8pm. In The Mirage, 3400 Las Vegas Blvd. S. ☎ **800/963-9634** or 702/792-7777. Tickets $100 (with tax and surcharge).

Folies Bergere **Ages 8 and up.** There is little difference between this show's 7:30pm performance and a Shakira or Britney Spears video—think G-strings, pasties, and some shimmying. That aside, the "family" version of Las Vegas's longest-running show provides a glimpse into the days of yore with beautiful women in sequined headdresses, plenty of dancing (including can-can and hoe down numbers), and some juggling thrown in for good measure. (The late show, which is for adults only, features topless dancers, which, oddly, are not that enthralling, but if you want to see an old-school Vegas show once you put the kids to bed, this might be the call.) Of course, depending on their age, your children may not enjoy watching scantily clad ladies prance about with you seated next to them; you too may feel a bit uncomfy for the 90 minutes the show is on, but rest assured that it's no worse than what's being shown on MTV these days. The dinner/show combo features a meal at Tuscano Italian Café, Mizuno, or Savanna and a ticket for the show, actually a bargain if you are thinking of making a night of it. Shows are Tuesday and Friday at 8:30pm and Monday, Wednesday, Thursday, and Saturday at 7 and 10pm. In the Tropicana Resort & Casino,

3801 Las Vegas Blvd. S. Ⓒ **800/829-9034** or 702/739-2411. www.tropicanalv.com. Tickets $57–$63 (including tax and surcharge), dinner and show special $58 and $68 (including tax and surcharge).

The Illusionary Magic of Rick Thomas   **Ages 5 and up.** This is a great show for families. Not only is it an incredible value, but its afternoon hours make it especially good for younger kids who might get tired at evening shows. Along with being a fine magician with, dare we say, plenty of tricks up his sleeve, Thomas delivers a warm, uplifting message about believing in yourself, following your dreams, and using your imagination, along with making tigers appear and disappear, doing card tricks, and levitating a showgirl. Plus, he includes a moving tribute to his mother, stressing how important she was in encouraging his dreams. (Moms, are you listening?) Handsome and charming, Thomas has been voted Stage Magician of the Year at the World Magic Awards and is considered the top matinee act in Las Vegas, and for good reason (though we think Mac King, see below, is his equal or maybe even a tad better). Thomas emphasizes that he himself developed his desire to be a stage magician at age 7 after being pulled out of an audience to assist in an act before pulling a child on stage to help him out. Charming!

A quick word about seating and the room itself: The tables and seats in the front are set up perpendicular to the stage, so you will have to rotate your chairs, or twist your neck for a straight-on view, and it may be hard for children to see around grown-ups seated next to them. The tables farther from the stage are small and round, and, again, require some maneuvering of chairs for a straight-on view of the stage, but they are on a raised level and have good sight lines. The booths on the floor are about $6 more per person, but offer greater seating comfort and more table space, as well as an awesome view. Shows are Monday through Saturday at 2 and 4pm. In the Tropicana Resort & Casino, 3801 Las Vegas Blvd. S. Ⓒ **888/826-8767** or 702/739-2222. Tickets $21 and $27 (plus tax and surcharge).

Lance Burton: *Master Magician*   **Ages 5 and up.** There are numerous magic acts in Vegas of varying degrees of charm and opulence, most of which rely on huge, bombastic effects and plenty of animals while ignoring the fine art of legerdemain—sleight of hand, close-up magic. If you want to see an evening magic show that won't leave you feeling like your pocket has been picked, this is the act to see. Burton, a true Southern gentleman via Lexington, Kentucky, offers low-key delivery and dry humor, along with producing dozens of ducks

---

Aloha, Las Vegas!

For those who want to take a brief detour to the South Pacific during their explorations of Paris, Egypt, Rome, and other exotic locales in Vegas, the **Imperial Palace,** 3535 Las Vegas Blvd. S. (Ⓒ **888/777-7664** or 702/731-3311; www.imperialpalace.com) provides an evening of island-themed entertainment and (naturally, this being Vegas) an all-you-can-eat island buffet with unlimited mai tais and piña coladas, and nonalcoholic fruit punch. Exotic drumming, hula dancing, torch lighting, conch blowing, and the wearing of flower leis are all part of evening fun here, Tuesdays and Thursdays, from April through October.

This is a sort of goofy fun evening (adults will welcome the free tropical drink to get them in the mood), but the dancing is amazing, and the drumming invigorating. A meal and show runs $38 for adults and $18 for children. Children under 4 are free.

American Superstars
(Stratosphere Las Vegas) **1**

Circus Circus Casino **2**

Elvis-A-Rama **4**

Riviera Comedy Club
(Riviera Hotel & Casino) **3**

Splash
(Riviera Hotel & Casino) **3**

Viva Las Vegas
(Stratosphere Las Vegas) **1**

out of nowhere and turning a dove into confetti. His work with coins, candles, and other objects is what won him his title as World Champion of Magic from Federation International Society de Magic, but he can make cars come and go with equal ease. The show is housed in a specially built theater, reminiscent of a Victorian music hall, but with modern touches; the comfy seats come with cup holders, an especially thoughtful touch for families. There really isn't a bad seat in the room, though you will want to be as close to the action as possible. Shows are Tuesday through Saturday at 7 and 10pm. In the Lance Burton Theater at the Monte Carlo Resort & Casino, 3770 Las Vegas Blvd. S. ✆ **800/311-8999** or 702/730-7777. www.lance burton.com. Tickets $60–$65 (plus tax and surcharge).

Legends in Concert **Ages 5 and up.** For more than 2 decades, this show has been pleasing crowds of all ages with impersonations of classic stars (Elvis, the Supremes, and more) to the more time-specific (Prince). Instead of lip-syncing, these impersonators—um, re-creations—actually sing and speak (and when called for, play instruments) just like the stars they're dressed up to be. Overall, they succeed on all counts. Acts are accompanied by a live band, and dancers of both genders do their darnedest in gauzy, skimpy outfits, dancing to different artist's greatest hits. The acts change seasonally (expect a more country flair during December's rodeo finals), but Elvis is always in the house here. Other re-creations have included Rod Stewart, Madonna, Prince, Bruce Springsteen, Little Richard, and Bette Midler—a sort of middle-of-the-road demographic spread that will appeal to everyone from grandparents on down through the generations. This 90-minute show has no age minimums, but kids over 5 will enjoy it the most. The dinner package includes a ticket to the Emperor's buffet dinner and a pass for the Imperial Auto Collections. Both this show and *American Superstars,* reviewed above, deliver solid entertainment. However, there is a slight rock edge at *Legends* (Bruce Springsteen, Rod Stewart, Little Richard), while *Superstars* goes more for the pop emphasis. That aside, the only real difference is location: *Legends'* home, the Imperial Palace, is Center Strip, while *American Superstars* is located on the North Strip at the Stratosphere. Shows are Monday through Saturday at 7 and 10pm. In the Imperial Palace, 3535 Las Vegas Blvd. S. © **888/ 777-7664** or 702/731-3311. www.imperialpalace.com. Tickets $40 adults (includes 2 drinks, tax, and gratuity), $25 children 2–12, free for children under 2; dinner package $45 adults, $30 children 2–12, free for children under 2 (includes tax and gratuity).

Mac King Comedy Magic Show **All ages.** Goofy, beguiling, funny, sweet, and, at under $20 a ticket, possibly the best show deal in Vegas—Mac King is the perfect show for children and adults. His costuming is straight off *Green Acres* (plaid suit, bowl haircut), his humor is broad, his tricks impeccable, and he seems so charmingly astounded when they work (when they don't he shrugs it off with, "That would have been cool, though," while working the "failed" trick into part of a larger scheme). At least one child will be called up on stage to help with a trick, while a pair of grown-ups will be drawn into a complex card trick involving the magician's cloak of invisibility. Whether turning himself into a white tiger (sort of) or playing with flying food, King makes every trick fresh, as though this is the first time he's tried it; and that sort of attitude is infectious. The hour-long show is brilliant, and a must see. Shows are Tuesday through Saturday at 1 and 3pm. At Harrah's Las Vegas, 3475 Las Vegas Blvd. S. © **800/392-9002** or 702/ 369-5000. www.harrahs.com/our_casinos/las/entertainment/mac_king.html. Tickets $19 (plus tax and gratuity).

Mamma Mia **Ages 5 and up.** Swedish pop group ABBA created some of the most infectious hits of the 1970s, and the group's songwriters, Benny Andersson and Björn Ulvaeus (the Bs in ABBA) have woven 22 of their tunes into this rollicking, frothy musical. Some parents may find the "plot" a little off-putting for children: Unsure of who her father might be, because mom was a bit wild, a bride-to-be invites the three likely men to her wedding on a Greek island. The music is the real draw, however, and the songs fit cleverly into the storyline. This 2-hour show could be a little long for younger kids, even if they do perk up during the music and dance; teens with a 1970s flair will especially enjoy it here. Shows are Monday, Thursday, Saturday, and Sunday at 5 and 9pm. At Mandalay Bay, 3950 Las Vegas Blvd. S. © **877/632-7000** or 702/632-7000. www.mandalaybay.com/entertainment. Tickets $45–$100 (plus tax and gratuity).

Penn & Teller **Ages 5 and up.** This is the show for cynical, bored teens, for know-it-alls, wiseacres, and, well, for anyone over 12. The Bad Boys of Magic, Penn and Teller (Penn speaks, Teller suffers) brought their bullets and wood chippers with them to this one. Penn & Teller deconstruct magic, explaining its

Value Feathered & Free

In the *Tropicana Bird Show,* starring Tiana Carroll, the talented animal trainer performs with her fine-feathered cast of amazing avians who sing, dance, ride a bicycle, fly through hoops on command, and juggle upside down. The action happens at the **Tropicana**, 3801 Las Vegas Blvd. S. (✆ **888/ 826-8767** or 702/739-2411; www.tropicanalv.com). The free shows take place daily at 11:30am and 1:30 and 2:30pm.

history, laying out its scams. Using cards, knives, and bullets, they'll perform an illusion, then do the stunt again, pulling the scales from the audience's eyes by explaining how the trick works, and then—when the audience thinks they have it all figured out—perform another, similar trick without explanation, leaving the audience gaping. This is a clever, smart show: It's irreverent, sarcastic, and, at times, disturbing (the bunny/wood chipper trick, plus other cool but gory effects, makes this a show for older kids, despite the hotel being willing to admit any paying customer aged 5 and up). But you will leave the theater after an hour and a half thinking about the nature of reality, illusion, and deception; and wanting to see the show again, just to see if you can catch the sleight of hand, the distraction, the wire, the false bottom, and maybe, maybe figure out how these two masters do it. Their loyal fans follow the duo on their website, **www. pennandteller.com**. All seats are good for this show, though, as in most cases with magic acts, closer is better. Shows are Wednesday through Monday at 9pm. In the Rio Hotel & Casino, 3700 Las Vegas Blvd. S. ✆ **888/746-7784** or 702/252-7777. www.play rio.com. Tickets $80 (includes tax and gratuity).

Steve Wyrick **Ages 5 and up.** This magic show features animals, birds, and some thrilling stunts involving a helicopter, the spinning engine blade of a 747 (very scary), and dancing girls, making it, all in all, a very Vegas experience. Some adults and older kids (especially those who have watched all those "Secrets of the Magicians Revealed" type shows) may find it a bit hokey—you know Wyrick won't be chopped to bits by the spinning blades, because if that were to happen, how would he do the second show?—but it's still cool to try and figure out how the heck he does some of his illusions. Aside from being quite handy with the big production stunts (including unshackling himself from restraints a second before a huge saw drops from above), Wyrick performs an excellent, extended card trick (which he claims took 7 months to perfect) involving a complex story and audience participation. Seating is at tables or at booths, but for the price difference, stick to the tables. *Warning:* There are explosions and stage smoke; the former may scare some children, while the latter could affect those with asthma. Shows are Wednesday through Saturday and Monday at 7 and 10pm, and Sunday at 7pm. At the Steve Wyrick Theater at the Aladdin/Planet Hollywood Resort & Casino, 3667 Las Vegas Blvd. S. ✆ 877/335-9474 or 702/736-1111. www.aladdin casino.com. Tickets $50–$90.

Tony 'n' Tina's Wedding **Ages 10 and up.** Tony and Tina are getting married, and you, plus the entire audience, are invited to participate in this unique interactive theatrical experience. Because the audience is indistinguishable from the cast, expect plenty of surprises and some unpredictable behavior from "guests" of the Nunzio and Vitale families during the ceremony and reception, where you'll feast at the wedding buffet (pretty darn good Italian food), eat cake, and dance during the two-and-a-half-hour production. Older children and teens will enjoy following the plot twists and the spontaneous interaction with the actors. This wacky, zany, and fun show is unlike any other in Vegas, and has been an off-Broadway classic since it debuted in the mid-1980s. Shows take place nightly at 7pm. At the Rio Hotel & Casino, 3700 Las Vegas Blvd. S. © **888/746-7784** or 702/252-7777. www.playrio.com. Tickets $87.

Tournament of Kings **All ages.** Galloping horses! Swordplay! Pounding the table! Singing! Shouting! Good vs. evil! Eating with your hands! *Tournament of Kings* is the big all-ages show at Excalibur. It's pretty darn fun for kids, and while a bit long for grown-ups, it definitely delivers plenty of live action.

As you enter the large arena surrounding a dirt floor, you'll take your assigned seat in sections named after countries and decorated with medieval flags and ye olde signage. Not to give away too much of the ending, but unless you like rooting for the loser, or want to be on the side of Ultimate Evil, avoid the Dragon section like the plague by asking in advance to sit elsewhere. If you want to back a winner, go for, say, France, Norway, or Ireland. If you prefer the "if you're not cheating, you're not playing" dictum, you might request Russia at the ticket booth.

The premise—as explained by Merlin the Magician, the minuscule court jester, and the Lord of Festival—is that you are all invited guests of King Arthur on the occasion of his son Christopher's 16th birthday. In his honor, the kings of various countries will be engaging in all sorts of jousting, swordsmanship, and medieval sporty-type activities. Never mind that Arthur didn't have a son named Christopher, as loudly pointed out by one child who had obviously read his *Knights of the Roundtable* near us on our last visit! Instead, get into the spirit and loudly cheer your champion! Beat your fists on the table! Tear apart your roasted game hen with your bare hands and wave its legs in the air! See why kids like it so much?

While the hour and a half of pageantry and spectacle is going on in front of you, you're getting fed a meal, because, after all, this is a dinner theater. The food is adequate, but barely so—pitchers of cola and salty cream of tomato soup with rolls, followed by a rather nicely cooked game hen, some dry potato wedges and a vegetable. (We got broccoli.) Dessert is a bland apple turnover. The very best

---

The Men Who Could Be (the) King

Las Vegas has cornered the market in fakery (note all the architecture that replicates other places and times), and much of its current low-cost entertainment is based on the art of illusions—and we don't mean just the magic acts. In addition to the female impersonator shows (not suitable for kids) and the full-production celebrity impersonators, there can be up to half a dozen Elvises in Las Vegas working the lounges at any one time. We prefer to catch our Elvis at the temple of all things Elvis, **Elvis-A-Rama,** 3401 S. Industrial Rd. (© **702/309-7200**), where a pseudo-Presley performs for three or four songs for free—a real bargain by any standard. If that's not enough for you, you'll have to pay from $15 to $20 ($22–$27, including museum admission) to see the Exhilarating Show, held daily at 7pm, or the Ultimate Tribute Show, playing Saturday through Thursday at 4pm. Expect to see '70s Elvis at the first show and a range of Elvis's music at the last, while the 4pm show includes Beatles and Bobby Darin impersonators. Kids will like the music; you'll enjoy the kitsch.

part—no utensils because this is the 12th century, and cutlery did not become popular for another 200 years or so.

Warning: The show features chemical fog, pyrotechnics, and dirt, as well as horses, so those with allergies or asthma should definitely take this into consideration before going. Also, this show might not be the best thing for younger children who could be upset by live fights (including a bloodless, simulated throat slitting), creepy masks, or by flames, explosions, and swirling spotlights. On the other hand, your young child may thrive on that sort of thing . . . Shows are nightly at 6 and 8:30pm. In Excalibur, 3850 Las Vegas Blvd. S. ✆ **800/933-1334** or 702/597-7600. Tickets $56 (includes tax and dinner).

Viva Las Vegas **Ages 7 and up.** If you are staying on, or visiting other attractions around the North Strip, this afternoon show could be a nice, inexpensive, hour-long diversion for your family, especially if they really want to see a typical Vegas show, and you'd prefer not to drop $50 a ticket. The show is inexpensive by comparison to most production shows, not too raunchy (though the raciness of the show depends on the demographic of the audience; the fewer the kids, the more off-color it can get—expect size, gender, and breast jokes), and has singing, dancing, some magic, and an Elvis impersonator—basically every Vegas routine that could be crammed on stage in 60 minutes. This is Las Vegas's longest running afternoon show, and while it's not the best show in town, or even the best afternoon show, it does provide some entertainment.

Note: Discount coupons are often found in those free magazines in your hotel room. Sometimes the discount gets you in free, with just the price of a drink; other deals include package discounts for a tower pass, the buffet, or other combinations. Shows are Monday through Saturday at 2 and 4pm. In the Stratosphere Las Vegas, 2000 Las Vegas Blvd. S. ✆ **800/99-TOWER** or 702/380-7777. Tickets $17 (plus tax and surcharge).

We Will Rock You **Ages 5 and up.** Originating in London's West End, *We Will Rock You* weaves 25 of rock band Queen's greatest hits around a thin story line. The plot takes place in a futuristic world where musical instruments are banned and conformity is strictly enforced. A group of rebels challenge the status quo blasting the establishment with the music of Queen. The 90-minute production is augmented by laser lights and images projected on six house-size plasma screens. Shows are at 9pm Monday and Friday; Tuesday, Wednesday, and Saturday at 7 and 10:30pm; and on Sunday at 5 and 9pm. At the Paris Las Vegas, 3655 Las Vegas Boulevard S., ✆ **702/946-4567**. www.paris-lv.com. Tickets $53–$114 including tax and gratuities.

3 Headliner Showrooms

Vegas entertainment made its name with its showrooms, though its glory days are somewhat behind it, gone with the Rat Pack themselves. For a long time, Vegas headliners were something of a joke; only those on the downhill side of fame were thought to play there, and children weren't welcome in them anyway. But with all the new performance spaces—and high fees—offered by the new hotels, Vegas suddenly has credence again, especially, in of all things, the rock scene. Both the Hard Rock Hotel's The Joint and the House of Blues are attracting very current and very popular acts who find it hip, rather than humiliating, to play Sin City, and some of those acts actually make it a point of catering to their fans by insisting that their shows allow all ages inside. However, the classic Vegas showroom itself does seem headed the way of the dinosaurs; many of the hotels have shuttered theirs. As for the remainder, one is pretty much like any other, with the exception of the Hard Rock and House of Blues (hence their detailed descriptions below), and, in any case, audiences go based on the performer rather than the space itself. Check with your hotel, or look in those free magazines in your room to see who is in town when you are and if the show is appropriate (and/or will be enjoyable) for your children.

Hard Rock Hotel's The Joint   Formerly just about the only game in town in terms of good rock bookings, The Joint, with a 1,400-seat capacity, now faces some stiff competition from the House of Blues. For example, when Alanis Morrisette came to town, she played the Hard Rock, but her opening act, Garbage, played the House of Blues. On the other hand, it was here that the Rolling Stones chose to do a show during their arena tour—this was the smallest venue the band had played in years, and, as you can imagine, it was one hot ticket. When the Hard Rock Hotel opened in 1995, The Eagles were the first act to appear. Since then, the facility has presented Ziggy Marley, Marilyn Manson, Tori Amos, the Black Crowes, Beck, the Rolling Stones, Tears for Fears, the Red Hot Chili Peppers, and Counting Crows, to name a few kid faves, along with Stephen Stills and Bob Dylan, who may be more appealing to adults.

The venue is not a preferred one, however; it's only worth going if a favorite performer is playing or if it's an opportunity to see a big artist play a smaller-than-usual room, or if there's an all-ages show, and you want to show your kid a good time. Though there's sometimes table seating, it's usually festival style, making personal space at a premium during a crowded show, and though the floor is slightly raked, this still makes for poor sightlines, especially for smaller kids. ("We get them as young as 6," said the helpful lady at the box office when asked about age limits.) The balconies upstairs, if you can get to them, aren't much better, as once the bodies are packed in about two deep, the stage is completely obscured. Unless you want to brave the crush at the very front (sure, you should—it's a rock show!), we suggest standing at the rail toward the back, which not only elevates you slightly above the crowd (improving those sightlines), but also protects one side of your body from the crowd. *Note:* Children must be accompanied by an adult here.

Showroom Policies: Smoking permitted for some shows; seating is either pre-assigned or general, depending on the performer. **Price:** $45 to $125, depending on the performer (tax and drinks extra). **Show Times:** 8:30pm (nights of performance vary, as do age requirements). **Reservations:** You can reserve up to 30 days in advance. In the Hard Rock Hotel & Casino, 4455 Paradise Rd. ℂ **800/473-7625** or 702/693-5000. www.hardrockhotel.com.

House of Blues   The House of Blues at Mandalay Bay goes head-to-head with The Joint at the Hard Rock Hotel. Probably the most comfortable and user-friendly place to see a rock show in Vegas, especially for children and teens, the House of Blues is a good, intimate room with a cozy floor surrounded by a bar area, and an upstairs balcony area that has actual theater seating. (The balcony might actually be a better place to see a show because the sightlines are unobscured, unlike down below, where posts and such can obstruct the view.) The Disney-bayou décor—with corrugated tin and weathered wood, plus walls covered in outsider/primitive/folk art from various Southern artists—can be a bit twee and overly nouveau-riche folksy, but kids do love to stare at all the stuff. The House of Blues has rock and blues shows just about every night, and, as mentioned, nationally recognized acts are flocking to the place: Billy Idol, X, Garbage, the B-52s, the Pretenders, the Wallflowers, Reverend Horton Heat,

Headliner Stadiums

Two arenas are worth a special mention because they often feature major entertainers and are open to all ages. **Sam Boyd Stadium,** the outdoor stadium for the University of Nevada, Las Vegas (UNLV) at 7000 E. Russell Rd., has been host to such major acts as Paul McCartney, U2, the Eagles, and Metallica. The **Thomas & Mack Center,** the university's indoor arena, located on the campus at 4505 Maryland Pkwy., has a more comprehensive concert schedule, which, in the past, has included Phish, Van Halen, Celine Dion, and Michael Bolton as well as shows such as Disney on Ice and the Ringling Bros. Circus. To reach either of the above, call ✆ **702/895-3900** or visit **www.thomasandmack.com**.

Ticketmaster (✆ **702/474-4000**) handles ticketing for concerts at these arenas, though tickets to some events can be purchased through the university (✆ **702/739-3267;** www.unlvtickets.com).

Etta James, Al Green, the Go-Gos, the Neville Brothers, and even the spoken word by Henry Rollins are just some of the acts who have performed here since the club opened.

Showroom Policies: Smoking permitted; seating is either preassigned or general, depending on the performer (some shows are all general admission, with everyone standing on the floor). **Price:** $15 to $100, depending on the performer. **Show Times:** Vary, but usually 8pm. Age requirements vary by acts. **Reservations:** You can buy tickets as soon as shows are announced; lead time varies with each artist. In Mandalay Bay, 3950 Las Vegas Blvd. S. ✆ **877/632-7400** or 702/632-7600. www.hob.com/venues/clubvenues/lasvegas.

4 Comedy Clubs

While Las Vegas is the proving ground for many comics and a place where visitors can catch both top-name and rising stars, unfortunately, most clubs are 21 and over. Below are the exceptions.

Riviera Comedy Club   Ages 12 and up. Featuring a rotating lineup of comedians, and designed to resemble a classic basement comedy club (rows of tables, a semicircular stage with a spot light and microphone), this is the only all-ages comedy spot in Las Vegas. Children 5 and older are welcome, though expect that they will hear some raunchy language and some off-color jokes, staples of comics and many PG-13 movies during the 1½-hour-long show; the 10pm show is even more "blue." Along with comics, hypnotists and ventriloquists occasionally share the bill. Dinner and show combos are also available. Performances are nightly at 8:30 and 10:30pm. In The Riviera, 2901 Las Vegas Blvd. S. ✆ **800/634-6753** or 702/734-5110. www.rivierahotel.com/entertainment_comedyclub.asp. Tickets $17, dinner/show combos $33 and $35.

Second City   Ages 12 and up. This wild troupe of improvisational comics goes for the laughs by skewering all manners of sacred cows. Expect at times to hear racial, sexual, and other jokes (think PG-13) as the audience shouts out suggestions and the cast works with the words and ideas to create skits and jokes. Second City, founded in Chicago in 1959, has spawned numerous comedians—many of the big-names cast in *Saturday Night Live* came from the troupe, including Bill Murray, Mike Myers, Gilda Radner, and John Belushi. Though the 75-minute show is open to ages 5 and up, the material is best suited for adolescents, and the early show is usually less raunchy. Performances are Thursday through Tuesday at 8pm; and Thursday through Saturday and Monday at 10:30pm. At The Flamingo, 3555 Las Vegas Blvd. S. ✆ **800/732-2111** or 702/733-3111. www.flamingolasvegas.com or www.secondcity.com. Tickets $30.

5 Spectator Sports

Las Vegas isn't especially well known for its sports teams. The only consistent spectator sports are those featuring teams from the University of Nevada, Las Vegas, while the rest of the city's sports teams, such as they are, resemble a bad soap opera, in which the characters get amnesia, disappear for years, or change their names and reappear as their twin. Sin City's minor league baseball team, the Stars, changed their named to the 51s and became a farm team for the Los Angeles Dodgers. The city's hockey team, the Thunder, took a powder break, and was replaced by the Wranglers.

A major venue for car racing, **Las Vegas Motor Speedway** draws major race events to Las Vegas, as well as providing a venue for demolition derbies, dirt biking, and go-kart races.

Because the city has several top-notch sporting arenas, there are important annual events that take place in Las Vegas, details for which can be found in the listings of major conventions (p. 22) and the "Las Vegas Calendar of Kid-Friendly Events" (p. 21). In addition to those listings, the **PGA Tours Las Vegas Senior Classic** is held each April in nearby Summerlin, and the **Las Vegas Invitational** takes place in Las Vegas each October. The **National Finals Rodeo** is held in UNLV's Thomas & Mack Center each December. From time to time, you'll also find NBA exhibition games, professional ice-skating competitions, or gymnastics exhibitions.

Finally, Las Vegas is well known as a major location for championship **boxing matches.** These are held in several Strip hotels, most often at Caesars or the MGM Grand, but sometimes, also, at The Mirage and Mandalay Bay. Tickets are hard to come by for these matches and are quite expensive. We suggest that if your children truly wish to watch a boxing match, you spring for the pay-per-view, rather than the insanity of the stadium during a match.

Tickets for sporting events at hotels are available either through **Ticketmaster** (✆ **702/893-3000**) or through the hotels themselves. (Why pay the service charges if you don't have to?)

PROFESSIONAL TEAMS

The 51s ★★ Las Vegas's local minor league team used to be known as the Stars, but after becoming the Los Angeles Dodgers' farm team, they took on this moniker, a tribute to alleged UFO spotting site, Area 51, located 90 minutes from Las Vegas. Their logo is an alien, and their fans truly love them. Home games are played at Cashman Field, which is also the site of preseason Major League exhibition games. Cashman Field, 850 Las Vegas Blvd. N. ✆ **702/474-4000**. www.lv51.com. General admission $7, reserved seating $8, plaza level $9, field level $11. Seasonal.

MAJOR SPORTS VENUES
OUTSIDE OF HOTELS

Las Vegas Motor Speedway ★★ The first new superspeedway to be built in the Southwest in over 2 decades, this venue seats 107,000. Included in the $100-million state-of-the-art motor-sports entertainment complex are a 1½-mile super-speedway, a 2½-mile FIA-approved road course, paved and dirt short-track

Las Vegas's Sports Venues, Stadiums & Local Performing Arts Venues

Washington Ave.
1 (8 miles)
2
3
Washington Ave.
Bonanza Rd.
93
15
Bruce St.
Eastern Ave.
95
Bonanza Rd.
← To The Meadows
Fremont St. Experience
515
95
93
599
Central Pkwy
Ogden Ave.
Fremont St.
Alta Dr.
Bonneville
Grand
Main St.
Casino Center Blvd.
DOWNTOWN
Las Vegas Ave.
Martin L. King Blvd.
Rancho Dr.
582
4
(1 mile)
Charleston Blvd.
GATEWAY DISTRICT
Charleston Blvd.
← To Red Rock Canyon/
Bonnie Springs Ranch
604
Oakey Blvd.
Main St.
Oakey Blvd.
0   0.5 mi
St. Louis Ave.
0   0.5 km
15
Sahara Ave.
Sahara Ave.
Sahara Ave.
Las Vegas Blvd. (The Strip)
Sahara
Monorail
Sahara Monorail station
Karen Ave.
Circus Circus Dr.
Joe W. Brown Dr.
Vegas Valley Dr.
Maryland Pkwy
La Canada St.
LV Hilton
Riviera Blvd.
Las Vegas Country Club
NORTH STRIP
Stardust Rd.
Convention Center Dr.
Desert Inn Rd.
Las Vegas Convention Center
Desert Inn Rd.
Industrial Rd.
LV Convention Center
Paradise Rd.
Fashion Show Mall
Treasure Island
Boulevard Mall
Las Vegas National Golf Club
Tram
Sands Expo
Sands Ave.
Swenson Ave.
Twain Ave.
Maryland Pkwy
Eastern Ave.
CENTER STRIP
5
6
Harrah's/Imperial Palace
Flamingo/Caesars Palace
605
Flamingo Rd.
Bally's & Paris
Flamingo Rd.
7 →
(4 miles)
Spencer St.
Frank Sinatra Dr.
Las Vegas Blvd. (The Strip)
Koval Ln.
Harmon Ave.
Paradise Rd.
UNIVERSITY OF NEVADA, LAS VEGAS
8
9
Maryland Pkwy
MGM Grand
Tropicana Ave.
10
Tropicana Ave.
Excalibur
Reno Ave.
To Henderson
SOUTH STRIP
Mandalay Bay Rd.
11
15
McCARRAN INTERNATIONAL AIRPORT
Russell Rd.
12 (12 miles)

Caesars Palace **6**
Cashman Field **3**
Charleston Heights Arts Center **4**
Cox Pavilion **9**
Henderson Promenade and Arts Center **12**
Las Vegas Motor Speedway **1**

Mandalay Bay **11**
MGM Grand **10**
The Mirage **5**
Reed Whipple Cultural Center **2**
Sam Boyd Stadium **7**
Thomas & Mack Center **9**
University of Nevada– Las Vegas **8**

Baby Bikers

Motocross, known colloquially as dirt biking, attracts many families, both as spectators and as participants. A women's league recently formed, and kids as young as 4 years old are racing on small bikes with 50cc (cubic centimeters; the engine size) engines called "teeny 50s." These peewee dirt bike competitions are held at Las Vegas Motor Speedway. Check out **www.dirt bikekids.com** for more information.

ovals, and a 4,000-foot drag strip. Also on the property are facilities for go-kart and Motocross racing, along with specialty racing opportunities such as Legends Car and Sand Drag. The new speedway is accessible via shuttle buses to and from the Imperial Palace hotel, though some of the other major hotels have their own shuttles to the Speedway. Free tours are offered. 7000 Las Vegas Blvd. N., directly across from Nellis Air Force base (take I-15 north to Speedway exit 54). ℂ 702/644-4443 for ticket information. www.lvms.com. Tickets $11–$262 (higher prices for major events).

University of Nevada, Las Vegas ★★ The university hosts three major sports venues: the Thomas & Mack Center, Cox Pavilion, and Sam Boyd Stadium. The Thomas & Mack Center, located on the campus at 4505 Maryland Pkwy., hosts the UNLV Running Rebels basketball team, as well as being the site of bull-riding championships, as well as concerts. The 3,000-seat Cox Pavilion, also on the campus, at 4505 Maryland Pkwy., is home to the UNLV volleyball teams and UNLV's Lady Rebels basketball team, as well as being the site of other indoor events. Sam Boyd Stadium, at 7000 East Russell Rd., is the site of UNLV Rebels' football games, as well as being a concert venue for bands like U2, the Eagles, and Metallica. Tickets for events at the Sam Boyd Stadium, Cox Pavilion, and the Thomas & Mack Center can be purchased through the campus's ticketing agency. 4505 Maryland Pkwy. and 7000 E. Russell Rd. ℂ 702/739-3267 for ticket information. www.thomasandmack.com for event listings at all UNLV venues. Tickets $10 and up depending on event.

MAJOR SPORTS VENUES
IN HOTELS

Caesars Palace (ℂ 800/634-6698 or 702/731-7110) has a long tradition of sporting events, from Evel Knievel's attempted motorcycle jump over its fountains in 1967 to Grand Prix auto races. Mary Lou Retton has tumbled in gymnastic events at Caesars, and Olympians Brian Boitano and Katarina Witt have taken to the ice, as has Wayne Gretzky. Additionally, well over 100 world-championship boxing contests (not the best place for children—under any circumstance) have taken place at Caesars Palace since the hotel opened.

The **MGM Grand's Garden Events Arena** (ℂ 800/929-1111 or 702/891-7777) is a major venue for professional boxing matches, rodeos, tennis, ice-skating shows, World Figure Skating Championships, and more.

Mandalay Bay (ℂ 877/632-7400) has been hosting a number of boxing matches in its 12,000-seat Events Center, and **The Mirage** (ℂ 800/627-6667 or 702/791-7111) also features occasional championship boxing matches. You may wish to avoid these hotels during boxing matches, as that type of sporting event can draw raucous, and according to *Los Angeles Times* reports, decidedly unsavory types to the area.

6 Local Performing Arts

The local performing arts scene in Las Vegas provides cultural events of all types, whether your tastes lean toward light musicals, classical music, or ballet. We've chosen the most family-friendly ones for you—the ones where a child asking questions about plot points or wanting to go to the restroom won't be frowned upon (usually).

Las Vegas Youth Orchestras   All ages. Sponsored in part by the Clark County School District and the City of Las Vegas, the Las Vegas Youth Orchestras consists of four divisions based on age and experience; the annual concert for all the orchestras takes place in December, with other concerts, including a performance by the Youth Philharmonic with the UNLV Philharmonic, take place throughout the year. The coaching staff, conductors, and other services are provided by the Clark County School District, while the City of Las Vegas provides a rehearsal hall and storage at Reed Whipple Center, sponsors one concert a year, and has commissioned music written specially for the LVYO. Reed Whipple Cultural Center, 821 Las Vegas Blvd. N. ℂ **702/229-6211** or 702/385-3828. www.lvyo.com. Tickets $6 adults, $3 children under 19, seniors, and visitors with disabilities.

Nevada Ballet Theatre   Ages 5 and up. This much-beloved ballet company is the beneficiary of funds raised at the annual All-You-Can-Eat Ice Cream Festival held in September in nearby Summerlin, where the theater stages a special performance. The company, whose season runs from December though May, offers performances geared toward the entire family, usually held at stages on the UNLV campus. Along with the much-adored *Nutcracker* (staged at the Rio Hotel's Samba Theatre), their 2002–03 season included the especially enlightening-for-kids *From Vivaldi to Pink Floyd* and *Peter Pan.* At University of Nevada, Las Vegas, 4505 Maryland Pkwy. ℂ **702/243-2623.** www.nevadaballet.com. Tickets $20–$60.

Nevada Shakespeare in the Park   Ages 7 and up, depending on play. Founded in 1987 and supported with donations and sponsorships by the Arts Council of Henderson, this annual event showcases local actors performing one of the Bard's works, staged for one weekend in October. Sword fights and costumes make the plays enjoyable for younger children, while older ones might actually get excited by the Shakespeare's words coming to life onstage. The 2004 season also included performances of *Winnie the Pooh, Little Shop of Horrors,* and *Tales from Hans Christian.* At Henderson Promenade and Arts Center, Liberty Point Park, 200 S. Green Valley Pkwy., Henderson, NV 89014. ℂ **702/221-7491.** www.artscouncilhenderson.org/pages/SpInthe Park.html. Tickets are free.

Look & Listen

Families interested in a one-stop cultural experience should check out the **Charleston Heights Arts Center,** 800 S. Brush St. (ℂ **702/229-6383**), a city-run facility that showcases both visual and performing arts, with events coordinated by the cultural affairs division of the city's Department of Parks and Leisure. Along with gallery space for national and regional artists, its concert halls feature anything from the Eastern European folk sounds of klezmer to jazz to classical music, and musicals such as the Rainbow Theatre's *Snoopy!* have been staged in the 375-seat theater.

Rainbow Company Youth Theatre   **Ages 4 and up, depending on play.**
This award-winning theater company, supported by the City of Las Vegas, is
housed at the Reed Whipple Cultural Center, and performs there and at other
locations including the Charleston Heights Arts Center (see "Look & Listen,"
above). Annually, the company stages five shows, which have included the musicals *Meet Me in St. Louis* and *Snoopy!,* and the drama *The Effect of Gamma Rays
on Man in the Moon Marigolds.* Thanks to city support and funding, ticket prices
are kept low, making this an affordable community resource. At the Reed Whipple
Cultural Center, 821 Las Vegas Blvd. N. ✆ **702/229-6211.** www.nevada.edu/~treed/rainbow.
Tickets $7 adults, $5 seniors and children 13–18, $3 children under 13. Combo show tickets, for all
5 shows are $12–$28; for 3 shows, $7–$18.

7 What to Do if You've Left the Kids with a Babysitter

It's Vegas! Do we really need to tell you what to do if you've made suitable
arrangements for your munchkins? You can't walk two steps in this town without finding something that will entertain you. Nevertheless, we've given you
some options below.

For information on babysitters and child-care services, see section 13,
"Babysitters & Child-Care Centers," of chapter 2 beginning on p. 60.

BARS

Eiffel Tower Bar   From this chic and elegant room, in the restaurant on the
11th floor of the Eiffel Tower, you can look down on everyone (in Vegas)—just
like a real Parisian! (Just kidding, Francophiles.) But really, this is a date-impress-
ing bar, and, because there's no cover or minimum, it's a cost-effective alternative to the overly inflated food prices at the restaurant. Drop by for a drink, but
try to look sophisticated. Then you can cop an attitude and dismiss everything
as *gauche*—or *droit,* depending on which way you are seated. Open daily until
1am. In Paris Las Vegas, 3655 Las Vegas Blvd. S. ✆ **702/948-6937.**

Venus and Tiki Bar Lounge   Venus is a see-and-be-seen place that mostly
attracts tourists, who don't seem to mind that there is a DJ spinning house music
but there is no dance floor and that you can't get near the balcony overlooking
the Strip thanks to all the other folks who are seeing and being seen. Check out
the painting by highly hip and collectible artist Shag at the entrance, and snag
some of the club's matchbooks with his cool design work. The tiki bar, located
just inside the club, on the left in a separate room, is truly swell—bamboo wall
coverings, framed tiki artwork, and a slew of mind-altering tropical drinks. The
tiki bar opens daily at 6pm and closes at 4am, while Venus is open Wednesday
through Sunday from 10:30pm until 4am. In The Venetian, 3377 Las Vegas Blvd. S.
✆ **702/414-1000.** No cover 5–10pm; after 10pm, cover varies (usually $10 and up).

VooDoo Lounge   In one of those amazing Vegas sleight of hands, this bar is
supposedly located on the 51st floor of the Rio, but, in reality, is on the 41st.
(The number 4 is considered unlucky in Chinese culture—it's a homophone for
"death"—and is thus avoided by casino hotels eager to draw Asian gamblers)
Numerical trickery aside, the view from the lounge's balcony is astounding—the
entire Strip is laid out glistening with neon. The lounge's tropical drinks—with
names such as Shrunken Head, High Priestess, and What the Witch Doctor
Ordered—are potent and pricey, and are made by handsome bartenders who flip
and toss the bottles with considerable showmanship and flair; they are almost as
much fun to watch as the sparkling lights of the Strip. The decor carries out the
voodoo theme with mysterious symbols and beaded flags covering the walls. The

dress code basically translates as no jeans or T-shirts. From 9:30pm on, there are live bands. Open daily 5pm to 4am. In the Rio All-Suite Hotel and Casino, 3700 W. Flamingo Blvd. ✆ **702/252-7777**. Cover $10 after 8pm.

CASINOS

What? You didn't come to Las Vegas for the Liberace Museum? We are shocked. *Shocked.*

Yes, there are gambling opportunities in Vegas. We've noticed this. You will, too. The tip-off will be the slot machines in the airport as soon as you step off the plane. And the slot machines in the convenience stores as soon as you drive across the state line. Let's not kid ourselves, gambling is what Vegas is about. The bright lights, the shows, the showgirls, the food—it's all there just to lure you in and make you open your wallet. (The free drinks certainly help ease the latter as well.)

You can disappoint them if you want, but what would be the point? *This is Las Vegas.* You don't have to be a high roller. You would not believe how much fun you can have at a nickel slot machine. You won't get rich, but neither will most of those guys playing the $5 slots, either.

Of course, that's not going to stop anyone from trying. Almost everyone plays in Vegas with the hopes of winning The Big One. That only a few ever do win doesn't stop them from trying again and again and again. That's how the casinos make their money, by the way.

But we're not going to give you a lecture here. Enjoy the time you have in the casinos while you can—because they are strict about not letting anyone under-age into their hallowed halls, so, if this is the only time you have away from your kids while you're in Las Vegas, this may be your only opportunity to take part in the gambling hoopla that Las Vegas is so famous for.

Casino choice is a personal thing. Some like to find their lucky place and stick with it, while others love to take advantage of the nearly endless choices that Vegas offers. Everyone should casino-hop at least once to marvel (or get dizzy) at the decor/spectacle and the sheer excess of it all. But beyond decoration, there isn't too much difference. You've got your slot machines, your gaming tables, and your big chandeliers.

Don't be a snob, and don't be overly dazzled by the fancy casinos. Sometimes you can have a better time at one of the older places Downtown, where stakes are lower, pretensions are nonexistent, and the clientele is often friendlier. Frankly, real gamblers—and by that we don't necessarily mean high rollers, but those who play to win regardless of the amount of said win—head straight for Downtown (and most often, straight for Binion's—128 E. Fremont St., between Casino Center Blvd. and 1st St.; ✆ **800/622-6468** or 702/382-1600; www.binions.com) for these precise reasons, caring not a whit about glitz and glamour. Even if you don't take your gambling as seriously as that, you may well want to follow their example. After all, it's getting harder and harder to find cheap tables (where you can play a hand of blackjack, for example, for less than $10) on the Strip—so take your hard-earned money to where you can lose it more slowly; or, lose it all in one fantabulous hand of a very glamorous poker game; whatever floats your boat.

SOUTH STRIP

Aladdin/Planet Hollywood   A financial basket case from the day it opened, the Aladdin, with its Arabian Nights/desert theme, was acquired in 2004 by Planet Hollywood. It's not certain how the new owners will blend their American pop theme with the camels and the bazaar, but where better to try than Las Vegas. For the moment the casino and hotel are decidedly closer to Lawrence of Arabia than

Arnold of Hollywood. Both the hotel and casino, as well as the adjoining Desert Passage Mall, project a whimsical desert style augmented with the prerequisite pinch of Strip neon. A two-story, football-field-long mural over the Strip entrance, for example, glitters with fiber-optic flowers, not something you'd be likely to see in the desert, even with a good buzz. The size of the mural typifies the oversized proportions of the casino and hotel public areas, where scale dominates detail. 3667 Las Vegas Blvd. S. ℂ 877/333-9474 or 702/785-5555. www.aladdincasino.com.

Excalibur   As you might expect, the Excalibur casino is replete with suits of armor, stained-glass panels, knights, dragons, and velvet and satin heraldic banners, with gaming action taking place beneath vast iron-and-gold chandeliers fit for a medieval castle fortress. This all makes it fine for kitsch-seekers, but anyone who hates crowds or is sensitive to noise will hate it. The overall effect is less like a castle and more like a dungeon. (We really only recommend it if you're staying there anyway, and even then, we advise you to look beyond this one.) Excalibur's 100,000-plus square feet of gaming facilities also include a race and sports book, a keno lounge, a poker room, blackjack, minibaccarat, Caribbean stud, Let-It-Ride, Casino War (like the game you played as a kid), craps, roulette, pai gow poker, Big Six, and slot/video-poker machines. 3850 Las Vegas Blvd. S. ℂ 877/750-5464 or 702/597-7777. www.excaliburcasino.com.

Luxor Las Vegas   More accessible than ever thanks to the air-conditioned people mover from Excalibur and the monorail from Mandalay Bay, Luxor has been completely remodeled and, in our opinion, improved immeasurably. You enter through a giant temple gateway flanked by massive statues of Ramses. Gone is the space-wasting central area that used to contain the bathrooms, cashiers, and casino offices. This additional space gives the casino a much more airy feel, which produces a low claustrophobia level—in parts, you can see all the way up the inside of the pyramid. King Tut heads and sphinxes adorn slot areas. The "One Club," a Mandalay Resorts slot-players' club, also valid at sister properties such as Excalibur, Mandalay Bay, Monte Carlo, Circus Circus, and others, offers rewards of cash, merchandise, meals, and special services to slot and table players. Sports action unfolds on 17 large-screen TVs and 128 personalized monitors in Luxor's race and sports book. Additional gaming facilities include a keno lounge, blackjack, craps, roulette, poker, baccarat, minibaccarat, pai gow, Big Six, Caribbean stud, and slot/video-poker machines. 3900 Las Vegas Blvd. S. ℂ 800/288-1000 or 702/262-4000. www.luxor.com.

Mandalay Bay   You'll find "elegant" gaming in a prefab, deliberate way, with a very high ceiling that produces a very low claustrophobia factor. It's definitely the place to go if you're looking for less hectic, less gimmick-filled play. The layout makes it look airy, and it's marginally less confusing and certainly less overwhelming than many other casinos. Because it is at the far south end of the Strip, there are fewer walk-in players, but the presence of the House of Blues and the increasing popularity of the rumjungle nightclub (p. 238) can mean a late-night influx of customers. There's a big, ultracomfortable sports book (what casinos call the room where you bet on sports), complete with armchairs that could well encourage a relaxed gambler to fall asleep, including a live daily sports-radio show. Other gaming available includes poker, blackjack, craps, roulette, baccarat, minibaccarat, Let-It-Ride, Caribbean stud, pai gow poker, Big Six, and slot/video-poker machines. Players can sign up for the "One Club," a Mandalay Resorts player-reward system also valid at sister properties such as Luxor, Excalibur, Circus Circus, and others. 3950 Las Vegas Blvd. S. ℂ 877/632-7000 or 702/632-7000. www.mandalaybay.com.

MGM Grand   Las Vegas's largest casino at 171,500 square feet—we've been to countries that were smaller!—is divided into four themed areas, in a futile attempt to make it seem smaller. Many of the *Wizard of Oz* decorations have been removed, but spend an hour in here and you may feel like Dorothy after she was whisked away by the twister. You will get lost at least once. One section features a high-roller slot area with machines that operate on coins valued at $100 and $500! The sports casino houses a big poker room, a state-of-the-art race and sports book, and the Turf Club Lounge. And the French Riviera–themed Monte Carlo casino has a luxurious marble-columned and gold-draped private high-end gaming area. Carousels of progressive slots unique to the MGM Grand include the very popular Majestic Lions high-frequency $1 slot machines that pay out more than $1 million daily, and the Lion's Share $1 slots, which are capable of jackpots exceeding $1 million each at any time. Additional gaming facilities include a keno lounge, blackjack, craps, roulette, baccarat, minibaccarat, pai gow, pai gow poker, Caribbean stud, Let-It-Ride, Casino War, Big Six, and slot/video-poker machines. This hotel takes part in the MGM Mirage "Players Club," which is also valid at sister properties such as The Mirage, New York–New York, and others. 3799 Las Vegas Blvd. S. ✆ **800/929-1111** or 702/891-7777. www.mgmgrand.com.

New York–New York   Another theme-run-wild place: tuxes on the backs of gaming chairs, change carts that look like yellow cabs, and so forth, all set in a miniature New York City. Crammed into the casino are such landmarks as Greenwich Village, Wall Street, Little Italy, and Times Square. The most obvious resemblance to the real New York, however, is the casino's virtually gridlocked pedestrian traffic. Simply put, avoid this place if you're a little claustrophobic. Even if you can handle jostling crowds, you're still in for a major case of sensory overload. Serious gamblers understandably may sniff at it all and prefer to take their business to a less congested venue, especially if they don't regard gambling as a contact sport. Everyone else should drop in and gawk for a couple of minutes. There's a keno lounge, blackjack, craps, roulette, baccarat, minibaccarat, pai gow, pai gow poker, Caribbean stud, Let-It-Ride, Casino War, Big Six, and slot/video-poker machines. NY–NY participates in the MGM MIRAGE "Player's Club," also valid at sister properties such as the MGM Grand and The Mirage. 3790 Las Vegas Blvd. S. ✆ **888/693-6763** or 702/740-6969. www.nynyhotelcasino.com.

Orleans   This is not a particularly special gambling space, though it does have a low claustrophobia level, but, if you're staying here and don't want to venture out of the hotel, it'll do. Another plus is that they sometimes play Cajun and zydeco music over the sound system, so you can two-step while you gamble, which can make losing somewhat less painful. It has all the needed tables—blackjack, craps, and so forth—plus plenty of slots, including the popular Wheel of Fortune machine, which works like those other roulette-wheel slots, but in this case, actually plays the theme song from the TV show. It will even applaud for you if you win. Because Orleans is popular with locals, there are lots of video-poker options. And because it's not on the Strip, you'll find better odds for craps and cheaper table minimums. 4500 W. Tropicana Ave. ✆ **800/675-3267** or 702/365-7111. www.orleanscasino.com.

CENTER STRIP

Bellagio   The slot machines here are mostly encased in marble and fine woods. How's that for upping the ante on classy? In all fairness, Bellagio comes the closest to re-creating the feel of gambling in Monte Carlo (the country, not the next-door casino), but its relentless good taste means that this is one pretty forgettable casino. After all, we are suckers for a wacky theme that screams "Vegas," and European class just doesn't cut it. Sure, there are good touches—we always like a high ceiling to reduce the claustrophobia index, and the place is laid out in an easy-to-navigate grid with ultrawide aisles, so walking through doesn't seem like such a crowded collision-course maze. Anyway, the cozy sports book has individual TVs and entirely denlike leather chairs—quite, quite comfortable. 3600 Las Vegas Blvd. S. ✆ 888/987-6667 or 702/693-7111. www.bellagio.com.

Caesars Palace   Caesars' casino is simultaneously the ultimate in gambling luxury and the ultimate in Vegas kitsch. Cocktail waitresses in togas parade about, as you gamble under the watchful gaze of faux-marble Roman statues. The very high ceiling in certain areas of the casino makes for a very low claustrophobia level. Although we love it, the casino has become somewhat confusing and unmanageable because of its size and meandering layout, like Caesars itself.

A notable facility is the state-of-the-art **Race and Sports Book,** with huge electronic display boards and giant video screens. (Caesars pioneered computer-generated wagering data that can be communicated in less than half a second, and has sophisticated satellite equipment that can pick up the broadcast of virtually any sporting event in the world.) The domed VIP slot arena of the Forum Casino (minimum bet is $5, but you can wager up to $1,500 on a single pull!) is a plush, crystal-chandeliered precinct with seating in roomy, adjustable chairs. Gamblers can accumulate bonus points toward cash back, gifts, gratis show tickets, meals, and rooms by joining a players club also valid at sister properties like Bally's and Paris. Club membership also lets you in on grand-prize drawings, tournaments, and parties.

The most upscale of the Caesars gaming rooms is the intimate, European-style casino adjoining the **808** restaurant. Total facilities in all three casinos contain craps tables, blackjack, roulette, baccarat, minibaccarat, Let-It-Ride, Caribbean stud, pai gow poker, two Big Six wheels, slot/video-poker machines, and a keno lounge. 3570 Las Vegas Blvd. S. ✆ 800/634-6661 or 702/731-7110. www.caesars.com.

The Mirage   Gamble in a Polynesian village in one of the prettiest casinos in town. It has a meandering layout, and the low ceiling makes for a medium claustrophobia level, but neither of these aspects is overwhelming. This remains one of our favorite places to gamble. Facilities include a plush European-style *salon privé* for high rollers at baccarat, blackjack, and roulette; an elegant dining room serves catered meals to gamblers there. Slot and table players can join the MGM MIRAGE Players Club, also valid at sister hotels such as Treasure Island and MGM Grand, and work toward bonus points for cash rebates, special room rates, complimentary meals and/or show tickets, and other benefits. The elaborate race and sports book offers theater stereo sound and a movie-theater-size screen. Other gaming facilities here: a keno lounge, 75 blackjack tables, craps, roulette, baccarat, minibaccarat, pai gow, pai gow poker, Big Six, and slot/video-poker machines. It's one of the most pleasant, and popular, casinos in town, so it's very crowded more often than not. 3400 Las Vegas Blvd. S. ✆ 800/627-6667 or 702/791-7111. www.themirage.com.

The Venetian   "Tasteful" is the watchword in these days of classy Vegas gaming, and consequently, with the exception of more hand-painted Venetian art re-creations on parts of the ceiling, The Venetian's casino is interchangeable with those found at Mandalay Bay, the Monte Carlo, and to a certain extent, Bellagio. All that gleaming marble, columns, and such is very nice, but after awhile, also a bit ho-hum. Besides, this is Vegas, and we want our tacky theme elements, by gosh. The lack thereof, combined with poor signage, may be why this casino is so hard to get around—every part looks exactly the same. It's not claustrophobic, but it can be confusing. Plus, there is no (at this writing) giant slot machine. On the other hand, you can access the casino directly from the St. Mark's Square re-creation out front. Facilities include a relatively small but comfortable sports book, poker, blackjack, craps, roulette, pai gow poker, baccarat, keno, and slot/video-poker machines. 3355 Las Vegas Blvd. S. ℂ **888/2-VENICE (283-6423)** or 702/414-1000. www.venetian.com.

NORTH STRIP

Circus Circus   This vast property has three full-size casinos that, combined, comprise one of the largest gaming operations in Nevada (more than 100,000 sq. ft.). More importantly, it has an entire circus midway set up throughout, so you are literally gambling with trapeze stunts going on over your head. The other great gimmick is the slot machine carousel—yep, it turns while you spin the reels. The Mandalay Resorts "One Club" offers slot/video-poker and table players the opportunity to earn points redeemable for cash, discounted rooms and meals, and other benefits at Circus or any of the sister properties such as Mandalay Bay or Luxor. The Circus Bucks progressive slot machines here build from a jackpot base of $500,000, which players can win on a $2 pull. Gaming facilities include a 10,000-square-foot race and sports book with 30 video monitors ranging from 13 to 52 inches, 40-seat and 89-seat keno lounges, poker tables, blackjack, craps, roulette, a Big Six wheel, Let-It-Ride, pai gow poker, dice, Caribbean stud poker, and slot/video-poker machines. Unfortunately, the casino is crowded and noisy, and there are lots of children passing through (making it more crowded and noisy). That, plus some low ceilings (not in the Big Top, obviously), makes for a very high claustrophobia rating, though the new commedia dell'arte clown motif (as opposed to the old garish circus motif) has upgraded the decor. 2880 Las Vegas Blvd. S. ℂ **877/224-7287** or 702/734-0410. www.circuscircus.com.

EAST OF THE STRIP

Hard Rock Hotel & Casino   This is where Gen X goes to gamble. The Hard Rock has certainly taken casino decor to a whole new level. The attention to detail and the resulting playfulness is admirable, if not incredible. Gaming tables have piano keyboards at one end; some slots have Fender guitar fretboards as arms; gaming chips have band names and/or pictures on them; slot machines are similarly rock-themed (check out the Jimi Hendrix machine!); and so it goes. The whole thing is set in the middle of a circular room, around the outskirts of which are various rock memorabilia in glass cases. Rock blares over the sound system, allowing boomers to boogie while they gamble.

A bank of slots makes gambling an act of charity: Environmentally committed owner Peter Morton (the Hard Rock's motto is SAVE THE PLANET) donates profits from specified slots to organizations dedicated to saving the rainforests. A Back Stage Pass allows patrons to rack up discounts on meals, lodging, and gift-shop items while playing slots and table games. The race and sports book here provides comfortable seating in leather-upholstered reclining armchairs. Gaming facilities (with selected nonsmoking tables) include blackjack, roulette, craps, Caribbean stud, minibaccarat, Let-It-Ride, pai gow poker, and slot/video-poker machines. All this is genuinely amazing, but the noise level is above even that of a normal casino. 4455 Paradise Rd. ℂ **800/473-ROCK (473-7625)** or 702/693-5000. www.hardrockhotel.com.

DANCE CLUBS

Cleopatra's Barge Nightclub This is a small, unique nightclub set in part on a floating barge—you can feel it rocking. The bandstand, a small dance floor, and a few (usually reserved) tables are here, while others are seated around the boat on "land." It's a gimmick, but one that makes this far more fun than other, more pedestrian, hotel bars. Plenty of dark makes for romance, but blaring volume levels mean you will have to scream those sweet nothings. Check out the bare-breasted figurehead on the ship's prow who juts out over the hallway going past the entrance. She could put someone's eye out. Open nightly from 10:30pm until 4am. In Caesars Palace, 3570 Las Vegas Blvd. S. ℂ **702/731-7110.** No cover, 2-drink minimum.

Monte Carlo Pub & Brewery *Finds* After 9pm nightly, this immense warehouselike pub and working microbrewery turns from a casual restaurant into something of a dance club. Rock videos blare forth from a large screen and 40 TV monitors around the room, while on stage, dueling pianos provide music and audience-participation entertainment. The Pub is cigar friendly and maintains a humidor. There's a full bar, and, of course, the house microbrews are featured. You can also order pizza. Open until 3am Sunday to Thursday, until 4am Friday and Saturday. In the Monte Carlo Resort & Casino, 3770 Las Vegas Blvd. S. ℂ **702/730-7777.**

rumjungle Now, normally our delicate sensibilities wince at such overkill, and we tend to write off such efforts as just trying a bit too hard. But surprisingly, rumjungle really delivers the great fun it promises. The fire-wall entrance gives way to a wall of water; the two-story bar is full of the largest collection of rum varieties anywhere, each bottle illuminated with a laser beam of light; go-go girls dance and prance between bottles of wine, to dueling congas; and the food all comes skewered on swords. It's all a bit much, but it works, it really does. A great deal of thought went into the various clever designs and schemes, and it's paid off. Almost instantly, rumjungle became the hottest club in Vegas, with lines of partiers out the door every night, ready to dance to live world-beat music. Get there early (before 10pm) to avoid lines/guest lists/the cover charge, and consider having dinner (served till 11pm); it's costly, but it's a multicourse, all-you-can-eat feast of flame-pit-cooked Brazilian food. For the amount of food and the waiving of the cover charge, dinner is a good deal. Then dance it all off all night long. (The club is open 'til 2am on weeknights, till 4am Thurs–Sat night.) In Mandalay Bay, 3950 Las Vegas Blvd. S. ℂ **702/632-7408.** Cover $10–$20.

MAJOR PRODUCTION SHOWS

Folies Bergere See listing earlier in this chapter, p. 219.

Jubilee! A classic Vegas spectacular, crammed with singing, dancing, magic, acrobats, elaborate costumes and sets, and, of course, bare breasts. It's a basic revue, with production numbers featuring homogenized versions of standards (Gershwin, Cole Porter, some Fred Astaire numbers) sometimes sung live, sometimes lip-synced, and always accompanied by lavishly costumed and frequently topless showgirls. Humorous set pieces about Samson and Delilah and the sinking of the *Titanic* (!) show off some pretty awesome sets. (They were doing the *Titanic* long before a certain movie, and recent attendees claimed the ship-sinking effect on stage here was better than the one in the movie.) The finale features aerodynamically impossible feathered and bejeweled costumes and headpieces designed by Bob Mackie. So what if the dancers are occasionally out of step, and the action sometimes veers into the dubious (a Vegas-style revue about a disaster that took more than 1,000 lives?) or even the inexplicable (a finale praising beautiful and bare-breasted girls suddenly stops for three lines of "Somewhere Over the Rainbow"?). Shows are Saturday through Thursday at 7:30 and 10:30pm. In Bally's Las Vegas, 3645 Las Vegas Blvd. S. ℂ **800/237-7469** or 702/739-4567. Tickets $60–$74 (excluding tax and gratuity).

La Femme!   *La Femme!* is part of Vegas's new, classy, adult entertainment resurrection. Allegedly the same show that has been running for years in a famous racy French nightclub, this show is just a bunch of pretty girls taking their clothes off. Except that the girls are smashingly pretty, with the kind of bodies just not found on real live human beings, and they take their clothes off in curious and, yes, artistic ways, gyrating on pointe shoes while holding on to ropes or hoops, falling over sofas while lip-syncing to French torch songs—in short, it's what striptease ought to be, and by gosh, if strip clubs were this well staged we'd go to them all the time. But $60 a ticket is a great deal to pay for arty nudie fun, especially when the routines, no matter how clever or how naked (the girls get down to a postage-stamp-size triangle covering the naughtiest of their bits, so they aren't "nude," but talk about a technicality), start to seem alike after a while. Shows are Wednesday through Monday at 8 and 10:30pm. In the MGM Grand, 3799 Las Vegas Blvd. S. ℂ **800/929-1111** or 702/891-7777. Tickets $59 (includes tax and gratuity).

Splash   They took out the mermaids and water tank that gave this show its name, froze the water, and added ice skaters and some increased production values. If the show is now the one in town that most closely resembles the guffaw-inducing extravaganza in *Showgirls,* it's nonetheless a considerable improvement over its previous incarnations. That may be because we are partial to ice skaters in any form, even if they are performing to the music from *Titanic* while topless dancers preen on a small version of the deck of the boat. The weird lip-syncing numbers, including a long tribute to Madonna that reenacts portions of *Evita,* even as clips from the real thing are shown on video screens, still remain, though improved and more ambitious choreography has been added. Expect up-close looks at bare breasts as the flashy and not terribly competent dancers parade through the crowd (sometimes in see-through filmy net catsuits that show less and are thus considerably more sexy—more topless shows should go this teasing route). Some "comedy gauchos" crack whips and insensitive jokes, and there's a truly talented trio of juggling brothers. Pass the time wondering if it's uncomfortable skating in a butt thong, and pondering the philosophical implications of a country's wretched political problems providing fodder for first the Andrew Lloyd Webber mill and now a Vegas topless revue. **Seating warnings:** Seats on the sides are so bad that fully three-quarters of the stage might be obscured. Shows are Tuesday through Thursday and Saturday at 8 and 10:30pm; Sunday and Monday at 8pm. In The Riviera Hotel & Casino, 2901 Las Vegas Blvd. S. ℂ **877/892-7469** or 702/734-9301. Tickets $70–$85 (includes tax and gratuity).

Zumanity   Zumanity is the first Cirque du Soleil production to chart a decidedly adult course. Celebrating love, both physical and emotional, in all of its myriad forms, *Zumanity* is the buzz of the Las Vegas show scene. If you're comfortable with sexuality, including your own, *Zumanity* will wash over you like a torrid desert wind. If not, you're in for an hour and a half of varying degrees of revulsion and a lot of squirming in your seat. *Zumanity* is zany, raucous, and decidedly outrageous. It is lovable in its humor and insightful in its understanding of sex. The visually hypnotic production seamlessly blends its challenging theme with Cirque du Soleil's signature music, color, acrobatics, and dance. *Zumanity* is sometimes very tender but at other moments quite hard-edged. Urging us to look at how we define human beauty and making a plea for the acceptance of differences, *Zumanity* delivers a powerful message. As the production unfolds, you witness an artful sequence of sexual vignettes celebrating heterosexual sex, gay sex, masturbation, sex between obese lovers, sex with midgets, group sex, sado-masochistic sex, and sex between the very old. As the name "Zumanity" implies, sex and the varied emotions we bring to it, is a defining element of our humanity. Sex is happy, sex is sad, sex is of the moment, sex is transcendent, sex is funny, sex is bewildering. And as *Zumanity* so ably demonstrates, sex is a window into our essential being. Shows are Friday through Tuesday at 7:30 and 10:30pm. In the New York–New York Hotel & Casino, 3790 Las Vegas Boulevard S. © 702/740-6815. www.nynyhotelcasino.com. Tickets range from $65 to $125 including tax and gratuity.

Side Trips from Las Vegas

From the strange desert formations of Red Rock and Valley of Fire to the pine trees and cool breezes of Mount Charleston, the area surrounding Las Vegas is rich with natural beauty. Whether you decide to take a guided tour or drive yourself, you'll discover that there is more to Las Vegas than just casinos and roller coasters (though those, too, can be found outside the city limits).

The city of Las Vegas is modern and overdeveloped, layered with concrete and minimalls. In stark contrast, the outlying deserts and mountains are raw, wild, and untamed. If you visit Las Vegas with your kids, you owe it to yourself, and to them, to see the natural wonders that lie less than an hour away from the artificial miracles of the Strip. Go ahead! Breathe some fresh air, frolic in the forest, or take a trip back in time. You'll be glad you did.

To interest the kids, let them know that, as different as Vegas the city is from its surrounding areas, they are deeply interconnected. For instance, the miles of lights, exploding volcanoes, and dancing fountains all over the city would not be able to exist were it not for Hoover Dam.

The excursions in this chapter, with the exception of the Grand Canyon trip, will take you anywhere from 20 to 60 miles outside of town for memorable family-travel experiences. In these surrounding areas, there are plenty of opportunities for outdoors recreation in truly astounding environments. (But, if you're really partial to gambling, riding thrill rides, and shopping, and haven't gotten your fill yet in Vegas, you can find those same opportunities outside of the city, in Primm.)

1 Hoover Dam & Lake Mead

30 miles SE of Las Vegas

You must take your kids to see the Hoover Dam (www.usbr.gov/lc/hooverdam). It is an engineering and architectural marvel, one of the wonders of the modern world, and, without it, Las Vegas, nay, the Southwest as we know it today, would not exist. Plus, most kids think that all that rushing water is cool. If your children appear antsy or bored at the visitor center, you may want to skip the actual tour of the dam, but, trust us, you should try to wheedle, connive, or bribe them into taking it: They'll learn something and see some amazing sights, including an up-close-and-personal view of the dam.

Be sure to wear comfortable shoes, as the tour involves quite a bit of walking, something that, unfortunately, your child may be too young to complete on their own. Those kids aged 6 years and up will enjoy it the most; any younger, and you'll probably be in for a struggle. For the most comfortable tour, try to arrive early in the morning, when the dam first opens; you'll not only beat the desert heat, but also the crowds, because 2,000 to 3,000 people visit the dam daily.

After touring the dam, you can have lunch in Boulder City, and, if you are up for a long drive, perhaps go back to Vegas the long way through **Valley of Fire State Park** (© 702/397-2088; www.parks.nv.gov/vf.htm), a landscape of wind and water-hewn formations of red sandstone, about 6 miles from Lake Mead. *Note:* Fill up your gas tank and buy drinking water before you start! Or, you can spend the rest of the day at Lake Mead—hiking, boating, or scuba diving in season. At Lake Mead, there's also the option of a steamboat tour. Alternatively, some families prefer to combine Hoover Dam with a trip to **Bonnie Springs Ranch** (© 702/875-4191; www.bonniesprings.com). For more on the ranch, see section 4, "Bonnie Springs Ranch/Old Nevada," later in this chapter.

GETTING THERE

Drive east on either Flamingo or Tropicana to U.S. 515 south, which automatically becomes I-93 and takes you right to the dam. This is a beautiful and dramatic drive; as you go through Boulder City, you come over a rise, and Lake Mead is suddenly spread before you. (Be aware that at this point, the road narrows to two lanes, and traffic can slow considerably, meaning that on busy tourist days, the drive can take an hour or more, just another reason to get an early start.) Go past the Lake Mead turnoff, and, as you near the dam, you will see a five-story parking structure to your left against the canyon wall. Parking there costs $5, cash only. (There is also free parking on the Arizona side of the dam, which is easily accessible.)

Coach USA (© 800/634-6579; www.coachusa.com) offers an organized bus tour that includes admission and a tour of the dam. Discount coupons for tours are often offered in the free Las Vegas tourist publications distributed throughout Vegas hotels. The 6½-hour **Hoover Dam Shuttle Tour,** which costs $42, departs daily at 7:30am and 11am, and includes pickup and drop off.

SUV or passenger van tours to and from Las Vegas are available through **Action Tours.** Tours include the 4½-hour **Express Tour** for $29; the 7½-hour **Deluxe Tour** (both hotel-to-hotel); and the **Hoover Dam and Lake Mead combo tour,** 7½-hours long, $62. Call © 702/566-7400 or visit **www.actiontours.com** for details.

THE HOOVER DAM 🎯🎯

Without the Hoover Dam, there would be no glittering lights and chiming slot machines in Las Vegas; its fountains would not dance nor would its swimming pools exist. In fact, the growth of the entire Southwest, not just Las Vegas, can be tied directly to the electricity generated by the dam, and the controlled water use it provides.

Before the dam was built, the Colorado River had run unchecked for millions of years, its turbulent waters carving out the Grand Canyon. When settlers came en masse and agriculture began as an industry, the river's natural behavior (drying up most of the year, then flooding when fed by the melting snow in the Rocky Mountains) caused severe hardships. Crops, lives, and property were consistently lost, progress was stalled, and so the powers that be, in this case Congress, stepped in.

In 1928, Congress—strongly urged by the seven states through which the Colorado runs during its 1,400 mile journey to the Gulf of California—authorized the construction of a dam intending that "A mighty river, now a source of destruction, is to be curbed and put to work in the interest of society." Construction began in 1931 and was completed in 1936, 2 years ahead of schedule and $15 million under budget. During those 5 years, more than 5,200 laborers worked 24 hours a day, and the project generated significant advances in engineering,

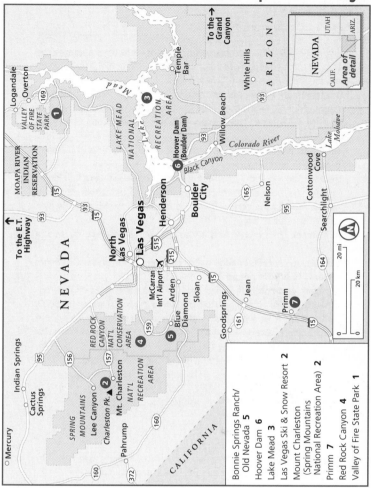

Bonnie Springs Ranch/
Old Nevada **5**

Hoover Dam **6**

Lake Mead **3**

Las Vegas Ski & Snow Resort **2**

Mount Charleston
(Spring Mountains
National Recreation Area) **2**

Primm **7**

Red Rock Canyon **4**

Valley of Fire State Park **1**

machinery production, and construction. The completed dam served its purpose, stopping the annual floods and conserving water for agricultural, industrial, and domestic use. Equally important, Hoover Dam, now one of the world's major electrical generating plants, provides low-cost, pollution-free hydroelectric power to neighboring communities. The cost of building the dam, $165 million, has been repaid by the sale of its electricity to a number of California cities and the states of Nevada and Arizona.

A massive curved wall, 660 feet at its base, tapering to 45 feet across at the top where the road crosses it, the Hoover Dam towers 726½ feet above the bedrock, acting as a plug between the canyon walls. The dam holds back up to 9.2 trillion gallons of water in Lake Mead, the reservoir created by its construction. Four concrete intake towers on the dam's lakeside drop the water down about 600 feet to drive turbines and create power, after which the water spills out into the river, continuing south to the Gulf of California.

> ### *Fun Fact* Did You Know . . .
>
> - Five million 8-cubic-yard buckets of cement were used to create the Hoover Dam—enough concrete to pave a two-lane highway between Miami and Los Angeles?
> - The minimum wage paid on the dam construction project was $4 a day? Comparatively, those wages of 50¢ an hour weren't bad because most of the workers' Depression-era peers were making an average of 5¢ per hour!
> - Ninety-six men died while building, excavating, blasting, and scaling mountains during dam construction, and on-the-job injuries totaled about 1,500 a month? However, though 96 workers were killed during the construction, contrary to popular myth, none were accidentally buried as the concrete was poured. (It was poured only at a rate of 8 in. at a time.)
> - In summer, the canyon rocks are so hot you can literally fry an egg on them?
> - Lake Mead contains enough water to cover the entire state of Pennsylvania to a 1-foot depth?
> - The dam was originally called Boulder Dam because of its first-designated canyon site, and then renamed Hoover Dam in 1930 to honor Herbert Hoover's years of work making the project a reality? Unofficially, it was renamed Boulder Dam by FDR, who did not wish to honor Hoover; it finally regained the name Hoover Dam under Truman, who, in 1948, asked the 80th Congress to find out just what the "dam" name really was. Both names are still in popular usage.
> - It took 6½ years to fill the lake created by the Hoover Dam?
> - Hoover Dam is 726½ feet high and weighs over 6,600,000 tons?

The dam has become a major sightseeing attraction along with Lake Mead, a huge local recreation site and the nation's largest artificial reservoir.

On your way to Hoover Dam, 7 miles to the west on U.S. 93, you'll pass through Boulder City, which was built to house the dam's managerial and construction workers. Boulder City's higher elevation offered lower temperatures than the area surrounding the dam, making it a more appealing location for a community. Within a single year, the city emerged from the wasteland, with a population of 6,000. By 1934, Boulder City was Nevada's third-largest town.

TOURING THE DAM
Things have changed at Hoover Dam since the September 11, 2001, terrorist attacks, and, for those with children, the tour itself has become much more manageable—you are left to discover the dam and its history on your own. Fans of the old tour may be disappointed by this truncated version, but newcomers won't miss a thing. Whereas before you were on a structured group tour, with a guide moving you at a steady pace, now the visit is self-guided, and you can linger or move on as the mood strikes you. The exchange for this is the ability to see what you want to see, and what your kids can handle, without being tied into a structured tour. If the children get bored watching one of the two movies at the Visitor Center, you can traipse right along and take the elevator to the fifth-floor observation

deck, without having to wait. Want to watch the water roar for 20 minutes? Go ahead, look as long as you like. If the kids are getting cranky or you're getting tired, you're free to cut the visit short and head on out for a snack.

Your tour begins at the Visitor Center, where your admission to the center, the exhibit hall across the street, and your self-guided sightseeing of the dam are covered in one admission price ($10 for adults, $5 for ages 7–16, and $8 for seniors; children under 7 are free).

The three-story **Hoover Dam Visitor Center,** built in 1995, features a rooftop overlook with an unobstructed view of Lake Mead, the dam, the power plant, the Colorado River, and the Black Canyon. This is one of the tour's many fabulous photo opportunities. The ground-floor Reception Lobby is the ticketing station as well as the place where exhibits, memorabilia, and photographs are displayed and where the two informational videos are screened continuously. By watching these, you'll learn more about the importance of water, the events leading up to the construction of Hoover Dam, and the many benefits it confers. The Plaza Level includes interactive displays on the environment, habitation, and development of the Southwest; the people who built the dam; and related topics. The third-floor Overlook Center provides an astounding view of Lake Mead, the dam, the power plant, the mighty Colorado River, and Black Canyon. Along with the awe-inspiring vista, there are (far less interesting to children) sculpted bronze panels demonstrating how Lake Mead and Hoover Dam benefit Arizona, Nevada, and California. Included in your ticket price is the exhibit center across the street, where a 10-minute presentation in a small theater focuses on a topographical map of the 1,400-mile Colorado River. This building also has a cafeteria.

While you are at the dam, make sure to take in all the exterior details, including the floors inlaid with the wheel of the zodiac, a compass, and the American eagle as well as the sculptural tributes to those who died building the dam, including the dam's mascot, a black dog who was killed when a truck inadvertently ran him over some years after the dam's completion. On the grounds of the dam, you may also be able to spot wildlife, including ravens, cormorants, an occasional bighorn sheep, and the lively antelope ground squirrels. When you return to your car, note the cactus garden at the top of the escalators, which was installed by the movie company who made the Chevy Chase movie *National Lampoon's Vegas Vacation* to make the location look more "desertlike." Hollywood being what it is, the plants they chose for their desert atmosphere are not native to this region, but they do look nice, especially when they bloom in the spring. *Tip:* It is highly recommended that persons with defibrillators do not take the tour. Additionally, some areas may be difficult to navigate with strollers and wheelchairs. For more information on the dam, surf over to its website at **www.usbr.gov/lc/hooverdam**.

Tips Travel Time

The least-crowded times to visit are during the first 2 hours of each day. Also, keep in mind that the busiest season is in the summer from Memorial Day until Labor Day. Spring break is also a busy time at the dam. The slowest months are January and February. When visiting, make sure to bring bottled water and wear a hat and sunscreen, as you will be outside for part of your explorations.

The self-guided tour around the dam begins with an elevator ride to the fifth-floor observation deck. You'll get to walk along the top of the dam, watch the water roil, and learn about this stupendous monument from the displays and the guides. Six guides, each with their own spiel, are strategically placed and are able to answer any questions you or your kids might have. The self-guided tour can take up to 2½ hours or as little as 30 minutes, depending on your family's level of interest.

LAKE MEAD NATIONAL RECREATION AREA ★★

The 1.5-million-acre Lake Mead National Recreation Area was created in 1936 around Lake Mead, a man-made reservoir lake resulting from the construction of Hoover Dam. Later, Lake Mohave, to the south, was formed with the construction of Davis Dam. The entire area is administered by the National Park Service, except for the dam itself, which is administered by the Bureau of Reclamation. Before the two lakes—comprising over 290 square miles—emerged, this desert region was brutally hot, dry, rugged, and unfit for human habitation. Today, it attracts about 9 million visitors annually, making it one of the nation's most popular playgrounds. At an elevation of 1,221½ feet, Lake Mead itself extends some 110 miles upstream toward the Grand Canyon. Backed by spectacular cliff and canyon scenery, its 550-mile shoreline forms a perfect setting for a wide variety of watersports and desert hiking.

Run by the National Park Service, the **Alan Bible Lake Mead Visitor Center,** 4 miles northeast of Boulder City on U.S. 93 at Nev. 166 (© **702/293-8990**), provides information on all area activities and services, and contacts for renting accommodations, boats, and fish equipment. There you can pick up trail maps and brochures, view informative films, and find out about scenic drives, accommodations, ranger-guided hikes, naturalist programs and lectures, bird-watching, canoeing, camping, lakeside RV parks, and picnic facilities. The center is open daily from 8:30am to 4:30pm. The center also sells books and videotapes about the area.

Seven Crown Resorts provides the accommodations, boat rentals, and fishing equipment for Lake Mead. You can make reservations with them either by calling © **800/752-9669** or visiting www.sevencrown.com.

You can also find information on the Lake Mead National Recreation Area on the Web at **www.nps.gov/lame**.

In May of 2000, the park service began to charge **entry fees** for the first time. $5 per vehicle (this covers all passengers in the vehicle) gets you entry that is valid for 5 days, or $3 per individual for 5 days.

LAKE MEAD & VICINITY'S OUTDOOR ACTIVITIES

This is a lovely area for scenic drives amidst the dramatic desert scenery. One popular route follows the Lakeshore and Northshore Scenic Drives along the edge of Lake Mead. From these roads, there are panoramic views of the blue lake set against a backdrop of the browns, blacks, reds, and grays of the desert mountains. Northshore Scenic Drive also leads through areas of brilliant red boulders and rock formations, and you'll find a picnic area along the way.

BOATING & FISHING   Under the auspices of Seven Crown Resorts (© **800/752-9669** or 702/293-3484; www.sevencrown.com), WaveRunners, fishing boats, patio boats, and personal watercrafts can be rented from at **Lake Mead Resort and Marina.** This store also carries groceries, clothing, marine supplies, sporting goods, water-skiing gear, fishing equipment, and bait and tackle. You can get a fishing license here ($51 a year or $21 for 3 days; $9 for children 12 to

Lake Mead & Vicinity

- Logandale
- Overton
- **15**
- MOAPA RIVER INDIAN RESERVATION
- **93**
- **VALLEY OF FIRE STATE PARK** ❶
- **169**
- Overton Beach
- **15**
- **93**
- N E V A D A
- Echo Bay
- Overton Arm

Inset map
NEVADA
Area shown
CA
UT
Las Vegas
AZ

- ← To Las Vegas
- **147**
- Northshore Scenic Drive
- BLACK MOUNTAINS
- **LAKE MEAD** ❷
- *Lake Mead*
- Boulder Canyon
- Lake Mead Pkwy
- Lakeshore Scenic Dr.
- *Boulder Basin*
- ❸
- BLACK MOUNTAINS
- **N A T I O N A L**
- Temple Bar
- Henderson
- ❹
- Hoover Dam (Boulder Dam) ❺
- **R E C R E A T I O N**
- **93 95**
- **Boulder City**
- **93**
- **A R E A**
- Black Canyon of the Colorado River
- **95**
- Willow Beach
- **A R I Z O N A**
- **165**
- *PACIFIC TIME ZONE*
- *MOUNTAIN TIME ZONE*
- White Hills
- Nelson
- **93**
- **95**
- 0 — 10 mi
- 0 — 10 km
- Cottonwood Cove
- *Lake Mohave*

Alan Bible Lake Mead
  Visitor Center **4**
Callville Bay **2**
Hacienda Hotel **5**
Lake Mead Lodge **3**
Valley of Fire State Park
  Visitors Center **1**

15; children under 12 may fish without a license). The knowledgeable staff can direct you to good fishing spots. Largemouth bass, striped bass, channel catfish, crappie, and bluegill are found in Lake Mead; rainbow trout, largemouth bass, and striped bass in Lake Mohave. You can also arrange here to rent a fully equipped houseboat at **Echo Bay,** 40 miles north.

Other convenient Lake Mead marinas offering similar rentals and equipment are **Las Vegas Bay** (✆ **702/565-9111**), which is even closer to Las Vegas, and **Callville Bay** (✆ **702/565-8958**), which is the least crowded of the five on the Nevada Shore.

CAMPING   Available on a first-come, first-served basis, all of the campsites along Lake Mead's shoreline are equipped with running water, picnic tables, and grills. They are administered by the **National Park Service** (✆ **702/293-8990;** www.nps.gov/lame), with a $10 per night charge at each campsite.

CANOEING   The **Alan Bible Lake Mead Visitor Center** (see "Lake Mead National Reservation Area," above) can provide a list of outfitters who rent canoes for trips on the Colorado River. There's one catch, however: A canoeing permit ($13 per person) is required in advance for certain areas near the dam and is available from the **Bureau of Reclamation**'s concessionaires, Black Canyon/ Willow Beach River Adventures, located inside the **Hacienda Hotel and Casino** on Nev. 93 (✆ **800/245-6380** or 702/293-5000; www.haciendaonline.com) in Boulder City. This fee includes a $3 national parks service fee. Call the bureau at ✆ **702/293-8204** or visit the website **www.usbr.gov/lc/hooverdam/paddlecraft/ canoenew.html** for information.

HIKING   The best season for hiking is November to March, as it's really too hot the rest of the year. The **Alan Bible Lake Mead Visitor Center** (see above) offers detailed trail maps. Three trails, ranging in length from .75 to 6 miles, originate at the Visitor Center. The 6-mile trail goes past remains of the railroad built for the dam project. Be sure to take all necessary desert-hiking precautions (see the "Take a Hike: Desert Hiking Advice" box on p. 252). From November to March, the park offers a number of free, ranger guided hikes; check its website at **www. nps.gov/lame** for information about upcoming hikes. You must call the visitor center to make reservations for these guided hikes (✆ **702/293-5907**).

LAKE CRUISES   A delightful way to enjoy Lake Mead is on a cruise aboard **Lake Mead Cruises** *Desert Princess* ⭐ (✆ **702/293-6180;** www.lakemead cruises.com), a Mississippi-style paddle-wheeler. Cruises depart year-round from a terminal near **Lake Mead Lodge** (see below). Enjoy the relaxing, scenic trip from an open promenade deck or from one of two fully enclosed, climate-controlled decks. The trip takes you through Black Canyon and past colorful rock formations known as the Arizona Paint Pots en route to Hoover Dam. Your best family bets would be either the buffet breakfast cruises ($33 adults, $15 children under 12) or the narrated midday cruises ($20 adults, $9 children), each of which are 1½ hours long. The cocktail/dinner cruises ($44 adults, $21 children) last 2 hours, and can include a spectacular view of Hoover Dam lit up for the night, depending on the time of year. The three sunset dinner/dance cruises with live music ($54 adults) are not recommended for kids. Meals (basic, decent food that's hardly gourmet, but you're there for the view) are served in a pleasant, windowed, air-conditioned dining room. Call ✆ **702/293-6180** for departure times. Reservations are strongly recommended.

RAFTING   Through **Black Canyon/Willow Beach River Adventures** (the Bureau of Reclamation's concessionaires), located in the Hacienda Hotel and

Casino, Nev. 93, Boulder City (© **702/293-8204;** www.blackcanyonadventures. com), you can take a flat raft trip down the Colorado River. Your flat raft (also known as a paddle craft, as the rafts are paddled), complete with guide, is launched below Hoover Dam, and you then slowly go downstream to Willow Beach, Arizona, where a bus will return you to your point of origination. During your 3½- to 4-hour ride on the water, your guide will discuss the history of Hoover Dam, the history and geography of the area, the Native American tribes, and the local flora and fauna. As this is a flat-water trip, you shouldn't get too wet in the summer, but in the winter, water-resistant jackets would be a sound idea. Sunblock and hats are advised no matter what the season. The cost is $73 for adults; $70 for 12- to 15-year-olds; $45 for 5- to 11-year-olds; those under 5 are free. Hotel pickups can be arranged for an additional cost of $33 per person. These rafting tours are offered year-round, weather permitting.

The best time to run the river is in the fall through December. The spring is prettiest with new green foliage seen on the beaches and in the side canyons. The spring, along with January and February, however, tends to be the windiest time of year. Headwinds can whip up 3-foot waves and make forward progress grueling. If winds of more than 15 miles per hour are forecast, go another day. Summers are hot, and the canyons tend to hold the heat. The 53°F (12°C) water, however, provides some natural cooling.

SCUBA DIVING   There's good visibility for scuba diving in Lake Mead October to April, lessened in summer months when algae flourishes. A list of good dive locations, authorized instructors, and nearby dive shops is available at the **Alan Bible Lake Mead Visitor Center** (see above). There's also an underwater, designated diving area near Lake Mead Marina.

WHERE TO STAY & DINE AROUND LAKE MEAD

In addition to the hotels listed below, there are a number of little hotels in Boulder City.

Hacienda Hotel and Casino   Located on Highway 93, 3½ miles south of Boulder City, the Hacienda is a standard gaming hotel, complete with nice rooms, a casino, and a four-screen movie theater showing first-run flicks, which is almost a necessity, as there is no cable for the in-room TVs. Double rooms have two queen beds; suites, a king with a couch or loveseat (neither folds out). This hotel, with a buffet and food court, is a safe bet for families looking to stay close to the lake. There's also a steakhouse if you feel like having a sit-down meal after a day of boating and sightseeing. The hotel can also arrange helicopter tours over Hoover Dam and Lake Mead, ranging from $29 to $99 (© **702/294-2200**).

Nev. 93, Boulder City, NV 89005. © 800/245-6380 or 702/293-5000. www.haciendaonline.com. 325 units. Sun–Thurs $49 and up double, $59 suite; Fri–Sat $59 double, $69 suite; holidays $79 double, $89 suite. Extra person $3. Children under 5 stay free in parent's room. Cribs $3, rollaways $5. AE, DC, DISC, MC, V. Pets accepted for $5 per animal. **Amenities:** 2 restaurants (buffet and steakhouse); food court; movie theater; outdoor pool. *In room:* A/C, TV (no cable).

Lake Mead Lodge (Value   This rustic and comfortable bungalow-style lodge is an easy drive from Hoover Dam. It's beautifully situated right on the lake, and surrounded on three sides by desert. The rooms are pleasant, with wood-paneled ceilings and walls of white-painted brick or rough-hewn pine, and all offer full private bathrooms. There is a suite with three rooms and a small kitchen, which might be good for families staying a few days. (There are plans to add a second suite.) The pool is rudimentary, but you might want to relax with a good book in one of the gazebos on the property. About a half-mile down the road is the marina, where you can while away a few hours over cocktails on a lakeside patio. The marina is the area's headquarters for boating, fishing, and watersports; it also houses a large shop (for details, see the "Boating & Fishing" section, above).

There's a nautically themed restaurant called **Tale of the Whale** (© 702/ 293-3484) at the marina, its rough-hewn pine interior embellished with various sea-faring iconography. It's open 7am to 9pm daily. (It closes an hour later during the summer.) The restaurant serves hearty breakfasts; sandwiches, salads, and burgers at lunch; and steak-and-seafood dinners. And Boulder Beach, also an easy walk from the lodge, has waterfront picnic tables and barbecue grills.

322 Lakeshore Rd., Boulder City, NV 89005. © 800/752-9669 or 702/293-2074. 42 units. Early Mar to late Nov $70 and up double; the rest of the year $60 and up double. Children under 5 stay free in parent's room, $6 per night per person over age 5. Rollaways $6. DISC, MC, V. Pets accepted for $5 per animal. **Amenities:** Outdoor pool; picnic area with barbecue pit. *In room:* A/C, TV w/basic cable.

BOULDER CITY

Consider poking around Boulder City on your way back to Vegas. Founded in 1936, Boulder City was the first planned community in the United States. The company town for those building Hoover Dam, it was created by the wives who came with their husbands and turned a temporary site into a real community, since aided by the recreational attractions and attendant businesses of Lake Mead. It doesn't look like much as you first approach it, but once you are in the heart, you'll discover that it's quite charming. The town has some antiques and curio shops, and a number of family-style restaurants as well as burger and Mexican joints, including **Totos,** a reasonably priced Mexican restaurant at 806 Buchanan Blvd. (© 702/293-1744); it's in the Von's shopping center.

2 Valley of Fire State Park ★★

60 miles NE of Las Vegas

In contrast to the modern developments in Las Vegas, much of the Mojave Desert around the city resembles a Martian landscape—a seemingly lifeless tundra where misshaped rock formations erupt from the vivid red earth. Shaped by time, climate, and subterranean upheaval, these majestic canyons, cliffs, and ridges provide a striking contrast to the man-made monuments of Sin City.

The 36,000-acre **Valley of Fire State Park** (© 702/397-2088; www.parks. nv.gov/vf.htm) typifies the mountainous red Mojave Desert. Deriving its name from the crimson sandstone formations created 150 million years ago by a great shifting of sand, the park continues to be shaped by the geologic processes of wind and water erosion. Mysterious, loaded with petroglyphs, and totally inhospitable, this was a sacred place for Native Americans, where only the men came as a test of their manhood; it is still a natural wonder that must be seen to be appreciated. The otherworldly rock formations, fiery outcroppings blazing under the relentless sun—are surreal, beautiful, and strange beyond comprehension. There is nothing green in the area and no plant life as far as the eye can see. No wonder this park has been used as a location for various sci-fi movies; it is unlike any other place on earth; studios, even with all the modern technology available to them, cannot reproduce Nature's handiwork in this case.

Although it's hard to imagine while you're driving through the park in the sweltering Nevada heat, for billions of years, these rocks were under hundreds of feet of ocean, which began to rise some 200 million years ago. The ocean's waters became shallower and shallower over time, until the sea made a complete retreat, leaving a muddy terrain traversed by ever-diminishing streams. Eventually, a great sandy desert covered much of the southwestern part of the American continent until about 140 million years ago. Over these eons, winds, massive fault action, and water erosion sculpted fantastic formations of sand and limestone. Oxidation of iron in the sands and mud—and the effect of ground water leaching the oxidized iron—in other words, rust on a huge scale—turned the rocks the many hues of red, pink, russet, lavender, and white that can be seen today. Logs of ancient forests washed down from faraway highlands and became petrified fossils, which can be seen along two interpretive trails.

The centuries between 2000 B.C. and 300 B.C., when human beings occupied the region, were much wetter and cooler than now. While these early residents didn't live in the Valley of Fire itself, the men of the tribes traveled here to hunt bighorn sheep for a source of food, clothing, blankets, and hut coverings, using a notched stick called an *atlatl* that is depicted in the park's petroglyphs, while the women and children caught rabbits, tortoises, and other small game.

In the Valley of Fire's next historical phase, from 300 B.C. to A.D. 700, the climate became warmer and drier. Bows and arrows replaced the atlatl, and the hunters and gatherers discovered farming. Corn, squash, and beans were cultivated by the Anasazi people, whose communities began replacing small nomadic family groups. These ancient people wove watertight baskets, mats, hunting nets, and clothing. Around A.D. 300, they learned how to make sun-dried ceramic pottery. Over time, other tribes, notably the Paiutes, migrated to the area, and by A.D. 1150, they had become the dominant group. Unlike the Anasazi, the Paiutes were still nomadic and used the Valley of Fire region seasonally. The Paiutes were the inhabitants found by white settlers when they entered the area in the early to mid-1800s. The pioneers diverted river and spring waters to irrigate their farmlands, destroying the nature-based Paiute way of life. Now about 300 descendants of those Paiute tribespeople still live on the Moapa Indian Reservation (about 20 miles northwest) that was established along the Muddy River in 1872.

Dedicated in 1935, Valley of Fire is Nevada's oldest and largest state park. Since that time, the park's notable rock formations have been named for the shapes they vaguely resemble—a duck, an elephant, seven sisters, domes, beehives, etc. You can have fun with your family by looking for these and renaming formations to suit your visions. Look for Mouse's Tank, named for a fugitive Paiute called Mouse who hid there in the late 1890s. It is a natural basin that collects rainwater (hence the "tank" appellation). You can hike to see Native American **petroglyphs** etched into the rock walls and boulders—some dating from as early as 3,000 years ago. These can be observed on self-guided trails. Petroglyphs at Atlatl Rock and Petroglyph Canyon are both easily accessible. It is unlawful to remove rocks, plants, or animals from the park; there is a $250 fine per object if you're caught. Make sure to tell your children about this law, so you don't encounter any problems. And, naturally, carving your initials on the rocks is also illegal. In summer, when temperatures are usually over 100°F (38°C), you may have to settle for driving through the park in an air-conditioned car.

Your first stop on your visit through this bizarre landscape should be the **Visitor Center** on Nev. 169, 6 miles west of North Shore Scenic Drive (© **702/397-2088;** www.parks.nv.gov/vf.htm). It's open daily 8:30am to 4:30pm and is worth a quick stop for information and a bit of history before entering the park. Exhibits on the premises explain the origin and geologic history of the park's colorful sandstone formations, describe the ancient peoples who carved their rock art on canyon walls, and identify the plants and wildlife you're likely to see. Postcards, books, slides, and film are on sale here, and you can also pick up hiking maps and brochures or have your park-related questions answered by rangers.

GETTING THERE

From Las Vegas, take I-15 north to exit 75 (Valley of Fire turnoff). However, the more scenic route is to take I-15 north, then travel Lake Mead Boulevard (exit 45) east to North Shore Scenic Road (Nev. 167), and proceed north to the Valley of Fire exit. The first route takes about an hour, the second, about 1½ hours.

There is a $6 per vehicle admission charge to the park, regardless of how many people you cram inside.

Plan on spending a minimum of an hour in the park, though you can spend a great deal of time more. It can get very hot in there (there is nothing to relieve the sun beating down on all that red and reflecting off it) and there is no water,

---

Tips Take a Hike: Desert Hiking Advice

Except in summer, when temperatures can reach 120°F (49°C) in the shade, the Las Vegas area is great for hiking. The best hiking season is November to March.

Hiking in the desert is exceptionally rewarding, but it can be dangerous. Here are some safety tips:

1. Don't hike alone.
2. Carry plenty of water and drink it often. Don't assume spring waters are safe to drink. A gallon of water per person per day is recommended for hikers.
3. Be alert for signs of heat exhaustion (headache; nausea; dizziness; fatigue; and cool, damp, pale, or red skin).
4. Gauge your fitness accurately. Desert hiking may involve rough or steep terrain. Don't take on more than you can handle.
5. Check weather forecasts before starting out. Thunderstorms can turn into raging flash floods, which are extremely hazardous to hikers.
6. Dress properly. Wear sturdy walking shoes for rock scrambling, long pants (to protect yourself from rocks and cacti), a hat, sunscreen, and sunglasses.
7. Carry a small first-aid kit.
8. Be careful when climbing on sandstone, which can be surprisingly soft and crumbly.
9. Don't feed or play with animals, such as the wild burros in Red Rock Canyon. (It's actually illegal to approach them.)
10. Be alert for snakes and insects. Though they're rarely encountered, you'll want to look into a crevice before putting your hand into it.
11. Visit park or other information offices before you start out and acquaint yourself with rules and regulations and any possible hazards. It's also a good idea to tell the staff where you're going, when you'll return, how many are in your party, and so on. Some park offices offer hiker registration programs.
12. Follow the hiker's rule of thumb: Take only photographs and leave only footprints.

so be certain to bring a liter, maybe two, per person. In the summer, consider a gallon per person. Without a guide, you must stay on paved roads, but don't worry if they end; you can always turn around and come back to the main road again. You can see a great deal from the car, but there are also hiking trails.

Char Cruze of **Creative Adventures** (p. 178) also offers a fantastic tour, which can be tailored to your family's interests (© **702/893-2051**).

The Valley of Fire can also be visited in conjunction with Lake Mead. From **Lake Mead Lodge,** take Nev. 166 (Lakeshore Scenic Dr.) north, make a right turn on Nev. 167 (North Shore Scenic Dr.), turn left on Nev. 169 (Moapa Valley Blvd.) west—a spectacularly scenic drive—and follow the signs. Valley of Fire is about 70 miles, approximately an hour, from Hoover Dam itself.

There are no food concessions or gas stations in the park; however, you can obtain meals or gas on Nev. 167 or in nearby **Overton** (15 miles northwest on Nev. 169). A fertile valley town replete with trees, agricultural crops, horses, and herds of cattle, Overton is quite a change in scenery from the Valley of Fire's looming ruddy formations. On your way in or out of the quaint burg, treat your family to a meal or snack at **Inside Scoop** ⚡, 395 S. Moapa Valley Blvd. (© **702/397-2055**), open Monday through Saturday 10am to 8pm, and Sunday 11am to 6pm. This sweet, old-fashioned ice cream parlor is run by extremely friendly people who offer a proper menu of fresh food and classic sandwiches, including a vegetarian option. Consider coming by here on your way into the park and picking up box lunches (perfect for picnicking in the park), and then coming by afterward for a much-needed ice cream.

You might also want to stop at the **Lost City Museum** ⚡, 721 S. Moapa Valley Blvd. (© **702/397-2193**), on the southern edge of town. This little museum, surrounded by reconstructed wattle-and-daub pueblos, displays artifacts dating back 12,000 years from the ancient Anasazi village that was discovered in the region in 1924. This village had reached one of the highest levels of Native American culture in the United States. Clay jars, dried corn and beans, arrowheads, seashell necklaces, and willow baskets of the ancient Pueblo culture that inhabited this region between A.D. 300 and 1150 are thoughtfully and informatively exhibited. You'll also find exhibits about Mormon farmers who settled the valley in the 1860s. In addition, there's a large collection of local rocks—petrified wood, fern fossils, iron pyrites, green copper, and red iron oxide. Kids seem especially fascinated by the purple glass bottles—manganese blown bottles turned purple by the ultraviolet rays of the sun. Admission is $3 for adults, $2 for seniors 65 and older, and free for children under 18. The museum is open daily 8:30am to 4:30pm. Closed Thanksgiving, December 25, and January 1.

There are **hiking trails, shaded picnic sites,** and **two campgrounds** in the park. Most sites are equipped with tables, grills, water, and restrooms. A $14 per vehicle per night camping fee is charged for use of the campground; if you're not camping, it costs $6 per vehicle to enter the park.

3 Red Rock Canyon ⚡⚡⚡

19 miles W of Las Vegas

If you need a break from Las Vegas and its overstimulating hustle and glow, soothe your senses and spend some family time at Red Rock Canyon, less than 20 miles away from the neonopolis's glittering Strip. A visit to this magnificent, unspoiled vista is a refreshing break from the hubbub and neon of Vegas. And what makes the canyon even more appealing is that you and yours can spend a good part of the day out here, taking in the unique natural wonders, and still make it back to your hotel in time for the Bellagio fountain show or the Blue Man Group. You can drive the panoramic 13-mile **Scenic Drive** (open daily 7am–dusk) or explore the park in more depth on foot, making it perfect for both athletes and armchair types. You'll find many interesting sights and trail heads along the drive itself, allowing you to get out and stretch your legs or just take in the views. The wider **National Conservation Area** offers hiking trails and internationally acclaimed rock-climbing opportunities (especially notable is the 7,068-ft. Mount Wilson, the highest sandstone peak among the bluffs). There are picnic areas along the drive and in nearby **Spring Mountain Ranch State Park,** 5 miles south, which also offers plays in an outdoor theater during the summer. Because Bonnie Springs Ranch (see the next section) is just a few miles away, it makes a great base for exploring Red Rock Canyon.

GETTING THERE

Just drive west on Charleston Boulevard, which becomes Nev. 159. Virtually as soon as you leave the city, the red rocks begin to loom around you. The Visitor Center will appear on your right.

You can also go on an **organized tour. Coach USA** (© **800/828-6699;** www. coachusa.com), among other companies, runs bus tours to Red Rock Canyon. A 7-hour tour costs $55 and includes lunch and the park fee. Inquire at your hotel tour desk.

Finally, the adventurous, in-shape family can go **by bike.** Not very far out of town (at Rainbow Blvd.), Charleston Boulevard is flanked by a bike path that continues for about 11 miles to the Visitor Center/Scenic Drive. The path is hilly but not difficult if you're in reasonable shape. However, exploring Red Rock Canyon by bike should be attempted only by exceptionally fit and experienced bikers. Bike equipment can be rented from **Escape Adventures/Las Vegas Cyclery,** 8221 W. Charleston Blvd. (© **702/383-6966;** www.escapeadventures.com), starting at $35 per day. They also offer guided tours (p. 266).

Just off Nev. 159, you'll see the **Red Rock Canyon Visitor Center** (© **702/ 515-5350;** www.redrockcanyon.blm.gov), which marks the actual entrance to the park. There, you can pick up information on trails and view history exhibits on the canyon. The center is open daily from 8:30am to 4:30pm. Red Rock Canyon can also be combined with a visit to Bonnie Springs Ranch.

ABOUT RED ROCK CANYON

Some 600 million years ago, the forces of nature began forming Red Rock Canyon. During most of its history, Red Rock Canyon was below a warm shallow sea. Then, about 225 million years ago, massive fault action and volcanic eruptions caused this seabed to begin rising. As the waters receded, sea creatures died and the calcium in their bodies combined with sea minerals to form limestone cliffs studded with ancient fossils. Some 45 million years later, the region was buried beneath thousands of feet of windblown sand. The landscape was as arid as the Sahara. As time progressed, iron oxide and calcium carbonate infiltrated the sand, consolidating it into cross-bedded rock.

Winds and water shaped the sandstone monoliths into arches, natural bridges, and massive sculptures, and painted them a stunning palette with gray-white limestone, pink and crimson oxidized minerals, dolomite, black mineral deposits, and orange and green lichen stains.

As shallow streams began carving the Red Rock landscape, logs washed down from ancient highland forests and gradually fossilized, their molecules replaced

Tips Wild Weather

Although it can get very hot in Red Rock during the summer, it can also get very cold there during the winter. A recent trip in March to Red Rock and Bonnie Springs found the latter closed—due to snow!

by quartz and other minerals, becoming petrified wood. These stone logs, which the Paiute Indians believed were weapons of the wolf god, Shinarav, can be viewed in the **Chinle Formation** at the base of the Red Rock Cliffs. About 100 million years ago, massive fault action began dramatically shifting the rock landscape here, forming spectacular limestone and sandstone cliffs and rugged canyons punctuated by waterfalls, shallow streams, and serene oasis pools. Even now, spring-fed areas of lush foliage contrast the harsh rocks and steep cliffs jutting 2,000 feet above the valley floors.

The seismic activity is exemplified by the **Keystone Thrust Fault,** dating back about 65 million years, where two of the earth's crustal plates collided, forcing older limestone and dolomite plates from the ancient seas over younger red and white sandstones.

Red Rock's valley is home to more than 45 species of mammals, including bighorn sheep, about 100 species of birds, 30 kinds of reptiles and amphibians, and an abundance of plant life. Ascending the slopes from the valley, you'll see cactus and creosote bushes, aromatic purple sage, yellow-flowering blackbrush, yucca and Joshua trees, and, at higher elevations, clusters of forest-green piñon, juniper, and ponderosa pines. In spring, this desert blooms with extraordinary wildflowers.

Archaeological studies of Red Rock have turned up pottery fragments, stone tools, pictographs (rock drawings), and petroglyphs (rock etchings), along with other ancient artifacts. They show that humans have been in this region since about 3000 B.C. (some experts say as early as 10,000 B.C.). You can still see remains of early inhabitants on hiking expeditions in the park. (It's the same, sad Anasazi to Paiutes to white settlers progression related in the Valley of the Fire section above.)

In the latter part of the 19th century, Red Rock was a mining site and later a sandstone quarry that provided materials for many buildings in Los Angeles, San Francisco, and early Las Vegas. By the end of World War II, however, as Las Vegas developed, many people became aware of the importance of preserving the canyon. In 1967, the Secretary of the Interior designated 62,000 acres as Red Rock Canyon Recreation Lands under the auspices of the Bureau of Land Management, and later legislation banned all development except hiking trails and limited recreational facilities. In 1990, Red Rock Canyon became a National Conservation Area, further elevating its protected status; its current acreage is 197,000.

WHAT TO SEE & DO

Begin with a stop at the **Visitor Center** (*©* **702/515-5350;** www.redrock canyon.blm.gov); not only is there a $5 per vehicle fee to pay, but you can pick up a variety of helpful literature: history, guides, hiking trail maps, and lists of local flora and fauna. There, you can also view exhibits that tell the history of the canyon and depict its plant and animal life. The center also has a fascinating video about Nevada's thousands of wild horses and burros, protected by an act of

Congress since 1971. Furthermore, you can obtain permits for hiking and back-packing there. Call ahead to find out about ranger-guided tours as well as inform-ative guided hikes offered by groups such as the Sierra Club and the Audubon Society. Also ask about the free *Junior Ranger Discovery Book* filled with fun fam-ily activities. Other books and videotapes are on sale here, including a guidebook identifying more than 100 top-rated climbing sites. The website for the park provides a special **Kids Korner** (www.redrockcanyon.blm.gov/kids), which has images available for printing and coloring and also lists the story time and crafts programs provide by the Las Vegas Library District.

The visitor center also offers astronomy programs, for those interested in stargazing; details can be found on the website or by calling the center. There is a campsite, located 2 miles past the visitor center, which has barbecue grills (bring your own fuel), picnic tables, trash pickup, and pit toilets. There is a park employee, called a campground host, on-site if you need any help. Campsites are on a first-come-first served basis, and cost $10 per night. Pets are permitted, but must be on a leash at all times.

The easiest thing to do with your family is to **drive the 13-mile scenic loop** ★★. It is a one-way loop and once you start, you are committed to driv-ing the whole thing, which can take as little as 40 minutes or as long as you like, depending on whether you stop and get out to admire your surroundings. Any-where along the way, you can stop the car to gaze at any number of fabulous views and sights, have a picnic, or to take a walk or hike. Point out to your kids how dramatically the milky-white limestone alternates with the iron-rich red rocks and show them the evergreen forest, which is a strange sight in the desert, through the limestone canyons.

For the most part, **hiking** is best left to in-shape adults and athletic young adults, who can read maps and enjoy clambering and climbing. However, if you're up to it, we can't stress enough that the way to really see the canyon is by hiking, as the trails are the best way to explore the park. Most of the trails are designated "easy," but that is fairly subjective. There is, however, a trail designed especially for children, the **Lost Creek Children's Discovery Trail,** which is .7 mile and suitable for all ages.

A trail appropriate for children 8 years and up is the **Moenkopi Trail.** Orig-inating at the Visitor Center and traversing undulating open terrain in a broad desert valley, the short loop trail takes a little more than an hour to walk.

All of the canyon's hikes involve a certain amount of effort, as you have to scramble over rocks on even the shorter hikes. Younger children, the out of shape, and the clumsy may wish to stand by the side and just take in the scenery. Be sure to wear good shoes as the rocks can be slippery and take a map along with you. You probably won't get lost forever without one (there are usually other hikers around to help you out—eventually!), but you can get lost, which could be very upsetting for all concerned. It is often tough to find a landmark, and once deep into the rocks, everything looks the same, even with the map. Consequently, give yourself extra time for each hike (at least an additional hour except for the two hikes mentioned above), regardless of its billed length, to allow for the lack of paths, getting disoriented, and simply slowing down and admiring the scenery. And please carry water with you, as much as a gallon per person during the summer. You can check out the hikes in advance at **www.redrockcanyon.blm.gov/activities/hiking.asp**.

As you hike, keep your eyes peeled for lizards, the occasional desert tortoise, herds of bighorn sheep, birds, and other critters. There are also minicaves to explore and rocks to climb. On trails along Calico Hills and the escarpment, look for "Indian marbles," a local name for small, rounded sandstone rocks that have eroded off larger sandstone formations. Look, but don't touch: *You should not take these or any other rocks with you as souvenirs, as it is illegal.* Petroglyphs are also tucked away in various locales, but don't be tempted to add your own: The park is a National Conservation Area controlled by the federal government. The fines—which vary by offense—are steep for desecrating the monuments, taking plants and rocks, and for harassing (trying to touch, chasing, etc.) the animals in the park.

Biking is another option for seeing the park; riding a bicycle would be a tremendous way to travel the loop. There are also terrific off-road mountain biking trails, with levels from amateur to expert. If you don't want to go on your own, **Escape Adventures** (✆ **702/383-6966;** www.escapeadventures.com) offers a half-day, 18-mile bike ride through Red Rock.

After you tour the canyon, drive over to Bonnie Springs Ranch (see below) for lunch or dinner.

4 Bonnie Springs Ranch/Old Nevada ✶✶

About 24 miles W of Las Vegas, 5 miles from Red Rock Canyon

Bonnie Springs Ranch/Old Nevada is a kind of Wild West theme park with a zoo, ghost town, accommodations, and a restaurant. Admission to the zoo and Old Nevada is covered in one low fee. If you're traveling with kids, a day or overnight trip to Bonnie Springs/Old Nevada is recommended, but it is surprisingly appealing for adults, too. It could even be a romantic getaway, offering horseback riding, gorgeous mountain vistas, proximity to Red Rock Canyon, and temperatures 5° to 10° cooler than on the Strip.

For additional information, contact **Bonnie Springs Ranch/Old Nevada** at ✆ **702/875-4191** or **www.bonniesprings.com**.

If you're **driving,** a trip to Bonnie Springs Ranch can be combined easily with a day trip to Red Rock Canyon; it is about 5 miles further on. But you can also stay overnight at the Bonnie Springs Hotel to make this destination more than just a day trip.

GETTING THERE

From anywhere on Las Vegas Boulevard South (the Strip), drive north to Charleston Boulevard, make a left onto Charleston Boulevard, and take it west for 25 miles (6 miles past the Red Rock Visitor Center). Bonnie Springs/Old Nevada will be on the right side. A wooden arch that says OLD NEVADA marks the entrance.

For those without transportation, there's a shuttle service, **Star Land Tours/ Bonnie Springs Shuttle** (✆ **702/296-4381** or 702/296-4972), which will pick you up at your Vegas hotel and take you out to Bonnie Springs for $30 round-trip per person. The shuttle fee includes admission to Old Nevada and the zoo.

WHAT TO SEE & DO AT BONNIE SPRINGS RANCH

For kids, the **zoo** (its admission is covered in the entrance fee to Old Nevada) is the big draw at Bonnie Springs Ranch, located right next door to Old Nevada, on the same property, at 1 Gunfighter Lane, with the same hours, daily 10:30am to 6pm from May to October, and 10:30am to 5pm October to May. In addition to the petting zoo with potbellied pigs, llamas, goats, and sheep, there are wire enclosures holding all manner of creatures, including wolves and bobcats.

Parents and some children may find this a bit prehistoric in comparison to the zoos located in large urban centers. However, the creatures are healthy and well cared for, and the ranch provides a home for wild horses, many of whom would starve to death if not rounded up and placed here.

The zoo includes an aviary, housing peacocks, Polish chickens, peachface and blackmask lovebirds, finches, parakeets, ravens, ducks, pheasants, and geese. Keep your eyes peeled for the peacocks roaming free; with luck, they will spread their tails for a photo op. With greater luck, some of the angelic, rare white peacocks will do the same. It may be worth dropping by just in the hopes of spotting one in full fan-tailed glory.

Riding stables offer guided trail rides into the mountain area on a continuous basis throughout the day (9am–3:15pm spring–fall, until 5:45pm in summer). Children must be at least 6 years old to participate. Cost is $25 per person for the hour-long guided ride through the surrounding hills. For more information, call ⓒ 702/875-4191.

WHAT TO SEE & DO IN OLD NEVADA

Old Nevada 🖈🖈 (ⓒ 702/875-4191) is a re-creation of an 1880s frontier town, built on the site of a very old ranch. Though a bit hokey, it's got a certain charm, and children up to age 12 (before teenage cynicism kicks in) will certainly get a kick out of the authentic-looking Western town (and you just might, as well!). Rustic buildings are entirely made of weathered wood, and the town lies right in front of beautiful mountains with layered red rock. Hollywood could not have done any better.

The block-long town, with its well-replicated places of business (a blacksmith shop, a working mill), a saloon, and a museum that has a potpourri of items from the Old West and Old Las Vegas (antique gaming tables and slot machines, typewriters, and a great display of old shoes including lace-up boots) also has (of course) an old-fashioned general store, which functions as a gift shop. Additionally, there's a wax museum, which pales beside the free **stage melodramas** that take place three times a day in the (all ages allowed) saloon. These melodramas (staged at 11:30am, and 2 and 4:30pm in the summer and 11:30am, and 1:30 and 3:30pm in the winter) are entirely tongue-in-cheek—the actors are goofy and know it, and the plot is hokey and fully intended to be that way. Somehow, however, all of these factors just heighten the fun you have while watching them. Kids will like the interactivity of the audience who, in response to cue cards held up by the players, boo and hiss the mustache-twirling villain, sob in sympathy with the distressed heroine, and laugh, cheer, and applaud as the cards instruct. It's hugely silly and hugely fun, provided you all play along. Kids love it, though younger ones might be scared by the occasional gunshot.

Immediately following each melodrama, a free **Western drama** is presented outside the saloon on the street, involving a bank robbery, a shootout, and the trial of the bad guy. A judge, prosecuting attorney, and defense attorney are chosen from the audience, the remainder of whom act as the jury. The action always culminates in a hanging, which some younger kids might find disturbing. None of this is a particularly polished act, but the dialogue is quite funny and the whole thing is performed with enthusiasm and affection.

Throughout the area, during the hours of operation, "cowboys" (costumed actors) continually interact with visiting kids, who, on the weekends, are given badges so that they can join a "posse" hunting for bad guys (also costumed actors). There are also ongoing, somewhat clumsy **stunt shootouts** on the street in this wild frontier town, staged by said actors, and some rather unsavory characters (more actors) occasionally languishing in the town jail, at least until their lunch break!

The town (in all of its block-long-pseudo-ghost-town glory) also has replicas of a turn-of-the-century church and stamp mill; the latter, having original 1902 machinery, was used for crushing rocks to separate gold and silver from the earth. In the **Old Nevada Photograph Shoppe,** on the main street, you can dress up in period costumes and have a tintype picture taken with a 120-year-old camera. You can also tour the remains of the **old Comstock Lode silver mine,** behind the saloon, though there isn't much to see there. And if you must, you can shop for a variety of "Western" souvenirs (though, to us, this is when the real tourist trap part of Old Nevada kicks in).

There is plenty of parking in Old Nevada; weekends and holidays, a free shuttle train takes visitors from the parking lot to the entrance. Admission to Old Nevada is charged by vehicle—$7 per car weekdays for up to 6 people in the car and $10 per car on the weekends. The park is open daily from 10:30am to 5pm November to April, until 6pm the rest of the year, and admission also includes entrance into Bonnie Springs Ranch, with its zoo.

WHERE TO STAY & DINE

Bonnie Springs Motel 🎯   This is really a hoot; a funky, friendly little place in the middle of nowhere—though nowhere is really a gorgeous setting. The motel is in two double-story buildings and offers regular rooms, "Western" rooms, "specialty theme" rooms, and kitchen suites.

Unfortunately, the specialty rooms (decorated in theatrical Chinese, Native American, Gay '90s, and Spanish themes) are off limits to kids, but children are allowed in the Calico West rooms and kitchen suites, which have sleeper sofas in the living room. The Western-motif Calico West rooms sleep four and are quite large, though long and narrow. All of these Calico West rooms have private balconies or patios, and mountain views. The family suites, which are also Western themed and sleep six, come with fully equipped kitchens, bedrooms, living rooms (with convertible sofas), and dressing areas; these are also equipped with two phones and two TVs and are available for long-term rentals. Videotapes and players are also available for rental, and there is even a tiny train that takes you around the grounds and on a short tour of the desert. The motel also offers a special breakfast and sunrise horseback ride package for guests, at a cost of $25. Guests of the motel receive free admission into Old Nevada.

1 Gunfighter Lane, Old Nevada, NV 89004. © 702/875-4400. www.bonniesprings.com. Fax 702/875-4424. 50 units. Sun–Thurs $60–$70 double, Fri–Sat $70–$80 double (4 people maximum); Sun–Thurs $120 fantasy suite, Fri–Sat $135 fantasy suite (4 people maximum); Sun–Thurs $95 family suite, Fri–Sat $100 family suite (6 people maximum). Extra person $5. $100 deposit required on family suites; $10 key and phone deposit for all rooms. Cribs/rollaways free, unless they are for an extra person, in which case the $5 extra person fee applies. AE, MC, V. **Amenities:** Outdoor pool. *In room:* A/C, TV w/pay movies, VCRs available to rent, coffeemakers.

Bonnie Springs Ranch Restaurant   This perfect family place has a lot of character, with a heavily rustic decor (complete with stone floors, log beams, raw wooden chairs made from tree branches, lanterns, a roaring fire in winter, and plenty of dead animals adorning the walls). It's a bit touristy, but small-town touristy. The food is basic—steak, ribs, chicken, burgers, and potato skins; pancakes and eggs for breakfast; most of it is greasy but good, with a children's menu featuring chicken fingers, steak, and other kid pleasers. For parents who want a break, there is also a cozy bar attached to the restaurant; its walls are covered with thousands of dollar bills with messages on them—what would be a classic neighborhood bar, if it were actually in a neighborhood!

n Bonnie Springs Ranch, 1 Gunfighter Lane. *©* **702/875-4191.** www.bonniesprings.com/restaurant.html. Highchairs, boosters. Main courses $15–$20; kids' menu $5.95–$13. AE, MC, V. Mon–Fri 9am–9pm; Sat–Sun 8am–10pm.

Miner's Restaurant   Inside Old Nevada, this is just a snack bar, but it is in a nice, quite-large room (with Western motif accessories, of course!), and it serves inexpensive fare (sandwiches, decent burgers, pizza, hot dogs, fresh-baked desserts, and soft drinks) that will surely be okay with your children's tastes. There are also tables out on the porch, so you can enjoy the West al fresco.

1 Gunfighter Lane (inside Old Nevada). *©* **702/875-4191.** www.bonniesprings.com. Highchairs, boosters. Snacks $3–$6. AE, MC, V. May–Oct daily 8am–11pm.

5 Spring Mountains National Recreation Area/Mount Charleston

25 miles NW of Las Vegas

Part of the 316,000-acre **Spring Mountains National Recreation Area** (known locally as Mount Charleston; www.fs.fed.us/r4/htnf/districts/smnra/index.shtml), this mountainous area offers stunning natural beauty year-round. Just half an hour from Las Vegas, Mount Charleston makes a quick, easy, and lovely getaway from the Strip. There are five separate eco-zones within the park, based on elevation. During the summer, it can be 30°F (–1°C) cooler here than on the Strip, and the green forests with pine trees beckon hikers. **Robber Roost,** 3 miles north of Nev. 157, on Nev. 158, is an 850-yard hiking loop (just under .5 mile), which weaves past caves, where, allegedly, real bandits hid out from lawmen. This is the easiest and shortest trail in the park, suitable for children 8 and over, with moderate athletic ability. Hiking trails, descriptions, and directions to each of the trails can be found at **www.fs.fed.us/htnf/smnratra.htm**.

From roughly Thanksgiving through Easter, depending on weather conditions, you can ski and snowboard at the **Las Vegas Ski and Snowboard Resort** (*©* **702/593-9500;** www.skilasvegas.com), located within the recreation area. The only snow sport facility in the Mount Charleston area, it rents equipment and clothing and also provides snowboarding and skiing lessons. There is also a snack bar on-site. The following information is for the 2004–05 ski season and may change during subsequent years. Call or e-mail the **Las Vegas Ski and Snowboard Resort** (ridenski@lvssr.com) to check for rate changes and get the most up-to-date information: Group rates for skiing or snowboarding lessons—based on groups of three or more—for an hour and a half of instruction are $25 per person providing their own equipment and lift ticket, $60 including tickets and equipment. Children must be over 8 years old for these lessons. All-day instruction, lasting 5 hours, for one or two people is $300, and each additional person is $100. Private instruction is also available hourly for $100 per hour, $25 for each additional person. There is also a special children's program for kids ages 4 to 12 from 9am to 3:30pm. The $90 fee includes equipment and lunch. The half-day children's program is $65 and goes from 9:30am to noon, and does not include lunch.

The all-day pass for adults is $33 and $25 for children 12 and under. Those 65 and over can ski or snowboard all day for $25.

Complete ski equipment rental (skis, poles, and boots) is $25 no matter whether they are rented for a full day or for the 3-hour afternoon session. Skis alone are $18 and poles are $5. Snowboards, either in a complete package (including boots) or with the board alone, can be rented for $25. The fee is the same whether rented for the full day or for the shorter afternoon session. Snow clothes can be rented as well; bib and jacket together are $15 for the full day. Rented separately they are $10 each for a full day.

GETTING THERE

Mount Charleston is easily accessible from the Strip. Take Las Vegas Boulevard north to Spring Mountain Road. Turn west on Spring Mountain and merge onto I-15 north. Take I-15 north to U.S. 95 north and follow that to Nev. 157 (Kyle Canyon). Turn left on 157, and the signs will announce your arrival in the recreation area.

WHERE TO STAY

Mount Charleston Hotel   This rustic-style hotel (think log walls and fire-places in the public areas) becomes a bustling ski resort during the winter months. During the summer, it provides an excellent, though slightly expensive, location for families who want to hike in the Mount Charleston area. Rooms are attractive, offering a pleasant place to rest up, and most have stunning views of the surrounding area. Suites sleep four with the pullout couch. The website lists room rate specials. The restaurant, featuring what staff calls "middle of the road, tasty" food (they're right), serves reasonably priced breakfasts, lunches, and din-ners, and provides a children's menu as well.

2 Kyle Canyon Rd. (Nev. 157), Mount Charleston, NV 89124. ✆ 800/794-3456 or 702/872-5500. www.mt charlestonhotel.com. 63 units. $95 double, $125–$225 suite. Extra person $5. Children under 12 stay free in par-ent's room. No cribs or rollaways. AE, DC, DISC, MC, V. **Amenities:** Restaurant (American); whirlpool; Jacuzzi; sauna; arcade. *In room:* A/C, TV w/pay movies, coffeemaker.

Mount Charleston Lodge   Located at the very top of Nev. 157, and designed primarily as a honeymoon and vacation getaway for couples, Mount Charleston Lodge provides rustic log cabins that sleep two to four people. Two cabins have full kitchens; all have whirlpool tubs and fireplaces. Designed mainly for skiers, the Lodge's rates go up approximately $15 during December and on all major holidays. On weekends, during September and October, the Lodge restaurant adds German food to its extensive menu (ostrich, elk, and buf-falo burgers in addition to beef, plus pizza, desserts, and breakfast) and throws a big Oktoberfest celebration.

1200 Old Park Rd., Mount Charleston, NV 89124. ✆ 800/955-1314 or 702/872-5408. www.mtcharlestonlodge. com. 23 units. $125–$250. Extra person $10. No cribs or rollaways. AE, DISC, MC, V. **Amenities:** 24-hr. restaurant (American). *In room:* A/C, TV w/pay movies in some cabins, coffeemaker, Jacuzzi, fireplace.

6 Primm

35 miles S of Las Vegas

Best known for its outlet shopping (p. 192), Primm is located half an hour south of Las Vegas, on I-15, right before the border with California. (It was formerly named Stateline.) There are four hotels, including a golf resort, in Primm, but, really, you're better off staying in Las Vegas.

Primm, in its entirety, can be found on the Web at **www.primadonna.com**.

Crime buffs will enjoy looking at Bonnie and Clyde's death car, Clyde's death shirt, and Al Capone's car at **Primm Valley Resort & Casino** (31900 Las Vegas Blvd. S.; ✆ **800/386-7867** or 702/386-7867), within walking distance from Buffalo Bill's.

However, the main reasons to come here with your family, aside from making sure that the heavily discounted clothes fit them, are the thrill rides at **Buffalo Bill's**

Resort and Casino (31900 Las Blvd. S.; ℂ **800/386-7867** or 702/382-1212; www.primadonna.com). There's the **Desperado,** a steep, exciting roller coaster that zips through the casino, dropping 225 feet and reaching speeds of 85 mph. And the **Adventure Canyon** log flume ride will definitely leave you sopping wet. If that's not enough for thrill lovers, there's the **Turbo Drop,** which will plunge you 170 feet in milliseconds. **MaxFlight 2002** allows you, through the miracle of virtual reality and motion simulators, to design your own roller coaster ride, then take it, and the **Vault,** another 3-D ride, offers you a series of interactive adventures.

To ride these, you must be over 48 inches, with the exception of the flume ride, which allows smaller children to ride with an adult. For those 36 to 48 inches, there's also a **Frog Hopper,** which raises riders 20 feet up in the air and gently brings them down; the ride is four cycles long.

Rides range from $5 to $6; the best buy, if you plan to stay awhile, is a wristband. For $33, you can ride everything all day long, plus see a feature movie in the casino's theater (generally screening G and PG family-oriented flicks), and get a small soda and popcorn. Alternatively, a $25 wristband is good for 3 hours, which might be plenty of time to get your child's ya-yas out. For $15, those under 48 inches can get a Little Wranglers wristband that's good for all-day Frog Hoppers, plus a movie, soda, and popcorn. For more information, call the recorded ride hot line at ℂ **702/679-7433.**

7 The Grand Canyon: Grand Canyon West

The Grand Canyon—the name is at once both entirely apt and entirely inadequate. How can words sum up the grandeur of 2 billion years of the earth's history sliced open by the power of a single river? Once an impassable and forbidding barrier to explorers and settlers, the Grand Canyon is today a magnet that each year attracts millions of visitors from all over the world. The pastel layers of rock weaving through the rugged ramparts of the canyon, the interplay of shadows and light, the wind in the pines, and the croaking of ravens on the rim—these are the sights and sounds that never fail to transfix the hordes of visitors who gaze awestruck into the canyon's seemingly infinite depths.

With more than four million people each year visiting the South Rim of the Grand Canyon, and traffic congestion and parking problems becoming the most memorable aspects of most people's trips, you might want to consider an alternative to the South Rim. For most travelers, this means driving around to the North Rim; however, it's open only from mid-May to late October and itself is not immune to parking problems and traffic congestion. Plus, it's pretty far away from Las Vegas.

So, if you want to go to the canyon on your own (not taking a tour), we recommend Grand Canyon West as your best option if you're going to the canyon as a "side trip" from Las Vegas. Visiting Grand Canyon West, on the Hualapai Indian Reservation, is favored by people short on time or who want to fly down into the canyon (something that isn't permitted within Grand Canyon National Park). Note that the drive to and from Grand Canyon West involves spending some 28 miles on gravel, so expect lots of dust and some rough stretches. Also remember that Grand Canyon West is particularly popular with tour buses from Las Vegas (because it's about the closest spot to Las Vegas that actually provides a glimpse of the Colorado River and Grand Canyon National Park), and the constant helicopter traffic here precludes any sort of tranquil canyon experience. That said, you're still at the Grand Canyon, which is pretty . . . well, awesome, no matter what.

Grand Canyon West & Environs

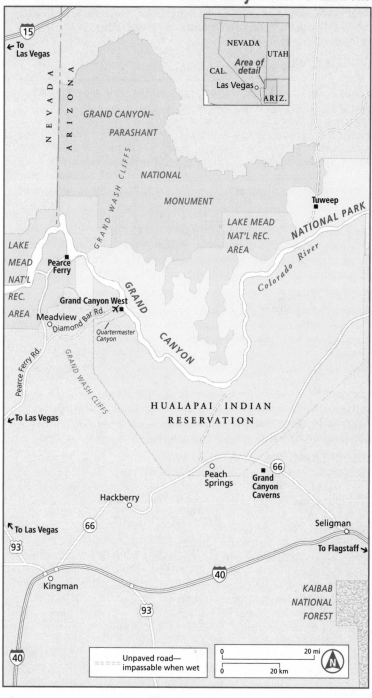

For information on Grand Canyon West, contact **Hualapai Reservations,** P.O. Box 538, Peach Springs, AZ 86434-0538 (© **888/255-9550** or 928/769-2230; www.hualapaitours.com).

GUIDED TOURS
Generally, tourists visiting Las Vegas don't drive the hundreds of miles to Arizona to see the Grand Canyon National Park from the North or South rims, but there are dozens of sightseeing tours departing from the city daily, which will bring you there. In addition to the Coach USA tours described on p. 242, another major operator, **Scenic Airlines** (© **800/634-6801** or 702/638-3200; www.scenic.com), runs deluxe, 8-hour, guided air-ground tours for $219 per person ($189 for children 2–11); the price for the tour which begins with a narrated flight over the canyon, includes a bus excursion through the national park as well as lunch. In addition to the full-day tours, the company offers overnight tours with hiking and flightseeing. Scenic also offers flight tours to other points of interest and national parks, including a 12-hour trip combining the Grand Canyon and Bryce Canyon in Utah (270 miles from Las Vegas), and a flight tour of Monument Valley, which is located on Navajo land straddling the border between Arizona and Utah (approximately 450 miles from Las Vegas, and a 12-hr. tour with Scenic). Ask for details when you call.

GETTING THERE
Be aware that at least 14 miles of the route heading to Grand Canyon West from Las Vegas features dirt roads, making a trip there almost impossible if it has rained recently. From Vegas, take Nev. 93, south, approximately 30 miles past Hoover Dam to Pearce Ferry Road (signed for Dolan Springs and Meadowview). Turn left onto Dolan Springs/Meadowview and continue for 28 miles on this road, then turn right onto gravel Diamond Bar Road, which is signed for Grand Canyon West. Another 14 miles down this road brings you to the Hualapai Indian Reservation, and onto the paved road, which demarcates the reservation. A little farther along, you'll come to the Grand Canyon West Terminal (there's actually an airstrip here), where visitor permits and bus-tour tickets are sold.

DISCOVERING THE CANYON
Located on the Hualapai Indian Reservation on the south side of the Colorado River, **Grand Canyon West** (© **702/565-8761;** www.grandcanyonwest.com) overlooks the rarely visited west end of Grand Canyon National Park. Although the view is not as spectacular as at either the South Rim or the North Rim, Grand Canyon West is noteworthy for one thing: It is one of the only places where you can legally fly down into the canyon. This is possible because the helicopters operate on land that is part of the Hualapai Indian Reservation. At this point, the south side of the Colorado lies within the reservation, while the north side of the river is within Grand Canyon National Park. Helicopter tours are operated by **Papillon Helicopters** (© **888/635-7272** or 702/736-7243; www.papillon.com), which charges $115 to $180 per person for flight tours to the bottom of the canyon; some tours also include pontoon boat cruises and meals—call for further information.

There are also guided **bus tours** along the rim of the canyon. These include time to do a bit of exploring at a canyon overlook. Tours stop at Eagle Point, where rock formations resemble various animals and people, and at Guano Point, where bat guano was once mined commercially. The tours to the South and West rims, which operate daily throughout the year, cost $110. No reservations are accepted, so it's a good idea to arrive around 9am, when Grand Canyon West opens.

If you'd just like to take in the view from this end of the canyon, head to **Quartermaster Point,** after first purchasing your sightseeing permit ($13) at the Grand Canyon West terminal. At Quartermaster Point, you'll find a trail that leads down a few hundred yards to a viewpoint overlooking the Colorado River.

While we can only recommend a trip out to Grand Canyon West as a side trip from Las Vegas or for travelers who absolutely must fly down into the canyon, the drive out here is almost as scenic as the destination itself. Along Diamond Bar Road, the dirt road that leads to the Hualapai reservation, you'll be driving below the Grand Wash Cliffs, and for much of the way, the route traverses a dense forest of Joshua trees.

OTHER AREA ACTIVITIES

If you long to raft the Grand Canyon but have only a couple of free days in your schedule to realize your dream, then you have only a couple of options. Here at the west end of the canyon, it's possible to do a 1-day rafting trip that begins on the Hualapai Indian Reservation. These trips are operated by **Hualapai River Runners,** P.O. Box 538, Peach Springs, AZ 86434 (© **928/769-2211;** www. grandcanyonresort.com), a tribal rafting company, and run between mid-March and late October. Expect a mix of white water and flat water (all of it very cold). Although perhaps not as exciting as longer trips in the main section of the canyon, you'll still plow through some pretty big waves (kids must be 8 or older to ride). Be ready to get wet! These trips stop at a couple of side canyons where you can get out and do some exploring. The trip lasts 10 hours and costs $285 per person, which includes transportation, equipment, vests, and a meal, plus a helicopter ride out of the canyon at the end of the trip. Groups of eight or more can also arrange a 2-day tour, if they wish.

Also in this area, you can visit **Grand Canyon Caverns** (© **928/422-3223;** www.gccaverns.com), just outside Peach Springs. The caverns, which are accessed via a 210-foot elevator ride, are open from Memorial Day to October 15, daily from 8am to 6pm, and other months, daily from 10am to 5pm. Admission is $12 for adults, $7.95 for children 4 to 12.

WHERE TO STAY & DINE
IN & NEAR PEACH SPRINGS

Grand Canyon Caverns Inn   As the name implies, this motel is built on the site of the Grand Canyon Caverns, which are open to the public (see above). The curio store, general store, and restaurant/bar are located on the same property, a mile up the road, while the pool and laundry are adjacent to the rooms. There's a real sense of Americana here, a classic motel just off historic Route 66. Book early; for most of the year, the motel is used by the Elderhostel travel group and thus stays very busy.

P.O. Box 180, Peach Springs, AZ 86434. © **928/422-4565.** www.gccaverns.com/GCCInn.html. 48 units. $49–$90. Rollaways $10. AE, DISC, MC, V. Pets accepted with $50 deposit. **Amenities:** Restaurant (American); lounge; outdoor pool; coin-op laundry. *In room:* A/C, TV.

Hualapai Lodge ☆ *(Finds*   Located in the Hualapai community of Peach Springs, this lodge is by far the most luxurious accommodation anywhere in the region. (Though that's not saying much!). Guest rooms are spacious and modern, with a few bits of regional decor for character. Most people staying here are in the area to visit Grand Canyon West, to go rafting with Hualapai River Runners, or to hike in to Havasu Canyon. The dining room is just about the only place in town to get a meal.

900 Rte. 66, P.O. Box 538, Peach Springs, AZ 86434. © **888/255-9550** or 928/769-2230. Fax 928/769-2372. www.hualapaitours.com. 60 units. $80–$90. Children under 12 stay free in parent's room. Extra person $10. Cribs/rollaways $10. AE, DC, DISC, MC, V. **Amenities:** Restaurant (American); concierge; tour desk; coin-op laundry. *In room:* A/C, TV, dataport.

8 Outdoor Activities & Tour Companies

CYCLING

Downhill Bicycle Tours (© **702/897-8287**) can take you on tours that span 18 miles and three different environments through areas surrounding Las Vegas. **Escape Adventures** (© **702/383-6966** or 800/596-2953; www.escapeadventures. com) rents bikes and biking equipment, starting at $30 per day, as well as providing guided and self-guided tours of Red Rock Canyon and Mount Charleston, which begin at $89 for a half-day self-guided tour and include the bike rental. These tours range from 7 to 23 miles and span experience and age levels, depending on your children's abilities. One that is definitely suited to children is a summer tour that's 18 miles and all downhill from the top of Mount Charleston (a shuttle takes you up the mountain).

HIKING

Desert hiking trails in the region include marked trails in both Red Rock Canyon and Valley of Fire. Keep in mind that in the summer, temperatures can soar to 120°f (49°C); the best time for exploring the beauty of the desert is November through March. If you'd prefer a guided hiking adventure in Red Rock, an experienced guide from **Grand Canyon Tours** (© **800/222-6966** or 702/655-6060; www.grandcanyontourcompany.com) will pick up at your hotel and drive you into Red Rock for lunch and an up-close walking tour of the formations for $160 to $215 per person (no discount for children). **Sky's the Limit** (© **800/733-7597** or 702/363-4533; www.skysthelimit.com) offers a tour called Hike of the Day, in either the morning or afternoon, where you'll explore a portion of Humboldt–Toiyabe National Forest, which includes Mount Charleston and Red Rock Canyon. The half-day hike includes lunch. You should be fundamentally fit and able to walk several miles to enjoy this excursion, which costs $100 per person. **Escape Adventures** (© **702/383-6966**; www.escapeadventures.com) offers a half-day guided hike through Red Rock for $89 per person. Guided tours are offered on a limited basis through the Red Rock Canyon visitor center, but reservations must be made in advance. There is a website specifically devoted to hiking in the Las Vegas area, www.hikinglasvegas. com, which provides an overview of local hiking sights. Also see the "Take a Hike: Desert Hiking Advice" box, on p. 252, for more information on hiking in the desert.

HORSEBACK RIDING

Cowboy Trail Rides (© **702/948-7061;** www.cowboytrailrides.com) offers a variety of rides and trails in Red Rock Canyon and on Mount Charleston (at the 12-mile marker), ranging in price from $89 to $139. The high end is for a Red Rock Canyon sunset trail ride; it's about 2 hours, with the canyon providing a glorious backdrop for the end of the day. Riders then return to camp for a barbecue dinner (including a 16-oz. T-bone steak), joined by the cowboys for sing-alongs and marshmallow roasting. They also offer hour-and-a-half rides at $70. There are also riding stables at **Bonnie Springs Ranch** (© **702/875-4191;** see section earlier in this chapter) that offer guided trail rides daily through the area close to Red Rock. Rates are $25 per person per hour. Wear tennis shoes, riding boots, or hiking boots and jeans for riding.

For children 11 years and up a real *City Slickers* experience is available at **Sandy Valley Ranch** (© 877/726-3998; www.sandyvalleyranch.com), located 45 minutes southwest of the Strip. Isolated from towns, roads, and just about everything else, you can follow existing trails or blaze new ones in 300 square miles (yes, that's square *miles*) of sage and mesquite rangeland. The terrain varies from flat valleys to foothills to canyons and mountains. Guest horses are carefully screened for responsiveness, gentleness, patience, and compatibility with other horses. The ranch offers overnight camping in sturdy, platform-mounted tents; excellent dinners in a modern but rustic dining hall; buckboard rides; and guided trail rides. Most fun of all, however, is playing with cattle (you'll want to take some home!). You can participate in an actual round-up where you scour the plains and canyons in search of cattle to herd back to the corral, or you can join friendly competitions in the rodeo arena. Partial day outings run from $60 to $138. All include preliminary training, a trail ride, and working with the cattle. The more expensive outings include a meal, cowboy skills games, and, in the evening, a campfire. The ranch also provides transportation from Las Vegas hotels.

ROCK CLIMBING

If you or your children are interested in learning to rock climb or in improving your skills, an excellent rock-climbing school and guide service called **Sky's the Limit** (© 800/733-7597 or 702/363-4533; www.skysthelimit.com) offers programs for beginning, intermediate, and advanced climbers. No experience is needed. The school is accredited by the American Mountain Guides Association. The beginning program ($200 per person) is a 1-day, entry-level experience suitable for those of all ages who are mobile and basically athletic. You are taken to Red Rock Canyon where you'll receive your guide's personalized attention and instruction in this challenging sport. You'll learn to climb and rappel; and by the end of the day, you'll not only have the terminology and basic skills of a rock climber, but you'll have a sense of accomplishment, plus be able to tie a really strong knot. For locations to practice rock climbing, check out some of the places listed on p. 187.

SKIING & SNOWBOARDING

From roughly Thanksgiving through Easter, depending on weather conditions, you can ski and snowboard at the **Las Vegas Ski and Snowboard Resort** (© 702/593-9500; www.skilasvegas.com). It rents equipment and clothing as well as provide lessons. Adult all-day passes are $33; children 12 and under $25; afternoon passes good from 1 to 4pm are $6 less. For more information see p. 260.

Appendix A:
For International Visitors

The pervasiveness of American culture around the world may make you feel that you know the United States pretty well, but leaving your own country still requires an additional degree of planning. This chapter will help prepare you for the more common issues you may encounter in Las Vegas.

1 Preparing for Your Trip

ENTRY REQUIREMENTS

Check at any U.S. embassy or consulate for current information and requirements. You can also obtain a visa application and other information online at the **U.S. State Department**'s website, at **www.travel.state.gov**.

VISAS The U.S. State Department has a **Visa Waiver Program** allowing citizens of certain countries to enter the United States without a visa for stays of up to 90 days. At press time these included Andorra, Australia, Austria, Belgium, Brunei, Denmark, Finland, France, Germany, Iceland, Ireland, Italy, Japan, Liechtenstein, Luxembourg, Monaco, the Netherlands, New Zealand, Norway, Portugal, San Marino, Singapore, Slovenia, Spain, Sweden, Switzerland, and the United Kingdom. Citizens of these countries need only a valid passport and a round-trip air or cruise ticket in their possession upon arrival. If they first enter the United States, they may also visit Mexico, Canada, Bermuda, and/or the Caribbean islands and return to the United States without a visa. Further information is available from any U.S. embassy or consulate. Canadian citizens may enter the United States without visas; they need only proof of residence.

Citizens of all other countries must have (1) a valid passport that expires at least 6 months later than the scheduled end of their visit to the United States, and (2) a tourist visa, which may be obtained for a minimum fee of $100 (some countries charge more) from any U.S. consulate.

To obtain a visa, the traveler must submit a completed application form (either in person or by mail) with a 1½-inch-square photo, and must demonstrate binding ties to a residence abroad. Usually you can obtain a visa at once or within 24 hours, but it may take longer during the summer rush from June through August. If you cannot go in person, contact the nearest U.S. embassy or consulate for directions on applying by mail. Your travel agent or airline office may also be able to provide you with visa applications and instructions. The U.S. consulate or embassy that issues your visa will determine whether you will be issued a multiple- or single-entry visa and any restrictions regarding the length of your stay.

British subjects can obtain up-to-date visa information by calling the **U.S. Embassy Visa Information Line** (© 09068/200-290, only available in the U.K.) or by visiting the "Consular Services" section of the American Embassy London's website at **www.usembassy.org.uk**.

Irish citizens can obtain up-to-date visa information through the **Embassy of USA Dublin,** 42 Elgin Rd., Dublin 4, Ireland (© 353/1-668-8777), or by checking the "Consular Services" section of the website at **www.usembassy.ie**.

Australian citizens can obtain up-to-date visa information by contacting the **U.S. Embassy Canberra,** Moonah Place, Yarralumla, ACT 2600 (© **02/ 6214-5600**), or by checking the U.S. Diplomatic Mission's website at **http://us embassy-australia.state.gov/consular**.

Citizens of **New Zealand** can obtain up-to-date visa information by contacting the **U.S. Embassy New Zealand,** 29 Fitzherbert Terrace, Thorndon, Wellington (© **644/462-6000**), or get the information directly from the "Services to New Zealanders" section of the website at **http://usembassy.org.nz**.

MEDICAL REQUIREMENTS   Unless you're arriving from an area known to be suffering from an epidemic (particularly cholera or yellow fever), inoculations or vaccinations are not required for entry into the United States. If you have a medical condition that requires **syringe-administered medication,** carry a valid signed prescription from your physician—the Transportation Security Administration (TSA) no longer allows airline passengers to pack syringes in their carry-on baggage without documented proof of medical need. If you have a disease that requires treatment with **narcotics,** you should also carry documented proof with you—smuggling narcotics aboard a plane is a serious offense that carries severe penalties in the U.S.

For **HIV-positive visitors,** requirements for entering the United States are somewhat vague and change frequently. According to the latest publication of *HIV and Immigrants: A Manual for AIDS Service Providers,* the Immigration and Naturalization Service (INS) doesn't require a medical exam for entry into the United States, but INS officials may stop individuals because they look sick or because they are carrying AIDS/HIV medicine.

If an HIV-positive noncitizen applies for a nonimmigrant visa, the question on the application regarding communicable diseases is tricky no matter which way it's answered. If the applicant checks "no," INS may deny the visa on the grounds that the applicant committed fraud. If the applicant checks "yes" or if INS suspects the person is HIV-positive, it will deny the visa unless the applicant asks for a special waiver for visitors. This waiver is for people visiting the United States for a short time (to attend a conference, for instance), to visit close relatives, or to receive medical treatment. It can be a confusing situation. For up-to-the-minute information, contact **AIDSinfo** (© **800/448-0440** or 301/519-6616 outside the U.S.; www.aidsinfo.nih.gov) or the **Gay Men's Health Crisis** (© **212/367-1000;** www. gmhc.org).

DRIVER'S LICENSES   Foreign driver's licenses are mostly recognized in the U.S., although you may want to get an international driver's license if your home license is not written in English.

PASSPORT INFORMATION
FOR RESIDENTS OF CANADA

You can pick up a passport application at 1 of 28 regional passport offices or most travel agencies. Canadian children who travel must have their own passports. However, if you hold a valid Canadian passport issued before December 11, 2001, that bears the name of your child, the passport remains valid for you and your child until it expires. Passports cost C$85 for those 16 years and older (valid 5 years), C$35 for children 3 to 15 (valid 5 years), and C$20 for children under 3 (valid 3 years). Applications, which must be accompanied by two identical passport-sized photographs and proof of Canadian citizenship, are available at travel agencies throughout Canada or from the central **Passport Office,** Department of

Foreign Affairs and International Trade, Ottawa, ON K1A 0G3 (© **800/567-6868;** www.dfait-maeci.gc.ca/passport). Processing takes 5 to 10 days if you apply in person, or about 3 weeks by mail.

FOR RESIDENTS OF THE UNITED KINGDOM

To pick up an application for a standard 10-year passport (5-year passport for children under 16), visit the nearest Passport Office, major post office, or travel agency. You can also contact the **United Kingdom Passport Service** at © **0870/571-0410** or visit its website at **www.passport.gov.uk**. Passports are £42 for adults and £25 for children under 16, with an additional £30 fee if you apply in person at a passport office. Processing takes about 2 weeks (1 week if you apply at the passport office).

FOR RESIDENTS OF IRELAND

You can apply for a 10-year passport, costing €75, at the **Passport Office,** Setanta Centre, Molesworth Street, Dublin 2 (© **01/671-1633;** www.irlgov.ie/iveagh). Those under age 18 must apply for a €25 5-year passport. Persons over 65 can apply for a 10-year passport at €25. You can also apply at 1A South Mall, Cork (© **021/272-525**), or over the counter at most main post offices.

FOR RESIDENTS OF AUSTRALIA

You can pick up an application from your local post office or any branch of Passports Australia, but you must schedule an interview at the passport office to present your application materials. Call the **Australian Passport Information Service** at © **131-232,** or visit the government website at **www.passports.gov.au**. Passports for adults are A$150 and for those under 18 are A$75.

FOR RESIDENTS OF NEW ZEALAND

You can pick up a passport application at any New Zealand Passports Office or download it from their website. Contact the **Passports Office** at © **0800/225-050** in New Zealand or © **64(4)/474-8100** outside of New Zealand, or log on to **www.passports.govt.nz/diawebsite.NSF**. Passports for adults are NZ$71 and for children under 16, NZ$36.

CUSTOMS
WHAT YOU CAN BRING IN

Every visitor more than 21 years of age may bring in, free of duty, the following: (1) 1 liter of wine or hard liquor; (2) 200 cigarettes, 100 cigars (but not from Cuba), or 3 pounds of smoking tobacco; and (3) $100 worth of gifts. These exemptions are offered to travelers who spend at least 72 hours in the United States and who have not claimed them within the preceding 6 months. It is altogether forbidden to bring into the country foodstuffs (particularly fruit, cooked meats, and canned goods) and plants (vegetables, seeds, tropical plants, and the like). Foreign tourists may bring in or take out up to $10,000 in U.S. or foreign currency with no formalities; larger sums must be declared to U.S. Customs on entering or leaving, which includes filing form CM 4790. For more specific information regarding U.S. Customs, contact your nearest U.S. embassy or consulate, or the **U.S. Customs** office (© **202/927-1770;** www.customs.ustreas.gov).

WHAT YOU CAN TAKE HOME

U.K. citizens returning from a non-EU country have a Customs allowance of: 200 cigarettes; 50 cigars; 250 grams of smoking tobacco; 2 liters of still table wine; 1 liter of spirits or strong liqueurs (over 22% volume); 2 liters of fortified wine, sparkling wine or other liqueurs; 60 cubic centimeters (ml) of perfume;

250 cubic centimeters (ml) of toilet water; and £145 worth of all other goods, including gifts and souvenirs. People under 17 cannot have the tobacco or alcohol allowance. For more information, contact HM Customs & Excise at © **0845/ 010-8500** (from outside the U.K., 020/8929-0152), or consult their website at **www.hmce.gov.uk**.

For a clear summary of **Canadian** rules, request the booklet *I Declare,* issued by the **Canada Customs and Revenue Agency** (© **800/461-9999** in Canada, or 204/983-3500; www.ccra-adrc.gc.ca). Canada allows its citizens a C$750 exemption, and you're allowed to bring back duty-free one carton of cigarettes, one can of tobacco, 40 imperial ounces of liquor, and 50 cigars. In addition, you're allowed to mail gifts to Canada valued at less than C$60 a day, provided they're unsolicited and don't contain alcohol or tobacco (write on the package "Unsolicited gift, under $60 value"). All valuables should be declared on the Y-38 form before departure from Canada, including serial numbers of valuables you already own, such as expensive foreign cameras. *Note:* The C$750 exemption can only be used once a year and only after an absence of 7 days.

The duty-free allowance in **Australia** is A$400 or, for those under 18, A$200. Citizens age 18 and over can bring in 250 cigarettes or 250 grams of loose tobacco, and 1,125 milliliters of alcohol. If you're returning with valuables you already own, such as foreign-made cameras, you should file form B263. A helpful brochure available from Australian consulates or Customs offices is *Know Before You Go.* For more information, call the **Australian Customs Service** at © **1300/363-263,** or log on to **www.customs.gov.au**.

The duty-free allowance for **New Zealand** is NZ$700. Citizens over 17 can bring in 200 cigarettes, 50 cigars, or 250 grams of tobacco (or a mixture of all three if their combined weight doesn't exceed 250g); plus 4.5 liters of wine and beer, or 1.125 liters of liquor. New Zealand currency does not carry import or export restrictions. Fill out a certificate of export, listing the valuables you are taking out of the country; that way, you can bring them back without paying duty. Most questions are answered in a free pamphlet available at New Zealand consulates and Customs offices: *New Zealand Customs Guide for Travellers, Notice no. 4.* For more information, contact **New Zealand Customs,** The Customhouse, 17–21 Whitmore St., Box 2218, Wellington (© **0800/428-786** or 04/473-6099; www. customs.govt.nz).

HEALTH INSURANCE

Although it's not required of travelers, health insurance is highly recommended. Unlike many European countries, the United States does not usually offer free or low-cost medical care to its citizens or visitors. Doctors and hospitals are expensive, and in most cases will require advance payment or proof of coverage before they render their services. Policies can cover everything from the loss or theft of your baggage and trip cancellation to the guarantee of bail in case you're

Impressions

For the grand debut of Monte Carlo as a resort in 1879 the architect Charles Garnier designed an opera house for the Place du Casino; and Sarah Bernhardt read a symbolic poem. For the debut of Las Vegas as a resort in 1946 Bugsy Siegel hired Abbott and Costello, and there, in a way, you have it all.

—Tom Wolfe

arrested. Good policies will also cover the costs of an accident, repatriation, or death. See "Insurance, Health & Safety" in chapter 2 for more information. Packages such as **Europ Assistance's Worldwide Healthcare Plan** are sold by European automobile clubs and travel agencies at attractive rates. **Worldwide Assistance Services, Inc.** (✆ **800/821-2828;** www.worldwideassistance.com) is the agent for Europ Assistance in the United States.

Though lack of health insurance may prevent you from being admitted to a hospital in nonemergencies, don't worry about being left on a street corner to die: The American way is to fix you now and bill the living daylights out of you later.

INSURANCE FOR BRITISH TRAVELERS　Most big travel agents offer their own insurance and will probably try to sell you their package when you book a holiday. Think before you sign. **Britain's Consumers' Association** recommends that you insist on seeing the policy and reading the fine print before buying travel insurance. **The Association of British Insurers** (✆ **020/7600-3333;** www.abi.org.uk) gives advice by phone and publishes *Holiday Insurance,* a free guide to policy provisions and prices. You might also shop around for better deals: Try **Columbus Direct** (✆ **020/7375-0011;** www.columbusdirect.net).

INSURANCE FOR CANADIAN TRAVELERS　Canadians should check with their provincial health plan offices or call **Health Canada** (✆ **613/957-2991;** www.hc-sc.gc.ca) to find out the extent of their coverage and what documentation and receipts they must take home in case they are treated in the United States.

MONEY

CURRENCY　The U.S. monetary system is very simple: The most common **bills** are the $1 (colloquially, a "buck"), $5, $10, and $20 denominations. There are also $2 bills (seldom encountered), $50 bills, and $100 bills (the last two are usually not welcome as payment for small purchases). All the paper money was recently redesigned, making the famous faces adorning them disproportionately large. The old-style bills are still legal tender.

There are seven denominations of coins: 1¢ (1 cent, or a penny); 5¢ (5 cents, or a nickel); 10¢ (10 cents, or a dime); 25¢ (25 cents, or a quarter); 50¢ (50 cents, or a half dollar); the newer gold Sacagawea coin worth $1; and, prized by collectors, the rare, older silver dollar.

Note: The "foreign-exchange bureaus" so common in Europe are rare even at airports in the United States, and nonexistent outside major cities. It's best not to change foreign money (or traveler's checks denominated in a currency other than U.S. dollars) at a small-town bank, or even a branch in a big city; in fact, leave any currency other than U.S. dollars at home—it may prove a greater nuisance to you than it's worth.

For the latest conversion rates see **www.x-rates.com.**

TRAVELER'S CHECKS　Though traveler's checks are widely accepted, make sure that they're denominated in U.S. dollars, as foreign-currency checks are often difficult to exchange. The three traveler's checks that are most widely recognized—and least likely to be denied—are **Visa, American Express,** and **Thomas Cook.** Be sure to record the numbers of the checks, and keep that information in a separate place in case they get lost or stolen. Most businesses are pretty good about taking traveler's checks, but you're better off cashing them in at a bank (in small amounts, of course) and paying in cash. *Remember:* You'll need identification, such as a driver's license or passport, to change a traveler's check.

CREDIT CARDS & ATMs　Credit cards are the most widely used form of payment in the United States: **Visa** (Barclaycard in Britain), **MasterCard** (EuroCard in Europe, Access in Britain, Chargex in Canada), **American Express, Diners Club,** and **Discover.** You'll also find that some Vegas vendors may also accept international cards like **enRoute, EuroCard,** and **JCB,** but not as universally as Amex, MasterCard, or Visa. There are, however, a handful of stores and restaurants that do not take credit cards, so be sure to ask in advance. Most businesses display a sticker near their entrance to let you know which cards they accept. (*Note:* Businesses may require a minimum purchase, usually around $10, to use a credit card.)

It is strongly recommended that you bring at least one major credit card. You must have a credit or charge card to rent a car. Hotels and airlines usually require a credit card imprint as a deposit against expenses, and in an emergency a credit card can be priceless.

You'll find **automated teller machines (ATMs)** on just about every block— at least in almost every town—across the country. Some ATMs will allow you to draw U.S. currency against your bank and credit cards. Check with your bank before leaving home, and remember that you will need your personal identification number (PIN) to do so. Most accept Visa, MasterCard, and American Express, as well as ATM cards from other U.S. banks. Expect to be charged up to $3 per transaction, however, if you're not using your own bank's ATM.

One way around these fees is to ask for cash back at grocery stores that accept ATM cards and don't charge usage fees. Of course, you'll have to purchase something first.

ATM cards with major credit card backing, known as "debit cards," are now a commonly acceptable form of payment in most stores and restaurants. Debit cards draw money directly from your checking account. Some stores enable you to receive "cash back" on your debit-card purchases as well.

SIZE CONVERSION CHART

Women's Clothing

American	4	6	8	10	12	14	16	
French	34	36	38	40	42	44	46	
British	6	8	10	12	14	16	18	

Women's Shoes

American	5	6	7	8	9	10		
French	36	37	38	39	40	41		
British	4	5	6	7	8	9		

Men's Suits

American	34	36	38	40	42	44	46	48
French	44	46	48	50	52	54	56	58
British	34	36	38	40	42	44	46	48

Men's Shirts

American	14½	15	15½	16	16½	17	17½
French	37	38	39	41	42	43	44
British	14½	15	15½	16	16½	17	17½

Men's Shoes

American	7	8	9	10	11	12	13
French	39½	41	42	43	44½	46	47
British	6	7	8	9	10	11	12

Tips **Travel-Document Tip**

Be sure to keep a copy of all your travel papers separate from your wallet or purse, and leave a copy with someone at home should you need it faxed in an emergency.

SAFETY

GENERAL SAFETY SUGGESTIONS   While tourist areas are generally safe, crime is a national problem, and U.S. urban areas tend to be less safe than those in Europe or Japan. You should always stay alert. It's wise to ask your hotel front-desk staff if you're in doubt about which neighborhoods are safe.

Avoid carrying valuables with you on the street, and don't display expensive cameras or electronic equipment. Hold on to your pocketbook, and place your billfold in an inside pocket. In theaters, restaurants, and other public places, keep your possessions in sight.

Remember also that hotels are open to the public, and in a large hotel, security may not be able to screen everyone entering. Always lock your room door—don't assume that once inside your hotel you are automatically safe and no longer need to be aware of your surroundings. In Las Vegas, many hotels inspect room keys at the elevators at night, providing some extra security. Many Las Vegas hotels also have in-room safes; if yours doesn't and you're traveling with valuables, put them in a safety-deposit box at the front desk.

DRIVING SAFETY   Driving safety is important too, and carjacking is not unprecedented. Question your rental agency about personal safety and ask for a traveler-safety brochure when you pick up your car. Obtain from the agency written directions—or a map with the route clearly marked—showing how to get to your destination. (Many agencies now offer the option of renting a cell-phone for the duration of your car rental; check with the rental agent when you pick up the car. Otherwise, contact **InTouch USA** at © **800/872-7626** or www. intouchusa.com for short-term cellphone rental.) And, if possible, arrive and depart during daylight hours.

If you drive off a highway and end up in a dodgy-looking neighborhood, leave the area as quickly as possible. If you have an accident, even on the highway, stay in your car with the doors locked until you assess the situation or until the police arrive. If you're bumped from behind on the street or are involved in a minor accident with no injuries, and the situation appears to be suspicious, motion to the other driver to follow you. Never get out of your car in such situations. Go directly to the nearest police precinct, well-lit service station, or 24-hour store.

Park in well-lit and well-traveled areas whenever possible—in the casino hotels, take advantage of the free valet parking. Always keep your car doors locked, whether the vehicle is attended or unattended. Never leave any packages or valuables in sight. If someone attempts to rob you or steal your car, don't try to resist the thief/carjacker. Report the incident to the police department immediately by calling © **911.**

2 Getting to the United States

THE MAJOR AIRLINES   A number of U.S. airlines offer service from Europe to the United States, though a number of those same airlines are having financial troubles, and may perhaps be in different shape by the time you read this. If they do not have direct flights from Europe to Las Vegas, they can book you straight through on a connecting flight. You can make reservations by calling the following numbers in the United Kingdom: **American** (✆ **0181/572-5555** in the U.K., 800/433-7300 in the U.S.; www.aa.com), **Continental** (✆ **01293/776-464** in the U.K., 800/525-0280 in the U.S.; www.continental.com), **Delta** (✆ **0800/414-767** in the U.K., 800/221-1212 in the U.S.; www.delta.com), and **United** (✆ **0845/8-444-777** in the U.K., 800/538-2929 in the U.S.; www.ual.com).

And, of course, many international carriers serve Los Angeles and/or San Francisco International Airport. From LAX or San Francisco International Airport, you can take a domestic airline to Las Vegas. Helpful numbers to know include **Virgin Atlantic** (✆ **01293/747-747** in the U.K., 800/862-8621 in the U.S.; www.virgin-atlantic.com), **British Airways** (✆ **0345/222-111** in the U.K., 800/AIRWAYS in the U.S.; www.british-airways.com) and **Aer Lingus** (✆ **01/886-8888**) in Dublin, 800/IRISH-AIR in the U.S.; www.aerlingus.com). **Qantas** (✆ **13-13-13** in Australia, 800/227-4500 in the U.S.; www.qantas.com.au) has flights from Sydney to Los Angeles and San Francisco; you can also take United from Australia to the West Coast. **Air New Zealand** (✆ **0800/737-000** in New Zealand, 800/262-1234 in the U.S.; www.airnewzealand.co.nz) also offers service to LAX. Canadian readers can book flights on **Air Canada** (✆ **800/776-3000;** www.aircanada.ca), which offers direct service from Toronto, Montréal, Calgary, and Vancouver to San Francisco and Los Angeles, and will book your final leg on a partner airline.

JetBlue (✆ **800/538-2583;** www.jetblue.com) is a highly rated low-cost carrier that operates out of a number of U.S. cities, and has daily direct service to Las Vegas out of New York City and Long Beach, California.

AIRLINE DISCOUNTS   The smart traveler can find numerable ways to reduce the price of a plane ticket simply by taking time to shop around. For example, overseas visitors can take advantage of the APEX (Advance Purchase Excursion) reductions offered by all major U.S. and European carriers. For more money-saving airline advice, see "Getting There" and "Planning Your Trip Online," in chapter 2. For the best rates, compare fares and be flexible with the dates and times of travel.

Operated by the European Travel Network, **www.discount-tickets.com** is a great online source for regular and discounted airfares to Las Vegas and other destinations around the world. You can also use this site to compare rates and book accommodations, car rentals, and tours. Click "Special Offers" for the latest package deals.

IMMIGRATION & CUSTOMS CLEARANCE   Visitors arriving by air, no matter what the port of entry, should cultivate patience and resignation before setting foot on U.S. soil. Getting through immigration control can take as long as 2 hours on some days, especially on summer weekends, so be sure to carry this guidebook or something else to read. This is especially true in the aftermath of the September 11, 2001, terrorist attacks, when security clearances have been considerably beefed up at U.S. airports.

People traveling by air from Canada, Bermuda, and certain countries in the Caribbean can sometimes clear Customs and Immigration at the point of departure, which is much quicker.

3 Getting Around the United States

BY PLANE   Some large airlines (for example, Northwest and Delta) offer travelers on their transatlantic or transpacific flights special discount tickets under the name **Visit USA,** allowing mostly one-way travel from one U.S. destination to another at very low prices. These discount tickets are not on sale in the United States and must be purchased abroad in conjunction with your international ticket. This system is the best, easiest, and fastest way to see the United States at low cost. You should obtain information well in advance from your travel agent or the office of the airline concerned, since the conditions attached to these discount tickets can be changed without advance notice.

BY CAR   Though you don't necessarily need to rent a car while in Las Vegas, the most cost-effective, convenient, and comfortable way to travel around the United States is by car. The interstate highway system connects cities and towns all over the country; in addition to these high-speed, limited-access roadways, there's an extensive network of federal, state, and local highways and roads. Some of the national car-rental companies include **Alamo/National** (℃ 800/462-5266; www.alamo.com), **Avis** (℃ 800/230-4898; www.avis.com), **Budget** (℃ 800/527-0700; www.budget.com), **Dollar** (℃ 800/800-3665; www.dollar.com), **Hertz** (℃ 800/654-3131; www.hertz.com), and **Thrifty** (℃ 800/847-4389; www.thrifty.com).

If you plan to rent a car in the United States, you probably won't need the services of an additional automobile organization. If you're planning to buy or borrow a car, automobile-association membership is recommended. **AAA,** the **American Automobile Association** (℃ 800/222-4357; www.aaa.com), is the country's largest auto club and supplies its members with maps, insurance, and, most important, emergency road service. The cost of joining runs from $63 for singles to $87 for two members, but if you're a member of a foreign auto club with reciprocal arrangements, you can enjoy free AAA service in America. See "Getting Around" in chapter 3 for more information on renting a car in Las Vegas.

BY BUS   Although bus travel is often the most economical form of public transit for short hops between U.S. cities, it can also be slow and uncomfortable—certainly not an option for everyone (particularly when Amtrak, which is far more luxurious, offers similar or slightly higher rates).

Greyhound/Trailways (℃ 800/231-2222; www.greyhound.com), the sole nationwide bus line, offers an **International Ameripass** that must be purchased before coming to the United States, or by phone through the Greyhound International Office at the Port Authority Bus Terminal in New York City (℃ 212/971-0492). The pass can be obtained from foreign travel agents and costs less than the domestic version. Passes are available for 7, 10, 15, 21, 30, 45, or 60 days; prices vary seasonally. Note that the opening page on Greyhound's website makes no mention of the International Ameripass. To obtain information and rates online, go directly to **http://greyhound.com/scripts/passes/step1.asp?passtype=2**. Special ticket rates are available for seniors and students. Information via phone is available by calling ℃ **212/971-0492** (2–9pm) or ℃ 402/330-8552 (all other times).

Though bus stations are often located in undesirable neighborhoods, the one in Las Vegas is conveniently located in a safe part of Downtown.

BY TRAIN   Amtrak (℃ **800/USA-RAIL;** www.amtrak.com) does not currently offer direct rail service, although plans have been in the works to restore the rails between Los Angeles and Las Vegas for years now. At press time, Amtrak wouldn't confirm a date, but various reports have indicated that at some point they will restore service using the Talgo. This European-designed "Casino Train" completes the trip from Los Angeles in about 5½ hours, with a wholesale seat price of $99 round-trip. (There's some talk that the train's route may continue on to Salt Lake City, but this had not been finalized at press time.) We still don't believe this is going to happen in our lifetime.

Much of the train will be presold to various hotels, so the final price to the traveler will depend on how you get the ticket. High rollers will probably end up with freebies, but the ticket will most likely be $99 if you purchase at the counter. In the meantime, you can take the train to Los Angeles or Barstow and Amtrak will get you to Vegas by bus.

FAST FACTS: For the International Traveler

Automobile Organizations Auto clubs will supply maps, suggested routes, guidebooks, accident and bail-bond insurance, and emergency road service. The **American Automobile Association (AAA)** is the major auto club in the United States. If you belong to an auto club in your home country, inquire about AAA reciprocity before you leave. You may be able to join AAA even if you're not a member of a reciprocal club; to inquire, contact AAA (✆ **800/222-4357**; www.aaa.com). AAA is actually an organization of regional auto clubs; so look under "AAA Automobile Club" in the White Pages of the telephone directory. AAA has a nationwide emergency road service telephone number (✆ 800/AAA-HELP).

Business Hours Offices are usually open weekdays from 9am to 5pm. Banks are open weekdays from 9am to 3pm or later, and sometimes on Saturday morning, although there's 24-hour access to the automated teller machines (ATMs) at most banks and other outlets. In Las Vegas, money is also available around the clock at casino cages—and every casino has at least one ATM. Shops, especially those in shopping complexes, tend to stay open late: until about 9pm weekdays and until 6pm weekends (including Sun).

Climate See "When to Go," in chapter 2.

Currency & Currency Exchange See "Money" under "Preparing for Your Trip," earlier in this chapter.

Drinking Laws The legal age for purchase and consumption of alcoholic beverages is 21; proof of age is required and often requested at bars, nightclubs, and restaurants, so it's always a good idea to bring ID when you go out, especially if you look young. Do not carry open containers of alcohol in your car or any public area that isn't zoned for alcohol consumption. The police can fine you on the spot. And nothing will ruin your trip faster than getting arrested for DUI ("driving under the influence"), so don't even think about driving if you've been drinking. Beer, wine, and liquor are all sold in all kinds of stores, pretty much around the clock; trust us, you won't have a hard time finding a drink in this town. It's even legal to have an open container on the Strip.

Electricity Like Canada, the United States uses 110 to 120 volts AC (60 cycles), compared to 220 to 240 volts AC (50 cycles) in most of Europe, Australia, and New Zealand. If your small appliances use 220 to 240 volts, you'll need a 110-volt transformer and a plug adapter with two flat parallel pins to operate them here. Downward converters that change 220–240 volts to 110–120 volts are difficult to find in the United States, so bring one with you.

Embassies & Consulates All embassies are located in the nation's capital, Washington, D.C. Some consulates are located in major U.S. cities, and most nations have a mission to the United Nations in New York City. If your country isn't listed below, call for directory information in Washington, D.C. (© **202/555-1212**) or log on to **www.embassy.org/embassies**.

The embassy of **Australia** is at 1601 Massachusetts Ave. NW, Washington, DC 20036 (© **202/797-3000**; www.austemb.org). There are consulates in New York, Honolulu, Houston, Los Angeles, and San Francisco.

The embassy of **Canada** is at 501 Pennsylvania Ave. NW, Washington, DC 20001 (© **202/682-1740**; www.canadianembassy.org). Other Canadian consulates are in Buffalo (New York), Detroit, Los Angeles, New York, and Seattle.

The embassy of **Ireland** is at 2234 Massachusetts Ave. NW, Washington, DC 20008 (© **202/462-3939**; www.irelandemb.org). Irish consulates are in Boston, Chicago, New York, and San Francisco.

The embassy of **Japan** is at 2520 Massachusetts Ave. NW, Washington, DC 20008 (© **202/238-6700**; www.embjapan.org). Japanese consulates are located in Atlanta, Kansas City, San Francisco, and Washington, D.C.

The embassy of **New Zealand** is at 37 Observatory Circle NW, Washington, DC 20008 (© **202/328-4800**; www.nzemb.org). New Zealand consulates are in Los Angeles, Salt Lake City, San Francisco, and Seattle.

The embassy of the **United Kingdom** is at 3100 Massachusetts Ave. NW, Washington, DC 20008 (© **202/558-6500**; www.britainusa.com). British consulates are in Atlanta, Boston, Chicago, Cleveland, Houston, Los Angeles, New York, San Francisco, and Seattle.

Emergencies Call © **911** to report a fire, call the police, or get an ambulance in Las Vegas. This is a toll-free call (no coins are required at public telephones).

If you have a medical emergency that doesn't require an ambulance, you can walk into a hospital's 24-hour emergency room (usually a separate entrance). For a list of hospitals, see "Fast Facts: Las Vegas" in chapter 3.

If you encounter serious problems, contact **Traveler's Aid International** (© **202/546-1127**; www.travelersaid.org) to help direct you to a local branch. This nationwide, nonprofit, social-service organization geared to helping travelers in difficult straits offers services that might include reuniting families separated while traveling, providing food and/or shelter to people stranded without cash, or even emotional counseling. If you're in trouble, seek them out. In Las Vegas there is an office at **McCarran International Airport** (© **702/798-1742**), which is open daily from 8am to 5pm. Similar services are provided by **Help of Southern Nevada**, 953 E. Sahara Ave., Suite 208, at Maryland Parkway in the Commercial Center on the northeast corner (© **702/369-4357**; www.helpsonv.org). Hours are Monday to Friday from 8am to 4pm.

Gasoline (Petrol) Petrol is known as gasoline (or simply "gas") in the United States, and petrol stations are known as both gas stations and service stations. Though prices were volatile and rising sharply throughout the first half of 2004, gasoline costs significantly less here than it does in Europe (about $2 per gal. in Vegas at press time), and taxes are already included in the printed price. One U.S. gallon equals 3.8 liters or .85 imperial gallons.

Holidays Banks, government offices, post offices, and many stores, restaurants, and museums are closed on the following legal national holidays: January 1 (New Year's Day), the third Monday in January (Martin Luther King, Jr., Day), the third Monday in February (Presidents' Day, Washington's Birthday), the last Monday in May (Memorial Day), July 4 (Independence Day), the first Monday in September (Labor Day), the second Monday in October (Columbus Day), November 11 (Veterans Day/Armistice Day), the fourth Thursday in November (Thanksgiving Day), and December 25 (Christmas). Also, the Tuesday following the first Monday in November is Election Day and is a federal government holiday in presidential-election years (held every 4 years, next in 2008).

Legal Aid If you are "pulled over" for a minor infraction (such as speeding), never attempt to pay the fine directly to a police officer; this could be construed as attempted bribery, a much more serious crime. Pay fines by mail, or directly into the hands of the clerk of the court. If accused of a more serious offense, say and do nothing before consulting a lawyer. Here the burden is on the state to prove a person's guilt beyond a reasonable doubt, and everyone has the right to remain silent, whether he or she is suspected of a crime or actually arrested. Once arrested, a person can make one telephone call to a party of his or her choice. Call your embassy or consulate.

Mail If you aren't sure what your address will be in the United States, mail can be sent to you, in your name, c/o General Delivery at the main post office of the city or region where you expect to be. (Call ✆ **800/275-8777** for information on the nearest post office.) The addressee must pick up mail in person and must produce proof of identity (driver's license, passport, and so forth). Most post offices will hold your mail for up to 1 month and are open Monday to Friday from 8am to 6pm and Saturday from 9am to 3pm.

Generally found at intersections, mailboxes are blue with a red-and-white stripe and carry the inscription U.S. MAIL. If your mail is addressed to a U.S. destination, don't forget to add the five-digit postal code (or zip code) after the two-letter abbreviation of the state to which the mail is addressed. This is essential to prompt delivery.

At press time, domestic postage rates were 23¢ for a postcard and 37¢ for a letter. For international mail, a first-class letter of up to ½ ounce costs 80¢ (60¢ to Canada and Mexico); a first-class postcard costs 70¢ (50¢ to Canada and Mexico); and a preprinted postal aerogramme costs 70¢. Point your Web browser to **www.usps.com** for complete U.S. postal information.

In Las Vegas the closest post office to the Strip is behind the Stardust Hotel at 3100 S. Industrial Rd., between Sahara Avenue and Spring Mountain Road (✆ **800/297-5543**). The **main post office** is at 1001 E. Sunset Rd. (same phone number). It's open Monday to Friday from 8:30am to 6pm. You can also mail letters and packages at your hotel, and there's a full-service U.S. Post Office in the Forum Shops in Caesars Palace.

Measurements See the chart on the inside front cover of this book for details on converting metric measurements to U.S. equivalents. See also the "Size Conversion Chart" on p. 273 in this chapter for clothing and shoe size equivalencies.

Taxes The United States has no value-added tax (VAT) or other indirect tax at the national level. Every state, county, and city has the right to levy its own local tax on all purchases, including hotel and restaurant checks, airline tickets, and so on. These taxes are not refundable and are not included in the price tags you'll see on merchandise. In Clark County (where Las Vegas is located), hotel room tax is 9% and sales tax is 7%.

Telephone, Telegraph, Telex & Fax The telephone system in the United States is run by private corporations, so rates, especially for long-distance service and operator-assisted calls, can vary widely. Generally, hotel surcharges on long-distance and local calls are astronomical, so you're usually better off using a **public pay telephone,** which you'll find clearly marked in most public buildings and private establishments as well as on the street. Convenience grocery stores and gas stations always have them. Many convenience groceries and packaging services sell **prepaid calling cards** in denominations up to $50; these can be the least expensive way to call home. Many public phones at airports now accept American Express, MasterCard, and Visa credit cards. **Local calls** made from public pay phones in most locales cost either 25¢ or 50¢. Pay phones do not accept pennies, and few will take anything larger than a quarter.

You may want to look into leasing a cellphone for the duration of your trip.

Most long-distance and international calls can be dialed directly from any phone. **For calls within the United States and to Canada,** dial 1 followed by the area code and the seven-digit number. **For other international calls,** dial 011 followed by the country code, city code, and the telephone number of the person you are calling.

Calls to area codes **800, 888, 877,** and **866** are toll-free. However, calls to numbers in area codes **700** and **900** (chat lines, bulletin boards, "dating" services, and so on) can be very expensive—usually a charge of 95¢ to $3 or more per minute, and they sometimes have minimum charges that can run as high as $15 or more.

For **reversed-charge or collect calls,** and for person-to-person calls, dial 0 (zero, not the letter O) followed by the area code and number you want; an operator will then come on the line, and you should specify that you are calling collect, or person-to-person, or both. If your operator-assisted call is international, ask for the overseas operator.

For **local directory assistance** ("information"), dial ☏ 411; for long-distance information, dial 1, then the appropriate area code and 555-1212.

Telegraph and telex services are provided primarily by Western Union. You can bring your telegram into the nearest Western Union office (there are hundreds across the country) or dictate it over the phone (☏ **800/325-6000**). You can also telegraph money, or have it telegraphed to you, very quickly over the Western Union system, but this service can cost as much as 15% to 20% of the amount sent. You can find a Western Union office at 1350 E. Flamingo Rd. (☏ **702/732-0024**).

Most Las Vegas hotels have **fax machines** available for guest use (be sure to ask about the charge to use it, as charges tend to be very expensive), and many hotel rooms are even wired for guests' fax machines. A less-expensive way to send and receive faxes is to do it at stores such as

Kinko's, a national chain offering computer and copying services. There is a Kinko's near UNLV at 4440 S. Maryland Pkwy. (© **702/735-4402**), and another branch is located Downtown at 830 4th St. (© **702/383-7022**).

There are two kinds of telephone directories in the United States. The so-called **White Pages** list private households and business subscribers in alphabetical order. The inside front cover lists emergency numbers for police, fire, ambulance, the Coast Guard, poison-control center, crime-victims hot line, and so on. The first few pages will tell you how to make long-distance and international calls, complete with country codes and area codes. Government numbers are usually printed on blue paper within the White Pages. Printed on yellow paper, the so-called **Yellow Pages** list all local services, businesses, industries, and houses of worship according to activity with an index at the front or back. (Drugstores/pharmacies and restaurants are also listed by geographic location.) The Yellow Pages also include city plans or detailed area maps, postal zip codes, and public transportation routes.

Time The continental United States is divided into four time zones, and Nevada is on **Pacific Standard Time (PST),** which is 3 hours earlier than on the U.S. East Coast. For instance, when it is noon in Las Vegas, it is 3pm in New York City (EST); 2pm in Chicago (CST), and 1pm in Denver (MST). Nevada, like most of the rest of the United States (but not all of it), observes **daylight saving time** from 1am on the first Sunday in April through 1am on the last Sunday in October. Daylight saving time moves the clock 1 hour ahead of standard time. This results in lovely, long summer evenings, when the sun sets as late as 8:30 or 9pm.

Tipping Tipping is so ingrained in the American way of life that the annual income tax of tip-earning service personnel is based on how much they should have received in light of their employers' gross revenues. Accordingly, they may have to pay tax on a tip you didn't actually give them.

Here are some rules of thumb:

In hotels, tip **bellhops** at least $1 per bag ($2–$3 per bag if you have a lot of luggage) and tip the **chamber staff** $2 to $4 per day (more if you've left a disaster area for him or her to clean up, or if you're traveling with kids and/or pets). Tip the **doorman** or **concierge** only if he or she has provided you with some specific service (for example, calling a cab for you or obtaining difficult-to-get theater tickets). Tip the **valet-parking attendant** $1 every time you get your car.

In restaurants, bars, and nightclubs, tip **service staff** 15% to 20% of the check, tip **bartenders** $1 to $2, and tip **checkroom attendants** $1 per garment. Tip the **doorman** only if he has provided you with some specific service (such as calling a cab for you). Tipping is not expected in cafeterias and fast-food restaurants.

Tip **cab drivers** $2 to $5 for short hauls, 15% of the fare for longer rides.

As for other service personnel, tip **skycaps** at airports at least $1 per bag ($2–$3 per bag if you have a lot of luggage) and tip **hairdressers** and **barbers** 15% to 20%.

Tipping ushers at movies and theaters, and gas-station attendants, is not expected.

Casino dealers usually get a few dollars if you've had a big win.

Toilets You won't find public toilets or "restrooms" on the streets in most U.S. cities, but they can be found in hotel lobbies, bars, restaurants, museums, department stores, railway and bus stations, and service stations. Large hotels, all of the casino hotels, and fast-food restaurants are probably the best bet for good, clean facilities. If possible, avoid the toilets at parks and beaches, which tend to be dirty; some may be unsafe. Restaurants and bars in resorts or heavily visited areas may reserve their restrooms for patrons. Some establishments display a notice indicating this. You can ignore this sign or, better yet, avoid arguments by paying for a cup of coffee or a soft drink, which will qualify you as a patron.

Appendix B:
Las Vegas in Depth

There has rarely been in a time in Vegas's post-Bugsy history when the city wasn't booming, but it's been on a particular roll for the past decade or so. A new megaresort seems to go up at least once a year, and each brings something new to the party: great works of art, five-star world-renowned chefs, rock clubs and arenas that attract significant and still-current acts—you get the idea. In other words, everything old is new again, and Vegas glamour is back, while the sightseeing, thrill rides, and animals continue as a draw for all ages.

1 A Look at the Past

For many centuries, the land that would become Nevada was inhabited only by several Native American tribes: the Paiute, Shoshone, and Washoe. It wasn't until 1826 that Europeans set foot in the future state, and not until 1829 that Rafael Rivera, a scout for Mexican traders, discovered a small spring in the middle of a huge desert valley and called it Las Vegas ("The Meadows"). From 1831 to 1848, these springs served as a watering place on the Old Spanish Trail for trading caravans plying the route between New Mexico and the California coast. Explorer, soldier, and pathfinder Col. John C. Frémont (for whom the main thoroughfare in Downtown is named) rehydrated at Las Vegas Springs on an overland expedition in 1844. A decade later, Congress established a monthly mail route through Las Vegas Springs.

In 1855, Mormon leader Brigham Young sent 30 missionaries to Las Vegas to help expand Mormonism between Salt Lake City and southern California. Just north of what is today Downtown (what would these missionaries think if they could see it now?), the Mormon colony built an adobe fort and dwellings. They raised crops, baptized Paiutes, and mined lead in the nearby mountains. However, none of

Dateline

- **1831–48** Artesian spring waters of Las Vegas serve as a watering place on the Old Spanish Trail.
- **1855** Mormon colony of 30 missionaries establishes settlement just north of today's Downtown. Unsuccessful in its aims, the colony disbands in 1858.
- **1864** President Lincoln proclaims Nevada the 36th state of the Union. Las Vegas, however, is still part of the Territory of Arizona.
- **1865** Gold prospector Octavius D. Gass builds Las Vegas Ranch, the first permanent settlement in Las Vegas, on the site of the old Mormon fort.
- **1880s** Due to the past 2 decades' mining fever and the fervor for westward migration, the population of Nevada soars to more than 60,000 in 1880. The Paiutes are forced onto reservations.
- **1895** San Francisco inventor Charles Fey creates a three-reel gambling device—the first slot machine.
- **1907** Fremont Street, the future "Glitter Gulch," gets electric lights.
- **1909** Gambling is made illegal in Nevada, but Las Vegas pays little heed.
- **1928** Congress authorizes construction of Boulder Dam 30 miles away, bringing thousands of workers to the area. Later, Las Vegas will capitalize on hundreds of thousands who come to see the engineering marvel.
- **1931** Gambling is legalized once again.

continues

these ventures proved successful, and the ill-fated settlement was abandoned after just 3 years.

The next influx into the area came as a result of mining fever in the early 1860s. Gold fever gave way to a fervor for land as pioneers moved ever westward. In 1865, gold prospector Octavius Decatur Gass homesteaded the 640-acre Las Vegas Ranch, using structures left by the Mormons as his base. Because Gass controlled the valley's water, he finally found "gold" offering services to travelers passing through. Gass planted crops and fruit orchards, started vineyards, raised cattle, established cordial relations with the Paiutes (he even learned their language), and served as a legislator. Thus was born the first significant settlement in the area. By 1900, the Las Vegas valley had a population of 30.

A TENT CITY IN THE WILDERNESS

The city of Las Vegas was officially founded in 1905, when the Union Pacific Railroad connecting Los Angeles and Salt Lake City decided to route its trains through this rugged frontier outpost, selected for its ready supply of water and the availability of timber in the surrounding mountains. On a sweltering day in May, 1,200 town-site lots were auctioned off to eager pioneers and real-estate speculators who had come from all over the country. The railroad depot was located at the head of Fremont Street (site of today's Plaza Hotel-Casino). Championing the spot was Montana senator William Clark, who had paid the astronomical sum (for that time) of $55,000 for the nearby Las Vegas Ranch and springs. The coming of a railroad more or less ensured the growth of the town. As construction began, tent settlements, saloons, ramshackle restaurants, boardinghouses, and shops gradually emerged. (The early tent hotels charged a dollar to share a double bed with a stranger for 8 hours!)

- 1932 The 100-room Apache Hotel opens Downtown.
- 1933 Prohibition is repealed. Las Vegas's numerous speakeasies become legit.
- 1934 The city's first neon sign lights up the Boulder Club Downtown.
- 1941 The luxurious El Rancho Vegas becomes the first hotel on the Strip. Downtown, the El Cortez opens.
- 1942 Last Frontier opens 2 miles south of El Rancho Vegas.
- 1946 Benjamin "Bugsy" Siegel's Flamingo extends the boundaries of the Strip. Sammy Davis, Jr., debuts at the El Rancho Vegas. Downtown (dubbed "Glitter Gulch") gets two new hotels: the Golden Nugget and the Eldorado.
- 1947 United Airlines inaugurates service to Las Vegas.
- 1948 The Thunderbird becomes the fourth hotel on the Strip.
- 1950 The Desert Inn adds country club panache to the Strip.
- 1951 The first of many atom bombs is tested in the desert just 65 miles from Las Vegas. An explosion of another sort takes place when Frank Sinatra debuts at the Desert Inn.
- 1952 The Club Bingo (opened in 1947) becomes the desert-themed Sahara. The Sands's Copa Room enhances the city's image as an entertainment center.
- 1954 The Showboat pioneers buffet meals and bowling alleys in a new area of Downtown.
- 1955 The Strip gets its first high-rise hotel, the nine-story Riviera, which pays Liberace the unprecedented sum of $50,000 to open its showroom. The Riviera is the ninth hotel on the Strip. A month later, the Dunes becomes the 10th.
- 1956 The Fremont opens Downtown, and the Hacienda becomes the southernmost hotel on the Strip.
- 1957 The Dunes introduces barebreasted showgirls in its *Minsky Goes to Paris* revue. The most luxurious hotel to date, the Tropicana, opens on the Strip.
- 1958 The 1,065-room Stardust opens as the world's largest resort complex with a spectacular show from France, the *Lido de Paris*.

By present-day standards, the new town was not a pleasant place to live. Prospectors' burros roamed the streets braying loudly, generally creating havoc and attracting swarms of flies. There were no screens, no air-conditioners, no modern showers or bathrooms (the town's bathhouse had but one tub) to ameliorate the fierce summer heat. The streets were rutted with dust pockets up to a foot deep that rose in great gusts as stagecoaches, supply wagons, and 20-animal mule teams careened over them. It was a true pioneer town, complete with saloon brawls and shoot-outs. Discomforts notwithstanding, gaming establishments, hotels, and nightclubs—some of them seedy dives, others rather luxurious—sprang up and prospered in the new railroad town. A red-light district emerged on Second Street between Ogden and Stewart avenues. And gambling, which was legal until 1909, flourished.

THE EIGHTH WONDER OF THE WORLD

For many years after its creation, Las Vegas was a mere whistle-stop town. That all changed in 1928 when Congress authorized the building of nearby Boulder (later renamed Hoover) Dam, bringing thousands of workers to the area. In 1931, gambling once again became legal in Nevada, and Fremont Street's gaming emporiums and speakeasies attracted workers from the dam. Upon the dam's completion, the Las Vegas Chamber of Commerce worked hard to lure the hordes of tourists who came to see the engineering marvel (it was called "The Eighth Wonder of the World") to its casinos. Las Vegas was about to make the transition from sleepy desert town to desert town that never sleeps. But it wasn't until the early years of World War II that visionary entrepreneurs began to plan for its glittering future.

- **1959** The Las Vegas Convention Center goes up, presaging the city's future as a major convention city. Another French production, the still-extant *Folies Bergere*, opens at the Tropicana.
- **1960** The Rat Pack, led by Chairman of the Board Frank Sinatra, holds a 3-week "Summit Meeting" at the Sands. A championship boxing match, the first of many, takes place at the Convention Center. El Rancho Vegas, the Strip's first property, burns to the ground.
- **1963** McCarran International Airport opens. Casinos and showrooms are darkened for a day as Las Vegas mourns the death of President John F. Kennedy.
- **1965** The 26-story Mint alters the Fremont Street skyline. Muhammad Ali defeats Floyd Patterson at the Las Vegas Convention Center.
- **1966** The Aladdin, the first new hotel on the Strip in 9 years, is soon eclipsed by the unparalleled grandeur of Caesars Palace. The Four Queens opens Downtown. Howard Hughes takes up residence at the Desert Inn. He buys up big chunks of Las Vegas and helps erase the city's gangland stigma.
- **1967** Elvis Presley marries Priscilla Beaulieu at the Aladdin.
- **1968** Circus Circus gives kids a reason to come to Las Vegas.
- **1969** The Landmark and the International (today the Hilton) open within a day of each other on Paradise Road. Elvis Presley makes a triumphant return headlining at the latter.
- **1973** The ultraglamorous 2,100-room MGM Grand assumes the mantle of "world's largest resort." Superstars of magic, Siegfried and Roy, debut at the Tropicana.
- **1976** Pioneer aviator Howard Hughes dies aboard a plane en route to a Houston hospital. Dean Martin and Jerry Lewis make up after a 20-year feud.
- **1978** Leon Spinks dethrones "The Greatest" (Muhammad Ali) at the Las Vegas Hilton. Crime-solver Dan Tanna (Robert Urich) makes the streets of *Vega$* safer, and better known.

continues

LAS VEGAS GOES SOUTH

Contrary to popular lore, Bugsy Siegel didn't actually stake a claim in the middle of nowhere—he just built a few blocks south of already existing properties. Development a few miles south of Downtown on Highway 91 (the future Strip) was already underway in the 1930s, with such establishments as the Pair-O-Dice Club and the Last Frontier.

And in 1941, El Rancho Vegas, ultraluxurious for its time, was built on the same remote stretch of highway (across the street from where the Sahara now stands). According to legend, Los Angeles hotelier Thomas E. Hull had been driving by the site when his car broke down. Noticing the extent of passing traffic, he decided to build there. Hull invited scores of Hollywood stars to his grand opening, and El Rancho Vegas soon became the hotel of choice for visiting film stars.

Beginning a trend that still continues today, each new property tried to outdo existing hotels in luxurious amenities and thematic splendor. In 1942, the Last Frontier (the Strip's second hotel) created an authentic Western setting by scouring the Southwest in search of authentic pioneer furnishings for its rooms, hiring Zuni craftsmen to create baskets and wall hangings, and picking up guests at the airport in a horse-drawn stagecoach. And with that, Las Vegas was on its way to becoming the entertainment capital of the world.

Las Vegas promoted itself in the 1940s as a town that combined Wild West frontier friendliness with glamour and excitement. As Chamber of Commerce president Maxwell Kelch aptly put it in a 1947 speech, "Las Vegas has the impact of a Wild West show, the friendliness of a country store, and the sophistication of Monte

- **1979** A new international arrivals building opens at McCarran International Airport.
- **1980** McCarran International Airport embarks on a 20-year, $785-million expansion program. Las Vegas celebrates its 75th birthday. A devastating fire destroys the MGM Grand, leaving 84 dead and 700 injured. Bally's takes over the property.
- **1981** Siegfried and Roy begin a record-breaking run in their own show, *Beyond Belief,* at the Frontier.
- **1982** A Las Vegas street is named Wayne Newton Boulevard.
- **1989** Steve Wynn makes headlines with his spectacular Mirage, fronted by an erupting volcano. He signs Siegfried and Roy to an unprecedented $57-million showroom contract.
- **1990s** The family-friendly medieval Arthurian realm of Excalibur opens as the new "world's largest resort" titleholder with 4,032 rooms, a claim it relinquishes when the MGM Grand's new 5,005-room megaresort/theme park opens in 1993, with a *Wizard of Oz* theme. Other properties geared toward families opened in the 1990s, most notably Luxor, with its pyramid and Egyptian motifs, and the pirate-themed Treasure Island. The rock-'n'-roll Hard Rock, Mandalay Bay, Bellagio, The Venetian, and Paris Las Vegas carried concept gaming resorts to new heights, while New York–New York was built with a roller coaster running around it. Celebrity chefs come to town.
- **2000** The new Aladdin opens. MGM Grand buys out Mirage Resorts; Steve Wynn buys the Desert Inn and promptly implodes it to begin building Wynn Las Vegas.
- **2001** The events of 9/11 hit Las Vegas especially hard; it takes nearly a year for the steamroller to build up a new head of steam.
- **2004** Strip Monorail debuts.
- **2005** Wynn Las Vegas, the first major new casino resort to open in 5 years, debuts on the Strip.

Carlo." Throughout the decade, the city was largely a regional resort—Hollywood's celebrity playground. Clara Bow and Rex Bell (a star of westerns) bought a ranch in Las Vegas, where they entertained the Barrymores, Norma Shearer,

Clark Gable, and Errol Flynn. The Hollywood connection gave the town glamour in the public's mind. So did the mob connection (something Las Vegas subsequently spent decades trying to live down), which became clear early on when the notorious underworld gangster Benjamin "Bugsy" Siegel (with partners Charles "Lucky" Luciano and Meyer Lansky) built the fabulous Flamingo, a tropical paradise and "a real class joint." In 1947, the Club Bingo opened across the street from El Rancho Vegas, bringing yet another new game to town.

A steady stream of name entertainers began to make their way to Las Vegas. In 1947, Jimmy Durante opened the showroom at The Flamingo. Other headliners of the 1940s included Dean Martin and Jerry Lewis, tap-dancing legend Bill "Bojangles" Robinson, the Mills Brothers, skater Sonja Henie, and Frankie Laine. (Future Las Vegas legend Sammy Davis, Jr., debuted at El Rancho Vegas in 1945.)

While the Strip was expanding, Downtown kept pace with new hotels such as the El Cortez and the Golden Nugget. By the end of the decade, Fremont Street was known as "Glitter Gulch," its profusion of neon signs proclaiming round-the-clock gaming and entertainment.

THE 1950S: BUILDING BOOMS & A-BOMBS

Las Vegas entered the new decade as a city (no longer a frontier town) with a population of about 50,000. Photographs remind us that Las Vegas celebrated a more formal nightlife in the 1950s than it does today. Men donned suits and ties, and women wore floor-length gowns to attend shows and try their luck in the casinos. The hotel growth of the time was phenomenal. The Desert Inn, which opened in 1950 with headliners Edgar Bergen and Charlie McCarthy, brought country club elegance (including an 18-hole golf course and tennis courts) to the Strip.

In 1951, the Eldorado Club Downtown became Benny Binion's Horseshoe Club, which would gain fame as the home of the annual World Series of Poker. In 1954, the Showboat sailed into a new area east of Downtown. Although people said it could never last in such a remote location, they were wrong. The Showboat not only innovated buffet meals and a bowling alley (at 106 lanes, the largest in Nevada for decades—till it closed in 2003), but offered round-the-clock bingo.

In 1955, the Côte d'Azur–themed Riviera became the ninth big hotel to open on the Strip. Breaking the ranch-style mode, it was, at nine stories, the Strip's first high-rise. And Liberace, one of the hottest names in show business, was paid the unprecedented sum of $50,000 a week to dazzle audiences in The Riviera's posh Clover Room.

The 15-story Fremont Hotel Downtown became the tallest building in Las Vegas, and the Hacienda extended the boundaries of the Strip by opening 2 miles south of the nearest resort.

Elvis appeared at the New Frontier in 1956, but wasn't a huge success; his fans were too young to fit the Las Vegas tourist mold. In 1957, the Tropicana joined the Hacienda at the far end of Las Vegas Boulevard. In 1958, the $10-million, 1,065-room Stardust upped the spectacular stakes by importing the famed *Lido de Paris* from the French capital. It became one of the longest-running shows ever to play Las Vegas.

Throughout the 1950s, most of the above-mentioned hotels competed for performers whose followers spent freely in the casinos. The advent of big-name Strip entertainment tolled a death knell for glamorous nightclubs in America; owners simply could not compete with the astronomical salaries paid to Las

Vegas headliners. Major '50s stars of the Strip included Rosemary Clooney, Nat King Cole, Peggy Lee, Milton Berle, Judy Garland, Red Skelton, Ernie Kovacs, Abbott and Costello, Fred Astaire and Ginger Rogers, the Andrews Sisters, and Marlene Dietrich. Two performers whose names have been linked to Las Vegas ever since—Frank Sinatra and Wayne Newton—made their debuts there. Mae West not only performed in Las Vegas, but also cleverly bought up a half mile of desolate Strip frontage between the Dunes and the Tropicana.

Competition for the tourist dollar also brought nationally televised sporting events such as the PGA's Tournament of Champions to the Desert Inn golf course (the winner got a wheelbarrow filled with silver dollars). And, in the 1950s, the wedding industry helped make Las Vegas one of the nation's most popular venues for "goin' to the chapel." (Nevada requires no blood test or waiting period.) Celebrity weddings of the 1950s that sparked the trend included singer Dick Haymes and Rita Hayworth, Joan Crawford and Pepsi chairman Alfred Steele, Carol Channing and TV exec Charles Lowe, and Paul Newman and Joanne Woodward.

On a grimmer note, the '50s also heralded the atomic age in Nevada, with nuclear testing taking place just 65 miles northwest of Las Vegas. A chilling 1951 photograph shows a mushroom-shaped cloud from an atomic bomb test visible over the Fremont Street horizon. Throughout the decade, about one bomb a month was detonated in the nearby desert.

THE 1960S: THE RAT PACK & A PACK RAT

The very first month of the new decade made entertainment history when the Sands hosted a 3-week "Summit Meeting" in the Copa Room that was presided over by "Chairman of the Board" Frank Sinatra with Rat Pack cronies Dean Martin, Sammy Davis, Jr., Peter Lawford, and Joey Bishop (all of whom were in town filming *Ocean's Eleven*).

The building boom of the '50s took a brief respite. The Strip's first property, the El Rancho Vegas, burned down in 1960. And the first new hotel of the decade, the first to be built in 9 years, was the exotic Aladdin in 1966. A year after it opened, the Aladdin hosted the most celebrated Las Vegas wedding of all time when Elvis Presley married Priscilla Beaulieu. In 1966, Las Vegas also hailed Caesar—Caesars Palace, that is—a Lucullan pleasure palace whose grand opening was a million-dollar, 3-day Roman orgy with 1,800 guests.

During the '60s, negative attention focused on mob influence in Las Vegas. Of the 11 major casino hotels that had opened in the previous decade, 10 were believed to have been financed with mob money. Attorney General Robert Kennedy ordered the Department of Justice to begin serious scrutiny of Las Vegas gaming operations. Then, like a knight in shining armor, Howard Hughes rode into town. He was not, however, on a white horse. Ever eccentric, he arrived (for security rather than health reasons) in an ambulance. The reclusive billionaire moved into a Desert Inn penthouse on Thanksgiving Day 1966 and didn't set foot outside the hotel for the next 3 years! It became his headquarters for a $300-million hotel- and property-buying spree, which included the Desert Inn itself (in 1967). Hughes was as "bugsy" as Benjamin Siegel any day, but his pristine reputation helped bring respectability to the desert city and lessen its gangland stigma. For a while, it worked.

Las Vegas became a family destination in 1968, when Circus Circus burst on the scene with the world's largest permanent circus and a "junior casino" comprising dozens of carnival midway games on its mezzanine level. In 1969, the Landmark and the dazzling International (today the Hilton) ventured into a

Farewell to Frank

Only a few times in its history have the lights of Vegas been turned off at night. Twice it happened in the '60s, for President Kennedy (when the casinos themselves actually closed) and for Martin Luther King, Jr. And it happened twice in the '90s; the Strip went completely dark for 10 minutes to honor the passing of Sammy Davis, Jr., and when Dean Martin died in 1996, the Strip dimmed again.

So when Frank Sinatra, the man who practically built this town, died in 1998, we were sure Vegas would do something big to honor the paramount Rat Packer. We were wrong. The Strip went dark, but for 1 lousy minute. (Did we mention Sammy got 10?) And some of the lesser casinos and buildings never shut off at all. Still, some of the hotels put up tributes to Frankie on their signs, while cars drove down the Strip honking their horns, and a few of the hundreds of tourists who lined the boulevard to watch this historic moment burst into applause for The Voice.

It was something. And it's unlikely we will ever see anything like it happen again. (Though, in 2004, the reaction when the Strip went dark again in honor of President Reagan, who'd performed in several casinos during his acting days, came pretty close.)

new area of town: Paradise Road near the Convention Center. That same year, Elvis made a triumphant return to Las Vegas at the International's showroom and went on to become one of the city's all-time legendary performers. His fans had come of age.

Hoping to establish Las Vegas as "the Broadway of the West," the Thunderbird Hotel presented Rodgers and Hammerstein's *Flower Drum Song*. It was a smash hit. Soon The Riviera picked up *Bye, Bye, Birdie*, and, as the decade progressed, *Mame* and *The Odd Couple* played at Caesars Palace. While Broadway played the Strip, production shows such as the Dunes's *Casino de Paris* became ever more lavish, expensive, and technically innovative. Showroom stars of the 1960s included Barbra Streisand, Phyllis Diller, Carol Burnett, Little Richard (who billed himself as "the bronze Liberace"), Louis Armstrong, Bobby Darin, the Supremes, Johnny Carson, Bob Newhart, the Smothers Brothers, and Aretha Franklin. Liza Minnelli filled her mother's shoes, while Nancy Sinatra's boots were made for walking on stage, and Tom Jones wowed 'em at The Flamingo.

THE 1970S: MERV, MIKE, MGM & MAGIC

In 1971, the 500-room Union Plaza opened at the head of Fremont Street on the site of the old Union Pacific Station. It had what was, at the time, the world's largest casino, and its showroom specialized in Broadway productions. The same year, talk-show host Merv Griffin began taping at Caesars Palace, taking advantage of a ready supply of local headliner guests. He helped popularize Las Vegas even more by bringing it into America's living rooms every afternoon. Rival Mike Douglas soon followed suit at the Las Vegas Hilton.

The year 1973 was eventful: The Holiday Inn (today Harrah's) built a Mississippi riverboat complete with towering smokestacks and foghorn whistle, which was immediately dubbed "the ship on the Strip." Dean Martin headlined in the celebrity room of the magnificent new MGM Grand, named for the movie *Grand Hotel*. And over at the Tropicana, illusionists extraordinaire Siegfried and Roy began turning women into tigers and themselves into legends in the *Folies Bergere*.

However, two major disasters hit Las Vegas in the 1970s. First, a flash flood devastated the Strip, causing more than $1 million in damage and sweeping away hundreds of cars in the raging waters. Second, gambling was legalized in Atlantic City, which caused Las Vegas's hotel business to slump as fickle tourists decided to check out the new East Coast gambling Mecca.

On a happier note, audiences were moved when Frank Sinatra helped to patch up a 20-year feud by introducing Dean Martin as a surprise guest on Jerry Lewis's 1976 Muscular Dystrophy Telethon at the Sahara, where Martin and Lewis hugged and made up.

As the decade drew to a close, Dan Tanna began investigating crime in glamorous *Vega$*, an international arrivals building opened at McCarran International Airport, and dollar slot machines caused a sensation in the casinos. Hot performers of the '70s included Ann-Margret, Tina Turner, Englebert Humperdinck, Bill Cosby, Sonny and Cher, Tony Bennett, Mel Tormé, Bobby Darin, Gregory Hines (with his brother and dad), Donny and Marie, the Jackson 5, Gladys Knight and the Pips, and that "wild and crazy guy," Steve Martin. Debbie Reynolds introduced daughter Carrie Fisher with a duet performance before a Desert Inn audience. Shirley MacLaine began an incarnation at The Riviera. And country was now cool: The names Johnny Cash, Bobbie Gentry, Charley Pride, and Roy Clark went up in marquee lights.

THE 1980S: THE CITY ERUPTS

Las Vegas was booming once again. McCarran Airport began a 20-year, $785-million expansion program. On a tragic note, in 1980, a devastating fire swept through the MGM Grand, leaving 84 dead and 700 injured. Shortly thereafter, Bally acquired the property and reopened newly named Bally's Las Vegas.

Siegfried and Roy were no longer just the star segment of various stage spectaculars. Their own show, *Beyond Belief*, ran for 6 years at the Frontier, playing a record-breaking 3,538 performances to sellout audiences every night. It became the most successful attraction in the city's history.

In 1989, Steve Wynn made Las Vegas sit up and take notice. His gleaming white-and-gold Mirage was fronted by five-story waterfalls, lagoons, and lush tropical foliage—not to mention a 50-foot volcano that dramatically erupted, spewing great gusts of fire another 50 feet into the air every 15 minutes after dark! Wynn gave world-renowned illusionists Siegfried and Roy carte blanche (and more than $50 million) to create the most spellbinding show Las Vegas had ever seen.

Stars of the '80s included Eddie Murphy, Don Rickles, Roseanne Barr, Dionne Warwick, Paul Anka, the Captain and Tennille, Donna Summer, Rich Little, George Carlin, Barry Manilow, Bernadette Peters, and Diahann Carroll. Country continued to be cool, as evidenced by frequent headliners Willie Nelson, Kenny Rogers, Dolly Parton, Crystal Gayle, Merle Haggard, and Barbara Mandrell. Joan Rivers posed her famous question, "Can we talk?" and bug-eyed comic Rodney Dangerfield complained he got "no respect."

THE 1990S: KING ARTHUR MEETS KING TUT

The decade began with a blare of trumpets heralding the rise of a turreted medieval castle fronted by a moated drawbridge and staffed by jousting knights and fair damsels. Excalibur's interior had so many stone castle walls that a Strip comedian quipped, "It looks like a prison for Snow White." Excalibur also reflected the early '90s marketing trend to promote Las Vegas as a family-vacation destination.

More sensational megahotels followed on the Strip, including the *new* MGM Grand hotel, backed by a full theme park (it ended Excalibur's brief reign as the world's largest resort), Luxor Las Vegas, and Steve Wynn's Treasure Island.

On October 27, 1993, a quarter of a million people crowded onto the Strip to witness the implosion of the 37-year-old Dunes Hotel. In true Vegas style, it went out with a bang. Later that year, a unique pink-domed 5-acre indoor amusement park, Grand Slam Canyon (now Adventuredome), became part of the Circus Circus hotel. In 1995, the Fremont Street Experience was completed, revitalizing Downtown Las Vegas. Closer to the Strip, rock restaurant magnate Peter Morton opened the Hard Rock Hotel, billed as "the world's first rock-'n'-roll hotel and casino." The year 1996 saw the advent of the French Riviera–themed Monte Carlo and the Stratosphere, its 1,149-foot tower the highest building west of the Mississippi. New York–New York arrived in 1997 and set a new Las Vegas standard for themed architecture.

Then, in 1998 and 1999, Vegas hastily repositioned itself (again) from "family destination" to "luxury resort," as several new hotels, once again eclipsing anything that had come before, opened up. Bellagio, created by Vegas visionary Steve Wynn, was an attempt to bring grand European style to the desert, while at the far southern end of the Strip, Mandalay Bay also charms, topped with floors entirely owned and run by the highly regarded Four Seasons (an *actual* luxury resort hotel in Vegas, which pampers children almost as well as it spoils adults). As if this weren't enough, The Venetian's ambitious detailed re-creation of everyone's favorite Italian city came along in May 1999, and was followed in short order by the opening of Paris Las Vegas in the fall of 1999.

And then everything got shaken up again when the MGM Grand purchased Steve Wynn's Mirage Corporation to become MGM MIRAGE, which led to a large number of the Strip's properties being placed under one corporate umbrella. Never one to rest, Wynn responded by purchasing the Desert Inn, then designing and building the $2.7-billion Wynn Las Vegas, poised to open in April 2005.

But that was hardly the end of the city's corporate wheeling and dealing. In 2004, Planet Hollywood took over the bankrupt Aladdin, Colony Capital bought the Las Vegas Hilton, Harrah's acquired and reopened Downtown's famous Binion's Horseshoe, and two 30-something dot.com superstars purchased the Golden Nugget. But the two biggest merger blockbusters came in the summer of 2004, when Harrah's Entertainment moved to acquire Caesars Entertainment, and MGM MIRAGE reached an agreement to merge with Mandalay Resort Group. Both of these pending deals require the approval of the Antitrust Division of the U.S. Department of Justice; if approved, the two surviving companies would control 16 of the 25 major Strip properties. Opponents of the acquisitions claim decreased competition will lead to spiraling room rates—not an unfounded worry. Word on the Strip is that the companies may be forced to divest some properties before the merger is approved—so look for more deals on the horizon. Clearly, no one can rest on their laurels in Vegas, for this is not only a city that never sleeps, but one in which progress never stops moving, even for a heartbeat.

2 Las Vegas Today

The Vegas-as-family-vacation experiment didn't quite meet corporate expectations, so much so that the city continues to repudiate the idea. Now, the powers that be are returning to the idea of Vegas-as-adult-fun with a vengeance—and, this time around, they're determined not only to recapture that long-ago Vegas elegance (if, indeed, it ever existed), but also to persuade potential visitors to view Vegas as a luxury resort destination. This means creating a place where lounging, recreation, and food are given greater emphasis than ever before—even, hotels owners say, over the sacred gaming tables.

But don't let any of this make you think that you shouldn't come to Vegas with your kids. Thankfully, there seems to be a tacit understanding in Sin City that many visitors do have children, and they like to go on vacation as a family. With that in mind, though hotels are hardly wooing families as hard as they did in the 1990s, they are in no way overlooking children either (hence, the arcades, rides, animals, and more).

Keep in mind that Vegas is, has been, and will always be first and foremost a gambling destination. After all, if they really didn't want you to gamble, they would have left the casinos out of the new "luxury resorts." But, as we stress, there is more to Las Vegas than the cling-clang bling-bling of the casinos: The city is surrounded by beautiful desert mountains; history comes alive at the city's many museums; and the income generated from the gaming resorts has helped build the city's arts and leisure activities—all of which are great for families.

Whether Las Vegas's current experiment in luxury will succeed remains to be seen, but its effects are already being felt. Vegas has the 10 largest hotels in the United States (MGM Grand is number one in size), with 37 million tourists filling all those rooms. Another big resort, the $1-billion Aladdin, opened in mid-2000, bringing another 3,000 rooms with it (it subsequently had to file for bankruptcy and the Aladdin was sold to Planet Hollywood in 2004), which makes you wonder just when the place will reach critical mass. But so far, so good: The occupancy rate is running at an impressive 90%. And for every new glistening hotel that goes up, another old-timer comes down, or undergoes a facelift because it looks so shabby next to its shining new neighbor.

The phenomenal growth in tourism is being paralleled by a population explosion. Las Vegas has had a 28% increase in its population over the last 5 years (it was the fastest-growing metropolis in the United States in 2004), and an average of 6,000 people are relocating into the area monthly, many of whom have families or are looking to start them. This is the only city in America where the phone book is published twice a year in order to keep up with all the changes and newcomers. Unfortunately, the highways can't expand as rapidly as the phone books, and school construction is lagging behind the population boom. For tourists, the town's all-too-rapid growth is most evident along the Strip, which is totally inadequate to accommodate such huge numbers of cars and people. While people movers and bridges have helped smooth pedestrian travel, and monorails and other traffic solutions are slowly being integrated, Strip traffic remains frustratingly bumper-to-bumper at almost all times.

Snarled traffic notwithstanding, families visiting Las Vegas will be awestruck by the variety of eye candy and amusements offered to them, and overwhelmed at times by the plethora of options for exploration, food, fun, attractions, and shopping. Each time something new opens up, you think, "They can't possibly top this." And yet they do. And one thing's for sure—somehow, they always will.

Index

See also Accommodations and Restaurant indexes, below.

GENERAL INDEX

A
AA (American Automobile Association), 276, 277
AARP, 36
Abercrombie & Fitch, 204
Abilities 2000, 34
Above and Beyond Tours, 35
Academy Fine Books and Antiques, 195
Access Adventures, 34
Access America, 29
Accessible Journeys, 34
Accommodations, 75–115.
    See also Accommodations Index
    around Lake Mead, 249–250
    avoiding the crowds, 82
    best bets, 8–11
    Center Strip, 90–97
    check-in time, 75
    East of the Strip, 101–110
    with a fridge in your room, 137
    guests-per-room maximum, 102
    landing the best room, 60
    Mount Charleston, 261
    North Strip, 97–101
    Old Nevada, 259–260
    outside of Las Vegas, 113–115
    package tours and, 53–54
    Peach Springs (AZ), 265–266
    room rates, 77–80
    saving on, 58–60
    shopping promenades, 192–195
    South Strip, 80–90
    "suite," meaning of, 106
    surfing for, 55–57
    tipping, 281
    West of the Strip, 110–113
Action Tours, 242
Adaptive Recreation Center, 188
Adventure Canyon (Primm), 262

Adventuredome, 151, 166, 187
Aer Lingus, 275
Afternoon tea, 128
Age of Chivalry Renaissance Festival, 24
AIDSinfo, 269
Air Canada, 38, 275
Airfares
    discounts for international visitors, 275
    surfing for, 54–57
    tips for getting the best, 41–42
Airlines, 38, 275–276
    bankruptcy and, 41
    from Europe, 274–275
    meals and snacks, 50–52
Air New Zealand, 275
Air Play at the Tropicana, 154
Air Tickets Direct, 41–42
Air tours, Grand Canyon West, 264
Air travel, 49–51
    children traveling solo, 47–48
    first-class experience in coach, 42–43
    safe seats for kids, 45–47
    security measures, 39–41
    toys and games, 50, 51
A. J. Hackett Bungy, 185
Aladdin/Planet Hollywood Resort & Casino
    casino, 233–234
    Desert Passage at, 10, 154
    entertainment, 154, 223
    restaurants and food court, 123, 127–128, 130
    shopping, 192–193
Alamo/National, 70, 276
Alan Bible Lake Mead Visitor Center, 246, 248
Alaska Airlines, 38, 52
Albertsons Food and Drugs, 207
Albion Books, 196
All-American Sports Park, 7
Allegiant Air, 38

The Alliance for Retired Americans, 36
All-You-Can-Eat Ice Cream Festival, 24
Aloha Air, 38
Along Came a Spider, 206
Alternate Reality Comics, 198
American Airlines, 52, 275
American Airlines Vacations, 52
American/American Eagle, 38
American Automobile Association (AAA), 277
American Express, 72
    traveler's checks, 18
American Foundation for the Blind, 34
American Golf, 186
American Superstars, 216
American Trans Air/Comair, 38
America West, 38, 52
Amtrak, 45, 276–277
Angel Park Golf Club, 186
Antique Sampler Shoppes, 196
Antiques and collectibles, 195–196
Antiques at the Market, 196
Arcades, 164, 173
    curfew in, 32
Armani Exchange, 206
Around the Clock Child Care, 61
Arts and crafts, 196
    Great Las Vegas Craft Festival, 24
Arts Factory Complex, 207
Asian Market, 207
ATMs (automated teller machines), 17, 18, 273
The Attic, 212
Auto Collections at the Imperial Palace, 168, 170, 179
Auto insurance, 30
Avis rental cars, 70, 276

B abies "R" Us, 196
Babysitters, 60–61
Bali Hai Golf Club, 186
Ballet, 231
Bally's Las Vegas
    entertainment, 239
    shopping, 193
    tennis courts, 187
Banana Republic, 204
Banks, 72
Barnes & Noble, 196
Bars, 232–233
Baseball, 228
BCBG, 206
B. Dalton, 196
Bebe, 206
Bellagio
    casino, 235–236
    entertainment, 154, 214,
        218
    shopping, 193
Bellagio Fountains, 154
Bellagio Gallery of Fine Art,
    170
Bell Book & Candle, 197
Bell Trans, 38
Bernini Collection, 208
Best Buy, 202
Bicycling, 184–185
    areas surrounding Las
        Vegas, 266
    Red Rock Canyon, 254, 257
BiddingForTravel.com, 55, 56
Big Shot, 7, 98, 168
Big-Top Acts and Midway at
    Circus Circus, 156
Bike World, 210
Black Canyon/Willow Beach
    River Adventures, 248–249
Black Mountain Golf &
    Country Club (Henderson),
    186
Blue Man Group: *Live at
    Luxor*, 216–217
BluWay, 35
Boating, Lake Mead and
    vicinity, 246, 248
Bonanza Gift and Souvenir
    Shop, 207
Bonnie Springs Ranch, 242
Bonnie Springs Ranch/Old
    Nevada, 257–260
Books, 25–27
    for adults, 63
    for kids, about flying or air-
        plane travel, 50
    on traveling with kids, 49
Bookstores, 196–198
Borders, 197

Boulder City, 242, 250
    accommodations and
        restaurants, 249
Boulder Station, 62
Boulevard Mall, 190
Bowling, 185
Boxing matches, 228
*Brain Quest for the Car:
    1,100 Questions and
    Answers All About
    America,* 51
Brats, 196, 206
British Airways, 275
Bucket shops, 41
Budget, 276
Budget rental cars, 70
Buffalo Bill's Resort and
    Casino, 261–262
Buffalo Exchange, 212
Buffets, 130, 145–149
    best, 11
Build-a-Bear Workshop, 211
Bungee jumping, 185
Business hours, 277
Bus tours, Grand Canyon
    West, 264
Bus travel, 276

C abs, 69
    tipping, 281
Cactus and wetlands garden
    (Henderson), 176–177
Caesars Forum Shops, 10
Caesars Palace
    attractions, 156–157, 173
    casino, 236
    entertainment, 5, 214,
        217–218, 238
    restaurants, 134, 136–138
    shopping, 193–194, 206
    sporting events, 230
Calendar of events, 21–25
Callville Bay, 248
Cameras, digital, 40, 57
Camping, Lake Mead and
    vicinity, 248
Candy, chocolate and
    sweets, 198
Canoeing, Lake Mead and
    vicinity, 248
Car rentals, 70–72, 276
    at the airport, 39
    insurance, 30
    surfing for, 56
Car travel, 276
    games, 51
    in Las Vegas, 69–70
    to Las Vegas, 45

    packing tips, 29
    safety suggestions, 71
Casey's Sports Cards, 210
Cashman Field Center, 72
Casino Legends Hall of Fame
    Museum, 170–171
Casinos, 233–237
    Center Strip, 235–237
Celine Dion: *A New Day,*
    217–218
Cellphones, 28
Center Strip, 66
    accommodations, 90–97
    casinos, 235–237
    restaurants, 132–138,
        147–148
Chamber of Commerce, Las
    Vegas, 15, 25, 64
Charleston, Mount, 14,
    260–261
Charleston Heights Arts
    Center, 231
Child-care centers, 61–63
Chinatown restaurants, 132
Chinese New Year, 21
Chinle Formation (Red Rock
    Canyon), 255
Chocolates, 198
Cinco de Mayo Festival, 22
CineVegas International Film
    Festival, 23
Circuit City, 202
Circus Circus
    arcade, 164
    Big-Top Acts and Midway
        at, 156
    casino, 237
    free attractions, 154
    restaurants, 136, 139, 148
    shopping, 194
Cirque du Soleil
    Mystère, 218
    O, 218
    Zumanity, 239–240
Cirrus network, 17
Citizens Area Transit, 69
Citysearch, 17
Clark County Marriage
    License Bureau, 74
Clark County Museum, 171
Clark County Parks and
    Community Services, 188
Clark County Parks and
    Recreation Department, 21
Clark County Rodeo and
    Fair, 22
Classes and workshops, 188
Cleopatra's Barge Nightclub,
    238

Climate, 20
Clothing
    baby and preschooler,
        196
    costumes, 200
    at department stores,
        200–202
    everyday, 204, 206
    fashion
        for children, 206
        for teens and adults,
            206
    men's, 208–209
    packing tips, 27
    sportswear, 210
    vintage and used, 212
Coach USA, 178, 242, 254
Comedy clubs, 227–228
Comics, 198–199
Commercial Center
    restaurants, 142
Comstock Lode silver mine,
    259
Coney Island Emporium
    Arcade, 164
Consolidators, 41
Consulates, 278
Continental Airlines, 38, 52,
    275
Continental Airlines
    Vacations, 52
Convention Center. See East
    of the Strip/Convention
    Center
Convention dates, major, 22
Conventions, 72
Cookware, 199
Cosmetics, 199–200
Cosmic Comics, 198
Costumes, 200
Craig Ranch Golf Club, 186
Creative Adventures,
    178, 253
Credit cards, 19, 272–273
    auto insurance, 71
Crime, 31–33, 74
Cruises, Lake Mead, 248
Cruze, Char, 178, 253
Cult Vegas (Weatherford), 25
Curfew, 31–32
Currency and currency
    exchange, 272
Customs regulations,
    270–271
Cybercafes, 57–58
Cycling, 184–185
    areas surrounding Las
        Vegas, 266
    Red Rock Canyon, 254, 257

D ance clubs, 238
Danny Gans: The Man of
    Many Voices, 218–219
Daylight saving time, 281
Dead Poet Books, 13, 197
Deep vein thrombosis, 43
Delta Airlines, 38, 52, 275
Delta Vacations, 52
Dentists, 72
Department stores, 200–202
Desert Brats, 206
Desert Cab Company, 69
Desert Outfitters, 210
Desert Passage, 206
Desert Passage at Aladdin/
    Planet Hollywood, 10, 154
Desert Princess, 248
Desert Rose Golf Club, 186
Desert Springs Hospital, 72
Desert tours, 178–180
Desperado, 262
De Witty, Gordon, 34
Dex, Officer, 98
Diesel, 206
Digital cameras, 40, 57
Digitalcity, 17
Dillard's, 200
Dining, 4, 116–150. See also
    Restaurant Index
    around Lake Mead,
        249–250
    best bets, 11–13
    buffets, 130, 145–149
        best, 11
    Center Strip, 132–138,
        147–148
    Chinatown, 132
    Commercial Center, 142
    by cuisine, 119–121
    Downtown, 144–145
    East of the Strip, 141–144,
        148–149
    hamburgers, 131
    hot dogs, 130–131
    menus for the blind, 34
    money-saving tips,
        117–119
    North Strip, 139–140, 148
    Old Nevada, 259–260
    Peach Springs (AZ),
        265–266
    pizza, 119, 138, 142
    price categories, 119
    reservations, 117, 134
    for romantic dining,
        149–150
    South Strip, 121–132,
        145–147
    tipping, 281
    West of the Strip, 144, 149

Dinosaurs, at the Las Vegas
    Natural History Museum,
    7, 159, 172
Dion, Celine, 217–218
Dirt biking (motocross), 230
Disabilities, travelers with,
    33–35
Disney Store, 211
DKNY, 206
Doctors, 72
Dollar rental cars, 70, 276
Dolphin Habitat, 7, 152, 162,
    163
Donna Beam Fine Art
    Gallery, 171
Doughnuts, Krispy Kreme,
    136
Downhill Bicycle Tours, 266
Downtown, 66
    area between the Strip
        and, 67
    brief description of, 67
    restaurants, 144–145
Drinking laws, 277
Driver's licenses, foreign,
    269
Driving safety, 71
    for international visitors,
        274
Drugstores, 72, 202
Dry cleaners, 72

E ast of the Strip/Conven-
    tion Center, 66–67
    accommodations, 101–110
    casino, 237
    restaurants, 141–144,
        148–149
Echo Bay, 248
Economy-class syndrome, 43
Eddie Bauer, 204
Eiffel Tower Bar, 232
Elderhostel, 36
Electricity, 277
Electronics, 202, 204
Elvis-A-Rama, 171
Embassies and consulates,
    278
Emergencies, 73, 278
Endangered Species Store,
    211
Enterprise rental cars, 70
Entertainment, 213–240
    for adults, 232
    casinos, 233–237
    dance clubs, 238
    headliner showrooms,
        225–227
    local performing arts, 231
    magic shows, 220–223

Entertainment *(cont.)*
major production shows, 215–225, 238–240
rides, 166–168
spectator sports, 228–230
tickets, 215
Entry requirements, 268–269
Equifax, 19
Escape Adventure Bike Shop and Tour Center, 185, 210, 257, 266
Escape Adventures/Las Vegas Cyclery, 254
Ethel M's Chocolate Factory and Cactus Gardens (Henderson), 175–177
Europ Assistance's World-wide Healthcare Plan, 272
Everything Coca-Cola Las Vegas, 154, 175
Excalibur
casino, 234
entertainment, 154, 214, 225
Krispy Kreme doughnuts at, 136
shopping, 189, 194
Expedia, 54, 55
Experian, 19

F actories and food, 175–178
Factory outlets, 189, 192
Family Film Fests, 5, 23
Family vacations, tips for having great, 26
Fantasy Toys, 211
FAO Schwarz, 14, 211
Fashions. *See* Clothing
Fashion Show Mall, 189, 190, 206
Fax machines, 280
Festivals and special events, 21–25
Field of Dreams, 173, 210
The 51s, 228
Film, flying with, 40
Film Festival, CineVegas International, 23
Film Festival, Family, 23
Fishing, Lake Mead and vicinity, 246
Fishing licenses, 183
Fitness centers, best, 9
Fitzgeralds, Krispy Kreme doughnuts at, 136
The Flamingo Las Vegas
entertainment, 227–228
shopping, 194
tennis courts at, 187

Flyaway Indoor Skydiving, 185
Fly-Cheap, 41
Flying Wheels Travel, 34
Folies Bergere, 219–220
Food
grocery stores and markets, 207–208
stocking up on staples, 119
Food courts, best, 11–12
Footlocker & Lady Footlocker, 209
Foreign visitors, 268–282
customs regulations, 270–271
entry requirements, 268–269
health insurance, 271–272
immigration and customs clearance, 275
medical requirements for entry, 269
passport information, 269
Forum Shops, 193, 206
Fountain Shows at the Forum Shops, 156–157
Fremont Medical Center, 73
Fremont Street, 5, 32
Fremont Street Experience, 154, 157
Frequent-flier clubs, 42
Frequent-gambling programs, 87
Friday Family Film Fest, 23
Frog Hopper (Primm), 262
Frommers.com, 55, 60
Frontier Airlines, 38

G allery of Legends, 210–211
Gambling, frequent-gambling programs, 87
GameKeeper, 212
Games, 211
in-flight, 51
GameWorks, 157–159, 173, 187
Gans, Danny, 218–219
Gap, 206
GapKids, 204
The Gardens at Springs Preserve, 181
Gasoline, 278
Gateway District, 67
Gay, lesbian, bi & transgender (GLBT) families
information and resources, 35
Pride Festival, 23

The Gay and Lesbian Community Center of Southern Nevada, 35
Gay Men's Health Crisis, 269
Gay Travel A to Z, 36
Gelato, 135
Gifts and souvenirs, 206–207
Giovanni's Room, 36
Gladstones Games to Go: Verbal Volleys, Coin Contests, Dot Duel, and Other Games for Boredom-Free Days, 51
Godiva, 198
Golden Access Passport, 33–34
Golden Age Passport, 36
Golf, 185–187
tournaments, 228
Gondola Ride, 159
Good Guys, 202, 204
The Grand Canal Shoppes, 10, 154, 159, 172, 206
Grand Canyon Caverns, 265
Grand Canyon Tours, 266
Grand Canyon West, 262–266
tours, 178
Grandma Dottie's Babysitting, 61
Grand Spa (MGM Grand), 83
Great Las Vegas Craft Festival, 21, 24
Greyhound/Trailways, 276
Grocery stores and markets, 207–208
Guggenheim and Guggenheim Hermitage Museums, 171–172
Gymboree, 204

H alloween Experience, 200
Hard Rock Hotel & Casino
casino, 237
entertainment, 226
Harrah's Las Vegas
entertainment, 214, 222
shopping, 194
Hawaiian Airlines, 38
Headliner showrooms, 225–227
Headliner stadiums, 227
Health concerns, 30–31
Health insurance, 29, 30
for international visitors, 271–272
Helicopter tours, Grand Canyon West, 264

Help of Southern Nevada,
278
Henderson
accommodations, 113–115
factories, 175–177
golf, 186
Heritage Park/Old Mormon
Fort, 183
Hertz rental cars, 70, 276
High Roller, 7, 98, 168
High tea, 128
Highway conditions, 73
Hiking
in the desert, 252, 266
Lake Mead and vicinity,
248
Red Rock Canyon,
256–257
Spring Mountains National
Recreation Area (Mount
Charleston), 260
Valley of Fire State Park,
253
History, 283–291
HIV-positive visitors, 269
Holidays, 279
Hoover Dam, 241–245
Hoover Dam Shuttle Tour,
242
Hoover Dam Visitor Center,
245
Horseback riding
Bonnie Springs Ranch, 258
Red Rock Canyon and
Mount Charleston,
266–267
Sandy Valley Ranch, 267
Hospitals, 73
Hot-Air Balloon Festival, Las
Vegas, 24
Hot dogs, 130–131
Hoteldiscounts.com, 55
Hotel Reservations
Network, 59
Hotels, 75–115. *See also*
Accommodations Index
around Lake Mead,
249–250
avoiding the crowds, 82
best bets, 8–11
Center Strip, 90–97
check-in time, 75
East of the Strip, 101–110
with a fridge in your room,
137
guests-per-room maximum,
102
landing the best room, 60
Mount Charleston, 261
North Strip, 97–101
Old Nevada, 259–260

outside of Las Vegas,
113–115
package tours and, 53–54
Peach Springs (AZ),
265–266
room rates, 77–80
saving on, 58–60
shopping promenades,
192–195
South Strip, 80–90
"suite," meaning of, 106
surfing for, 55–57
tipping, 281
West of the Strip, 110–113
Hotels.com, 55, 59
Hot lines, 73
Hotmail, 58
Hotwire, 54–56
Houdini Museum, 172
Houdini's Magic Shop, 208
House of Blues, 226–227
Howard W. Cannon Aviation
Museum, 172
Hualapai Reservations, 264
Hualapai River Runners, 265
Humana Medical Center, 31

I **GLTA (International Gay**
& Lesbian Travel
Association), 35
The Illusionary Magic of
Rick Thomas, 220
I Love Las Vegas
(website), 15
Imperial Palace
auto collections at, 179
entertainment, 214,
220–222
India Bazaar, 207–208
Information sources, 15–17,
64–66
Insurance, 29–30, 41
car-rental, 30, 71–72
Intellicast, 56
International Ameripass, 276
The International Gay & Les-
bian Travel Association
(IGLTA), 35
International Mariachi
Festival, 23–24
International Marketplace,
7, 208
International visitors,
268–282
customs regulations,
270–271
entry requirements,
268–269
health insurance, 271–272

immigration and customs
clearance, 275
medical requirements for
entry, 269
passport information, 269
Internet access, 57–58
InTouch USA, 28, 274

J **apan Airlines, 38**
Jazz Festival, Las Vegas, 23
Jazz in the Park, 22–23
Jester's Stage, 154
JetBlue, 38, 275
Jet lag, 44
Jimmy Choo, 209
Jo-Ann, 196
The Joint, 226
Jubilee!, 238–239

K **enneth Cole, 209**
Keystone Thrust Fault (Red
Rock Canyon), 255
KidQuest, 10, 62
Hawthorn Suites, 10
Kids' Castle, 206
Kids' Karnival, 206
Kids Kloset, 212
Kids "R" Us, 204
King, Mac, 222
King, Martin Luther, Jr.,
Parade, 21
King Tut's Tomb & Museum,
159, 162
Kmart, 200
Krispy Kreme doughnuts,
136

L **a Femme!, 239**
Lake Mead and vicinity,
241–250
Lake Mead Cruises, 248
Lake Mead National Recre-
ation Area, 246
Lake Mead Resort and
Marina, 246
Lance Burton: Master
Magician, 220–221
Las Vegas Advisor (website),
15–16
Las Vegas Bay, 248
Las Vegas Bugle, 35
Las Vegas Chamber of
Commerce, 15, 25, 64
Las Vegas Convention and
Visitors Authority (LVCVA),
2, 15, 22, 25, 64
Las Vegas Convention
Center, 72

Las Vegas 51s, 8
Las Vegas Hot-Air Balloon Festival, 24
Las Vegas Invitational, 228
Las Vegas Jazz Festival, 23
Las Vegas Kids (website), 15
Las Vegas Mercury, 17, 73
Las Vegas Mini Grand Prix, 179, 184
Las Vegas Motor Speedway, 179, 228, 230
Las Vegas Museum of Natural History, 7, 159, 172
Las Vegas National Golf Club, 187
Las Vegas Outlet Center, 192
Las Vegas Premium Outlets, 10, 192
Las Vegas Review-Journal, 17, 73
Las Vegas's Chinatown, 132
Las Vegas Ski and Snowboard Resort, 260–261, 267
Las Vegas Strip Monorail, 7, 66, 68
Las Vegas Strip Trolley, 68–69
Las Vegas Sun, 73
Las Vegas Valley Bicycle Club, 184
Las Vegas Youth Orchestras, 231
Layout of Las Vegas, 66–67
Learning Is Fun, 197–198
Legal aid, 279
Legends in Concert, 221–222
Liberace Museum and Center for the Arts, 173–174, 179
Liberty Travel, 53
Lied Discovery Children's Museum, 5, 162, 188
Lion Habitat, 155, 158
Liquor and gambling laws, 73
Lorenzi Park, 183
Lost children, 32–33
Lost City Museum, 253
Lost Creek Children's Discovery Trail (Red Rock Canyon), 256
Lost-luggage insurance, 29–30
Lost or stolen wallet or credit cards, 19
Lucky Brand, 206
Luggage, lost-luggage insurance, 29–30
Luxor Arcade, 164

Luxor Las Vegas
    Blue Man Group: *Live at Luxor*, 216–217
    casino, 234
    entertainment, 214
    restaurants, 124, 129–130, 145–146
    shopping, 189, 194

McCarran International Airport, 278
    getting into town from, 38–39
Mac King Comedy Magic Show, 222
Macy's, 200
Madame Tussaud's Celebrity Encounter, 162
Magic and gags, 208
The Magic Shop, 208
Magic shows, 220–223
Mail, 279
Mail2web, 58
Malls, 190
Mamma Mia, 222
Mandalay Bay
    boxing matches, 230
    casino, 234
    entertainment, 214, 222, 226–227, 238
    restaurants, 123–126
    Shark Reef at, 7, 159, 164–165
    shopping, 194
M&Ms World, 154, 175, 198
Manhattan Express, 166
Mapquest, 56
Marjorie Barrick Museum, 159, 174
Marshalls, 200
Martin Luther King, Jr., Parade, 21
Masquerade in the Sky, 155
MasterCard
    ATM Locator, 56
    traveler's checks, 18
MaxFlight 2002 (Primm), 262
Mead, Lake, 242. *See also* Lake Mead and vicinity
    cruises, 248
The Meadows, 190
Meals and snacks, air travel and, 50–52
MEDEX International, 29
MedicAlert Identification Tag, 30
Medical insurance, 29, 30
    for international visitors, 271–272

Medical requirements for entry, 269
Menorah Lighting Ceremony, 24
Men's Wearhouse, 208–209
Mervyn's, 200–201
Metro Pizza, 8, 12, 119, 142
MGM Grand
    casino, 235
    entertainment, 155, 158, 230, 239
    Garden Events Arena, 230
    restaurants and food court, 11–12, 121–122, 124, 128–129, 131, 135, 146
    shopping, 194
Midwest Express, 38
The Mirage
    attractions and entertainment, 155, 158 162–164
    boxing matches, 230
    casino, 236
    entertainment, 218–219
    shopping, 189
    volcano in front of, 155
Moenkopi Trail (Red Rock Canyon), 256
Moment's Notice, 42
Money matters, 17–20
    for international visitors, 272–273
Money-saving tips
    accommodations, 58–60
    restaurants, 117–119
Monorail, 7, 66, 68
Monte Carlo Hotel & Casino, tennis courts at, 187
Monte Carlo Pub & Brewery, 238
Monte Carlo Resort & Casino
    entertainment, 214, 220–221, 238
    restaurants, 126–127, 131, 132, 146
    shopping, 194
The MossRehab Hospital, 34
Motocross (dirt biking), 230
Mount Charleston (Spring Mountains National Recreation Area), 260–261, 266
Mount Charleston Resort, 23
Mousesavers (website), 16, 56
Movies, recommended, 25–27
Music stores, 209
Mystère (Cirque du Soleil), 218

Napoleon, 209
NASCAR-replica vehicles, 7, 166, 179, 184
National Conservation Area (Red Rock Canyon), 254
National Finals Rodeo, 24–25, 228
National Vitamin Company Factory, 175
Nature walks, 181, 183
Neiman Marcus, 201
Nevada Ballet Theatre, 231
Nevada Commission on Tourism, 15, 25, 34, 66
Nevada Shakespeare in the Park, 24, 231
New Balance, 209–210
Newspapers and periodicals, 73
New York-New York
  attractions and entertainment, 164, 166
  casino, 235
  restaurants, 125–127
NFR Cowboy Christmas Gift Show, 25
Niketown, 210
North Strip, 66, 237
  accommodations, 97–101
  restaurants, 139–140, 148
Northwest Airlines, 38, 52
Now, Voyager, 35

O (Cirque du Soleil), 218
Odysseus, 36
Oktoberfest, 23
Old Comstock Lode silver mine, 259
Old Las Vegas Mormon Fort, 174
Old Nevada, 257–260
Old Nevada on the Bonnie Springs Ranch, 14
Old Nevada Photograph Shoppe, 259
Open World Magazine, 35
Orbitz, 54
Orleans bowling alleys, 185
Orleans casino, 235
Out and About, 35
Outdoor activities. *See* Sports and activities
Outlet shopping, 189, 192
Overton, 253

Pacific Standard Time (PST), 281
Pacifiers, 50–51

Package tours, 52–54
Packing tips, 27–29, 49
Papillon Helicopters, 264
Parents Without Partners, 35
Paris Las Vegas
  bar, 232
  entertainment, 215, 225
  free attractions, 155
  restaurants, 134, 138
Parking, 70, 73
Parks and playgrounds, 183
Party City, 200
Passport information, 269–270
Payless rental cars, 70
Peach Springs (AZ), 265–266
Penn & Teller, 222–223
Performing arts, 231–232
Petroglyphs (rock etchings), 250, 251, 255, 257
Petrol, 278
Pets, traveling with, 10, 37–38
PGA Tours Las Vegas Senior Classic, 228
Pharmacies, 72
Pirate Battle at Treasure Island *(Sirens of TI),* 5, 12, 16, 155
Pizza, 119, 138, 142
  best, 12
Playgrounds
  indoor, 184
  outdoor, 183
PLUS network, 17
Police, 73
Post office, 73–74
Powerhouse Indoor Climbing Center, 187
Prescription medications, 30
Presley, Elvis, Elvis-A-Rama, 171
Priceline, 54–56
Pride Festival, 23
Primm, 261–262
Primm Valley Resort & Casino, 261
Psychic Eye, 198

Qantas, 275
Quartermaster Point (Grand Canyon West), 265
Quikbook, 59–60

Race and Sports Book, 236
Rafting, 248–249
  Grand Canyon West, 265
Rainbow Company Youth Theatre, 232

Red Rock Canyon, 253–257, 266
Red Rock Canyon Visitor Center, 254
Red Rooster Antique Mall, 196
Renaissance Festival, Age of Chivalry, 24
Rental cars, 70–72, 276
  at the airport, 39
  insurance, 30
  surfing for, 56
Reservations
  hotel, 59
  restaurant, 117, 134
Reservations Plus, 53
Restaurants, 4, 116–150. *See also* Restaurant Index
  around Lake Mead, 249–250
  best bets, 11–13
  buffets, 130, 145–149
    best, 11
  Center Strip, 132–138, 147–148
  Chinatown, 132
  Commercial Center, 142
  by cuisine, 119–121
  Downtown, 144–145
  East of the Strip, 141–144, 148–149
  hamburgers, 131
  hot dogs, 130–131
  menus for the blind, 34
  money-saving tips, 117–119
  North Strip, 139–140, 148
  Old Nevada, 259–260
  Peach Springs (AZ), 265–266
  pizza, 119, 138, 142
  price categories, 119
  reservations, 117, 134
  for romantic dining, 149–150
  South Strip, 121–132, 145–147
  tipping, 281
  West of the Strip, 144, 149
Restrooms, 282
Rides, 166–168
  Adventure Canyon (Primm), 262
  Big Shot, 7, 98, 168
  Desperado (Primm), 262
  High Roller, 7, 98, 168
  Manhattan Express, 166
  Primm, 262
  Speed-The Ride, 166
  Speedworld, 166–167
  Star Trek: The Experience, 7–8, 167–168

The Rio, shopping, 195
Rio All-Suite Hotel and
    Casino
    bar, 232–233
    entertainment, 155, 215,
        223, 224
Rite Aid, 202
The Riviera
    entertainment, 227
    shopping, 195
Riviera Comedy Club, 227
The Riviera Hotel & Casino
    entertainment, 239
    tennis courts at, 187
Robber Roost, 260
Robinson's May, 201
Rock climbing, 187
    Red Rock Canyon, 267
Rockreation Sport Climbing
    Wall, 187
Rodeo and Fair, Clark
    County, 22
Rodeos
    Clark County Rodeo and
        Fair, 22
    National Finals Rodeo,
        24–25, 228
Ron Lee's World of Clowns
    (Henderson), 178
Royal Links Golf Club, 187
Royal White Tiger Habitat,
    7, 155, 158, 163
rumjungle, 238

S afety, 31–33, 74
    air travel, 49
    for international visitors,
        274
Sahara Hotel & Casino, rides,
    166–167
Saks Fifth Avenue, 201–202
Sam Boyd Stadium, 227
Sam's Town & Gambling
    Hall, 185
Sandy Valley Ranch, 267
San Gennaro Feast, 24
Sav-On, 72, 202
Scandia Family Fun Center,
    184
Scenic Airlines, 178, 264
Scenic Drive (Red Rock
    Canyon), 254
Scuba diving, 249
Sears, 202
Seasons, 20
Seats, airplane, 45–47,
    49–50, 56
Second City, 227–228
Secret Garden, Siegfried &
    Roy's, 162–163
Senior travel, 36–37

Sephora, 199–200
Serge's Showgirl Wigs, 200
Seven Crown Resorts, 246
Shakespeare in the Park,
    Nevada, 24
Shark Reef at Mandalay Bay,
    7, 159, 164–165
Sharper Image, 204
Shelby American Sports Car
    Museum and Assembly
    Area, 179
Shoes, 209–210
Shopping, 189–212
    best hotels for, 10
    districts, 190–195
Showcase Mall, 207
SideStep, 54
Side trips from Las Vegas,
    241–267
Siegfried & Roy
    Royal White Tiger Habitat,
        7, 155, 158, 163
    Secret Garden, 162–163
Sights and activities,
    151–180. See also Sports
    and activities
    for animal lovers, 158–159
    arcades, 164
    art galleries and history
        museums, 168–174
    factories and food,
        175–178
    free, 154–155
    for kids, 156–165
    for race car fans, 179
    suggested itineraries,
        152–153, 156
    tours, 178–180
Silver Cactus Comics, 199
Single parents, 35
Sirens of TI (pirate battle),
    5, 12, 16, 155
Site59.com, 54
Size conversion chart, 273
Skiing, Las Vegas Ski and
    Snowboard Resort,
    260–261, 267
Sky's the Limit, 266, 267
Slot clubs, 87, 93
Smarter Living, 54
Snapfish, 57
Snowboarding, Las Vegas
    Ski and Snowboard
    Resort, 260–261, 267
The Society for Accessible
    Travel and Hospitality, 34
Song, 38
The Southern Nevada Center
    for Independent Living
    Program, 34
Southern Nevada
    Zoological-Botanical
    Park, 159

South Strip, 66
    accommodations, 80–90
    casinos, 233–235
    restaurants, 121–132,
        145–147
Southwest Airlines, 38, 53
Spartacus International Gay
    Guide, 36
Special events and festivals,
    21–25
Spectator sports, 173,
    228–230
Speed-The Ride, 166
Speedworld, 166
Spirit Airlines, 38
Splash, 239
SportCenter, 173, 179, 184
Sporting goods and
    sportswear, 210
Sport Logo, 210
Sports and activities,
    173, 181
    bicycling, 184–185
    bowling, 185
    bungee jumping, 185
    classes and workshops,
        188
    family fun centers and
        indoor playgrounds, 184
    golf, 185–187
    Grand Canyon West,
        266–267
    Lake Mead and vicinity,
        246, 248–249
    nature walks and botanical
        gardens, 181, 183
    parks and playgrounds,
        183
    rock climbing, 187
    running and walking,
        181–183
    for the special-needs child,
        188
    tennis, 187
Sports Hall of Fame,
    155, 173
Sports memorabilia,
    210–211
Spring Mountain Ranch
    State Park, 254
Spring Mountains National
    Recreation Area (Mount
    Charleston), 260–261
Star Land Tours/Bonnie
    Springs Shuttle, 257
Star Trek: The Experience,
    7–8, 167–168
Steve Wyrick, 223
Stratosphere Las Vegas
    entertainment, 215, 216,
        225
    shopping, 195
    Thrill Rides, 168

The Strip, 66. *See also* East
    of the Strip/Convention
    Center; Center Strip; South
    Strip; West of the Strip
    area between Downtown
        and, 67
Strollers, 27
Sun exposure, 30
Sunrise Hospital and
    Medical Center, 73
Sunset Park, 13, 24, 37, 183
Sunset Station, 62
Sur la Table, 199
Syringe-administered
    medications, 269

Talbots, 206
Target, 202
Taxes, 74, 280
Taxis, 69
    tipping, 281
Teens, best hotels for, 11
Telegraph and telex services,
    280
Telephone, 280–281
Temperatures, average, 21
Tennis, 187
Texas Station Gambling Hall
    & Hotel, 62
Theater, 231–232
Thomas, Rick, 220
Thomas & Mack Center, 227
Thrifty rental cars, 70, 276
Thrill rides. *See* Rides
Ticketmaster, 215
Tickets2Nite, 215
Time zones, 74, 281
Tipping, 281
TI-Treasure Island Las Vegas
    Cirque du Soleil's *Mystère*,
        218
    entertainment, 215
    Krispy Kreme doughnuts
        at, 136
    restaurants, 133, 136, 148
    shopping, 195
    Sirens of TI (pirate battle),
        5, 12, 16, 155
Tix4Tonight, 215
T. J. Maxx, 202
Toddlers, best hotels for, 10
Toilets, 282
Tony 'n' Tina's Wedding,
    223–224
Tourist information, 15–17,
    64–66
Tournament of Kings,
    224–225
Tours, 178–180
    Grand Canyon West, 264
    Hoover Dam, 242

package, 52–54
    Red Rock Canyon, 254,
        256
Tower Records/Video/Books,
    209
Toys
    for air travel, 50
    shopping for, 189,
        211–212
Toys "R" Us, 212
Trader Joe's, 207
Train travel, 276–277
Transportation, 67–72
    by car, 69–72
    by public transportation,
        68–69
    by taxi, 69
Transportation Security
    Administration (TSA),
    39–41
TransUnion, 19
Travel agencies, 53
    for disabled travelers, 34
    for gay, lesbian, bi &
        trans-gender (GLBT)
        families, 35
    online, 54
    for seniors, 36
Travel Assistance
    International, 29
Travelaxe.com, 16, 55
Travel clubs, 42
Travelers Advantage, 42
Traveler's Aid International,
    278
Traveler's checks, 17–18, 272
Travelex Insurance
    Services, 29
Travel Guard International,
    29
TravelHub, 42
Traveling
    around the United States,
        275–277
    to Las Vegas, 38–45
        by car, 45
        by plane, 38–44
        by train, 45
    to the United States,
        274–275
Travel insurance, 29–30, 41
Travel Insured International,
    29
Travelocity, 54, 55
Treasure Island. *See* TI-
    Treasure Island Las Vegas
Tree and Menorah Lighting
    Ceremonies, 24
Trip-cancellation
    insurance, 29
Trolleys, 68–69

Tropicana Bird Show,
    155, 223
Tropicana Resort & Casino
    bird show, 5, 155, 223
    entertainment, 154, 215,
        219–220
    restaurants, 125, 129–131
Turbo Drop (Primm), 262

United Airlines, 38, 52,
    275
United States Tour Operators
    Association, 53
United Vacations, 52–53
Universal Currency
    Converter, 56
University Medical
    Center, 73
University of Nevada,
    Las Vegas, 181
    sports venues, 230
    tennis courts at, 187
US Airways, 38, 52
US Airways Vacations, 53

Vacation Fun Mad Libs:
    *World's Greatest Party
    Game*, 51
Vacation Together, 53
Valley of Fire State Park,
    242, 250–253
Vault (Primm), 262
Vegas4Visitors, 17
Vegas.com, 17
Vegetarian and vegan meals,
    43, 51–52
The Venetian
    bar, 232
    casino, 236–237
    food court and restaurants,
        131, 133, 135, 137, 150
    Krispy Kreme doughnuts
        at, 136
    shopping (Grand Canal
        Shoppes), 10, 70, 154,
        159, 172, 195, 206
Venus and Tiki Bar Lounge,
    232
Veterinarian, 74
Videotape, flying with, 40
Vintage and used clothing
    shops, 212
Virgin Atlantic, 275
Virgin Atlantic Airways, 38
Virgin Megastore, 13, 198,
    209
Visa
    ATM Locator, 56
    traveler's checks, 18

Visas, 268–269
Visa Waiver Program, 268
Visitor information, 15–17,
    64–66
Visitor's Guide, 15
Visit USA, 276
Viva Las Vegas, 225
VooDoo Lounge, 232–233

Waldenbooks, 13, 198
Walgreens, 72, 202
Wallet, lost or stolen, 19
Wal-Mart, 202
We Are Family (website), 35
Weather, 20–21, 74, 76
Weather.com, 56
Weatherford, Mike, 25
Websites
    for disabled travelers,
        34–35
    for family travel, 37
    for single parents, 35
    traveler's toolbox, 56
    travel-planning and
        booking, 54–58
Weddings, 74
Western Union, 19
West Flamingo Animal
    Hospital, 74
West of the Strip, 67
    accommodations, 110–113
    restaurants, 144, 149
Wetlands Nature Preserve,
    181, 183
We Will Rock You, 225
Wheelchair accessibility,
    33–35
Whirlpool, 95
White Cross Drugs, 72
White Tiger Habitat, 7, 155,
    158, 163
White-water rafting,
    248–249
Whittlesea Blue Cab, 69
Wizard's Arcade, 164
Worldwide Assistance
    Services, 272
Wynn, Steve, 76–77
Wyrick, Steve, 223

Yahoo! Mail, 58
Yellow/Checker Cab/Star
    Company, 69

Zoo, Old Nevada,
    257–258
Zumanity, 239–240

ACCOMMODATIONS

Aladdin/Planet Hollywood
    Resort & Casino, 81–82
AmeriSuites, 101
Atrium Suites, 101–102
Bellagio, 10, 88
Best Western Mardi Gras
    Inn, 107
Boardwalk Hotel & Casino,
    10, 86–87
Bonnie Springs Motel (Old
    Nevada), 259
Budget Suites of America,
    110, 112
Caesars Palace, 9, 90–92
Candlewood Suites, 107
Carriage House, 102, 104
Circus Circus, 8, 10, 98–100
Clarion Hotel & Suites Emer-
    ald Springs, 108
Courtyard by Marriott, 104
Desert Paradise, 110
Emerald Suites, 112
Excalibur, 8, 10, 87–88
Fairfield Inn by Marriott,
    9, 108
The Flamingo Las Vegas,
    9, 10, 94
The Four Seasons, 9, 61, 80
Grand Canyon Caverns Inn
    (Peach Springs, AZ), 265
Green Valley Ranch, 9, 113
Hacienda Hotel and Casino
    (Boulder City), 249
Hard Rock, 11
Hard Rock Hotel and Casino,
    10, 104–105
Hawthorn Suites, 105
Hotel San Remo, 88
Hualapai Lodge (Peach
    Springs, AZ), 265–266
Imperial Palace, 88–89
Lake Mead Lodge (Boulder
    City), 249–250
La Quinta Inn, 105–106
Las Vegas Hilton, 108–109
Luxor Las Vegas, 9, 89–90
Mandalay Bay, 9, 10, 89
Marriott Suites, 106
MGM Grand Hotel/Casino,
    10, 82–84
The Mirage, 95
Monte Carlo Resort &
    Casino, 9, 11, 84–85
Motel 6, 109
Mount Charleston Hotel,
    261
Mount Charleston Lodge,
    261
New York-New York Hotel &
    Casino, 9, 85

Orleans Hotel & Casino, 8–9,
    62, 112–113
Paris Las Vegas, 92–93
Residence Inn by Marriott,
    106
Rio All-Suite Hotel &
    Casino, 89
Sahara Hotel and Casino, 97
St. Tropez, 106–107
Sam's Town Hotel & Gam-
    bling Hall, 109
South Coast Hotel &
    Casino, 62
Stratosphere Las Vegas,
    9, 98
Sunset Station (Henderson),
    114–115
Terrible's, 109–110
TI-Treasure Island Las Vegas,
    95–97
The Tropicana Resort &
    Casino, 10, 85–86
The Venetian, 9, 11, 93–94
Westward Ho Hotel &
    Casino, 100–101

RESTAURANTS

Alizé, 13, 150
America, 12, 125–126
Arizona Charlie's, 130
Bally's Big Kitchen Buffet,
    147–148
Boardwalk Casino & Hotel,
    146
Bonnie Springs Ranch
    Restaurant, 259–260
Border Grill, 123–124
Border Grill Cantina, 126
Bouchon, 150
Buccaneer Bay Club,
    12, 132–133
California Pizza Kitchen,
    12, 138
Calypsos, 10, 86, 129
Capriotti's, 139
Cheesecake Factory,
    135–137
Chin Chin, 12, 126
Chinois Café, 137
Cocolini Gelato, 135
Delmonico Steakhouse,
    11, 133
Dragon Noodle Co., 126–127
Dragon Sushi, 132
Ellis Island, 131
El Sombrero, 11, 145
Emeril's New Orleans Fish
    House, 121–122
ESPN Zone, 127, 173
Excalibur's Round Table
    Buffet, 147

The Flamingo buffet, 11
Flamingo Paradise Garden
    Buffet, 148
Gold Coast buffet, 130
Gold Coast Casino hot dogs,
    131
Grand Lux Café, 13, 137
Grand Wok and Sushi Bar,
    124
Hamada, 124
Harbor Palace, 132
Hard Rock Cafe, 141
Harley-Davidson Cafe, 127
House of Blues, 125
In-N-Out Burger, 11, 129
Inside Scoop (Overton), 253
Key Largo, 131
La Salsa, 129–130
Las Vegas Hilton buffet,
    11, 149
Legends Deli, 130–131
Lenôtre, 138
Lotus of Siam, 12–13,
    141–142
Lutèce, 150
Luxor buffet, 11
Luxor's Pharaoh's Pheast
    Buffet, 145–146

Main Street Station buffet,
    130
MGM Grand Buffet, 146
Miner's Restaurant, 260
The Mirage Cravings Buffet,
    147
Mizuno's, 125
Mon Ami Gabi, 13, 134, 149
Monte Carlo Buffet, 146
Monte Carlo Pub & Brewery,
    131–132
Mr. Lucky's 24/7, 10, 11, 131,
    142
NASCAR Cafe, 139, 179
Nathan's Hot Dogs, 13
Nob Hill, 122
Nobu, 141
Olio Gelato, 12, 135
168 Shanghai, 132
The Orleans buffet, 130
Paris's Le Village Buffet, 147
P.F. Chang's China Bistro,
    127–128
Pho, 132
Picasso, 149
Pink Pony Cafe, 10, 100, 139
Pink Taco, 144

Rainforest Cafe, 10, 128
Rio's Carnival World Buffet,
    149
Roxy's Diner, 12
Royal Star, 135
Sam's Town Firelight Buffet,
    149
Schrafft's, 12
Second Street Grill, 144–145
Slots A Fun Casino hot dogs,
    131
Spago, 134
Stage Deli, 138
Stivali, 139
Tale of the Whale (Boulder
    City), 250
Tiffany's Cafe at White Cross
    Drugs, 11, 12, 140
Todai, 122–123
Totos (Boulder City), 250
Treasure Island Buffet, 148
Verandah, 11, 128
Voodoo Café, 144
Westward Ho Hotel & Casino
    hot dogs, 130–131
Wolfgang Puck Cafe, 12,
    128–129

For families who want the ultimate in fun and convenience

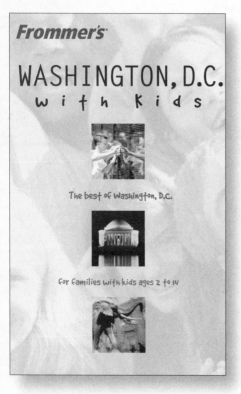

Frommer's

WASHINGTON, D.C.
with Kids

The best of Washington, D.C.

For families with kids ages 2 to 14

The guide with family-friendly information on where to stay, eat, shop, and visit.

- Frommer's Chicago with Kids
- Frommer's Las Vegas with Kids
- Frommer's New York City with Kids
- Frommer's Ottawa with Kids
- Frommer's San Francisco with Kids

- Frommer's Toronto with Kids
- Frommer's Vancouver with Kids
- Frommer's Walt Disney World® & Orlando with Kids
- Frommer's Washington, D.C. with Kids

Frommer's

WILEY

Frommer's Complete Guides

The only guide independent travelers need to make smart choices, avoid rip-offs, get the most for their money, and travel like a pro.

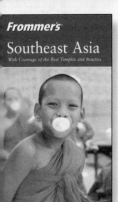

Frommer's
Southeast Asia
With Coverage of the Best Temples and Beaches

Frommer's Alaska
Frommer's Alaska Cruises & Ports of Call
Frommer's Amsterdam
Frommer's Argentina & Chile
Frommer's Arizona
Frommer's Atlanta
Frommer's Australia
Frommer's Austria
Frommer's Bahamas
Frommer's Barcelona, Madrid & Seville
Frommer's Beijing
Frommer's Belgium, Holland & Luxembourg
Frommer's Bermuda
Frommer's Boston
Frommer's Brazil
Frommer's British Columbia & the Canadian Rockies
Frommer's Brussels & Bruges with Ghent & Antwerp
Frommer's Budapest & the Best of Hungary
Frommer's California
Frommer's Canada
Frommer's Cancun, Cozumel & the Yucatan
Frommer's Cape Cod, Nantucket & Martha's Vineyard
Frommer's Caribbean
Frommer's Caribbean Cruises & Ports of Call
Frommer's Caribbean Ports of Call
Frommer's Carolinas & Georgia
Frommer's Chicago
Frommer's China
Frommer's Colorado
Frommer's Costa Rica
Frommer's Cuba

Frommer's Denmark
Frommer's Denver, Boulder & Colorado Springs
Frommer's England
Frommer's Europe
Frommer's European Cruises & Ports of Call
Frommer's Florence, Tuscany & Umbria
Frommer's Florida
Frommer's France
Frommer's Germany
Frommer's Great Britain
Frommer's Greece
Frommer's Greek Islands
Frommer's Hawaii
Frommer's Hong Kong
Frommer's Honolulu, Waikiki & Oahu
Frommer's Ireland
Frommer's Israel
Frommer's Italy
Frommer's Jamaica
Frommer's Japan
Frommer's Las Vegas
Frommer's London
Frommer's Los Angeles with Disneyland® & Palm Springs
Frommer's Maryland & Delaware
Frommer's Maui
Frommer's Mexico
Frommer's Montana & Wyoming
Frommer's Montreal & Quebec City
Frommer's Munich & the Bavarian Alps
Frommer's Nashville & Memphis
Frommer's Nepal
Frommer's New England
Frommer's Newfoundland & Labrador
Frommer's New Mexico
Frommer's New Orleans
Frommer's New York City
Frommer's New Zealand
Frommer's Northern Italy
Frommer's Norway
Frommer's Nova Scotia, New Brunswick & Prince Edward Island
Frommer's Oregon

Frommer's Ottawa
Frommer's Paris
Frommer's Peru
Frommer's Philadelphia & the Amish Country
Frommer's Portugal
Frommer's Prague & the Best of the Czech Republic
Frommer's Provence & the Riviera
Frommer's Puerto Rico
Frommer's Rome
Frommer's San Antonio & Austin
Frommer's San Diego
Frommer's San Francisco
Frommer's Santa Fe, Taos & Albuquerque
Frommer's Scandinavia
Frommer's Scotland
Frommer's Seattle
Frommer's Shanghai
Frommer's Sicily
Frommer's Singapore & Malaysia
Frommer's South Africa
Frommer's South America
Frommer's Southeast Asia
Frommer's South Florida
Frommer's South Pacific
Frommer's Spain
Frommer's Sweden
Frommer's Switzerland
Frommer's Texas
Frommer's Thailand
Frommer's Tokyo
Frommer's Toronto
Frommer's Turkey
Frommer's USA
Frommer's Utah
Frommer's Vancouver & Victoria
Frommer's Vermont, New Hampshire & Maine
Frommer's Vienna & the Danube Valley
Frommer's Virginia
Frommer's Virgin Islands
Frommer's Walt Disney World® & Orlando
Frommer's Washington, D.C.
Frommer's Washington State

Frommer's

⊛ WILEY

Available where.

theUnofficial Guides

For travelers who want more than the official line.

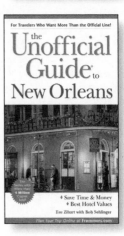

- Beyond Disney
- California with Kids
- Central Italy: Florence, Rome, Tuscany & Umbria
- Chicago
- Cruises
- Disneyland®
- England
- Florida
- Florida with Kids
- Inside Disney

- Hawaii
- Las Vegas
- London
- Maui
- Mexico's Best Beach Resorts
- Mini Las Vegas
- Mini Mickey
- New Orleans
- New York City
- Paris

- San Francisco
- Skiing & Snowboarding in the West
- South Florida
- Walt Disney World®
- Walt Disney World® for Grown-Ups
- Walt Disney World® with Kids
- Washington, D.C.

Now you know.

wiley.com

Available at bookstores everywhere.

DARE TO BE...

...Different

Irreverent Guide to Las Vegas

Irreverent Guide to London

Irreverent Guide to Paris

Irreverent Guide to Boston

Irreverent Guide to Los Angeles

Irreverent Guide to Rome

Irreverent Guide to Seattle & Portland

Irreverent Guide to Vancouver

Irreverent Guide to Washington, D.C.

Irreverent Guide to Chicago

Frommer's®
A Branded Imprint of ⊛WILEY
Now you know.

Available at bookstores everywhere.

Destinations in a Nutshell

- Frommer's Portable Acapulco, Ixtapa & Zihuatanejo
- Frommer's Portable Amsterdam
- Frommer's Portable Aruba
- Frommer's Portable Australia's Great Barrier Reef
- Frommer's Portable Bahamas
- Frommer's Portable Berlin
- Frommer's Portable Big Island of Hawaii
- Frommer's Portable Boston
- Frommer's Portable California Wine Country
- Frommer's Portable Cancun
- Frommer's Portable Cayman Islands
- Frommer's Portable Charleston
- Frommer's Portable Chicago
- Frommer's Portable Disneyland®
- Frommer's Portable Dominican Republic
- Frommer's Portable Dublin
- Frommer's Portable Florence
- Frommer's Portable Frankfurt
- Frommer's Portable Hong Kong
- Frommer's Portable Houston
- Frommer's Portable Las Vegas
- Frommer's Portable Las Vegas for Non-Gamblers
- Frommer's Portable London
- Frommer's Portable London from $90 a Day
- Frommer's Portable Los Angeles

- Frommer's Portable Los Cabos & Baja
- Frommer's Portable Maine Coast
- Frommer's Portable Maui
- Frommer's Portable Miami
- Frommer's Portable Nantucket & Martha's Vineyard
- Frommer's Portable New Orleans
- Frommer's Portable New York City
- Frommer's Portable New York City from $90 a Day
- Frommer's Portable Paris
- Frommer's Portable Paris from $90 a Day
- Frommer's Portable Phoenix & Scottsdale
- Frommer's Portable Portland
- Frommer's Portable Puerto Rico
- Frommer's Portable Puerto Vallarta, Manzanillo & Guadalajara
- Frommer's Portable Rio de Janeiro
- Frommer's Portable San Diego
- Frommer's Portable San Francisco
- Frommer's Portable Savannah
- Frommer's Portable Seattle
- Frommer's Portable Sydney
- Frommer's Portable Tampa & St. Petersburg
- Frommer's Portable Vancouver
- Frommer's Portable Vancouver Island
- Frommer's Portable Venice
- Frommer's Portable Virgin Islands
- Frommer's Portable Washington, D.C.

Frommer's

WILEY

Avai... ...rywhere.

FROMMER'S® COMPLETE TRAVEL GUIDES

Alaska
Alaska Cruises & Ports of Call
American Southwest
Amsterdam
Argentina & Chile
Arizona
Atlanta
Australia
Austria
Bahamas
Barcelona, Madrid & Seville
Beijing
Belgium, Holland & Luxembourg
Bermuda
Boston
Brazil
British Columbia & the Canadian
  Rockies
Brussels & Bruges
Budapest & the Best of Hungary
Calgary
California
Canada
Cancún, Cozumel & the Yucatán
Cape Cod, Nantucket & Martha's
  Vineyard
Caribbean
Caribbean Ports of Call
Carolinas & Georgia
Chicago
China
Colorado
Costa Rica
Cruises & Ports of Call
Cuba
Denmark
Denver, Boulder & Colorado
  Springs
England
Europe
Europe by Rail
European Cruises & Ports of Call

Florence, Tuscany & Umbria
Florida
France
Germany
Great Britain
Greece
Greek Islands
Halifax
Hawaii
Hong Kong
Honolulu, Waikiki & Oahu
India
Ireland
Italy
Jamaica
Japan
Kauai
Las Vegas
London
Los Angeles
Maryland & Delaware
Maui
Mexico
Montana & Wyoming
Montréal & Québec City
Munich & the Bavarian Alps
Nashville & Memphis
New England
Newfoundland & Labrador
New Mexico
New Orleans
New York City
New York State
New Zealand
Northern Italy
Norway
Nova Scotia, New Brunswick &
  Prince Edward Island
Oregon
Ottawa
Paris
Peru

Philadelphia & the Amish
  Country
Portugal
Prague & the Best of the Czech
  Republic
Provence & the Riviera
Puerto Rico
Rome
San Antonio & Austin
San Diego
San Francisco
Santa Fe, Taos & Albuquerque
Scandinavia
Scotland
Seattle
Shanghai
Sicily
Singapore & Malaysia
South Africa
South America
South Florida
South Pacific
Southeast Asia
Spain
Sweden
Switzerland
Texas
Thailand
Tokyo
Toronto
Turkey
USA
Utah
Vancouver & Victoria
Vermont, New Hampshire &
  Maine
Vienna & the Danube Valley
Virgin Islands
Virginia
Walt Disney World® & Orlando
Washington, D.C.
Washington State

FROMMER'S® DOLLAR-A-DAY GUIDES

Australia from $50 a Day
California from $70 a Day
England from $75 a Day
Europe from $85 a Day
Florida from $70 a Day
Hawaii from $80 a Day

Ireland from $80 a Day
Italy from $70 a Day
London from $90 a Day
New York City from $90 a Day
Paris from $90 a Day
San Francisco from $70 a Day

Washington, D.C. from $80 a
  Day
Portable London from $90 a Day
Portable New York City from $90
  a Day
Portable Paris from $90 a Day

FROMMER'S® PORTABLE GUIDES

Acapulco, Ixtapa & Zihuatanejo
Amsterdam
Aruba
Australia's Great Barrier Reef
Bahamas
Berlin
Big Island of Hawaii
Boston
California Wine Country
Cancún
Cayman Islands
Charleston
Chicago
Disneyland®
Dominican Republic
Dublin

Florence
Frankfurt
Hong Kong
Las Vegas
Las Vegas for Non-Gamblers
London
Los Angeles
Los Cabos & Baja
Maine Coast
Maui
Miami
Nantucket & Martha's Vineyard
New Orleans
New York City
Paris

Phoenix & Scottsdale
Portland
Puerto Rico
Puerto Vallarta, Manzanillo &
  Guadalajara
Rio de Janeiro
San Diego
San Francisco
Savannah
Vancouver
Vancouver Island
Venice
Virgin Islands
Washington, D.C.
Whistler

FROMMER'S® NATIONAL PARK GUIDES

Algonquin Provincial Park
Banff & Jasper
Family Vacations in the National
  Parks

Grand Canyon
National Parks of the American
  West
Rocky Mountain

Yellowstone & Grand Teton
Yosemite & Sequoia/Kings
  Canyon
Zion & Bryce Canyon

FROMMER'S® MEMORABLE WALKS

Chicago
London

New York
Paris

San Francisco

FROMMER'S® WITH KIDS GUIDES

Chicago
Las Vegas
New York City

Ottawa
San Francisco
Toronto

Vancouver
Walt Disney World® & Orlando
Washington, D.C.

SUZY GERSHMAN'S BORN TO SHOP GUIDES

Born to Shop: France
Born to Shop: Hong Kong,
  Shanghai & Beijing

Born to Shop: Italy
Born to Shop: London

Born to Shop: New York
Born to Shop: Paris

FROMMER'S® IRREVERENT GUIDES

Amsterdam
Boston
Chicago
Las Vegas
London

Los Angeles
Manhattan
New Orleans
Paris
Rome

San Francisco
Seattle & Portland
Vancouver
Walt Disney World®
Washington, D.C.

FROMMER'S® BEST-LOVED DRIVING TOURS

Austria
Britain
California
France

Germany
Ireland
Italy
New England

Northern Italy
Scotland
Spain
Tuscany & Umbria

THE UNOFFICIAL GUIDES®

Beyond Disney
California with Kids
Central Italy
Chicago
Cruises
Disneyland®
England
Florida
Florida with Kids
Inside Disney

Hawaii
Las Vegas
London
Maui
Mexico's Best Beach Resorts
Mini Las Vegas
Mini Mickey
New Orleans
New York City
Paris

San Francisco
Skiing & Snowboarding in the
  West
South Florida including Miami &
  the Keys
Walt Disney World®
Walt Disney World® for
  Grown-ups
Walt Disney World® with Kids
Washington, D.C.

SPECIAL-INTEREST TITLES

Athens Past & Present
Cities Ranked & Rated
Frommer's Best Day Trips from London
Frommer's Best RV & Tent Campgrounds
  in the U.S.A.
Frommer's Caribbean Hideaways
Frommer's China: The 50 Most Memorable Trips
Frommer's Exploring America by RV
Frommer's Gay & Lesbian Europe
Frommer's NYC Free & Dirt Cheap

Frommer's Road Atlas Europe
Frommer's Road Atlas France
Frommer's Road Atlas Ireland
Frommer's Wonderful Weekends from
  New York City
The New York Times' Guide to Unforgettable
  Weekends
Retirement Places Rated
Rome Past & Present